The
Peasant Prince

THE
PEASANT PRINCE

Thaddeus Kosciuszko and the Age of Revolution

Alex Storozynski

THOMAS DUNNE BOOKS
ST. MARTIN'S GRIFFIN
NEW YORK

THOMAS DUNNE BOOKS.
An imprint of St. Martin's Press.

THE PEASANT PRINCE. Copyright © 2009 by Alex Storozynski. All rights reserved.
Printed in the United States of America. For information, address St. Martin's
Press, 175 Fifth Avenue, New York, N.Y. 10010.

Design by Susan Walsh

www.thomasdunnebooks.com
www.stmartins.com

The Library of Congress has cataloged the hardcover edition as follows:

Storozynski, Alex.
    The peasant prince : Thaddeus Kosciuszko and the age of revolution /
Alex Storozynski.
        p. cm.
    Includes bibliographical references and index.
    ISBN 978-0-312-38802-7
    1. Kosciuszko, Tadeusz, 1746–1817. 2. Generals—Poland—Biography.
3. Statesmen—Poland—Biography. 4. United States. Army—Officers—
Biography. 5. United States—History—Revolution, 1775–1783—Campaigns.
6. Poland—History—Partition period, 1763–1796. 7. Poland—History—
1795–1815. I. Title.
    DK4348.K67S76 2009
    973.3092—dc22
    [B]

                                                                2008044625

ISBN 978-0-312-62594-8 (trade paperback)

First St. Martin's Griffin Edition: August 2010

10 9 8 7 6 5 4 3 2 1

*Dedicated to all Polish soldiers
who have fought,
"For your freedom and ours."*

Contents

Acknowledgments

ICOULD NOT HAVE WRITTEN THIS BOOK WITHOUT THE LOVE, SUP-
port, and critical eye of my wife, Agnieszka, whom Americans prefer to call
Angie. She read early versions of the manuscript and was invaluable during the
translations of Polish memoirs that were written two centuries ago. If Kosciuszko
had had a partner like her, Poland would have won its freedom much earlier. I
also have to thank my agent, Carol Mann, for believing that we could sell a book
about a hero with an unpronounceable name, and my editor, Rob Kirkpatrick,
who immediately saw the duality of Kosciuszko as an American and a European
revolutionary. My son, Nicholas, deserves praise for his patience as a young boy
while I dragged him to places like West Point, Fort Ticonderoga, Philadelphia,
and the Saratoga battlefield to research "that Polish guy," as he put it.

In researching Kosciuszko's life I received invaluable help and access to re-
search libraries and archives in the United States and Europe. My thanks go to
Joseph Gore and Tom Pniewski of the Kosciuszko Foundation; Krystyna Baron,
Janina Gromada Kedron, and Krystyna Olszer of the Polish Institute of Arts and
Sciences in New York; Wojciech Siemaszkiewicz of the Slavic and Baltic Divi-
sion of the New York Public Library; Suzanne Christoff, archivist of the Special
Collections and Archives Division of the U.S. Military Academy at West Point;
Anna Berkes, research librarian at Thomas Jefferson's Monticello; Jeremy Dibbell,
assistant reference librarian at the Massachusetts Historical Society; Robert Gi-
annini, museum curator of the Kosciuszko home in the Independence National
Historical Park in Philadelphia; Jan Lorys of the Polish Museum of America in
Chicago. I also want to thank Ed Waszak for his help in finding archival materials

in Chicago; Barbara Allen, curator of the Stockbridge Library Historical Collection in Stockbridge, Massachusetts; the archivists of the New-York Historical Society; and the librarians at the YIVO Institute for Jewish Research in New York.

Much of the research was done on several trips to Poland, and when I hit dead ends, Polish consul general Krzysztof Kasprzyk and consul Ewa Ger in New York helped find answers to my questions from museums and archives in Poland, and assisted in obtaining permission to use paintings for the book.

In Poland I received a great deal of help from the Czartoryski Foundation in Krakow; the Library of Polish Academic Sciences in Krakow; and the National Library in Warsaw. I received great encouragement and assistance from Professor Janusz Cisek of the Museum of the Polish Army in Warsaw; Ewa Wierzynska of the Museum of Polish Jews in Warsaw; and Romuald Nowak of the National Museum in Wroclaw, Poland, which is home to the breathtaking *Raclawice Panorama*.

I must also acknowledge the help from Mariola Sigrist in the archives of the Polish Museum in Rapperswil, Switzerland, and Dr. J. A. Konopka of Geneva for providing me with facsimiles of Kosciuszko's letters from Soleure, Switzerland.

My warmest appreciation goes to several historians who have researched aspects of Kosciuszko's life and who proofread my manuscript and provided important feedback. They are: Professor James Pula of Purdue University; Professor and Colonel James Johnson, U.S. Army (Ret.), military historian of the Hudson River Valley National Heritage Area, and former chief of military history, U.S. Military Academy at West Point; Professor Izabella Rusinowa of the University of Warsaw, and Gary Nash of UCLA.

Writing history is like doing detective work, and hopefully future historians will uncover more evidence and documentation about the fascinating life and character of Thaddeus Kosciuszko.

Introduction

As a child growing up in Brooklyn and Queens, I often saw portraits of Pulaski and Kosciuszko at Polish army veterans' events where old warriors bemoaned Poland's oppression behind the Iron Curtain. My father fought with the Polish, French, and English armies during various World War II campaigns against the Germans and Russians before he was exiled from his homeland, so he made sure that I spoke Polish and learned the history of Poland. I heard about Kosciuszko in the American Revolution, his failed insurrection against czarist Russia, and his last will and testament, leaving his salary from the American Revolution to purchase and liberate black slaves.

I learned more about this hero of two worlds in 1985, when the Kosciuszko Foundation awarded me a scholarship to attend the Columbia University Graduate School of Journalism. The foundation's president, Joseph Gore, gave me two volumes by Miecislaus Haiman, published by the Polish Institute of Arts and Sciences in the 1940s, one of which reprinted Kosciuszko's last will, in which he told Thomas Jefferson that African slaves deserved freedom and to know "the duty of a citizen in a free government," and that they should be educated and "make themselves happy as possible."

I hiked around the hills of West Point, where George Washington ordered Kosciuszko to build forts; traveled to Kosciuszko's home in Philadelphia, where Thomas Jefferson visited him for discussions on politics and slavery; and went to Krakow, where Kosciuszko launched a revolution to free the peasants of Poland. I also visited Stockbridge, Massachusetts, to see the grave of Kosciuszko's black orderly, Agrippa Hull, and learned of an amusing story: When Hull secretly tried on Kosciuszko's Polish uniform and drank his wine, rather than flog him, which was customary at the time, Kosciuszko made Hull drink more alcohol until he got sick.

Knowing my obsession with Kosciuszko, my wife, Agnieszka, suggested that I write a book. But was there anything new to be found? To my surprise, other than Haiman's works the only biographies printed in the United States were Francis Kajencki's self-published *Thaddeus Kościuszko: Military Engineer of the American Revolution*, and James Pula's *Thaddeus Kościuszko: The Purest Son of Liberty,* published by a small ethnic press. Both are wonderful books that focus on Kosciuszko's career in America. Polish historians, on the other hand, uncovered little about Kosciuszko's life in America, but more surprisingly, they ignored important parts of his life in Poland. The most important book in Polish was *Kościuszko: Biografia z Dokumentów Wysnuta* (Kościuszko, A Biography Derived from Documents), by Tadeusz Korzon in 1894. With a foot in both worlds, I tried to bridge the works of American and Polish historians, while delving deeper into the original sources.

As a journalist rather than a historian, I have the benefit of interviewing live people rather than reading words of the deceased. But as I sifted through Kosciuszko's letters and the memoirs of people who knew him, it turned out that there was much that has not been known about Kosciuszko. Journalists have an inherent skepticism about the truthfulness of politicians and public figures, so I tried to figure out what historians were not telling me as I read their books along with the original sources, deciphering quotes, stories, and legends about Kosciuszko.

For starters Polish historians have claimed that Kosciuszko must have come to America with a letter of recommendation written by his mentor, Prince Czartoryski, to Gen. Charles Lee of the Continental Army. This is not true. I found an article from 1825 written by Kosciuszko's personal secretary, Jozef Pawlikowski, for a publication called the *Weteran Poznański*, The Poznan Veteran. Pawlikowski relayed the story that Kosciuszko told him about his first steps in Philadelphia, and his unannounced visit to Benjamin Franklin. It is a fascinating account that has been overlooked.

Another point historians have missed is that it was Kosciuszko's plans for West Point that Benedict Arnold tried to sell to the British in what remains the most infamous case of treason in U.S. history. Kosciuszko warned that the tallest hill at West Point, Rocky Point, was the fort's Achilles' heel, so he built Redoubt No. 4 on it to protect the other nearby forts. When Washington sent the Pole to fight in the Carolinas, Arnold ordered most of the men out of Redoubt No. 4 and told the British that this was the best route to sneak into the fort to capture it.

Kosciuszko's relationship with the Jews has also been ignored, which is surprising, because a Jewish horse salesman named Berek Joselewicz called

Kosciuszko a "messenger from God," and founded a Jewish cavalry in 1794 to fight alongside the Poles against czarist Russia. It was the first Jewish military unit since biblical times.

I have also found an incredible painting of Jean Lapierre, a black man who made his way to Poland in 1794 and was at Kosciuszko's side as he led a revolt to try to free white serfs who were enslaved by feudalism. As far as I know, this will be the first time the Lapierre painting is reproduced in any book.

Historical books are not always accurate when typeset from the original handwritten sources. Sometimes this was the fault of an innocent typo, but other times it was censorship for political reasons, or matters of discretion. For example, I found one historian who claimed that a letter by Kosciuszko warned a friend not to catch "a cold," when in fact Kosciuszko's original handwriting makes it clear that he warned his friend not to catch "the clap."

Sex is an important part of life, yet many historians avoid or diminish the relationships of historical figures, even when their romantic lives have a strong relevance to the subject matter. Poland and the United States were then religious countries, so these things were not talked about openly. But to understand Kosciuszko's era, it is crucial to know that Stanislaw Augustus Poniatowski became king of Poland by sleeping with Russian czarina Catherine the Great. It is also important to know that Prince Adam Jerzy Czartoryski was the illegitimate son of Russian ambassador Nikolai Repnin and Polish princess Isabella Czartoryski. The irony is that the offspring of this illicit affair became the biggest promoter of Polish interests in the Russian court and was a pivotal player in Kosciuszko's life. Casanova's lechery in Poland is relevant because it shows that in addition to having the fruits of their labor taken from them, peasants had the chastity and dignity of their wives and daughters taken as well.

My editor advised me to make sure that this book was not a hagiography, so I searched for Kosciuszko's shortcomings as well as his virtues. In his politics and respect for all people, however, it was tough to find blemishes on Kosciuszko's character. The deeper I delved into his words and actions, I began to feel that historians have missed the real man. He was obsessed with republicanism, or democracy as we call it today. But his deep sense of respect extended to all races, religions, classes, genders, and nationalities. His well-known will urging the freeing of black slaves was brilliant. But he also spoke up for peasants, Jews, American Indians, women, and everyone else who was being discriminated against. He was a true prince of tolerance.

But his personal life—with its failed love affairs, visits to a beautiful Greek prostitute, and rumors of adulterous liaisons with married women—demonstrates that he was a flawed individual like all of us. There were also rumors of his fathering a child out of wedlock. These rumors came from sources that knew him, so I mention them only in passing, without making a judgment on whether they are true. (Most likely there is no definitive answer, unless someone could trace the lineage and conduct DNA tests, as was the case with Thomas Jefferson and Sally Hemings.)

While Kosciuszko may have been a brilliant strategist on the battlefield, which allowed him to challenge much larger armies, his political tactics and unwillingness to compromise got in the way of his goals—a free Poland and liberty for all.

The Peasant Prince begins with Kosciuszko's attempt to elope with Ludwika (Louise) Sosnowska, which was interrupted by her father, Lord Sosnowski. This account comes from three men who knew Kosciuszko and spent time with him, including a Swiss writer, Karl Falkenstein, who interviewed Kosciuszko toward the end of his life. Polish historians have given various versions of this failed love affair, doubting Falkenstein, even though the Swiss writer interviewed Kosciuszko and the Zeltner family, whom he lived with in Soleure, Switzerland. While Falkenstein did make some mistakes, Polish historians have no problem quoting other parts of his book as fact.

There is evidence that Falkenstein was right about the elopement. Kosciuszko's close friend and confidant Julian Ursyn Niemcewicz also wrote that Kosciuszko tried to run away with Louise, as did Dr. James Thacher, who knew Kosciuszko at West Point. And in his biography of Kosciuszko, Korzon writes that Lord Sosnowski gave a man named Wojewodzki a house and land "for intervening in the elopement of Lady Louise and Kosciuszko."

Despite the fact that Kosciuszko's rejection as a suitor for the daughter of an aristocrat was the pivotal moment in his life, it has been completely underplayed by historians.

In the end, when forced to make a choice on which sources to give more credence, I chose the memoirs of people who knew Kosciuszko and witnessed him in action over those who wrote about him later.

A brief note on spelling: I use the English versions of Polish names because this book is aimed at English readers. Some Polish letters do not exist in English, so for the name Kołłątaj, I use Kollontay, a phonetic spelling found in British books about Poland. Two more examples are Wiridianna, which translates roughly as Vera-Diana, and Ludwika as Louise. These forms make the book more accessible to people who do not speak Polish.

ONE

Broken Hearts and Greek Role Models

THE HORSE BUGGY RACED OVER A BUMPY DIRT ROAD AS THE TWO passengers were jostled from side to side. It was a chilly autumn night, clouds hiding most of the stars, while the moonlight peeked through the dimness to expose a village in the distance. The couple wanted to find a priest who would marry them.[1]

Before the wagon reached town several horsemen galloped up and latched on to the steeds, dragging them to a stop at the side of the road. Twenty-nine-year-old Capt. Thaddeus Kosciuszko leaped to the ground from his seat at the reins and drew his sword, ready to fight. The talented alumnus of the king's royal military academy could have fought off the first two or three of Lord Sosnowski's rural guards.[2]

On the passenger side was Sosnowski's daughter Louise, who wanted to elope with the captain after her father arranged for her to marry Prince Lubomirski to forge a dynasty between two clans of rich land magnates. While her lover was also part of the landed gentry, his family estate was small and struggling, in part because the Kosciuszkos were much easier on the serfs who farmed their land. Feudalism served these children of the nobility well, but the idealistic pair opposed the bondage of peasants. Lord Sosnowski denied Kosciuszko's request for Louise's hand, saying, "Pigeons are not meant for sparrows and the daughters of magnates are not meant for the sons of the common gentry."[3]

As Kosciuszko held his sword between himself and Sosnowski's guards, he looked past its long blade and saw that the lord was among them. Rather than engage in a clash that could harm Louise's father before her eyes, he stood down.

When he slid the saber back into its sheath, the sentries attacked and knocked him unconscious.[4] They dragged Louise, kicking and screaming, back to the estate. When he came to several hours later, he found a white handkerchief that Louise had dropped in the scuffle. He stood up, stuffed the piece of linen into his pocket, and began the long walk home.[5]

Such was the legend of Kosciuszko's failed elopement with the love of his life. While historians question the circumstances of just how far the escape plan actually went, three men who knew Kosciuszko, from three different countries, wrote similar accounts of his attempt to run off with Louise.[6]

It was one of the first days of fall 1775, and the hats of peasants would have been visible through tall stalks of golden grains as their scythes swished back and forth through tall spires of grain swaying and bending over from the weight of the blond hulls that were ready to harvest. The blades made a rustling sound as they sliced through the slender shoots that tumbled to the ground. All around, vast fields of wheat, rye, and hops stretched as far as the eye could see across the flat *pole*, or prairie lands, from which Poland gets its name.

The greedy land barons of the eighteenth century got rich off the brawn and sweat of the peasants who toiled in these fertile plains. These lords established a plutocracy to elect a king, and dictated the terms of government to him and to the rest of society.

European serfdom was not as vicious as American slavery, but peasants were bought and sold with the land they tilled. Troublesome serfs were whipped and hanged if they tried to revolt. British colonies exploited slaves for tobacco, rice, indigo, sugar, and cotton, while Poland capitalized on serf labor to drive the grain trade. These vassals slogged away in the fields and lived in abject poverty, while the land magnates who abused them grew fat off the land. The peasants were subject to the whims of landowners such as Lord Sosnowski, who could beat them for infractions.[7]

This was the world into which Thaddeus Kosciuszko was born on February 12, 1746.[8] He grew up on a midsize estate where 31 peasant families worked the land that belonged to his family. His father, Ludwig Kosciuszko, was well off but not wealthy.[9]

Their comfortable wooden manor house had fireplaces and a tile stove where Kosciuszko's mother, Tekla, would serve a typical Sunday dinner (prepared by the servants) of pork chops and peas, chicken soup, or borscht and kielbasa, accompanied by a mead-honey wine and, on special occasions, coffee. The elder Kosciuszko was easier on his farmhands than most landlords and taught his sons, Joseph and Thaddeus, and his daughters, Anna and Catherine, that treating the peasants fairly and providing them with a greater share of the fruits of their labor would make them more productive.[10] Ludwig was a loving husband, father, and landlord who believed that all people were entitled to hope and happiness.

Thaddeus, the youngest child, was idealistic and took his father's philosophy to heart. He played with peasant children, sometimes leading them to his favorite perch, a huge boulder where he would squat and observe the world around him.[11] When he turned nine he was sent to the Catholic Piarist Fathers College at Lubieszow, near Pinsk.

There he followed a new syllabus set up by Father Stanislaw Konarski, the Piarist leader of a cadre of reformist priests who were revolutionizing Poland's school system. They instituted a curriculum that included lessons about British philosopher John Locke's theory of a social contract, in which the people of a nation consent to be governed in exchange for social order.[12] The Poles had already experimented with their own form of democracy, but Father Konarski's educational reforms were laying the groundwork for a political enlightenment in Poland.

Consumed by the Piarist teachings, Kosciuszko was fascinated by the ancient Greeks and the Roman Empire. The works of Tacitus, Plutarch, and Aristides engrossed him and he was riveted by a biography of Timoleon, the Greek statesman and general who freed his fellow Corinthians and the Sicilians from the tyranny of Carthage. Kosciuszko explained his hero worship saying, "He overthrew tyrants, set up republics and never demanded any power for himself."[13]

The quixotic student drew parallels between Timoleon's Greece and Poland's subjugation by czarist Russia, whose army was growing more assertive in controlling Polish affairs. He saw in Timoleon a lesson in freeing his own people from Russian domination. Kosciuszko realized early on that Europe's unjust class structure and agrarian economy allowed the rich to get richer by exploiting the peasants. To him the notion of happiness meant self-determination.

The modest Kosciuszko estate was in the Brest region of the Polish-Lithuanian Commonwealth, a confederation of two nations that united in the fifteenth century to defend themselves from foreign invaders, such as the German Roman Catholic order of the Teutonic Knights. In recent years it had been a kingdom in decline because of foreign meddling in legislative affairs.

While the Kosciuszkos were part of the well-heeled top ten percent of society known as the *szlachta*, there was also the top one percent, the upper echelon of land magnates made up of wealthy families that employed small armies to protect their dynasties. There were clans such as the Czartoryskis, known as *Familia*, "the Family," who had close ties with the Russians; the Potockis, who were allied with Saxony; and the Radziwills, who had long-standing connections to Lithuania.

The decentralized government and divisive alliances of the aristocrats destabilized Poland, creating a tumult in the Commonwealth. When the last king of the Jagiellonian dynasty died without an heir in the late sixteenth century, the magnates experimented with elections, creating a new system in which the nobility voted on the monarch.

The Polish lords chose a French prince, Henri de Valois, to be king, but they required him and future monarchs to sign the "Henrician Articles." These included a stipulation that the monarchy was not hereditary but elected, and that the king must call a session of the legislature, the Seym, every two years. The king could not declare war or collect taxes without approval of the Seym, and was bound by the Articles of Agreement, in which he promised to abide by his campaign promises.[14]

This libertarian system hailed its "Golden Freedoms," such as freedom of religion, which could not be taken away by the king. While most Poles were Catholics, Eastern Orthodox, Protestants, Jews, and Muslims were also free to build churches, synagogues, and mosques and worship as they pleased. Poland's kings provided sanctuary to Jews who were persecuted elsewhere and stopped priests who wanted to convert them to Christianity. As a result Jews flocked to Poland and formed the core of the merchant class. While Jews were not allowed to own land, they could lease it and own businesses. They ran the royal treasury and the mint and helped establish the banking system. Some early coins had names of Polish princes etched in Hebrew lettering or engraved names of Jewish minters, such as Abraham, son of Isaac Nagid.[15] The Catholic magnates used the Jewish bankers and traders to compound their wealth and create an export system that turned Poland into the breadbasket of Europe. While this allowed Jewish culture to thrive, the lords also gave the Jews the unpopular tasks of collecting taxes, tariffs, and interest on loans, helping the magnates to camouflage their exploitation of the serfs.[16]

This multicultural society was protected by the Hussar Knights, master horsemen whose spooky armor gave them a supernatural appearance that struck fear into the hearts of their enemies and earned them the appellation "Winged Hussars." Attached to the back of their metal vests were wings made of wooden frames covered with eagle, crane, or ostrich feathers. They draped pelts of leopards, tigers, bears, or wolves over their chest plates, and wore steel and brass helmets. The Hussar cavalries stretched the Polish-Lithuanian Commonwealth's borders from the Baltic to the Black Sea.

The country had a small Muslim population of Asian Tatars, who initially arrived as invaders, starting in the fourteenth century. These nomadic horsemen, descended from the Mongol army of Genghis Khan, drank horse milk mixed with blood and ate raw meat that they kept under their saddles to cushion their ride and tenderize their steaks. The Hussars defeated the Tatar warriors, and some of the vanquished were allowed to settle in Poland, where they freely practiced their Sunni religion.[17]

The Winged Hussars once again faced the Muslims in the late seventeenth century, when the Ottoman Empire swallowed Greece, the Balkans, Hungary, and much of Austria. The Turkish Grand Vizier Kara Mustafa Pasha and his army surrounded Vienna and were on the verge of capturing the Danube River, the commercial gateway to Europe. With the Muslims on their doorstep, the German-speaking kingdoms, Austria and Prussia, pleaded with King John Sobieski to send the hussars to repel the marauding army.

Sobieski's hussars led an army that routed the Turks in the Battle of Vienna in 1683. He was hailed as the savior of Europe who rescued the Christians from Muslim invaders. But after Sobieski's death in 1696, Poland's influence began to dwindle. In the election for king after his demise, three candidates emerged: Sobieski's son Jacob, French prince François Louis, and Friedrich Augustus Wettin of Dresden. Augustus did not win the election but rushed to Poland and, with the support of Austria and Russia, declared himself king, establishing a Saxon dynasty.

Rather than challenge the status quo, the land magnates made perfidious deals and took bribes from foreign agents who meddled in Polish affairs. The result was bedlam, and the gluttonous oligarchs ushered in a period of decadence with the slogan, "Under the Saxon king, eat, drink, and loosen your belt."[18]

While the Saxons carted Poland's treasury back to Dresden, the mutual distrust among the Polish nobles in the Seym led to the creation of a parliamentary procedure called the *liberum veto*. This unitary veto allowed a single representative to block any legislation unless there was unanimous consent. This pleased foreign powers who wanted to tie up the legislature with gridlock.[19]

In this era of chaos Kosciuszko's life would be influenced greatly by the exploits of a young Polish count who set out abroad in the 1750s in search of adventure. Stanislaw Augustus Poniatowski, the son of a Krakow nobleman and a daughter of the Czartoryski *Familia*, spent years studying in Berlin, Vienna, Paris, and London before arriving in St. Petersburg, where he became secretary to the British ambassador, Sir Charles Hanbury-Williams. The charming count quoted Shakespeare and became a popular figure on the social circuit in the Russian capital.

One night as he twirled across the dance floor during a party, Poniatowski caught the eye of the German-born Grand Duchess Sophia Augusta Frederica.[20] Sophia had been delivered to the royal court to marry the naive and immature heir to the Russian throne, Duke Peter III. Both remained virgins during the first years of the marriage, until the duchess erupted like a sexual volcano bursting through a chain of steamy affairs with paramours discreetly known as her "favorites" in the royal court.

The Chevalier d'Eon, a cross-dressing spy sent by French king Louis XV to keep tabs on the Russian court, wrote: "The Grand Duchess is romantic, ardent, passionate; her eyes like those of a wild beast. Her brow is high; and, if I mistake not, there is a long and awful future on that brow. She is kind and affable, but when she comes near me, I draw back with a movement, which I cannot control. She frightens me."[21]

Another observation likened the grand duchess to a predator with a gaze that was "fixed and glassy, like that of a wild beast tracking down its prey."[22]

Hanbury-Williams noticed that Sophia lusted after his blond and hazel-eyed assistant and became a matchmaker to advance Great Britain's interests.

On a frigid December night in 1755, the Polish count left his apartment and was picked up by Lev Naryshkin, the gentleman of the royal bedchamber, who whisked Poniatowski through the snow on a sleigh to the side entrance of the Winter Palace, and escorted him past the guards for a secret rendezvous.[23] The twenty-six-year-old duchess was tall and thin, with black hair, a porcelain complexion, and pinkish cheeks. She complained that the harsh Russian winters numbed her body and turned her face "blue as a plum."[24] Yet underneath this delicate exterior was a red-hot sexual being.

Sophia's confidant Naryshkin would signal by meowing like a cat outside her bedroom door, waiting for her whispered reply when the coast was clear. The twenty-three-year-old Poniatowski was led into the royal chambers, shivering at the thought of exile in a frozen Russian prison if he was caught. Poniatowski recalled in his memoirs that the sight of Sophia in a simple white gown trimmed with lace and pink ribbons was so enticing as to "make one forget the very existence of Siberia."[25]

Poniatowski spent many nights dressed incognito, tiptoeing through the corridors of St. Petersburg's Winter Palace on his way to and from secret trysts with the grand duchess. Sophia wrote in her memoirs, "Count Poniatowski always put on a blonde wig and a cloak before leaving my room and when the sentries asked him: 'Who goes there?' he replied: 'The Grand Duke's musician.' "[26]

He visited Sophia's chambers so often that her dog betrayed their relationship to a visitor who noticed that the pet greeted Poniatowski. Poniatowski's friend, the Swedish count Horn, told him, "My friend, there is no worse traitor than a little Bolognese dog. The first thing I always did with the women I loved was give them one, and it was from these dogs that I always knew if there was someone more favored than I. The dog wanted to eat me, whom it did not know; where as it only rejoiced when it saw you again, surely this is not the first time it has seen you here."[27]

Poniatowski fell head over heels in love with Sophia, writing in his memoirs that her "eyes were bluest and merriest in the world, subjugating all who came within her orbit," she had "a mouth that seemed to beg to be kissed."[28]

The affair was one of the most political sexual liaisons in history. After a trip home Poniatowski returned to Russia as "ambassador" of the Polish-Lithuanian

Commonwealth. The count continued his dalliance with the grand duchess, and wrote, "Such was the mistress who would become the arbiter of my destiny."[29]

Poland's destiny was also determined between the sheets warmed by these political bedfellows. Eventually the dissolute duchess grew tired of Poniatowski, and he returned to Poland. She continued hiding her liaisons until Duke Peter became czar. The new monarch grew tired of his wife, but was assassinated in a coup staged by her supporters, who installed her as czarina. She became known as Catherine the Great and no longer lurked in the shadows with her love affairs.

Catherine continued the expansion of Russia begun years earlier by Ivan the Terrible. One month after ascending to the throne, she wrote to Poniatowski, "I am sending at once Count Keyserling as Ambassador to Poland to declare you king after the death of the present monarch."[30]

By the time the last Wettin king died in 1764, the Poles were fed up with foreign intervention. The oligarchs agreed to restore a Pole to the throne. The leading candidate was Poniatowski's maternal cousin, Prince Adam Casimir Czartoryski, a Renaissance man who studied eighteen languages and traveled throughout Europe conducting research in the sciences, literature, history, politics, military history, and the arts. But the prince was reluctant to wear the crown, preferring to occupy himself with intellectual pursuits. Eventually Kosciuszko would be caught up in the politics between Poniatowski and Prince Czartoryski.

In a twisted web of intrigue, Catherine conspired with the Polish aristocrats to prop her infatuated lover on the throne in Warsaw so that she could pull his strings from the Winter Palace in St. Petersburg. To ensure that the election went her way, Catherine sent sixty thousand troops into the woods surrounding the fields outside Warsaw, where the wealthy landowners gathered to choose their king. With Russian soldiers watching, the Poles elected Poniatowski king. He would rule as Stanislaw Augustus.

The czarina sent another of her "favorites," Prince Nikolai Repnin, to Warsaw as her ambassador to keep an eye on Stanislaw. But from his lofty perch the new king did not dance on the marionette strings as well as Catherine had hoped, especially after she made it clear that their love affair was over. Pining for the czarina, the jilted king went on a sex spree through the salons of Warsaw, making sure that his bed was never cold. The Polish capital became a lascivious party town under Stanislaw, and the promiscuous king lived out his fantasies, setting up chambers in his palace and nearby residences for various ladies of the nobility, actresses, and women of lesser prominence.[31]

The game of rotating bedfellows took a strange turn when Prince Czartoryski, busy with his own affairs, drove his wife, Princess Isabella, into the arms of the king. Using Catherine the Great's bedroom tactics, Stanislaw treated members of the opposite sex as pawns. He encouraged Princess Isabella to seduce

Minister Repnin and to whisper pillow talk into his ear that would help persuade the czarina to allow Poland to change its laws and expand its military. The patriotic princess did it for her country.

The king was not the only Pole to go through a sexual awakening as the libertine era heated up Europe and French literature and tales of *l'amour* and erotic theater gained popularity in Warsaw.[32] The elite held risqué costume balls and salacious carnivals in the Saxon Gardens near the royal castle that lured the legendary Venetian lothario Giacomo Casanova to carouse Warsaw's racy nightlife with the Polish king. In his memoirs Casanova wrote, "The carnival was a brilliant one. All Europe seemed to have assembled at Warsaw to see the happy being whom fortune had so unexpectedly raised to a throne."[33]

The infamous playboy had a grand time in Poland and took advantage of all the cold and brutal practices that feudal society had to offer. Impoverished serfs had to slave away in the fields, but they also suffered indignities for their families. The loathsome *droit de seigneur*, the lord's right to deflower virgins, was still common practice in Europe. Visiting one of the Czartoryski palaces, Casanova wrote, "A peasant girl who came into my room pleased me, and she ran away crying out one morning when I tried to do something with her."[34]

The caretaker came running to check on the commotion and told Casanova to go about it in "the straightforward way." When Casanova asked what he meant by "the straightforward way," the caretaker replied, "Talk to her father, who is here, and ask him amicably if he will sell you her maidenhead."

The go-between suggested a price of fifty florins, to which Casanova replied, "You are jesting. If she is a maiden, and gentle as a lamb, I will give him a hundred."

Casanova paid the peasant girl's father the fee, but the would-be sex slave was not willing to succumb to the oppression forced on her and "ran away like a thief."

In addition to satisfying the carnal desires of his court, Stanislaw invested in universities and invited foreign artists and scholars to Warsaw to stimulate a renaissance in Poland. Italian painters such as Marcello Bacciarelli and Canaletto's nephew, Bernardo Bellotto, filled canvases with scenes of Warsaw's castles and churches.

The king, longing to restore the glory of the Hussar Knights, established a military academy known as the Knights' School to educate and instill chivalry and patriotism in a new generation of officers. Stanislaw chose his cousin Prince Czartoryski to develop a curriculum and head the new military academy, which was the perfect job for the erudite Czartoryski. The king and the prince began a nationwide search for intelligent and patriotic cadets for their new academy.

When word spread that Poland had opened a new military academy, another colorful character to show up in Warsaw was British colonel Charles Lee. Lee was a restless British officer who lived in the American colonies where he fought in the French and Indian War, the American theater of the Seven Years' War. He was adopted by the Mohawk tribe and married the daughter of a Seneca chief and was dubbed *Ounewaterika*, meaning "boiling water," or "the spirit that never sleeps."[35]

Upon returning to London, Lee was denied his petition to become a general in the British army, so he sought greater experience by obtaining a post in the Polish army. The Poles were in no position to expand their military, so Lee agreed to serve as Stanislaw's aide-de-camp. Starting in 1764, he served for several years in the royal court in Warsaw. Lee was given a seat at the king's table and an apartment in Prince Czartoryski's palace. The English officer was so taken by Stanislaw that he wrote home asking that his prized possession, a sword once owned by Oliver Cromwell, be delivered to Warsaw so he could present it to the king as a gift.[36]

When Lee returned to London, King George III still deemed his foreign experience and social status insufficient to merit promotion in the British army. So before the outbreak of the American Revolution, the disappointed Lee again sailed for the colonies, where he enlisted in the Continental Army and was finally commissioned as a general.

Like Lee, King Stanislaw was also upset about the chain of command that forced his hand. Outwardly it appeared as though the king was in charge, but in reality he was trapped between Poland's wealthy land magnates, the Catholic Church, idealistic political reformers, and the Russian agent in Warsaw, Prince Repnin, who was calling the shots.

While the richest nobles were living it up in Warsaw, the rest of the nation was floundering. The Kosciuszkos were among those who struggled financially. Originally of Lithuanian-Ruthenian stock, their tongue-twisting name came from "Konstanty [Constantine] son of Teodora," and evolved into *Kost-iuszko*, the diminutive of "small bone." They spoke Polish and identified with Poland's culture to earn acceptance by the nobility, becoming so patriotic that in 1509 the Polish monarch presented them with an official coat of arms, dubbing them the Roch clan and later granting them the villages of Mereczowszczyzna and Siechnowicze.[37]

Ludwig Kosciuszko had the ceremonial rank of colonel and the title "Swordbearer of Brest."[38] But by the mid-eighteenth century the Hussar Knights were merely a memory of Poland's former glory, and much like the historical war reenactments of modern times, on holidays the Polish nobles would dust off the Hussar armor and weapons in museums and dress up and parade around.[39] These reenactors and their woebegone celebrations of the nation's military heritage stirred the imagination of Thaddeus Kosciuszko, who dreamed of joining the military.

After his father's death the family's financial difficulties forced Kosciuszko to leave the Piarist school and his studies of ancient Greece, to return to the family estate for homeschooling.

Kosciuszko's mother, Tekla Ratomska, ran the homestead after the death of her husband. She managed the work of the peasants on the Kosciuszko estate, which was spread out across several hamlets, and had to ensure the peasants made optimal use of the numerous plows and farming tools to get the most out of the plantation's fruit orchards, vegetable gardens, wheat fields, bakery, brewery, malthouse, grain silos, dairy, cheese-making cribs, chicken coops, pigsties, and barns stocked with horses and cows.[40]

As her elder son would receive the largest inheritance, Tekla made sure her younger son kept up his studies with an uncle and a priest who was a friend of the family. Kosciuszko excelled in geometry and in drawing, and his artistic talents were noticed early on by the priests in his school.

Kosciuszko was eighteen when Stanislaw Augustus Poniatowski became king of Poland. He lived far from the excitement of the Polish capital, but got the chance of a lifetime when he learned that Prince Czartoryski was looking for talented recruits for the Royal Knight School. The priests and local noblemen recommended Kosciuszko, and Prince Czartoryski arranged for a scholarship to send him to Warsaw, where he enrolled in the military academy's inaugural class.

The cosmopolitan Czartoryski used his foreign contacts to recruit talented scholars to teach at the academy, such as the famous barrister from Oxford, John Lind, the French military tactician Le Roy de Bosroger, and Prussian military experts Friedrich Gunther, and Antoni Leopold Oelsnitz. Oelsnitz lectured on the ancient treatise of Roman warfare written by Flavius Vegetius Renatus during the waning days of the Roman Empire. It was a manual for military training, logistics, and supply lines.

And while two centuries earlier the Catholic Church had denounced as heresy the heliocentric theory developed in Poland by astronomer Nicolaus Copernicus, Czartoryski pushed for more scientific research by purchasing a "planetary machine" in Britain that showed how the planets orbit around the sun.[41]

Kosciuszko was so eager to get a jump on his studies that before going to bed he tied a string to his hand, leaving the other end out in the hallway. He asked the night watchman to tug on it to wake him at 3:00 a.m. during his rounds to stoke the furnaces.[42] In addition to learning about fort construction and topography, his classes included practical geography for mapmaking, trigonometry, drawing, and engineering.

The ambitious student dedicated his mind and body to becoming a Sobieski-type Hussar Knight. He aggressively practiced swordsmanship with his classmates, sometimes even drawing blood. Although he was one of the most physical students at the academy, rather than bullying the weaker students, he became one of the most popular cadets because he was unpretentious and likable. He studied with equal gusto. One lesson was about Swedish king Charles XII, the savvy tactician whose success fighting the Russian troops of Peter the Great made him a popular role model for the officer corps. Kosciuszko's physical endurance and identification with the Scandinavian leader earned him the nickname "the Swede" among the cadets.[43]

When a pompous governor from one of the provinces insulted a cadet at a reception in Warsaw, it was "the Swede" who was chosen by his school chums to visit the royal castle and restore their honor by informing the king of the slight. Kosciuszko was so persuasive that the king ordered the arrogant official to apologize to his cadets. King Stanislaw was impressed with Kosciuszko and invited him to visit the castle periodically to provide progress reports about the new school.

After Kosciuszko's visit to the royal palace, the king had a greater interest in the academy. These future military leaders had their intellectual, spiritual, and physical needs catered to at the academy, and in the libertine atmosphere of the era of Stanislaw Augustus, this included allowing them to fulfill their erotic desires. Prostitution was rampant in the capital, and with the blatant sexuality exhibited in the arts, the cadets had a good time, often attending the same bawdy banquets as the noble class.[44]

While the king's public persona was that of a playboy who was loyal to Catherine the Great, behind the scenes he was trying to build an infrastructure to challenge Russia's dominance. But with the czarina's ambassador-provocateur, Prince Repnin, breathing down his neck, Stanislaw had to show discretion.

Several of the noble families did not see the patriotic side of Stanislaw, however, viewing him as a mere puppet of the Russian czarina. On February 29, 1768, they met in southern Poland in a town called Bar, where they established a confederate government. The Bar confederates were led by Joseph Pulaski, a nobleman whose son, Casimir, led a cavalry in several successful skirmishes against the Russians, taking control of several Polish provinces in the South.

French king Louis XV sent a spy, Charles François Dumouriez, to Poland to help the Bar confederates, and Austria allowed the rebels use of its territory. King Stanislaw was sympathetic with issues raised by the confederates and considered making peace, or even joining them, until Dumouriez denounced him as a tyrant and a traitor.[45]

A civil war erupted, and Poles were forced to take sides. Kosciuszko had worked his way up to lieutenant and was employed at the academy as an instructor, which led to a promotion to captain of the artillery because of his mathematical skills and ability to project accurately the range and line of fire for cannons.

When fighting broke out Kosciuszko had the difficult choice of joining Pulaski's confederates, who wanted to overthrow the king and drive out the Russians, or supporting his patrons, the monarch and the Czartoryski family, who favored a gradual strategy of shaking off Russian domination. In either scenario he would fight his own countrymen in a lost cause. Believing that the king had Poland's best interests at heart, Kosciuszko and his friend Capt. Joseph Orlowski avoided the cross fire between Poles by taking advantage of a scholarship for advanced studies in Paris.

In the autumn of 1769 Kosciuszko and Orlowski arrived in Paris, where they checked in to the Hotel Luxembourg and enrolled at the Royal Academy of Painting and Sculpture. Their real goal was to acquire military expertise, but as foreigners they could not officially attend the École Militaire or the military engineering academy at Mézières, so they tracked down professors from the military schools to tutor them privately.

Kosciuszko learned the war strategies of Marshal Sébastien le Prestre de Vauban, Europe's foremost authority on building and besieging forts. He studied architecture with Jean-Rodolphe Perronet, the civil engineer who had built the most beautiful bridges, roads, and buildings in Paris.[46] When not in class Kosciuszko spent time in cafés swilling coffee and soaking up the political ideas that were brewing before the French Revolution.[47] He read Montesquieu, Voltaire, and Jean-Jacques Rousseau, whose idea of a social contract between government and the people especially influenced him.

But the biggest impact on his life was that of a new philosophy called physiocracy, developed by the economist François Quesnay. Physiocrats held that land was the only true source of wealth, and agriculture the key to prosperity. They believed that only those who owned or leased land should be taxed. They opposed forced labor for serfs and argued that peasants should be able to migrate to find work. They advocated a natural law under which government took a hands-off, laissez-faire approach to economics. They opposed taxes on farmers and their harvest and argued that free markets would bring individual liberty and economic security. Physiocracy had major implications for Poland because it would essentially end feudalism.[48]

While becoming more cosmopolitan, Kosciuszko never forgot that his real mission was to soak up as much engineering knowledge as the French could offer. "As it pertains to soldiering, as your highness has advised," Kosciuszko wrote to Prince Czartoryski from Paris, he was studying French "construction of bridges, flood gates, roads, dams, canals, etc."[49]

After his schooling in Paris, Kosciuszko traveled to Holland to learn how the Dutch built dikes so he could help solve the water management issues of the swamps and marshlands in Poland. He also visited England, Switzerland, Saxony, and the ruins of ancient Rome before heading home. This added perspective convinced him that his political idealism was well founded. Many years later he said of his early travels, "Throughout my five years in foreign lands I studied in order to become proficient in economics and military matters, for which things I had a native passion, so as to discover what was necessary to attain durable government and the due happiness of all."[50]

During Kosciuszko's absence from Poland one of the Bar confederates hatched an ill-advised plot to kidnap King Stanislaw and force him to join the fight against Russia. At first Pulaski opposed the plan but changed his mind once he was assured that the king would not be harmed. The rebels hijacked the king's carriage and took him into custody. But before they could move him to a safe place, Stanislaw escaped.

Rumors spread that Pulaski had tried to assassinate the king, and he was convicted in absentia of regicide. A Polish court ruled that the crime was so heinous that if Pulaski was caught, his head was to be chopped off and his body quartered, burned, and the ashes thrown to the winds.

Russia and its Polish puppets crushed the Bar Rebellion, but news of the botched kidnapping sent shivers down the spine of monarchs across Europe. Poland's neighbors took advantage of its internal strife. On February 19, 1772, meeting in Vienna—the city Sobieski's knights had rescued from the Ottoman Empire—Russia, Prussia, and Austria each signed a pact to carve out a piece of the commonwealth's territory for themselves. In August the armies of these nations attacked the Commonwealth from all sides, and each annexed a piece of its land. Poland, weakened by civil war, was in no position to resist. It was the first of three partitions in which Poland would be attacked by its neighbors.

Stanislaw reached out for help to Britain's King George III, who replied, "Misfortunes have reached the point where redress can be had from the hand of the Almighty alone, and I see no other intervention that can afford a remedy."[51] A similar call for help to France's King Louis XV was completely ignored, as the French aristocrats ironically refused to help what they called "a country of nobles."[52]

By the time Kosciuszko returned to Poland in 1774, his two sisters had married and his brother, Joseph, had squandered the inheritance from their parents and mortgaged much of the estate. Frustrated that his knowledge from abroad could not be put to service for his country because officer commissions in the shrinking army had to be purchased, Kosciuszko searched for another career, migrating between the homes of his sisters and his uncle. On occasion he traveled to Warsaw to see his friends. One evening he joined his fellow graduates and the students of the Knights' School, who were invited to a formal ball in honor of the king given by Count Zamoyski. It was there that Kosciuszko met the love of his life.

Louise Sosnowska was not the prettiest belle at the ball, but she was the brightest. A gleaming light of awareness beamed from her big round eyes, and she had an intellect well beyond her years. Kosciuszko, who met many women during his travels in Europe, was drawn to her sharp mind. Louise was the daughter of Joseph Sosnowski, one of the richest noblemen in Kosciuszko's region. With the Slavic title "hetman," Lord Sosnowski was chieftain of the district. Years earlier Sosnowski had been one of those who recommended Kosciuszko as a candidate for the new military academy.[53]

Lord Sosnowski once again helped Kosciuszko by hiring him as a tutor for his daughters, Catherine and Louise. The twenty-nine-year-old captain spent several hours each day giving the hetman's girls lessons in history, mathematics, and art. The teacher grew enchanted with Louise, and the two souls developed a strong intellectual bond. As Kosciuszko proudly lectured Louise and her sister about what he had learned in France, including Quesnay's theories, he was stunned to learn that they had been the first to translate a book by Quesnay about physiocracy and agricultural reform from French into Polish.[54]

Louise and Kosciuszko were kindred spirits. The passion beating in his chest for the rights of the peasants melded into romantic love for Louise as he discovered that the worldviews of the hetman's feisty daughter were similar to his own. The tutoring sessions grew longer each day, and the two Francophiles shared their secrets during flirtatious strolls through the willowy gardens of the Sosnowski estate. The young people on the homestead knew of the budding romance and covered for the two lovers whenever they sneaked off through the hedges to be alone.

Kosciuszko's heart ached to ask the nobleman for his daughter's hand, but after conversations with Louise's mother, he realized that his financial situation did not make him an attractive suitor. Looking for support in his amorous endeavor, he rode to the Czartoryski palace in Pulawy for an urgent meeting with his benefactor, the prince.

The prince welcomed Kosciuszko, who explained the predicament. The passionate officer confessed that he was considering abducting Louise to take her away from her father. Czartoryski detailed the politics of marriage among the noble classes and suggested that Kosciuszko take his case to King Stanislaw, whom he considered an expert in these matters. Czartoryski vowed that whatever the outcome, he would support his infatuated protégé.[55]

Seeking the king's blessing, Kosciuszko raced to Warsaw, where the former star cadet obtained an audience in the royal castle. Stanislaw, remembering his own disastrous affair with the czarina, advised the young captain to dismiss his silly romantic notions. The king explained that he could not offer a captain protection against the wishes of a powerful nobleman. Kosciuszko bowed his head as the king expressed his disapproval.

The sullen Kosciuszko left the castle to visit his compatriots at the military academy. In the familiar circle of his school friends, he found the reassurance he was looking for and plotted his elopement with Louise. One of the younger students at the knight's school who saw Kosciuszko when he came to visit was Julian Ursyn Niemcewicz. "He came to the military academy to visit his old pals," Niemcewicz wrote. "He had big eyes, a pleasant build, but a melancholy and pale face, with a black ribbon tying a thick braid of natural hair into a pony tail."[56]

Years later Niemcewicz became one of his nation's most prolific writers and one of Kosciuszko's closest confidants. But on that day it was Kosciuszko's fellow alumnus of the academy's inaugural class who helped him concoct an elaborate plan to find a comfortable carriage, fast horses, a priest willing to marry them, and ways to cover their tracks and find safe houses in which to hide in the forests and mountains. But the former cadets were so indiscreet in their conniving that rumors of Kosciuszko's intentions made their way back to the king. Upset that his cadet had not listened to his advice, King Stanislaw warned Lord Sosnowski, who had his own plans.[57] Sosnowski wanted his offspring to climb up the social ladder, not take a step down.

The opportunity presented itself when he added more acres to his huge estate by winning a card game with Prince Stanislaw Lubomirski. Frustrated by the gambling debt, Lubomirski suggested that if Louise married his son, Prince Joseph, the vast expanse of countryside would be kept in the family. A deal was struck.[58] There would be no more talk of physiocracy on the Sosnowski estate.

Competing with a wealthy prince, Kosciuszko could not have timed things worse. Sosnowski's comparison of pigeons and sparrows to gentry and land magnates was his way of giving Kosciuszko a lesson in society's pecking order.

Once the dust had cleared after the failed elopement, Sosnowski turned the whole affair into a matter of honor and sought revenge against the captain whom he had welcomed into his home and entrusted with the education of his daughters. The painful reality of class distinction grew even harsher once Kosciuszko realized that he had not only lost the love of his life but also faced the loss of his life: Lord Sosnowski wanted him dead.

Lord Sosnowski confined Louise to a convent to prepare for her wedding and wanted to prosecute the romantic scoundrel for the abduction. As the most powerful land magnate in the area, Sosnowski could have prosecuted Kosciuszko for ravishing his daughter.[59] The outraged hetman was so influential and vengeful that Kosciuszko, broke and broken hearted, was forced to flee his homeland.

In October 1775 he got his affairs in order. He borrowed 8,820 zlotys from his brothers-in-law, Peter Estko and Karol Zolkowski, and an uncle, Faustyn Kosciuszko. He gave his beloved sister Anna and her husband, Peter, power of attorney to handle his affairs while he was away. Kosciuszko tracked down Prince Czartoryski, who was staying in the village of Slawatycze on the Bug River, and told his mentor that he was setting out on a quest for glory. He did not want to leave his homeland forever, and planned his absence from Poland to last varying periods of time. The first option was to find work in the Saxon court of Dresden, which was acquainted with Polish affairs. The second was to apply for a position in France's military. It's not clear how well he planned his third option, sailing to America. Some historians have speculated that Kosciuszko would not have sailed across the Atlantic without a letter of introduction from Prince Czartoryski. But as the judgment of the lovelorn is often blurred, no one knows what this hopeless romantic was truly thinking.

During their visit in the hamlet of Slawatycze, Prince Czartoryski gave his protégé five hundred ducats for traveling expenses. Czartoryski's stable master, Jerzy Soroka, witnessed the meeting and recalled in his memoirs that Kosciuszko said that in America "[I will] either distinguish myself, or end my misery." Kosciuszko wanted to travel to America because "Pulaski and many other Poles are already there."[60] But Casimir Pulaski had not yet crossed the Atlantic. A wanted outlaw with a price on his head, unwelcome in the monarchies of Europe, he was secretly hiding in France. Kosciuszko did not know this and believed that the Bar confederate who had fled the country three years earlier was already in the American colonies.

During their meeting in Slawatycze, Czartoryski may have suggested that his protégé look up his friend Charles Lee if he made it to America.[61]

On October 19, 1775, as Kosciuszko prepared to leave for Dresden, he wrote a letter to the nobleman Jerzy Wandalin Mniszech, in which he said, that his main goal, "Is to some day be of service to our country and to pay her back with the obligations of citizenship, but currently in Poland, even though I am so inclined, I can not find a way to offer her any happiness."[62]

The word "happiness" frequently appeared in Kosciuszko's letters. To him happiness and freedom went hand in hand. His growing opposition to feudalism, and the impact of Lord Sosnowski's class bias against him, made Kosciuszko even more attuned to tolerance. The affair with Louise Sosnowska had a clear effect on his psyche, and for the rest of his life he was drawn to the underprivileged, as well as those who were willing to help them. As he began his journey Kosciuszko hoped to find liked-minded people whose rhetoric matched the ideals to which he was drawn.

Kosciuszko did not find what he was looking for in Saxony, and by December he returned to Paris to look up friends from his university days. The French capital was abuzz over the rebellion against Britain in the thirteen colonies, and Kosciuszko spent time in the cafés and salons of Paris searching for the right opportunity to which to devote his skills. The story of the Boston Tea Party in 1774 was already known in Europe, and the latest news was of the "shot heard round the world" fired by the Massachusetts minutemen on the British at the battles of Lexington and Concord in April 1775. The French were openly giddy over the misfortunes of their greatest enemy, England.

Banging the drum for the French to support the Americans was the multitalented Pierre Augustin Caron de Beaumarchais, a writer, musician, inventor, watchmaker, publisher, revolutionary, and would-be spy. His plays *The Barber of Seville* and *The Marriage of Figaro,* would be turned into operas, and his revolutionary polemics were shaking up Paris. Beaumarchais wrote daring letters to the French foreign minister, Charles Gravier, Comte de Vergennes goading King Louis XVI into taking a moral stand in world affairs.

Beaumarchais boldly criticized Louis XVI for not opposing slavery in the new world, or the land grab by Poland's neighbors: "How can you allow your vessels [*sic*] to take by force and bind suffering black men whom nature made free and who are only miserable because you are powerful? How can you suffer three rival powers to seize iniquitously upon and divide Poland under your very eyes?"[63]

These issues resonated with the Polish engineer, and he enlisted in the effort to assist the Americans. Kosciuszko was not the only Pole in Paris, as many of the Bar confederates who fled Poland after the failed civil war had also sought refuge in the French capital. (Pulaski, however, was nowhere to be found because the French police in Marseille had thrown him into debtor's prison.)

Kosciuszko may have met Beaumarchais through Princess Maria Sanguszko, who moved to Paris after divorcing an influential member of the Potocki clan in Poland.[64] An incandescent beauty, Sanguszko was drawn to freethinking artists and mercenaries, and orbited in the same social circles as Kosciuszko. Elegant and graceful, the articulate princess was a shining star in the salons of Europe, where she mingled with nobles, intellectuals, and artists.[65]

Through the friends he made while studying in Paris, Kosciuszko found the opportunity he was looking for. The American colonists were reaching out to England's adversaries, and a Virginia diplomat, Arthur Lee, wrote to Beaumarchais pleading, "We need arms, powder and above all engineers."[66]

After receiving this request Beaumarchais again wrote to the king's foreign minister: "The Americans are in as good a situation as they can be. Army, fleet, food supplies, courage—everything is excellent. But without gunpowder and without engineers, how can they be victorious or even defend themselves? Are we going to let them perish rather than lend them one or two millions?"[67]

The appeal worked. On June 10, 1776, the French government loaned Beaumarchais one million livres to create a shell corporation under the alias Roderigue Hortalez & Co.[68] Its mission was to smuggle weapons and ammunition to the Americans. Spain secretly matched that amount, and by the end of June, Kosciuszko was on a ship sailing across the Atlantic with the Frenchman Charles

Noel Romand, Sieur de Lisle, and Nicolas Dietrich, Baron von Ottendorf, a nobleman from Saxony.

These were but the first foreign officers that Beaumarchais' shell corporation sent to the new world. The same month the American diplomat and secret agent Silas Deane arrived in France to buy cannons, muskets, and tents to supply the Continental Army. Deane and Beaumarchais would establish a covert operation to send more Frenchmen to aid America's Continental Army.

TWO

~~~⟡~~~

A Rebel Joins the Cause

THE BRITISH BLOCKADE OF AMERICAN PORTS FORCED THE clandestine ship carrying European mercenaries to sail south through the Caribbean islands for the French colony of Saint Domingue, which later became Haiti. The schooner bearing Kosciuszko and the other foreign fighters set sail from Le Havre toward the warm waters of the Caribbean in June 1776, right at the beginning of hurricane season.

The ship was being tossed about on the waves when America's Founding Fathers signed the Declaration of Independence. The long voyage across the choppy waters of the Atlantic took a heavy toll on the sailing vessel, and after two months on the high seas it was blown off course by a tropical storm and smashed on the coral reefs near the coast of the island of Martinique.

The following year, on April 16, 1777, the Polish newspaper *Nowiny* published an account of the wreck as relayed by Kosciuszko in a letter to Prince Czartoryski. Kosciuszko and five other Poles—former Bar confederates—planning to enlist in the American army rescued themselves from the powerful Gulf Stream currents by clutching the ship's mast and kicking to shore.[1]

The bustling slave trade in the French Caribbean colonies gave Kosciuszko his first exposure to the horrors suffered by Africans, who were kidnapped from their villages, dragged onto ships in shackles, and auctioned off as slave laborers in the new world. After a brief stay on Martinique, Kosciuszko and the other volunteers boarded a small fishing vessel that sailed to the Bahamas and then along North America's coast.[2]

When the trawler docked in the port of Philadelphia in late August 1776, the

Pennsylvania city had displaced Boston as the epicenter of the Revolution. With thirty thousand people, it was the most populous city in America and a bustling center of commerce, as farmers, artisans, craftsmen, traders, and representatives of the thirteen colonies all brought their business to its packed markets and taverns. When Kosciuszko disembarked, the capital was still pulsating with excitement over the Declaration of Independence and the idea that a new nation had just been created. The Polish volunteer did not know anyone in America, and Prince Czartoryski's friend Gen. Charles Lee was five hundred miles away in command of the Southern Army in Charleston, South Carolina.

Many years later Kosciuszko recounted his first steps in the new world to his personal secretary. He explained that after getting off the boat he went to visit the shop of the most famous American—Benjamin Franklin. When Kosciuszko walked through the door, the old sage of Philadelphia peered through the top half of his bifocals at the unannounced visitor.[3]

In broken English before switching to French, Kosciuszko introduced himself, explaining that he wanted to offer his services to the new nation. Thinking that America's armed forces were as structured as those in Europe, Kosciuszko asked to take the officer's placement exam so that he could enlist in the Continental Army.

Franklin was well attuned to the political situation in Poland and understood that the Poles were more radical about democratic principles than their neighbors. He asked, "Do you have any letters of recommendation?"

Kosciuszko replied, "I don't have any. A talented person should be able to show his worth, and not letters of recommendation. I want to show my competence by taking your placement exam."

About to embark for Paris to lobby France for military assistance, Franklin interrogated the French-educated engineer about news from Europe. The Founding Father pressed Kosciuszko about his own background and political views to get a better sense of the convictions of the foreign volunteer.

Satisfied with the answers, the seventy-year-old Franklin rose to his feet and said, "I am convinced of your clear and noble intentions." With that he leaned over and kissed the thirty-year-old volunteer on the forehead before saying, "But you have to admit, young man, that it was pretty unwise to travel two thousand miles without any commitments or connections?"

Franklin then asked Kosciuszko exactly what type of test it was that he would like to take. The Pole responded, "Engineering, military architecture, etc."

The elder statesman laughed at the idea that a new nation of farmers and merchants would have such expertise. Quite amused, Franklin said, "Who would proctor such an exam when there is no one here who is even familiar with those subjects? However, we do have a person who knows a little about geometry. We can have him give you a geometry exam."[4]

That person was most likely David Rittenhouse, a craftsman, surveyor and expert with scientific instruments who was working with Franklin on the Delaware River defenses.[5]

When Kosciuszko did well on the exam, Franklin personally recommended the Pole to Congress. On August 30, 1776, Kosciuszko went to the Pennsylvania State House (later renamed Independence Hall) to present his military credentials to Congress and the Board of War.

Franklin headed the Pennsylvania Committee of Safety, which was in charge of preventing the British navy from sailing into the Delaware River's shipping channels. Worried about a possible attack on Philadelphia, Franklin hired Kosciuszko as his chief engineer and put him to work designing the fortifications.

The British army had just routed George Washington's troops in the Battle of Long Island and captured New York. Maj. Gen. William Howe moved across northern New Jersey and forced Washington's troops to flee across the Delaware River into Pennsylvania. If the British navy in New York sailed its warships into the Delaware they would be within firing distance of the rebel capital.

The Americans desperately needed engineers to prepare for the coming attack. The French engineer assigned to work with Franklin's committee to secure Philadelphia, Col. Gilles-Jean-Marie Kermorvan, was instead sent to Perth Amboy, New Jersey. But Kermorvan could not get along with the workers and the Continental Army officers, and ultimately returned to France.[6]

That left Franklin and Kosciuszko to outline an elaborate network of defenses for Philadelphia.[7] The Polish engineer and his shipmate, the French artillery officer Romand de Lisle, reported for duty to the local commander of the city's forces, Gen. Israel Putnam. Thousands of Philadelphians were put to work ,on a massive fort-building project to prepare for the British attack.

On the shores of the Delaware River at Billingsport, New Jersey, Kosciuszko drafted plans for a 180-foot-square redoubt with parapets for soldiers and stations for eighteen cannons. To protect the fort from an inland assault, he laid out breastworks and a deep moat with a row of abatis (sharpened logs) facing out to deter an assault. The fort at Billingsport was meant to provide cover for underwater obstacles known as chevaux-de-frise. These interconnected wooden beams were sharpened at the top, capped with iron tips, and sunk into the river so that they would puncture and tear open the bottom of any British vessel sailing toward Philadelphia.

The brigades of soldiers at Kosciuszko's disposal floated 239 sturdy hemlock timbers, up to twenty inches thick, to Gloucester, New Jersey, where they were tied together to form giant crates sixty feet long. Iron tips were hammered onto the sharpened logs, some as long as seventy feet, and tied together at angles. The crates were floated into the shipping channel and loaded with thirty tons of rocks to sink them below the waterline. There were seventy sets of chevaux-de-frise, creating a treacherous underwater obstacle course sixty feet wide and eight miles long.[8]

Kosciuszko was already making a name for himself in Philadelphia when Gen. Charles Lee returned to the capital from the south. On October 7 Lee went to Congress to take care of his personal affairs and resume his duties with the Pennsylvania Line. There is no record that he spoke up for the Pole, but shortly after Lee's arrival, Congress commissioned Kosciuszko as an American officer.

On October 18, 1776, the president of the U.S. Congress, John Hancock, wrote to Kosciuszko: "We reposing especial Trust and Confidence in your Patriotism, Valour, Conduct and Fidelity, Do by these Presents, constitute and appoint you to be An Engineer with the Rank of Colonel in the Army of the United States, raised for the Defence of American Liberty, and for repelling every hostile Invasion thereof . . . and we do strictly charge and require all Officers and Soldiers under your Command to be obedient to your Orders as Engineer."[9] Congress set his salary at sixty dollars a month, which he declined to collect during the entire course of the war.

The Pennsylvania delegates were grateful for Kosciuszko's work, and on October 24 the Committee of Safety issued an order "in favor of Monsieur Thaddeus Kosciuszko for 50 pounds, as a reward for his services" at Billingsport.[10]

Three days later Franklin set sail for Paris, and soon there was a scramble to see whom Colonel Kosciuszko would work for next. Kosciuszko was a skilled engineer, and his services were in demand. But because his French was better than his English, many Americans mistook him for a Frenchman, including George Washington, who had yet to meet Kosciuszko but knew of his reputation.

On December 9 Washington wrote to Hancock: "If the Measure of fortifying the City should be adopted, some skillful person should immediately view the Grounds and begin to trace out the Lines and Works. I am informed there is a French Engineer of eminence in Philadelphia at this time. If so, he will be the most proper."[11]

The engineer in Philadelphia was Kosciuszko. While Washington did not know his name, Gen. John Armstrong (father of Maj. John Armstrong, a friend of Kosciuszko), figured out who he was and wanted to hire the talented engineer everyone was talking about. The threat of a British attack on Philadelphia was growing every day, and Armstrong asked the Board of War to send the Pole to assist him in Trenton Falls. Armstrong wrote, "I had without consulting the General written for Colonels Kosciuszko and Ramond; but as General Putnam is sent down for purpose on their way near town, I suppose they can't be sent here."[12]

Rather than send Kosciuszko to Washington's headquarters, Putnam sent the engineer downriver to set a trap for the British in the shipping channel. There

Kosciuszko built Fort Mercer on a forty-foot-high cliff in Red Bank, New Jersey, armed with heavy guns facing out over the Delaware. This elevation put it out of firing range of British ships that might try to navigate between the underwater obstacles meant to sink them.[13]

On the other side of the river was Fort Mifflin, whose cannons provided cover from the western bank. Kosciuszko ordered the orchards north of the fort cut down to clear a line of fire at any approaching enemy. His men also dug deep trenches outside the fort's walls and another row of breastworks along the river bluff. These were filled with another row of abatis to deter an infantry attack.

Washington wrote to Hancock again on December 20 from his camp at Trenton Falls, and it was obvious that he was growing frustrated with the Frenchmen Congress had been sending his way. Washington wrote, "For want of some establishment in the department of Engineers. . . . None of the French Gentlemen whom I have seen with appointments in that way, appear to me to know anything of the Matter. There is one in Philadelphia whom I am told is clever, but him I have never seen."[14]

While Washington worried about the British, his subordinate Gen. Horatio Gates, an ally of John Adams and the New England delegates, was lobbying members of Congress to reappoint him as commander of the Northern Department, a position he had held the year before. As Gates sauntered from one delegate to the next, pursuing his own interests, he heard about the new engineer whose defensive schemes would keep the British fleet from sailing into the Delaware.

Gates took command of the forces around Philadelphia when General Putnam was reassigned in February. Gates was one of several officers in the Continental Army who were more interested in pursuing promotions in the halls of Congress than on the battlefield. His polar opposite was Gen. Benedict Arnold, who distinguished himself in combat. Arnold led an expedition into the frontier of northern New York in 1775 and, along with Ethan Allen and the Green Mountain Boys, captured the outpost of Fort Ticonderoga from the British. Arnold also traveled hundreds of miles through the wilderness in the winter to attack the British stronghold of Quebec, Canada, where an English musket ball shattered his ankle. And it was Arnold who supervised the construction of a fleet of gunboats that patrolled Lake Champlain and repelled an invasion of Redcoats during the autumn of 1776.

Yet despite Arnold's brave actions in keeping the British north of Champlain, Congress appointed Gates commander of the Northern Army. Gates was jealous of Arnold's resourcefulness and in a letter to Congress took credit for the actions of the small navy on Lake Champlain.[15]

Making enemies of the officers he climbed over, Gates needed allies and befriended the Polish engineer. Like Kosciuszko the English-born Gates was not

wealthy and joined his country's military through the patronage of a noble mentor. Gates was rumored to be the illegitimate son of a nobleman. His parents
were servants to the Duke of Bolton.[16] His mother had previously worked as a
maid for the Duke of Leeds, who may have been his real father.[17]

Gen. Edward Cornwallis, the "Founder of Halifax" and governor of Nova
Scotia, was Gates's guardian angel. He was also the uncle of Gen. Lord Charles
Cornwallis, who would play a significant role in Gates's later years. The young
Gates became a captain in the British army and served in Prussia during the War
of the Austrian Succession. Unable to obtain a permanent position in the royal
army, Gates immigrated to America and fought in the French and Indian War
before settling in Virginia.

In 1775, upon hearing of the fighting at Lexington and Concord, Gates
rushed to Mt. Vernon and offered his services to George Washington. Washington recommended Gates and his friend Charles Lee, the only two colonial officers with any battle experience, to be commissioned as generals. But the two
former English officers were envious of Washington, and at one point Lee wrote
a letter to Gates disparaging the commander in chief, saying, "Between us, a certain great man is damnably deficient."[18]

Kosciuszko, who was still learning to speak English and how to navigate the
local political scene, would not have known about all the backbiting. Given their
similar backgrounds and class distinction, Gates and Kosciuszko, who commu-
nicated in French, became friends. When Gates was given command of the
Northern Army, he appointed the Pole his engineer. The political power play by
Gates did not sit well with his other chief rival, the man whom he replaced, Gen.
Philip Schuyler.

Schuyler was a wealthy New Yorker who owned huge tracts of land as well as
numerous mills along the Hudson River and a mansion in Albany. Gates and
Schuyler were constantly maneuvering to undercut each other, and resentment
by the displaced New Yorkers was to be expected when Gates, Kosciuszko, and
his new entourage arrived in Albany to take command of the Northern Army in
the spring of 1777.

In Canada, British general John Burgoyne was amassing British and Hessian
troops to launch a three-pronged attack to converge on Albany, New York.
"Gentleman Johnny," as his troops called him, was an infamous gambler. Before
he left London he made a wager with a friend that he would be home with a victory by Christmas.

The British "gentlemen" ridiculed New Englanders with a song called "Yankee Doodle." A "doodle" was a simpleton, and as the rebellion spread to New
York, a colony of many Hollanders, the name Janke, Dutch for "little Jan," was
used derisively. The rebels wore the name Yankee as a badge of honor, and

turned the song around, rewriting the lyrics to praise their bravery. It became a battle hymn to tease the snooty Brits.[19]

Burgoyne had a plan to mislead the "doodles" of the Continental Army with a diversion by sending a small unit led by Col. Barry St. Leger east from Oswego along the Mohawk River valley toward Albany, while Burgoyne's main army swept down from Canada, and General Howe's forces marched north from New York City. This would hit the rebels from three sides. If properly executed the invasion would give the royal army control of New York and split the rebellious colonies in two.

But first Burgoyne had to retake Fort Ticonderoga, planted on a sliver of land between the Adirondacks and the Green Mountains at the confluence of Lake George and Lake Champlain. Named for an Iroquois word meaning land between two waters, the massive star-shaped stone fort was built by the French in the 1750s during the seven-year French and Indian War. The British took it in 1759 and held it until the outbreak of the Revolution.

The fort needed to be reinforced if it was to withstand an attack by the well-armed British royal army. In the summer of 1776 Gates was at Fort Ticonderoga when Col. John Trumbull (an engineer whose paintings are some of the most revered images of the American Revolution) suggested mounting cannons on nearby Sugar Loaf Hill, which overlooked the fort.[20] While Arnold agreed with Trumbull, the other officers present ridiculed the idea, arguing that it would be impossible to drag a cannon up the steep slopes of the 750-foot-high rocky hill.[21]

On May 8, 1777, Gates sent Col. James Wilkinson to this northern outpost "with instructions to examine and regulate the chain of communication with Ticonderoga."[22] Gates, who was present when Trumbull pointed out the fort's Achilles' heel, asked Kosciuszko to join Wilkinson to examine Ticonderoga's vulnerabilities and decide whether it was possible to position cannons on the cliffs of Sugar Loaf Hill.[23]

In a letter to the fort's commander, Gen. John Paterson, Gates wrote: "Col. Kusiusco accompanies Wilkinson, he is an able Engineer, and one of the best and neatest draughtsman I ever saw. I desire he may have a Quarter assigned him, and when he has thoroughly made himself acquainted with the works, [I] have ordered him to point out to you, where and in what manner the best improvements and additions can be made thereto; I expect Col. Baldwin will [give] his countenance and protection to this Gentleman, for he is meant to serve not supersede him."[24]

Col. Jeduthan Baldwin, the incompetent engineer stationed at Fort Ticonderoga, disagreed with Trumbull's idea and was instead building pointless wooden towers near the fort.[25] As soon as Kosciuszko arrived he saw that Trumbull was right: It was a mistake to leave Sugar Loaf Hill undefended. After climbing to the summit and making some mathematical calculations, the former captain of the Polish artillery pointed out to General Paterson that the hill was within firing range of the fort, and that a cannon should be mounted on it to provide cover against the approaching British army.

But Baldwin's inertia killed new ideas.[26] After surveying the area Kosciuszko wrote a detailed report (in French) to Gates pointing out several flaws in the work under way. He drew a map of the terrain around the fort, explaining to Gates, "What appears in black is what actually remains; what you see in red is my scheme." Kosciuszko wanted to put cannons on the hills overlooking the fort to cover the land and lake approaches to deter a British attack. He wrote that while Paterson and the other officers were polite and "extremely friendly," he hinted that someone had a problem with his "nationality." His plan received a cool reception from Colonel Baldwin, and he asked Gates, "My General, I request the favor you would not give me orders to proceed before your arrival. . . . I love peace and want to be on good terms with the whole world if possible." If not, he said he would rather "return home and plant cabbages."[27]

A few days later a frustrated Kosciuszko again wrote to Gates, saying that in addition to being vulnerable by not using his "model" to fortify Sugar Loaf Hill, they needed to install obstacles "to prevent the passage of shipping." He said that Fort Ticonderoga was not only "an excellent place to resist the enemy, but beat them." However, much of what was being done was unnecessary, and there was little progress on a much-needed footbridge of floating logs between the main fort and Fort Independence on the other side of a channel that connected Lake Champlain and Lake George.

Instead Kosciuszko wrote: "We are very fond here of making Block houses and they are erected in the most improper places. Nevertheless Genl, we shall prevail under your Excellency's leadership. Our steady attachment to you will be a great inducement added to the Sacred Duty which has engaged us to Defend this Country."[28]

Maj. John Armstrong watched as Kosciuszko calculated his plans to fortify Sugar Loaf Hill and agreed with the Polish engineer's assessment. Armstrong wrote that even though the sides of the hill were steep, with "strong fatigue parties" they would "permit the ascent of the heaviest cannon . . . [and] furnish a good site for a battery." He added that "a battery so placed, from elevation and proximity, would completely cover the two forts, the bridge of communication and the adjoining boat harbor."[29]

The other officers at Ticonderoga were too busy jostling for position to follow the advice of the new recruit with the unpronounceable name. Kosciuszko's surname was so mangled by colonials that some of them started calling him "Kos." Writing his name was just as difficult, and George Washington spelled it eleven different ways. Kosciuszko took it all in stride and purportedly joked that

"Knickerbocker" and "Schenectady" didn't exactly roll off his tongue either.[30] The Pole did not want to make waves and was not forceful in pushing his ideas. Colonel Baldwin began ridiculing his observations that cannons should be placed on top of the nearby hill.

Gates's other emissary, Colonel Wilkinson, who also felt strongly about pro-tecting Sugar Loaf Hill (renamed Mount Defiance), was shocked that the rebels did not follow Kosciuszko's proposal. Wilkinson wrote to Gates in Albany, "I wish to heaven that you or General St. Clair was here for a few days. Colonel Kosciuszko is timidly modest; Baldwin is inclosing the lines on a plan of his own."[31]

Frustrated, Kosciuszko rode south to Albany to provide Gates with a progress report at the fort. While he was gone Wilkinson wrote a desperate plea to Gates, "The works are now pushed on Baldwin's unmeaning plan. For God's sake, let Kosciuszko come back as soon as possible, with proper authority."[32]

Agreeing with Wilkinson, on May 28 Gates wrote to Paterson recommend-ing that "Kosciuszko's plan be immediately put in Execution, doing the most de-fensible parts first. Colonel Baldwin will gain my Affection; and Esteem, by Cultivating the Friendship of that Capable Young Man."[33]

Kosciuszko returned to Fort Ticonderoga on June 6 with orders from Gates to fortify the hills, but Baldwin became even more resentful of the Polish engi-neer and refused to budge. On June 7 Kosciuszko took several officers to recon-noiter the area around the fort. Baldwin wrote in his diary that they "rode over [to a peninsula south of the fort] Mount Independence. Laid out long lines be-tween the redoubts that I hope never will be finished as they are Staked now."[34]

Kosciuszko's plan had another setback when Schuyler convinced Congress to reinstate him over Gates as head of the Northern Army. As an upper-crust New Yorker, Schuyler was more concerned about his rank and social standing than an attack from the hill overlooking the fort's western flank.

The embittered Baldwin stalled the plan of putting cannons on Mount Defi-ance, so the Polish engineer pushed forward with the work on the floating bridge to Mount Independence, where he supervised one hundred soldiers in building three redoubts to provide cover for Ticonderoga's southern exposure.

With his ideas ignored, Kosciuszko requested a transfer in a letter to Gates praising his superior officer's love for his country and his "Great Military knowl-edge and true merit." He asked Gates to take him into battle: "I am not moti-vated by Interest, other than the ambition of signalizing myself in this War. And I seek an opportunity, which I am of opinion can never be better than under your Auspices."[35]

Out of genuine admiration, respect for the chain of command, and similar political views, the Pole became a sycophant when dealing with Gates. Wilkinson was also disturbed by Gates's demotion and saw it as a philosophical difference between members of Congress. "Wilky," as his brothers-in-arms called him, the spoiled son of a rich Maryland property owner, figured out that the South did not support Gates. "I really begin to love the New England men," Wilkinson wrote of those who supported Gates, because, "[their feelings] marked their countenances on the late astonishing revolution." The others, Wilkinson wrote, were "ingrates, assassins, and double faced villains."[36]

Unfortunately for Wilkinson his toadying letter never made it to Gates, and when Schuyler reached Fort Ticonderoga on June 17, the new commander admitted that he opened it because Gates had already left Albany when it arrived.[37] Schuyler assured Wilkinson that he would not hold it against him, but more distressingly, the reinstated New York commander expressed doubts on whether his army could withstand an attack by the British. After assembling a council of officers and crafting a ten-point declaration asking Washington for more men, Schuyler put Gen. Arthur St. Clair in charge of Ticonderoga and withdrew south to Fort Edward.

The decision on Kosciuszko's plan to fortify Mount Defiance was left to St. Clair, who was trapped between conflicting orders. He decided to follow Schuyler's decision to leave the hill exposed, "reasoning that no Engineer hitherto, French, British, or American, had believed in the practicality of placing a battery on Sugar loaf hill [Mount Defiance], was not disposed to embarrass himself or his means of defense by making the experiment."[38]

The embarrassment came from not placing a cannon on that nearby hill.

General Burgoyne arrived in lower Lake Champlain on July 1, 1777, with eight thousand troops, including British and Hessian soldiers and a few hundred Canadians, Tories, and Indians. Uneasiness descended on the fort with the news that the Indians had cut up the rebel reconnoitering parties that had tracked the approaching enemy.

Scouting the area, Burgoyne's chief of artillery, Gen. William Phillips, immediately recognized the tactical advantage of having guns mounted atop Mount Defiance. When the English troops also whined about the physically draining task, Phillips gave a direct order saying, "Where a goat can go, a man can go, and where a man can go, he can haul up a gun."[39]

The Americans woke up the next morning, after celebrating the first anniversary of the Declaration of Independence, to find soldiers in crimson jackets perched atop Mount Defiance aiming a cannon down on them. By noon six twelve-pound artillery pieces were pointed at Fort Ticonderoga. The British opened fire at a rebel boat in the lake.[40] One cannonball landed inside the fort. They also set fire to Colonel Baldwin's blockhouses.

St. Clair called a war council, and the officers decided that they had no choice but to evacuate. At ten o'clock in the evening the colonial soldiers and militiamen began quietly sneaking out of the fort. Luckily Kosciuszko's men had finished the floating log bridge just in time for the rebels to escape and retreat south toward Albany, avoiding the enemy troops that were converging on them from the north, east, and west.

The evacuation started smoothly, but an alcoholic Frenchman, Gen. Matthias Alexis Roche de Fermoy, bungled his job of protecting the rear guard. Fermoy passed out in a drunken stupor without telling his men to pack their gear and prepare to pull out. When he finally stirred from his slumber with a hangover, he left his troops in disarray and ignored St. Clair's orders to keep all lights out. Instead the fermented Fermoy torched his quarters. The fire spread quickly through the fort, lighting up the night sky and revealing shadowy silhouettes fleeing from Ticonderoga.[41]

The British and Hessians were in hot pursuit, shooting at the rebels as they ran. The next day English General Simon Fraser's unit caught up with the colonials in Hubbardton, Vermont, and captured two hundred of them. The rest fought their way out and escaped.

That's when Burgoyne unleashed his secret weapon, a reign of terror over the fleeing rebels. The Americans had asked the Indian tribes to stay neutral in the war, but the British stirred up the Iroquois nations against the colonials. The Oneida and Tuscarora nations stayed with the Americans, while the Mohawk, Onondaga, Cayuga, and Seneca sided with the king.[42] British and American generals often fed their troops rum to infuse them with bravery, and Burgoyne did the same with the Iroquois. The British promised that the "King across the Great Waters" would pay them handsomely for each scalp of an American soldier.[43]

The fleeing colonials were terrified by the whooping Indian scouts who chased them through the woods, picking off soldiers on the periphery, slicing open their heads with knives and tomahawks. The rebel army turned into a chaotic mob with no one clearly in charge. Some soldiers simply cut and ran, deserting to head home.

Schuyler was forty miles to the south at Fort Edward when Ticonderoga was abandoned. A week later he caught up to his retreating troops and tried to restore order. He regretted not listening to Kosciuszko's advice to arm Mount Defiance. Schuyler relieved Fermoy of his job of hindering the British advance and ordered Col. Morgan Lewis to ride north to inform Kosciuszko that he was to take charge of holding off the Redcoats so the Continental Army could escape.

On July 16 Schuyler wrote to Kosciuszko: "I have sent one of the Quartermasters to Saratoga and the post below to bring up all the axes which can be collected, and to deliver them to you. Col. Lewis has my orders to send you a horse immediately. I will give the orders for moving General Fermoy's and General Paterson's Brigade tomorrow and dispose of them in the manner you wish."[44]

Schuyler reassigned hundreds of soldiers and put them under Kosciuszko's command. Lt. Col. Henry B. Livingston issued the order: "The fatigue party, till further orders . . . is to proceed . . . and receive orders from Colo. Kosciuszko, Engineer."[45]

The Pole rallied the troops to delay the enemy's pursuit. With Adirondack blackflies biting the backs of their necks and arms, and timber rattlesnakes nipping at their feet, three hundred wool-clad, sweating Continental soldiers under Kosciuszko's command toiled in the heat to chop down trees to block roads and destroy bridges over streams as soon as the rebel troops had crossed them. They rolled boulders into Wood Creek to make it unnavigable and rerouted streams to flood roadways and trails.[46]

The long train of British supply wagons was stopped in its tracks. Lt. Thomas Anburey complained that the British had to rebuild bridges and wait "till the roads are cleared of the trees which the Americans felled after their retreat . . . every ten or twelve yards great trees are laid across the road."[47] Another British soldier mentioned that "the felled trees were as plenty as lampposts upon a highway about London."[48]

The colonials also drove away cattle and set fire to fields of grain and corn, forcing the British to subsist on the rations that they could carry. As a result the unwieldy English supply line was stretched north all the way to Canada. Kosciuszko's diversionary tactics worked: It took the British army twenty days to travel twenty-two miles.[49]

With the rebels scattered in the woods, Kosciuszko raced everywhere on his horse trying to find safe campsites. Wilkinson wrote in his memoirs, "Thaddeus Kosciuszko was at that time our chief engineer, and for months had been the companion of my blanket: he selected a position for a fortified camp about four miles below Fort Edward, at Moses Creek, where the waters of the Hudson river are separated by an island."[50]

After a rest at Moses Creek, where the Indians threatened the position, Kosciuszko moved the troops to Van Schaick's Island, which offered the rebels a place to regroup and plan their next move. He put up batteries that commanded the pass along the river while also providing the rebels a barrier from any attack. Maj. John Armstrong wrote, "In the retreat of the American army, Kosciuszko was distinguished for activity and courage and upon him devolved the choices of camps and posts and everything connected with fortifications."[51]

The showdown in northern New York State was put off for a few more weeks, and St. Clair was made the scapegoat for the Fort Ticonderoga fiasco. Under fire for abandoning the massive fort, he wrote to Washington, "Our whole camp on the Ticonderoga side was exposed to fire."[52]

Even though this was the same point Kosciuszko had made before the British attack, the Pole stood by his besieged commander. Schuyler also faced consequences for the defeat. He lost the support of Congress, which removed him from his post. Upon hearing the news of the retreat from Ticonderoga, the fort that he had taken from the British, General Arnold raced north from Pennsylvania, hoping that he would finally be given the command that he had earned. But alas Arnold's nemesis Gates was once again reinstated as commander of the Northern Army. The Continental Army would regroup and stand to face the British. This time the decision on where to place cannons would be left to Kosciuszko.

THREE

Turning Back the British Tide:
The Battle of Saratoga

A FTER LOSING THE ENORMOUS STONE CITADEL THAT WAS FORT Ticonderoga, the colonials sank into a deep malaise and camped in the mud on Van Schaick's Island. Scouts reported that Indian scalping parties were still on the prowl in the woods, and after clearing the obstructions that Kosciuszko's unit placed over the roads, the British were again on the march.

The chorus among the soldiers and members of Congress grew louder in calling for General St. Clair's head. He faced a court-martial and at the rebel campfires, his former soldiers blamed him for their defeat. Kosciuszko refused to allow St. Clair to become the fall guy. In a letter to the besieged general, Kosciuszko wrote: "If the retreat from Ticonderoga has drawn upon you many talkers and some jealous persons have furnished the occasion of under-mining you, even to the point of saying yesterday at dinner, that it is necessary that someone be sacrificed for the public good, it seems to me rather for their own. Therefore my General, it is necessary to take care and try to shut their mouths. I offer you my services."[1]

Morale was boosted at the rebel camp when General Gates arrived on August 19, 1777, and ordered the army to march back up the Hudson. Gates announced that they would find a spot to confront General Burgoyne's army. The troops received more encouragement two weeks later when General Arnold and General Ebenezer Learned's brigade arrived with reinforcements.

By September, Gates had marched the army up to Stillwater, along the Hudson a few miles south of Saratoga, where he ordered Col. Morgan Lewis to set up camp. Kosciuszko trotted his horse up to the field in the floodplain of the river where Lewis was positioning the army and told him that the place chosen by Gates was commanded by hills on every side and that the wide meadows along the river made the spot indefensible.[2] According to Lewis, Kosciuszko pointed to the nearby elevation and said in his heavily accented English, "From Yonder Hill, on the left, your encampment may be cannoned by the enemy, or from that on our right they may take aim at your shoe-buckles."[3]

Lewis knew that the engineer was right, but he was hesitant to challenge Gates's judgment. Kosciuszko brought Wilkinson to see Gates and voiced his objections. With the general's approval, the Polish engineer rode north with Lewis and Col. Udney Hay until he found the perfect vantage point to make a stand. When they reached an elevated pasture above the road to Albany along the Hudson, Kosciuszko's eyes lit up and he galloped his horse around in circles on the hill and exclaimed, "This is the spot!"[4]

Bemis Heights looks down on a bottleneck that the British would have to squeeze through between the hills and the river. The bluffs, named after a tavern run by Jotham Bemis, overlook the Hudson and steep sloping fields with four parallel crevasses carved into them by Mill Creek and its tributaries. The British would have to cross those open fields and deep ravines if they planned to mount an attack. Below the cliffs to the east was a narrow riverside passage running south to Albany. To the west were hills with thick forests that would keep the British from outflanking the Continental Army.

As a cadet at the Warsaw military academy, Kosciuszko had studied the legendary ancient Greek battle at Thermopylae, in which three hundred Spartans faced a much larger Persian army. The Greeks made clever use of topography to their advantage and held out for several days against the Persian invaders. While the Spartans lost the battle, it inspired Greeks from various other city-states to unite and stand up to the Persians. Americans from different states would have to do the same and stand up to their invaders.

Lewis later recalled that Kosciuszko "inquired the number of divisions in the Army and their names, took a piece of paper from his portfolio, and drew in pencil the plan of the camp, and assigned the location of several regiments and in conformity with that plan they were speedily marched to the ground and they proceeded to erect breastworks and fortifications."[5]

Positioning the Continental Army on Bemis Heights, Kosciuszko ensured that the British would have an uphill battle in every sense. The Pole was put in charge of one thousand soldiers who carried out his plans for redoubts, batteries, bivouacs, and roads to coordinate the proper placement of the army. Lewis reported that each night "every division, brigade and regiment was placed in the quarter allotted" according to Kosciuszko's plan.[6]

The downtrodden rebels awoke with a new sense of purpose once they got back to work. In a letter to a friend Colonel Hay wrote: "From this miserable state of despondency and terror, Gates' arrival raises us, as if by magic. We began to hope and then to act. Our first step was to Stillwater, and we are now on the heights called Bhemus', looking the enemy boldly in the face. Kosciuszko has selected this ground, and has covered its weak point, (its right) with redoubts from the hill to the river."[7] Wilkinson, who had respected the Pole's judgment ever since Ticonderoga, also felt more secure with the new position knowing that "Kosciuszko has selected it."[8]

The Americans had several lucky breaks that swung the battle in their favor. Rather than march north to attack Gates's rear, General Howe turned south to attack Philadelphia instead. And the rebels in the Mohawk River valley, led by General Arnold, stopped St. Leger's army at Fort Stanwix in Rome, New York. St. Leger's confused troops hightailed it back to Canada. Most of the Iroquois scouts abandoned the British after the murder and scalping of a British officer's fiancée, Jane McCrea. The savage killing of McCrea became a rallying cry for the rebels and more colonials enlisted in Gates's army.

As volunteers streamed into the hills over the Hudson from various directions of the countryside, there was a growing feeling of confidence among the rebels. But while they were there to unite against the British, the competitiveness between the officers from different backgrounds and states never went away.

Gates, hunched over, with thinning gray hair, chubby ruddy cheeks, and spectacles perched at the tip of his nose, looked older than his fifty years and was called "Granny Gates" by his men. Burgoyne also belittled Gates by referring to him as "an old midwife."[9]

But Kosciuszko saw in Gates a commitment to the same ideals that brought him to America in the first place. The feeling was mutual, and years later Gates would tell a friend, "Kosciuszko is the only pure republican I ever knew. He is without any dross."[10]

The two men with humble beginnings had the same sense of purpose and opinion of what the Revolution was all about—freedom for all classes. Both believed that slaves should be allowed to join the army to fight for their freedom. The inclusion of black soldiers in the Continental Army became a major issue after Virginia's royal governor, Lord Dunmore, issued a proclamation on November 7, 1775, stating that "all indentured Servants, Negroes" willing "to bear arms, they joining his Majesty's troops," are to be declared "free."[11] One in five colonial Americans was black, but the Southern plantation owners were reluctant to arm African slaves.

As a Southern plantation owner who personally owned more than one hundred slaves (three hundred when those of his wife, Martha, were included), Washington was outraged by the proclamation and said Dunmore should be "crushed." Six days later, on November 13, 1775, Washington responded, giving the order, "Neither Negroes, Boys unable to bare Arms, nor old men unfit to endure the fatigues of the campaign, are to be enlisted."[12]

In the two years after Lord Dunmore's proclamation, Washington sent conflicting signals on what the Continental Army should do regarding black recruits. Each state had its own laws regarding slavery, and as the Revolution progressed, it became standard practice that slaves could be recruited with written permission of their masters.

Some colonists avoided the war by ordering their slaves to fight in their place. However, Gates allowed black men who escaped their owners to enlist under their own names. When Israel Ashley of Westfield, Massachusetts, attempted to sign up his slave Gilliam as a substitute, he was aghast to discover that his servant had already enlisted as himself. Ashley protested to Gates, but the general refused to return Gilliam to his master, saying that state laws were unclear and that he sympathized with the "slaves who have or will assist us in securing our freedom at the risk of their own lives."[13]

Gates owned slaves at his Virginia plantation, called Traveller's Rest, but seeing the horrors of the wicked institution during the Revolution, he freed them in an emotional and teary-eyed farewell after the war.[14] Gates clearly made an impression on the African Americans he knew because at his funeral, a former slave named Uncle Robert threw himself on Gates's coffin as it was being lowered into its grave and honored "with grateful tears the author of his liberty and happiness."[15]

This concern for human rights also extended to Native Americans. Prior to the war Gates wrote: "As to the Indians, the behaviour of certain of the White people is beyond all comparison abominable towards those unhappy Natives."[16]

While many colonists agreed with Gates about trying to live in harmony with the Indians, it was the British army that had riled up the Native Americans to attack the colonial settlers. By the time the British had reached Saratoga, most of the Indians were no longer providing reconnaissance for Burgoyne's troops.

Instead of a three-pronged attack Gates would face only Burgoyne's army. The overconfident Gentleman Johnny and his officers were camped near Saratoga, drinking champagne, gambling at cards, and taking pleasure with the services of the petticoat battalion that traveled with the army to entertain the officers.[17] The hedonistic Burgoyne indulged himself in the arms of Madame Rousseau, the wife of his commissary.[18]

As the British caroused and frolicked nearby, waiting for reinforcements that would not arrive, Kosciuszko and his men built a series of defensive positions—parapets, trenches, and redoubts—that were unassailable from below. The Mill Creek ravines and steep grassy approaches gave the rebel positions a clear shot on the path the enemy would have to take. Kosciuszko set an additional trap by pointing cannons at the Hudson River passage one hundred feet below Bemis

Heights. The only other access point was along the fields near the thick woods, which meant the attacking soldiers would be sitting ducks.

Of all the units that Gates had at his disposal, the most important was a team of backwoods riflemen sent to him by George Washington. Col. Daniel Morgan's sharpshooters were just as good as the Indians in scouting out the enemy's movement and causing havoc in their rear.

Daniel Morgan was raised in New Jersey before moving to the frontier of the Shenandoah Valley in what would become West Virginia. He was a bear of a man who worked clearing land driving a team of oxen and horses, and as a wagoner moving supplies into the wilderness. He had a voracious appetite for drinking and gambling and held a terrible grudge against the British army. At the outbreak of the French and Indian War, Morgan had a confrontation with a British officer, which resulted in Morgan being stripped, tied up, and whipped five hundred lashes. When his punishment was done, the skin on his back hung down in bloody flesh tags. Morgan wanted revenge.[19]

The rebels were prepared, but petty bickering between generals nearly sidetracked the battle. Arnold, who was thirty-six and full of energy, resented the gray-haired Gates's leadership and defensive style of warfare. Arnold remained loyal to his friend General Schuyler, who was now a subordinate of Gates. Gates resented this disloyalty and was cool toward Arnold.

The aggressive Arnold wanted to "march out and attack."[20] Arnold's overly aggressive tactics led to disaster in his Canadian mission, and Gates wanted to take advantage of his strong position to force the Redcoats to climb the hills in their parade formations and enter the trap. The friction between the two generals was so heated that eventually Arnold was banned from Gates's staff meetings.

While Kosciuszko held Arnold in high "esteem," they parted ways when it came to respecting the chain of command.[21] Kosciuszko was one of Gates's confidants who dined with him, advised him, and was at the commander's side during most of the campaign. This inner circle included Col. Robert Troup, who when the war broke out was studying law with the future Chief Justice of the United States, John Jay, and Colonel Wilkinson, who hated Arnold.

Gates's staff did occasionally challenge him, but the three colonels often used shameless adulation to vie for his attention. Troup called them Gates's "family" and wrote that during the entire campaign Wilkinson and Kosciuszko "were about General Gates's person and indeed they messed [ate] with him." Troup wrote that while Wilky was a young man of "moderate abilities" and "a gross flatterer," Kosciuszko was "a young man—of unassuming manners—of grave temper—of abilities exceeding those of Wilkinson . . . [and] was skillful in the use of delicate flattery where it could be used to advantage."[22]

When the British assault finally came, on September 19, Burgoyne's army could not challenge Kosciuszko's fortifications. The Redcoats were forced to march around the redoubts and ended up in the woods, where the rebels ambushed them.

The first skirmish was known as the Battle for Freeman's Farm. For most of the day General Gates was holed up in his tent swilling a "strong drink," complaining about Arnold, and commanding the battle from his headquarters.[23]

As two British columns and one Hessian column marched up the embankment through the woods, Arnold, who had also been dipping heavily into the rum barrel, shouted at Gates to signal for an attack. Gates waited until the British marched deeper into the trap before sending Morgan's sharpshooters into the field.

Morgan's Virginia riflemen wore hunting shirts and leggings, and had bullet pouches hanging from their waists and gunpowder flasks made from ox horns strapped over their shoulders. They climbed trees to get a better shot at the enemy. These snipers were armed with the shorter and lighter Pennsylvania rifle, which was deadly accurate at one hundred yards and could still hit a target three hundred yards away, losing only some of its precision. Unfortunately they took longer to load and had no bayonets.

For regular infantrymen on both sides, the British "brown Bess" was so inaccurate that it inspired the phrase "can't hit the side of a barn."[24] Soldiers could get off three shots a minute, and in hand-to-hand combat the musket was superior because its bayonet with a triple blade could stab and slice open enemy soldiers.

Morgan's marksmen could easily focus their sights on the bright red jackets in the nearby wheat fields and woods. The rebels were out of range of the British muskets, and Morgan's snipers picked off the English officers in the front lines. With the royal army's leaders falling and the troops in disarray, Morgan's men attacked the main column. After their initial success, however, they came upon the full strength of the British, which began firing back in steady volleys.

Determined to cover himself in glory, Arnold broke out from behind the barricades and charged the British on horseback with reinforcements. During the course of the afternoon Arnold personally led his men in charging the British lines, galloping up and down the field yelling, "Come on, boys. Hurry up, my brave boys!"[25]

About six hundred Redcoats were killed or wounded, yet Gates was not able to finish off the British army. He had good reason to hold back. The rebel army's ammunition had been exhausted, and each of Morgan and Arnold's soldiers had only about a single shot left. If Burgoyne had known this, he would have sent his men charging into the mix with their deadly bayonets, and the battle might have finished differently. It was not until the next day that General Schuyler arrived with a fresh supply of gunpowder and lead taken from windowpanes from houses in Albany that could be melted down for bullets.[26]

In his official report to Congress, Gates excluded any mention of Arnold's role in the battle. Arnold felt slighted and got drunk, openly badmouthing Gates to anyone who would listen. The insubordination became a distraction in the rebel camp. Kosciuszko was put off by this challenge to the commander's authority and viewed Arnold's behavior as "rash" and "drunken," and suggested that Gates should "order him out of the field."[27]

A few days later, when it was announced that Morgan would no longer be under Arnold's command, leaving the hero of the first battle without a unit to lead, Arnold stormed over to Gates's tent and the two began shouting and cursing at each other. In the argument that erupted, "Gates was irritating, arrogant and vulgar; Arnold indiscreet, haughty and passionate."[28]

Even though the first phase of the battle went well and the Americans had half as many casualties as the British, Gates was furious that Arnold had usurped his authority and was envious of his bravery on the battlefield. Arnold was indignant that Gates would receive credit for the victory. Schuyler, who had been superseded by Gates, wrote that his replacement was "so very sure of success that he did not wish the other [Arnold] to come in for a share of the glory he may acquire" from a victory.[29] Gates relieved Arnold of his command.

Over the next few days the British were licking their wounds and burying hundreds of dead soldiers in shallow graves near the battlefield. The stench of death wafted through the hills. Wolves caught the scent and began howling in the night in the nearby mountains. Shivers crawled down the spines of soldiers on both sides as large wolf packs bolted down the hills in the darkness and began gnawing on the bones of the dead. The growling intensified, and they dug up the bodies from their shallow graves, causing English lieutenant William Digby and his men to worry about the plague.[30]

Rather than wait for disease to set in, two weeks after the first skirmish Burgoyne struck again. This time the British troops swung even farther west into the forest to avoid Kosciuszko's defenses on Bemis Heights.

Arnold, ignoring the fact that Gates had taken away his command, jumped on his steed and charged with the rebel troops directly toward the British position. One of Morgan's snipers killed Gen. Simon Fraser, causing the approaching column to fall apart. The Continental Army inflicted heavy losses on the enemy, and Arnold led the charge into Breymann's Redoubt until he fell from his horse when he was shot in the leg. The horse collapsed on top of him and nearly crushed him.

Morgan continued the fight, and his unit outflanked the Redcoats to the north, gunning down hundreds of British soldiers. Burgoyne was beaten, and within days his entire army was surrounded. On October 17 the British were forced to surrender. The rebel band needled the enemy as drums rattled and fifes whistled out "Yankee Doodle Dandy" when the Redcoats were forced to put down their muskets and march out of camp. The same day Gates wrote to his wife: "Burgoyne and his whole army have laid down their arms, and surrendered themselves to me and my Yankees. . . . If Old England is not by this lesson taught humility, then she is an obstinate old slut, bent upon her ruin."[31]

Although Kosciuszko had set the stage by planning and constructing the defensive positions, Arnold's bravery became legendary, and Gates received the glory for the Battle of Saratoga. Yet Gates was willing to share the credit with his Polish friend.

The following year, when Dr. Benjamin Rush of Philadelphia visited his headquarters, the lucky general brushed off the praise for his victory at Saratoga. "Stop, Doctor, stop," said Gates. "Let us be honest. In war, as in medicine, natural causes not under our control, do much. In the present case, the great tacticians of the campaign were hills and forests, which a young Polish Engineer was skilful enough to select for my encampment."[32]

The magnitude of the victory was enormous. It was the first time in history that an entire British army had been captured. It was the turning point of the Revolution.

On December 4, 1777, a Boston sea captain, Jonathan L. Austin, arrived in Paris with the news that Burgoyne's army had been captured. Franklin and his delegation had new ammunition to persuade King Louis XVI to commit to an official treaty of alliance with the United States.[33]

FOUR

French Egos and Colonial Conspirators

KOSCIUSZKO'S DIVERSIONARY TACTICS DURING THE RETREAT from Ticonderoga and his battle plan for Saratoga earned him a reputation as an adroit field strategist among the troops. Soldiers often had to lobby Congress for promotions, but Kosciuszko's awkward English and lack of political skills kept him from leveraging his achievements for advancement. And as France was helping the United States with guns and soldiers, French recruits overshadowed him.

The Polish rebel focused on his job in the field. He understood that the job of a clever military engineer was to come up with a strategy and a battle plan. Engineers had to decide where to position the troops by using math and physics to figure out how far cannonballs could fly and the firing range for muskets. They had to organize troop movements quickly, coordinate safe campsites, and select defensible positions. The military engineer was a crucial part of the war effort.

This is precisely why Benjamin Franklin had asked the French to send engineers. Franklin advanced the recruitment campaign in Paris that was started by Beaumarchais and Silas Deane, and negotiated an agreement to commission four of the king's military engineers for service in America. But rather than give up his seasoned war veterans, King Louis XVI sent four recent graduates from the French military academy.

Before sending these raw cadets on a mission abroad, the king promoted Capt. Louis Duportail to major, Louis de la Radiere and Jean Baptiste Joseph de Laumoy to captain and Jean Baptiste de Gouvion to lieutenant in the French army. It was February 1777 and, unsatisfied with the king's gesture, Major Duportail demanded that before they set sail for America, Congress must also agree to promote all the engineers again by one additional rank.[1]

By March, when Duportail learned that they would have to sail through the Caribbean to avoid the British blockade, he complained to Franklin about having to make "such a detour." When the envoys of the French king finally disembarked in Philadelphia in July 1777, they were furious to learn that one of their countrymen, another engineer who had arrived before them, Maj. Philippe Tronson du Coudray had climbed the ranks in America to major general.[2] They were also piqued when the nineteen-year-old Marquis de Lafayette arrived and was appointed general.

Duportail thought very highly of himself, and before the French king's engineers lifted a gun or stuck a shovel in the ground in support of America's Revolution against the British king, the new arrival wrote a letter to Congress complaining that he and his "Royal Engineers . . . [are] Demanding for me the rank of Brigadier-general, for Mr. de la Radiere of Colonel, for Mr. de Gouvion the rank of Lt. Colonel." In addition to promotions the French officers wanted more money, and Duportail issued a memorandum to Congress demanding higher pay for his engineers, servants to wait on them, two horses for each of his engineers and three for himself, declaring that these things were "absolutely necessary for our service."[3]

The French engineers presented a quandary for George Washington. Two decades earlier France had been Washington's enemy in the French and Indian War and after surrendering at the Battle of Fort Necessity; his reputation was nearly destroyed when he was tricked into signing a truce written in French, which he did not understand. It said that he had "assassinated" a French officer named Jumonville. But with France funding the rebellion against the British, Washington had to appease Duportail as best as he could.

Washington also had a problem with Gates. The decisive victory over the British at Saratoga inflated Gates's ego and put him in a position to challenge Washington's authority as commander in chief. While Gates's celebrity was on the rise after he turned the tables on the British, Washington was on the run after losing the Battles of Brandywine and Germantown. When the Redcoats attacked Philadelphia, Congress fled west and set up shop in York, Pennsylvania. Washington was the scapegoat. Driven from their capital, several New England delegates believed that the commander in chief should be replaced.

John Adams was openly critical of Washington's "Fabian strategy," named after the Roman dictator Fabius Maximus, who used delaying tactics and harassment against his enemy Hannibal rather than seek a decisive battle. Adams wrote, "Washington has a great body of militia assembled and assembling, in addition to a grand Continental army. Whether he will strike or not, I can't say. He is very prudent, you know, and will not unnecessarily hazard his army. . . . I am sick of Fabian systems in all quarters. The officers drink, [to] a long and moderate war. My toast is, a short and violent war."[4]

In a shot across Washington's bow, on October 17, 1777, Congress reestablished the Board of War to oversee his handling of the military. For their sneaky maneuvering, the anti-Washington faction became known as "the Conway cabal."[5]

It was named after Gen. Thomas Conway, an Irishman who had served in the French army. He did not like Washington, and after the Battle of Saratoga, Conway wrote a congratulatory letter to Gates in which he took a dig at the commander in chief, saying, "Heaven had determined to save our country, or a weak general and bad counselors would have ruined it."[6]

The letter would have gone unnoticed, but Colonel Wilkinson blabbered on about the news of Conway's disparagement of Washington. Gates sent Wilkinson to York to deliver the official dispatch of Burgoyne's surrender to Congress. Wilkinson took his time and instead of rushing to deliver the news of this victory. The twenty-year-old Wilky lollygagged through the countryside, taking eleven days to travel the 285 miles from Albany to York, which he should have covered in half that time.[7]

Wilky spent a few days with his fiancée, Ann Biddle, in Easton, Pennsylvania. Next, he dawdled in Reading, Pennsylvania, where he got drunk and indiscreetly talked about Conway's letter about replacing Washington with Gates. By the time he made it to York, Wilkinson acted as if the war were over, proclaiming to Congress: "The whole British army have laid down their arms, at Saratoga; our own, full of vigor and courage; expect your orders: it is for your wisdom to decide where the country may still have need for their services."[8]

Congress was so impressed with the success at Saratoga that it presented Gates with a gold medal, minted expressly in commemoration of this glorious victory.[9] And on November 27 Congress fired another salvo at the commander in chief's leadership and expanded the Board of War, adding Washington's biggest critic, Gen. Thomas Mifflin, along with the commissary general Joseph Trumbull and a lawyer, Richard Peters. Adding insult to this injury, Gates was named president of the board.

Washington's enemies were a malcontented group of officers and officials who had been passed over for higher positions. They were allied with John Adams, who thought Washington might try to take over as a military dictator. Rumors of the Conway cabal made it into the press. A Tory newspaper, *Rivington's Royal Gazette*, reported: "A junto is formed at Philadelphia, and said to consist of Generals Mifflin, Thompson, Arnold, and Sinclair; their object is the removal of George Washington from the chief of command of the rebel army. The Generals Lee and Gates, with all the Yankees who have resolution enough to declare themselves of a party wish well to this enterprise."[10]

That Arnold would be involved in a "junto" with his nemesis Gates was preposterous. But the legend of the cabal spread through the ranks of the military.[11] Washington was furious over the gossip that Wilkinson had spread about him being a "weak general." He confronted Conway, but the Irishman issued a declaration saying that he never wrote the offending line.[12] Washington weathered the storm and reestablished his authority over the army.

When Gates heard that Washington learned about the Conway letter through Wilky's gossip, he berated his chatty colonel. Gates aggravated the situation by claiming that the letter had been stolen from his camp. The disagreement between the general and his subordinate spun out of control, and Wilkinson challenged Gates to a duel with pistols. But when Wilky showed up, a teary-eyed Gates took his protégé by the hand and said, "I, injure you, it is impossible, I should as soon think of injuring my own child."[13]

While York was engulfed in political chaos, Kosciuszko was posted 250 miles away in Albany trying to hold together the ragged Northern Army and build redoubts to protect New York from another attack. Kosciuszko stayed loyal to Gates on a personal level, but because of his rudimentary English and lack of contact with Congress in York, he was out of the loop of the machinations of military politics.

The "cabalists" were trying to push their own agenda, but Washington had a war to fight. Even though he had not met Kosciuszko, he acknowledged the Pole's growing reputation. On November 10, 1777, when Washington wrote to Congress requesting promotions for Duportail and the French officers who were threatening to "quit the service," he also asked for a promotion for Kosciuszko: "While I am on this subject, I would take the liberty to mention, that I have been well informed, that the Engineer in the Northern Army (Cosieski, I think his name is) is a Gentleman of science and merit. From the character I have had of him he is deserving of notice, too."[14]

When Congress promoted Duportail to general, and each of the French engineers by an additional rank, Kosciuszko's friends argued that he should be promoted as well. One of these was Col. Robert Troup, who was with Gates in York. Kosciuszko responded to Troup, saying: "I am far from possessing such Qualities as you mention. . . . My dear Colonel if you see that my promotion will make a great many Jealous, tell the General that I will not accept of one because I prefer peace more than the greatest Rank in the World."[15]

A cold winter set in and the snowfall in northern New York sent many of the rebels home to seek shelter. Kosciuszko tried to keep his work crew in Albany busy, fed, and paid so that the Northern Army would not fall apart. He signed a memorandum with Capt. Jedidiah Thayer of Massachusetts, who promised to raise a company of 80 carpenters to work through the winter without leave.

Kosciuszko promised that the captain would be paid "Fourteen Shillings each Day, One Lieutenant Twelve Shillings, two Foremans Eleven Shillings each, the Quarter Master Seven Shillings and each Private Nine Shillings per Day New York currency, for each day he Shall be in Actual Employment, that each man Shall Receive one and half Ration of Provisions, and one half pint of Rum a man per Day."[16]

The standard of living in the colonies was higher than in England because of all of the successful farmers and merchants. While the soldiers had a plentiful bounty on their tables at home, the fare served by the Continental Army usually consisted of gruel, or Scottish "bannock cakes" made of oats, water, salt, and lard mashed into small patties and fried on a hot griddle. When oats were lacking, Indian cornmeal was used. So keeping the men in the field, when they could fill their bellies at home, was no easy task. The lack of food made spirits all the more important, and rum was the best way to keep the rebels from abandoning their posts. Without an alcoholic stimulant, some men refused to fight, and soldiers demanded their daily ration as a foodstuff. But with supplies dwindling, the size of the Northern Army began to shrink.

Boredom in the dark winter months was an additional problem, and the Continental Army needed a crusade for inspiration. For many, Quebec was the prize that captured the imagination. It would stop the Redcoats from using Canada as a base for future attacks on New York and New England, and Kosciuszko was eager to take part in the raid. Gates often spoke with his inner circle about an invasion of Canada, and Kosciuszko viewed his mentor as the obvious choice to lead such a mission.

The charming Pole used every method he could to try to join that mission. He had a good rapport with the opposite sex and was not above using coquetry to get his way. A handsome man with a medium build, brown flowing hair, he was a notorious flirt and at his best when stroking women's egos with platonic banter.

Kosciuszko was a good friend of Mrs. Gates, and from Albany he wrote to her in French, "I suppose that you and I both enjoy the same advantages of good society: I should like to see you, Madam, during the journey taking out biscuits from your portable magazine where they are so neatly stored, and distributing them among your Family and saying: my son, Here, this is for you; come Troup, take this Biscuit, it is very good; and then I should like to see General Gates how he takes one and says, indeed they are good for nothing. O! Madam how I should laugh."[17] But the real reason for the buttery letter to Mrs. Gates was to persuade her to rely on her "good heart" to remind her husband of the "recommendation before Congress" to include Kosciuszko in the Canadian campaign.

Around this time the Polish rebel Casimir Pulaski finally made it to America. He was in Pennsylvania with Washington trying to form a European-style cavalry.

One of Pulaski's cavalrymen from Poland, Jan Zielinski, contacted Kosciuszko after Zielinski was struck in a confrontation with an Irish officer, Col. Stephen Moylan. Pulaski sided with his countryman, but after a court-martial Moylan was acquitted, even though the evidence showed that he had lost his temper and struck Zielinski in a hotheaded rage because he could understand neither his English nor his French.

On January 17, 1778, Kosciuszko wrote to Washington asking "protection for me and my Countryman Mr. Zielinski, if his side is right as he informed me: But if it is not, tell him Sir that he had better return to his Country than make confusion to me and others. I should be very sorry to see him Conduct bad in this Country. I beg more of your favour Sir to have me always under your Command and believe my sincere attachment to you."[18] This is the first known communication between Kosciuszko and Washington, and with his expression of loyalty to the commander in chief, the Polish officer made it clear that he was not involved with the rumored cabal.

Lafayette, worried that as a foreign officer he might not be respected by American soldiers, also expressed concern about the Moylan verdict in a letter to Washington: "Count De Pulaski was much affronted by the decision of a court martial entirely acquitting Colonel Molens [sic]. However, as I know the English customs I am nothing else but surprised to see such partiality in a court martial."[19]

When Pulaski arrived in America he delivered a letter to Lafayette from his wife, and the two foreign officers developed a mutual respect. Lafayette became one of Washington's closest friends, and the conspirators who wanted to replace the commander in chief searched for a way to drive a wedge between the two.

Gates was in control of the Board of War and attempted to get the long-stalled invasion of Canada back on track. The board appointed Lafayette to lead the mission and appointed the controversial Conway as his second in command. The rationale was that the French-speaking population of Montreal would welcome Lafayette as a liberator who could help them shake off the British yoke. Lafayette had heard the rumors of the Conway cabal, and seeking Washington's approval, he demanded that the German general Johann de Kalb be second-in-command of the invasion.[20]

Once Lafayette was ready to leave for Albany, the board held a party and toasted him with wine and flattery, promising that he would be met by an army of three thousand regulars, as well as John Stark and one thousand rebels known as the Green Mountain Boys from Vermont. Lafayette sat placidly listening to the festivities, and when he rose to speak, there was a breathless silence in the room. The young general reminded his hosts that there was one toast they forgot to make. He lifted his glass and proposed that they drink to the health of Washington.

The historian John Fiske wrote, "The deep silence became still deeper. None dared to refuse the toast, but some merely raised their glasses to their lips while others cautiously put them down untasted."[21] The officers bowed to each other and parted ways. Lafayette mounted his horse and began his 300-mile trek to Albany.

Kosciuszko greeted Lafayette in Albany on February 17, 1778. The French general gave Kosciuszko a firsthand account of Pulaski's efforts to raise a cavalry unit in Pennsylvania, and the Polish engineer gave Lafayette an update on the sorry state of the Northern Army.

Instead of the promised thousands, there were fewer than twelve hundred soldiers in Albany. They were dressed in rags and not equipped or ready to make the long march north to Canada. Arnold was bedridden with the wounds from Saratoga and facing the possibility that his leg might be amputated. When Lafayette went to visit him, Arnold went on a tirade claiming that Gates was a coward and "the greatest poltroon in the world."[22]

Lafayette felt that he had been duped. He wrote an emotional letter to the president of Congress, Henry Laurens, complaining about the "hell of blunders, madness, and deception I am involved in," referring to the planned invasion as a "ridiculous and schoking [sic] affair a piece of folly or a piece of villainy beyond all expressions." He said Arnold was "an inveterate enemy to General Gates and calls him the greatest poltroon in the world and many other genteel qualifications of that kind. . . . I am reduced to wish to have never [set] foot in America or thought of an American war."[23]

Once it became obvious that the Canadian incursion would not take place, and probably hoping to meet with Pulaski and the other Poles in Pennsylvania, Kosciuszko set out for York. Lafayette asked Kosciuszko to deliver his letter to Congress, but the day after Kosciuszko left Albany, Lafayette rethought his angry rant and sent a less emotional, toned-down draft of the letter. Lafayette's express rider made it to York before Kosciuszko, and the angry letter was read after the calmer correspondence had been delivered. Gates opened the letter from Lafayette and the mixup caused even more frustration for the French general.

Kosciuszko arrived in York three days after the argument between Gates and Wilkinson. By then plans for an invasion of Canada had completely fizzled, so Kosciuszko asked for a new posting. He was itching to prove himself in battle, but because of the shortage of engineers he was deployed to the highlands of New York's mid–Hudson Valley to prevent a battle from taking place.

Around this time Pulaski was trying to persuade Congress to form a cavalry that could storm the British positions and cause havoc in their rear. As the leader of dragoon battles against a Russian army that outnumbered his, and a veteran of the Turkish war, Pulaski had more combat experience than anyone in the Continental Army. He met Ben Franklin in Paris, who recommended him to Washington, writing: "Count Pulaski of Poland, an officer famous throughout Europe for his bravery and conduct in defence of the liberties of his country against the three great invading powers of Russia, Austria and Prussia . . . may be highly useful to our service."[24]

Pulaski presented his recommendation to Congress and rode to Washington's headquarters at Valley Forge, where he showed off his horsemanship and adroit handling of weapons. At a full gallop Pulaski would drop his hat to the ground and circle back, hanging from his horse, to pick it up. Charging through the field on his mount, he would flip his pistol into the air and catch it after completing complicated maneuvers on the horse.[25] The point of Pulaski's rodeo stunts was to show the superiority of a cavalryman over an infantry soldier. In a garbled mix of broken English, French, and Polish he tried to explain that troop mobility is key during combat. In mainland Europe and on the steppes of Asia, the cavalry reigned supreme.

On September 11, 1777, Pulaski proved himself when British general Howe's army attacked Washington's troops on the Brandywine River between Baltimore and Philadelphia. As a ruse Howe sent some troops ahead to give the appearance that the attack would come along the river, while his main army traveled upstream, crossed the river, and outflanked Washington's troops, much the same way they had at the Battle of Long Island. The Continental Army collapsed and started to retreat as Howe moved in for the kill. But Pulaski persuaded Washington to allow him to lead the general's thirty mounted bodyguards in a counterattack.

Paul Bentalou, a French captain in the Continental Army, wrote: "Pulaski, with his usual intrepidity and judgment led them to the charge and succeeded in retarding the advance of the enemy—a delay which was of the highest importance to our retreating army. Moreover, the penetrating military *coup d'oeil* of Pulaski soon perceived that the enemy was maneuvering to take possession of the road leading to Chester, with the view of cutting off our retreat, or at least, the column of our baggage. He hastened to General Washington, to communicate the information, and was immediately authorized by the commander in chief to collect as many of the scattered troops as he could find at hand, and make the best use of them. . . . Pulaski, who, by an oblique advance upon the enemy's front and right flank, defeated their object, and effectually protected our baggage, and the retreat of our army."[26]

Pulaski's quick reaction kept the British from wiping out Washington's army. Word of Pulaski's horse sense and military prowess made it to York, and four days after the Battle of Brandywine, Congress commissioned him the country's first "commander of the horse," with the rank of brigadier general. Yet even

after the father of the American cavalry showed the colonials how mounted soldiers were more effective than foot soldiers, Pulaski's dragoons were still considered a reconnaissance troop or diversionary unit, while the infantry was the
primary fighting force.

After rescuing Washington's men at Brandywine, Pulaski became famous,
while the humble Kosciuszko, whose efforts had a greater impact on the overall
Revolution, was still a colonel. Although Pulaski arrived in America a year later
than Kosciuszko, his proximity to Washington and Congress put him in a better
position for advancement, while Kosciuszko's connection to Gates and Lee, who
were sniping at the commander in chief, relegated him to the shadows.

This would soon change.

Washington understood that the British wanted to divide and conquer the
American colonies by controlling the Hudson, then called the "North River."
Their plan was to separate New England's troublemakers from the Southern
states, where a larger share of the population was still loyal to King George. For
the British, keeping the "Yankee" revolution from flowing from the North to the
South became critical.

The Hudson was first explored in 1609, when Henry Hudson sailed upstream
for the Dutch East India Company. Five years later Dutch settlers founded Fort
Orange, which was later expanded and renamed Albany. The river became a major trade route for raw materials such as Indian furs, agricultural goods, flour,
timber, and livestock heading south from upstate to New York City, and finished
products north from the city.

In addition to the Hudson, which flows south for 315 miles from the Adirondacks past Albany, New York City, and into the ocean, New York's vast network
of waterways includes the Mohawk River, which pours into the Hudson from the
west, and the St. Lawrence River, which connects the Atlantic Ocean from the
north to the Great Lakes and to Lake Champlain. Washington was so impressed
by these water routes that he called New York "the seat of empire," giving it its
nickname, the Empire State.[27] His understanding of the potential for inland
navigation, showed great foresight, because several decades later, when these
waterways were connected by the Erie Canal, New York became an economic
powerhouse with commerce and immigration flowing through its harbors.[28]

But, Washington lacked a real navy. Without help from the French navy, the
best chance the Americans had to destroy the British fleet was when it was close
to shore. The best spot from which to defend America's busiest inland water
route was in the highlands of the Hudson Valley. He outlined this strategy, writing, "It is the only passage by which the Enemy from New York or any part of
our Coast, can ever hope to Cooperate with an Army that may come from
Canada . . . the possession of it is indispensably essential."[29]

On December 2, 1777, he wrote to Gen. Israel Putnam: "The importance of the North River in the present contest and the necessity of defending it, are subjects which have been so frequently and so fully discussed and are so well understood, that it is unnecessary to enlarge upon them." Washington wrote that if the Continental Army was "to preserve the communication between the Eastern, Middle and Southern States" and keep the "chief supplies of flour" flowing to feed the troops, Putnam had to use all his forces to erect "works and obstructions as may be necessary to defend and secure the River against any future attempts of the Enemy."

Since autumn 1777 the British had burned Kingston, New York, and its wheat fields to the ground, Washington worried that the Redcoats would try to destroy all the houses, mills, and towns in the Hudson Valley. "Unless proper measures are taken to prevent them," he wrote Putnam, "they will renew their Ravages in the Spring, or as soon as the season will admit, and perhaps Albany the only Town in the State of any importance remaining in our hands, may undergo a like fate and a general havoc and devastation take place."[30]

The French engineer Colonel Radiere was ordered to report to General Putnam in the Hudson Highlands and design the defenses for West Point as the Americans saw fit. But as soon as he arrived, the Frenchman clashed with Putnam and the other officers. Kosciuszko, who worked with Putnam on the defenses for Philadelphia, would soon be sent to take Radiere's place. But Gates and the Board of War made the switch without telling Washington.

The Continental Army was still at Valley Forge in the winter of 1778, when Pulaski was putting together his proposal for an independent cavalry unit, which he would present to the Board of War. Before he made up his mind on whether to fund the horse unit, Gates would have asked his Polish engineer, Kosciuszko, what he knew about his famous countryman. As Kosciuszko had never met the Bar confederate, he could only talk about Pulaski's reputation, so he would probably have been eager to meet him.

In March, Kosciuszko was riding north to Albany from York, and Pulaski was about to travel south to the temporary rebel capital. The historian Miecislaus Haiman believed that their paths must have crossed near Valley Forge in mid-March 1778.[31]

While there is no evidence that the encounter took place, the two Polish revolutionaries appear to have had a common friend in Haym Salomon, a Polish Jew who helped finance the American Revolution. The financial broker's son, Haym M. Salomon, said that his father was an "intimate associate" of Pulaski and Kosciuszko.[32] Most likely Pulaski met Salomon in 1778, while he was raising money to outfit his cavalry legion. Kosciuszko probably met Salomon later.[33]

Salomon left Poland because of Russia's subjugation of Poland and the heavy taxes imposed on Jews.[34] He worked as a merchant, banker, and currency trader in Holland and France before coming to New York City around 1775, where he began courting fifteen-year-old Rachel Franks. Her father, Moses B. Franks, was a successful merchant, who with his brother, Jacob, ran the commissary for the British during the French and Indian War.[35] Rachel's brother, Isaac, was a major in the Continental Army, who served with Kosciuszko at West Point.[36] Her cousin Maj. (later Col.) David Salisbury Franks was aide-de-camp to Benedict Arnold.[37]

In 1776 Salomon loaded a horse cart with provisions and traveled to Fort Ticonderoga, where he pitched a tent and ran the commissary for the troops. General Schuyler discouraged "suttling," or peddling, to his soldiers, but a New York legislator wrote a letter of recommendation to the Northern commander: "Mr. Haym Salomon tells me he has laid in stores to go Suttling. . . . I can inform the General that Mr. Salomon has hitherto sustained the character of being warmly attached to America."[38]

Salomon returned to New York City and hung his shingle at 22 Wall Street, where he became an auctioneer and broker of "every species of merchandise . . . and every branch of business."[39] Arrested by the English as "a spy," he escaped to Philadelphia in 1778 and began trading foreign currencies out of a coffee shop. Salomon sent for his wife and child and moved them into a house on Front Street. The coffee shop became Philadelphia's de facto stock market, and Salomon loaned money to the Founding Fathers. Salomon also met the French ambassador, the Chevalier de La Luzerne, who hired him as broker, paymaster, and supplier of the French troops.

The superintendent of finance for the United States, Robert Morris, had to find creative ways to fund the war. At first Morris preferred to deal with brokers of his own faith, but as Salomon's reputation grew as a financial backer of the Revolution, his cooperation with Morris grew as well. More than seventy-five notations in Morris's records outline some of Salomon's financial transactions obtaining money, provisions, and raw materials from rich colonials who supported the Revolution.[40]

The American navy was virtually nonexistent, so it relied on privateers, such as John Paul Jones, who were given prize money for raiding British ships. Called "pirates" by King George, these seamen captured more than three thousand English merchant vessels carrying commercial goods, money, and supplies such as muskets and gunpowder that were transferred to the rebel army.[41] Morris, Salomon, and other merchants helped auction off the booty captured by these raiders of British ships.

Salomon joined Philadelphia's Jewish congregation and donated money to build a synagogue. He also led the fight to repeal Pennsylvania laws that prohibited non-Christians from serving in public office. One of Salomon's friends, James Madison, became a champion of freedom of religion, and for those who were true to the noble cause, the broker was not so quick to call in the loans, if at all. Madison realized this when he wrote to Representative Edmund Randolph in 1782: "I have for some time been a pensioner on the favor of Haym Salomon, a Jew broker."[42]

A month later Madison again wrote to Randolph, "The kindness of our little friend in Front street, near the coffee-house, is a fund which will preserve me from extremities, but I never resort to it without great mortification, as he obstinately rejects all recompense."[43]

Madison was but one of the politicians to whom Salomon lent money without asking for repayment. Salomon subsidized those with enlightened views, advancing funds to Thomas Jefferson, General St. Clair, Gen. Baron von Steuben, Col. Dan Morgan, and at least one receipt showed that he lent Kosciuszko $142.[44] While Pulaski transferred some of his own funds from Poland for the "Pulaski Legion," Salomon probably assisted him with his connections in French and Dutch banks to finance Pulaski's independent cavalry.

When Salomon died in 1785 at age forty-five, he had no will, but left receipts at the Register's Officer in Philadelphia for various loans and state and treasury certificates totaling $353,744 to the U.S. government. Unfortunately many of the records concerning Salomon were destroyed when the British burned Washington, D.C., during the War of 1812.[45] In 1850, however, the U.S. Senate issued a report that said: "Haym Salomon gave great assistance to the government by loans of money, and advancing liberally of his means to sustain the men engaged in the struggle for independence at a time when the sinews of war were essential to success."[46]

Salomon's contribution to the American Revolution showed Kosciuszko that the Jews were willing to take part in the struggle for liberty against a monarchy and the old system of government. This would have ramifications for the coming struggle for liberty in Poland as well.

FIVE

Washington's West Point Architect

AFTER LEAVING PENNSYLVANIA, KOSCIUSZKO RETURNED TO
Albany, picked up his belongings, and bade farewell to his friends before
riding back down the Hudson to his new post. Colonel Troup wrote to Gates:
"Kosciuszko left this, for West Point, on Monday. When I cease to love this
young Man, I must cease to love those Qualities which form the brightest &
completest of characters."[1] This was in sharp contrast with the French engineer
Kosciuszko was about to replace. His predecessor in the Highlands, Radiere,
seemed to offend everyone he worked with.

From the start of the war in 1775, Washington had a hard time finding an architect to devise a strategy to protect the Hudson. Fifty miles north of New York
City, West Point juts out into the river where it narrows and turns ninety degrees
through rocky escarpments and mountains called the Hudson Highlands. The
Americans wanted to arm vantage points from which they could fire on British
ships that passed. The bend in the river has steep cliffs on its western bank,
marshland near the shore of its eastern bank, and a hill in the middle of the river
known as Constitution Island. Any vessel that tried to navigate these waters had
to slow down to make the sharp turn and squeeze through the channel between
the island and the cliffs of the highlands, through which treacherous air currents
often blew.

New York first hired Bernard Romans, a Dutch-born surveyor, mapmaker,
and botanist, but after drawing lavish plans that were ineffective, Washington,
dismissed him in January 1776, when one general concluded: "Upon the whole,
Mr. Romans has displayed his genius at a very great expense and to very little

public advantage."[2] The state then recruited New York City's chief engineer, William Smith, who outlined three forts on Constitution Island but left before construction began. For the rest of 1776 and 1777 the Americans focused on building Forts Montgomery and Clinton farther down the Hudson.

In early January 1778 Major General Putnam, Gen. Samuel Holden Parsons, and his construction brigade trudged up the hills through two feet of snow to the frozen rocks of West Point to break ground on a new fort overlooking the Hudson. Maj. David Humphreys wrote, "Want of covering for the troops, together with want of tools and materials for the works, made the prospect truly gloomy and discouraging."[3]

Washington was relieved when the thrice-promoted French engineers finally agreed to get to work and Radiere was sent to the Hudson Highlands. But Radiere was still complaining about his rank when he arrived at West Point, and argued with the Americans over their plans. Frustrated with Radiere, on January 13 General Putnam wrote to Washington, "The place agreed upon to obstruct the navigation of Hudson River was at West Point. Previous to that, I had been with Governor Clinton, his brother, the French Engineer and several others, to view that place, it was the opinion of all except the Frenchman that it was the best, and only effectual [spot] on the river."[4]

Radiere told the Americans they were in the wrong place and asked for more time so he could design a massive Vauban-style fort downriver near Forts Montgomery and Clinton, which had been captured and then abandoned by the British. While Radiere worked on his plans, Putnam appointed a reconnoitering committee that unanimously determined West Point to be the best place for the fort. Radiere drew impressive diagrams of a stone fortress that looked like a European castle, but he couldn't actually get anything built.

"I have directed the Engineers to lay out the Fort immediately," Putnam told Washington, adding that Radiere "seems greatly disgusted that every thing does not go as he thinks proper, even if contrary to the judgment of every other person. In short he is an excellent paper engineer, and I think it would be as well for us if he was employed wholly in that way—I am confident if Congress could have found business for him, with them, our works, would have been as well constructed and much more forward than they now are."[5]

Radiere refused to follow orders and went over General Putnam's head, writing directly to Washington and to Congress, complaining, "It was resolved to fortify a place called West Point . . . this was done contrary to my advice." Radiere's correspondence complained that the officers in New York also disputed his command when he sought to court-martial a captain of artillery. "For me the case is not open to doubt," Radiere wrote, "otherwise we, whom you have treated as legitimate children would be bastards in the military state."[6]

Radiere failed to realize that Washington himself had suggested West Point years earlier when he sailed through the canyons of the Hudson.[7] The commander in chief also became exasperated with the French engineer and responded to Radiere: "As the Majority of the Council were for erecting the new works upon West Point, in preference to the place upon which Fort Clinton was built, I desire that they may be carried on with all dispatch. If we remain much longer disputing about the proper place, we shall lose the winter, which is the only time that we have to make preparations for the reception of the Enemy."[8]

The Frenchman also fought with General Parsons, who was overseeing construction, so Parsons wrote to Washington: "Col. La Radiere [is] finding it impossible to compleat the Fort and other Defences intended at this Post in Such Manner as to effectively withstand the Attempts of the Enemy."[9] Parsons said Radiere told him that he did not want to "hazard his reputation" on a fort so small. The Americans overruled Radiere's grandiose ideas because their focus was not to protect themselves, but to provide cover for the huge iron chain that they had stretched across the river to block navigation.

Radiere became such a distraction that New York governor George Clinton complained to the Board of War: "The works in this Quarter for the defence of the Country and Security of the River go on very tardily indeed, it can hardly be said (with strict propriety) they have yet Commenced. . . . I fear the Engineer who has the direction of the works is deficient in point of practical Knowledge; without which altho possessed of ever so much scientific I need not mention to you Sir, how unfit he must be for the present Task, the Chief Direction & Management of which requires a Man of Business & Authority."[10]

On March 5, 1778, Gates and the Board of War issued a direct order stating that Radiere must accommodate Clinton's "plans & mode of constructing the Batteries & Forts, to the Nature of the Country and Material, Time & Number of Men; in all which he is absolutely to be directed by Governor Clinton or the Commanding Officer of the Army in which he acts who are best acquainted with these circumstances . . . it will be improper for Col. Radiere to command the Troops."[11]

The order also directed Kosciuszko to report to the highlands under the command of General Putnam as engineer of West Point. But Putnam left to attend to personal business in Connecticut, so Kosciuszko reported to Governor Clinton in Poughkeepsie. The governor was impressed with the Pole and wrote a letter to Parsons: "Colo. Kuziazke who by Resolve of Congress is directed to act as Ingeneer at the Works for the Security of the River will deliver you this: I believe you will find him an Ingenous Young Man & disposed to do every Thing he can in the most agreeable Manner."[12]

By the time Kosciuszko arrived at West Point in late March, Radiere had so annoyed everyone that the Americans were relieved to have an agreeable engineer. Parsons worked well with Kosciuszko.[13] Like Radiere, Kosciuszko also studied Vauban's theories. Since it would take years to build a massive stone fort, and as time was of the essence to stave off a British attack to keep commerce and military transports flowing on the river, the rebels began throwing up works of earth and rocks. Masonry and stones would be added later.

By tradition forts were named after the officer who built and defended them. As the governor's brother, Col. James Clinton, and his brigade would build the main fort, it was to be named after him. Behind Fort Clinton was a grassy plateau. A few hundred yards to the west were a thick forest with two elevations, Rocky Point and Crown Hill, that loomed over the fields and the fort. These hills made the fort vulnerable to attack from land, and just as he did at Fort Ticonderoga, Kosciuszko pointed out that the hills should be fortified with cannons.

But first Parsons and Kosciuszko focused on pointing cannons at the shipping lanes below Fort Clinton, leading to the chain. They agreed that the British would not be able to climb the sheer descent of rock to the east and north that were hundreds of feet above the river, so they built up the southern and western sides of Fort Clinton, constructing walls that were nine feet high and twenty feet thick. Kosciuszko placed eight cannons to provide cross fire against an inland British infantry assault, and strategically laid out plans for batteries to cover the chain and the Continental Army's dock on the river.[14]

The Polish engineer was introduced to the talented and resourceful Capt. Thomas Machin, who was foreman of the construction crews and keeper of the chain. Machin was the backbone of the operations at West Point, and he and Kosciuszko designed a huge capstan on Constitution Island in the middle of the river. This rotating spindle was used to reel in the chain whenever it needed to be stored.[15]

Machin had built cannon batteries along the river's edge to fire upon anyone who came near the chain, and Kosciuszko added two more: the Lanthorn Battery at Gee's Point, to force ships away from the chain and to cover the point, and also the Knox Battery on a cliff above the river, to cover the South Dock. Kosciuszko also designed plans to protect Fort Clinton from the southern landside approaches along the river with three redoubts and batteries that were dubbed Forts Meigs, Wyllys, and Webb.

When the disgruntled Radiere showed up at the camp in Valley Forge, Washington was shocked that he had abandoned his post. Unaware that the Board of War had already replaced him, and concerned about alienating the French at a time when Franklin was in Paris asking for more money and military support, Washington listened to Radiere's complaints and sent him back to West Point. Washington also sent Gen. Alexander McDougall, a Scotsman, to take General Putnam's place and speed up construction of the fort.

Upon his return to West Point, Radiere was surprised to find another engineer at work and fought with Kosciuszko just as he did with the Americans. He refused to follow orders from the Polish colonel, who by the date of his commission and direct orders from the Board of War outranked him. Arguing that he answered only to General Duportail, Radiere continued drafting plans, but by that point he was no longer welcome.

Major Humphreys described the situation: "The estimates and requisitions of Colonel la Radiere, the Engineer who laid out the works altogether disproportioned to our circumstances served only to put us in mind of our poverty, and, as it were to satirize our resources. His petulant behaviour and unaccommodating disposition added further embarrassments."[16]

Conversely, Kosciuszko got along with the rebels and got the job done. Jared Sparks, the eminent historian who interviewed veterans of the American Revolution, wrote that the Pole had an impact on the base as soon as he arrived: "Gen. McDougall took the command on the 28th of March. Two days previously Kosciuszko arrived, who had been appointed engineer in place of Radiere. From that time on the works were pressed forward with spirit. To the scientific skill and sedulous application of Kosciuszko, the public was mainly indebted for the construction of the military defences at West Point."[17]

Frustrated to learn that there were two engineers at West Point, Washington wrote to McDougall, "The presence of Colonel de la Radiere rendering the Services of Mr. Kosciouski, as Engineer at Fishkill, unnecessary, you are to give him orders to join this Army without loss of time." Yet in the same letter the commander in chief wrote, "P.S. However desirous I am that Mr. Kosciousko should repair to this Army, if he is specially employed by order of Congress or the Board of War, I would not wish to contravene their Commands."[18]

This did little to clarify the situation, and McDougall had to separate the Pole and the Frenchman until he could resolve this quandary. The consensus at camp about who should stay was obvious to everyone but McDougall. General Parsons made the case for the officers, writing to their new commander: "Inclosed are the Resolutions of Congress and Board of War respecting this Post and the conduct o the Engineer employed. Colo. Kosciuszko sent to this Place is particularly agreeable to the Gentleman of this State and all others concerned at this Post. . . . As we are desirous of having Col. Kosciuszko continue here and both cannot live upon the Point, I wish your Honor to adopt such Measures as will answer the Wishes of the People and Garrison; and best serve the public Good."[19]

General McDougall had to figure out himself which engineer was more proficient. It would not take long. Two weeks after taking command of the highlands, McDougall, who was still relying on Radiere as his engineer, set out with the Frenchman and other officers on a reconnaissance mission of the high ground overlooking their position. On the summit of Crown Hill the Frenchman convinced the officers that the British would never be able to drag cannons up the steep incline. And even if they did, Radiere argued, it would be too far away to threaten the main fort. As none of the Americans had engineering experience, they accepted Radiere's educated opinion.

That night, April 10, McDougall wrote in his diary, "Genl. Parson, Clinton and Col. Delaradiere went with me to View the Rock & Crown Hills in the rear of our works. They all agreed it was inexpedient to make any works on those hills, and the direction of cannon from there would be very uncertain." McDougall ordered Radiere "to report a proper plan to finish the works & the probable places the Enemy will land at on the west side" of the river.[20]

Kosciuszko had an eerie feeling of déjà vu when the colonial officers told him of their decision. Once again the rebels would be sitting ducks if they did not protect the hills to their rear. The Pole convinced the other officers that Radiere was wrong about not covering the high ground.

The Scotsman was paranoid about not repeating St. Clair's mistake at Fort Ticonderoga, so the next day he changed his mind after hearing that the other officers agreed with Kosciuszko. Radiere was furious at being made to look like a fool, and Kosciuszko went to work drafting blueprints for the defenses of Crown Hill. The Pole's design incorporated the existing steep cliffs by adding stone walls directly up the rock face, making the cliffs impossible to scale.

McDougall's turnaround could not have been more complete. A day after writing that it would be "inexpedient" to arm the hill, he suddenly wanted to arm all the hills around West Point. Col. Rufus Putnam, "Old Put's" younger cousin, had sailed down the Hudson with three hundred men crowded onto four sloops carrying fresh-cut lumber for the forts.[21] Colonel Putnam and Kosciuszko served together in the Saratoga campaign, and Putnam's brigade went to work building what would become Fort Putnam.

On April 11 McDougall wrote to Parsons, "The hill which Col. Putnam is fortifying is the most commanding and important of any that we can now attend to . . . the eastern-most face of this work must be so constructed as to command the plain."[22] The Scottish general changed his tactics and told his officers that the most important part of their battle plan would be to defend Forts Putnam and Clinton.

After the Frenchman's imprudent assessment on Crown Hill, McDougall wrote to Washington on April 13, 1777: "The heights near it are such at the Fort is not tenable if the enemy possess them. For this reason we are obliged to make some work on them." McDougall added that he needed five thousand men to complete the job, and that the men already there would prefer to work with Kosciuszko than Radiere. "Mr. Kosciuszko," he wrote, "is esteemed by those who have attended the works at West Point, to have had more practice than Col. Radiere, and his manner is more acceptable than that of the latter; which induced Gen. Parsons and Gov. Clinton to desire the former may be continued at West Point."[23]

Washington was fed up with the situation and recalled Radiere to Valley Forge, writing to McDougall on April 22: "I think it will be best to order La Radiere to return, especially as you say Kosiusko is better adapted to the genius and temper of the people."[24]

The pace of work at West Point stepped up after Radiere was sent packing, and more men and resources began arriving at West Point to build the defenses that Kosciuszko was designing. The remnants of the Northern Army that was supposed to take part in the aborted invasion in Canada began marching south from Albany to help.

With new arrivals pouring into the camp, Kosciuszko drew plans for the hundreds of blacksmiths, carpenters, and soldiers required to build forts, storehouses, a commissary, and barracks for six hundred men. The sleeping quarters had nine bunk beds in each room, so each room could sleep thirty-six men.

Accommodations, provisions, and horses were scarce, and when Lafayette pulled into camp on his way to Valley Forge after the Canadian mission was scrapped, McDougall commented in his diary that the "Marquis de Lafayette arrived here at 5 P.M. with 7 horses. And four Domestics." It seemed quite an extravagance for one man during wartime, and the next day McDougall noted that the elegant entourage "left us, after taking some replenishment."[25]

The Continental Army was strapped for resources and every cent had to go toward the war effort. The previous year the soldiers stretched an iron chain across the river. The links were one and half inches thick. But in the winter of 1778 Governor Clinton had to scrape together $92,000 to pay a blacksmith, Peter Townsend of Sterling Ironworks in Warwick, New York, to forge a new chain. Each link was two and quarter inches thick and two feet long and each weighed about 140 pounds. The entire chain was about fifteen hundred feet long and weighed 186 tons.[26]

The heavy iron links were kept afloat on huge logs and removed during the winter so that they wouldn't be broken by the ice floes. It took forty men four days to move the chain. Kosciuszko's capstan eased its removal, and he used tar and a burned lime plaster to refurbish the logs. The previous engineers had failed to motivate the troops, and the Pole was receiving praise for keeping the various construction projects moving. Colonel Troup wrote to Gates: "I have not seen the Works erecting at West Point, but it is said, They are in great Forwardness. Kosciuszko has made many Alterations, which are universally approved of; & I am happy to find he is esteemed as an able Engineer."[27]

McDougall also lauded the progress at the fort, and Governor Clinton, who had complained about Radiere, wrote that the work was "in good forwardness."[28]

When Dr. James Thacher was transferred to the highlands to become resident surgeon of the camp, he wrote in his diary: "We have a most interesting view of the fortress and garrison of West Point. Fort Putnam, on its most elevated part, the several redoubts beneath, and the barracks on the plain below, with numerous armed soldiers in active motion, all defended by the most formidable machinery of war."[29]

With the Conway affair fading into history, Gates requested to be sent back to active duty and resigned his post at president of the Board of War. After conferring with Washington at Valley Forge, on April 15 Gates was once again named the commander of the Northern Army to be stationed in the highlands. McDougall, who had sought a more active post, was being replaced. For Kosciuszko it meant that his mentor would be about twenty miles away, across the river in Fishkill at the highlands headquarters.

In late April whoops and hurrahs roared through the camps of the Continental Army as news spread that France had signed a treaty with the United States. After hearing about the victory at Saratoga, King Louis XVI officially sanctioned France's support of the war. The French navy was sailing for Boston. To celebrate, Deputy Quartermaster Hugh Hughes announced that a party would be held in the highlands: "A number of the friends to freedom and independence, chiefly New Yorkers, have agreed to spend a day in social festivity on account of the aforesaid intelligence, for which purpose they have provided an ox which is to be roasted whole." The feast was planned for May 2 in Fishkill, New York, and Hughes wrote, "In particular, I would beg that Capt. Machin & Col. Cusyesco may be of the party."[30]

The colonial soldiers spent the day gorging on roast beef, swilling grog, and toasting the French king, their independent states, their commander in chief, and whatever else popped into their drunken heads. That Kosciuszko would be an honored guest at the festivities celebrating France's entry into the war stuck in the craw of Radiere, who still wanted control over Washington's pet project. With France as an official ally of the United States, General Duportail began a coordinated campaign to undermine the Pole and reinstate Radiere as the architect of West Point.

Still hobbled from the musket ball that shattered his leg at Saratoga, on May 11, 1778, Benedict Arnold gimped into West Point to visit his friend General McDougall before he continued on to Valley Forge. McDougall briefed Arnold on the various projects under way, and as neither officer was too thrilled about having "Granny Gates" take command of the highlands, they came up with the perfect way to embarrass the old man before he even arrived. As Arnold was the true hero of Saratoga, McDougall decided to honor this victory and rename Fort Clinton after him. McDougall and Arnold must have had a good laugh, relishing the thought of Gates being forced to complete the construction of "Fort Arnold" while serving in the highlands.[31]

After Arnold showed up the Scotsman's attitude toward Kosciuszko also changed. One month earlier McDougall was making changes to West Point based on the Pole's suggestions and praising his work to Washington, writing that the fort "is so enclosed as to resist a sudden assault of the Enemy."[32] Yet the day Arnold arrived in camp, something changed, and McDougall fired off an angry letter to Governor Clinton: "I am far from being pleased with Mr. Korsuasco's constructing the Batteries, and carrying on the works, and I fear they will not answer the expectation of the Country."[33]

The Pole was caught in the backlash against his mentor. The ambitious Gates was making enemies among the officer corps, and he added a new foe when he replaced Col. John Lamb as commander of the artillery in the northern department with a junior officer. Lamb, who had more experience, was bitter and wrote to Gates's latest adjutant general, Col. William Malcom, complaining about favoritism. Lamb's biographer, Isaac Q. Leake, wrote: "The consequence of this predilection of Gates for particular officers had the usual effect of souring the minds of those who happened to be on the shady side of the General's favor, and of exciting strong prejudices against the more fortunate individuals who enjoyed the sunshine."[34]

Kosciuszko was one of the officers who basked in Gates's "sunshine," which stirred Arnold and Lamb's resentment. A week after Arnold's visit to West Point, Gates walked the grounds with McDougall and Kosciuszko to inspect the works. That's when McDougall gleefully informed his successor that the main garrison had been named "Fort Arnold." The Scotsman took the following week off, in which time he polished off "four and a half gallons of rum."[35]

Gates, who had faith in Kosciuszko's work, was pleased to see that his protégé had done so much in so little time. Yet a few weeks after Gates left for Fishkill, his aide Colonel Malcom denounced the project. Malcom, another rebel of Scottish descent, took a cursory look at Fortress West Point and griped to his friend Lamb: "I was sent to this command; which I found in just as bad order. . . . The works are not worth a farthing."[36]

Malcom's denigration of the works came when an attack on West Point by the Redcoats was becoming a growing possibility. The British commander in North America, Sir William Howe, was made the scapegoat for the loss of Burgoyne's army and recalled to London. With France joining the war against England, the new British commander, Sir Henry Clinton, was ordered to send five thousand troops to protect the British Crown's sugar plantations in the Caribbean. This forced him to withdraw from Philadelphia and consolidate his army in New York City, which was the more strategic position.

Washington followed the British north through New Jersey, and fought them in Monmouth before moving his main army to the highlands to get ready for the battle over New York. Duportail saw this as his chance to unseat Kosciuszko and reinstall Radiere as the architect of West Point. Not aware of the relationship between Gates and the Pole, Duportail wrote to Gates complaining about Kosciuszko and cautioning him not to risk "his reputation for a gentleman who does not know his duty."[37]

The British moved troops from Long Island and Staten Island north into Connecticut and from Philadelphia to northern New Jersey, ostensibly to search for provisions. Gates, at Washington's behest, responded by sending more resources to Gen. John Glover, the temporary commander at West Point, saying, "I must beg you to give your whole Attention to the completing of, first the Out Works at West Point, and then the Body of the Place; Col. Kusciuzsco cannot be too vigilant in this important service."[38]

Capts. Jedidiah Thayer and Jacob Low, and the carpenter companies that were under Kosciuszko's command in Albany, made it to West Point, along with a company of blacksmiths led by Capt. Ezra Eaton.[39]

Temperatures soared above one hundred degrees during the steamy summer of 1778, and the crews toiled in the heat to prepare for a possible attack. General Glover ordered the work details to begin at 5 a.m. and work until 10 a.m., with a break until 3 p.m. during the hottest point of the midday sun. The work in the afternoon continued until sundown. With the food stocks and materials running low, Glover sent out a search party to gather provisions. On July 4 Glover ordered a captain and forty men "used to boats" to take two days' rations and search for supplies. Glover wrote, "They will take orders from the engineer, Col. Kosciuszko."[40]

The site of French sails fluttering in the wind off the coast of New York stirred anticipation in the rebels that the war would finally come to a head. Adm. Count Charles Hector d'Estaing positioned his fleet for a naval battle with the British ships in the Hudson Bay. The liberation of New York would be a huge boost for the American war effort. The opportunity for a decisive confrontation had finally arrived.

Washington rushed to the highlands to take command. On July 16, 1778, *Thatcher's Military Journal* reported, "His Excellency the Commander in Chief visited West Point, to take a view of the works which are constructing there. His arrival was announced by the discharge of thirteen cannon, the number of the United States."[41]

It was the first meeting between Kosciuszko and Washington. The Polish engineer gave the commander in chief a tour of the fortifications at West Point. Washington did not stay long but apparently liked what he saw. After hearing about Colonel Malcom's griping, Washington wrote to him: "Colo. Kosciuszko was left at the Fort as Acting Engineer and I have always understood is fully competent to the Business. I do not therefore see why another is necessary."[42]

When Duportail and Radiere arrived in the highlands with Washington's army, they stepped up their harassment of Kosciuszko. The Pole wanted to get back into action rather than stay where he thought he was not appreciated. As Quebec was still the staging area for the British army, the idea of a foray into Canada had never completely died, and Washington appointed a team of officers to study the feasibility of an invasion.

One of those pushing the idea was Lafayette, who salivated at the notion of being able to restore Quebec to the French monarchy.[43] But the commander in chief, seeing through this, wrote to Congress: "As the Marquis clothed his proposition when he spoke of it to me, it would seem to originate wholly with himself; but it is far from impossible that it had its birth in the Cabinet of France and was put into this artful dress, to give it the readier currency."[44]

Deep down Washington knew that the French could not be totally trusted, and that by inviting Louis XVI's army into Canada, the Americans would exchange one monarch for another, and that "hatred to England may carry some into an excess of Confidence in France." He knew that his friend Lafayette was trying to pull a fast one, and that by giving France control of Quebec, in addition to the islands it already controlled in the Carribean, the United States would be surrounded by French colonies that would try to monopolize commerce across the Atlantic and dominate the American continent.

The commander in chief's letter to Congress described his "alarm" and "fear" at the proposal, saying, "I am heartily disposed to entertain the most favourable sentiments of our new ally and to cherish them in others to a reasonable degree; but it is a maxim founded on the universal experience of mankind, that no nation is to be trusted farther than it is bound by its interest."

Washington was right to be alarmed by the proposal. The French king was not helping America's war against the British king out of love for liberty or fraternity, or out of altruism. For Louis XVI, the war was strictly business.

Duportail made this clear when he wrote to the French minister of war, the Comte de Saint-Germain, "It is necessary that France, if she wishes to assist this revolution, furnish the people with everything that they need and not experience too great privations—it will cost France several millions, but it will be amply repaid by the destruction of the maritime power of England . . . Her commerce in consequence will pass to France, which will no longer have a rival among the European powers." Some Americans may have sensed Duportail's plan, because he added: "This people here, although at war with England, hate the French more than they do the English (we prove it every day) . . . if we pass before the line, the soldiers who do not love the French, and even some ill-bred officers give us bad language."[45]

Gates also had a selfish motive for keeping the adventure into Canada alive, and the Polish engineer bought into it. Kosciuszko wanted to prove that Gates was a military genius and that he could succeed where Arnold had failed—capturing Quebec. The Pole wrote to Gates: "You must think Sir [of an] Expedition for Canada, which will be your Conquest no doubt and will add to you Honour, your Reputation and your Habilitus [qualification] of [the] Surrender [of] Burgoyne. Believe me Sir, if we have not Canada, Britain will be very Trubbelsom."[46]

Washington wanted to drive the British out of New York. He moved his army across the Hudson and camped near the Connecticut border to prepare for a coordinated attack on New York when the French fleet attacked the British navy. But d'Estaing was afraid that his ships would run into the sandbars off New York Harbor and hoisted anchor, sailing to Newport, Rhode Island. Washington ordered Gens. Nathanael Greene and Lafayette to meet up with Gen. John Sullivan's army and the New England militia to attack the British fleet in Newport Harbor. The Americans amassed ten thousand troops, but the French sailors who went ashore looked on them with disdain. D'Estaing's dispatcher, the Chevalier de Pontgiband, said: "I have never seen a more laughable spectacle; all the tailors and apothecaries in the country must have been called out, I should think;—one could recognize them by their round wigs. They were mounted on bad nags, and looked like a flock of ducks in cross-belts."[47]

While the French chortled about the Americans, d'Estaing gave Sullivan daily assurances that the French would enter the harbor and land three thousand troops in a coordinated attack against the British on Conanicut Island. Confident that the French were ready, Sullivan landed his troops on the east side of the island. But rather than attack the western shore as agreed, d'Estaing pouted that Sullivan had "insulted France" by moving too quickly. Sullivan responded by calling d'Estaing a "traitor." The two generals nearly fought a duel.[48] One historian wrote that d'Estaing, "was more punctilious than wise, and, as the result proved, sacrificed the whole expedition to a point of etiquette."[49]

When more British ships arrived on the horizon, the French sailed to engage them. But after two days of maneuvering a rough storm roared, and the masts of several French ships were damaged. Rather than carry out the invasion of Newport, d'Estaing retreated to Boston to repair his vessels. The American forces were left stranded, and the British counterattacked the Continental regiments, forcing them to flee.

New Englanders were disgusted, and a riot broke out between French and American sailors on the wharves of Boston.[50] Washington had to make peace and stationed his forces in between the two most important military objectives in America: Fortress West Point in the New York Highlands, and the French navy in Boston Harbor.

Washington explained: "There are but two capital objects, which they [the enemy] can have in view . . . the Highlands, by which the communication between the eastern and southern states would be cut off, and the destruction of the French fleet at Boston. . . . I have, therefore, in order to do the best that the nature of the case will admit, strengthened the works, and reinforced the garrison in the Highlands, and thrown the army into such positions, as to move eastward or westward as circumstances require."[51]

As the officer in charge of the works, Kosciuszko had become a key player, and in the summer of 1778 Gates tried again to persuade Congress to promote him to brigadier general. When Radiere learned of this, he wrote to Congress on August 3 demanding a promotion for himself: "It is reported here that Congress will appoint several Brigadiers generals five or six days hence. . . . I am in the right to beg the Congress to be appointed Brigadier general in this promotion. . . . The right of my claim is so plain that I think it is not necessary to insist upon the subject."[52]

Rather than promote Kosciuszko and the American colonels who were in line for advancement ahead of Radiere, Congress tabled the promotions in order not to cause a stir with the French.

With the added importance placed on the highlands by the commander in chief, the position of architect of West Point became one of the most important jobs in the army. Duportail, who had Washington's ear, kept trying to get rid of Kosciuszko.

A year and a half after the Board of War, and Washington, asked that Radiere be replaced by Kosciuszko, Duportail wrote to Congress on August 27, 1778 complaining that Kosciuszko was not subservient to his men: "There happened some difficulty about it—A Col. Engineer, would not acknowledge Mr. de la Radiere, Col. of the Engineers, for his Superior. It is a matter of importance, Sir, that these things should be determined, and I beg you to your endeavors to have them as soon as possible."[53]

Four days later Washington finally put the issue to rest by writing to Congress, "I think it right to observe, that it cannot be expected that Colo. Cosciusko, who has been a good while in this line and conducted himself with reputation and satisfaction, will consent to act in a subordinate capacity to any of the French Gentlemen, except General Portail."[54]

There was nothing Kosciuszko could do about Duportail's constant badgering, so he focused on his work. When he saw that the soldiers were storing gunpowder in ships docked along the river below the cliffs or in sheds aboveground, he started work on a bombproof magazine inside Fort Arnold. And as the work on Fort Putnam hummed along, he grew more concerned about nearby Rocky Hill, which loomed three hundred feet above them.

In the sweltering summer sun Kosciuszko scaled the steep cliffs and looked down on the masons and carpenters in Colonel Putnam's detail. A cannon would have a clear shot into the fort and also threaten the plateau and Fort Arnold to the east. He pulled out his pencil and began sketching out the first draft of a plan for a redoubt.

The front line of the war had moved to New York, so Washington moved his headquarters to White Plains to get closer to the British, and sent Duportail to check on progress at West Point. Well aware of the animosity that the French engineers felt toward Kosciuszko, he asked Duportail his opinion on any necessary improvements, but, "In doing this, you will of course consider the labor and expense which have been already incurred, the advanced season of the year and the resources of the Country for carrying any plan which may be formed into execution."[55]

In short Washington was telling the Frenchman to be realistic.

But Duportail could not hide his resentment of Kosciuszko when he showed up at West Point in September 1778 for an inspection. The vainglorious Frenchman was not liked because he was cold and reserved toward the other officers.[56] The historian Paul K. Walker wrote in his *Documentary History of the Army Engineers in the American Revolution*, "Down to the several misspellings of Kosciuszko's name, the report reflected genuine animosity toward Kosciuszko, who after all, had sharply criticized Duportail's associate, Radiere."[57] And in *The River and the Rock: The History of Fortress West Point*, Dave Palmer wrote, "The professional competence of the report is marred by the thread of pettiness running through it."[58]

Duportail did make a wise observation when he pointed out that there was only one battery on Constitution Island protecting the chain from the eastern bank of the Hudson, but he also had less advisable ideas, such as sinking the heavy iron chain three feet under water rather than floating it with logs as Captain Machin had done.

The French engineer also belittled Kosciuszko's plan to fortify Rocky Hill, saying, "It would be very difficult for an enemy, even when master of it to bring heavy cannon there. Besides it would be too far to make a breach."[59]

Once again a French engineer was making the same misguided argument about not fortifying the high ground. Duportail could find little wrong with Kosciuszko's work, but his report was written in a haughty tone that nitpicked at the projects under construction. To make matters worse, Kosciuszko was not present during his visit. The Polish engineer had kept his promise to General St. Clair to testify on his behalf at his court-martial. Kosciuszko traveled to White Plains to speak up for his former commanding officer.

When he crossed the river Kosciuszko ran into some unfinished business left over from the Conway mess. Wilkinson and Gates were also at the trial in White Plains, and the feud that had begun earlier in the year in York once again flared up. Wilky renewed his challenge to duel with Gates. This time the general accepted.

Gates asked Kosciuszko to act as his second.

For a duel the confrontation in the woods was a humdrum affair, with both men firing or attempting to shoot at each other three times. After the sun went down everyone agreed that chivalry had been served, and a certificate of honor was prepared by Wilkinson's second, a man named John Baker Church who had fled England under shady circumstances and changed his name to John Carter. In the darkness Carter scribbled out an account of the duel and gave it to Kosciuszko to sign.

Carter beguiled the trusting Pole into signing the piece of paper, which said that Wilkinson had behaved as a gentleman during the Conway affair. However, the note made no mention of Gates's behavior. Later that night, after realizing that he had been duped, Kosciuszko jumped on his horse and raced over to General Schuyler's quarters where the conniver was lodging.

According to Maj. John Lansing and Col. Lewis Morris, who witnessed the encounter, the Polish officer demanded to see Carter's copy of the certificate. He then folded the paper and put it in his pocket, explaining that because of his poor knowledge of the English language he had misinterpreted the document when he signed it in the dark. As the general's second, Kosciuszko said that unless it was rewritten to attest to Gates's integrity as well, he would not return it, and he "would rather lose the last drop of his blood than consent to a measure which would tend to its prejudice." After a heated argument, Carter and Kosciuszko agreed to resolve the matter the following morning with Gates and Wilkinson present.[60]

The feud escalated the next day when Gates refused to give Wilkinson any written account of their flimsy skirmish in the woods unless he also signed a statement testifying to Gates's honor. The bombastic battle of honor spun out of control for days, with the principals exchanging accusations of impropriety and cowardice, and with Carter calling Kosciuszko a thief for taking back the certificate of the duel "under false pretenses."

The Pole challenged Carter to a duel, and when he refused Kosciuszko angrily threatened to resolve the matter "with my sword." Rather than accept the challenge, Carter published a letter in a Fishkill newspaper, the *New York Packet*, attacking Kosciuszko for threatening, "to redress the injury with his sword" and likening him to "a midnight robber, who steals a purse, or an assassin, . . . a mad-man."

The ugly affair overshadowed St. Clair's trial when Carter showed up in the courtroom with a pistol and threatened to shoot Kosciuszko. Guards cleared the court, and Carter raced away on his horse before he could be apprehended for threatening an officer at a military tribunal. The newspapers ran competing letters between the two men, with Kosciuszko calling Carter "a scoundrel and a coward" for drawing a pistol on him when he was unarmed.[61]

In trying to defend Gates's honor, Kosciuszko allowed himself to be dragged into a petty clash with Carter that had degenerated into silly name-calling. The officers in the courtroom defended the Polish colonel's actions in regard to Carter, but the whole affair got the best of Kosciuszko and filled him with frustration and anger. The list of people who were disrespectful of his mentor was growing, and because of his loyalty and protectiveness toward Gates, Kosciuszko's temper had reached its boiling point.

When the court-martial resumed, Kosciuszko vouched for his former commander, General St. Clair, who was charged with abandoning Fort Ticonderoga and failing to secure it properly to withstand an attack. Kosciuszko asserted that when the British showed up with eight thousand troops to challenge a fort that could hold only one thousand soldiers, St. Clair had no choice but to retreat. Even though Kosciuszko's suggestions to arm Mount Defiance were not followed, the Pole believed that his commander had done all that he could.

As a witness Kosciuszko testified that the rebels would have run out of water because "the spring would have been exposed to the fire of the enemy." He also said that the British were about to encircle the Americans and that "the communication with Lake George was cut off."[62]

As a result of Kosciuszko's testimony, St. Clair was acquitted of all charges. The silliness over the duel subsided, and Kosciuszko returned to his post across the Hudson. Little did the Polish engineer realize, however, that waiting for him at West Point was Duportail's vengeful report criticizing his work.

With the French engineers constantly badgering him, Kosciuszko had had enough. He volunteered for what he thought would be a new mission to strike the British staging ground in Canada. The Pole was no different from most of the American officers who did not want to serve in the remote Hudson Highlands. There was no glory in the laborious routine, and the action always seemed to be someplace else. West Point was a cluttered construction site.

Yet somehow Kosciuszko brought order to this confusion, and Washington realized that the industrious Pole was transforming the rocks over the Hudson into an unassailable position. Washington was circling his troops around New York City and ordered Gates to head east, into the Connecticut River valley, and set up camp in Danbury.

Gates wrote to Washington: "I earnestly entreat your Excellency will be pleased to permit Colo. Kuscuiusco to be The Engineer to serve with the troops marching under my Command. If I had not an affectionate regard for this amiable foreigner, I should upon no account have made this my request."[63]

Washington denied the request. West Point was the fulcrum of the arc around New York, and the Polish engineer was the point man. The commander in chief replied to Gates: "I am always willing to grant requests where I think the good of the service will admit of it. . . . However, in the present instance of your application, I cannot do it with any degree of propriety, as I conceive. Colo. Kosciuszko has had the chief direction and superintendence of the Works at West Point, and it is my desire, that he should remain to carry them on. New plans and alterations at this time, would be attended with many inconveniences, and protract the defences of the River. These possibly in some degree, might take place in case of his absence, under the management of Another Engineer."[64]

Kosciuszko was stunned. His shot at glory, the conquest of Quebec, was slipping away. He wrote to Gates, "My happiness is lost," and added that if the invasion to the north were revived, he would go "as a volunteer for the next expedition to Canada."[65]

With Gates heading east, McDougall was once again sent to command the highlands, and Colonel Malcom stayed on as commander of the camp at West Point. Now that Malcom was responsible for finishing the forts, he complained that he did not have enough workers. (Part of the problem was of his own making, because he started a policy of granting furloughs to his soldiers.)

Malcom jumped on a suggestion by Governor Clinton to use Tory prisoners in the custody of local magistrates to help with the construction, but he treated them as slave laborers to work at West Point for three-month terms. Malcom called them "boobies" and "miscreants" and used them as free labor for the state before sending them on their way, telling them that they've been "white washed." When some magistrates and slave laborers got upset about his tactics, Malcom tried to cover his rear by warning Governor Clinton that they might complain, suggesting that the governor "only amuse your stupid Justices that they may not torment me with their foolish demands & we shall make a Good Fort."[66]

Morale plummeted even further when Colonel Malcom meted out harsh punishment for troublemakers by whipping and chaining them to wheelbarrows.

Lonely and miserable, the Pole complained to his friend John Taylor, an Albany merchant and banker who supported the Revolution: "I am the most enhappy [sic] man in the World, because all my Jankees [Yankees] the best Friends is gone to Whit Plains or to [the] Eastern [department] and left me with the Skoches or Irishes impolites as Saviges." He also grumbled that Washington would not allow him to join Gates in the Eastern Department and whined about a lack of good company, adding, "my respect to Mistris Skayler and miss Kayler do not forgive, to your lady and to all my Friends give my Compliments. You must remember that if I go to Albany I must be in your hause, Your Friend, Thad. Kosciuszko."[67]

The object of Kosciuszko's affections in Albany was the dark-eyed Betsy Schuyler, daughter of Gen. Schuyler. As Schuyler was also one of the wealthiest men in New York, once again the Polish officer had become enamored of a woman out of his league. A year later Betsy Schuyler was engaged to Washington's chief of staff, Alexander Hamilton.

Kosciuszko would have to make do without "miss Kayler" or his "Jankee" friends. He was learning about the different views that his Yankee buddies had of the world. Even at this early stage of the American Republic he understood that Northerners and Southerners viewed the Revolution quite differently.

One of Kosciuszko's associates, West Point's surgeon, Dr. Thacher, wrote in his diary: "Since the troops from the Southern states have been incorporated and associated in military duty with those from New England, a strong prejudice has assumed its unhappy influence, and drawn a line of distinction between them. Many of the officers from the South are gentlemen of education, and unaccustomed to that equality which prevails in New England. . . . Hence we too frequently hear the burlesque epithet of Yankee from one party, and that of Buckskin, by way of retort, from the other."[68]

The Yankee notion of equality stemmed from republicanism—that belief the supreme power of a government stems from its citizens in elections. Gates was a staunch republican and pushed for the states to sign America's first constitution: the Articles of Confederation. To the governor of Connecticut, Jonathan Trumbull, he wrote: "We entered into this war to preserve our Freedom & to establish that Republican Equality, without which, Freedom is but a Name,—in my Opinion, The British Fleet, & Army will leave Our Coast the Moment they can do it with a good appearance of Safety,—but Confederation is not Signed."[69]

Gates also considered himself a Yankee, a term that later became synonymous with abolitionist. The New England states would be the first to abolish slavery, Vermont in 1777, Massachusetts and New Hampshire in 1783, and Rhode Island and Connecticut in 1784. Kosciuszko was clearly in the Yankee camp. For him "equality" was not just a buzzword; it was important to treat everyone as equals.

As the Pole yearned for acceptance from American officers, he did not realize that he was the one engineer who had been able to keep the work crews motivated at West Point by treating the men with respect. However, the commander in chief did realize this and knew that he had to find a way to keep the Pole happy, while at the same time keeping the teetering French alliance intact.

On September 19, 1778, Washington rode up the hill to West Point to follow up on Duportail's inspection. Kosciuszko once again gave the commander in chief a complete tour of the garrison. Washington examined every fort and redoubt, tested the chain, and checked the positions of the cannons. As a former surveyor attuned to the tools of his day, Washington would have even peered through Kosciuszko's theodolite to gauge the line of fire that his Polish engineer projected for the artillery.

After his own inspection Washington sat down in Fort Arnold and wrote a response to Duportail's report: "I have perused the memorial, which you delivered relative to the defence of the North River at this place, and upon a view of them highly approve what you have offered upon the Subject, Colo. Kosciousko who was charged by congress with the direction of the forts and batteries, has already made such progress in the construction of them as would render any alteration in the general plan, a work of too much time, and the favorable testimony which you have given of Colo. Kosciousko's abilities prevents uneasiness on this head; but whatever amendments subordinate to the general disposition shall occur as proper to be made, you will be pleased to point out to Col. Kosciousko that they may be carried into execution. The Works proposed on the peninsula not being subject to the abovementioned inconvenience, you will desire Colo. Kosciousko to shew you his plan for approbation before he proceeds to the construction or have them traced in the first instance conformably to your own ideas."[70]

Anyone who could read English could see that Duportail's report did not give any "favorable testimony . . . of Colo. Kosciousko's abilities." In fact the four times that Duportail did mention the Pole in his report it was always derisively.

The commander in chief was showing support for Kosciuszko while at the same time making it clear that Duportail was still the chief engineer of the Continental Army. Washington's response to the Duportail report was a stroke of brilliant diplomacy because both Kosciuszko and the Frenchman thought that they had won.[71]

When Washington inspected West Point and praised the Polish engineer for his complex redoubt and fort system, Kosciuszko was quite pleased, and in his Slavic grammar, wrote to Gates: "His Excellency was here with General Portail to see the works after all Conclusion was made that I am not the worst of Inginier."[72] The commander in chief also took the Pole aside and spoke with him privately, because the letter to Gates shows that Kosciuszko understood that Washington wanted "to show me that I have superior . . . [Duportail] above me."

As for Duportail, the Pole questioned his judgment as an engineer, writing to Gates, "I discover in Conversation that this Gentlemen . . . [had little experience] because he believe that it is the same thing upon the paper as upon the Ground. We must always have the works according to the Ground and Circumstance but not as the paper is level and make the works accordingly."[73]

As the saying goes, "The best laid schemes of mice and men . . . often go awry." Sketching a blueprint is one thing; Kosciuszko proved that actually getting a fort built is another story.

SIX

A Rock, an African Prince, and America's Traitor

L IFE IN THE BOONDOCKS OF THE HIGHLANDS WAS MONOTONOUS and the workload heavy. Initially the Polish engineer worked long hours and stayed in the nearby boardinghouse of Mrs. Sarah Warren.[1] But once the threat of a British attack was no longer imminent, and the frenetic pace of construction slowed down, he built a log cabin near the fort to serve as his quarters.

Kosciuszko also planted a garden on a granite ridge overlooking the Hudson. The secluded ledge was naturally carved into the cliffs and could be reached only by descending the rocks from Fort Arnold. He lowered soil with ropes and buckets down the precipice to plant a flower patch encircled with stones, and crafted a marble basin that was naturally filled by a waterfall that trickled down the escarpment. Just like the huge rock that Kosciuszko climbed as a child, the crag hidden beneath Fort Arnold offered him solace and a place to meditate.

The garden became one of the camp's attractions, and Dr. Thacher, who climbed down the rock face to the engineer's secret spot, described it in his diary: "Colonel Thaddeus Kosciuszko, a gentleman of distinction from Poland . . . amused himself while stationed on this point, in laying out a curious garden in a deep valley, abounding more in rocks than soil. I was gratified in viewing his curious water fountain with jets and cascades."[2]

It was probably here that Kosciuszko told Dr. Thacher about his botched elopement with Louise Sosnowska. And it was here during his moments of solitude that Kosciuszko pondered the predicament of the subjugated peasants in his own country, and the plight of America's citizen militia and the African slaves in the United States.

Also living in the highlands during this time was Burgoyne's captured army, and in late November they were shipped across the river to a camp north of West Point. Kosciuszko showed compassion for the English prisoners of war, and even though the rebel soldiers had little food, he shared his own meager rations with the captives. (Many years later a Polish traveler to Queensland, Australia, fell ill with yellow fever and was nursed back to health by a local shopkeeper. The Australian brought the sick Pole to his home and cared for him, explaining that his grandfather would have starved to death as a prisoner during the American Revolution, if not for a Polish soldier named Kosciuszko who shared his bread.)[3]

The gold- and rust-colored leaves of the surrounding forest had floated to the ground when Kosciuszko's good karma blew back to him in the fall of 1779. Lt. Col. Philip Van Rensselaer sent him a bed from the Albany armory for his cabin.[4] The log shanty in the highlands had become a home, and with winter approaching and the necessities of war as they were, the Pole allowed some visitors to share the bed with him.

One of his houseguests, Capt. Samuel Richards from Connecticut, wrote in his diary: "I quartered a considerable time with Kosciuszko in the same log hut, and soon discovered in him an elevation of mind which gave fair promise of those high achievements to which he attained. His manners were soft and conciliating and, at the same time, elevated. I used to take much pleasure in accompanying him with his theodolite, measuring the heights of the surrounding mountains. He was very ready in mathematics."[5]

Another guest was Gen. John Paterson, one of Kosciuszko's closest associates from the Saratoga campaign. Seeing that Colonel Malcolm needed help to maintain the workflow, Washington reassigned Paterson to take command of West Point. Kosciuszko first served with Paterson at Fort Ticonderoga. The two athletic officers often wrestled and played practical jokes on each other. Sometimes when Paterson won their grappling matches, he would hold Kosciuszko across his knee until the Pole would beg to be released, calling him "a cruel man." The two officers became so close that—as was customary with friends in the frigid winter months of upstate New York during the Saratoga campaign— they sometimes shared the same blanket.

The close bond that Kosciuszko had with Paterson also extended to Paterson's black servant, Agrippa Hull. While slavery was still legal in the North before the Revolution, Hull, whom everyone called Grippy, was a free man. A witty raconteur, Grippy told stories about his father, who he said was a prince in Africa. His Polish friend cherished this legacy and the verbal history passed down from his ancestors about his roots in Africa. As an ardent student of ancient Rome and Greece, Kosciuszko knew that Agrippa was also the name of a Roman statesman and general and probably would have discussed this with the son of an African prince.

Paterson, seeing the bond between the two, presented his servant to Kosciuszko, and Grippy happily served as the Polish officer's confidant and aide-de-camp.

Often scouting the terrain and approaches to the Hudson Highlands, on one occasion when Kosciuszko set out to reconnoiter the positions on the east side of the river, he left Grippy to watch over his quarters high above the bend in the river, close to where a statue of the Polish revolutionary now stares out over the Hudson. Kosciuszko told his aide that he was headed downstream to cross the river and that he would be gone for two or three days. Grippy took advantage of his officer's absence and threw a party in the cabin, inviting all the slaves and free black men at the camp.

The guests drank wine and enjoyed the show put on by Grippy, who paraded around the cabin in the Polish officer's dress uniform, featuring a navy blue jacket with a crimson collar, golden epaulets, and a four-cornered cap adorned with nodding ostrich plumes. Kosciuszko was wearing his boots when he rode out of camp, so Grippy shined his own legs with black shoe polish to resemble riding boots.[6]

Grippy left the windows open but hung a screen over the door to hide the party from passersby. For some reason Kosciuszko unexpectedly returned the same night, and when he heard the hoopla and laughter reverberating from his quarters, he dismounted from his horse and sneaked inside, where he found the slaves toasting Grippy and calling him "Kosciuszko."

The stunned revelers acted as if they had seen a ghost or, worse, "Satan himself," when the real Kosciuszko stepped among them. Expecting to be beaten by the white officer, several of the black men jumped through the windows, and the rest stampeded out the door. Terrified, Grippy fell at Kosciuszko's feet, cowering and crying, "Whip me, kill me, Massa; do anything with me Mr. General."[7]

Kosciuszko took Grippy by the hand and said, "Rise, Prince. It is beneath the dignity of an African prince to prostrate himself at the feet of anyone." He made Grippy wear the plumed hat and marched him across the camp to General Paterson's quarters. A black man wearing a flashy uniform with ostrich feathers in his cap caught the attention of the soldiers and drew a crowd that followed Kosciuszko as he dragged his servant toward the other officers to mete out punishment for stealing wine and violating his personal belongings.[8]

The soldiers expected that the black man would be whipped for his indiscretions, but Kosciuszko introduced the nattily clad Grippy as a prince from Africa who had come to join the fight. The Pole was so convincing in his introduction that some of the soldiers believed that Grippy was in fact a prince.

The officers built an impromptu throne for Grippy, proffering toasts and forcing him to swill wine, brandy, and a cocktail called Hollands, made from Dutch gin distilled from rye, barley, and flavored with juniper berries.[9] The assembled partygoers smoked a peace pipe in honor of their royal guest. Rather than waking up with bloody slash marks on his back from whipping, which was the normal punishment in those times, Grippy woke up with a terrible hangover from all the alcohol he had drunk.

After the war, Agrippa Hull settled in Stockbridge, Massachusetts, started a catering business, bought land, and built a house. For many years Grippy fondly retold this embarrassing story, explaining how his hangover from the forced binge drinking was akin to being crucified. Kosciuszko also gave Grippy one of his prized possessions, a flintlock pistol made by one of Poland's eminent gun makers for the royal cadets.[10] Like many other black men in the north, Grippy was a free soldier in the Continental Army.

Life for Kosciuszko became easier at West Point under Paterson, but he wanted to fight the British. He wrote to Gates, "I am pretty Happy with General Paterson, but not so as I should be with you. You promise me Sir if you go to Canada to take me with you."[11]

But Washington realized that Kosciuszko had the best plans for West Point, and had no intention of allowing the Polish engineer to go elsewhere. Washington even sent the most junior of the Royal French engineers, Lieutenant Colonel Gouvion, to West Point to be Kosciuszko's assistant. Gouvion was more personable than Duportail or Radiere, and willing to follow orders. Once the snow began to fall most of the forts that Kosciuszko had designed were completed or under construction, and work was under way for the redoubts that Duportail had recommended for Constitution Island.

Yet conditions and morale at West Point were abysmal. Supplies were scant and food was scarce. McDougall was growing frustrated with his administrative duties as the commander of the highlands and wanted a change of command. "I am unhappily left in this Department," he wrote to Governor Clinton. "My Condition is not much better, than the Israelites in Egypt, who were ordered to make Brick without Straw. But I am determined it's the last Winter I shall be imprisoned in the Highlands to be a Drudge for others."[12]

Worried that the British would try to attack during his watch, McDougall grew increasingly paranoid and instructed Gouvion to play devil's advocate and pretend that he was a British general in charge of seven thousand men about to attack the highlands. McDougall asked the French engineer, "What would be your plan to reduce the works or to remove or pass the chain?"[13]

But rather than propose any real improvements, Gouvion simply made inventory lists and progress reports of the work under way. On New Year's Eve 1778, McDougall ordered him to travel down the Hudson to King's Ferry, where he spent the winter working on a redoubt and barracks for forty men.[14]

Washington was puzzled when he learned of Gouvion's redeployment and wrote to inquire whether Kosciuszko was still overseeing the work. He told McDougall: "From the manner in which you speak of employing Mr. Gouvion in this business, I am in doubt whether Col. Koshiosko still remains at West Point, or not. As he has not been removed by my order or permission, I should imagine he is still there. If Koshiosko be still at West Point, as he is a senior officer he must of necessity have the chief direction."[15]

The Polish engineer had been working judiciously, without fanfare, throughout the winter. A note in Kosciuszko's handwriting left with McDougall shows that he was finishing Fort Putnam and building a bombproof shelter and cistern to catch rainwater; erecting a stone wall around the Webb redoubt and putting in a bombproof storage magazine; building a redoubt and bombproof shelter on Matters Rock Hill; finishing another battery along the river overlooking the chain; and building one redoubt and designing another on Constitution Island.[16]

Kosciuszko also ordered replacement logs for those that were rotting under the mammoth chain and "50 Barrels of Tar" to grease the new logs so they would float up and down with the tides rather than freeze and break.

In addition he finished blueprints for Rocky Hill. When Kosciuszko first proposed arming Crown Heights, he also wanted to defend Rocky Hill, which is three hundred feet higher than Fort Putnam and within firing range of the plateau and Fort Arnold. The Pole sketched out a redoubt on the summit, protected on the three sides that had steep ridges with projecting spikes of chevaux-de-frise, and an elevated gun parapet to cover the downward-sloping valley to the west.

But the Pole was having problems getting the tools and raw materials he needed to get the job done. On February 6 he presented McDougall with his sketches and wrote: "As it is very difficult to procure fascines [bundles of bound sticks to begin construction for a fort] near that Place, I think that the Parapet can easily be done in Timber for the Bombproof immediate. I am in great Want of a Whip saw and Cannot get it from Fishkill. Should be the Favor of having one from a Maj. Campbell."[17]

· McDougall responded to Washington's inquiry as to the whereabouts of the Pole with a simple "Colo. Kusciasco has been undisturbed in his Line at West Point."[18]

Construction slowed down over the winter, in part because the disruptive Colonel Malcom, who was upset that Paterson had replaced him as commander, was more focused on writing letters to Washington and Governor Clinton griping about his predicament than on the work at hand. Kosciuszko was trying to solve problems of Malcom's making, such as his granting leave to skilled workers and replacing them with Tory slave laborers. The engineer's team of craftsmen shrank from several hundred to five officers and 105 men.[19]

Trying to hold his work crews together, Kosciuszko complained to McDougall.

"As Confusion has taken place respecting the artificers since Col. Malcom took the Command at the Post," Kosciuszko wrote that he needed "a daily report" to know how many men would report for work and that "furloughing the men is attended with bad Consequences, they ought to be given by the Commander of the Garrison with my consent."[20]

When Captain Machin left West Point in late summer, the responsibility of maintaining the chain fell by default to Kosciuszko. Washington was the only one authorized to order the chain out of the river, and the Pole had suggested as early as November that it might be time to remove the links and restore the logs to keep them from trapping chunks of ice flowing downriver, which could snap them.

On November 5, 1778, Malcom had asked Washington for his opinion: "With respect to the Chain & Boom, I have asked the Engineer about them and he agrees with me that in a short time both ought to be taken on shore lest the Ice carry them away. Does your Excellency choose to have it done ere the Winter sets in severe?"[21]

Washington replied, "You may, if you think it is proper, put all things in readiness to take up the Chain and Boom. I do not think there is any danger of a Visit from the Enemy this Fall, but still there is no need of running any Risque by taking it up before there is a necessity for it."[22]

The autumn weather was warmer than usual, and Malcom didn't follow up on the order, nor did he inform General Paterson that Washington wanted the chain pulled out of the river. But by mid-December, a deep frost descended from the north, and the rotting logs and heavy iron links were caught in the ice flowing down the river. The entire garrison rushed down the cliffs, and men jumped into boats in the freezing water to tow the floating timbers and massive chain to shore.

Malcom's hesitation and antipathy for General Paterson nearly cost the rebels the most effective tool they had to keep the British navy out of the Hudson. Perhaps it was the seclusion or the mountain air, but West Point became known as a post infamous for its infighting. West Point superintendent Dave Palmer wrote, "Washington, if he bothered to recount all the personality problems that had erupted at the peculiar bend in the river, might have wondered if it was just human nature or if the location itself somehow bred dissension."[23]

With the construction work moving along, Kosciuszko clung to his hopes that he would soon be able to leave for the front lines. He wrote to Gates, who was then in Boston: "West Point is as barren of news as the mountains that surround it." Again showing his allegiance to the Northerners he served with, Kosciuszko wrote: "I must beg the favor of you to promote the interest of the Yankees at Court, this request is formed on principles of real justice as well because I suppose to be myself at this time more than half a Yankee."[24]

At the time, Gates was being asked to take on a battle that he was none too thrilled about. The Native American tribes in western New York were raiding colonial towns, and Washington wanted Gates to lead an attack on the Seneca. Fighting the Indians was a treacherous mission. On top of that Gates wanted to remain on good terms with the Oneida, who called him "brother Arahoiktea."[25] Using his age (fifty) as an excuse, Gates declined Washington's request, writing, "The Man who undertakes the Indian Service, should enjoy Youth and Strength; requisites I do not possess."[26]

Instead Washington sent General Sullivan into the wilderness. His troops burned forty villages and 160,000 bushels of corn. As a result the Indian chief named Cornplanter dubbed Washington "the Town Destroyer."[27]

Gates was not the only friend Kosciuszko missed. With spring fever in the air, on March 3, 1779, the lonely bachelor wrote a risqué letter to his friends who were with Gates in Boston, teasing them that they were neglecting their friendship because they were too busy behaving like soldiers on leave. To Maj. John Armstrong he wrote: "I do not tax you with want of Friendships in not writing to me knowing that you have a good reason to give, that the handsome Girls ingross the whole of your Time and attention, and really if I was in your place I should Chose do the same."

To Gates's aide, William Clajon, Kosciuszko added, "But you Col. Clairjon can give me no Reason but your Laxiness. I have been told that you are about [to] marry a Young girl and mean to exert yourself so the name of Clairjons may not be extinguished." He asked Colonel Troup to be "a good officer of the Artillery" and make good use of "your Cannon on the wedding Day of Col. Clairjon." And to ensure that Clajon had the procreative powers of the Greek god of fertility, he asked Dr. James Brown to use "all your Surgical Faculties to promote so laudable a design for the interest of Mr. Clairjon and administer such Medicine as will make him Strong and Famous as Priapus."

As for Gates's son, Bob, Kosciuszko offered a warning that he not get into the same trouble as another soldier who caught a venereal disease, saying, "Take example from the misfortune of Mr. Bucks and not be so imprudent as to get the clap."[28]

However, the amorous adventures of his pals in Boston were not the only thing on Kosciuszko's mind as the weather warmed up. With the ice melting and the spring rains replenishing the tributaries of the Hudson, the navigational season was also approaching, and it was time once again to spread the chain across the river.

The focus was put back on restoring the logs for the chain, but Kosciuszko still lacked a sufficient crew and the "two large coils of cable and one sloop" needed to stretch the chain across the river.[29]

Sir Henry Clinton was biding his time in New York City during the winter months, hoping to send his navy up the Hudson to carry out the mission in which Burgoyne had failed—cutting the colonies in two and containing the Yankee Revolution in New England. With a break in the cold weather, by April 5 Kosciuszko was able to tow the chain across to the new redoubts on Constitution Island, and he sketched out a map to show McDougall its position.

The Pole also managed to keep up to date on news from both sides of the Atlantic by reading any newspapers and correspondence he could get hold of. The scandal of the day involved the American spy Silas Deane, who arrived in Paris in 1776 around the time that Kosciuszko and the first foreign mercenaries were leaving for the United States on Beaumarchais' secret ships.

Deane took credit for funds that had been funneled to the rebels before he ever arrived in Paris. Things got sticky when Beaumarchais asked for repayment of a loan that the French had said was a gift, and several of Deane's dispatches were intercepted. Congress was also unhappy that Deane was signing lavish contracts and making promises that could not be honored. He was also charged with commingling his own funds with public money, which he claimed he was using only for his cover as a merchant to keep his true mission a secret.

When Deane was recalled to provide an explanation, he returned to America under a cloud, and the author of *Common Sense*, Thomas Paine, became his greatest critic. The proceedings became "the sport of parties in Congress," and Paine chronicled the whole affair in a newspaper, the *Pennsylvania Packet*.[30]

In a cryptic comment on the affair, Kosciuszko wrote to Deputy Quartermaster Gen. Henry Wells: "Mr. Deane is now out of date and take no more the public notice . . . as for Common Sense, [he] seems that he have lost his Sense. . . . My best compliments to all my friends of the Yankee species."[31]

While the Pole continually tried to show solidarity with his Yankee friends, the French had still not given up trying to undermine him. Duportail spent the winter in Philadelphia lobbying Congress to create an army corps of engineers, also arguing that he should run the new corps. After months of negotiations he persuaded Congress to appoint him "Commandant of the Corps of Engineers and Sappers and Miners."

One of Duportail's first acts in his new post—without even checking on the status of the projects at West Point—was to renew his tirades against Kosciuszko, writing to Congress on May 11, complaining that even though he had given directions to the "officer [Kosciuszko] entrusted with the fortifications of that place . . . unhappily, I have heard, that almost nothing has been done."[32]

By this point the Frenchman's attacks on Kosciuszko had become so frequent and transparent that they were simply ignored. The commander in chief had faith in the Pole, and that was all that mattered. Besides, there was a more pressing issue to deal with: The Redcoats were finally making their move toward the highlands.

In early May 1779 the British raided several towns in Virginia to disrupt the supply lines and force the Southern states to keep their militias in place defending the home front so that they would be hesitant about sending their troops to Washington's main Continental Army.

Later that month Gen. Henry Clinton sent a warship, the HMS *Vulture,* up the Hudson while his infantry marched upriver to attack Stony Point, twelve miles south of West Point, and Fort Lafayette, on Verplanck's Point on the eastern side of the river. By capturing these two peninsulas, the British closed King's Ferry, a major crossing point on the Hudson.

With the Redcoats on the move, a sense of urgency fell over West Point.

Washington remembered Kosciuszko and McDougall's earlier warnings about the hills overlooking Fort Arnold. On May 28 he wrote to McDougall: "The completion of the works at Westpoint has prudently made a principal part in our system; and I am persuaded every thing has been done by you for this purpose. In one of your former letters you intimate your fears of a spot of ground opposite the Fort, should it be possessed by the enemy. Can it be possessed by us to advantage?"[33]

Work had been under way all winter on Fort Putnam atop Crown Hill. The hill that Radiere had said not to worry about would be the centerpiece of the battle if the British did scale the plateau of West Point. And while Duportail had belittled Kosciuszko for suggesting that cannons could be mounted above it on Rocky Hill, the Pole was still pushing ahead with what would become Redoubt Number 4.

On June 8 Washington showed up at West Point to check Kosciuszko's progress. The Polish engineer gave him a tour of the works, and confident that the fort was in good hands, the commander in chief rushed back to his headquarters to devise a plan to recapture Stony Point. He was in such a hurry that there was a glitch as he mounted, and one of the spurs fell off his boot.

The next day posters were hung around the fort: "Lost yesterday, reconnoitering with his Excellency General Washington, a spur, with treble chains on the side, and a single one under foot, all silver, except the tongue of the buckle and the rowel. Whoever has found, or shall find it, and will bring it to Colonel Kosciuszko or at head-quarters, shall have ten dollars reward."[34]

Washington's missing spur was a minor problem compared to the thorn in his side of the enemy parked on a peninsula twelve miles south of West Point. The fort at Stony Point had water on three sides, guarded by the sloop *Vulture,* and marshland on the fourth. The British quickly threw up redoubts and abatis around the camp, making it a tough objective to capture.

Capt. Allen McLane staked out Stony Point for two weeks and even slipped

inside the British camp disguised as an old woman visiting her Tory son. He reported the fort's vulnerabilities, and two weeks later the Continental soldiers
crept up to the enemy camp. Along the way the rebels quietly killed every dog
within three miles so that barking would not arouse the British.[35] McLane arrested "the Widow Calhoun and another widow going to the enemy with chick-
ens and greens. Drove off twenty head of horned cattle from their pasture."[36]

A group of gritty commandos known as "forlorn hope" went on a suicide
mission in July 1779, chopping their way through the abatis with axes, while
hundreds of other soldiers who had sloshed through the marshland charged into
the holes they made in the fort. The operation was led by Gen. "Mad Anthony"
Wayne, who was seeking revenge against the British for the 1777 Battle of Paoli
where some of his men were bayonetted and hacked to pieces with swords as
they tried to surrender.

The *New Hampshire Gazette* hailed the victory, crowing, "Nothing can exceed the spirit and intrepidity of our brave countrymen in storming and carrying
the British fortress at Stony Point. It demonstrates that the Americans have soldiers equal to any in the world: and that they can attack and vanquish the Britons
in their strongest works."[37]

The British forces were driven back down the Hudson, but they torched and
ransacked towns along the way. It was clear that they would once again try to
capture the highlands, and Washington stepped up his efforts to make West
Point invincible. The commander in chief issued general orders from his headquarters at New Windsor, New York: "All those soldiers who are Masons by
trade in the line are immediately to be drawn out and sent to the Fort for a special and temporary service. They are to take their orders from Colonel
Kosciuszko."[38]

Though it was the first time that the commander in chief had actually spelled
his Polish engineer's name correctly, it was more than a matter of penmanship.
The initial ambivalence that he had felt toward Gates's friend and ally had
evolved into trust and respect for the architect of West Point, which Washington
called "the most important Post in America."[39]

As the summer progressed Kosciuszko also began to feel closer to Washington, and when he had yet to receive the promised reinforcements several weeks
later, the Pole unloaded his frustrations directly to the commander in chief: "I
have only two Masons as yet come from the Main Army, and do not expect any
more, the Officers being unwilling to part with them," Kosciuszko wrote. "I am
out of lime . . . I have twenty Carpenters sick by raison of drinking Water in this
hot Weather they suppose that one Half Gill remedy the Evil. Col. Stewart was so
good as to let me have a Stone Cutter from his Regiment for One Week. I wish to
have him for a Month having much to do and know not where to find another."[40]

Concerned that the British might once again make a move on the main rebel garrison, Washington decided to take over the highlands personally, and ordered McDougall to join Mad Anthony at Stony Point, writing to General Wayne, "I propose either this evening or tomorrow to pitch my Tent some where near West point."[41]

Kosciuszko once again had face time with Washington to reiterate the importance of Rocky Hill. At long last the commander in chief himself commented on "the long Hill in front of Fort Putnam at the extremities of which the Engineer is commencing some works."[42]

To Washington, Kosciuszko's concerns were obvious. Two decades earlier, when he was trying to stave off an attack by the French at Fort Necessity during the French and Indian War, Washington was forced to surrender when the French fired into the fort from an elevated position. He completely understood his engineer's concerns. Ironically General St. Clair, who ignored Kosciuszko's advice at Fort Ticonderoga and was acquitted at his court-martial thanks to the Pole's testimony, was put in charge of building Redoubt No. 4 on the high ground of Rocky Hill.

After a tour of the camp Washington made sure that this time St. Clair would follow the orders: "The possession of this Hill appears to me essential to the preservation of the whole post and our main effort ought to be directed to keeping the enemy off of it . . . Make yourself completely master of its defence . . . you will have an eye to the works to be erected to hasten their completion as fast as possible."[43]

Duportail was also present at West Point when Washington reversed the Frenchman's previous orders to leave Rocky Hill unmanned. Palmer wrote: "General Duportail might have seen a smirk flash across Colonel Kosciuszko's face when Washington made that decision."[44] The commander in chief vindicated Kosciuszko over the naysayers who had doubted his ideas for the past three years.

With Washington firmly ensconced in the Highlands, on August 19, 1779, the *New York Packet* teased the British commander with a scathing satire called "Sir Henry Clinton's Soliloquy. . . .

> What dread ideas fill my tortured brain!
> West Point still rises to my troubled view!
> Unnerves my heart! and damps my ardent passion
> For the charge! There proud America's undaunted host
> With vict'ry flush'd, and pulses beating high,
> Unfurl their glitt'ring ensigns to the air,
> And claim, impatient claim, the promis'd fight!
> There god-like Washington triumphant stands,
> Smiles at my losses and defies my power![45]

Having seen the conditions at West Point for himself, the commander in chief also had a better understanding of the need for more tools and building supplies. There was also no food for the workhorses and livestock. The year before, McDougall had complained about the conditions: "Cattle have been for three days eating their mangers; others dying for want."[46]

There was a new commitment to keeping the construction workers happy, and on September 9, Washington wrote to Kosciuszko: "Sir: In consequence of yours of this morning I have ordered the Commy Genl. to procure a supply of Rum if possible for the Men upon fatigue. I shall be glad to know whether there has been any special agreement to give the Artificers draughted from the line any thing extraordinary for their Work. If there has, they must be paid in Rum (if that was the agreement) or an equivalent in Money when they do not get Rum. They must not at any Rate think of returning to their Regiments while their services are waiting."[47]

In late October 1779 news reached West Point that General Pulaski had been killed leading a cavalry charge against the British in Savannah, Georgia. He was trying to regroup the French troops of Admiral d'Estaing that were fleeing from the battlefield. After his failed naval actions in the north, d'Estaing sailed south and attacked Savannah. But when the French marched in the morning fog toward the barricades surrounding the city, they gave away their position by banging on war drums and firing before they were within range of the enemy.

The British easily repulsed the attack, and d'Estaing was peppered with musket fire. The second and third columns fared no better than the initial advance, and under heavy fire the confused French troops fled into the nearby woods.[48]

The aide at Pulaski's side during the battle, French captain Bentalou, wrote: "Aware of the fatal effects which such a disaster was likely to produce on the spirits of French soldiers—and hoping that his presence would reanimate them, Pulaski rushed on to the scene of disorder and bloodshed."[49]

Pulaski bolted into the melee on his black charger to restore order and encourage the French to return to the battle. As he tried to squeeze past the barricades, he was hit in the arm by musket fire and a cannon blast sent a golf-ball-size grapeshot ripping into his thigh, sending his horse stumbling into the ground. Pulaski was carried from the battlefield to the American ship the *Wasp*, where he died from his wounds.[50]

Dr. David Ramsay, who served as field surgeon in the Revolution before becoming a U.S. representative and a historian, wrote about Pulaski: "He was a thunderbolt of war, and always sought the post of danger as the post of honor."[51]

Washington found a way to honor Pulaski and at the same time make a gesture to boost the morale of Kosciuszko and the Poles serving in his army. Washington was staying at Moore House, his headquarters in West Point, when he gave the sentries a new password to distinguish between friend and foe. On November 17, 1779, he set the parole (query) and countersign (password) for crossing military checkpoints as "Pulaski" and "Poland."[52]

General Pulaski's heroic death enshrined his name in American history. It also made Colonel Kosciuszko the highest-ranking Pole in the Continental Army, and made him even more eager to prove himself in battle as a master tactician. But first he had to finish his grand construction project.

Much of the work had been carried out with a skeleton crew, and many of the forts looked like skeletons themselves. The first layers of the various redoubts were done with wood, dirt, and rocks, and when masons were available, stone walls were added to strengthen them. With winter approaching, Washington was confident enough in the designs that he wanted the remainder of the forts to be solidified in stone, and on November 21 he issued the following order: "The commanding officers of corps in the four Massachusetts brigades are desired to draught all the Masons in their respective regiments and send them to Col. Kosciuszko immediately, for the purpose of completing the barracks as expeditiously as possible."[53]

The push from Washington inspired the men to finish Fort Putnam, and the rest of the redoubts and forts that were also close to completion. General Gates was quite impressed with his protégé's work when he arrived at West Point for a brief visit on November 24. (Gates was traveling with his family to Traveller's Rest for a short leave to get his personal affairs in order.)

Washington was also impressed with the progress at the fort and left the camp on November 28, 1779, naming Maj. Gen. William Heath of Massachusetts as the new commander of the highlands. That same day Col. Israel Angell of the Second Rhode Island Regiment described West Point in his diary: "This Morning I got up by break of Day and went to view the forts. The first was Fort Putnam on a high Mountain, which may be properly Called the American Gibraltar, the next I went to was fort Arnold in both these forts was bumb [sic] proof Suficient to hold what men it would take to man the lines there was a fort on Every Emminence Some Distance round."[54]

Kosciuszko's Parisian art school education had equipped him to draw more than blueprints, and he was popular with the ladies, who wanted him to draw their portraits. Colonel Richard Varick of New Jersey, who had gotten to know Kosciuszko when both served in the Saratoga campaign, spent some time at West Point as inspector general. When Varick told his friend that he would not be spending the winter with him, Kosciuszko wrote back, "I am very sorry that your business will not permit to pass winter Quarters with me. I send you your picture which when you will give to your Sister pray not forget to pay my best respects to her and tell her that I propose to make her picture, I suppose will be very good resemblance if I make the handsomest feature of the fair creature that I am only able with my genius mind."[55]

It was already cold, and with winter approaching, Kosciuszko told Varick that he was going to keep his blankets until he came to retrieve them. It was just as well. The winter of 1780 was one of the coldest on record. Four feet of snow fell on West Point, and the water in the Hudson, even though it is a tidal basin, froze solid all the way south to New York City.[56]

The soldiers huddled together in their barracks covered in every blanket and article of clothing they could find. The men were so reliant for survival on the fireplaces in their huts that on several occasions they accidentally set fire to their quarters. Kosciuszko would have to organize crews to repair the torched barracks.

It was a harbinger of things to come, as 1780 would be the darkest year of the Revolution. Nature was even playing tricks on the wildlife in New York. When the spring thaw came, moles were found lying dead aboveground, shellfish had been destroyed, and nearly two-thirds of frog species had been killed off.[57]

During the coldest days of winter Kosciuszko was putting the finishing touches on Fortress West Point, and he searched for feedback. His cabin buried in the snow, he made copies of the blueprints of West Point that he sent to Washington once the roads were passable.

Thinking that he would finally be reassigned after two years in one place, he wrote to Gen. Nathanael Greene, giving recommendations for several of his men who were the most active and honest. He also asked Greene to take a look at the plans he had sent to Washington: "I have sent the Commander in Chief the Plans of Fort Putnam and at the Point, [Fort Arnold] with the respective profiles as I propose them to be finished. I beg you would see and give me your opinion. Conscious of your Extensive abilities, I am certain will afford as well as to the public good, as to my own improvement."[58]

The engineer grew concerned after he did not hear back about his blueprints, and on March 23 he wrote to Col. Richard Kidder Meade, Washington's acting secretary, asking if the drawings had "come to hand." In the same letter he asked for help to find forage for the work animals as well as shoes and clothing for his men.[59]

Meade replied that the sketches had "not yet come to hand" and said Kosciuszko had to "make application" for the shoes for his barefoot masons through official channels.[60]

Nearly two months went by and none of the officers in the highlands was able to find any more shoes, uniforms, or sufficient food for the workers at West Point.

When the French engineers wrote to Congress, it was often to seek promotions or for political manuevering. After four years of serving in the Continental Army, when Kosciuszko finally wrote to Congress, it was to ask for clothes for his men. As Duportail, the head of the Army Corps of Engineers, had been captured by the British in Charleston, Kosciuszko took his case to Gen. Philip Schuyler, who was then in Congress: "As you are the only Person in Congress with whom I have the Honor to be acquainted, that knows the system of the whole Army and its several Departments, you will forgive me the trouble I am about to give you in favor of the Corps of Engineers. We beg that the Honorable Congress would grant us clothing in appointed manner as for the Army. Why should all Departments receive and we be excluded?"[61]

Kosciuszko was not the only one reaching out to Schuyler in May 1780. Benedict Arnold called on Schuyler in Philadelphia as well.

Arnold's motive was treachery.

Greed had bubbled beneath the surface of Arnold's soul for years. In 1777 he was accused of looting Montreal during his invasion of Quebec. After the British withdrew from Philadelphia in 1778, Washington appointed Arnold military governor of the city to protect the crucial port, warehouses, and transportation network of the country's commercial hub. But once again Arnold was accused of abusing his authority and put on trial for malfeasance when it was discovered that he ran a corrupt speculation scheme by which he took control of many of the city's commodities and price gouged the war-weary population. He was acquitted, but he needed another source of income to keep him and his new wife, Peggy Shippen, living in the lap of luxury that they had grown accustomed to living among Pennsylvania's high society.

Arnold called on Schuyler to ask him to talk to Washington about giving him a new military command. The hero general pouted that as his wounded leg made it tough for him to engage in battle or ride a horse; he sought an administrative post, such as command of the Hudson Highlands.

Schuyler wrote to Arnold on June 2, "I had conversed with the General on the subject which passed between us before I left Philadelphia . . . [and] he expressed himself with regard to you in terms such as the friends who love you could wish."[62]

What Schuyler did not realize was that Arnold had already set in motion a plan to sell Kosciuszko's plans for West Point to the British. Arnold reached out to the British spy, Joseph Stansbury, a prominent merchant in Philadelphia to be his secret emissary with the enemy. Stansbury became Arnold's go-between with British major John André.

Major André had courted Miss Shippen before she married Arnold. After the wedding it was André who presented Arnold with the Faustian bargain for the wealth that he was after.

Arnold traveled to Washington's headquarters on June 12 to plead his case to be named commander of West Point. Washington was planning to invade New York City and wanted to bring Arnold along. But Arnold, who was limping around on a large built up red shoe that compensated for the two inches that he lost in his leg after the Battle of Saratoga, explained that he was no longer fit for battle.

On June 16 Arnold once again stopped at West Point to visit Gen. Robert Howe of North Carolina, who was the garrison's latest commandant. Arnold asked Howe for a tour of the redoubts at West Point, which, he claimed untruthfully, "I never saw before." The Southerner complied with the request, showing off all the fortifications. Later Howe would recall that Arnold "spoke so particularly of the Rocky Hill work [Redoubt No. 4] and with what ease it would be taken as struck me oddly even then, though I had not the least suspicion of him."[63]

As soon as he limped out of the meeting with Howe, Arnold scribbled a letter to André outlining how the British could capture West Point: "General Howe tells me there is not ten days provisions for the garrison—a quantity is on the way from Connecticut and soon expected, but if the English were to cut off the communication with Pennsylvania" the rebels would be starved of food and supplies. "The Heights called Rocky Hill, which commands all the other works, is about half a mile from Fort Putnam, which is strong," he continued. "On Rocky Hill there is a small redoubt to hold two hundred men and two six pounders pointed on the other works. The wall [is] six foot thick and defenseless on the Back, and I am told the English may land three miles below and have a good road to bring up heavy Cannon to Rocky Hill."[64]

Arnold's plan was set.

Rocky Hill, which Kosciuszko had warned all along was West Point's Achilles' heel, would be the focal point of the British attack. From there the Redcoats could fire down on the rebel soldiers in West Point, and then like dominoes, the redoubts would tumble downhill to Fort Arnold, to the chain redoubts and finally to the iron links that stretched across the Hudson River. If Arnold's plan were to succeed, the colonies would be divided in two, with New York's "North River" as the borderline.

Throughout the summer Arnold stepped up his lobbying efforts to be named commander of the highlands and worked to finalize his deal with the British. On July 15 he wrote to André: "If I point out a plan of cooperation by which Sir Henry [the British Commander in America] shall possess himself of West Point, the Garrison, etc. etc. etc. twenty-thousand pounds Sterling I think will be a cheap purchase for—an object of so much importance."[65]

Arnold's efforts to sell out West Point would inadvertently be assisted by an unlikely source, his former nemesis—Gen. Horatio Gates. On June 13 Congress appointed Gates to take command of the Southern Army after Gen. Benjamin

Lincoln, Duportail and thousands of Continental soldiers were surrounded and captured by the Redcoats in Charleston, South Carolina. Gates, who was at Travellers Rest, his plantation in Virginia, scrambled to put together an effective team to help him fight the British. Gates once again wrote to Washington asking for permission to take the Polish engineer with him.

Referring to the Southern Army in shambles, Gates wrote to Washington: "As all appearances from that Quarter are exceeding Gloomy, I could wish Your Excellency would somewhat Brighten the Scene, by indulging me in my request, to Obtain Colonel Kuscuiusco for my Chief Engineer. His Services with me in the Campaign of 77 and of High Opinion I entertain of his Talents, and His Honor, induce me to be thus importunate with your Excellency, to let me have the Colonel for my Chief Engineer."[66]

Trying to round up his posse from the Saratoga campaign, Gates also wrote to Kosciuszko's close friend, Maj. John Armstrong: "I am destined by the Congress to command in the South. In entering on this new and (as Lee says) most difficult theatre of the war, my first thoughts have been turned to the selections of an Engineer, and Adjutant-General and a Quarter-Master-General, Kosciuszko, Hay and yourself, if I can prevail upon you all, are to fill these offices, and will fill them well. The excellent qualities of the Pole, which no one knows better than yourself, are now acknowledged at head-quarters, and may induce others to prevent his joining us. But his promise once given, we are sure of him."[67]

Kosciuszko, who had buckled down through two and a half years of monotonous construction duty, was eager to find glory. He was itching once again to go into battle with Gates, and on July 30 Kosciuszko wrote to Washington begging to go to the front lines: "I beg your Excellency to give me permission to leave the Engeneer Department and direct me a Command in the light Infantry in the Army under your immediate Command or the Army at the Southward agreeable to my ranck I now hold. Your Excellency may be certain that I am acquiented with the Tactic & discipline and my Conduct to Joind with a small share of ambition to distinguish my self, I hope will prove to the Contrary."[68]

By the summer of 1780 Kosciuszko had transformed the highlands into "Fortress West Point," an impregnable stronghold. The sixteen enclosed positions and ten major battery sites formed three defensive rings around the chain that guarded the bend in the Hudson.

For the French engineers, the Marquis de Vauban's theories of solitary massive stone forts were gospel, while Kosciuszko's ideas of taking advantage of existing terrain and scattering forts and redoubts on various hills were heresy. Of all the foreign engineers who studied fort construction in France, "only Kosciuszko appears to have recognized Vauban's flexibility," Walker wrote in *Engineers of Independence*.[69]

The French wanted to build an eighteenth-century fort, while the Pole created a sophisticated nineteenth-century megafortress that twentieth-century Colonel Palmer called, "a splendid prototype for the system of fortifications which were to be built in Europe in the next century."[70] The prominent nineteenth-century American historian George Bancroft wrote: "Until 1778, West Point was a solitude, nearly inaccessible; now it was covered by fortresses with numerous redoubts, constructed chiefly under the direction of Kosciuszko as an engineer, and so connected as to form one system of defense, which was believed to be impregnable."[71]

An alumnus of the military academy in Warsaw, and a former student who audited classes at the military academy in Paris, Kosciuszko suggested that Americans establish a military school to train their officers.[72] After his death American cadets at the officer school raised money for a column on which a statue of Kosciuszko now stares out over the Hudson River where the chain once blocked British navigation.

Convinced of Kosciuszko's importance to West Point, Washington wanted to keep him there. But he was also desperate to win back the South, which required a military tactician who could figure out the lay of the land and place the Continental Army on a firm footing. Kosciuszko had proven that he could quickly move the rebels into defensible positions. On August 3 Washington wrote to the Pole in West Point: "As there is a necessity for a Gentlemen in the Engineering department to remain constantly at that post, and as you from your long residence there are particularly acquainted with the nature of the Works and the plans for their completion, it was my intent that you should continue. The Infantry Corps was arranged before the receipt of your letter. The southern Army, but the captivity of Genl. du portail and the other Gentleman in that branch is without an Engineer, and as you seem to express a wish of going there rather than remaining at West Point, I shall, if you prefer it to your present appointment, have no objection to your going."[73]

This was the chance Kosciuszko had been waiting for. While his skills were needed on the battlefield, his absence at West Point would be more critical than anyone realized. The same day that Washington approved Kosciuszko's transfer, he accepted Benedict Arnold's petition to be the new commanding officer of West Point.

On August 6, 1780, Washington wrote to Arnold, "Colo. Kosciuszko having permission to join the Southern Army, Major Villefranche has direction to report to West Point and take upon him the Superintendence of the Works. . . . P.S. If Genl. Howe has not left you a plan of the Works, Maj. Villefranche will be able to furnish you with one."[74]

Maj. Chevalier de Villefranche was the latest French engineer sent to West Point. Before he arrived Kosciuszko had pondered what to do with a chest full of detailed plans that he had drafted during his two and a half years working on the citadel. The Polish engineer did not know who his successor would be, so he left the valuable renderings at the boardinghouse of Mrs. Warren for safekeeping. For the British the chest might as well have been filled with gold, because it would have provided them with a secret roadmap of how to sneak in and capture West Point.

When Villefranche arrived at the fort, Kosciuszko invited him to lodge at his log cabin. He even left Villefranche a book by Philip Stanhope, the Earl of Chesterfield, and asked that he return it to its owner when he was done. But Kosciuszko was in such a hurry that he left without telling the Frenchman where he left his sketches. Without the original blueprints, Villefranche had to draw from scratch a map of the river, the chain, and the military base with all its forts and redoubts. Kosciuszko's haste to get back into battle is what delayed Arnold's plot to hand the British the plans for West Point.

Rushing off to thank the commander in chief for sending him back into battle, Kosciuszko left the fortress and rode to Washington's headquarters in Orange Town. The Pole asked Washington for permission to bring along Agrippa Hull, and by the second week of August, Kosciuszko and Grippy were headed south.

The Southern campaign was to reunite Kosciuszko with his mentor, and Washington gave him a letter to deliver to Gates: "I have taken the opportunity of writing by Colo. Kosciuszko, with whom I part reluctantly, as I have experienced great Satisfaction from his general conduct, and particularly from the attention and zeal with which he has prosecuted the Works committed to his charge at West Point."[75]

As the new chief engineer for West Point, Major Villefranche took over the burden of making sure that the work continued and that the logs under the chain were buoyant enough to float the heavy metal links. He also went to work drawing a map and compiling a full inventory of the works at the garrison to give to Arnold.

Even before he took command of the garrison, Arnold informed the British that he would provide them with a "drawing of the works on both sides of the river done by the French Engineer."[76]

Unaware that Arnold was using him as a pawn, Villefranche compiled a list of the redoubts and tallied up how many soldiers were needed to man each fort.[77] Arnold folded the list and stuck it in his pocket. Kosciuszko had left before Arnold arrived, and the new commander had not yet figured out where the Polish engineer had stashed his blueprints. The traitor inspected the various works and wrote a description of each one, outlining the strengths and weaknesses of Kosciuszko's projects.

Over the next month Arnold began undoing all the work Kosciuszko and his crews had done at West Point over the past two and a half years. In a letter to André, Arnold wrote that he weakened the chain by ordering one of the links to be removed under the pretense that it needed repairs.[78]

While Arnold was living in comfort on the eastern bank of the Hudson at the Beverly Robinson House, a wood-and-brick mansion that had been confiscated from one of the richest landowners in the highlands, he cut back on the soldiers' food rations and peddled wine and meat to his hungry troops.[79] He also reassigned units from various redoubts and sent them on bogus reconnaissance missions and wild-goose chases for more supplies.

During these first weeks of Arnold's command, the whole base was transformed into "a wild Tartar camp" that was run by an "ungovernable and undisciplined militia."[80] Once he had achieved this state of pandemonium, Arnold prepared to open the back door to West Point so that the British could march right in.

Kosciuszko planned for two hundred men to be stationed in Redoubt No. 4 that he had designed on Rocky Hill, and Villefranche's memo to Arnold specifically noted that it would take one hundred soldiers to "man the works" on that redoubt.[81] Yet on September 5, 1780, Arnold issued orders "in case of an alarm," which stated that only "a non-commissioned officer and three men" would be stationed on Redoubt No. 4.[82]

This would immediately have raised a red flag with Kosciuszko, who argued for two years with the French engineers about the tactical significance of defending Rocky Hill. But he had already left to take part in the Southern campaign.

One officer who did sense something was amiss was Maj. Sebastian Bauman, West Point's commander of artillery. Ten days after Kosciuszko was reassigned, Bauman wrote to Washington's aide Alexander Hamilton, explaining that it was a mistake to transfer the Polish engineer and that the fort would face "bad consequences" unless "an officer is fixed to this post, and who ought to be a competent judge of fortifications."

Major Bauman, worried about what would happen next, wrote: "Let General Arnold have all the sagacity imaginable, it will take him some time to get himself well acquainted with the position and defence of this post, and the very engineer is transferred from hence, on who he, in some measure could have depended for information, with regard to the weakest and strongest parts of this fortress."[83]

That was the point. Unknown to Bauman, Arnold was already aware of the weak link in the fortress. In fact, Arnold was doing all he could to make it even weaker.

With the troops hungry and disorganized, Arnold's next step was to get them drunk. The first line of defense for the highlands was the river crossing at King's Ferry, several miles down the Hudson. If any British ships passed that point north of New York City, an alarm would be sent to West Point.

On September 8, 1780, from their comfortable perch in the Robinson House, Arnold's aide Col. Richard Varick ordered Major Bauman to send "Gin to the Officer commanding the Post" at Kings Ferry, "By Command of M. Gen'l Arnold."[84]

Arnold even provided the boat to deliver the gin.

After hearing that Varick had been transferred to West Point, Kosciuszko wrote to the colonel to express regret that they had not had a chance to say good-bye. Kosciuszko wrote to Varick, who was from New Jersey, that when he stopped at a prominent house in Morristown, "Your name was mentioned by one hand-some Lady, which gave me great pleasure to hear so well spoken and everything in your favor." The ladies in Morristown were "too amiable" and greeted the Pole with hospitality, inviting him to "stay the night."

While Kosciuszko did not care for Arnold's heavy drinking and disrespect for authority, the Pole did appreciate his military skill, and told Varick to send "My Best respect to General Arnold. I will always esteem him. Remember to pay my respects to all ladys at West Point and particularly to Mistress Bauman, Jackson." He even asked Varick to remind Villefranche to return the book he had lent him to its owner when he was done reading it.[85]

By the time Arnold was ready to make his move and hand over the key to West Point to the British, Kosciuszko was 350 miles away in Richmond, Virginia, where he stopped off to deliver correspondence to Gov. Thomas Jefferson. Jefferson was helping the Southern Army by funding the construction of boats to transport troops. Kosciuszko had been traveling with Hull, a free black man, and was surprised to learn that the man who wrote that "all men are created equal" owned slaves.

On September 21, 1780, Arnold crept out of West Point to set his plot in motion, meeting with André, who had rowed to shore in a boat launched from the HMS *Vulture*, which had sailed up the Hudson. The turncoat handed over Ville-franche's memo and several other documents outlining Kosciuszko's fortifications and troop deployments at West Point. But before André could row back to the *Vulture*, guns from Teller's Point began firing on the British warship, forcing it to sail downstream, out of firing range.

André was forced to take an overland route to return to the British-occupied zone. Arnold wrote a pass for André to cross the American lines and demanded that the spy put the secret plans inside his boot. The traitor mounted his horse and rode back to West Point, thinking that he would soon be twenty thousand pounds richer.

On September 25, with several guests eating breakfast at his quarters in the Robinson house, Arnold was reading the dispatches of the day when he came across a report that had been accidentally sent to him instead of Washington. It revealed that a spy going by the name of John Anderson [André], dressed in civilian clothes, had been searched at a checkpoint. He was arrested with clandestine documents in his boot, along with a pass from Arnold.[86]

Stunned by the realization that the plan had fallen apart, and that he was about to be caught, Arnold quietly limped upstairs to his bedroom to speak with his wife. Within minutes Col. Franks knocked on the door to announce that Washington's servant had ridden up. Arnold knew that the commander in chief would not be far behind. The traitor hobbled down the stairs, jumped on his horse, and raced down to the river, where he found a whaleboat with eight British soldiers who rowed him to the *Vulture* to make his escape.

About forty minutes later "a great rumbling and trampling of horses" stormed up to the Robinson house, wrote Massachusetts militiaman Alpheus Parkhurst, "a great smoke of dust, the weather being dry, and in a few moments General Washington with 160 horse rode up." When he learned that Arnold was gone, Washington and his entourage raced off to West Point to assess the damage.[87]

Paranoia spread through the highlands, and a witch hunt began for those who were close to Arnold. Colonels Franks and Varick were suspected but cleared. In the investigation to uncover what the British had learned during Arnold's plot, the Continental Army collected all the documents concerning West Point.

The search was on for Kosciuszko's missing blueprints.

Washington wrote to Gen. William Heath: "I am informed by Gen. Irvine, a Chest belonging to Col Kosciuszko containing principally Papers of a public nature; which General Greene had determined to have removed from Mrs. Warrens to a place of more security; but in the hurry of business might have omitted. If the chest still remains at West Point, you will be pleased to take it into your charge, or have it removed to a place of safety. As the Drafts and Papers are of service to the Public."[88]

Heath inquired into the chest's whereabouts and replied to Washington, "I have sent for Colo. Kosciuszko's chest; it was left without lock. Mrs. Warren says upon the detection of Arnold, she burnt the plans lest their being found with her should raise a suspicion to her disadvantage. I shall order a further inquiry into the matter."[89]

While the story of the infamous traitor Benedict Arnold is taught in schools across America, the prize he was trying to sell to the British, Kosciuszko's handiwork of two and a half years in the Hudson Highlands, has been but a footnote in history books.

Two days after the treasonous affair was uncovered, Maj. Samuel Shaw was at the Robinson house and wrote about the "horror" of "Arnold's villainy." On October 1, 1780, Shaw wrote: "West Point and its dependencies constitute the palladium of American independence; and, this grand link in the chain of our union, once being broken, we may bid adieu to peace, liberty and safety. . . . The enemy would, had the treason succeeded, have had entire possession of the country from New York to Ticonderoga. This, with the impression they have already made on the Southern States, would have reduced us to an extremity from which nothing, in the present spirit of the times, but a creating power could have extricated us."[90]

Thanks to Kosciuszko's help the British were not able to break the chain between New York City and Fort Ticonderoga. Extricating the British army from the Southern States, where most of the wealthy plantation owners supported the British king, would be a completely different battle.

SEVEN

A Polish Yankee Goes South

GATES'S SECRETARY DURING THE NORTHERN CAMPAIGN, WILLIAM Clajon, saw Kosciuszko when he stopped in Philadelphia to report to the Board of War and pick up his orders. As a newlywed, Clajon wanted to settle the matter of his back pay and secure extra rations before joining the Southern Army.[1]

Clajon told the engineer that Gates's son, Bob, was suffering from tuberculosis, and perhaps dying. He was being treated at the general's plantation in Virginia. The Pole couldn't help but make a detour to see his dying friend at the Gates's homestead. Kosciuszko consoled Bob and Mrs. Gates and tried to cheer them up by drawing blueprints for a more stately home than the modest accommodations that the Gates family had been accustomed to. Clajon wrote to General Gates in South Carolina letting him know that Kosciuszko would stop to see Bob before continuing south.[2]

Before Kosciuszko arrived Gates jumped the gun and ordered his troops to march directly on the British camp in Camden before he had enough provisions, supplies, or even a battle plan. Gates expected to fight Gen. Lord Francis Rawdon-Hastings, but was surprised when Gen. Lord Charles Cornwallis showed up with reinforcements.

Gates carried a heavy burden of emotional baggage from the name "Cornwallis" when he left England to cross the Atlantic. Lord Cornwallis was the nephew of Gates's former mentor in London, Gen. Edward Cornwallis. But Gates had a terrible falling-out with the Cornwallis family, and resented that early in his life he had been forced to rely on the Cornwallis "Hard Hand of Power."[3] This time another Cornwallis would wield "a hard hand" against Gates. The British forces overran the Southern Army at the Battle of Camden on August 16, 1780.

Gates tried to rally his men, but on that hot summer day in the South, clouds of gunsmoke hung in the hazy air, and the disoriented general, thinking that his men had retreated, turned and fled, leaving the troops in disarray to be slaughtered on the battlefield. Gates hightailed it 180 miles in three days to Hillsborough, North Carolina. The scene that he left behind was a bloodbath, with nine hundred Americans killed and one thousand captured.[4]

It was the end of combat duty for Gates, and his reputation never recovered. Alexander Hamilton wrote: "Was there ever an instance of a general running away, as Gates has done, from his whole army? And was there ever so precipitous a flight? One hundred and eighty miles in three days and a half. It does admirable credit to the activity of a man at this time of his life. But it disgraces the general and the soldier. I have always believed him to be very far short of a Hector, or a Ulysses. All the world, I think will begin to agree with me."[5]

While this was taking place, Kosciuszko was on his way to Richmond, Virginia, to deliver money from Gates to Gov. Thomas Jefferson.[6] Jefferson briefed Kosciuszko about the state of the military in Virginia and discussed logistics about helping the Southern Army. Jefferson, who was concerned about strengthening his state militia in case of an invasion of Virginia, offered to help the Continental Army with construction of twelve boats to transport troops along the rivers in the Carolinas and to deliver bread, corn, beef, and guns to the rebels.

A marked difference in the South was the role that African Americans played in the Revolution. In Pennsylvania slaves made up less than 1 percent of the population, and in New York, where slaves were 6 percent of the population, black men were allowed to serve in the militia. Rhode Island had an entire regiment of more than two hundred armed black soldiers that had been given their freedom.

But in Virginia, Kosciuszko could not help noticing that 40 percent of the population was black, and in Richmond the percentage was even higher. Southern plantation owners cowered at the notion of arming slaves, and Jefferson, a slave owner who claimed to be opposed to slavery, straddled the fence as a politician, saying, "Slaves are by the laws excluded from the Militia," especially when it came to carrying a gun.[7] However, he encouraged the military to use blacks as laborers.

Kosciuszko could not understand how the author of the Declaration of Independence was able to sacrifice his views on human rights for the sake of politics and economics. After the Revolution the two men became close friends, and the Pole held Jefferson's feet to the fire over slavery.

But first there was a war to fight.

In October the Pole caught up with the remnants of Gates's tattered army, which was trying to regroup in Hillsborough, North Carolina. Traveling through the South, Kosciuszko saw enough of the local culture to understand that blacks were treated worse than in the North. Careful not to offend his Southern hosts, Kosciuszko began politely advocating for fairness for African Americans writing kind words about a young slave named Billy to his master, Dr. William Read.[8] Kosciuszko also demanded a pair of shoes for Agrippa Hull, who of his own free will accompanied him to slave country in the Carolinas.[9]

There was little food or supplies for the Continental regulars, and as the autumn chill set in, there was only one blanket for every five men. Kosciuszko and Dr. Read shared Gen. Isaac Huger's cloak as their only form of bedding.[10]

Gates held a war council on November 25 with his officers in New Providence to determine where the army should move to search for provisions. The troops marched to Charlotte in late November, and on December 2 Gen. Nathanael Greene arrived with orders from Congress to replace Gates as the new commander of the Southern Army. Gates, who was humiliated at Camden and facing a possible court-martial, respectfully stepped aside and returned to his Virginia homestead to comfort his grieving wife over the death of their only son.

While Gates's life was in disarray, Greene devised a plan for the Southern Army before he even arrived in North Carolina. He understood that troop movements were a major problem in the South because the army had few horses or wagons at its disposal. On his way to take charge of the army, he wrote to Washington: "I intend to have all the rivers examined in order to see if I cannot ease this heavy business by water transportation."[11]

Greene had confidence in his engineer's abilities after seeing his work at Fortress West Point. Greene had been sent there to restore order after Arnold's attempt to weaken the fort and hand it over to the British. On December 8 the new Southern commander ordered Kosciuszko to take a guide, "and examine the country from the mouth of the Little River, twenty or thirty miles down from the Pedee, and search for a good position for the army." He was also to report back on the availability of produce and drinking water and the navigability of the river and its creeks and fords.[12]

Kosciuszko and his scout paddled down the Pee Dee River in a canoe to find a new base camp. Greene sent other officers in different directions to survey the Yadkin and Dan rivers. After not hearing from the Pole for a week, some of the soldiers grew anxious about moving out from their current position. But Greene refused to move his army until he heard back from the Pole.

On December 15 Greene wrote to Col. Thomas Polk, North Carolina's commissary general, saying that it was "impossible to leave this Camp as early as I intended as Col. Kosciuszko has made no report yet respecting a position upon Pedee."[13]

When Kosciuszko returned the next day, Greene followed his advice to move the army to a position at Cheraw Hill, where Hick's Creek poured into the Pee Dee River. The new camp turned out to be a strategically wise position, from which Greene's forces had the options of attacking Camden, marching on Charleston, or aiding Gen. Francis "Swamp Fox" Marion and his South Carolina militia.[14]

Once the engineer finished fortifying the camp, Greene informed Washington that, "Kosciuszko is employed building flat-bottomed boats to be transported with the army."[15] On New Year's Day 1781 Greene ordered Kosciuszko to move to Cross Creek and take all of the officers he could find "to assist you in procuring a number of tools suitable for constructing a number of boats [and] . . . engage all the carpenters you can find you may think necessary to dispatch to the construction of the boats. Confiding in your zeal and activity I persuade myself you will make all the dispatch the business will admit as the safety and support of the Army depend upon your accomplishing this business."[16]

Throughout January, Kosciuszko worked on building the small fleet of boats that could be carried overland from one river to another. These light watercraft became critical after Greene sent Daniel Morgan's unit into South Carolina, where the rebels routed the British cavalry and infantry unit of Col. Banastre Tarleton at the Battle of Cowpens on January 17, 1781.

While Morgan's brilliant and decisive victory boosted the morale of the Southern Army, it infuriated General Cornwallis, whose troop strength still outnumbered Greene's. The Americans were not ready for a fight to the finish. They needed more time. Once Cornwallis figured out where the Southern Army was hiding, the British set out in pursuit of Greene, and the two opposing forces played a game of cat and mouse, with the rebels fleeing from the Redcoats on their tail.

Kosciuszko charted the course ahead of the Americans as Cornwallis hunted the rebels in a swirling two hundred-mile diversionary race through the Carolinas to the Dan River. The portable flatboats were used strategically to evade the British with quick river crossings.

The historian James Pula wrote, "Kosciuszko appeared to be everywhere, handling the myriads of details necessary for success, planning lines of march, gathering and dispatching crucial boats, and seeking little known shortcuts."[17]

While Kosciuszko was blazing the path in front of the rebels, covering their rear were the troops of Col. Otho Williams of Maryland. At times the Redcoats were so close that to relieve their hunger, Williams's men would hold the bridles of their horses with one hand while with the other they would attempt to roast a piece of bacon stuck on the point of a stick, ready to run before it was even cooked.[18]

A cold February rain mixed with snow made the march to the Dan miserable and slippery. Kosciuszko rejoined Greene at Guilford, North Carolina.[19] The troops were so exhausted that the general considered making a stand on a hill near an isolated courthouse.[20]

The Pole always touted the benefits of using the high ground to one's advantage and was ready to assemble barricades, but with little time to prepare for battle, Greene decided to move on and sent Kosciuszko ahead to prepare for a crossing at Irwin's Ferry on the Dan River. There the Polish engineer got the boats ready and threw up breastworks to provide sniper cover for the passage of the American army.[21]

Cornwallis, who was only a few hours' march behind Greene, believed that he was poised to wipe out what was left of the Southern Army. The Continentals made it to the rushing river and crossed in the boats Kosciuszko had built for them. As the last of the soldiers drifted to shore, Cornwallis arrived to find Greene's men heckling him and thumbing their noses at the Redcoats from the northern bank of the Dan.

Many of the Continental soldiers were barefoot and had bloody feet after the long march. Greene wrote to Jefferson that he and his men were "almost fatigued to death, having had a retreat to conduct for upwards of two hundred miles."[22]

Their next step was not so clear. Cornwallis could not cross the river and his army pitched camp to rest after the two hundred-mile race. Greene ordered Kosciuszko to head to Halifax on the Roanoke River to "see if it is practicable to fortify it in a short time and whether it may be garrisoned with a small force." The general told Kosciuszko to use his judgment and ask the North Carolina legislature for men and tools if he decided that this would be the place to make a stand, adding, "as Lord Cornwallis's movements are rapid I recommend the greatest dispatch . . . you will report to me the situation of things that I may know as early as possible how to make my measures."[23]

If the British captured Halifax they would be knocking on Virginia's door.

Greene was convinced that Halifax was Cornwallis's target. He wrote to Washington, "I imagine [Cornwallis] will file off for Halifax, and endeavor to establish a post there; to prevent which I have sent Colonel Kosciuszko to fortify it. That position would greatly awe Virginia, and almost totally subject North Carolina."[24]

With a mangy old horse that eventually gave out, forcing him to walk part of the way, it took Kosciuszko two days to travel the eighty miles through hostile Tory country to Halifax. Once he arrived and surveyed his options, Kosciuszko wrote to Greene that as he would have to build at least six redoubts to defend the city, it made more sense to move the stores of provisions across the river to nearby Taylor's Ferry, where there were a "thousand good militia" who "could cover entirely Halifax and the adjacent Country."[25]

The engineer sketched out a map of Halifax and sent it to Greene.[26] But the threat to Halifax abated when Cornwallis broke camp and turned south after a few days of rest. Greene recrossed the Dan in the flatboats and gave chase from behind. The rebels shooed off Tory reinforcements that tried to join Cornwallis and harassed the foraging parties of Redcoats as they searched for food.

Getting word that the two armies had moved away from the Dan, Kosciuszko caught up with Greene's army at Guilford Courthouse. Just as they had at Saratoga, American volunteers began trickling in to join the Continental Army. Greene's forces soon outnumbered the British troops by more than two to one. But most of Greene's 4,300 men, positioned in three lines of defenses on the hills near the courthouse, were raw militiamen who had never seen action.

The frost was melting in the rising sun on the morning of March 15, 1781, when Lord Cornwallis sent his professional force of nineteen hundred British and Hessian infantrymen to attack the Americans. The bloody battle lasted several hours. Both sides had heavy losses, and Cornwallis grew desperate. He ordered his cannons packed with grapeshot, canvas bags stuffed with cast-iron balls that resembled a bunch of grapes as they hurtled toward the enemy like a massive shotgun blast. When the British artillery blasts scattered into the fracas, these small iron orbs tore through the flesh of British and American soldiers alike.

By using his own troops as cannon fodder, Cornwallis drove the Continental Army back. Even though victory was within his grasp, Greene was not willing to sacrifice his own men in a similar fashion and signaled for a retreat.

The British suffered more than 532 dead and wounded, while the American losses were 78 killed and 183 wounded. Even though he lost one-fourth of his men, Cornwallis declared himself the victor of the Battle of Guilford Courthouse. When the English politician Charles James Fox heard this, he proclaimed in Parliament that, "Another such victory would ruin the British Army."[27]

Fox's public indictment of the war harked back to Plutarch's quote of King Pyrrhus of Epirus, who suffered horrible casualties in his triumph over the Romans and said, "Another such victory, and I shall be undone."[28] That Britain's victory was Pyrrhic became obvious once Cornwallis abandoned his wounded and ran for cover toward the seacoast. The "vanquisher" of Guilford courthouse ran so fast toward the Tory outpost of Wilmington, North Carolina, that Greene's army could not catch him.

While the British and the Loyalists controlled much of the coastline between Wilmington and Charleston, South Carolina, Greene decided to focus on the inland British garrisons of South Carolina. With Cornwallis licking his wounds, the Continentals had to contend with Lord Rawdon, who held Camden.

Lord Rawdon was tall, dark, and ugly. In fact he was called the "ugliest man in England."[29] Born to a noble Irish family, Rawdon commanded the Volunteers of Ireland, a group of newly arrived recruits from Ireland, as well as Irish deserters from American units who were holding Camden.

Rawdon also had an ugly reputation as a ruthless pillager who was so amused by his troops' raping the local girls on Staten Island, New York, in 1776 that he wrote: "The fair nymphs of this isle are in wonderful tribulation, as the fresh meat our men have got here has made them as riotous as satyrs. A girl cannot step into the bushes to pluck a rose without running the most imminent risk of being ravished."[30]

The British had heavily fortified Camden after defeating Gates, so Greene did not risk attacking the town head on and camped out nearby at Hobkirk's Hill. Rawdon was worried that more volunteers would show up to join Greene, so on April 25 he took the initiative and sneaked out of Camden creeping up to the rebel camp along a swampy bog near a row of pine trees. The Continental encampment was laid out in battle formation along a ridge. Greene was having breakfast when he heard his sentries fire on the approaching enemy. As Rawdon's troops charged, the rebels fired cannons loaded with grapeshot that tore the British front lines to pieces.

In a firsthand account given by Col. Guilford Dudley, this was followed up by a blaze of musket fire led by Greene and "every officer exhorting all the bravery and energy of his soul, the general himself, with his cool intrepidity risking his invaluable person in the thickest of battle."[31]

The battle devolved into a bloody clash of slashing bayonets, and Kosciuszko and Greene's aide-de-camp Maj. William Pierce were sent to the right wing just as it began to give way.[32] Greene again ordered a pullback. Both sides lost about 250 men, and the British again claimed victory. But while the British bragged that they had won the battle, Greene was actually beginning to win the war.

Rawdon, concerned that he could no longer hold Camden, followed Cornwallis's strategy and retreated toward the seaport of Charleston. Camden was liberated.

Greene refused to be discouraged and wrote to the French minister to the United States, the Chevalier de la Luzerne: "We fight, get beat, rise, and fight again."[33] He also thanked Luzerne for sending Lafayette to help out in Virginia.

Lafayette, in turn, told Washington that as he was taking a new posting in the South, he would like to take Gouvion along as his engineer. Washington, who had kept track of Kosciuszko's work in the Southern campaign and had a favorable opinion of his effectiveness, denied Lafayette's request, pointing out that this "would interfere with Colo. Kosciuszko who had been considered as the commanding Engineer with the southern Army."[34]

The Pole had finally earned his stripes in the field. But he would soon face his first major failure. On May 22, 1781, Greene's army of about one thousand soldiers reached the village called Ninety-Six and its star-shaped earthen fort, which was a Loyalist outpost in the South Carolina wilderness. The prosperous Tory village was given its unusual name by merchants from Charleston who thought that it was ninety-six miles from the Cherokee village of Keowee, near the Blue Ridge Mountains, where they traded their goods for animal pelts with the Indians.

The fort was defended by Lt. Col. John Harris Cruger and about 550 Loyalists.

Greene and Kosciuszko reconnoitered the trenches and rows of abatis that circled the village and its star-shaped fort. They decided that the best strategy was to blast their way directly into the fort, which was raised on a dirt mound that commanded the entire area. Kosciuszko devised a plan using Vauban's siege craft techniques that he had learned in French military schools and ordered his men to dig a Z-shaped trench leading up to the British outpost. The plan was to tunnel under the fort and pack barrels of gunpowder into a mine to blow a hole through the wall of the defensive positions.

Unfortunately the Pole chose a starting line for the trench that was too close to the fort, only about two hundred feet away. As the digging went on outside the walls, Cruger had his men put up a platform inside the fort, from which they fired cannons at the Continentals. The artillery fired on the soldiers who were digging, and then about thirty Tories stormed out of the fort and began bayoneting the men in the ditch. Kosciuszko and his men were caught by surprise and had to flee without their entrenching tools.

The rebels pulled back, and Kosciuszko ordered his men to continue digging from three hundred yards away where they were out of firing range. They built a rolling wooden shield to defend themselves from gunfire.[35] They also shot flaming "African arrows" into the British fort to set the buildings on fire. Cruger responded by having his men rip the shingles off the roofs so they wouldn't catch fire.[36]

Because of the rock-hard ground, it took the rebels about a week to dig their way to the spot where the original trench started. Each day the rebel groundhogs got closer to the fort and the gunfire from inside the fort grew more intense. To provide cover for the work detail, Kosciuszko had his men put up a thirty-foot Maham tower, from which sharpshooters could fire into the fort. The concept was named after Lt. Col. Hezekiah Maham, who had developed it earlier during the Revolution. The tower was made from freshly cut green wood so it could not be burned down. Cruger's Tories defended themselves from the tower's sharpshooters by placing sandbags on top of the wall, leaving small openings from which they could fire their muskets.

On June 8, Col. "Light Horse" Harry Lee and his unit arrived at Ninety-Six to assist in the siege and assailed Kosciuszko for aiming the trenches toward the strongest part of the enemy's defenses. He also criticized the Pole for not cutting off the fort's access to drinking water from a stream on the western edge of the village.

Lee's unit camped on the west side of the village near the creek, and during the day they fired upon any Loyalists who tried to collect water. What Lee didn't realize was that once the sun went down, naked black slaves crawled out of the fortified village to fetch water under cover of the night.

On June 9, while Kosciuszko was investigating the mine near the fort's wall that was almost ready to be packed with gunpowder, Tory scouts sneaked out from the fort and overwhelmed him. As he turned to flee, his pursuers stabbed him in the buttocks with a bayonet and shot several of his men. The British were delighted by the engineer's wound, and it might be said that he soon became the butt of their jokes.

Roderick Mackenzie of the British army wrote in his report, "Never did luckless wight [a person] receive a more inglorious wound, upon any occasion, than Count Koziusco did on this—it was in that part which Hudibras has constituted the seat of honour, and was given just as this engineer was examining the mine which he had projected!"[37]

Hudibras was a seventeenth-century satire mocking Puritans and Cromwellians by the royalist writer Samuel Butler. Given Oliver Cromwell's struggle in favor of republicanism over monarchy, Kosciuszko would have been amused to be placed in such lofty company by his English foes. The Pole went back to work as soon as Dr. Read treated his wounds, and as the historian Lynn Montross noted "neither pain nor ribald jest kept him from duty."[38]

As the mine tunnels edged closer to the fort, Greene worried that the promised six hundred pounds of gunpowder that were supposed to be delivered from Augusta might never arrive. Without the powder they would not be able to blast through the wall.[39]

Kosciuszko's plan of attack was starting to unravel.

Greene saw that he had an even bigger problem when a rider inconspicuously galloped into camp and began greeting the Continental soldiers and catching them off guard. The rambler then jammed his spurs into his horse and raced toward the fort's main gate, waving a letter in his raised hand. The rebels fired at the lone horseman but the gate quickly swung open and then shut just as fast after he raced in behind the barricades. The dispatcher had arrived with news for Colonel Cruger that General Lord Rawdon would arrive in a few days with two thousand British reinforcements to save the Loyalists.[40]

There was no time to lose. Kosciuszko's trench had taken too long to build, there were not enough explosives to blow through the wall, and no one did anything to cut off the fort's drinking water until Lee had arrived.

On June 18, Greene gave the order to storm the star fort at Ninety-Six. He sent in a "forlorn hope" team of axmen to chop away at the abatis on top of the fort, while another team of daredevils charged ahead with pole-hooks and began pulling down the sandbags stacked atop the walls.

Lee's troops focused on Holmes Fort, an outpost of the village made from three barns that had been transformed into a stockade to protect the stream. It was connected to the village via a caponier, a covered ditch with firing ports to provide passage.

On the day of the battle Lee's men easily took the stockade because the Tories who sneaked out the night before through the caponier had abandoned it.[41] Yet Lee held back from advancing on the village or the fort. This proved to be disastrous when Cruger sent two parties of about thirty men each out of the back of the fort to surround the perimeter from opposite directions. The Tories stormed with fixed bayonets into the Continental lines and stabbed and killed dozens of the rebels. Standing over the ditches, the Redcoats jabbed their rifle blades into the rebel soldiers who were trying to make their way through the unfinished trenches.

One hundred and forty-seven Continental soldiers were killed during the twenty-eight-day siege on Ninety Six. Greene had decided that enough was enough. After the longest siege in the American Revolution, Greene decided to flee across the Saluda River before Lord Rawdon arrived with his reinforcements the following day.

In his own notes on the Siege of Ninety Six, Kosciuszko wrote that "blind fortune [did] not always keep pace with Courage and Good Cause." He praised his own men for their "valor . . . fortitude, perseverance, courage and exertions," while also acknowledging the enemy "for their vigilance, frequent judicious sallies and proper means to counteract the assailant measures."[42]

The bitter loss at the doomed siege of Ninety Six turned out to be Kosciuszko's greatest failure during the American Revolution. Colonel Lee blamed the Pole for the defeat, writing in his memoirs, "Kosciuszko was extremely amiable, and, I believe, a truly good man, nor was he deficient in his professional knowledge; but he was very moderate in talent,—not a spark of the ethereal in his composition. His blunders lost us Ninety Six; and general Greene, much as he was beloved and respected, did not escape criticism, for permitting his engineer to direct the manner of approach."[43]

General Greene disagreed, writing in his orderly book on June 20: "The General presents his thanks to Colonel Kosciuszko chief Engineer for his Assiduity, perseverance and indefatigable exertions in planning and prosecuting the approaches which he is persuades were judiciously designed and would have infallibly gained success if time had admitted of their being completed."[44]

Greene was not the only officer who was confident that Kosciuszko's plan would have worked, given more time. Three days after the failed siege, Greene's chief of staff, Col. Otho Williams, wrote a letter to his brother, Elie: "Col. Kosciuszko, a young gentleman of distinction from Poland who left his native country to follow the banners of Liberty in America, superintended the operations, and by his Zeal, assiduity, perseverance and firmness promoted the business with . . . expedition."[45]

After the retreat Kosciuszko wrote to Gates telling him that, "Any Circumstance in the world will never change my Esteem, Friendship and respect for you." The Pole now also had a defeat under his belt and lamented, "You had information so far as to our Blockade of Ninety Six I suppose, in which we were unlucky, the Ground was so hard that our approaches could not go but very slow, had Lord Roudon gave us four days more we should blow up Theirs Works and take Six Hundred men in it."[46]

Once again Greene had lost a battle but taken another step toward winning the war in the South. The siege was not a complete loss because it forced the Redcoats to abandon the outpost of Ninety Six.

Lord Rawdon's troops marched back to Charleston in their heavy wool uniforms under a burning summer sun through clammy swamps infested with mosquitoes. Along the way dozens of his Irish troops died from heat stroke, and Rawdon contracted malaria and was forced to retire. He boarded a ship to England that was hijacked by pirates, and he was handed over to the French.

The Continental Army was sick of eating the frogs and alligators they had been subsisting on, so Greene moved them to search for food and rest.[47] The Polish engineer set up camp on the High Hills of the Santee under shady trees near the pure water of several rivers. The breezy hills and nearby fields of grain and fruit trees made it the perfect place to rest for the next six weeks.

As the troops rested Kosciuszko grew jittery. He was not a big drinker and ate little, but he did have one addiction—caffeine. When an expected shipment of coffee from Charleston did not arrive, Kosciuszko found "great mortification" by the bad news and wrote to Dr. Reed, "I cannot live without Coffee . . . I beg you to send me six pounds of Coffee, with Sugar in proportion."[48]

As Greene contemplated his next move in the Carolinas, he also had to figure out what to do about the situation in Virginia, where Benedict Arnold had led a raid of British troops into the capital and captured Richmond. He even came close to abducting Thomas Jefferson at Monticello.

The Continental Army wanted nothing more than to catch their worst traitor. At one point Arnold asked a rebel captain whom he was holding prisoner what the Americans would do if they captured him. After first balking at the question, the captain replied, "If my countrymen should catch you, I believe they would first cut off that lame leg, which was wounded in the cause of freedom and virtue, and bury it with the honors of war, and afterwards hang the remainder of your body in gibbets."[49]

Concerned about the British troops in neighboring Virginia, North Carolina governor Thomas Burke asked Greene for an engineer who could design defenses to protect against enemy raids on his military stores. Greene replied, "I will send to your assistance Colo. Kosciuszko, our principal engineer who is a Master of his profession, and will afford you every aid you can wish."[50]

Virginia remained unscathed by the war until 1779, when Lord Dunmore burned Norfolk. Lord Dunmore had created problems for the South ever since his proclamation early in the war to free slaves. Dunmore also created an Ethiopian Regiment to fight for the King with the words "Liberty to Slaves" embroidered on their uniforms. While the Ethiopian regiment did not last long, many blacks still served in the British army.

As the war pressed on, opposition to blacks serving in the Continental Army had subsided in the North but continued in the South. Maryland was the only Southern state that allowed slaves to enlist. During the course of his numerous defeats in the South, Greene grew increasingly frustrated by these circumstances. On September 8, he lost the Battle of Eutaw Springs against British colonel Alexander Stewart's troops. Greene was also unable to pursue Lord Cornwallis, who had fled to Yorktown, Virginia, for supplies and reinforcements.

While Greene lost every battle that he had fought in the South, he won the war by keeping his army intact. Kosciuszko's role was significant because he helped Greene's army to elude Cornwallis, buying the rebels enough time for reinforcements to arrive.

Ultimately Greene's campaign of harassment in the South drove Cornwallis north, directly into line of fire of the French navy and George Washington, and the main forces of the Continental Army.

Greene's goal of finishing off Cornwallis would have to be left up to others.

The French army did little fighting in support of the American Revolution during the first six years of the war. While France supported the rebels secretly before officially joining the war, most of the time French troops avoided fights with the Redcoats. France's biggest contribution was providing 90 percent of the gunpowder that the rebels used to shoot at the British army. This would soon change, as French troops would play a major role in the largest battle of the war.

In September, French admiral François de Grasse sailed twenty-four battleships to Virginia and took control of Chesapeake Bay away from the British navy. Lord Cornwallis had his access to the sea cut off, and several weeks later, ten thousand French troops and 8,500 Continental Army soldiers under the command of George Washington showed up to surround the British army. After three weeks of shelling damaged his army, Cornwallis had no choice but to surrender.

The alliance with France had finally paid off.

Yet even after Yorktown, the British still held on to the seacoast near the port of Charleston. As 1781 drew to a close Greene once again raised an issue he had touched on early in the Revolution. He believed that black slaves should be able to fight for their freedom.

Greene was surprised when he learned that out of South Carolina's 248,139 inhabitants, 120,000 were black.[51] Greene wrote to the state's governor, John Rutledge: "The natural strength of this country in point of numbers, appears to me to consist much more in the black, than the whites. . . . That they would make good soldiers I have not the least doubt." He added the British could be driven out of "this country, when they find they have not only the whites, but the blacks also to contend with."[52]

Greene was a Quaker, who were America's first abolitionists. Like Kosciuszko many of Greene's officers were opposed to slavery. Greene's aide, Maj. Lewis Morris, wrote about life in South Carolina, "I envy everything I see, except the poor unhappy blacks who, to the disgrace of human nature, are subject to every species of oppression while we are contending of the rights of liberties of mankind."[53]

The most outspoken of Greene's staff was Col. John Laurens, whose father, Henry Laurens, was president of the Continental Congress.[54] The elder Laurens was a South Carolina plantation owner who had abandoned the slave trade in 1770, and on one occasion, wrote to his son, "I am devising means of manumitting many of them and for cutting off the entail of slavery."[55]

The younger Laurens was even more outspoken in opposing slavery and became the Continental Army's leading advocate for allowing African Americans to fight for their freedom by joining the army. "I have long deplored the wretched state of these men, and considered their history, the bloody wars excited in Africa to furnish America with Slaves—the groans of despairing multitudes toiling for the luxuries of merciless tyrants," wrote Laurens to his father.[56]

Kosciuszko had found men of like thinking in Laurens, Greene, and Morris. The plight of the African slaves was even more desperate than that of the serfs who tilled the land for their masters in his native Poland. Kosciuszko had always been close to the peasants who farmed the plantations in his homeland, and with Grippy at his side during much of the Southern campaign, Kosciuszko also developed a rapport with slaves in the United States. Thousands of black men fought on the American side, but in his units in South Carolina and Georgia, Greene would have to settle for using black men as unarmed laborers.

By 1782 the war in the South had settled into a battle of containment. The British controlled Savannah and Charleston, but Greene gradually tightened the ring around Charleston. He moved his army from the high hills to a camp in an area of rice plantations called Round O, between the Pon Pon and Ashepoo rivers. The fertile region was full of things that the soldiers had not seen in some time, including poultry, wild game, fruit—and young women.

By the time spring arrived the soldiers' minds turned to the fairer sex. Morris was excited by the "fine girls, the patriotic fair of the country."[57]

The ranking officers were given lodging in some of the finer homes in the area, and Kosciuszko and his friend Col. Williams stayed in the house of Mrs. Susan Hayne. As the pace of the war slowed, Williams, who had been suffering from battle wounds, decided to return home to Baltimore to recuperate.

With little to report about the war, his Polish friend kept Williams up to date on romantic gossip of his former unit. "Everybody is in love," Kosciuszko wrote to Williams in March, "Colo. Morris fancy himself to be with Miss Nancy Eliot in love."[58]

About a week later the Pole gave Williams another update about the antics of his brothers-in-arms, joking that Morris fell in love, Maj. Edmund Burnet turned out to be pretty "gallant" with women, Maj. William Pierce was beginning to "catch sentimental visions" and their friend Capt. Nathaniel Pendleton proposed to become "a Priest."

Kosciuszko was popular with the ladies because he played piano and sang in French at the parties in the stately homes and used his Parisian art school education to sketch portraits of smitten damsels. He informed Williams that he "was frightened out of my Soul" when several Southern belles accosted him at a party to "make their pictures." He playfully declined, saying, "that I cannot make them handsome judge pray without partiality" because of their "natural propensity to cruel acts."

The ladies, who had been drinking rum, gave Kosciuszko a wicked tongue-lashing, and one even came at him with a shovel. He gave in and sketched their portraits, so the women "approached me with very smiling countenances, kissed me half a dozen times each, and begged I would instantly draw them but handsome—such unexpected change put me almost to extasy." The alcohol consumption continued, and the women grew more aggressive until Kosciuszko ran away "as they could not follow me one step without falling down [as] so much rum affected their poor heads."[59]

The women in the South were not the only things heating up the soldiers of the Continental Army. The summer of 1782 was miserable, and troops were getting bitten by mosquitoes and catching malaria. The hazy, hot, and humid air that lingered over Charleston and the surrounding area meant that the British troops were also suffering from the oppressive summer heat, leading to a stalemate.

The Polish engineer took on a new role after Col. Laurens was killed on August 27 in a cavalry skirmish with British troops searching for food.

Kosciuszko was disgusted when he saw the rebel soldiers strip Laurens's dead body of valuables and divide the possessions among themselves. The Pole wrote to Greene saying that it was "mean, low thinking," to take Laurens's belongings, and that "the Devil himself would not take from him."[60] Kosciuszko followed up with another letter to Greene suggesting that Laurens's clothes be given to his black aides because the "two negroes belonging to L.C. Laurence . . . are nacked they want shirts, jackets, Breeches and their skin can bear as well as ours good things."[61]

The death of his friend Laurens created an opening for a field commander, a post that Kosciuszko had long sought. The Polish patriot was given the command of Ashley Ferry, about nine miles north of Charleston. His mission was to keep an eye on the last remaining British stronghold between Savannah and New York.

As a favorite son of South Carolina, Laurens had developed a network of spies that let him know who in Charleston was allied with the rebel cause, and who was helping the British. Kosciuszko's rapport with the slaves allowed him to continue using Laurens's clandestine channels of black men who were liaisons shuttling information back and forth between Charleston and the rebel camp at Ashley Ferry.

Kosciuszko made contact with Edmund Petrie, the son of a silversmith, and with several mysterious men who went only by the names W, P, and X. These agents delivered intelligence about British troop movements.

This allowed the rebels to set traps for the Redcoats, and in one clash Kosciuszko and twenty of his men took sixty horses away from the British cavalry. With two squads of cavalry and an infantry made up of Delaware and Pennsylvania Continentals, Kosciuszko's unit won several battles with the Redcoats on the outskirts of Charleston. They ambushed English patrols, interrupted the supply line, captured horses, and harassed the British every chance they had.

The Pole's mounted units also moved to starve out the Redcoats in Charleston by driving the cattle and other livestock in the nearby pastures behind the Continental Army lines. Kosciuszko was able to capture one of the largest sources of the British food supply when Petrie visited the Pole to tell him that the English were hiding their livestock in Charleston Neck. He wrote to Greene informing him that Petrie "told me that there is about a thousand cattle including Beef, Sheeps and hogs that in the night [are brought] to the Works and at day break let out to pasture."[62]

On September 20, 1782, Kosciuszko sneaked across the Ashley River to meet with "Mr. W" who told him that Maj. Thomas Fraser and one hundred British cavalrymen had crossed the Cooper River on the other side of Charleston to rendezvous with an infantry to attack the South Carolina militia to "beat General Marion to atoms," and bring cattle and rice back to their base camp. Kosciuszko warned General Greene about this expedition force and then planned to attack the British on his own doorstep at James Island. Kosciuszko asked "Mr. W" for a scout who could sneak onto James Island. A black man named Prince was recommended for the job because he had just been on the island and was familiar with the British redoubts and campsites.[63]

With their food supply shrinking, the Redcoats were growing more desperate by the day. Each week about thirty deserters fled their ranks. The Pole learned from his underground network that only about five hundred English soldiers remained on James Island, and that many of them were sick with malaria.

British general Alexander Leslie created a unit of black dragoons known as the "Negro Horse," which hunted down the fugitives.[64] Kosciuszko welcomed black men into his unit, but fought them when they donned British uniforms. On November 4, Sgt. Maj. William Seymour was out on patrol with Kosciuszko and reported that their unit fell into battle with a platoon of the Negro Horse and killed eight of them.[65]

Ten days later Kosciuszko led a rebel unit in what turned out to be the last military skirmish of the Revolutionary War. A slave came to see Kosciuszko and told him that the British would be cutting wood near Fort Johnson on James Island at daybreak. The Polish colonel and sixty of his men took position on the island at 2 a.m.

When the British cavalry arrived, the rebels fired, killing several of the enemy during intense fighting. The English dragoons were pushed back, but the sixty Americans who pursued them were met by an additional three hundred Redcoats with a field cannon. The Continental soldiers were hit by a barrage of bullets and cannon shells and forced to pull back. Kosciuszko was carrying a spontoon, a half-pike blade with a pointed crossbar at its base, which shattered in his hand when it was hit by English gunfire. Four musket balls pierced his coat, yet he escaped unhurt.[66] These are believed to be the last shots fired during the American Revolution.[67]

As his troops captured a British officer named Stancliffe, Kosciuszko negotiated a prisoner swap, asking for the return of one of his men, "William Smith, a Mulatto soldier who was wounded in the shoulder." The Pole carried out his end of the deal, but was furious when the British failed to keep their word and did not free Smith. Kosciuszko wrote a letter to General Leslie scolding the British for this "disgrace," of which they should be "ashamed," saying, "I appeal to your feelings . . . [as] a man of honor and have no doubt you will be pleased to order the man Smith should be sent to me."[68]

It was all for naught. The British replied, "The Mulatto wounded in the shoulder is dead."[69]

British ships began withdrawing Tories from Charleston, and by December, Kosciuszko knew from his spies that the British were about to evacuate Charleston. On December 9 he wrote to Greene, "Just now a Negro Came from the Town with the inclosed, and say that the British Burnt Mud Fort . . . [and] that the Enemys will leave the town tomorrow."[70]

The war was over. On December 14, 1782, Greene's army marched triumphantly into Charleston. Nathanael Greene had not won a single battle in the South, but he had won the war by persevering and outlasting the British.

Greene's wife, Caty, rode into Charleston in a carriage with other prominent women. Within days she was planning a grand ball and, along with Kosciuszko, decorated the hall with magnolia leaves and paper cutouts of flowers.[71]

Kosciuszko's troops set up camp on James Island across the harbor from Charleston, where they feasted on the stone crabs, fish, and oysters that were plentiful in the local waters. The soldiers also took turns dining with General Greene at his house in the city as the troops began to enjoy leave. The early months of 1783 were for rejoicing and wedding bells. Morris and several other officers of the Southern Army left the military and married rich widows and young girls who had inherited plantations. In April news of the peace treaty signed by Benjamin Franklin with the British in Paris reached the South. Kosciuszko, who learned about pyrotechnics at military school in France, prepared a fireworks exhibition to celebrate the end of the American Revolution.[72]

On April 23 the ladies and gentlemen of Charleston were ferried across to James Island for a grand party and dinner dance that was followed by a bonfire and artillery display, a *feu de joie* (fire of joy).[73]

Joy also shot out from Kosciuszko's pen as he expressed his motives for serving in the Revolution in a letter to his friend Colonel Williams in Baltimore: "O! how happy we think our Self when Conscious of our deeds, that were started from principle of rectitude, from conviction of the goodness of the thing itself, from motive of the good that will Come to Human Kind."[74]

The close relationship that the Polish engineer had developed with Greene and his general staff was noteworthy, given that Greene had denounced the recruitment of foreign officers for the Continental Army. Greene wrote several letters to Congress early in the war including one that said: "I have no wish to see such a large proportion of important offices in the military department in the hands of foreigners. I cannot help considering them as so many spies in our camp."[75]

Yet Kosciuszko was different. Just as he did with Gates, the Polish volunteer had formed a special bond with Greene. The two officers said their warm goodbyes in Charleston when Kosciuszko set sail for Philadelphia.

After he left Greene wrote to Gen. William Irvine: "Among the most useful and agreeable of my companions in arms, was Colonel Kosciuszko. Nothing

could exceed his zeal for the public service, nor in the prosecution of various objects that presented themselves in our small but active warfare, could any thing
be more useful than his attention, vigilance and industry. In promoting my views
whatever department of the service directed, he was at all times, a ready and able
assistant. One, in a word, whom no pleasure could seduce, no labor fatigue and
no danger deter. What besides greatly distinguished him was an unparalleled
modesty and entire unconsciousness of having done anything extraordinary.
Never making a claim or pretension for himself and never omitting to distinguish
and commend the merits of others. This able and gallant soldier has now left us
for the North; intending to return directly to his own country, where he cannot
fail to be soon and greatly distinguished."[76]

EIGHT

Love and Rockets

KOSCIUSZKO SET SAIL ON A SHIP FROM CHARLESTON HARBOR IN late May with Major Pierce and a Mr. Godin. They arrived in Philadelphia about ten days later. During his seven years in the Continental Army, the Polish officer had not drawn any of his salary and lived off the same paltry rations as his men. Upon arriving in the capital he attempted to pick up his back pay and inquire about the status of his promotion to general, which Gates had requested years earlier.

These tasks proved to be more difficult than expected, as soldiers who had not been paid besieged the capital. About eighty deserters from the Pennsylvania unit in Lancaster stormed into Philadelphia threatening to kidnap congressmen and break into the bank holding federal deposits. They got drunk and aimed their muskets at the windows of the Pennsylvania Statehouse, shouting vulgarities at the legislators inside. The delegates were forced out of the building through a gauntlet of two rows of menacing rogues who hurled obscenities and threats at them.[1]

Congress was forced to adjourn and flee to Princeton, New Jersey, where the Founding Fathers reconvened. Gen. Robert Howe was sent to Philadelphia with fifteen hundred troops to quash the mutiny.[2]

Kosciuszko rode to Princeton with the legislators, where he was asked by Congress to prepare a fireworks display for July 4, 1783, to mark the first Independence Day celebrating the end of the Revolution.

He was supposed to meet his friend Williams in Elizabethtown, Pennsylvania, to commemorate the nation's birthday, but explained that he could not because, "Congress having intention to make Illumination on the fourth of July, they have made Choice of me as nobody is better for the execution of it. It was in vain to say that I was engaged to go to Elisabeth Town, to join my friend. They insisted upon [it], judge but favorably that [it] is not my fault."

Kosciuszko suggested that Williams come to Princeton to join the festivities, but if he could not, the Pole asked that he pass along his compliments to all his friends that he served with, "at west point, particularly General Washington, Colo. Nicolas, Colo. Jackson, Colo. Brooks and Mrs. Brooks, tell her that I come see her when ever she will be able to receive me in a Silk Gown."[3]

Oddly enough, while Kosciuszko had failed miserably in his own love life, his friends relied on his advice in dealing with the fairer sex—and their parents. Williams, who like Kosciuszko was having trouble with the father of a young woman he was courting, asked the Pole for guidance.

"It surprise me . . . of so nonsensical disposition of her parents and do not know whether I sense right that the mother is in love with you," Kosciuszko wrote, suggesting that his friend try to elope. "I would marry her, and after, beg [the] parents pardon."[4]

It was this kind of humor and, "go get 'em" attitude that made Kosciuszko popular with the officers he served with. Maj. Michael Jackson of Massachusetts was so upset when he learned that Kosciuszko would not join the veterans gathering in Elizabethtown that he wrote to Williams, "Liberty is nothing without a Pole. . . . His presence here is essential—The Illumination—the rockets—and the racket are lost without him."[5]

While his colleagues were charmed by his personality and impressed with his devotion and skill, the bean counters in Congress were trying their best to pay off the war's debts as cheaply as possible. Kosciuszko was one of the first foreign officers to enlist his services with the colonial army in 1776, and during the war, he never sought advancement for himself, even when others spoke up for him. But when the war ended, he put in a request for his back pay and the promotion that he had earned.

The Continental Army's top brass wrote letters in support of his request.

On July 10, 1783, Greene, still in Charleston, wrote to the president of Congress, Elias Boudinot: "Col. Kosciuszko who has been our Chief Engineer in the Southern department and with the Northern Army at the taking of Burgoyne, and whose zeal and activity have been equaled by few and exceeded by none, has it in contemplation to return to Europe. To enable him to do this and bring his affairs with the public to a close in this Country he wishes to have such pay and emoluments as he is entitled to from the rank he holds in the Army and the services he has performed for the accomplishing of our independence put upon such footing as to enable him to reduce it all to ready money.

"From this peculiar situation, I beg leave to recommend his case to Congress;

and if the thing be practicable, that the Financier [Robert Morris] be desired to settle and accommodate the matter with him. My friendship for the Col. must apologize for the singularity of this recommendation. My feelings are warmly interested in his favor; but I presume not to judge of the difficulties attending to the business."[6]

The original of Greene's letter in the papers of the Continental Congress is endorsed with the words, "In favor of Kosciuszko," in Washington's handwriting.[7]

Greene's letter was followed up on August 8, by Gen. Benjamin Lincoln, then secretary of war, who wrote to Congress making the case that Kosciuszko deserved to be promoted to brigadier general because he had served longer than Duportail and the French engineers and because he had received "notice and applause of all under whom he has served."[8]

In late September, Greene arrived in Philadelphia and traveled with Kosciuszko to Trenton, where they met up with Washington. The three officers rode to Princeton, and the Polish engineer asked the commander in chief for his blessing. Washington, Greene, and Kosciuszko had dinner with Boudinot to discuss various issues, one of them being Kosciuszko's promotion.[9]

In one of his last official acts as general, Washington interceded with Congress in favor of Kosciuszko, writing: "From my knowledge of his Merit and services, and the concurrent testimony of all who know him I cannot but recommend him as deserving the favor of Congress."[10] Washington wrote to Kosciuszko assuring him, "I heartily wish your application to meet with success."[11]

Yet even with George Washington and the other generals lobbying Congress on his behalf, Kosciuszko did not get the merit promotion that he deserved. Instead, on October 13, 1783, Kosciuszko was advanced to brigadier general by brevet, in a mass promotion given to all officers who had served in the Revolution, meaning that it did not come with a pay raise and the privileges of advancement for merit.[12]

To soften the slight, Congress issued the following statement: "Resolved, That the secretary of war transmit to colonel Kosciuszko, the brevet commission of brigadier general; and signify to that officer, that Congress entertain a high sense of his long, faithful, and meritorious services."[13]

While he was finally made a general, Kosciuszko was still broke. He was not alone. Congress was struggling to pay the soldiers who had delivered America's independence from the British. Dr. Thacher noted in his journal: "Painful indeed was the parting scene, no description can be adequate to the tragic exhibition. Both officers and soldiers, long unaccustomed to the affairs of private life, turned loose on the world to starve and to become prey to vulture speculators."[14]

The U.S. superintendent of finance, Robert Morris, wrote to Congress that while "the merit of Col. Kosciuszko is great and acknowledged," a law passed in 1781 stipulated that foreign officers were to receive one-fifth of the amount due, and four-fifths in bank notes with interest.[15] Morris wrote a glowing letter about Kosciuszko to Congress, but left the matter up to the legislature, which stalled on paying all soldiers.

Morris even wiggled out of paying Kosciuszko the one-fifth that was due him, yet when Duportail and the French engineers came knocking several weeks later and demanded their pay, he dutifully found a way to come up with their money.

While Kosciuszko eventually did get a few months' pay from Congress, it was the banker from the coffee shop on Front Street in Philadelphia who came to his rescue.[16] Haym Salomon was feeding some of the hungry soldiers, as well as delegates to the Continental Congress. He also lent (and even gave) many of them money from his own bank account. One notation in Salomon's records showed that he lent Kosciuszko $142 in 1783.[17] The money was probably put aside for his voyage back to Poland.

Worried that he, too, might become a man without a country, Kosciuszko related to Salomon and the Diaspora that scattered Jews throughout the world. Kosciuszko noted to Greene that he might not be allowed to return to Poland and end up a nomad. He wrote that he, and the other homeless and unpaid American officers from every state, are, "in the situation of the Izraelits . . . perhaps I will be obliged to ramble on for two years more and this is my misfortune."[18]

As the new government was still setting up its treasury and unable to pay him, General Kosciuszko was given a certificate for $12,280 bearing interest at 6 percent starting on January 1, 1784. The interest payments were to be sent to him through Paris.[19] And in case he wanted to settle in the United States, Kosciuszko was entitled to five hundred acres of land.

Throughout his service in the American army, Kosciuszko remained close friends with his commanding officers Gates and Greene. To show his appreciation for the Pole's service in the Continental Army, Washington gave Kosciuszko two pistols and a sword with the Latin engraving: *America cum Vashington suo Amico T. Kosciuconi* (America and Washington are joined with our friend T. Kosciuszko), and on the back, *Mater Dei ora pro nobis* (Mother of God, pray for us).[20]

Kosciuszko was one of the officers invited to dinner at Fraunces Tavern in Lower Manhattan when the commander in chief bade farewell to the troops on December 4, 1783. A teary-eyed Washington was clearly moved by what this group of men had achieved and said, "With a heart full of love and gratitude, I now take leave of you. I most devoutly wish that your latter days may be as prosperous and honorable." Washington raised a glass of wine, took a drink, and added, "I cannot come to each of you, to take my leave, but shall be obliged if each of you will come and take me by the hand." Starting with General Henry Knox, each officer in succession stepped toward their leader, grasped his hand, and embraced him. No one spoke a word.[21]

When it was Kosciuszko's turn Washington pulled off the cameo ring, given to him as a member of the Society of Cincinnati, and slid it onto Kosciuszko's finger.[22] The cameo bore the image of the Roman farmer Lucius Quinctius Cincinnatus, who left his farm to lead an army against foreign invaders before becoming the temporary dictator of Rome. The inner circle of America's top officers had founded an order named after Cincinnatus, and Kosciuszko was invited to join.

The order's motto was, "He gave up everything to serve the republic."

Little did those in attendance realize that in giving Kosciuszko that cameo ring and engraved sword, Washington was passing the baton to the next farmer-general who would lead his nation against foreign invaders in the name of liberty.

It was a lonely moment for soldiers who had put their lives on the line for one another. They filed out of the tavern and followed Washington in a silent procession to the Whitehall wharf, where a barge was waiting to take him to New Jersey. From there he would continue his journey south to resign his commission as commander in chief before returning home to Mount Vernon. The officers fanned out to their states, and Kosciuszko was invited to spend the winter with General Greene and his wife, Caty, at their home in Newport, Rhode Island.

Among the loneliest of the soldiers was Otho Williams, who had also been promoted to general. He had returned to his home in Baltimore before the war ended, and on Kosciuszko's advice decided to elope with "the fascinating Sophia." While Sophia promised Williams "that she would never be the wife of another man," she backed out of their secret plan to marry because of the objections of her father. Williams was devastated.

"I have suffered the extremity of mental misery," Williams wrote in a long and woeful letter to Greene on January 14, 1784. Not realizing that the Pole was at Greene's house in Rhode Island, Williams wrote, "Kosciuszko will be petrified at all this if he hears it, but where he is, or how to let him know it (if I wanted to make a Statue of him) I cannot imagine, for in his last he promised to be here a month ago."[23]

In the spring, the Polish rebel visited his fellow war veterans in New York and Philadelphia, but he did not make it to Baltimore. Like Williams, Kosciuszko was also still heartbroken over his lost love, but even more anguished over the subjugation of his homeland.

The news from Poland was not good. The libertine writer Tomasz Kajetan Wegierski arrived in the United States with stories of Russia's increasingly belligerent treatment of Poland. Wegierski had been banished from Warsaw because of his burlesque satires of Czarina Catherine and King Stanislaw. Like Kosciuszko, Wegierski had been educated by Jesuits, but he could no longer tolerate the political situation in Poland and spoke his mind.[24]

Wegierski's plight made it clear to the engineer that after helping America to win its liberty, it would take some time to readjust to living in a country with an absolute monarchy. Kosciuszko was concerned about how he would be greeted by King Stanislaw after taking part in a revolution to overthrow the British king in America.

The education Kosciuszko had received at the Royal Cadet Academy in Warsaw and universities in Paris paled in comparison with his experiences in the American Revolution. In the United States he was further enlightened by the great minds of people like Jefferson, Adams, Washington, Franklin, and the other Founding Fathers.

As Kosciuszko saw it, the revolution of farmers and citizen-soldiers was a perfect model for his own country. Americans had cut their ties with a distant monarch and were about to govern themselves. The Polish rebel thought that with slavery on its way out in the Northern states, if all went well, the Yankee philosophy of freedom for all would spread to the South. If the American states in the North could free their slaves, then surely Europe could free its serfs.

During Kosciuszko's absence from his homeland, his sisters suffered as their older brother, Joseph, squandered much of the estate and creditors tried to seize the rebellious officer's portion of the estate as well. In 1778 the sisters inquired about their brother's whereabouts in America, and Prince Czartoryski requested one of his agents in Paris to look into it but heard nothing.

In October 1781, Kosciuszko's sister Anna Estko asked Princess Elizabeth Sapieha to ask her contacts in France to try to find her brother, but still there was no news. She then wrote to Benjamin Franklin, telling him that creditors were trying to foreclose on her brother's property unless she could prove that he was still alive. Estko asked Franklin for an affidavit stating that her brother was still serving in the army, adding: "I would like to take this occasion to pay my homage to you, that your virtues and your great name have inspired to us; and though we are inhabitants of a distant land, ignored by the rest of the Universe, we do share with the rest of Europe, our admiration for you, and O, that we would have a Franklin who would deliver us from oppression."[25]

After Franklin looked into the matter, the French Comte de Murinais responded in February that "This Gentleman named Cosciuscko was still alive after the affair at York[town]." Murinais added that he would try to find out more about Kosciuszko so that his sister could hold off the creditors.[26]

Apparently Kosciuszko's sisters were not the only ones trying to track him down. It appears that his beloved Louise also wrote to him in America.

In his 1866 book, *A Stroll Through America*, the Polish writer Jakob Gordon quoted a letter from Louise to Kosciuszko that outlined in depressing detail how her father stashed her away in a convent to await the arranged marriage to Prince Lubomirski. In the dramatic letter, dated May 17, 1781, Louise said she had written to the king, asking that she be allowed to die in the convent rather than marry someone she did not love. She proclaimed to Kosciuszko that she loved him with her "heart and soul."[27]

Polish historians have debated the authenticity of Louise's billet-doux. It appears that the letter did exist, but most likely whoever translated it from French into Polish took some poetic license. It had been eight years since Kosciuszko had seen Louise, and he would probably have heard that she had married Lubomirski.

Having left Poland under a cloud, Kosciuszko would have wondered whether Lord Sosnowski ever dropped the kidnapping charges over the "abduction" of his daughter. His failed love affair with Louise and the political situation in Poland weighed heavily on his mind as he prepared to return to his homeland.

The Pole booked passage on a ship across the Atlantic and wrote to his friends bidding them adieu. On July 4, 1784, he wrote to Maj. Evan Edwards, "At a distance I am more bold to express the intention of my heart, which gives sensible pain, to show it in the presences we have esteem, or friendships for." Expressing "love" and "affection" for his friends, he ended by saying, "Give my sincere thanks to Jackson, Carlton and Armstrong for their friendship for me, assure them of my reciprocity equal if not great to theirs tell the same . . . may you all prosper."[28]

The day before his departure Kosciuszko wrote to Greene to thank him for his hospitality. He was concerned about his future where "events are uncertain . . . Drawing the tickets in the lottery of chance for so many years, I am too well acquainted to depend upon probabilities where even certainties are so often doubtful." Asking his friend and former commander to keep him up to date about his family and events in the United States, Kosciuszko added, "By long staying here, I have a partiality for this country and for its inhabitants, and would equally within, wherever I should be, feel the sentiment of good Patriot upon every occasion."[29]

Having served longer in the American Revolution than any other foreign officer, Brigadier General Kosciuszko boarded the ship *Courier de l'Europe* in New York City on July 15, 1784 and set sail for the port of Lorient in France. Also sailing on that ship was his friend Col. David Humphreys, who had served with the Pole at Saratoga and West Point. Congress had appointed Humphreys secretary to the commissioners to negotiate commercial treaties in Europe.[30]

The prevailing winds of North America carried the ship across the Atlantic to Lorient in twenty-four days. When they disembarked Kosciuszko and Humphreys shared a carriage ride to Paris. Humphreys was excited about going to the theater to see his first "French Comedy," while Kosciuszko was at once grim and eager to learn the latest news about the tragedy that had befallen Poland.[31]

Waves of French soldiers, such as Lafayette, who had fought in America also returned to Paris, and the capital was full of veterans with stories of the new type of republic being forged in the new world. It was a natural progression for them also to question the monarchy in their own country. Kosciuszko looked up some of his old friends and wrote letters to his new friends in the United States. The interaction with various ideas and ethnic groups during his years in Paris and the United States had made a big impression on him, and Kosciuszko was beginning to develop his own philosophy, which moved him to speak up for tolerance.

After returning to Poland, Kosciuszko wrote to Greene: "Are we ought to like only our Compatriots, [with] no allowance to be made for one sort of Strangers; from your Philosophical turn of mind I would expect of enlarging the limits of our affection contracted by prejudice and superstition towards the rest of mankind, and more so for whom we have a Sinceier Esteem, let him be Turck, or Polander, American or Japon."[32]

It was a theme he would expand upon over the years in his words and deeds.

NINE

Fiddling Lords and Enslaved Hordes

D EBAUCHERY AND DUPLICITY WALKED HAND IN HAND IN THE courts of the European monarchies of the eighteenth century. Kosciuszko returned to Poland in late 1784 as its political landscape was about to undergo a seismic shift under the feet of a voluptuous Italian courtesan. Marie-Therese Neri, aka "Baroness de Lautenbourg," was a dark-haired femme fatale who had conned noblemen in Venice, Bruges, Berlin, and Hamburg before charming her way into the salons of Warsaw's nobility. The sexy con artist married a Russian army major named Dogrumov, giving her a new moniker, Madame Dogrumova, and entrée into the social circles of the Polish capital.

Dogrumova scrutinized the city's elite, seeking an easy mark for her next scam. Warsaw's high society was soon buzzing over a series of salacious sex scandal/murder plots that dripped from the lips of the gossiping charmer. The Italian siren started at the top with her first scheme, trying to convince King Stanislaw's aides that Prince Czartoryski was plotting to murder the king and take the throne. The king told his men to give the nasty vamp the brushoff. She tried selling the tale to Archbishop Michael Poniatowski, the king's brother, but he, too, steered clear of the scheming temptress.[1]

Kosciuszko arrived in Warsaw just as the scandals were about to explode. His patron, Prince Czartoryski, greeted the veteran of the American Revolution as a hero and invited him to stay at his palace. While Dogrumova's murder plot was bogus, Czartoryski and his cousin King Stanislaw had drifted apart by the mid-1780s because of disagreements over political reforms and growing unease over Russia's meddling in Polish affairs.

The Czartoryskis had homes all over the country, but the prince moved his base of operations from his Pawazki estate outside Warsaw to his palace in Pulawy, seventy miles south on the Wisla River. (Ironically the Lubomirski family, Louise's new clan, had once owned the Pulawy Palace.) By then Kosciuszko's great love had become Princess Louise, borne Prince Lubomirski three children, and moved to the town of Rovno, near the Russian border.

As a battle-tested general, Kosciuszko wanted to serve his country and visited the royal palace to ask for a post in the military. King Stanislaw was eager to hear the latest news from across the ocean and granted his famous cadet an audience.

Kosciuszko met with Stanislaw in the greeting parlor of the castle, and as they talked about the new system of government being set up in the United States, the king could not help notice the medallion of the Order of the Cincinnati that Kosciuszko had hanging around his neck. The king examined the medal and read the inscription out loud: *Omnia reliquit servare rem publicam* (He gave up everything to save the state).[2]

Stanislaw seemed offended by the medal and said, "Methinks this inscription savors somewhat of fanaticism,"[3] adding that the citizens of a nation had other obligations in addition to public affairs.

Kosciuszko replied that a citizen's duty to his nation's public affairs was foremost and encompassed all his other duties as well. After quietly listening to his subject's arguments, the king turned his back and left the room in a huff. The American brigadier's commission as an officer in the Polish military was not to be.

Before returning to his own meager estate, Kosciuszko visited the Czartoryski Palace in Pulawy, which had become a magnet for poets, painters, and intellectuals. While the prince was the star attraction at Pulawy, his wife, Isabella, was the hostess many came to see. The princess had a pockmarked face, but with her large beautiful eyes and an inimitable grace, men were drawn to her.[4]

The couple married in 1761 when the prince was twenty-seven and Isabella a small skinny girl of fifteen. It was a cold political relationship, and both took lovers. Of their seven children, only two were the offspring of Prince Czartoryski. In the 1760s the prince actually delivered Princess Isabella to the royal castle for her liaisons with his cousin, King Stanislaw, which produced a daughter, Maria Anna. Isabella's affair with the Russian minister Repnin produced a son, Adam Jerzy, who bore a striking resemblance to Repnin's daughter.[5]

After the first partition of Poland in 1772, Princess Isabella moved to London and then Paris for several years, where she had an affair with the Duc de Lauzun, which produced another son, Constantine. During these years abroad Princess Isabella became a democratic thinker in her own right after meeting Benjamin Franklin in London and Jean-Jacques Rousseau and Voltaire in Paris. She purchased numerous books and artworks that she sent to Poland. On a visit to Stratford-upon-Avon she bought a chair once owned by William Shakespeare. By the mid-1780s the princess had turned a new leaf and focused on her family and political affairs. She adorned the Czartoryski palace near Warsaw in the French rococo style of elegant paintings and statues, with baroque furniture, flowing tapestries, and ornamental mirrors.

Isabella decorated the palace at Pulawy in a more rustic style, that of a tranquil English country estate. The palace had parlors with fireplaces and bars, a billiard table, and a library with thousands of books. Princess Isabella became the hostess at this center for the royal opposition, and Prince Czartoryski joined his wife at the country palace full-time after the Dogrumova affair temporarily forced him off the national stage.

Thwarted in her attempts to scam the king, Madame Dogrumova shifted her attentions to Prince Czartoryski. She brought in an accomplice, an English con man named Taylor, and told Czartoryski that the king's men had asked her to seduce him and stab or poison him while they were in flagrante. The prince did not believe her, but Dogrumova showed him the "poison powder." To prove her story, the grifter set up an elaborate trap inviting the nobleman Ignacy Potocki and Taylor to hide in her closet while she invited into her home the king's chamberlain, who had proposed the murder.

Dogrumova lured the chamberlain, Francis Ryks, into her apartment by claiming she had new proof of a plot to kill Stanislaw. With Potocki and Taylor hiding in her wardrobe, the double-dealing Dogrumova vaguely chattered away to Ryks about a dark "conspiracy" that involved "poison and daggers."

While Ryks thought she was talking about the cabal against Stanislaw, Potocki was convinced that she was referring to "the plot" to kill the prince. Taylor jumped out of the closet and pointed a pistol at Ryks. With Potocki tagging along, Taylor dragged Ryks to the home of Prince Czartoryski's sister, and burst into a crowded salon shouting that he had caught Ryks plotting to murder the prince. Marshals were summoned, and Ryks was arrested.

It was the night of January 16, 1785, and King Stanislaw and hundreds of Warsaw's fashionable elite were at the opera house attending the premiere of a production of *King Theodore*. A whisper swooshed through the audience that Ryks had tried to poison Prince Czartoryski. When the news reached the king's box, Stanislaw got up and stormed out of the theater. Within days an anonymous pamphlet was steaming up the parlors of the rich across the city with licentious accusations about the king's cabal.[6]

Ignacy and his brother Stanislaw Potocki accused the king's staff of using the seductress to beguile the prince and slip him a deadly powder. Dogrumova was their star witness, and the Potockis stirred up the intrigue, using the ridiculous ruse to mobilize opposition against the king.

The absurd affair spun out of control into a political circus. Czartoryski fell into the trap and demanded that the king's aides be prosecuted, while Ryks and the king's men demanded legal action against Dogrumova and Taylor. An investigation found that "the potion" that was supposed to be fed to the prince was nothing more than an aphrodisiac. The plot was proved to be a hoax, and Czartoryski was humiliated. Dogrumova was sentenced to life in prison, but first she was bent over with her head and hands shackled into a wooden pillory in the market square, where she was branded with a red-hot poker on her bare buttocks.[7]

The bizarre scandal shadowed Polish politics for the next several years, dividing the noble class into two camps. Czartoryski resigned as commander of the royal military academy and temporarily withdrew from public life.

With his two patrons, the king and the prince, at loggerheads, Kosciuszko's chances of securing the command of a cavalry regiment were dashed. He returned to his family plantation in Siechnowicze, where his brother, Joseph, had bungled the finances and mortgaged much of the estate, bankrupting himself in the process. Creditors had come after Kosciuszko's share of the property as well, but his sister Anna and her husband, Peter Estko, paid off the loans and back taxes so that the general could make a living when he returned from America.

He took up residence in an old house with a thatched roof and walls that were so dilapidated that only two rooms were inhabitable. The engineer went to work renovating the homestead, starting by partitioning one of the rooms to form a small bedroom and wardrobe. It was furnished meagerly, with a bed, a table, a dresser, and a desk that was stacked with books and papers. Kosciuszko enjoyed carpentry and built a table out of wood from an old apple tree to keep a tray for serving coffee, his greatest extravagance.

An aunt named Suzanne cooked and managed the household, which included a butler and a wagon driver. Behind his home were a garden, a fruit orchard, and a fishpond that was the mating area for several families of wild ducks.[8]

The manor house was in bad shape for a respected member of the landed gentry, but as a landlord Kosciuszko was more frustrated about the conditions in which his serfs lived and worked. There were nine peasant cottages on his land, and the families that lived in them were bonded to him. Even though European serfs were better off than the black slaves he had seen in America, Kosciuszko could not get used to the fact that the people on his land were his vassals.

The central instrument for holding down Europe's indentured servants was the corvée—days of unpaid labor forced upon serfs who farmed the land of feudal landlords. In Poland the corvée requirement was six and sometimes seven days per week. Serfs were not allowed to leave the estate, and if they did they were whipped with a knout, a lash with numerous strips of rawhide. Peasants who misbehaved were severely beaten and even faced medieval torture. Many estates of the landed gentry included dungeons with chains, shackles, stocks, and hooks to punish unruly serfs.[9]

Disgusted with feudalism, Kosciuszko wrote, "Serfdom is a word that must be cursed by all enlightened nations."[10]

However, he was in a quandary because his sister, Anna, and her husband had used their own money to save his farm from foreclosure. He walked a fine line as he tried to find a way to end forced labor for the serfs on his land while not losing the generous investments made by his sister. He also had to make sure he was able to pay the estate's bills, loans, and fees, such as the chimney tax the government imposed on the number of flues for each house.

There had to be a way to give his peasants more freedom to acquire their own wealth without creating more financial problems for his family. Kosciuszko counted on receiving the interest payments from his salary in the Continental Army.

The money never arrived.

With no signs of his situation improving, on January 20, 1786, an exasperated Kosciuszko grumbled in a letter to Greene: "It surprises me very much that to this time, I have not one line from you, I am alarmed and my friendship for you puts thousands [of] disagreeable thoughts into my head. Who knows, you may be sick or dead." He wrote that he was concerned about the United States and informed Greene of his meeting with King Stanislaw, adding that he was "very unhappy of the situation in my Country, which I believe *nulla redemptio* [unredeemable]."

Kosciuszko ended the letter on a light note, asking his former commander to pay his respects to his wife, as well as to the former Miss Nancy Elliott of Charleston, who married his friend Major Morris. "Tell her I propose to marry her when her husband dies"; however, if he was still alive, Kosciuszko added, "My best compliments to him."[11]

The forty-year-old bachelor lived a lonely existence in the countryside, and as a local nobleman, Kosciuszko made the rounds among his neighbors. He became close friends with Michael Zaleski, an attorney who made a fortune representing the region's richest land magnates. Zaleski's political connections earned him a seat in the Seym and a seat on the local treasury board.

The gallant general spent a great deal of time at the Zaleski estate, and grew quite fond of Zaleski's wife. "Ah, that I would be able to find such a wife," Kosciuszko teased his friend. "She's an example for thousands. She delights her husband and her in-laws. You won't see that in Warsaw. . . . Please don't be jealous, that I, a nobody, kiss her hand several times."[12]

As frustrated as he was in his personal life, Kosciuszko was even more disheartened by the political situation in his country. After several years of running his farm, he still could not get a post in the army because the commissioned officers were those with political connections or enough money to buy their rank.

Occasionally the peasants in the eastern Ukrainian provinces were overworked and treated so badly by their masters that they would fight back. In early 1789, when a peasant rebelled and killed a nobleman who abused him, some of the land magnates wanted to send troops to exact retribution on the serfs in the area.

Zaleski and a group of army officers were chosen to judge the rebellious peasants. The serfs feared that the soldiers would brutalize them, and they often hid their farming tools and bread when the army was passing through, for fear that their farms would be plundered. Kosciuszko was outraged by the bloodlust for revenge. "My God, how few real citizens we have. I'm sitting here in the country trying to produce as much hay as we can for your cavalry," he wrote to Zaleski, asking him to "show mercy."

The treatment of serfs was abhorrent to Kosciuszko, and he pleaded for a fair trial for the peasants. "I've run out of patience with the fact that officers have the power to interrogate people charged with rebellion and that they shall judge who will remain incarcerated and who will go free." This authority, he argued, should be in the hands of a civil court. "A republican government should be very careful about the power that it gives to its military," Kosciuszko wrote, adding that in civilized countries, marauding "officers should themselves be arrested."

Kosciuszko was disgusted by his country's corrupt military system. He explained to Zaleski that Poland should have a professional army, and denounced, "the bartering and selling of officer ranks from one to another, now at a time when the Republic needs a committed military service that is accountable, advanced and functional like it was in the old days. Who allows this to go on, if not the Seym?"[13]

Growing restless on his farm, he caught up on the issues affecting his country and read books by Poland's intelligentsia. The National Education Commission was the world's first ministry of education. Created by King Stanislaw, it had spurred the growth of Poland's university system and given rise to homegrown philosophers such as the priests Hugo Kollontay, who pushed for more rights for the burgher townspeople of Poland's cities, and Stanislaw Staszic, who advocated for more rights for peasants.

While Philadelphia had been shaken up by Thomas Paine's anonymous pamphlet *Common Sense*, Warsaw was stirred by a series of "Anonymous Letters" addressed to the speaker of the Seym, Stanislaw Malachowski. The letters denounced the treatment of serfs as livestock, and called for a democratic constitution to end class distinction and create a strong central government to revive Poland.

One of the letters read in part: "We know full well that the worker on the estates of the gentry became a possession of the manor-house and by an incomprehensible violation of humanity ceased to be an individual, contrary to the obvious laws of nature. Given over into the custody of the lord, left in his legal, if one may say so, bondage, regarded no better than cattle . . . Oh truth! . . . enter today into the hearts of free Poles, enlighten their minds and inspire them with a magnificent attachment to freedom!"[14]

Kosciuszko was thrilled that people of like mind were finally speaking up. While the king was offended by the "fanaticism" of his Cincinnati medal, others were fascinated by it. In Warsaw, Kosciuszko met Rev. Kollontay and others who were captivated by his stories of the American Revolution and his ideas about republicanism. Kollontay offered Kosciuszko a post as a lecturer at the Kraków Academy, the Jagiellonian University, where he had served as rector. The general politely declined.[15]

Instead he became a political activist and tried to convince those who did not agree with his democratic ideals. Kosciuszko tried to eke out a living together with the serfs that worked his land, and wrote to Zaleski denouncing serfdom: "It takes centuries to enlighten people, and it's even more difficult for us, where people need permission from their master even to take a breath, and they have no legal rights, even to move from where they live . . . even if they could run away, where would they go? To Moscow? Everyone has taken away the rights of the serfs."[16]

If the government was not going to help the peasants, Kosciuszko argued, the "Russified" Orthodox Christian peasants in the eastern provinces should be "Polonized" and instilled with "the Polish spirit" that wanted to abolish serfdom. Then the Ukrainian and Belarusian peasants would understand that it was in their best interests to be loyal to the Polish-Lithuanian Commonwealth rather than to Moscow.

Kosciuszko began to think more and more like a Deist, believing that God does not interfere in free will to change the course of one's life. But the church, he believed, could step in to ease the suffering of peasants. He proposed changing the calendars of the Catholic and Orthodox Churches to "unite all of the holidays, theirs and ours, into one calendar. If we can convince the Orthodox Pope to allow masses to be said in Polish," the existing "hatred toward nationalities" could be turned into a dislike of tyranny and oppression so people could be steered "toward the universal good."[17]

The proposals for a unified Christian calendar were too radical for the church, and even naive. And as far as governments were concerned, they were in the business of taking over people by force, not by winning their hearts and minds.

The idealistic veteran of the American Revolution wanted Poland to take the lead in freeing Europe's serfs. By 1788 the winds of change that blasted through the United States and swirled around France were hovering over Poland. Just as America's Founding Fathers left their farms to convene the Continental Congress in Philadelphia to cut ties with the British monarch, Polish and Lithuanian landlords left their farms to convene the Seym in Warsaw's royal castle to cut ties with the Russian monarch.

The author of the "Anonymous Letters" turned out to be Kollontay, who incited the reformers by writing, "Who does not see the similarities between an unhappy Poland, that is ruled by a foreign power and magnates in a hideous manner, to the situation that once divided America? That nation searched for freedom and independence."[18]

The Founding Fathers had just finished the U.S. Constitution, which created a presidency without term limits. Thomas Jefferson, then ambassador to France, wrote to John Adams that the office of president was "a bad edition of a Polish king. He may be elected from four years to four years to life." This, Jefferson lamented, could create a situation open to foreign meddling as in Poland, except that the "intrigue, bribery and foreign interference" would be coming from France and England. "It will be of great consequence to have America governed by a Galloman, or an Angloman."[19]

For Poland the timing was right for change when Russia went to war again with the Turks. The Ottoman Empire was in decline, and Russia, looking for a warm-water port to its south, sent troops to the Black Sea to capture the Crimean Peninsula. By 1783 one of the czarina's "favorites," Gen. Grigory Aleksandrovich Potemkin, annexed Crimea and was rewarded with vast estates and thousands of serfs. He was put in charge of colonizing southern Ukraine for Mother Russia, and of building a port and a Black Sea fleet.

When the czarina decided to tour Russia's new southern seacoast in 1787, Potemkin decorated the villages along the Dnieper River, and according to many historians he even put up theatrical sets and phony facades to make the colonized territory look more developed from the river as Catherine's flotilla of galleys sailed downstream to the Black Sea.[20]

Stanislaw heard of the czarina's visit to her new territories and dashed out of Warsaw in the February frost. He raced across the snowy plains of southern Poland on a sled covered in furs and crossed freezing rivers in rowboats to meet with her on her yacht in the middle of the Dnieper River, near the Polish border town of Kaniow. Stanislaw proclaimed his alliance to Russia in case of war with the Turks and asked for permission to amend Poland's constitution and to expand his army.[21]

Catherine denied his request. One militarized neighbor was enough.[22]

The Turks were furious over Russia's expansion, and the following year they sent troops to retake Crimea. Potemkin succeeded at pleasing the czarina, but did not fare as well as a naval commander. The navy was not the star branch of Russia's military forces, and Catherine searched for experienced sea captains.

The czarina's refusal to allow Stanislaw to reform his government and increase the size of his army did not stop him. There was no turning back for the Polish king, because the political activists would force his hand.

A group of writers and intellectuals began meeting at the home of Rev. Kollontay, and the informal gatherings became known as "Kollontay's forge."

Consensus was building among the land barons that it was time to shake off Russia's meddling control. But while the magnates wanted to climb out from under the thumb of Catherine the Great, they were less interested in loosening their own grip over the serfs whose free labor made them rich. There had to be a compromise, and with Russia preoccupied with the Ottoman Empire, the Poles had their chance. Russia pulled its soldiers out of Poland and sent them to the Turkish front. Over time the Poles began to pursue policies that made it clear that the czarist troops were not welcome back.

"Whilst the Russian cat was away at the Turkish War," wrote the British historian Norman Davies, "the Polish mice began to play with fire."[23]

On October 6, 1788, King Stanislaw called to order a session of the Seym. As Stanislaw was still perceived to be a pawn of Russia and a defender of the status quo, a new party known as the Patriots was formed to push for change.

Stanislaw's chief opponents, Ignacy Potocki and Prince Czartoryski, who were seeking a treaty with Prussia to offset the Russians, led the conservative wing of the reform movement. Kollontay and his "forge" led the liberal wing of the movement, while the speaker of the Seym, Stanislaw Malachowski, was a moderate who was seeking a compromise among the various factions.

To change Poland's system of government, they had to get around the ludicrous *liberum veto*, which gave every delegate the authority to cancel, postpone, or reject legislation. The French writer Guillaume Thomas Francois Raynal declared that in Poland "everyone has the power to prevent action, and no one the power to act. There the will of any individual may thwart the general will; and there alone a foolish, a wicked, or an insane man is sure to prevail over a whole nation."[24]

The Patriots found a loophole. They wisely called the proceedings to order under rules of confederation, meaning that the *liberum veto* did not apply. A simple majority would decide all issues. This gave the reformers an advantage over those who wanted to throw the Seym into gridlock so they could keep the status quo.[25]

With so much at stake during the long session that would become known as "the Great Seym," the spectators' gallery was packed with observers, such as Princess Isabella and ladies of the nobility who cheered when the Patriots made their points and jeered at those who disagreed with them. Kosciuszko, who traveled to Warsaw with his friend Zaleski, also attended one session and sat at the end of the bench with the delegates from the Brest region. To show that he still had respect for the king, Kosciuszko presented Stanislaw with an engraving.

Another observer in the legislative chamber was the Russian ambassador, Baron Otto Magnus von Stackelberg, who was in Warsaw to do Catherine's bidding.

On October 16 it became clear that Poland was on a collision course with Russia, when its "protector," Jan Suchorzewski, a representative from a small town near Warsaw, addressed the king from the floor of the Seym. He said that its three powerful neighbors would never respect Poland until it raised an army "in proportion to all other European Countries. We've decided to raise an army of 100,000. Let this thought for the good of the fatherland, not sadden the king; because they are courageous, they'll be victorious, and lift the country from the depths to which it has sunk."[26]

Roars of approval rose from the floor of the Seym and its gallery. The king realized that the government's coffers did not have enough money to pay for such a large army, much less the equipment, barracks, and forts needed to support such a fighting force. Stanislaw's concerns over how to pay the soldiers were mistaken as subservience to Russia. In a burst of enthusiasm over the thought of a new army, the delegates passed Poland's first-ever income tax on the nobility.

Another point of contention was Potocki's proposal for an alliance with Prussia. Stanislaw objected because the Prussians had always been enemies of the Poles, dating back centuries, to the invasions by the Teutonic Knights. Nothing had changed. In exchange for a treaty, the Prussian king wanted to annex the cities of Gdansk and Torun, the hometown of the Polish astronomer Copernicus. The talks stalled.

In late 1788 a dark mysterious figure appeared in the spectators' balcony above the Senate chamber of the Seym: He would change the balance of power in Poland.

The Marquis Girolamo Lucchesini was a skinny man with an olive complexion and one large black eye, the other having been lost in a chemistry experiment.[27] Years earlier the Italian aristocrat had arrived at the Prussian court in Berlin and offered his services to King Frederick the Great, who asked, "How often, sir, will the Marquises of Italy be base enough to sell themselves to the Monarchs of Germany?"

The marquis replied, "So long, your Majesty, as the Monarchs of Germany are fools enough to pay them." Lucchesini's crafty retort so pleased Frederick that he hired him as an envoy to negotiate with the Vatican. He had found the unscrupulous agent he needed to do his bidding.[28]

During an election for archbishop, Lucchesini disguised himself as a jeweler, sliding across the marble floors and under the hallowed domes of Saint Peter's Basilica handing out gemstones to bishops so that they would vote for the Prussian king's candidate. The Italian marquis was a witty and charming diplomat, a perceptive listener, and a shrewd operator.[29] Lucchesini's new mission was to tear the Poles away from their loyalty to Russia and convince them that the Prussians had their best interest at heart.

Lucchesini's meddling also bore fruit in Poland for Frederick the Great's successor, King Frederick William. Russia needed the grain from Polish farms to fuel its soldiers and horses fighting the Turks. With hatred of the czarina growing, some landowners suggested cutting off wheat shipments to the Russian army. As this would cut profits and hurt the gentry's ability to pay taxes, the idea was contested in the Seym. But the conniving Lucchesini convinced the delegates at least to pass a temporary ban.

"In spite of it being against the interests of the oligarch families," Lucchesini wrote to the Prussian king, "Without it being noticed, I was able to limit the shipments of Polish grain."[30] The Austrian chargé d'affaires in Warsaw reported back to Vienna, "Withholding food shipments could have very harmful consequences for the Russian army."[31]

As Lucchesini worked the Patriots on one side of the aisle in the Seym, Russia's Stackelberg worked the other side with the king and his royalists. Russian general Potemkin told Stackelberg to inform the Seym that if the Poles did not sell them wheat, the Russian army would stop all of Poland's grain trade on the Dnieper River. Tensions were mounting, and when the Russian ambassador's demands were too much to take, his chair was removed from the Seym's spectators' gallery.

The capital was engaged in a full-fledged political campaign. Warsaw's grande dames wined, dined, and entertained the Patriots, and King Stanislaw asked shopkeepers to sell ribbons embroidered with the words, "The king with the nation, and the nation with the king." The king's supporters even launched hot-air balloons with "Patriot" painted on the sides, inviting the public to watch as they floated around in the air above the city before being blown in different directions.[32]

Hearing about the Seym's decision to expand the army, Kosciuszko traveled to Warsaw to follow the debate. He applied for a post in the military, referencing his experience in the United States, which he praised as a model for a citizen army of farmers and town dwellers. The local legislature in Brest told its representatives to the Seym to request that its favorite son, Kosciuszko, be given a military commission.[33] Other nobles also lobbied the king to appoint the hero of the American Revolution to the Polish army.

Kosciuszko's disastrous attempt to elope with the daughter of a rich nobleman had a major impact on his political thinking and his relationships with women. The feelings that he still had for his former lover, Louise, were mutual.

Princess Louise penned a heartfelt but secret note to King Stanislaw: "Your Royal Majesty is well aware of the relationship long ago between myself and Mr. Kosciuszko, which for a long time caused him unhappiness and forced him to leave this country. I now feel obligated to make amends for his misfortune. That is why I respectfully request that your Royal Highness appoint him to the army, an issue that is now being addressed. In America he served honorably as a professional, and if he served so eagerly for foreigners, imagine how much more useful he will be to his own fatherland. I ask Your Highness for leniency if my appeal seems too audacious, and I keep my lips sealed, to keep this request a secret, and knowing the good will of Your Majesty, I flatter myself that this request will not be futile."[34]

In the spring of 1789 a letter from America arrived for Kosciuszko from his friend Maj. Elnathan Haskell, with whom he had served in the South. The grim news was that their former commander, General Greene, had died.

"He is gone, my good friend Greene—rain begins to fall heavy from my eyes whenever I think of [him]. You ought to make a statue or a mausoleum for his memory," Kosciuszko replied to Haskell.[35] Kosciuszko was so moved that he sent money to his friend David Humphreys, asking that he commission an artist to make engravings from a portrait of Greene and send it to his friends in the United States.

More troubling news arrived when Kosciuszko learned that the "Kontradmiral Pavel Ivanovich Dzhones," commanding Russian warships on the Black Sea, was none other than John Paul Jones, the hero of the American navy. Kosciuszko was stunned that a rebel who had fought so gallantly for freedom could serve a tyrannical monarch. Kosciuszko wrote to Haskell: "The brave Paul Jones is at Petersburg. I am sorry he is in the service of Russia, a Republican and American." Kosciuszko also explained to Haskell that Poland was in the process of drafting "Established Laws" that would help his nation "to be more respectable abroad."[36]

The Scottish born Jones had earned world renown for turning the tide in a 1779 naval battle against British captain Richard Pearson of the HMS *Serapis*. With the battle-scarred American ship, the *Bonhomme Richard*, on fire and taking on water, Captain Pearson asked Jones to surrender. In his Scottish brogue Jones was famously quoted as saying, "I have not yet begun to fight."[37] After a daylong battle in which Jones captured the enemy's ship, the *Bonhomme Richard* sank off the coast of England, and Jones and his crew sailed away on the *Serapis*.

After the Revolution, Jones was out of work and went to France in search of a commission. When war broke out with the Turks, Russia's minister in Paris asked Jefferson about securing the services of the legendary naval officer. Jones accepted the czarina's offer and left for Russia.[38]

Despite being given a fleet of clunky and leaky Russian ships, over a three-week campaign in the Black Sea, Jones fought four naval battles, destroying or capturing thirteen Turkish ships and helping to capture the Ottoman fortress of Otchakoff. He served brilliantly and was awarded the Medal of Saint Anne.[39]

Potemkin felt threatened by the American admiral and did everything he could to undermine him, referring to him as a "pirate" with "a black soul." Potemkin downplayed Jones's contributions to the war and wrote in a letter to the czarina: "The sleepy Admiral Paul Jones has missed the transports to Otchakoff, and could not burn the ship which the Don Cossacks burned. He was brave when he was a pirate, but he has never been at the head of many ships. No one consents to serve under him."[40]

With Sweden building up its navy on the Baltic Sea to challenge Russia, Jones was sent back to St. Petersburg to meet with the czarina. But the cutthroat Russian officers were plotting against him, and rather than being allowed to serve in the Baltic, he was accused by his enemies of raping a young girl.[41] Catherine had no choice but to give him a two-year shore leave. Soon after, Jones left for Warsaw.

Kosciuszko was on his farm in late May 1789, when Princess Louise risked her marriage by sending him a letter advising that he should return to the Polish capital because the Seym was about to commission officers for the new army.

"As your best girlfriend, I advise you to make sure that you will be in Warsaw, because those who are not present, don't have the right." Princess Louise wrote: "Please believe that no one under the sun has a more real and intense interest in your fate than I do. I cannot think about you without a certain movement within my heart and soul. It is quite clear: My soul is not ungrateful that you were the first one to unravel my feelings of love and tenderness. Your misery is always alive in me and I want with my own luck to buy your happiness and satisfaction."[42]

Princess Louise recalled in her letter that while she was in Warsaw, Kosciuszko's name came up in a conversation with the king, who spoke emotionally about him and mentioned the engraving that Kosciuszko had given him as a gift. The brigadier general took his former lover's advice and traveled to Warsaw in the summer of 1789 to yet again apply for a position in the new army.

Warsaw was full of visitors during the years of the long legislative session of the Great Seym, and by chance, Kosciuszko ran into his beloved Louise in person at one of the gatherings in the capital. The chance meeting was so "stirring" and "both were so intensely emotional that they could not even speak to each other, and they simply withdrew to the corner of the apartment and cried."[43]

There was nothing that the two lovebirds—"the pigeon and the sparrow," as Louise's father once called them—could have done to rekindle their long-lost relationship. Louise was married to Prince Joseph Lubomirski, an aristocrat who held the rank of general in the army only by virtue of his social status.

The Seym was looking for real officers to train the army. And on October 1 Kosciuszko was one of five major generals officially approved by the legislature. By then John Paul Jones had arrived in Warsaw, where, he wrote to a friend, "I was treated with the greatest politeness by the king and people of fashion."[44] The admiral also wrote the czarina to pledge his dedication to her and to set the record straight about the Russian officers who were trying to tarnish his image. But spies sent by Potemkin to follow Jones to Warsaw intercepted the letter to Catherine.

Jones and Kosciuszko had not met during the American Revolution, but in

Warsaw the two famous veterans became friends.[45] Kosciuszko, who was convinced that after the war with the Turks, Russia would turn on Poland, pleaded
with Jones not to continue his service for the despotic czarina. He tried to
arrange for a commission for Jones in the Swedish Navy.

Potemkin's spies had followed Jones so closely that they informed Catherine
that Kosciuszko had persuaded the American to accept an offer from Sweden
before any official deal had been struck.[46]

The admiral considered the idea and traveled to Holland to conduct some
business. As he was leaving Warsaw, Jones wrote to Kosciuszko: "As I shall be in
relation with our friends in America, I shall not fail to mention on all occasions
the honourable employment and the respect you have attained in your own
country, and the great regard you retain for the natives of America, where your
character is esteemed, and your name justly beloved for your services."[47]

Kosciuszko wrote to Jones in Holland to let him know that he had contacted
the Swedish ministers in Amsterdam and The Hague on his behalf. The Polish
rebel pleaded with the American that he wished "with all my heart" that the
Swedes would meet his financial expectations so that he would join the "fight
against oppression and tyranny."[48]

Offended when a firm offer from Sweden was delayed, the American naval
hero never reached an agreement with Stockholm. Potemkin made sure that the
admiral never returned to Russia. John Paul Jones returned to Paris, where he
died two years later.

TEN

Europe's First Constitution and
the Polish Revolution

KOSCIUSZKO WAS SENT TO TRAIN A BATTALION OF DISORGA-nized troops in the small town of Wloclawek, toward the northern end of the Wisla River near Prussia. He needed to recruit officers, so he often returned to Warsaw to visit his alma mater, the Knights' School, in search of talented cadets.

Kosciuszko crossed paths with another alumnus of the school, Julian Ursyn Niemcewicz, who was also a protégé of Prince Czartoryski. Niemcewicz was a journalist, playwright, and editor of a newspaper called the *National and Foreign Gazette,* which ran articles in support of reforming the government. His comedy *The Envoy's Return* lambasted the greed and selfishness of Poland's nobility as the root of its political problems. And, as a member of the Seym, Niemcewicz was allied with Kollontay's reformers, and Kosciuszko soon fell into the same orbit.

Like Kosciuszko, Kollontay was a physiocrat who believed that the greatest source of wealth was land. Kollontay also studied the British economist Adam Smith and had a prescient sense of the emerging Industrial Revolution. Poland had begun building blast furnaces to modernize its ironworks, which spurred the coal-mining and textile industries. Warsaw became an international trade center, and new banks opened that financed businesses beyond the grain trade.

Kollontay was the main instigator of the democratic reforms, and on November 24, 1789, a group of 269 representatives from 141 cities across the Polish-Lithuanian Commonwealth arrived in the capital to sign "the United Cities Act." Kollontay helped the townsfolk draft a proclamation demanding that they be allowed to own land and elect representatives to the Seym. They were inspired by the rise of the "third estate" in France, where burgher townspeople and rural peasants were demanding new rights.

On December 2 the burghers, led by Warsaw mayor, Jan Dekert, dressed in black and marched down Senator Street to the royal castle to present their demands to the king and the Seym. The "Black March of the Burghers" was harshly received and called "impertinent" by the nobles in the Seym.[1] It also shook the other monarchs of Europe, who sat up and took notice.[2] Between two bookends, France in the west and Poland in the east, the entire continent of Europe seemed to be on the verge of revolution.

The march of the burghers was most troublesome for Prussia. The French bourgeois class was on the verge of solidifying new rights, and if the Polish burghers also won legal rights and seats in the Seym, the Prussian middle class would have no reason to stay in Prussia, where they were disenfranchised.

Three days after the march on the castle, Lucchesini wrote to Prussian king Frederick William: "Trying not to be obvious, I am quietly working to interfere with the burgher cause. Until now, the oppression under which the Polish nobles have held down this class of townspeople (most of whom are of German descent), has kept foreigners from moving here to establish factories. But if this class gets rights to participate in the nation's administration, then many burgers from other countries will probably move to Poland, and this example would be most infectious for neighboring countries."[3]

The Prussian king, concerned about losing his own industrial class, encouraged Lucchesini to continue: "It's good that you are secretly trying to interfere. Because if the Polish cities manage to regain these ancient privileges, manufacturers from my country will start moving to Poland."[4]

Kollontay became the voice of the burghers, and Kosciuszko, who supported the democratic revolution, allied himself with the reformers. Kollontay took an immediate liking to Kosciuszko and later wrote of his "love, respect and admiration" for the general, whose "speeches personify my own heart and way of thinking."[5]

The general and the priest shared an abhorrence of feudalism, and Kosciuszko related stories of the horrors of the slavery he had seen in America. The African slave trade inspired Kollontay to write a comparison of slavery and serfdom: "The French islands, the Dutch and the English colonies mete out much worse treatment to the Negroes, these unfortunate citizens of two worlds. . . . [But] Whether he be a white or a black slave, or whether he moan under the violence of unjust laws or of chains, he is a human being and in no way differs from us! . . . What kind of government do we desire in our country? Do we want a genuine republic or an oligarchy? Do we want to restore freedom to Poland or only to a few families ruling over the rest of the slaves?"[6]

Kosciuszko saw the Polish reform movement as a continuation of the American Revolution, and hoped that it would not stop until all slaves, serfs, and oppressed peoples were treated as equals. With the French Revolution also gathering momentum, Europe was poised for war as monarchs created alliances to defend themselves in a cross-continental chess match.

The Polish rebel laid out a plan for defending the nation: "A regular army recruited by force, made up mostly of peasants with no legal rights or government protection of their persons or their property will not feel ties to our country, and not be interested in our common good. . . . What would be most effective is the formation of a militia, with an infantry and a cavalry. Officers should be chosen by local legislatures. Each foot soldier should have a patron to supply scores of bullets, and for the cavalry, horses and other requisites such as uniforms of their counties, and two Sundays each year, this militia should gather in their counties to practice and drill, left, right, march, aim, fire . . . especially nobles should be represented in the same proportions as peasants, Jews, and those with no complete legal ties to the country."[7]

It was an egalitarian notion that the various classes should enlist in the army in the same proportions as to the population as a whole. At the time Poland's 8.7 million people were roughly: peasants 73 percent, Jews 10 percent, nobility 8 percent, burghers 6 percent, Eastern Orthodox, Muslims, and foreigners 2 percent, and clergy 1 percent.[8]

By mentioning the Jews in the same context as the peasants, Kosciuszko made it clear that he would stand up for the two largest disenfranchised groups in Polish society. He reasoned that these groups could not be expected to defend the nation if they did not have equal rights. Kosciuszko wrote that if Jews and peasants were given legal status, they would enlist in a militia to supplement the regular army because each group "would be fighting for its own property, legal rights and happiness."[9]

There was a lot of historical baggage weighing down Kosciuszko's proposal to arm the peasants and Jews. There had not been a Jewish army since the days of the Roman Empire, so initially the concept did not elicit much of a reaction.

Most noblemen thought Kosciuszko's plan to give guns, ammunition, and freedom to the peasants was a bad idea. Just as Southern plantation owners in America did not want to arm black slaves, the land magnates frowned upon the idea of a peasant militia. The serfs hated the Catholic noblemen who oppressed them, and they also hated the Jews who worked for the feudal lords.

Kosciuszko's observations turned out to be correct, because when the army tried to recruit serfs into the military by force, they dropped their scythes and fled the fields. The mere sight of the cavalry riding into the countryside caused stampedes of ragged serfs running into the woods. About ten thousand peasants fled from central Poland to Prussia rather than being forced into serving as cannon fodder in the infantry.[10]

Like the peasant class, the Jews of eastern Europe in the eighteenth century did not fall under the jurisdiction of the court system. Jews in Poland had their own state within a state, with an autonomous government.[11] Some integrated with their Christian neighbors, but most lived in separate villages, shtetls, where they established their own governing bodies, called *kahals*. These communes elected their own judges, legislators and conducted their own administrative affairs in Yiddish and Hebrew.[12] The Polish Jews referred to this haven as Canaan, "the Promised Land."[13]

Jews were present in Poland from its inception as a Catholic nation in 966, but many more arrived after 1264, when Prince Boleslaus the Pious issued the Statute of Kalisz, which established the *kahal* communes that granted Jews the freedom to worship, conduct business, and travel, and run their own autonomous government. It imposed monetary penalties on Christians who harmed Jews and instituted the death penalty for those who killed Jews. It also set up a legal process to prosecute Christians who accused Jews of blood libel.[14]

Subsequent waves arrived when Jews were offered asylum after the Crusades and the Spanish Inquisition. In the early 1500s the Jagiellonian dynasty reasserted Poland's commitment to Jewish autonomy, passing a charter in 1551 that became known as the "Magna Carta of Jewish self-government."[15]

While Catholic nobles were Poland's upper class and the peasants were the lower class, Jewish merchants filled the void to make up the middle class. Jews moved into Polish cities where they were traders and shopkeepers and represented about half of the artisans such as shoemakers, tailors, furriers, goldsmiths, carpenters, stonecutters, and barbers. Jewish merchants helped make the Polish landlords richer by managing the grain export business for them. The Jewish historian Simon Dubnow wrote: "As regards commerce, the Jews figured in it in the following proportions: 75% of the whole export trade of Poland and 10% of the imports lay in their hands."[16]

Most alcohol distillers and tavernkeepers were also Jewish. This was a boon to the king and the noblemen, because the liquor traffic was heavily taxed. And when downtrodden serfs were drunk, they couldn't offer resistance. With the peasants angry with the Jews, they had less time to be mad at their landlords. As Dubnow wrote: "The final stage in the economic breakdown of the peasant was reached at the door of the tavern, and the Jewish liquor dealer was looked upon as the despoiler of the peasant."[17]

A symbiotic relationship and a state of relative tolerance existed between the Polish noblemen and the Jews. But when the Polish-Lithuanian Commonwealth expanded eastward into Ukraine in the seventeenth century, the Cossacks and peasants, who were Orthodox Christians, resented the Catholic Poles moving onto their lands. Jews were not allowed to own land in areas where Polish noblemen had farms, but they could lease land farmed by Ukrainian serfs. When the Ukrainian Bohdan Khmelnytsky fought with a neighbor and was offered no relief by the Polish court, he started a rebellion that massacred Polish Catholics and Jews. In 1648 Khmelnytsky's army burned and looted property, killing hundreds of Poles, including priests and nuns. Khmelnytsky's forces were more vicious against the Jews, slaughtering tens of thousands of men (including rabbis), women, and children.[18]

The Poles and Lithuanians withdrew from most of the Ukraine, and the Russians came to dominate the region. The Jews found relative safety in their Polish shtetls, which became incubators for Ashkenazic culture. This segregation gave these villages a medieval texture and isolated them from the outside world.[19]

By the end of the eighteenth century nearly a million Jews lived in Poland, yet they also faced discrimination in the country that was their sanctuary. While the peasants had to contend with the corvée, the Jews had to pay a poll tax for each member of their families. They also paid higher rates than Christians on the chimney tax. There were also inequalities within Jewish communities, and sometimes the Talmudic scholars and wealthy leaders at the top of the *kahal* hierarchy imposed unfair tax burdens, such as the *korobka*, a kosher meat tax that weighed more heavily on the poor.

While Catholics felt threatened by Calvinism and Lutheranism, Polish Jews were concerned about the differences among Orthodox Jews, Karaite Jews, and Frankists, and about the rise of Hasidism, a mystic form of Judaism whose adherents wore black silk robes, large fur hats, long beards, and side curls, *payess*. Some rabbis saw the Hasidic movement as a threat to their authority, and because they dressed differently from Jews who wore wool clothes, the Hasidic Jews were called "Men of Silk" in some Jewish locales. Gradually this pious religious sect grew to dominate Jewish society in Poland.[20]

The German Jewish philosopher Solomon Maimon wrote in the 1790s: "There is perhaps no country besides Poland where religious freedom and religious enmity are to be met with in equal degree. The Jews enjoy there a perfectly free exercise of their religion and all of their civil liberties; they even have a jurisdiction of their own. On the other hand, however, religious hatred goes so far that the name of Jew has become an abomination, and the abhorrence, which had taken root in barbarous times, continued to show its effects."[21]

It was not a perfect world for the Jews, but compared with other European countries, it was their best option. After the first partition of Poland in 1772, Prussia and Austria expelled Jews from the annexed territories and sent them deeper into Poland to be resettled.[22] When Catherine the Great took the throne in a coup, Jews were banned from living in Russia. Her mentor, Czarina Elizabeth, declared, "From the enemies of Christ, I desire neither gain, nor profit."[23]

Kosciuszko's idea for peasant and Jewish militias was unrealistic. Jews had served in other countries' armies, but there had not been a wholly Jewish military brigade since biblical times. The Jews had no reason to join the army of a regime that did not allow them to participate in government affairs. They were banned from living in Warsaw and required to pay a tax if they wanted to stay overnight in the capital.[24] The exception was when the Seym was in session, so that they could do business with the assembled noblemen. With the ban lifted during the term of the "Great Seym," of 1788–91, Jewish merchants flocked to Warsaw. Some delegates argued that it was time for Jews to be given Polish citizenship with full rights under the commonwealth's laws. Mathias Butrymowicz, a legislator from Pinsk, drafted a policy paper that urged the Seym "to give Jews an estate, and transform them from eternal wanderers into citizens of this country, in which until now they were guests," adding that doing so "should be the very first aim."[25]

Butrymowicz wrote: "Our laws regarding the Jews are wrong. Their situation, as an outside class, is wrong. It is wrong to place the power over them in the hands of private individuals or special Jewish bureaucrats. It is wrong to consider them a bad nation and to offer them no fatherland. Worst of all is that we allow them to live with special laws and customs. Owing to this, they appear as a state within a state; in view of the fact that Jewish laws and rites are different from ours, such a state of affairs causes conflicts, confusion, mutual distrust, contempt and hatred."[26]

Some legislators declared that while Jews could keep their own religion and beliefs, they should be required to learn Polish, the official language of the country. Others demanded that Jews be assimilated and forced to cut off their side curls and wear modern clothes. The political writer Joseph Pawlikowski, who would become Kosciuszko's secretary, argued against forced assimilation: "We have agreed to be tolerant of their religion. By what logic, then, shall we now interfere with it, with its holidays, with its fasts? Why should we be toward them like the Spaniards of old? Let us not force them to change their garb! Let us instead act toward them so as not to make them feel aggrieved but happy with being Poles."[27]

As the legislative session stretched into its third year, thousands of Jewish artisans, such as goldsmiths, tailors, hatmakers, and furriers, set up booths and shops all along Senator Street, crowding the theater square and area around the Church of the Holy Trinity, a few blocks from where the Seym was meeting. Business was booming along Senator Street while nearby shops were empty.[28]

By March 1790 the burghers were losing customers, and an angry mob of merchants marched on city hall to demand that the magistrate reinstate the ban on Jews living full-time in the capital.[29] If not, the crowd threatened to take matters into their own hands. The Jews were asked to move back beyond the city limits, and they complied.

By May, Jews began moving back into the city. A burgher tailor named Fox spotted a Jewish clothier walking down the street in Warsaw carrying apparel that had just been sewn. Fox grabbed at the garment bag and yelled that he would report the tailor to the trade union. The Jewish merchant was startled and ran away. Fox and two boys chased him into a building where Jewish outfitters were sewing clothes. When Fox tussled with the garment workers, they locked him in an alcove to calm him down. The boys ran into the street shouting that the Jews had killed Fox. A riot broke out, and Jewish stores were plundered. Marshals rushed in to break up the melee, but they were pelted with rocks. It was not until soldiers on horseback appeared that the frenzied crowd dispersed.[30]

Poland's burgher class was in an uproar. The townspeople could not compete with Jewish merchants, and because they could not own land, they could not compete with Catholic land magnates. The competing interests of the various classes were coming to a head. The reformers had opened a Pandora's box. The burghers, Jews, and peasants were all clamoring for expanded rights, while the land magnates tried to keep the lid on what had become an explosive situation.

Kollontay viewed the Catholic burghers and Jewish merchants as allies, because they were the middle class stuck between the nobility and the peasants. Kollontay wrote, "The human rights of Jews are to be respected no less than the rights of any other human beings."[31] On June 22, 1790, after the urging of Kollontay and others, the speaker of the Seym, Stanislaw Malachowski, created the Commission on Jewish Reform to resolve the differences between the burghers and the Jews.[32]

The chairman of the commission, Jacek Jezierski, addressed the Seym pointing out the crucial role that the Jews played in Poland's grain trade, saying: "Jews are useful Polish citizens and merchants like no others in Poland. In my book, a good merchant is one who exports products from our country, and not just one who with gallantry transports products in, and then carries out money. A good administration of Jews will increase revenues into the treasury and facilitate the circulation of money in the millions."[33]

Parliamentarians such as Kollontay, Butrymowicz, Jezierski, and Thaddeus Czacki, another reformer who advocated for civic rights for Jews, ran the committee and sought input from a group of doctors, rabbis, and other Jewish leaders who presented various petitions to the Seym on what they would like to see in the constitution. But the opinions of these Jewish leaders varied from calls for full integration into Polish society, to civic emancipation without dissolving the *kahals*, and even to a rejection of any change whatsoever in the status quo of Jewish life.[34]

As some delegates tried to resolve Jewish issues, most members of the Seym focused on trying to please the burghers and to persuade the greedy land magnates to compromise. The biggest issue was still what form of government would replace the Russian-dominated plutocracy that ran the commonwealth.

The Seym delegates had a sword of Damocles hanging over their heads because the Russian czarina was not pleased with Poland's quest for self-determination. After the Bar confederates tried to drive out the Russians in 1772, Catherine convinced Prussia and Austria, that along with Russia, they should each annex a piece of Polish territory. This three-pronged attack on Poland in 1772 cost the commonwealth 29 percent of its land and 36 percent of its population.[35]

Once the czarina finished off the Ottomans Turks, it was clear that Russia would attack Poland again. The Poles had to avoid another attack from three sides.

Austria sided with Russia in its war against Turkey, causing the Prussians to grow more concerned about the Russian-Austrian alliance. The Prussians wanted to pull Poland into Berlin's sphere of influence, but they didn't hide their opinion of Poles and had a slogan that said: "Poland is the hell of peasants, the paradise of Jews, the purgatory of burghers, the heaven of nobles, and the gold mine of foreigners."[36]

Prussia forced Poland to sign a treaty, and Lucchesini squeezed King Stanislaw, saying, "If you do not sign the alliance, not only will we keep on wronging you, but we will increase our wrongdoing, and you, without an ally, not only will be forced to endure it, but Poland will become a battleground and finally the peace prize."[37] Stanislaw signed the treaty on March 29, 1790. It was a shaky alliance at best.

With the Prussian threat temporarily diminished, Kosciuszko had to come up with a battle plan for the Russians. He was homesick for his Lithuanian farm and wrote to his sister Anna that she should get his favorite jelly doughnuts ready in case he had a chance to visit her during Easter. His financial constraints eased by his new general's salary, he let his sister know that he would put aside money to pay the bills and the taxes, taking some of the pressure off her.[38]

Kosciuszko was transferred to Lublin, where he spent the summer on maneuvers with his troops on the plains between the Wisla and Bug rivers. Years of corruption by which officer commissions were bought and sold like real estate created an army of lazy aristocrats. They would face a larger and battle-hardened Russian army with combat experience fighting the Ottoman Empire. The Poles were undisciplined and in such bad shape that he had to start with the basics, drilling the recruits in bayonet thrusts, shooting, marching in columns, attack formations, and covering withdrawals.

Although the forty-four-year-old Kosciuszko was the only general with significant battle experience, the king's twenty-six-year-old nephew Prince Joseph Poniatowski was named commander of the military. Joseph's mother was from an aristocratic Austrian family and his father, Andrew Poniatowski, King Stanislaw's brother, died when the boy was ten. With no children, Stanislaw became his nephew's guardian and doted on his beloved Pepi. The prince was raised in Vienna and served in the Austrian military, briefly taking part in the war against the Turks.

Pepi may have been only a prince, but among the aristocracy he was king of the dance floor and master of the boudoir. The handsome ladies' man began considering himself a Pole only after Stanislaw invited him to Warsaw to lead the army. Prince Joseph devoted himself to modernizing Poland's military, but as the commander, politics often forced him to travel to the capital. The frequent trips to Warsaw complicated preparations on the front. The prince realized that Kosciuszko's military knowledge and experience were greater than his own, so he made the rebel his deputy and left him in charge during his absence.[39]

Kosciuszko struggled to get enough uniforms, ammunition, and feed for the horses and to establish lines of communication. But he was trying to bring order to a disorganized army. Things were so bad that one night the drivers of an artillery transport from Warsaw got drunk and accidentally crossed the border into a sliver of the Austrian Empire that jutted into Polish territory. They were so inebriated that they ran the horses off the road and flipped over the wagon, sending the cannons spilling onto the ground. It became a minor international incident.

Kosciuszko once again pushed his plan for American-style militias and reserve units that could be called up when needed. "The American Revolution serves as an example for how to fight a war for eight years without any money," he wrote. "If only the government has the care to supply uniforms and boots to its soldiers."[40]

But with the military bureaucracy firmly in place, he couldn't even get the resources he needed for the troops that he did have. He was often moving around Poland to train and inspect various units, and in late 1790 he stayed in a village in the Southeast called Miedzyboza, where most of the six thousand residents were Jewish, with a spattering of a few noble Catholic families.

His friend Gen. Joseph Orlowski was commander of Kamieniec Podolski, a giant stone fortress built in the fourteenth century on Poland's southeastern frontier to serve as an outpost to defend against Ottoman and Tatar invasions. It had a castle with minarets and high walls, on top of a hill surrounded by a moat. It overlooked lush fields of wheat and fruit trees. A river encircled the nearby village. Orlowski was headed to Warsaw for the winter and suggested that Kosciuszko ask for the command of the castle while he was away.

"My beloved friend, I hear from everyone that you can't sit in one place for a couple of hours and that you roam around like a Tatar," Orlowski wrote. "You write that you are in search of a wife. . . . I see you have a sense of urgency. You know that command of a fort can rarely be obtained."[41]

It was not a comfortable post that Kosciuszko was after, and while he was very lonely, the general was trying to whip the troops into shape. When an officer quickstepped out of his quarters in the village, a young woman wrote to Kosciuszko saying that he was impolite, and too tough on his soldiers.

Tekla Zurowska was the eighteen-year-old daughter of a nobleman who had two separate estates in Poland. The Zurowskis were visiting a renowned Dr. Hakenszmit for treatment, and they were staying in a house next to Kosciuszko's quarters. Young Tekla spent much of her time gazing out the window watching events unfold at the famous general's headquarters.

The commander replied to Tekla's letter, saying, "I greeted [the officer] beautifully and politely. He left quickly because he saw a pile of paperwork that I needed to finish." Tekla had a cousin, who by chance was also named Tekla. Kosciuszko became close to both of them. In a letter "To the two Teklas," Kosciuszko wrote: "I don't know whom I should write to, the first Tekla, or to the second, but I do know that I am in love with the first one, and great friends with the second."[42]

Kosciuszko and Tekla exchanged flirtatious letters and began teasing each other. They developed an understanding, and soon they were seen kissing and petting. Marriages with such an age difference were frequent in eighteenth-century Europe, and Tekla was smitten with the general. The feeling was mutual, and they fell in love.

"How did you sleep?" Kosciuszko wrote to Tekla on one occasion, "and what did you dream about?" When he set out to drill his soldiers, he wrote: "I kiss your hands, and your mother's feet. I'll have to content myself with this."

Out in the field on maneuvers, Kosciuszko wrote: "Tekla, when you write, send me one of the pearls that is hanging around your neck. Let providence and a coat of complete happiness wrap themselves around you, and you may be convinced of my stable, amiable respect and conviction."[43]

While Tekla's mother approved of Kosciuszko, her father, the wealthy Lord Zurowski, was not pleased about the romance. Tekla fell at her father's feet, crying and proclaiming her love and devotion for Kosciuszko. It was such a moving moment that even her father broke down in tears.

When Kosciuszko heard about this, he wrote to Tekla, "I also give you my sprinkled tears. . . . I embrace your heart with my own heart. I tremble not from the cold, but from internal uneasiness . . . open your breast so that I can kiss your heart. Hold out your lips, delicately, and do not be offended by my affectionate kisses. . . . I kiss you one more time. I take my leave, because in my conscious thoughts I am always beside you."[44]

Lord Zurowski proved to be just another greedy landlord trying to move his way up the feudal food chain, and Kosciuszko tried to impress him by applying to leasehold some farmland to provide for the nobleman's daughter.[45] He told Zurowski that he did have a small estate in Lithuania, and asked him to check his references with the Seym in Warsaw. He appealed to aristocrats such as Lord Ignatius Potocki to speak up in his favor.

It was all to no avail. Kosciuszko wrote a letter officially asking Lord Zurowski for his daughter's hand, but once again, his lack of a substantial estate turned the father of his beloved against him. And when Dr. Hakenszmit began gossiping about Kosciuszko's previous attempt to elope with Louise Sosnowska, Lord Zurowski accused the general of plotting to kidnap his daughter.

The general replied to the nobleman, "My God! Let me drop dead, if I even allowed shadows of such thoughts over a struggle to unite us in holy matrimony."[46] To Tekla's mother, he wrote, "What a cruel thought that I, against the laws of nature, would go against the father to tear my beloved from her home."[47]

Kosciuszko wrote a long respectful letter to Zurowski explaining that he loved Tekla and would not do anything against her father's wishes. But Lord Zurowski did not believe Kosciuszko and left the village with his family, surrounded by a cordon of guards, and headed back to his estate in Galicia.

With more than ten thousand soldiers at his disposal, Kosciuszko was offended by the nobleman's defensive escort. If he were going to kidnap Zurowski's daughter, or misuse his authority as a general, an entourage of a few men would not be able to stop him. It was yet another failed love affair, and the Polish rebel lamented that he would rather be "brave in battle like our knights, than be tender and loving like our priests."[48]

As Kosciuszko tried to restore order to the army, the legislative reformers kept the momentum going to draft Europe's first written democratic constitution. The debate heated up, and Kollontay said that if the choice was between a "noble revolution, or a mob, rabble revolution," he preferred the former. The lapsed priest argued that unlike France, the Seym's delegates were civilized enough to conduct a "gentle revolution."[49]

The session dragged on for two years with no agreement, and by 1790 it was time for a new election. It was unlikely that the nobles would reelect the reformers, and with no guarantee that a new session would continue under the confederation guidelines of majority rule, the *liberum veto* could again block any changes to the system of government.

The reformers had to find a way around their predicament. The first partition of Poland by its three neighbors shrunk the number of deputies in the Seym from 235 to 181. So rather than backtrack on the progress already made, in November the Patriots used a political trick to elect another set of 181 delegates, instead of putting the entire legislature up for reelection.[50]

Disgusted with the legislative gamesmanship and the direction the nation was taking, Kosciuszko's neighbor Zaleski quit the Seym after the election. As an attorney who made his living representing the rights of feudal lords who were allied with the Russians, he was upset about the debate over civil rights for serfs and voting powers for burghers. When Kosciuszko heard of his friend's resignation, he wrote to Zaleski saying that as a talented lawyer, he was abandoning the nation in its time of need.

"We need to unite with the same goal, to free our fatherland from foreign powers that want to enslave and even ruin the name of Poles. Believe me, that I always think the same, I always breathe as the soul of a free Republican citizen, and when our government will be on par with the English government, the bells will ring and our citizens will stand at attention," Kosciuszko wrote to Zaleski. "You demand tolerance from me, yet I don't understand your need, my esteemed Sir, no one has a more tolerant soul than I, with aspirations for universal harmony, unity, and friendship good wishes for our country."[51]

While Kosciuszko could not persuade his friend to use his legal skills for the benefit of the people, Kollontay and the reformers had been working on King Stanislaw to switch sides from the Muscovite Party to the Patriots.

An Italian priest named Scipione Piattoli became the linchpin in Stanislaw's shift to the Patriots. Rev. Piattoli was a tutor to children of aristocratic families and often traveled with them through Europe. The Italian scholar became an ally of the Patriots and was the go-between for the reformers and the king. He also introduced Stanislaw to another Italian who played a major role in Polish politics of the eighteenth century.

Philip Mazzei was an Italian doctor who in the 1770s journeyed to Virginia, where he taught Thomas Jefferson to cultivate grapes. The two opened a vineyard, and in 1779 Mazzei returned to Italy to buy guns for the American rebels. After the Revolution, Mazzei was in Paris, where Piattoli asked him to take a job as King Stanislaw's liaison in Paris. Diplomatic relations between France and Poland had broken off when Stanislaw took the crown, and in 1788 he was looking for a trusted agent to restore ties after the long hiatus.

Worried that the Americans would be upset if he served a European monarch, Mazzei consulted Jefferson, who was then the American ambassador in Paris. "Jefferson assured me to the contrary," Mazzei wrote in his memoirs, "saying that the King of Poland was better known in America than in Europe, that he was the head of a republic and not a despot, and that he was considered the best citizen of his kingdom."[52]

Mazzei took the job and learned a secret code to correspond with the king in Warsaw. The timing for hiring an agent in Paris was impeccable because the French Revolution was about to explode. Mazzei kept Stanislaw informed about the events unfolding in Paris. An angry French mob had stormed the Bastille, stolen thousands of muskets, decapitated its governor, and paraded around the city with his head stuck on a pike. The gruesome details emerging from Paris encouraged the king to work with the reformers in Warsaw in order to avoid a similar fate.

After an agreement that the new government would be a constitutional monarchy similar to that of England, Stanislaw wrote the first draft of the constitution, which had contributions and edits from Kollontay, Malachowski, Potocki, Niemcewicz, and others.

The impact of Kosciuszko's stories about America's Founding Fathers influenced his friends, and the notion of "no taxation without representation" began to reverberate among the reformers who represented the burghers, peasants, and Jews.

On April 2, 1791, Niemcewicz gave a rousing speech to the Seym challenging the legislative body full of noblemen: "Imagine for a moment, that our government was not so wonderful and the king or the Senate levied taxes on you unjustly?" Denouncing the birthrights of the aristocracy and trying to goad the delegates into action, Niemcewicz said, "No one knows who Washington's father was, or whether Franklin's forefathers had to be reckoned with. But everyone knows, and their descendents will know, that Washington and Franklin freed America!"[53]

Prussia's worst fears were about to become reality, and Lucchesini must have squirmed in his chair as Niemcewicz continued, declaring that Poland would become the land of opportunity if burghers were given property rights and laws were passed to encourage business. "Watch as they come from all parts of the world, burghers to settle under the rule of our sweet government," he said. "They will come and bring craftsmen and businesses that are now settled in foreign countries."

The "Black March of the Burghers" had forced the Seym to cave in to the demands of the townspeople, and on April 18, 1791, a law was passed giving the bourgeois class the right to elect twenty-four representatives to the Seym who could debate and vote on matters concerning cities, industry, and commerce. By passing this act the Seym was able to secure the burghers' support for the constitution.

The real battle, however, was over land—who could own it and thus have the right to vote. Burghers, Jews, and peasants were not allowed to own land—that right was left for the aristocracy. And while most nobles owned land, some did not. The rallying cry among those who did not want to give the right to vote to everyone became: "Birth can produce a nobleman, but only property turns him into a citizen."[54]

The Muscovite party was opposed to changes in the status quo, and with Easter approaching, a two-week recess was called on April 24 so they could go home for the holiday. The Patriots stayed behind in Piattoli's chambers to hammer out the final details of the constitution. When they approved the final draft, Stanislaw sent couriers to summon the delegates who supported the plan back to the capital for a vote to take place on May 5. About sixty people were involved with the secret negotiations, most under the age of thirty. Piattoli called the constitution "the glory above all of the Polish youth."[55]

News of the surprise session leaked out to the Muscovites, and as Patriot supporters rushed back to the capital to cast their votes, the Russian ambassadors sprang into action. Yakov Bulgakov, the czarina's former agent in Constantinople, had replaced the dour and heavy-handed Stackelberg, who failed to keep the Poles from pulling away from Russia. Bulgakov spent time in Turkish prisons for spying, where he learned much about underhanded dealing.

At his house in Warsaw the roly-poly Russian gave lavish parties for the legislators, where rare wines were uncorked and French chefs served sumptuous meals on luxurious porcelain with sparkling silver. The naive guests always came back for more, because shockingly, even noblemen who were terrible gamblers always won big when playing cards with Bulgakov. Some of these Polish legislators "never left the table without winning 200 or 300 red zloties."[56]

On May 2, Bulgakov once again invited the greediest land magnates to his home, but this time it was to devise a plan to disrupt the proceedings in the Seym. They spread gossip, and that night burghers in Warsaw's pubs and coffeehouses were chattering about rumored death threats sent to the king and members of the Patriot Party.

Across town King Stanislaw and the conspirators gathered in the baroque-style Radziwill Palace, where the constitution was read aloud to fewer than one hundred chosen members of the Seym. All those present promised their support. To throw the Russians off balance, Stanislaw moved the vote up to the next day.

On the morning of May 3, 1791, the townspeople of Warsaw were woken by the clopping hooves of cavalry horses trotting down Krakowskie Przedmiescie Street, known as "the Royal Route." People asked if Stanislaw had died or a revolution was under way. Kollontay spread the word to his burgher allies that something momentous was about to happen, and thousands of people flocked through Warsaw's streets and alleys and began walking toward the castle.[57]

Prince Joseph, who had left Kosciuszko on the eastern front to guard the Russian border, circled his cavalry and infantry around the royal castle. The army rolled cannons in front of the entrance as the cobblestones rattled with the sound of horse carriages carrying delegates through the portal into the castle courtyard, where they disembarked and walked to the legislative chamber. The artillery was supposedly brought in for a heavy-gun salute to celebrate the approval of the constitution, but it was clear that no disruptions would be tolerated.[58]

It was a coup d'état against Russia's supporters in the Seym. Prince Joseph and his officers marched into the Senate while the soldiers mingled with the crowds of people gathering outside. After the bizarre 1790 elections the Seym had two parliamentary speakers, Malachowski, and Kazimierz Sapieha. They took their seats across from the king's throne, each holding a large ebony staff. Cheers greeted King Stanislaw when he walked into the chamber, wearing opulent robes. He looked ebullient as he sat down on his throne, shimmering with embroidery and gold. On the king's right was the archbishop holding a tall silver staff, with a large cross draped around his neck and another crucifix next to him. Behind them were four levels of benches full of various bishops, generals, and cabinet members. They all faced the Senate floor.[59]

The speakers banged their staffs on the floor and called the session to order. Several delegates explained the importance of the new constitution. The document hailed: "We publish and proclaim a perfect and entire liberty to all people."[60] It was not a strict democracy because it preserved the dominance of the aristocracy. The compromise mostly benefited the burghers, opening the door for them to buy land and become members of the gentry.[61] It also provided them with *neminem captivabimus*, a form of habeas corpus to protect against arbitrary arrest.[62] While the new laws offered less for the peasants and the Jews, it promised them protection by the courts.

The status of serfs changed only marginally. "This agricultural class of people, the most numerous in the nation consequently forming the most considerable part of its force, from whose hands flows the source of our riches, we receive under the protection of national law and government."[63] Serfs won their rights "after having fulfilled the obligations [they] may have voluntarily entered into." While it was a tall order for indentured servants to pay off their debts and become free, it was possible.

Kosciuszko's hopes for ending serfdom were dashed. However, peasants who fled other countries were offered sanctuary. "Any person coming into Poland, from whatever part of the world," the constitution read, "as soon as he sets his foot on the territory of the Republic, becomes free and at liberty to exercise his industry, wherever and in whatever manner he pleases." Poland's neighbors worried that this would create an escape route for runaway serfs.

The Seym did not reorganize the Jewish state within a state or further integrate Jews into society because of burgher opposition, the greed of the aristocracy, and disagreement among Jews over how best to resolve the issue.[64] The constitution did, however, reiterate their rights to political autonomy and religious freedom.

It established Roman Catholicism as the "dominant national religion," but "as the same holy religion commands us to love our neighbors, we therefore owe to all people of whatever persuasion, peace in matters of faith, and the protection of government; consequently we assure, to all persuasions and religions, freedom and liberty, according to the laws of the country, and in all dominions of the republic."[65]

Executive power was vested in the king, but his power was checked by a Council of Inspection, cabinet ministers who could be impeached by the Seym if they went against the will of the people. The new system outlined a separation of powers with a bicameral legislature and a judicial branch. It abolished the *liberum veto* and reestablished majority rule. Recognizing that it was not a perfect document, the new constitution required a special legislative session every twenty-five years to examine amendments required to "perfect it."

Some nobles were opposed to a hereditary monarchy, but others saw it as a compromise to end foreign meddling in Polish affairs. Even with the establishment of an ancestral kingdom, the checks and balances of the new constitution were a giant leap forward when compared to the autocratic monarchies that ruled throughout Europe.

The legislative leader, Stanislaw Malachowski, took the floor and pronounced, "There are two republican governments in this century: the English and the American which has corrected the faults of the first. But the one which we intend to establish today will be finer than both, since it will combine in itself all that is most relevant in each to our own circumstances."[66]

But the Muscovites who made their way into the chamber did not agree, and a heated debate raged for seven hours. By the end of the afternoon the delegates were exhausted, and one deputy rose to ask the king to take a solemn oath to abide by all the reforms and constitutional protections for his subjects.

King Stanislaw stood up on his throne, turned to the archbishop and said, "I swear before God that I won't regret it. I ask that whoever loves the fatherland should come with me to the church to take the same oath!"[67]

The Patriots roared in approval, and the constitution was passed by acclamation. A wave of cheers rolled out of the chamber along the crowds in the hallway, down the stairs, and into the crowd waiting outside. The members of the Seym carried King Stanislaw on their shoulders along the narrow cobblestone street to Saint John's Cathedral, where he swore before God that he would make the new power-sharing arrangement work.

The bells of the cathedral clanged away as the assembled multitudes began to sing the Catholic hymn, *Te Deum Laudamus*, reserved for praising monumental occasions. More than twenty thousand people had gathered in front of the castle, and the bells of all the city's churches began ringing. Crowds of burghers gathered on the streets waved flags and cheered, "Long live the King! Long Live the Constitution, Long live Kollontay!"

At the end of the day Stanislaw turned to his secretary, Piattoli, and said with a smile, "Well! Not even a bruise, not a drop of blood. The greatest damage suffered today, was suffered by me, for I lost my hat in the crowd."[68]

Unlike Paris, where angry masses took matters into their own hands and turned against the noble class, in Warsaw the aristocracy began its own transformation toward democracy. The Polish revolution had begun. It was the first constitution in Europe, second in the world only to that of the United States. In Paris the Legislative Assembly continued to fight over whether France would have a constitutional monarchy or a republic.

To Kosciuszko's way of thinking, the Polish constitution did not go far enough. He was a republican who wanted a direct democracy descending from the people—all the people. While the great debate raged in Warsaw, he was charged with guarding the Russian border. The Polish rebel was in Miedzyboza when he received an order from the military commission in Warsaw to swear an oath to protect the constitution. It was not the full democracy he had hoped for, but the May 3 Constitution represented progress and hope for a democratic Poland. Kosciuszko signed it and asked ten of his fellow officers also to pledge their allegiance to the new system of government.

While Kosciuszko had mixed feelings on his country's reforms, reaction to the May 3 Constitution in London, Paris, and Philadelphia was much more enthusiastic. The world was stunned that such a bold document could emerge from feudal Europe. It was considered a major step forward by political thinkers of the day. The king had, after all, willingly given up much of his own power.

On July 20, 1791, George Washington, serving his first term as president, wrote to his representative in Europe: "Poland, by the public papers, appears to have made large and unexpected strides towards liberty, which, if true, reflects great honor on the present King, who seems to have been the principal promoter of the business."[69]

A member of the British House of Commons, the Irish statesman and philosopher Edmund Burke called the Polish constitution a "masterpiece of political wisdom" and "a glory to humanity."[70] Burke said that the Poles' quest for "liberty" went from "anarchy to order," while the French had gone from "order to anarchy."[71]

The *Times* of London wrote, "Such is this excellent Constitution dictated by equity, enlightened by understanding, and founded on the imprescriptible rights of man" that Poland "will become one of the happiest nations in the Universe."[72]

Scoffing at the "chaos" among the revolutionaries in Paris, Horace Walpole wrote, "Poland ought to make the French blush."[73] The French may not have blushed, but they were ready to break out the rouge. On May 10 the influential

Gazette de Leyde, Europe's newspaper of record, noted, "This truly Republican spirit of equality that comes out of the blue not only gives the representatives of Poland the upper hand, it is also one of religious and civil tolerance."[74] Because France did not have a free press, the *Gazette* was published in Leyden, Holland and on May 20 it gushed over the new constitution and the Polish Revolution, saying, "If there is a century of miracles, in the East it is the opera in Poland," thanks to "the wisdom of the king."[75]

In Philadelphia, *Dunlap's American Daily Advertiser* wrote: "In the history of mankind there are but few instances to be found, where kings, unsolicited and unintimidated, have made a voluntary surrender of their power. There are many great sayings of great acts; but we read of none that deserves to be preferred to the late conduct of the King of Poland. The form of the new constitution of Poland, is not merely sanctioned by the King, but dictated, framed, and fashioned in the exalted superiority of his own mind, affords a new lesson to the world."[76]

In America the constitution was associated with Kosciuszko. David Humphreys, serving as a trade representative in Lisbon, wrote to Kosciuszko that he was "delighted with the conduct of the King of Poland." Humphreys wrote a poem that said in part,

> New laurels brings to thee, great Stanislaus!—
> Thy glorious name shall stand unrivaled on the rolls of fame. . . .
> Thy voice pronounced to free the rights of man. . . .
> Thy Godlike voice, that op'd the feudal graves, Call'd to new life innumerable Slaves. . . .
> Thy generous Nobles made those Vassals free, Hail blessed example! Happy Poland hail! . . .
> No more shall Slavery sterilize thy soil, But fruits, that prompt, shall pay the Peasants toil. . . .[77]

King Stanislaw soaked in all the accolades. Thomas Jefferson sent him a copy of his book *Notes on the State of Virginia,* which the king read as he basked in the sun in the lush Lazienki Gardens.[78]

In the United States, Kosciuszko was the most famous Pole, so his friends viewed his association with the constitution positively: "Your acquaintances and friends in America all remember you with great affection," Humphreys wrote. "And the more so from the honorable agency you had in assisting to establish the Independence of that Country—a Country, which now, in reality begins to enjoy the fruits of its Revolution."[79]

The constitution put Poland on the political map, for better and worse. While it was looked upon positively in France, Britain, and the United States, the enthusiasm for the peaceful Polish revolution proved to be premature. The Russian, Prussian, and Austrian monarchs all viewed these reforms as a threat. It would be only a matter of time before they stepped in to quash the reforms.

After the constitution was passed Prince Joseph and his entourage rode to the village of Niemirow, near the eastern border, which had become the headquarters for the Polish army. Kosciuszko and the prince held joint maneuvers. Stanislaw promised to visit the front to inspect the troops, but when the prince realized that his uncle would not come, he asked that he at least send a member of the Seym to assess the needs of the army. A small delegation was sent, but after they left Prince Joseph learned that four of the observers of his army's war games were Russian officers dressed incognito in civilian clothes.[80]

In November 1791 Prince Joseph once again traveled to Warsaw for the winter, and Kosciuszko was again put in charge of the troops at the front. The two generals kept in touch via secret correspondence. Kosciuszko ordered Lt. Seweryn Bukar to draw maps of all the camps along the front, showing the number of troops and their positions, which he then sent to the military commission in Warsaw. Copies of these maps reportedly found their way into the hands of the Russians.[81]

King Stanislaw tried to keep his finger on the pulse of the Russian court by exchanging letters with his representative in St. Petersburg, August Antoni Deboli. The king kept him abreast of events and on November 19 wrote that the prince had returned to Warsaw: "The command has been left to Kosciuszko, now in the camp at Braclaw, who has shown his skills, and has a well-known reputation earned in the American war. But Prince Joseph will race from here to the Ukraine at the slightest sign of any brewing mischief by the Muscovites."[82]

By the end of the year several rich families that were not willing to give up power began conspiring with Russia. They printed propaganda denouncing the reforms and smuggled it into eastern Poland. Kosciuszko found copies of a brochure called *Observations on the Constitution and Revolution of May 3*, which claimed that the movement was a "conspiracy" pushed by enemies of the aristocracy.

Kosciuszko sent Prince Joseph a copy of the pamphlet saying, "This book is resounding everywhere. . . . It is written well, but there are few who can distinguish between these delusions and detach themselves from them and put on the robes of real freedom that rely on government and not the imagination or the likes of everyone."[83]

Even though a few of the land magnates were upset over ceding rights to the burghers, in February elections were held for a new Seym. The vote was seen as a referendum on the constitution. It won by a landslide.

This infuriated the greediest of the land magnates and during preparations for the constitution's anniversary, once again rumors of coup attempts and death threats to the king spread through Warsaw.

On May 3, 1792, the capital held a joyous festival to toast the first year of the new government. At eight in the morning, five thousand soldiers in colorful dress uniforms from various units assembled near the royal castle for a parade. A fraternity of merchants was clad in navy dress jackets and azure blue pants. Stanislaw's coach was lavishly decorated in bronze and crystal panes of glass, and two servants behind him carried his crown. In front of the king's carriage were wagons with the archbishop and bishops, and while priests in long frocks walked in front carrying a large crucifix, courtiers on horses dressed for a pageant rode alongside.[84]

Prince Joseph and his officers rode behind the king on horses adorned with shiny bridles, while the army marched with them. Buildings were decorated with flowing banners, and bands heralded the marchers with patriotic music as senators, priests, and the king's cabinet promenaded to the baroque Church of the Holy Cross across the street from the Royal Knight School.

There were a celebratory mass and the recital of a new *Te Deum* written specially for the occasion. Poland's Jews also commemorated the day. After the constitution passed, King Stanislaw invited Jewish leaders to the castle to resolve the issues affecting their rights under the new codes. Kollontay, Piattoli, and other delegates were debating proposals from various *kahals* on how to reform the Jewish governing system. There were still areas of disagreement, but negotiations continued in good faith because Stanislaw was adamant that Poland continue the policies set by previous kings to have good relations with the Jews.

To show their appreciation the Jews wrote a hymn in Hebrew that began:

"Gloomy sorrow has disappeared, and joy prevails;
the redeemed nation uses its sweet freedoms;
there is happiness, and no yoke is crushing the Poles.
Our kind-hearted God has professed, 'I have chosen you a king
I have instilled him with resourceful wisdom, in the illumination of Stanislaw,
you will find o' nation, happiness and your salvation.' "[85]

After the day's festivities Stanislaw invited honored guests to his "palace on the water" in the Lazienki Gardens for dinner and aristocrats held sumptuous parties and balls. At nine o'clock at night, dazzling fireworks displays exploded over the city. The celebrations went off without any problems as the nobility and bourgeois classes partied on into the night.

Prince Joseph was one of the day's star attractions. He spent the winter and spring lobbying the Seym for more support for the army and secured a promotion to lieutenant general. The young and handsome prince had a good time in the capital in the company of "easy women." The other officers who had traveled to Warsaw with him also enjoyed themselves, and during the first anniversary of the constitution, "hordes of the king's officers could be seen in the windows of bordellos."[86]

While Warsaw was celebrating, the frontline officers near the border with Russia were uneasy about the rumors that some of the noblemen in eastern Poland, Francis Branicki and Felix Potocki, from a disgruntled line of the Patriot family, were cozying up to the Russians. Kosciuszko and his troops ran border patrols to follow Russian troop movements and track the status of their war with Turkey.

The Polish field soldiers were also looking for ways to get their mind off the coming war. Before the beginning of Lent and its fasting period, Kosciuszko arranged for parties so his soldiers could celebrate Carnival. Taking a break from his military maneuvers, Kosciuszko took up quarters in a large house in the village of Niemirow. Bukar wrote in his memoirs: "We always had a flock of ladies to dance with, together with the wives and daughters of officers quartered in the nearby countryside."[87]

One of the women in this group was the wife of Col. Matthew Szyrer. Mrs. Szyrer was very pretty, educated, and played the violin beautifully. As her husband was frequently in the field with his regiment, she stayed in Niemirow, and Kosciuszko invited her to lodge in one of the many rooms in the house that served as his headquarters. "From what I remember," Bukar wrote, the colonel's wife "entertained" Kosciuszko "pretty vigorously."[88]

Mrs. Szyrer was not the only married woman to attract Kosciuszko. Zofia Glavani was the daughter of a Greek prostitute who had spent her early years in a Turkish harem in Constantinople. Zofia was a stunning raven-haired beauty with large dark eyes and curves that caught the attention of men wherever she went.[89] The lovely and intelligent femme fatale was the wife of Gen. Joseph Witt. When the couple lived in Warsaw as newlyweds, King Stanislaw paid the rent on their apartment out of the royal treasury so that he could have sex with the Greek goddess.[90] At one point before ending up in Niemirow, Mrs. Witt was even the lover of Russian general Potemkin.

"In such a small village, every new arrival is important and this Hellenist captured all the attention," Bukar recalled, "and the respected General Kosciuszko popped in after work for a little relaxation."[91]

Bukar also apparently enjoyed Mrs. Witt's "services." After he nursed Kosciuszko back to health from a fever, the general stopped by Bukar's quarters to thank him. Seeing the books in the room, Kosciuszko picked one up and noticed that it had a blessing written in it from Bukar's mother. Smiling, Kosciuszko teasingly scribbled his own message underneath: "So that he prays every day, does not frequent the Greek woman, and perfects his talents."[92]

Felix Potocki of the Muscovite Party, who had a palace in Niemirow, also fell in love with Mrs. Witt. Potocki, who was not pleased that the aristocracy had given away its power in the new constitution, wrote to Potemkin: "We have lost our liberty and our neighbors will soon lose their tranquillity. Every good Pole who is not seduced by the cabal of the Prussians and of the king is convinced that our country can be saved only by Russia."[93]

A few years later Potocki forced Witt to divorce the Greek beauty so that he could marry her himself. The rapacious Potocki and his greedy land-magnate friends simply took whatever they wanted.

It did not stop with women.

ELEVEN

~⟨✦⟩~

The "Noble" Traitors

THE CZARINA'S BLOOD BOILED WHEN SHE LEARNED THAT KING Stanislaw had clipped the marionette strings that she pulled from Russia. And when the constitution was ratified by the local legislatures, Catherine summoned Poland's ambassador to her palace and screamed, "What a constitution! Being surrounded by three powerful neighbors to declare freedom for peasants who come to Poland! What an Idea! That will lure most of the peasants of Belarus to Poland and the rest of my serfs will dilly dally."[1]

The promise of sanctuary for runaway serfs was a jab at the feudal system that bestowed great wealth on Europe's monarchs. The czarina called the constitution "an act of war." The royal tyrants had to do something before their peasants found out that they would be free if they made their way to Poland.

Prussian king Frederick William was also furious that his "ally" had given burghers the right to vote and a say in business affairs. He wanted the emerging Industrial Revolution to flourish in his country. The new constitution would encourage German entrepreneurs to move to Poland, lured by democracy and free-market economics.

Once the war with Turkey ended, Russian troops marched north. Kosciuszko sent a spy into the Ukraine to gather information on the number of soldiers, artillery pieces, and supplies that the enemy had. The news was not good. There was a massive troop buildup on the Polish frontier. Kosciuszko sent a message to Warsaw that said: "The Muscovite regiments are spreading out on our border."[2]

Kosciuszko's friend Niemcewicz noticed during the winter of 1792 that the ambassadors of Russia and Prussia were suddenly smiling at each other.

Lucchesini and Bulgakov were even seen visiting each other's homes in War-saw.[3] This struck fear into the hearts of the Seym delegates, who were still meet-ing to resolve unfinished business concerning the peasants, the Jews, the economy, and the government's budget.

During the American Revolution, Kosciuszko faced the treason of Benedict Arnold, who sold his plans for West Point to the enemy. Now, as he prepared for an imminent attack by the Russians, Kosciuszko's army would face the treason of a group of Poles who would sell out their country to the enemy. The keys to the castle would be given away by stingy Polish land magnates who would risk losing their entire country to retain control over their profits from the grain trade.

While the Patriots were celebrating the new constitution, in April 1792, Fe-lix Potocki, Seweryn Rzewuski, Francis Branicki, and several other collaborators traveled to St. Petersburg to meet with Catherine the Great in her palace to plot the overthrow of Poland's democratic government. Turning reality on its head, the traitors allowed the czarina's minions to draft the Act of the Targowica Con-federation, claiming that an international conspiracy had been hatched with rev-olutionary France, and that Russia needed to send its army to protect the security and freedom of Poland.

The defectors coordinated the timing of the invasion with the Russian army and then rushed to the small town of Targowica in southeastern Poland to issue their proclamation. On May 14, 1792, the traitors made their goals known: They had officially declared war on the constitution.

Prince Joseph was still in Warsaw in early May, and Kosciuszko had been the de facto leader of the army for six months. He had visited most of the camps along the border and had a better feel for the terrain than did the prince. The flat plains of Poland offered few defensible positions, and Prince Joseph wanted to keep all his units concentrated in one area, whereas Kosciuszko wanted the army to stretch out in a chain of outposts to patrol the border. Kosciuszko had written dispatches to Prince Joseph over the winter, explaining his tactics.

Rapid troop movements were the secret to Kosciuszko's success in the Bat-tles of New York and the Carolinas during the American Revolution, and he sug-gested having several lines of defense that could fall back when the massive Russian army attacked. He argued that the first line should be the cavalry, which could charge the invading troops on horseback, fight them on the run to slow their progress, and then retreat to a second line of infantry and artillery that could face the main thrust of attack.

When Prince Joseph finally arrived at the front on May 11, he broke up the Polish army into three divisions. Each was expected to defend a different border crossing against separate Russian divisions that would greatly outnumber them.

Kosciuszko said that this was a mistake and wrote to the prince that the Poles should fight as a tightly knit coordinated unit, because "each one of these Russian divisions is as large as the entire Polish Army." For the sake of morale, the experienced rebel told the prince that "the best way for an inexperienced army to acquire bravery" is to get the first victory under its belt by beating one of the Russian divisions before they knew what hit them.[4] Then the Poles could string together a number of smaller victories, rather than taking on the entire Russian army at once. The prince replied that this was not possible because the Poles had no reserves.

On May 18, 1792, a Russian army of 98,000 battle-hardened veterans of the war with Turkey began pouring over the Dnieper River and into Poland. It was twice the size of the Polish army and three times the size of the actual Polish fighting forces at the front. In the north the czarina's troops easily captured Lithuania. On the southern front in Ukraine, Prince Joseph and Kosciuszko's army of about 17,000 men were attacked on three sides by Russian general Mikhail Kachowski's army of 64,000 soldiers. Alongside the Russians were Cossack tribesman, adroit horsemen who rode across the Ukrainian steppes in baggy pants, sheepskin hats and fur vests.[5]

The Poles were forced to retreat, and just as he had been during the American escape from the British at Fort Ticonderoga, Kosciuszko was put in charge of covering the rear, sabotaging the enemy's pursuit and knocking down bridges so the army could get away. Over the next month the cautious defensive war that Prince Joseph was fighting had lost much of Poland's Ukrainian territory to the Russians.

One of the officers under Kosciuszko's command was Prince Joseph Lubomirski, who had married his great love, Louise. His brother, Michael Lubomirski, was in charge of the gunpowder and ammunition reserves that the king sent from Warsaw to the eastern town of Dubno.[6] The Lubomirski brothers had risen through the military's chain of command not through their talent as officers but through the nobility's old-boy network of backscratching and bribery.

The king was planning to visit the Lubomirskis and their troops at Dubno to personally deliver the new uniforms, provisions, and ammunition, but canceled his trip over concerns that he would not be able to find "decent cuisine" at the front.[7]

While Stanislaw was worried about fancy feasts, Kosciuszko had to figure out how to put boots on the feet and bread in the bellies of his troops. The army's quartermasters were not delivering wheat to his hungry troops. Kosciuszko wrote in his report on the campaign: "They did not deliver uniforms for the whole army, tents, provisions or other equipment even though they were warned" that supplies were running out.[8]

General Prince Joseph was pulling his regiment farther back into Poland and ordered Michael to meet him near the town of Zielence. Kosciuszko had covered the army's southern flank, but one regiment of the Russian army, led by Gen. Arkadi Markov, raced forward so quickly that it overshot its supply line across the middle of the front and came face-to-face with Prince Joseph's troops.

Markov's unit had chased the Poles through a swamp and ended up in a valley between two small hills. The Russian cannons opened fire on the Poles, and one of their units ransacked and burned the village of Zielence. After several hours of artillery exchanges and cavalry skirmishes, about one thousand Poles were dead, but twice as many Russians were killed. The Poles came out on top and even captured one of the enemy's flags. Markov ran away over a hill, but rather than pursuing the Russians and finishing them off, Prince Joseph allowed them to escape.

Once again Prince Joseph moved his army back.

Kosciuszko was holding off Russian divisions to the south of the main battle. He was frustrated that the Poles were once again retreating and complained that Prince Joseph had missed an opportunity to "capture 8,000 of the Russian army's best soldiers."[9]

The Poles had bloodied the czarina's troops so badly at Zielence that the Russians had to rest for ten days to regroup. Prince Joseph sent the captured banner of the enemy to his uncle Stanislaw in Warsaw and decided to make a stand on the Bug River. Seeking to justify the choice of his young nephew Pepi as commander of the army, the king hailed the Battle of Zielence as a great victory, and even created a new Medal of Military Virtue, or the *Virtuti Militari*, to honor the prince. Given that the Battle of Zielence was another step backward for the Poles, the honorifics were premature.

Most of the soldiers had been wearing the same uniforms for more than a year. Many of their jackets were ragged and their shoes worn out. With all the marching and riding he had done, even the soles of Kosciuszko's boots had worn all the way through, exposing his bare feet. At one point the army did get a shipment to help them get their minds off their hunger and defeats. Prince Joseph provided each soldier with three small packages of tobacco, and their worries temporarily went up in smoke.[10]

The retreating army got by as best as it could. The infantry usually slept in the woods or the fields, and one morning Kosciuszko gave commendations to three officers who managed to purchase food for his troops. Some days the soldiers were lucky enough to stumble upon a *karczma*, an old Polish tavern that served platters of meat and kielbasa, and tankards of ale or mead. One night they camped out near a brewery. But there was never enough to satisfy a hungry army of thousands.[11]

Some of the starving soldiers tried to run away. The penalty for desertion was execution, but often captured runaways were pardoned. And despite the frequent cannon fire from the Russians, even on the run they managed to hold religious processions or even put up a tent so a priest could say mass on Sundays.

Unable to hold off the invaders, Prince Joseph kept retreating deeper and deeper into Poland. He moved his army closer to the town of Dubno to collect the gunpowder the king had sent him. The prince wrote to Stanislaw, "Every step backwards my heart is breaking, and God knows that I am not hallucinating."[12]

Joseph would suffer even greater heart palpitations and delusions when his army tried to pick up the supplies at the Dubno storage facilities.

On July 1 Kosciuszko wrote in his journal: "Part of our arsenal is in Dubno, including uniforms and coats for our entire standing army. Prince Michael [Lubomirski] ordered them to be hidden in his palace and promises that the Muscovites won't take it."[13]

Lubomirski was lying. He had secretly defected to the enemy and stashed away the contents of the ammunition depot. Hoping to curry favor with the czarina, Lubomirski shipped the gunpowder to the Russians.[14]

Kosciuszko was furious. First Joseph Lubomirski had caused his greatest heartache by taking away his woman and marrying Louise. Now the brother, Michael Lubomirski, had stabbed his army in the heart by stealing their ammunition, provisions, and even their shoes.

"Dubno represented hope for the soldiers that they would be able to rest comfortably," Kosciuszko wrote. "In Dubno the soldiers expected to rest and be supplied with shoes that they lacked, along with their meals, their victuals that had been promised to them by the king himself." Instead, he added, "The ammunition was imprudently taken piecemeal across the border to Austria, and the Dubienka magazines plundered and given to the Muscovites. This great loss must never be forgotten by zealous citizens."[15]

The nearly barefoot general had counted on picking up a pair of boots in Dubno, but all the new footwear was given to the Russians. Russian ambassador Bulgakov and Prussian ambassador Lucchesini were becoming increasingly belligerent with Stanislaw in Warsaw, and the king was afraid to leave the capital to rally the troops. In fact, at one point, they even threatened that if Stanislaw left Warsaw, they would publicly announce that the king had abdicated.

Felix Lubienski, one of the Patriot Seym delegates, took it on himself to travel to the war zone to see how the troops were faring. Lubienski was shocked when he noticed Kosciuszko's feet sticking through the bottom of his boot leather and gave the rebel a pair of his own boots.

King Stanislaw could not admit that the Poles were losing because of his own failure to put the right people in charge of the army. On July 14 he wrote to his minister in London: "The condition of our army has fallen so terribly due to mismanagement of the storehouses, that they are hungry and lacking uniforms and boots, to such a state that even our excellent Kosciuszko, had to accept a cherished present, a pair of shoes from Lubienski." Stanislaw was in denial about Michael Lubomirski, claiming the supplies were mishandled, saying, "I don't think it was treason."[16]

Eventually, Prince Joseph relieved Lubomirski of his command.

The king had bungled the war from the beginning. Unbeknownst to the other generals, Stanislaw had ordered Prince Joseph to protect the line of communication with Warsaw at all costs. It was better to retreat than fight to the finish. After all, someone had to protect the king and the capital.

Because his unit covered the rear, Kosciuszko's men were usually closest to the enemy. His soldiers, and even the Russians, noticed his fearlessness. After a battle in a town called Wlodzimierz, one eyewitness said, "I was at the front line of the infantry with Kosciuszko. The Russians have a real appetite to get him. Several of our horses were standing next to each other when they started firing twelve-pound artillery directly at us. Ten steps away from us, a shell landed, wounding an artilleryman. Kosciuszko is an uncommon person, it's as if he was promenading under fire, judicious, brave, beloved and respected by his own men, and the enemy."[17]

The Bug River was the last natural boundary the Poles could take advantage of before the enemy would have a straight march on the capital, about 150 miles away. It was the traditional boundary line between Roman Catholic and Christian Orthodox populations, and the Poles could expect help from the noblemen and peasants behind them.

Kosciuszko was ordered by Prince Joseph to make a last stand near Dubienka, a small farming town on the river. With a much larger Russian army heading for Dubienka, it was considered a suicide mission. There were many deserters.

The architect of West Point had relied on his military engineers during much of the campaign until this point, and he gave them advice on how to improve their work. But with the battle of his life upon him, Kosciuszko rode along the river to scout out positions to use to his advantage. He was to hold a three-mile stretch between the Russian army approaching from the east, and the Austrian border to his south. He picked a spot just above the town, where a slight incline would favor the Poles. The river was on his left flank, and a thick forest was to the right, leaving marshy bogs in the path of the enemy planning to attack him.

The Polish forces under Kosciuszko's command numbered 5,300. He sent out scouts to spy on the approaching army. They came back with news that Russian general Kachowski was marching on their position with an army of 25,000.

They were also outnumbered in firepower. Kosciuszko's division had two twelve-pound cannons, half a dozen six-pound artillery pieces, and two mortars. The Russians were rolling up fifty-six cannons, some as big as twenty-pounders.[18]

Controlling the bridge over the river was crucial so that the Russians could not cross with their artillery. A few days before the battle, Kosciuszko saw about seventy Cossack horsemen riding along the other side of the river, so he ordered "the supports for the bridge to be filled with flammable material and greased with tar" and that it be set on fire before the Russians could cross.[19] He had his men dig trenches and put up batteries with mounted artillery. They set underwater booby traps of iron thorns and pikes in the shallow fords where the enemy would try to wade through the river. Teams of riflemen with bayonets were situated in strategic places.

At three o'clock in the afternoon on July 18, 1792, General Kachowski's army appeared before Kosciuszko's position. The Russians rolled out pontoons to cross the river where the Poles had burned down the bridge. Kachowski unleashed three columns from his massive infantry directly at the Polish position above Dubienka. An hour later the Russian cannons began bombarding the Poles from two sides.

The Russian infantry ran toward Kosciuszko's well-fortified positions, but hundreds of them got caught in the deep muck along the river and were slain by grapeshot fired from the cannons. They were sitting ducks. But they kept coming.

A cavalry charge led by Russian colonel Palembach galloped right up to the Polish batteries. The dragoons hurtled up the hill, and the first wave was torn to shreds by clusters of cast-iron grapeshot balls. The second wave ran right into a sea of bayonets. Palembach was killed, and his men were driven back in hand-to-hand combat.

"At the head of the cavalry," Kosciuszko wrote in his battle report, "was a very brave soldier, who hit the battery, but was killed and his command almost returned. The Muscovite infantry tried three times to move us from our place."[20]

After five hours of intense bloodshed, the Polish army had held their ground. The Russians could not take Kosciuszko's position, and four thousand of the czarina's troops were strewn dead on the battlefield or floating in the river. The Polish battalion had lost nine hundred men under the barrage of heavy cannon fire. Yet even with all their casualties, the invaders kept coming.

"It was not until the Palembach attack that Kosciuszko began to think about retreat," wrote Lieutenant Bukar, who fought at Dubienka. "They were trying to flank us with larger forces."[21]

As night fell Kosciuszko noticed that thousands of Russians were crossing into Austria just south of the Polish position. It was clear that they were trying to surround Kosciuszko's army. Despite the heavy losses in the enemy's divisions, they still had four times as many men as the Poles.

Kosciuszko knew that he could not hold Dubienka. If the road were cut off to the west, the Poles would run out of ammunition and provisions, which they were already short on. Kosciuszko was not willing to let his men be slaughtered. Under cover of darkness, he began an orderly withdrawal. The Russians quickly began burying their dead in mass graves to hide the magnitude of their casualties.

A few days earlier, in Warsaw, Niemcewicz left behind his work at the Seym, dusted off his old uniform from the royal cadet academy, and went to see Stanislaw.

"He was wearing a white robe, and had thick gray curls rolling down onto his shoulders," Niemcewicz recalled about his meeting with the king. "He looked heavily depressed and uneasy. His face was very pale and he probably would have squeezed out a few tears, if not for the attention that his own weakness was at fault for this sad position." The king gave Niemcewicz a package to take to the front for Prince Joseph, and said, "Tell him that I will soon rush to the camp."[22]

Niemcewicz took a small postal carriage and drove it to Prince Joseph's camp near the Bug River, where he found the top officers sniping at one another. There was intense shooting all along the Bug for several days. When Niemcewicz learned that Kosciuszko could not hold back the huge Russian army, he caught up with the retreating troops in a small town called Kumow. Many of the horses were so beat up with gashes and bullet wounds that they had to be put down.

Prince Joseph's division to the north also pulled back, and the various Polish divisions headed toward the city of Chelm to regroup. Word spread quickly that Kosciuszko had given the czarina's army a thrashing at the Battle of Dubienka, and his reputation skyrocketed. This made Prince Joseph's general staff, which was selected through nepotism, jealous of Kosciuszko's new fame, and they began grumbling over his retreat and tried to blame him for losing the war. But the reality overshadowed the controversy: More Russian invaders were killed at the Battle of Dubienka than at any other point in the war.

In his official report on the battle, Russian general Kachowski wrote to St. Petersburg: "I must stress that the enemy soldier fought with extreme persistence, skill and doggedness." He added that Kosciuszko's "extraordinary sound choice of position, by all measures made our mission difficult . . . after a month of actions with the Polish armies, this is the first time that I have stood against an adversary working in great unison with such a passionate plan to repulse our attacks and stubbornly defend themselves, which explains the great number of losses in our detachments."[23]

King Stanislaw also acknowledged Kosciuszko's achievement and awarded him and his officers with the *Virtuti Militari*. Even Prince Joseph, who disagreed with Kosciuszko over the battle preparations, filed a report admitting that it was "the good and foresighted disposition of General Kosciuszko that our retreat was unbroken, orderly and continuous, while the enemy, which sustained losses, especially to their cavalry and Cossacks, had to pull back, before they were able to cut us off at the Bug River, or injure us as we crossed."[24]

Yet by the end of the campaign Kosciuszko felt that King Stanislaw had duped him into fighting a pointless defensive war simply to protect Warsaw, while leaving the rest of Poland at the mercy of the Russians.

In his notebook after the campaign, Kosciuszko wrote: "All of this made it clear to the soldiers that in the king's mind, his plan was for the army to constantly retreat. It appears to be resonating that he put the army at risk and exposed the citizens to the revenge and plunder of the panting enemy. Others understood that the king had a deal with the enemy which insured the loss of the fatherland, while he sat calmly in his walled-in bathroom."[25]

Until then Kosciuszko had been convinced that the victories over the Russians in the swamps at Zielence and Dubienka would be the turning point of the war, just as the Battle of Saratoga had changed the course of the American Revolution.

But King Stanislaw was starting to feel the heat. He had written to the czarina proposing a truce. She was enraged over the thousands of Russian soldiers that she had already lost in the war. On July 21 he received his response from Catherine the Great. It was an ultimatum demanding that he, and his entire army, accede to the Targowica confederation or suffer the consequences. On July 23 the king buckled and signed the papers joining the Targowica traitors.

When the news broke, crowds in Warsaw splashed walls with graffiti criticizing the king and smashed windows in the homes of his supporters. A drunken nobleman climbed onstage at the National Theater and offered to give his estate to anyone who would assassinate the king.[26]

Even Stanislaw's beloved nephew Pepi was disgraced by the surrender. Prince Joseph wrote to the king, speaking for all his comrades at the front, condemning the "sordidness of lowering yourself to the traitors of our fatherland which would be the death of us. These are the feelings your Majesty . . . that I am honored to deliver."[27]

Prince Joseph was informed of the king's submission to the Targowica confederation by Princess Isabella, so along with Kosciuszko and several other officers, he raced to the Czartoryski Palace in Pulawy, the center of Poland's opposition movement. The former head of the military academy, Prince Adam Czartoryski, was in Vienna, desperately trying to persuade Austria to support the Poles, and Princess Isabella became a mentor to her husband's former royal cadets.

It had been two decades since Casimir Pulaski and the Bar confederates tried to kidnap King Stanislaw and persuade him to join the reformers. Princess Isabella told the new generation of patriotic Polish officers gathered in her palace that it was time to dust off the old plan, drag the king to their camp, and bring him to his senses.[28] It is not clear if the officers realized that Isabella and Stanislaw were once lovers, but after considering the abduction plan, Prince Joseph decided not to challenge his uncle.

The other officers even offered to make Joseph dictator of Poland if only he would keep up the fight for independence, but it was all for naught. The Prussian and Austrian monarchs also opposed the radical notions of liberty and democratic reforms hatched on their doorstep, and were threatening to invade Poland themselves. King Stanislaw wrote letters to the prince explaining that they had no choice. The king ordered his troops to surrender to General Kachowski.

Kosciuszko escorted Prince Joseph to the cease-fire meeting at the Russian camp. Afterward, in a letter to Princess Isabella, he wrote that he was unimpressed with their officers: "After shaking hands, I thought, how easy it would be to beat them, if our country had the energy and sense of its own freedom and the real enthusiasm of its citizenry. I left disgusted, with tears in my eyes."[29]

The rest of the Polish army crossed the Wisla River and spent a few days in Pulawy in limbo. The entire military was disgusted with the king, and they had nowhere to turn. On July 30, 1792, Kosciuszko wrote to the king: "Your royal highness. As the situation of the nation contradicts the oath which I have taken and my internal convictions, I honorably request that your highness kindly sign my resignation."[30]

Twenty officers submitted their resignations along with Kosciuszko, and soon another two hundred followed. "My God! Why won't Thou give us the means of rooting out the brood of adversaries of the nation's happiness," Kosciuszko wrote to Isabella, adding, "I shudder to think what end may befall our country."[31]

Kosciuszko and his adjutant, Maj. Stanislaw Fiszer, traveled to Warsaw for a meeting at the king's palace in the Lazienki Gardens to personally hand Stanislaw their resignations. The king pleaded with him not to resign, but the hero of Dubienka reiterated that he could not serve under a government run by the Targowica traitors.

Stanislaw often used sexual pawns to persuade his friends and adversaries, and as he knew of Kosciuszko's loneliness and weakness for women, the king asked young socialites to coax the rebel into continuing his service in the military.

Fiszer described how one by one, King Stanislaw sent his female allies to try to persuade Kosciuszko not to resign. Ladies Zamoyska, Branicka, Potocka, and Grabowska, all dames of the aristocracy, tried to charm and beguile Kosciuszko into serving under the new regime. It was no use. Kosciuszko would not budge on his principles and was even offended by the king's gesture.[32]

"The king has strongly insisted, sought to persuade, cajoled and finally sent ladies known to be in relationships with him, to convince us not abandon him and tender our resignation," Kosciuszko wrote to Princess Isabella about his meeting at the palace. "But I always unwaveringly replied, and shot down all arguments, that sometimes he was even embarrassed to reply. Finally, with tears in my eyes, I told him that we earned the consideration, fighting for our country, that his royal highness should never make us go against our principles and our honor."[33]

Stanislaw asked Kosciuszko to at least have dinner at the royal castle. Once he was there the king signed a proclamation promoting him to the rank of lieutenant general. Over the next several days Stanislaw met with his former general several times and Kosciuszko gave the king his opinion on which of the remaining officers were loyal to Poland and deserved to be promoted to fill the void left by the two hundred officers who had resigned.

On August 5, Kosciuszko and Fiszer stared out the windows of the royal castle and watched as the Russian army marched along the opposite riverbank and pitched camp in the waterfront neighborhood, Praga.[34] Kosciuszko agreed to stay on temporarily to keep order among the troops until a replacement could be found. As the Targowica traitors slinked into Warsaw, the next day Kosciuszko left the capital to say farewell to his beaten troops and lift their morale.

The demoralized Polish army was camped not far from the Czartoryski Palace at Pulawy, where Kosciuszko learned from his forlorn officers that one of the Targowica leaders, Felix Potocki, had threatened to demote and discharge any officers caught wearing the *Virtuti Militari* awarded during the war against Russia.

As the army's provisional commander, Kosciuszko fired off a letter to Potocki. "If this ban takes effect," he wrote, "I will go to the New World, my second fatherland to which I have earned a right by fighting for her independence. Once there, I shall beseech Providence, for a stable, free and good government in Poland, for the independence of our nation, for its virtuous, enlightened and free citizens."[35]

The Polish soldiers ripped the citations from their chests and sent the blue ribbons to Princess Isabella's palace so that the women of Pulawy could decorate their hair with patriotic ponytails.

Potocki replied to Kosciuszko that the king had no right to hand out "illegal medals," because the government run by the aristocracy had never agreed to decorate veterans of "a war fought against the Polish Republic." And while, "Sir, you valiantly fought in America, you were backed by foreign troops from France, and if you fought against the French, you would have never received the Order of the Cincinnati."[36] With twisted logic the Targowica ringleader added that liberties granted by Catherine the Great surpassed those won by the American colonies.

Ironically, while Potocki was using the French to poke Kosciuszko in the eye, the French Legislative Assembly had just voted to give Kosciuszko the distinction of "Honorary Citizen of France." He was one of eighteen people, along with the likes of George Washington, James Madison, Alexander Hamilton, Thomas

Paine, and others who were praised for serving the cause of liberty. As only citizens could vote in Europe, the French revolutionaries bestowed the title of "Citizen" on all the activists.

Newspapers throughout Poland praised Kosciuszko. On September 26 *The Warsaw Correspondent* reported that, "His honor made it to Praga to visit the sick soldiers wounded in the war." The next day the paper wrote, "Lt. General Kosciuszko, by visiting the wounded, sweetened their bitter state with kind words and deep interest in their health conditions, which for many was the very gesture that they needed to hear to help them recover."[37]

The Leyden *Gazette* "praised Kosciuszko's courage to the heavens."[38] However, the tribute from the democratic "mob" in Paris was just the excuse his enemies needed to paint him as a radical. The Russian czarina used the certification of Kosciuszko as a French citizen to designate him a dangerous Jacobin.

The rebel leader had become a national icon whose popularity was growing among all of Poland's classes. This made him persona non grata for the new regime. In Warsaw, Kosciuszko stayed at the Czartoryski's "Blue Palace," and crowds peered into the windows to try to catch a glimpse of the legendary war hero.

With his future unclear, Kosciuszko sent his belongings to his sister Anna, writing, "I am sending my horses and things, if you can find room for them. The horses you can sell, all of them except for the one chestnut, which I would like to keep. I might come see you this winter."[39]

Kosciuszko turned down something he had always lacked—a comfortable living with a hefty salary as lieutenant general, and status as a member of the aristocracy. He joked that he would rather work as a gardener among the hedges of the sprawling Czartoryski Palace. He also declined a gift from a rich widow who wanted to present him with a plantation where the serfs raked in substantial farm revenues. His refusal to accept the offers only enhanced his reputation.

Still hopeful that he could somehow serve his country, Kosciuszko wrote to Isabella: "My Princess, be assured of my heart, my mind, citizenship, allegiance, affection and appreciation. . . . I was faithful to the fatherland, I fought for it, and I would sacrifice my life a hundred times for it. But I think that the end of my service is near and that maybe this uniform that I wear, will be a mark of dishonor. . . . I bid farewell to the princess, who all adore for her virtue and devotion, I kiss her hands, which have wiped away the tears that I wept for the country. I ask, that you all remember me."[40]

After turning in his general's uniform, Kosciuszko signed over his Lithuanian estate to his sister Anna. He had thought that he could fight to end feudalism, and that Poland would free the serfs. As this was not the case, he tried to set an example by doing it on his own. He loosened the corvée of the peasants farming his land to two days a week, so that they would at least pay for the use of the property. He allowed them to work for themselves the rest of the time and totally abolished forced labor for women.

"Permit me, my Sister, to hug you, and because this may be the last time that I can ensure that you should know my will, I bequeath to you my Siechnowicze," he wrote to Anna. "However under one condition . . . the peasants from every house in the whole estate shall not be required to do more than two days of forced labor for the men, and for the women none at all. If this were another country where the government could ensure my will, I would free them entirely, but in this country, we must do what we are sure that we can to relieve humanity in any way, and always remember that by nature, we are all equals, that riches and education constitute the only difference."[41]

Most Poles could not believe that the constitution passed by the Seym and ratified in local elections could be wiped out by a handful of traitors. Kosciuszko came to personify the independence movement, and crowds thronged to see their hero when he visited friends in southern Poland.

Prince Adam Czartoryski and his wife, Princess Isabella, were taking a tour of their holdings in Galicia, a territory captured by Austria during the first partition of Poland. Czartoryski was thinking about spending a year or two in Pisa, Italy, and wrote to Mazzei, who had retired there, asking what it would cost to lodge his family and an entourage of about twenty people who could meet to discuss Poland's future.[42]

Czartoryski invited Kosciuszko to his palace in Sieniawa, ostensibly for a "name day" party to celebrate the feast of Saint Thaddeus on October 28, 1792. Kosciuszko and his longtime mentor had a teary reunion as former military officers and democratic noblemen from around Poland traveled to attend the party. As Sieniawa was in Galicia, not all the Patriots were welcome in the region. Those who could not attend sent letters of praise that were read aloud before the honored guests.

The Austrian police kept a close eye on the gathering of rebellious aristocrats. They were worried because the Poles called Kosciuszko the greatest Polish hero since King John Sobieski, whose Hussar Knights rescued Christian Europe from Kara Mustafa's Ottoman invasion during the Battle of Vienna.

Kosciuszko was lauded and greeted by women in white dresses adorned with black and azure blue sashes. Some tied their curly locks with the ribbons from the banned war medals. They placed a crown on Kosciuszko's head that was made of branches and leaves from an oak tree planted one hundred years earlier by King Sobieski.

Princess Isabella built up Kosciuszko's reputation as much as she could and even toyed with the idea of having him marry her daughter Sofia. But the famous general was pulled in all directions by various ladies of the nobility, which he began to view as a distraction from his mission. Another Czartoryski daughter, Maria, sketched a portrait of Kosciuszko with an inscription underneath that read: "Tadeusz Kosciuszko. Good and courageous, but unhappy."[43]

The revelers sang songs and read poetry written specially for the occasion. These cult-worshiping pieces of propaganda about Kosciuszko would soon be leaked to the press and disseminated throughout the country. Poland's underground reformers needed a chivalrous figure behind whom the nation could rally. They had found their man.

While Austrian and Russian spies followed Kosciuszko's every move in southern Poland, the real planning for the coming rebellion was taking place nearly five hundred miles away in Dresden and Leipzig, in Saxon Germany. That's where Kollontay and the other Patriots who fled Warsaw were conspiring to resuscitate the revolution.

After a few days at the Czartoryski's Sieniawa palace, Kosciuszko visited Lwow, one of Poland's largest cities before the Austrian Empire annexed it and renamed it Lemberg. The population was still mostly Polish, and Kosciuszko's arrival nearly caused a riot. Women threw themselves at him and began ripping buttons off his clothes and cutting off locks of his hair as souvenirs. Artists penciled his silhouette, portraying his upturned pointy nose, and the sketches sold like hotcakes.[44]

The *Warsaw Correspondent* sent a reporter to Lwow to cover Kosciuszko's trip, and dispatches were sent back to the Polish capital.

After ten intense days of parties in Lwow, Kosciuszko was invited to Zamosc, a Renaissance town, where once again a possible love interest emerged in his life. But this time, rather than the parents objecting to him seeing their daughter, it was a priest.

Rev. Stanislaw Staszic was one of the political writers whose essays in the 1780s helped spark the Polish Revolution. In Zamosc, Staszic worked as a tutor for the aristocratic Zamoyski family that owned the town. When Constance Zamoyska offered to give her daughter Anna's hand to the general, even though it had been promised to the son of a prince, the smitten maiden was ecstatic about the idea of being married to a hero.

But Rev. Staszic convinced the mother that Anna was better off marrying the rich prince than an unemployed, impoverished former general.[45] It appears that Kosciuszko was not heartbroken by yet another lost chance at love, because, as Anna's son later recalled in his memoirs, "Kosciuszko always recalled his first love, Hetman Sosnowski's daughter [Louise], and he did not want to think about other relationships."[46]

The Russians trailed Kosciuszko wherever he went and spread rumors about his disloyalty to the republic. Some of the myths were so outlandish that even the lookouts became paranoid and superstitious.

When he took a side trip from Zamosc to a small village near the Polish border, a Russian colonel called for a full alert, ordering his unit to be ready to move in case the rebel tried anything. That night a Russian guard began shooting into the darkness, and the entire regiment stormed out of the barracks with their rifles locked and loaded. When an officer asked the spooked sentry what he was shooting at, the dimwit replied that Kosciuszko had appeared before him, but when he tried to shoot him he eerily turned himself into a cat and darted into the black of night.[47]

The rebel's presence in the annexed Polish territory of Galicia concerned the Austrians greatly, and the Russians did not want him to come back to Poland. In Zamosc, Rev. Staszic gave Kosciuszko a tour of the city's baroque architectural splendors. The rebel and the priest debated politics and the best way to save Poland as they strolled down the cobblestone streets. Staszic argued that a constitutional monarchy was best for Poland, while Kosciuszko favored a republic, similar to that of the United States.[48]

The pragmatic Staszic respected Kosciuszko but thought that Poland needed someone more like Gen. Lucius Sulla, a tyrant who became dictator of the Roman Empire thanks to his strong spirit, which was half fox and half lion. In his sixteenth-century work *The Prince*, Machiavelli praised this combination because a lion cannot defend himself against snares, while a fox cannot defend himself against wolves.

Staszic commented about Kosciuszko, "This is a man who is righteous and brave, but he knows little about Poland, and even less about Europe. He wants to be the head of the army like Washington, but that won't save Poland; we need someone like Sulla."[49]

To take on Catherine the Great and her Machiavellian allies, Kosciuszko would have to transform himself into a prince like Sulla, half fox and half lion.

After tailing him for a month, the Austrians could not figure out what Kosciuszko was up to. The government in Vienna offered him a position in their army, but he declined it. Finally, after the officers shadowing him filed a report about his travels, Austrian general Dagobert-Sigismond de Wurmser issued an order giving Kosciuszko twelve hours to leave the country.

The *Warsaw Correspondent* reported the Austrian government's excuse: "The acknowledgement of the title of French citizenship from the National Assembly, with whom we are at war, and his refusal to enter our service, and above all, the impression made by the mob, the crowds following Mr. Kosciuszko in Lwow wherever he showed himself, would be enough reason for our government to deport him from this country."[50]

Worried about revenge, the Patriots began their exodus from Warsaw the same night that King Stanislaw signed the Targowica confederation. Kollontay, Piattoli, Ignacy Potocki, and dozens of other reformers left Poland, fanning out across Europe to find allies for their cause.

The czarina, increasingly impatient with Kosciuszko's growing fame, and fearing his power as a potential rallying point, had a warrant issued for his arrest. He had already left for Pulawy when he learned that the Russians had also set up a secret operations office to open all the mail sent by and delivered to the Patriots. He said his good-byes to the Czartoryskis and chose a pseudonym for future correspondence: "Mister Baron Misery."[51]

From Leipzig and Dresden, where they were planning their next move, the émigrés looked to France for help. Paris had exploded into full-scale revolution. The French rebels called for all nations to rise up against ancient regimes run by monarchs. This led to war with Prussia and Austria, and the French National Convention proclaimed: "The Convention declares in the name of the French people that it grants fraternity and succor to all those nations who seek to recover their freedom, and orders its generals to defend those citizens who have suffered or may suffer in the cause of liberty."[52]

With the same goals, and the same enemies, the Poles saw the French as their natural allies. The Patriots were swept up by the revolutionary propaganda spilling out of Paris about a worldwide struggle and saw the French as their brothers-in-arms in the quest for *Liberté, Egalité, Fraternité*.

They needed someone to send to Paris to make a connection with the revolutionaries. As he had been named an honorary citizen of France, Kosciuszko was the perfect candidate. After a short stay in Krakow, he traveled to Leipzig in early January 1793 and met with the Patriots to discuss the goals of his mission to Paris. He told a group of Polish students in the Saxon city that for him living under occupation "would have been a life on the cross."[53]

The Patriots in Leipzig had a Frenchman in their inner circle. Pierre Parandier, a lawyer from Lyon who wrote to the French minister of interior, Jean-Marie Roland: "Citizen Minister! The entire hope of the Polish Patriots gathered here depends on your care for the fate of their savagely oppressed nation. . . . Their choice in Kosciuszko to represent them should please you. When Europe suffered from the pains of violence, Kosciuszko, as a young adult, yearned for freedom and learned in America what needs to be done. The simplicity of his soul, his resolute conduct, moderation, and pure feelings as a sensitive person are even more precious than the military skills he possesses."[54]

The French wanted the Poles to open a second front against Prussia in eastern Europe. The Poles in turn asked France to provide loans, guns, and naval support in the Baltic Sea against Russia. Both sides had unrealistic expectations of what the other could deliver to ignite a full-scale democratic revolution to rid the Continent of tyrannical monarchies.

"Citizen Kosciuszko" left Leipzig with a wish list from his countrymen for military assistance, and a memorandum that said: "A revolution in Poland would unleash a nation which, by its topographical position, its kindred spirit, customs and language, by the armed forces it could muster, would be the only one able to rapidly spread Republicanism through Russia, of planting and flowering the tree of liberty even in the ice of Petersburg."[55]

The mission to Paris was doomed even before he arrived. Prussia had vowed to restore the French monarchy, but while Kosciuszko was on the road to Paris, the revolutionary council tried King Louis XVI and condemned him to death for conspiring with the enemies of France to return him to the throne. Paris was in a complete state of chaos, and the French were in no position to help anyone.

Along the way Kosciuszko stopped in Belgium, where he met with French revolutionary general Charles Dumouriez, who was fighting the Prussians. Dumouriez was considered an ally of Poland ever since the 1770s, when he tried to help Pulaski and the Bar confederates to drive out the Russians, so Kosciuszko shared his secret plans for a French-Polish alliance. Unfortunately Dumouriez was about to defect to the enemy and spill the beans.[56]

Kosciuszko arrived in Paris just in time to witness one of the most infamous events in French history. On January 21 an angry mob had gathered in the Place de la Concorde, between the Champs-Élysées and the Tuileries Gardens, to see a new device built by Dr. Joseph-Ignace Guillotin. Louis XVI was led to a platform above the jeering crowd, and his head was locked into a yoke. A heavy sharp blade slid down and sliced off his head. With the blood still gushing from it, the severed head was lifted for all to see. The use of the French national razor would not stop with the king.

The situation in Warsaw was also bleak. Russia and Prussia carried out the second partition of Polish territory. Czarina Catherine carved out another chunk of Poland's eastern territory, and King Frederick William annexed Gdansk, Torun, and the region known as Greater Poland.

"I trust in God, that these whales will not eat Poland," Kollontay wrote, citing the Bible. "They'll have to cough it up, just like Jonah."[57]

The diplomatic effort to persuade the French to deliver more than just angry words against Russia was unrealistic, but since Kosciuszko was an honored French citizen, leading revolutionaries including Maximilien Robespierre welcomed meetings with him.[58] He also had several discussions with the revolutionary French foreign minister Pierre Lebrun, who wrote: "The French Republic is actively occupied with the great measures that may release this interesting nation [Poland] from the odious yoke that oppresses it. . . . Courage, energy, and perseverance, and Poland will be saved."[59]

Lebrun, originally a journalist from Belgium, believed that the French should pursue a foreign policy that encouraged the Czechs and Hungarians to rebel against the Austrian Empire, which had swallowed their nations, and to persuade Turkey to join with Poland in fighting against Russia.

Thomas Paine was also in Paris. He was so excited about the May 3 Constitution that he considered applying for Polish citizenship.[60] Paine's friend, the poet and diplomat Joel Barlow, wrote to King Stanisław expressing his "congratulations" and "admiration" for Poland's democratic reforms. Barlow was opposed to the enslavement of serfs, whether it be by the government or the church, and wrote: "The tyrannies of Europe, whether civil or ecclesiastical, are all aristocratical and feudal . . . [and] detestable."[61]

Barlow and Paine were disappointed about the eradication of the May 3 Constitution. Paine had also become disillusioned with the American and French Revolutions because he believed that they touted freedom only for the elite and wealthy classes, and because he spoke out against the execution of the king, the Jacobins tossed Paine into prison.

The French revolutionaries chided the Poles for not going far enough with their constitution. Kosciuszko agreed and told the French that the Polish Patriots were willing get rid of the aristocratic system and end serfdom. They were also willing "to abolish royal power" and to "abolish the higher clergy."[62]

It was a dangerous promise to make. The American Revolution resulted in a guarantee of freedom of religion, but the French revolutionaries were lashing out at the influence of the Catholic Church. The May 3 Polish Constitution had promised freedom of religion, but it codified Catholicism as the official state religion to persuade the church to support the reforms. Pledging to put an end to the influence of the aristocracy, royalty and clergy were playing with fire.

One day Kosciuszko was sipping coffee in the Café de la Rotonde with his friend Count Thaddeus Mostowski, when they heard that an artist named Gilles-Louis Chrétien was nearby in the Palais Royal working with a new invention, an engraving device called a physionotrace. Kosciuszko, an art school graduate, wanted to see the apparatus. After Chrétien made his first few strokes of Kosciuszko's profile, the Pole joked that it looked accurate, but with his long hair, he looked more like "a prince than a soldier."

Count Mostowski replied, "That's easily remedied. Because you will still be fighting for the nation, the general needs a sword in his hand." Chrétien handed Kosciuszko a sword that was standing in the corner of the room and asked him to hold it with both hands in front of his face. When the count was told that the new etching mechanism used a pantograph drawing aid to make a small copperplate from which numerous prints could be made, he said, "Because this image will make it to Poland, we need to engrave a slogan underneath it, 'God! Allow me to fight once again for the Fatherland!' "[63]

Prints of the rebel holding the sword were sent across Europe and into Poland to promote the coming battle. While Paris did much for his image, there was a noticeable shift in the atmosphere in the city. The Jacobins were fighting among themselves.

After months of negotiations with the rebels in Paris, Kosciuszko grew weary of the French Revolution, which had started out as a democratic movement but was degenerating into a quest for revenge. The Jacobins and Girondists were at one anothers' throats. The Polish rebel came to the conclusion that the French revolutionaries were only interested in how a Polish diversion would benefit their own cause. Citizen Kosciuszko left Paris empty handed.

After he left the Jacobins unleashed the Reign of Terror. Death lists were compiled of those deemed enemies of the Revolution, and the guillotine was used to murder thousands of French citizens. Blood was literally running through the streets of Paris, and even the battle-hardened veteran was disgusted by the reports of decapitations of civilians.

Catherine the Great began her own reign of terror in Warsaw. Her spy service arrested enemies and dragged them into the basement of the Russian Embassy on Miodowa Street near Poland's royal castle.[64] Those still supporting the constitution were sent to Siberia. Valuables were looted and sent to Russia, including sentimental items such as the chairs from the Senate chamber that were used by the Seym.

The exiled Polish Patriots in Leipzig and Dresden grew desperate to start an uprising to drive out the Russians. They had come to the realization that Kosciuszko was the only person who could rally the country. But Kosciuszko did not believe that they were ready for a battle on all fronts against Russia, Prussia, and Austria. He did not want to fight another quixotic war, and wrote a manuscript outlining the details and mistakes of the 1792 war in defense of the constitution.

Trying to persuade him to lead a rebellion, on July 18, 1793, Kollontay wrote to Kosciuszko: "What I write is felt by unhappy Polish soldiers, today who are asked to fight against Prussians, and they, glowing with bravery and courage only grumble, you don't have Kosciuszko! The truth cannot be destroyed by oppression, hide wherever you want, but the nation will not forget about you. . . . The nation still trusts you."[65]

The nation was in worse shape than ever. Catherine the Great was moving to make her conquest official. She ordered King Stanislaw to convene a session of the Seym in the Lithuanian town of Grodno. Coerced elections were held to seat a puppet legislature that abolished the May 3 Constitution and ceded Poland's eastern territories to Russia. Under threat of being sent to Siberia, delegates were forced to pass an "eternal alliance" with Russia, allowing the czarina to station troops in Poland, ban the *Virtuti Militari* medal, and prohibit any treaties without the czarina's consent.

Kollontay wrote in his diary: "In order to avoid the unfortunate pitfalls of the French Revolution, we agree that an insurrection in Poland should be led under the dictatorship of one man who could inspire universal trust. The whole nation was pointing to Kosciuszko."[66]

But stroking Kosciuszko's ego would not be enough. He needed an army, horses, and guns. During the summer of 1793 he spent time with Ignacy Potocki in Leipzig, and learned that an underground network had already been formed in Warsaw and Vilnius that was preparing for an uprising. At the end of August two messengers from the Polish underground arrived in Leipzig to ask Kosciuszko if he would take command of the uprising. They were planning to start fighting on November 19.

Gen. Joseph Zajaczek, who had fought alongside Prince Joseph in the war to defend the constitution, was laying the groundwork in Warsaw for the Polish army to turn on the Russians as soon as they were given the word. The underground was providing guns to four thousand Warsaw burghers who were forming an insurgency. Just as the French had stormed the Bastille for guns, the Poles were planning on breaking into the Russian armory in Warsaw. They naively asked when the French army would arrive.

"Citizen Kosciuszko" was not optimistic that they could rely on the French.

To see what the plotters had prepared for the uprising, in early September Kosciuszko sneaked across the border into Poland. Using the pseudonym "Milewski," he traveled to Wroclaw and the foothills of Krakow to meet with the rebels.[67] As he gauged the discussions about arms, finances, and persuading Turkey to join the fight against Russia, it was clear that more work needed to be done.

He was also concerned that the plan concentrated too much on the capital. "Warsaw is not all of Poland," he told them.[68] Kosciuszko stressed the scheme that worked in the American Revolution, reinforcing the army with local militias across the country that could be called up as reserves, and "Minutemen" who could be ready to fight at "a minute's notice." He set conditions to be met before he would lead the revolt. "In every county, one citizen, who should be elected locally to take on the role of major general who will secretly gather people to the insurrection," Kosciuszko wrote.[69]

Charles Wojda, an administrator on the revolutionary council, wrote in his memoirs: "Kosciuszko's greatest wish was to return Poland to its former borders and to reinstate the May 3 Constitution; and then, if he could, to depart from it in the future to form a government similar to the one in America. Already the organization of the National Council was to mimic the actions of the American Revolution."[70]

Although he would not admit it publicly, Wojda said, Kosciuszko's "conduct toward this goal" was no secret to anyone.

The general pointed out that in 1792 Poland was invaded by one hundred thousand Russian troops. This time, he said, Prussian troops would march in from the west and the north, and Austria might attack from the south. The Poles needed at least one hundred thousand troops to start the uprising, and twice that once the fighting started. The Polish Army had only 52,000 soldiers when the war ended in 1792. Half of those were in the Ukraine, which was annexed by Russia, and the Grodno Seym had just reduced the size of the remaining forces to 14,500.[71] There was no guarantee that all those soldiers would join the insurrection.

Kosciuszko argued that they would need to empower an untapped resource—the peasants. He urged the plotters to work harder on persuading France, Sweden, and Turkey to join the fight against Russia because it had infringed on the interests of those nations.

One of those present, Pawlikowski, was convinced that the aristocrats and burghers would throw their support behind the revolution. Kosciuszko expressed doubts. When the discussion turned to the political system they would install after they won, the revolutionaries expressed a consensus that the new government should grant even more freedoms than those outlined in the May 3 Constitution.

Pawlikowski asked Kosciuszko his opinion. Kosciuszko took him by the hand and said, "I will not fight *only* for the nobility. I want freedom for the entire nation, and only for them will I risk my life."[72]

The current plan put all their lives at risk because the insurgents did not have enough troops, ammunition, or resources at their disposal. This became even more obvious after General Zajaczek sent a letter stating that Warsaw was not ready to begin the uprising. The organizers promised Kosciuszko that they would continue the preparations, and they all agreed to put off the insurrection for a few months. And apparently the secret meeting of the rebels near Krakow was no secret to the Russians, because czarist dragoons were sent to search the hills.[73]

Kosciuszko was once again on the lam, in search of allies. The rebel leader, who took a liking to Pawlikowski, confided in him that he was headed to Pisa.

In October he arrived in Italy, where he found Niemcewicz camped out in Florence writing a satire called *The Targowica Bible*, which parodied the political situation in Poland. Niemcewicz ran into many Poles in exile in Italy, but was surprised to see Kosciuszko.

"They want me to be the commander," Kosciuszko told him, "but until I see that we can afford to start, and then maintain ourselves, I don't want to bring any more unhappiness on myself or on the nation."[74]

The two friends spent time catching up, and two days later Kosciuszko left for a secret trip to Rome. But first he stopped in Pisa, an Italian university town where another faction of exiled Poles was meeting.

Kosciuszko ran into Mazzei after he checked in to the Locanda dell'Ussero, a famous inn where many of the Polish Patriots were staying. Mazzei was upset about the situation in Poland, and Kosciuszko told him that he still wanted to fight for his homeland but did not want to be seen as a "mercenary." His Italian friend suggested that he could go back to America, "where a large tract of land was due him for his contribution, as a general, to the establishment of independence."[75]

The Polish rebel considered the idea and even spoke with Mazzei about which ports he could sail from back to America. But instead Kosciuszko chose to travel down to Rome to see if he could figure out another way to serve his country.

One night Niemcewicz was in his room reading Machiavelli's *History of Florence,* under the light of an oil lamp when he heard the door creak open and a voice in Polish say, "Praise the Lord Jesus Christ. How are you brother?"

It was an old friend from the Seym, Constantine Jelski from Lithuania. The two compatriots hugged, and Niemcewicz asked, "What are you doing here?"

"I have come for you, and Kosciuszko," Jelski replied. "We're getting ready to start the revolution."[76]

Jelski and Maj. Antoni Guszkowski were sent to escort Kosciuszko back to Poland. They tracked down their leader in Rome, but he was not pleased by the visit. Kosciuszko had been secretly lobbying the Vatican to help Poland. He made friends in Vatican hierarchy and nearly became head of the Pope's army, but conservative cardinals viewed his participation in the American Revolution as too radical.[77]

Kosciuszko was angry that Jelski and Guszkowski had blown his cover in Rome and that the rebels had failed to make any progress in planning the revolt. He could not return to Poland before the fighting started because he was a wanted man and would be arrested immediately. He sent instructions to the underground leaders that said: "Such a praiseworthy goal, to lift up the nation from the yoke of slavery, among the most difficult obstacles must be well thought out, and not carried out in the haste of public spirit, but with cold reason, considering everything, so as not to endanger the country with even greater doom than before."[78]

The plotters had yet to make enough progress raising troops, and Kosciuszko demanded that unless they guaranteed one hundred thousand soldiers, the battle would be pointless. He asked them to send him a list showing the number of people and guns, and the amounts of ammunition and provisions, that they had at their disposal, as well as the number of enemy soldiers and garrisons stationed in Poland.

He promised that he would return to Saxony to meet with the exiled political leaders only after he received the information that he needed to reassess the situation.

In early February 1794 a barrister from Warsaw named Francis Barss arrived in Paris as the representative of the Polish revolutionaries. He was once again trying to form an alliance with France, and presented a memorial to the French foreign minister saying that "a revolutionary army" had been formed in Poland under the leadership of Kosciuszko to restore independence. This revolution would have a different character than the war in defense of the May 3 Constitution.

"This is not about returning a constitution grounded in silly principles of royalty, or aristocracy," Barss wrote. "It is about returning to people their right to independence and autonomous self-government."

To reiterate that it was a grass-roots movement, Barss continued: "Finding uniforms will not be hard, as general Kosciuszko has said, he does not need a higher rank, and only the robes of a Polish Peasant."[79]

Kosciuszko in peasant hat and robe, wearing the medal of the Order of the Cincinnati, given to him by George Washington, and the Virtuti Military cross for bravery given to him by Polish King Stanislaw Augustus. By Jozef Grassi, courtesy of Kosciuszko Foundation.

Ludwika (Louise) Sosnowska, later Princess Lubomirska, by Jozef Grassi, Muzeum Narodowe w Warszawie (MNW), The National Museum in Warsaw.

The Royal Knight's School in Warsaw, the former Kazimierzowski Palace, by Zygmunt Vogla, (MNW).

King Stanislaw Augustus Poniatowski, by
Marcello Bacciarelli, Muzeum Narodowe
Lubelskie (MNL).

Prince Adam Kazimierz Czartoryski, by
Tadeusz Kosciuszko, The Czartoryski
Foundation, Krakow (CF).

Tadeusz Kosciuszsko,
by Jozef Grassi
(1792), Instytut
Sztuki Polskiej
Adademii Nauk w
Warszawie.

Kosciuszko's plan for
the Battle of Saratoga
(the American
position is marked
"A" and the British
position, "B").
Archives at
West Point.

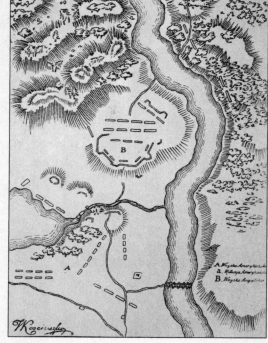

*Kosciuszsko, at West
Point*, by Boleslaw
Jan Czedekowski,
Kosciuszko
Foundation, New
York.

Kosciuszko, by Jozef Grassi, Polish Embassy, Washington, D.C.

Map of Kosciuszko's works at West Point drafted by a French engineer. *(These were the secret plans that Benedict Arnold tried to sell to the British.)* Archives at West Point.

Agrippa Hull, Kosciuszko's aide, from the Historical Collection of the Stockbridge Library, Stockbridge, Massachusetts.

Kosciuszko Takes the Oath in the Market Square in Krakow, by Michal Stachowicz, courtesy of the National Gallery in Krakow. On March 24, 1794, Kosciuszko was named "Commander in Chief" of the Polish nation.

Army at Prayer Before the Battle of Raclawice, by Jozef Chelmonski, National Museum at Wroclaw.

The Raclawice Panorama, this painting, housed in a circular museum in Wroclaw, is 50 feet tall and 374 feet around. It was painted by Jan Styka and Wojciech Kossak. They were assisted by Ludwik Boller, Tadeusz Popiel, Zygmunt Rozwadowski, Teodor Axentowicz, Wlodzimierz Tetmajer, Wincenty Wodzinowski, and Michal Sozanski.

Jean Lapierre, "Domingo," by Jan Jozef Sikorski, (MWP). Kosciuszko's aide-de-camp during the Polish Insurrection.

Berek Joselewicz, (artist unknown), courtesy of the National Museum in Krakow. Joselewicz was a merchant who started a Jewish cavalry to fight alongside Kosciuszko's rebels against the Russian Army. It was the first wholly Jewish military brigade since biblical times.

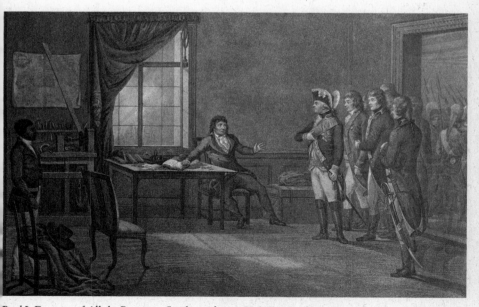

Paul I, Emperor of All the Russians, Condescending to Visit Kosciuszko in Prison, by Thomas Gaugain, courtesy of the Kosciuszko Foundation. (Standing at left is Jean Lapierre.)

Thomas Jefferson, by Rembrandt Peale, Collection of The New-York Historical Society, No. 1867.306. Jefferson is seen here wearing the fur given to him by Kosciuszko.

Chief Little Turtle, Indiana Historical Society. The chief gave Kosciuszko a combination tomahawk–peace pipe as a sign of friendship.

Kosciuszko, by R. R. Reinagle, Courtesy of the Kosciuszko Foundation. The Polish commander in chief in the last year of his life, while in exile in Switzerland.

TWELVE

Kosciuszko's Rebels: Peasant Scythemen,
a Burgher Militia, and a Jewish Cavalry

M EDIEVAL KRAKOW WAS SURROUNDED BY A RED GRANITE WALL,
eight feet wide and twenty feet tall, and a moat filled by the Wisla River. It
had thirty-nine lofty baroque towers and eight gates with drawbridges dispersed
along the bulwarks around the city. A covered passage led to an island in the
canal, where a brick barbican with turrets and mounted cannons provided cover
from invaders. The city was Poland's capital until 1596, when King Sigismund
III moved to Warsaw so he would be halfway between Krakow and the commonwealth's Lithuanian seat, Vilnius.

Dominating Krakow's bustling square, the towers of Saint Mary's Church
served as a lookout over the nearby foothills and provided a vantage point from
which a bugler blew his horn to welcome the dawn and warn when the gates
were about to be closed at dusk. In the center of the town square was a long
hall where merchants hawked wares from local artisans and fabrics from the silk
routes of Asia. The smell of fresh rye bread, bagels, hams, and smoked kielbasa
wafted from the bakeries and meat shops around the square.

On an island in the river was Kazimierz, the Jewish quarter, with flourishing
shops, restaurants, and several synagogues. Christians also shopped in the Jewish bazaar and frequented the local taverns that served roast duck with horse-
radish, garlic pickles, potato pancakes, and strong plum brandy called slivovitz.

Over the years the city had fallen into decay after Polish kings moved their
primary residence from the colossal limestone castle soaring above it on Wawel
Hill. According to legend, a fire-breathing dragon lived in a cave underneath. The
city captured the imagination of artists and political thinkers alike.

Philip Lichocki had just finished his first year as mayor of Krakow when he was shaken from a lazy slumber on the morning of March 24, 1794, by one of his servants who had just returned from the town square. The mayor of Krakow was an aristocrat chosen to run the medieval city that no longer had all the headaches of the national bureaucracy.

The anxious servant told the mayor that the army had pulled up the drawbridges over the moat. People were allowed in, but no one was allowed to leave. Mayor Lichocki got dressed and sent one of his guards to investigate the ruckus. Soon a nervous merchant rushed into the mayor's quarters and told him that a "storm was brewing in town."[1]

The stalled uprising was under way. A Polish army messenger arrived and ordered the mayor to gather the town council and all his deputies at city hall within the hour. There was going to be an announcement that Gen. Thaddeus Kosciuszko has been named commander in chief of the nation.

Two nights earlier, before the drawbridges were pulled up, Kosciuszko had walked across one of the spans, leading a single horse pulling a wagon with his baggage, uniform, and weapons. He had spent the previous night in a barn a few miles away, and his arrival was a surprise because he had been expected a few days earlier. On the eve of the uprising he inconspicuously pulled his horse and wagon to the stately home of Gen. Joseph Wodzicki, where he met with a group of revolutionaries to plan the next day's coup d'état.[2]

After more than a year of being prodded by various intellectuals, aristocrats, soldiers, and fawning women, Kosciuszko finally agreed to lead an uprising to oust the foreign armies from his country. He had never been a fluid writer, so when the time came to issue his tour de force, The Act of Insurrection, the writing was left up to Kollontay, whose essays inspired the Seym to pass a democratic constitution. Kosciuszko objected that the principles in the act were too similar to those of the May 3 Constitution. He wanted the "country to be formed on the same model as the American republic."[3]

Kosciuszko gave Kollontay's draft to another Patriot, a Lithuanian attorney named Joseph Weyssenhoff, who convinced Kosciuszko that, as in America, the form of democracy should be left up to the people to decide after the revolution.

After being tweaked and edited the act began with the words: "The wretched state in which Poland finds itself is known to the universe; the indignities of two neighboring powers, and the crimes of traitors to their country have sunk this nation into an abyss of misery." It proclaimed that "in the spirit of Patriotism, good citizenship and fraternity" rebel forces would fight for "the deliverance of Poland from foreign troops."[4] Kosciuszko was appointed commander in chief of the nation, and he vowed to convene a body called the Supreme National Council to oversee administrative affairs.

Before Kosciuszko sneaked into Krakow, the Russians and Prussians made another preemptive move, once again ordering Poland to demobilize half its army. This brought the total number of troops to about 15,449, with 8,865 stationed in Poland and the rest in Lithuania and Ukraine.[5]

Gen. Antoni Madalinski, a former Bar confederate who served under Pulaski, was visited by a courier from Kosciuszko, so he ignored the order to disarm and rushed his brigade of 1,500 troops toward Krakow. The Russian garrison stationed there raced out of the city to attack them, foiling any attempt by Kosciuszko and his men to surprise them and take their weapons.

Early in the morning on March 24, Kosciuszko and General Wodzicki attended mass at the monastery of Capuchin monks who were dedicated to preaching and missionary work. They placed their swords on the steps of the altar, in front of a statue of Mary, to be blessed by the priest.

After the service Kosciuszko and the officers returned to Wodzicki's house, where Mayor Lichocki met them. The mayor tried to compliment the nation's new leader, but General Wodzicki interrupted, stamping his feet, saying, "You knew that the Muscovites were leaving and you didn't tell me."[6]

Lichocki replied that while he had heard some of the women in town gossiping that the Russians might leave, he thought it was speculation. Kosciuszko sat with his face in his hands as the officers berated the mayor for not being more forthcoming.

With the Russian officers scheduled to attend a concert, the rebels planned to disguise themselves as peasants who were supposed to deliver a shipment of firewood to their garrison. Soldiers were poised to hide in basements and on rooftops to strike at the enemy when their officers were away. They would have struck earlier had they known that the Russians were pulling out to attack General Madalinski's renegade unit.[7]

Kosciuszko stood up and approached the mayor, saying, "Your honor! I won't concern myself with how you treated the Muscovites, but I expected that for me, you would be courteous. How can this be? Sir, did you invite your cabinet and the people to come to city hall?"[8]

The mayor nodded. In fact, the city hall bell tower was clanging away to summon the populace to the square. Kosciuszko told the mayor to lead the way. At 10 a.m., Kosciuszko stepped out into the town square where people were wearing sashes bearing such slogans as, Freedom or Death, Equality and Freedom, Long Live Kosciuszko, Unity and Independence, For Krakow and the Fatherland.[9]

There was a crowd of thousands, including soldiers, noblemen, townspeople, Jews, and peasants. A large number of young people were holding banners, some emblazoned with the image that Chrétien had made in Paris, of Kosciuszko holding a sword. Women were leaning out windows to get a glimpse of their leader.

As the mayor walked in front of Kosciuszko, some people tried to shove Lichocki and some whispered into his ear, "It's the guillotine for the mayor!"

Others yelled, "Here it is going to be different!"[10]

It was an unseasonably warm and sunny day. Kosciuszko was wearing tight riding pants, a red vest, and an overcoat with green and gray stripes. The officers draped a ceremonial general's sash over his shoulder and across his chest.

As soon as Kosciuszko began to speak, his words made it clear that his uprising would not tolerate vengeance, but rather celebrate unity: "Honorable sirs, in defense of the fatherland, equality will prosper in my eyes, and that is why Jews, peasants, aristocrats, priests and burghers have equal respect from me, the many citizens and land magnates who have been invited to participate in today's events."[11]

With all the different sectors of society in one place, it was an incredible show of harmony. The Act of Insurrection was read aloud by Krakow's Seym representative as the crowd listened attentively. There was a great rumble of applause when he finished, and the mass of people assembled in the square cheered in approval.

After a drumroll the crowd fell silent as the new "commander" stepped forward. He publicly vowed before the gathered multitude: "I Thaddeus Kosciuszko, swear before God to the whole Polish nation that I will not use the power vested in me to oppress anyone, but only for the defense of the integrity of the borders, to regain the nation's sovereignty, and the solid establishment of universal freedom. So help me God and the innocent passion of His Son."[12]

The crowd began to chant, "Long live Poland! Long live Kosciuszko!"[13]

The gathered soldiers took an oath of allegiance to Kosciuszko. The officers and government officials all filed into city hall. One of the angry burghers suggested that they take down the portrait of King Stanislaw hanging on the wall and throw it away. The consensus was that it would be a petty act, so Stanislaw's face was left on the wall, staring down on them as they plotted his overthrow.[14]

One after another they all took the quill pen, dipped it into the inkwell, and signed their names under the Act of Insurrection. Copies were sent out to foreign newspapers and the governments of France, England, Sweden, Denmark, Turkey, and the United States.[15]

Kosciuszko moved his headquarters into a gray stone row house directly facing the town square. The nation's newly appointed commander and his advisers began organizing the revolution. That afternoon he issued written appeals that were sent out across the country to the Polish and Lithuanian army, the nation's citizenry, the clergy, and to Polish women.

"We have sworn, my friends more than once, to be faithful to the fatherland," he wrote to the army. "Let us raise our country out of slavery. . . . I take with you, my beloved friends, this pledge: Death or Victory!"[16]

To the citizens Kosciuszko wrote: "My fellow citizens! Summoned by you to save our beloved country, I stand by your will at the head, but I will not be able to break this outrageous yoke of slavery if I do not receive the speediest and most courageous support from you." He begged for them to make sacrifices and provide the army with recruits, guns, horses, boots, clothes, canvas for tents and provisions, adding, "The first step in casting off slavery is to take a risk to be free. The first step to victory is to know your own strength."[17]

Kosciuszko needed the clergy to spread the message of the uprising from their pulpits, and he asked the priests to share the church's "enlightenment, fortunes and whatever wealth it could contribute" to freeing the fatherland.[18]

And even in wartime Kosciuszko could not help flirting. He was that type of Polish gentleman who liked to display exaggerated sentimentality by bending over to kiss a woman's hand as she entered the room and then lavish her with flattery. The women of his day enjoyed the attention, especially because he genuinely respected their opinions. But as a lifelong bachelor, he could not hide his attraction to the opposite sex.

In his appeal to women he wrote: "O' beautiful gender, the fairer sex! I honestly suffer at the site of your restless anxiety about the fate of our brave endeavor, which Poles are undertaking to free their fatherland. Your tears caused by your caring hearts, my fellow female citizens, are overwhelming for your countryman who is joyously devoting himself to a fight for the happiness of the nation." Kosciuszko needed women to run the hospitals once the fighting began, and said, "I ask you, for the love of humankind, to make bandages for the army. Such a sacrifice by your beautiful hands should ease their suffering and encourage bravery."[19]

The commander's appeals were printed and sent to cities and churches around Poland. As a Catholic he could not tell the rabbis what to do, so he went to the Jewish quarter in Kazimierz and walked into Krakow's Old Synagogue on Szeroka Street to ask Rabbi Hirsh David Lewi and his congregation to support the uprising.

Kosciuszko promised the Jewish community that his new government would address their grievances. Years later Rabbi Lewi recalled his conversation with the rebel leader. "I want nothing for myself," Kosciuszko told the rabbi. "This is about the deplorable state of the fatherland, rescuing the nation and bringing happiness to its residents, and yours are counted in this. That is the only goal of my undertaking."[20]

To allay the fears of aristocrats who worried that the rebellion would lead to chaos on their plantations, and the concerns of the Catholic Church that the rebels would usurp their authority and confiscate their property as in France, Kosciuszko had to be careful that his uprising was not seen as a Jacobin revolution. The Polish Patriots needed to distance themselves from the savage revolution that was taking place in Paris, where the motto was *Liberté, Egalité, Fraternité.*

Kosciuszko had a stamp made with the slogan Liberty, Unity, and Independence, which was impressed onto correspondence and written on banners. The commander sent spies to Warsaw and other cities across Poland to plan the war. Letters were sewn into pillows and camouflaged in other creative ways to get them past Russian checkpoints.

So that he could focus on the military aspect of the campaign, Kosciuszko convened a Commission for Order in Krakow to deal with the nobility and the clergy. The commission decided to recruit every healthy male between the ages of eighteen and twenty-eight, and passed an income tax to raise money for the troops.[21]

The commission asked the noblemen and serfs in surrounding villages to send recruits with rifles and ammunition, or eleven-foot pikes and axes, and a hat, two shirts, a good pair of shoes, a thick blanket, and enough biscuits to feed them for six days.

Over the next several days Kosciuszko took inventory of how many soldiers he had at his disposal and welcomed peasant volunteers shuffling into town with the scythes and sickles they used to harvest wheat. They bent the curved blades straight up to create long, sharp weapons. The peasant infantry were dubbed the "scythemen."

Contributions also started to flow in. One of the first benefactors was a nobleman named Gabriel Taszycki, who arrived with a bag full of coins and silver worth 20,756 zlotys.[22] The Czartoryski family and the bishop of Krakow, Felix Turski, sent Kosciuszko thousands of zlotys.[23] Women sold their jewelry, and farmers brought in horses, livestock, scythes, and guns. At Kosciuszko's suggestion the gold cross in the Krakow Cathedral was sold, and brought in 180,000 zlotys to help fund the army.[24]

On March 26 Kosciuszko received great news from Gen. Jan Manget, who was sent out on a reconnaissance mission to find the brigade of three hundred Russians who had escaped Krakow. Manget had given them a thrashing and sent four wagons of captured guns and supplies to Krakow.[25]

The rebels had only about a week of preparations when they learned that Russian general Fiodor Denisov was marching on Krakow with an army of five thousand. If the enemy surrounded Krakow and besieged the city, the uprising would be finished before it had a chance to spread through Poland. The commander realized that he would be better off if he could link up with the units of Generals Madalinski and Manget that had been harassing the enemy in the field.

On April 1 Kosciuszko marched out of Krakow with a ragtag army of 850 regular soldiers, two hundred young volunteers with horses, and four hundred-peasant scythemen with pikes and axes.[26] Over the next few days Manget, Madalinski, and other straggling military units and peasant volunteers joined the commander, bringing the size of his army to about five thousand men.[27]

Czarina Catherine had anticipated that this day might come. Several months earlier she had sent a Russian general of Swedish descent named Iosif Andreyevich Igelström to Warsaw to crack down on any rabblerousers. Igelström ordered his troops to sleep in their uniforms on the floor of the Russian Embassy in Warsaw, and demanded that King Stanislaw issue a statement condemning Kosciuszko. On April 2 the newspapers in Warsaw carried a statement from the king saying that the rebels were "behaving like criminals, like mutineers outside the rigors of the law."[28]

The "outlaw" and his rebels were already on the march. General Denisov located Kosciuszko's position and devised a plan to attack the Poles from two sides to wipe them out. On the morning of April 4 the Poles were passing a nearby village near Krakow called Raclawice. When his advance units clashed with the approaching Russian army, which blocked their forward progress, Kosciuszko took position on a nearby hill. With General Zajaczek on his left flank and General Madalinski on his right, Kosciuszko held the center with an army of peasants.

Russian general Alexander Tormasov, with about 3,000 men, was waiting for the remaining 2,500 troops to arrive. But by 3:00 p.m. Tormasov was growing impatient. General Denisov was to attack from the south, while another unit circled the forest to the north to attack the right flank. Tormasov's unit marched toward the main position, and the Polish artillery opened fire.

Tormasov's troops climbed the hill and took a higher position. They drove back the Polish cavalry and infantry on two sides. The Russians rolled their cannons up the incline and were about to blast away at the Polish army when Kosciuszko galloped up on his horse to the peasant brigade, yelling, "My boys, take that artillery! For God, and the Fatherland! Go forward with faith!"[29]

Waving their pikes and scythes in the air, three hundred peasants let out horrible shrieks as they charged the enemy position. Racing in front of them on his horse, Kosciuszko waved them on and shouted out their names, "Szymku, Macku, Bartku, keep going!"

The Russians fired one or two cannon blasts, killing some of the attacking serfs, but when a peasant named Wojciech Bartosz reached another cannon about to fire, he took off his hat and extinguished the sparkling fuse. The scythemen struck so quickly that the stunned Russians could not get off any more rounds as the peasants tamped out the fuses and began hacking away with scythes, axes, and pikes. The serfs slaughtered the czarist soldiers in savage hand-to-hand combat.

The scythemen resembled the grim reaper of pagan folklore, and some of the terrified Russians tried to surrender, begging for their lives, screaming, "Pardon!" But the peasants did not understand the French plea for forgiveness and kept savagely chopping away at the enemy troops. The first group of serfs captured three twelve-pound cannons, and a second wave captured eight more artillery pieces.[30] Young Polish cavalry volunteers raced in on their horses, pushing back the Russians and capturing the enemy flag.

Kosciuszko raced over to the left flank, where the infantry was firing on the enemy brigade marching up the hill. Once again Kosciuszko took the lead and ordered the infantry to charge the Russians with their bayonets. After intense combat the enemy broke ranks and ran into the forest, where they were followed by the scythemen, who showed no mercy and took no prisoners. General Denisov ordered a retreat. The hill was covered with dead soldiers and dismembered bodies.

Under the military tradition of the time, Polish commanders donned the uniform of their most effective unit in combat. To the delight of the serfs Kosciuszko ripped off his general's uniform and put on a *sukmana*, a peasant robe made from woven sheep's wool. The serfs shook their weapons in the air and roared in approval as their new peasant prince officially declared the scythemen infantry a separate branch of Poland's military. "They feed and defend," became their motto.

The commander in chief promoted Madalinski and Zajaczek to lieutenant general. Kosciuszko also received permission from Wojciech Bartosz's noble landlord to grant him his freedom, and the heroic peasant was promoted to standard-bearer. He was also awarded a tract of land and dubbed a nobleman. Bartosz assumed his mother's maiden name, becoming Duke Glowacki.

The peasants fought at Raclawice as if they had the least to lose—and the most to gain. In all, 800 Russians had been shot or hacked to death. Kosciuszko estimated that he lost about 100 soldiers with another 100 wounded, but in reality the Battle of Raclawice cost the Poles between 200 and 250 lives.[31]

Kosciuszko marched his army back to Krakow for a victory parade before pitching camp just outside the city in the fields of Bosutow. A bench under three large oak trees became the commander in chief's perch, from which he could see Krakow's church tower as he issued orders. An officer pulled out a knife and etched a large cross so deeply into the bark of one of the oaks that it was still visible decades later.[32] It was there that Kosciuszko wrote a "Report to the Polish Nation on the Victory at Raclawice."[33]

Just as a group of American farmers had chased the British army from their land, it looked as if Polish farmers could drive the Russian czarist army out of Poland. News of the peasants' actions spread across Poland. The nation's commander wanted to send pleas to the noble lords asking them to suspend the corvée on serfs for the duration of the war of independence, but the Commission for Order in Krakow argued that he was going too far, too fast. Some Polish lords even appeared at the camp claiming that their serfs had joined the army without permission, and some peasants disappeared "into the smoke" rather than go back to their plantations.[34]

The camp in Bosutow was full of energy as more peasants and deserters from the Polish army swarmed in to join the uprising. Because Kosciuszko was wearing a *sukmana,* the peasant robe became a uniform of honor, and the serfs were treated with respect in camp. The serfs even wrote patriotic military songs, urging more peasants to fight on with their pikes and scythes.

The sight of armed serfs frightened some of the land magnates, and many priests were ambivalent about the uprising. When the Jacobins in France took away the church's power to tax farmers, priests lost much of their influence, and their land and property was confiscated by the new regime. To Kosciuszko the right to be free was as important as freedom of religion. He needed the priests and the aristocrats to use all their money, power, and influence.

A Polish nobleman who visited the camp wrote about Kosciuszko: "He's a simple man, quite modest in his speech, manners and dress. The utmost firmness and enthusiasm for the chosen cause is coupled with a coolness and sensibility. . . . Especially in the details, nothing is left to chance everything is calculated and planned. Maybe he's not the most transcendental mind, or even nimble in politics. But he has enough of a natural common sense to assess the situation and make the best choice from the first glance."[35]

A week after the commander sent officers to the city of Sandomierz, there was still no action. He was subtle in suggesting that even though the church might not be helping as much as it could, God was on their side. On April 17 Kosciuszko sent a letter calling on them join the fight: "My countrymen! This is not the time to guard formalities and take lazy steps toward a National Uprising. To arms Poles, to arms! God has already blessed our weapons, and His powerful Providence has manifested itself in the manner that this country must free itself."[36]

Kosciuszko was growing frustrated. He was not sure if people were listening. Unbeknownst to him, that same day the uprising in Warsaw had been set in motion.

When General Igelström heard about Kosciuszko's victory at the Battle of Raclawice, he ordered the arrest of several Patriots and the disarming of the last Polish garrison in Warsaw, run by Gen. Stanislaw Mokronowski. Bishop Joseph Kossakowski, a collaborator with the Russians, suggested that their army surround the churches on Holy Saturday and arrest the dissidents as they left mass.

When a drunken Russian soldier leaked news of the imminent clampdown, the Poles got ready. As the czarina's soldiers appeared to empty out the arsenal, they were caught by surprise when the Polish guards opened fire on them. The guards handed out guns to civilians, and the burghers helped drive Russian troops away from the arsenal.

Mokronowski's units spread out, and several battles raged around the city. A cobbler named Jan Kilinski rallied the burghers and led a militia against the Russians. The Poles broke into the Russian Embassy and knocked down the painting of Catherine the Great, smashing it to the ground, stomping on it, and tearing it to shreds. They raided the secret archives in the basement outlining all of the czarina's clandestine activities in Poland since Stanislaw was named king, including files listing collaborators.

After two days of intense block-by-block fighting in the streets, most of the czarina's troops had been killed, captured, or driven out of the city. Warsaw's new leaders issued a proclamation announcing that they were joining the Kosciuszko insurrection. Similar uprisings sprang up against czarist troops in cities and towns across the country. The revolt had become a full-fledged revolution.

The Austrian ambassador to Poland, Benedict de Cache, lived on Miodowa Street, near the royal castle, right in the center of the action. Cache warned the foreign minister in Vienna about "a very dangerous uprising that has exploded among the people." Cache wrote that while there were a small number of regular soldiers involved, "they were joined by large groups of people armed with swords, pistols, rifles and other weapons taken from the arsenal. The number of these people grew to nearly 40 thousand people. Among them you could even see armed Jews."[37]

The Swedish emissary was also surprised to see Jews join the fight. Johan Christopher Toll had been sending updates on the situation in Warsaw to Prince Charles, Duke of Sodermanland. On April 19 he wrote: "A revolution has erupted here that cannot be compared to any you will find in history books. The Polish garrison, with about 2,000 soldiers, and the town's population, early in the morning, began a fight against the Russian garrison of 5,000 soldiers. The arsenal, with weapons and ammunition was opened. Even armed Jews took part in the battle."[38]

The Jews had heeded Kosciuszko's calls to arms. They too were worse off under czarist rule. The Jewish community was inspired by Kosciuszko's philosophy and backed his insurrection. Initially they contributed money and supplies, and eventually soldiers. In Warsaw they collected 80,450 zlotys for the army, and fought alongside the burgher militia. A doctor recruited forty Jews to put on army uniforms, and more would follow.[39]

On Easter Sunday, April 20, King Stanislaw attended mass in the Warsaw Cathedral, where he witnessed the top brass of his army and the cadets of the royal military academy he had founded take an oath of allegiance to his former cadet, the nation's new leader and commander in chief, Thaddeus Kosciuszko.

Three days later rebels in the Lithuanian capital of Vilnius expelled the Russian army from the city and issued a proclamation joining the Kosciuszko insurrection. In addition to the burghers and peasants who joined the fight in Lithuania, Dr. Salomon Polonus persuaded the Vilnius *kahal* to raise 25,000 zlotys to help fund the uprising. Dr. Polonus said that a victory would be possible through the "grace of God," and issued a proclamation, "An appeal to the Israelite people," to support the revolution. The doctor was so convincing that the Jews of Vilnius fought bravely against the czarist troops, and even women and children took part in the battle.[40]

The historical axis among Krakow, Warsaw, and Vilnius had been restored. Other cities around Poland would soon join the rebellion.

Kosciuszko left about two thousand soldiers and peasants to guard Krakow and marched his army along the left bank of the Wisla River toward Warsaw. On the right bank of the river was former Polish territory annexed by Austria. He had to be careful not to incur the wrath of three great powers at once, so Kosciuszko sent a message to Francis II, emperor of Austria, explaining that his fight was not with Austria. And as Austria was at war with France, Kosciuszko also had to assure the emperor that the Polish revolution did not have a Jacobin nature.

It was not until April 25, when Kosciuszko set up camp at a spot called Igolomi, that a courier arrived with the news that Warsaw had been liberated. Rev. Kollontay asked, "Is the king alive?" Disappointed when the messenger said yes, the priest told the commander, "In that case we and our revolution are done for; the army will fight for a few months and then Poland will fall and the king will sign her death warrant."[41]

But Kosciuszko was more interested in overturning the government and driving out the Russians than in executing the monarch. He was thrilled that the burghers had played such a vital role in the revolt and changed the policy of military promotions. Rank would no longer be based on connections but on merit.

"Henceforth, in considering the promotion of officers I will give greater weight to worthiness than to seniority," Kosciuszko wrote to General Mokronowski in Warsaw. "Any man from the ranks can become an officer if he merits it." The nation's commander told Mokronowski that he "should immediately bestow the rank of officer on at least a few of those soldiers who have behaved sensibly and showed courage."[42]

The shoemaker Jan Kilinski was made a colonel for his role in the uprising.

Unfortunately the Russians intercepted Kosciuszko's letters to Vilnius, so he did not know what was happening in Lithuania.

Austria was holding its fire against the Polish rebels, but Prussian king Frederick William sent his army into Poland to assist the Russians. The Poles had to contend with a war on two fronts, and with a shortage of weapons, ammunition, and regular soldiers, the commander in chief was getting desperate.

On April 30 Kosciuszko issued a letter to the Catholic Church: "All precious treasures in the churches owned by priests and secularists, including those living on alms, should be given up into the hands of the Krakow Commission for Order, for the current needs of the republic, . . . I solemnly swear that those church treasuries will be returned with respect, from the treasury of the republic once it gets freed from the enemy."[43]

Prince Eustachy Sanguszko, who was sent with soldiers and wagons to collect the funds, wrote in his memoirs that the coffers "were filled with substantial contributions from Krakow's citizens, wealthy people from Galicia as well as silver from churches."[44]

Kosciuszko's army marched up the Wisla and pitched camp on a hill south of the town of Polaniec. The camp was between the Wisla and one of its tributaries, the Czarna (Black) River. There he drilled his peasant army and regular soldiers so that they could work as a team in the next battle. Gradually the noble lords were starting to realize that they would no longer be able to keep the peasants down on the farm once they had seen the light of freedom.

The predicament of the serfs at Polaniec was similar to that of slaves in the American Revolution, where different states had different laws, and slave owners had varying opinions about who could be a soldier. At Saratoga, Israel Ashley tried to reclaim his slave, Gilliam, who enlisted without his master's approval. Kosciuszko's mentor, General Gates, thwarted Ashley's attempt to repossess Gilliam, and allowed him and other slaves to remain in the army. With Polish noblemen complaining that their serfs had joined the army without permission, it was Kosciuszko's turn to take a stand.

Together with his advisers Kollontay and Ignacy Potocki, the commander drafted the most radical proclamation of the war.

On May 7, 1794, in a field outside the village of Polaniec, Kosciuszko issued the Proclamation of Polaniec, granting civil rights to Poland's peasants and cutting their corvée. Kosciuszko's preamble criticized those noblemen who had a "criminal spirit of self love and selfish prospects, added with mixed up stubbornness, delay and the tendency to unite with outsiders, ending in ignoble submission to them."

The commander issued fourteen points, the first of which gave serfs the same rights as everyone else "under the laws and protection of the national government." The second declared that "every peasant is personally free, and free to move where he wishes, provided he notifies the Commission for Order of his County as to his whereabouts, and provided he has paid his debts and national taxes."[45]

As he had done with his own serfs, Kosciuszko cut the work requirement of the corvée in half, and by two-thirds for some. The remaining points reduced the bureaucratic restrictions that made it impossible for serfs to acquire their own wealth, capital, and happiness. It provided opportunities for peasants who worked for the manor to obtain their own land. The commander boldly ordered the clergy to read the proclamation "from the pulpits of the Catholic and Orthodox churches for the next four Sundays," and for the towns to spread the word to their residents.

The Proclamation of Polaniec would be the death knell for feudalism that Russia, Prussia, and Austria wanted to avoid. The same day at the camp in Polaniec, Kosciuszko issued an appeal to the clergy of all religions in Poland, and specifically to the Russian Orthodox chaplains in the eastern provinces: "Join your hearts with the Poles, who defend our freedom and yours."[46]

Polish revolutionaries loved the phrase, turning it around to, "For your freedom and ours," and making it Poland's unofficial motto. But the Orthodox clergy also did not want to unleash the strength of the serfs in Russia and Ukraine.

The commander in chief needed a strong leader in Lithuania, and on April 12 he promoted Prince Francis Sapieha to lieutenant general. To make sure Sapieha understood that the revolution would not follow standard procedures, he wrote: "Our war has a specific character which must be understood properly. Its success depends above all on spreading a universal fervor in all or inhabitants and arming everyone in our land. To this end, it is necessary to arouse a love of one's nation in those who until now did not even know they had a fatherland."

Kosciuszko explained that because their enemies had larger armies, they needed to discard the conventional methods of war and get the nobility and the clergy to inspire the peasants to assist the army in a guerrilla war against foreign invaders. He wrote: "Who would believe that with two companies of infantry and three hundred people with scythes . . . we could break the Muscovite infantry at Raclawice. That is why the people must be tied to public matters. That is why easing up on the corvée is necessary."[47]

But the nation's commander had overestimated the commitment to his cause from the aristocracy and the church. Poland's economy was based on slave labor, and getting rid of the corvée would be a disaster for the nobility. The aristocrats had contributed vast sums of money to the cause, and the church had given up much of its gold and silver, but the Proclamation of Polaniec meant that they would have to give up future income as well. The priests of the Catholic Church, who also had their own serfs, did not want to free the peasants who provided them with cheap labor and a steady income.[48]

It was an act of abolition, akin to the issue of the Declaration of Independence, the Bill of Rights, and the yet-unwritten Emancipation Proclamation all at once. Publicly Poland's priests and aristocrats backed the insurrection, but privately they were stewing that the commander of the nation had gone too far by granting freedom to the serfs with a stroke of the pen.

It was a promise that could not be kept.

The land magnates were even more worried after the publication of a fifteen-page anonymous brochure called *The Peasant Voice*, which praised Kosciuszko's Proclamation of Polaniec for "freeing the peasants from their handcuffs." However, the paper added, the peasants would not be satisfied "until they are in a position where they will no longer be afraid of their masters and they have in their own hands the power to protect themselves from the use of force." It asked that the peasants be represented and given a seat at the table alongside the noblemen and priests appointed to the new commissions and tribunals that were being created.[49]

While the peasants in the countryside were demanding more power, the burghers in the cities began flexing their new muscles. A vengeful group of Poles formed a Jacobin Club in Warsaw and established an insurrectionary tribunal. Jan Kilinski had uncovered records in the basement of the Russian Embassy which revealed that the Russians had been paying Bishop Kossakowski for his collaboration. Less than a month after he had urged the Russians to surround Polish churches and arrest the Patriots, the bishop was put on trial and hanged from a gallows set up across the street from a Bernardine church near the royal castle. Three delegates of the Grodno Seym, Peter Ozarowski, Joseph Ankwicz, and Joseph Zabiello, were convicted as traitors for approving the second partition of Poland, which ceded territory to Russia. They, too, were hanged before a cheering crowd of onlookers.[50]

Kosciuszko was not yet aware of the bloodlust in Warsaw. He was still in Polaniec, where on May 10 he finally appointed the Supreme National Council that was called for in his Act of Insurrection. The revolutionary council was led by Kollontay, who was appointed minister of the treasury, and Potocki, who was minister for foreign affairs. Others were chosen for the ministries of justice, security, military needs, provisions, national affairs, and the office of administrative affairs.

The new council decided to coin its own money. King Stanislaw's face would be taken off the new zloty coins, and replaced with the words "Freedom, Unity, Independence—The Republic, 1794."

Fearing he was to be taken to the gallows or, worse, face a guillotine like King Louis XVI, Stanislaw summoned his nephew, the former general, Prince Joseph, who was in Brussels, to come to Warsaw.[51] Stanislaw also wrote to Kosciuszko expressing his willingness to abdicate. Stanislaw's onetime star cadet replied respectfully, pointing out that the king had lost the public's trust by joining the Targowica confederation, but "I assure Your Royal Majesty of my deep respect."[52]

The commander in chief spared the king's neck.

With their new authority Kollontay and Potocki left Kosciuszko's camp in Polaniec and arrived in Warsaw on May 24. Kollontay, a hero in Warsaw ever since he helped organize the "Black March of the Burghers," was greeted by the crowds like a returning conqueror.

Kollontay and Potocki began setting up a Supreme National Council to run the revolution, but burghers demanded to be included. King Stanislaw called the rebels outlaws when the insurrection began, but when he saw the tide had turned, he too wanted a role in the new regime. Kosciuszko replied that first he was focused on chasing out the enemy, and only then would the temporary council form the government.

"Don't be deceived," Kosciuszko told the king. The council "is composed of virtuous citizens and friends of the people, and when I nominated them, I did not want to think about whether they are peasants, burghers or aristocrats."[53]

As the commander in chief continued his march toward Warsaw, the king's nephew, Prince Joseph, arrived at the base camp in the village of Jedrzejow. In an uncharacteristic display of rudeness, Kosciuszko barked at his former commanding officer, "What do you want, Prince?"

Prince Joseph replied, "To serve an upright soldier."[54]

Still upset over the defensive war that Prince Joseph had led in 1792, Kosciuszko offered him command of the army in Lithuania. But, claiming that he did not know the territory, the prince declined. Instead he was sent to report to the militia in the Polish capital.

To the outside world the hangings in Warsaw looked as if the Polish revolution had taken a turn toward Jacobin mob rule, while the commander in chief was busy issuing proclamations and appeals. When even his dear friend Princess Isabella Czartoryska wrote to criticize him, Kosciuszko felt he had to respond.

"How wrongly you judge me princess, if you don't yet know what is in my heart, you hurt my feelings and way of thinking," Kosciuszko replied. "Men may blacken me and our uprising, but God sees that we are not starting a French revolution. I want to destroy the enemy. I am giving some temporary orders, but I leave the framing of the laws to the nation."[55]

To make sure his soldiers knew what they were fighting for, Kosciuszko took care that each day's password and countersigns for those crossing checkpoints reflected the democratic nature of their cause. June 1 the parole was "Republican" and the countersign was "Soldier." The next day it was "Free" and the reply, "Lawmaker." On June 3 it was "Serf" and the reply, "Slave."[56]

By then General Denisov had regrouped and, with reinforcements from Russia, had amassed an army of nine thousand soldiers. The Russians burned all the villages, manor houses, peasant shacks, and barns with food stocks to limit the provisions available to the Polish army. There was a lack of potable water, and what little was available was fouled by the cavalry horses. About six thousand peasants had joined Kosciuszko's army, in addition to the cavalry and an army of about nine thousand; he was confident that he would be able to fend off the attack. But the commander in chief was caught off guard when Gen. Francis Favrat joined Denisov with a Prussian army of 17,500 to finish off the Polish army before it could reach Warsaw.[57] The enemy had fooled the Poles by hiding their tents and sleeping under the open sky so that spies would not see them. Kosciuszko, who had received assurances that Prussia would stay neutral for the time being, was in complete denial that the Prussians would attack him.

On the morning of June 6, General Wodzicki rode his horse to the top of a small hill near the village of Szczekociny and pulled out his telescope. Peering into the distance, he said, "It is impossible that Denisov could have amassed such an army. My eyes must be wrong, but I can see Prussians."[58]

Even then Kosciuszko was convinced that it was probably only a few Prussians scattered within the Russian ranks. He was wrong. The Polish officers tried to talk their commander in chief out of facing the combined army of 26,500 Prussian and Russian soldiers, but Kosciuszko felt that he had no choice and refused to retreat.

Cannonballs of various sizes began raining down on the Poles from three sides.

General Wodzicki yelled out to his troops, "Children, don't take a single step backward unless I say so! Remember!"[59]

At that moment a twenty-four-pound cannonball tore off his head and exploded, cutting his adjutant in half. The scythemen rushed forward but were slaughtered as they ran into Prussian cannons filled with grapeshot that shredded them to pieces. The hero Bartosz Glowacki was mortally wounded, and Kosciuszko had two horses shot out from under him. A sergeant, Francis Derysarz, had both of his legs blown off by a cannonball, crying out his dying words as he bled to death, "Brothers! Defend the fatherland! Defend bravely and win!"[60]

The gruesome scenery was later described in memoirs.

"Riding off of the battlefield," wrote General Sanguszko, "I saw a rider checking the field watching over the action without his sword. A hard rain began to fall in front of them all. It was Kosciuszko in his gray peasant overcoat on a bay horse, which was killed. Because of this I did not recognize him right away and mistook him for a chaplain giving last rites to the dying."

Sanguszko asked him, "Commander, what are you doing here?"

"I want to die here," Kosciuszko replied.

Sanguszko grabbed hold of the commander's glove and began to pull him away from the battle, which the Poles were losing badly. A cannonball tore through the hindquarters of Kosciuszko's horse, killing two soldiers next to them, and wounded the commander's leg. Sanguszko pulled Kosciuszko onto his own horse and rode him to have his leg bandaged.[61]

More than twelve hundred Poles were killed at the Battle of Szczekociny, and General Sanguszko led an orderly retreat. Enemy losses were minimal.

The Prussians did not give chase as Kosciuszko's rebels marched north toward Warsaw. Once again Julian Niemcewicz rushed to his friend's camp after a huge battle. Niemcewicz, who had returned from Italy, joined the commander and became his secretary.

The provisional government was trying hard to find allies to join the cause. France was at war with Prussia and Austria, and Sweden and Turkey had battled with the Russians off and on for the past several years. The Polish government kept working its foreign liaisons to create an alliance among France, Sweden, Poland, and Turkey, but the reign of terror in Paris made diplomacy impossible.

The Polish emissary in Paris, Francis Barss, could not persuade the French to lend money or military support to the uprising. The French Jacobins wanted the Polish revolutionaries to put up guillotines or gallows in their capital to get rid of the "aristocrats" and the "priests."[62]

At the same time Lucchesini had goaded the Austrians into joining the fight and opening a third front against the Poles in the south. Kosciuszko believed that Austria was the least vicious of Poland's neighbors, and instructed his officers in Krakow to surrender to the Austrian army if they could not defend the city.

But on June 15 it was the Prussian army that arrived at the walls of Krakow ready for a siege. Col. Ignacy Wieniawski, who was left in charge, fled the city, and the small contingent that remained lowered the drawbridges and gave up without a fight. A few days later Austria invaded Poland from the south and began to gobble up more territory. Once again Poland was facing three powerful enemies.

The fate of the entire Polish nation depended on its ability to defend Warsaw.

Like the rebels in the French capital, the Poles were beginning to fight among themselves. Polish Jacobins ran amok and erected gallows in the square between the royal castle and Saint Anne's Church.

On June 28 they broke into the jail and dragged out Bishop Ignacy Massalski, who had collaborated with the Russians and embezzled money from the public coffers. The rabid crowd strung up the bishop and cheered as his neck snapped. Six other prisoners were also hanged. A defense attorney who tried to stop the hangings without a trial, and a prosecutor delivering legal papers, were also beaten and hanged.

The gang was so anxious to kill the most notorious of the Targowica traitors, Felix Potocki, that when they could not find him, they hoisted his portrait on the gallows, stringing him up in effigy.

King Stanislaw and his brother, Michael, the archbishop of Poland, sat cowering in the castle as the drunken mob outside sang, "We Krakowians, with these ropes around our waists, will hang the King and the Primate!" Stanislaw dashed off a letter to Kosciuszko pleading that he come to Warsaw defend him and restore order.[63]

The commander in chief replied to the king, "the personal safety of Your Majesty concerns me in the highest degree."[64]

Kosciuszko was outraged by the lynch mob and demanded that the murderers be arrested. He issued a statement, "To the People of Warsaw," which he asked the newspapers to print: "What happened in Warsaw yesterday filled my heart with bitterness and sorrow. The desire to punish the guilty was right, but why were they punished without a court verdict? Why were the authority and the sanctity of laws violated? Why was the one [prosecutor] sent to you in our name hurt and covered with wounds? Why was the life of this innocent public official disgracefully taken away? . . . Those who do not obey the laws are not worthy of liberty."

As if to burden the residents of Warsaw with guilt and inspire them at the same time, he added: "Once the war takes a turn for the better and allows me to leave my dedicated duties for a moment, I will stand among you. Maybe you will enjoy the sight of a soldier who every day risks his life for you; but I don't want to spoil this moment with any grief engraved on my face."

The commander in chief ordered the Supreme Council to speed up the legal process to "prosecute the prisoners, sentence the guilty and free the innocent. And by fulfilling the demands of the public justice, I strictly prohibit the public, for its own good, from any unwarranted actions, such as breaking into prisons, capturing people and punishing them with death."

Kosciuszko adamantly declared that those who did not bring their grievances to the government "in a lawful way, will be considered mutineers destroying the public peace and will be punished." Seeking to harness the public's anger toward the real enemy, he added, "Those of you, whose heated courage wants to be active for your fatherland, join me in my camp."[65]

The message was clear: The Kosciuszko uprising would not be a French revolution. The stern words from the commander put an end to the mob rule and drew more recruits to his camp, including a cavalry of twelve hundred horsemen led by Peter Jazwinski. Kilinski, the shoemaker that had been promoted to colonel under Kosciuszko's new merit promotions, rounded up six thousand lazy "slackers" and led them to the commander in chief's camp.[66]

Swedish ambassador Toll reported back to Stockholm: "General Kosciuszko is more trusted and popular in Poland than anyone in the whole world so far, like Washington, under whom he served."[67]

Indeed, the nation hung on Kosciuszko's every word and trusted his judgment. About one hundred people were put on trial for the lynchings, and seven of them were hanged for murder. He had refocused the vengeance of the people on the enemy just in time. Warsaw was about to become the front line in the war.

But while the Poles were happy with their leader, the French revolutionaries were angry that Kosciuszko had prosecuted the Jacobins who built gallows and hanged traitors. The French viewed the Warsaw hangings as a positive development.

The Polish emissary in Paris, Barss, was given a statement that read: "The French government will not grant a single piece of gold, will not send a single soldier, to support a revolution which would aim at retaining aristocratic or royal governments in which using the term 'revolution' would lead only to a change in government that would not be based on the principles that are rudimental for truly Republican constitutions."[68]

By July the war had moved to Warsaw. Kosciuszko's forces beat the Russians in a series of skirmishes around the capital, and he ordered the city to dig in for the coming siege. The Poles did not have enough guns, cannons, and ammunition to defend the city, so once again he rallied the peasants. He asked a professor of architecture and hydraulics, Chrystian Piotr Aigner, to develop a series of scythes and pikes that were specifically designed for warfare. Aigner put out a military manual called, "A short lesson on pikes and scythes," to teach the peasants how to use their farming instruments as weapons.[69] Barns in the towns surrounding the capital were scoured for farming instruments that could be used to defend the city.

The rebels also began putting out their own newspaper, the *Government Gazette*, which became the propaganda organ of the revolution, informing the citizens of the city about their responsibilities.

From the west, Prussian king Frederick William II led an army of 25,000 soldiers to attack Warsaw. From the east, Russian general Ivan Fersen led an army of 41,000 to strike the Polish capital.[70] The city was surrounded.

The Poles had 16,000 regular soldiers and about 18,000 peasants armed with scythes and pikes. There were also 15,000 armed burghers ready to defend their city.[71]

On July 7 Kosciuszko positioned most of his army on the left bank of the Wisla River outside the city limits to defend against the armies approaching from the west. He took responsibility of guarding the central neighborhood, Mokotow, and sent Generals Zajaczek, Mokronoski, Dabrowski, and Prince Poniatowski to guard his flanks.

The commander in chief and the mayor of Warsaw, Ignacy Zakrzewski, secretly went to visit the king at the Lazienki Palace. Seemingly unaware of just how unpopular he was, and ungrateful that Kosciuszko had saved his life from the Jacobins, Stanislaw whined that he was not allowed to address the troops.

Kosciuszko had come to get a copy of the engineering maps of Warsaw, which were in the king's possession, so he could plan the city's defenses.

"If I still had diamonds, I would rather give them up than these maps," Stanislaw declared, still in denial over how dire the situation actually was.[72] The commander and the mayor were adamant, and Kosciuszko promised to bring the maps back in a few days.

The entire city came out to work on the redoubts that the commander in chief designed. Michael Starzenski, a nobleman who enlisted in Kosciuszko's army, wrote: "All of Warsaw was buzzing with activity. Thousands of burghers, servants, workers, soldiers, priests, monks, plain women and elegant ladies had gathered singing and waving flags, working to dig and pour the ramparts."[73]

The siege of Warsaw began on July 13, and the Prussian and Russian armies bombarded the city with cannonballs, shells, and incendiary devices. Kosciuszko and his army were able to keep the enemy out of range of most of the city, but many buildings on the outskirts were set ablaze in an attempt to terrorize the inhabitants of the capital. But the fires were calmly put out. When cannonballs did land inside the city, they were collected and given to the army. "Kosciuszko, worried that he might run out of powder and ammunition, put a price on every cannonball, unexploded shell, and bomb that was brought to camp," Starzenski wrote. "Boys and poor people raced to collect these things, sometimes coming 100 steps from the redoubts."[74]

The patchwork of armed forces held out for weeks, frustrating the attempts of the professional armies that were trying to capture Warsaw. After a lieutenant held off a strong attack from the Prussians with his incredibly accurate artillery fire, Kosciuszko took out his gold watch and chain and gave it to the officer as a reward. With no medals to hand out, Kosciuszko awarded rings and jewelry for bravery.[75]

While the west bank of the Wisla River in Warsaw was home to Christian burghers, the east bank was called Praga, a neighborhood with a large Jewish community. Its most prominent resident was Szmul [Samuel] Zbytkower, a successful merchant who was King Stanislaw's supplier for the castle. He ran a butcher shop, a tannery, a brickyard, a textile factory, and a bank, and he collected taxes and fees from the Jewish community for the king. He was a respected member of the Jewish community and held a position of authority in the synagogue. For his service, Stanislaw awarded him land in Praga, which became known as "Szmulowizna" among the locals.[76]

Zbytkower was commissioned by the Russians to make uniforms during their occupation of Warsaw, but once the insurrection began, his garment factory was requisitioned to make Polish uniforms.[77] The commander ordered merchants to produce more breeches and jackets "because there are not enough for the army" and instructed, "All the fabrics that can be used should be picked up from the churches."[78]

Even though many Jews were willing to take up arms for Poland, city hall bu-
reaucrats still demanded that they pay the tax levy to live in Warsaw. A group of
Jews went to see Kosciuszko, and he agreed it was time to abolish the poll tax on
Jews.

Kosciuszko wrote to the mayor, "On two occasions, they [the Jews] presented me with their requests and complaints about the levies that were imposed
on them, the ticket payment in particular. It's no wonder that under the former
government, with all these improprieties, the ticket payment was detested. But
today, when the fatherland is presenting itself equally to all as a mother, it should
grant everyone the same justice. It is indecent and inappropriate that this class of
citizens, that are equally useful like others, and even equally devoted to public
defense like others, should be more distant from the privileges of our government."[79]

His willingness to take up any issue for the people, and his modesty and
good nature did wonders to keep morale high in a city that was constantly under
cannon fire. The neighborhood where he was stationed was near the Lubomirski
Palace, owned by the family of his beloved Louise. But rather than sleep in the
comforts of the glorious mansion, he pitched a small tent nearby. He never took
off his peasant robe, even sleeping in it, so that he could jump up when the enemy bombarded during the night. He ate his meals under a tree with his officers
and drank old Hungarian wine and was constantly swilling coffee whether it was
hot, cold, or even icy.[80]

Kosciuszko attracted numerous volunteers in Warsaw. One of them was an
elegant black man named Jean Lapierre.[81] The Poles nicknamed him
"Domingo," so he may have had a connection to the French slave colony in Saint
Domingue. He made his way to Poland, where he later worked as a bookkeeper
for the nobleman Dominick Radziwill, who gave him a small share of his estate.[82]
Lapierre, who was well read and had traveled quite a bit, picking up several languages including French and Polish, became Kosciuszko's personal assistant. He
was tall, handsome, and well dressed.[83]

Lapierre was not the only example of the multicultural nature of Kosciuszko's
army. In addition to serfs and burghers Kosciuszko's army had six Muslim Tatar
regiments, and some of his Polish divisions were up to 20 percent Jewish.[84]

By his constant pronouncements proclaiming that everyone in the new
Poland would be equal, Kosciuszko created an atmosphere of camaraderie despite the relentless bombardment of the city throughout the summer.

On August 2 King Frederick William wrote to Kosciuszko and King Stanislaw demanding that the city surrender. The commander in chief laughed it off
and replied, "The city of Warsaw is not in a position that it needs to surrender."[85] Stanislaw also told the Prussian king that they would not give up.

The Prussians were growing frustrated, and a few weeks later, one of their leaders, General Johann Mannstein, asked to meet with one of his colonels whom the Poles had taken prisoner. The request was denied, but Polish general Zajaczek met with Mannstein and joked about the constant bombing: "What beautiful music you gentlemen have been playing for the past few weeks."[86] Zajaczek also teased his enemy about his Prussian king being a traitor for reneging on his alliance with Poland.

During the siege Kosciuszko galloped to all corners of the city, making sure the fortifications were secure, and that the egos of his officers and various spheres of society were not injured. "Our commander Kosciuszko was everywhere," Starzenski wrote. "He answered every call, wherever there was a threat of danger."[87]

Because of his leadership, focusing the people on keeping the enemy at bay, Warsaw bravely held out. On September 6 the *Government Gazette* reported the good news. The frustrated Russians and Prussians had withdrawn their troops. The only question was how many would return—and when.[88]

For the first time in months Kosciuszko was able to take off his peasant robe and settle in for a full night's rest in his tent. The next day the Supreme Council suggested some sort of celebration, but it was left to the churches to hold masses to give thanks.

"The spirit of liberty begins to shew itself in other regions," wrote America's representative in Paris, James Monroe, to his predecessor Thomas Jefferson. "Geneva has undergone revolution—the people have taken the gov't into their hands, apprehended the aristocrats & executed seven of the most wicked. And in Poland, under the direction of Kosciuszko who acted with us in America, a formidable head has been raised against Prussia and Russia."[89]

Some rebels in Warsaw also wanted to hang wicked aristocrats, and once the enemy withdrew the Jacobins again reared their ugly heads. The streamlined court process Kosciuszko ordered when he banned mob hangings resulted in new verdicts.

The convicted were sentenced to whippings and hard labor in government factories. But Bishop Wojciech Skarszewski, who collaborated with Russia against the constitution and sided with the Targowica traitors and the Grodno Seym, was found guilty of treason and sentenced to be hanged, his church possessions confiscated.[90]

Rev. Kollontay, who had been the voice of reason, speaking of "a gentle revolution" during the four-year Seym, had grown vengeful as the leader of the court council and emerged as "the Polish Robespierre." But the commander in chief had become uncomfortable with the death penalty, and on the advice of Niemcewicz and others, he commuted the bishop's sentence to life in prison. Starzenski, who watched the proceedings, wrote in his diary, "Kosciuszko said that he does not approve and will not take responsibility for all of these hangings, imprisonments and hot-headed violence, imitating the French Revolution. . . . He said that first and foremost we must strengthen the nation's army."[91]

Kollontay and the Jacobins accused Kosciuszko of being soft on the aristocracy and the church.[92] One of the court officials, Gabriel Taszycki, wrote a letter of resignation: "Commander in Chief! I used to look at you as the greatest republican. Yet today you spoke with lips of a despot. If decisions of our court are not in line with your thoughts, then for those of us who were part of the court, we see no choice but to ask you to relieve us of these sensitive responsibilities."[93]

Rev. Staszic was right. Kosciuszko was neither a Sulla nor the ruthless Machiavellian prince the Jacobins had hoped for. Even George Washington executed traitors and deserters during the American Revolution, but the peasant prince was soft on civilians, and even prisoners of war. He asked an Orthodox church to hold mass for the Russian prisoners, and a Lutheran minister to hold services for the Prussian soldiers who were captured during the siege of Warsaw. He freed Czech and Hungarian prisoners who served in the Prussian army, saying that they too deserved their own countries.

Kosciuszko did not want to make more enemies. He was looking for allies. He also had more urgent problems than rekindling the witch hunt for traitors. During the siege of Warsaw, the Russians had captured Vilnius, the Austrians took the Polish city of Lublin, and the Prussian army burned fifty villages on their march back toward Berlin.[94] As the summerlong siege of Warsaw kept the peasants from working in the fields, the fall harvest would not produce much wheat for bread or hay for horses.

One of the heroes who emerged in the siege of Warsaw was Gen. Jan Henryk Dabrowski, a talented cavalry leader. Kosciuszko sent General Dabrowski and his brigade west to the city of Poznan to recruit more soldiers to fight the Prussians before they could return. Dabrowski's dragoons won a series of quick battles against the Prussians, giving hope to the leader of the insurrection. Kosciuszko sent other officers to Lithuania and other parts of Poland to mobilize more troops across the country.

Berek Joselewicz, a Jewish merchant who sold horses, and his associate, Joseph Aronowicz, asked Kosciuszko if they could form a Jewish cavalry regiment to fight alongside the Polish troops. Kosciuszko was thrilled. The idea of peasant and Jewish militias went nowhere when he first suggested it several years earlier, and finally the time was right. He praised the initiative and appointed Joselewicz a colonel, and ordered the Supreme Council to give Joselewicz three thousand zlotys from the national treasury to help recruit and supply volunteers.[95]

It would be the first wholly Jewish brigade formed since biblical times.

To announce the formation of the Jewish cavalry, Kosciuszko wrote in the September 17, 1794 issue of the *Government Gazette*: "Nothing will convince other nations of the sanctity of our cause and the justness of our revolution than the fact that we set aside the different religions and traditions of those who support our uprising, and that, of their own free will, they offer to lay down their lives."

Kosciuszko outlined the troubles that the Jewish nation had faced after being "dispersed all over the world from the time they left their ancestral land," and lamented that they had been "despised and shunned by the rest of mankind, this nation was pronounced unable to protect its rights and property, and was kept around only for the sake of autocrats."

Citing examples from the Old Testament, Kosciuszko pointed out that Jews were "filled with love and a desire for freedom," and that there were "admirable heroic achievements of Jewish soldiers such as those who broke through enemy lines to eagerly bring King David a drink of water. Fearless Jesse, Abner, Joab and others terrified their enemies. Even Hebrew women set an example of courage and prowess for our era."

He also praised their involvement in the Polish revolution, saying, "On April 17 and 18, when Warsaw underwent a bloody battle with its Russian invaders, Jews living in the city rushed to get involved, bravely faced the attackers and proved to the world that when humankind can benefit, the Jewish people will not spare their lives."

The commander in chief proclaimed: "There is no resident of Poland who would not fully dedicate himself to the creation of this nation, seeing his freedom and happiness in it. Brimming with noble motives, Berek Joselewicz and Joseph Aronowicz, men of the Old Testament, remembering the land they were born in and that along with others they will benefit from Poland's regaining her freedom, have conveyed to me their need, and desire to form a Jewish light cavalry division. Having praised their devotion, I hereby allow for a draft to the given division and a collection of required arms, so that they should join the Polish army and engage the enemy as soon as possible."[96]

After Kosciuszko's proclamation, Colonel Joselewicz reached out to his community, writing in the *Government Gazette*: "Listen, children of the tribes of Israel! Ye, who have in their heart implanted the image of God Almighty, all that are willing to help in the struggle for the fatherland, we people should act, the time has come to consecrate all of our strength. This is how it is my faithful brothers! Awaken the love for your country, to bring new life to our nation whose blood has for years been sucked dry by poisonous snakes. . . . It will be easier now that our guardian, Thaddeus Kosciuszko, who is indeed a messenger from God Almighty, has given his full support for the creation of a Jewish regiment."

Praising the commander in chief, Joselewicz wrote: "He is the great savior of numerous great men who already have many liberties, yet nevertheless yearn for more freedom and to reclaim their country. Why should we not labor to obtain our freedom, which has been promised to us, just as firmly and sincerely as it has been to others in this world? But first we must show that we are worthy of it. . . . Let us fight for our country as long as a drop of blood is left in us! Though we ourselves may not live to see this freedom, at least our children will live in tranquility and freedom, and will not roam about like wild beasts. My beloved brothers! Awaken then like lions and leopards."[97]

Colonel Joselewicz and Aronowicz rode through Praga trying to raise money, supplies, and recruits. The Jewish community was skeptical of the idea, just as Kosciuszko's scythemen and burgher militiamen had been thought of when they started.

Praga was a poor neighborhood, and Joselewicz approached artisans and craftsmen and tried to teach them how to fire guns and fight with swords on horseback. It was not easy, but eventually Joselewicz had persuaded hundreds of Jews to trade in their gabardine coats for the black uniforms that had been designed. For religious reasons they did not want to shave, so they became known as the "bearded" army.

The first few volunteers were Marek Jakubowicz, Mayer Herszkowicz, Chaim Judkiewicz, Mordko Wolfowicz, Josel Abrahamowicz, Jacob Epstein, and Herszek Lewkowicz.[98] It took a few weeks, but eventually Colonel Joselewicz raised a dragoon unit of five hundred Jews.[99]

While the Jews were training and preparing to protect Praga against the inevitable return of the czarist troops, Kosciuszko learned that an army of Russian reinforcements was marching in from the east.

Kosciuszko's rebels would once again face overwhelming odds.

THIRTEEN

Poland Is Wiped Off the Map

CZARINA CATHERINE WAS ONCE AGAIN FURIOUS WITH THE POLES, but this time the scourge of her territorial ambitions was Kosciuszko. She put a price on his head, and offered "a great reward" for his capture, dead or alive.[1]

Seeing that General Fersen could not quash the uprising, Catherine wrote to her most talented commander, Gen. Alexander Vasilievich Suvorov, explaining why he had to join the fight, "I am sure you know about the rebel Kosciuszko, fomenting sedition in Poland, with his contacts with the monsters governing France he intends to widen the revolt to hurt Russia."[2]

General Suvorov was a wiry old man with stringy white hair combed over the top of his head. Even though he was sixty-four, his motto was still "Speed, assessment, and attack," a philosophy that served him well in campaigns that crushed the armies of Turkey and Sweden, and Casimir Pulaski's Bar confederates. "One minute decides the outcome of battle, one hour the success of a campaign, one day the fate of empires," Suvorov said. "I operate not by hours but by minutes."[3]

Dressed incognito in his woolen peasant frock, Kosciuszko traveled twice through the backwoods of Lithuania into territory controlled by Cossacks to find the shattered remains of his forces there. With Vilnius in the hands of the Russians, the battered brigades hiding in the surrounding forests were in no position to challenge the enemy, so he ordered them to march to Warsaw.

The Polish general in the east, Charles Sierakowski, who had about four thousand soldiers and peasant scythemen, sent a spy and four Tatar horsemen to reconnoiter the enemy forces on the Russian border. Suvorov's twelve thousand troops were marching on a course for Warsaw. Sierakowski tried to stop them from crossing the Bug River and fought them at Krupczyce and Terespol. He suffered heavy losses but managed to slow down the Russians.

South of Warsaw, Polish general Adam Poninski was following Fersen's fourteen thousand troops, recuperating after the failed siege on Warsaw. When couriers arrived in the capital with news that the two Russian generals were marching toward each other, Kosciuszko decided that he had no choice but to strike at Fersen before he could combine his troops with Suvorov's to form one massive army.

Chilly autumn rains had soaked much of Poland, so Kosciuszko finally agreed to move his army headquarters into the Mokotow Palace, the Warsaw residence of his beloved Princess Louise, who was at her estate in Ukraine.

On Sunday night, October 5, the commander in chief ordered two foot regiments to march out of Warsaw to join the armies in the east. He then attended a dinner party at the mayor's house until 1:00 a.m., with Kollontay, Potocki, and several more of the insurrection's leaders. As Kosciuszko was a marked man, he told only Kollontay and General Zajaczek, whom he left in charge of the army, that he was rushing out to attack the Russians before they could reach the capital. With the sun rising on the morning of October 6, Kosciuszko and Niemcewicz secretly slipped out of Warsaw, riding across the bridge into Praga before heading east.[4]

It was a crisp sunny day, and they galloped hard and switched horses whenever the legs gave out on the ponies they were riding. Mostly they rode on peasant nags, with girthless saddles and ratty ropes as bridles and bits. After riding for ten hours they caught up with General Sierakowski seventy miles away in the village of Okrzei.

The commander in chief held a war council with General Sierakowski and Gen. Poninski, who left his army twenty-six miles away to attend the meeting. Sierakowski had a little more than 5,000 soldiers at his disposal and Kosciuszko's adjutant, Major Fiszer, was expected to arrive with the two regiments marching from Warsaw in a few days. But even that would give Kosciuszko only about 7,000 troops. Fersen was leading an army of 14,000. Rather than order Poninski to retrieve his 4,000 troops, the commander in chief sent him back to his camp to await further instructions.[5] It would be the most disastrous miscalculation of Kosciuszko's life.

The next day, without waiting for the reinforcements from Warsaw or summoning Poninski's unit, Kosciuszko gave chase to Fersen, following the trail of scorched earth that was left behind. The Cossacks had plundered the surrounding villages and after a day of marching, Kosciuszko, Niemcewicz, and the officers found a lord's house, where they spent the night. Chairs, desk, dressers were smashed, and old books and newspapers were strewn on the floor.

The rains returned on the eighth, turning the marshy bogs even wetter. The soggy fields were filled with mud puddles, making movement difficult. Rather than force his troops to continue slogging through the muck, Kosciuszko let them stop and rest.

One of their advance teams captured ten Russian cavalrymen who had forced a Polish engineer to chart a course for Suvorov to reach Fersen. The engineer was interrogated and ordered to draw a map outlining the Russian camp, showing the number of troops and cannons. The sketch revealed that Fersen's army heavily outnumbered the Poles, but with Suvorov approaching, Kosciuszko felt compelled to strike as fast as he could.

With a short break in the rain, Niemcewicz took a walk with a friend from his days at the royal military academy with whom he studied the works of Titus Livius, a historian who lived in the days of Christ and wrote volumes on the Roman Empire.

"Do you remember your Livy?" his friend asked. "These ravens are on our right, it is a bad omen."

"It would be for the Romans," Niemcewicz replied, "but not for us. We shall beat the Muscovites."[6]

The rain stopped the following day, and the reinforcements from Warsaw finally caught up with Kosciuszko's troops. They were starving and exhausted, but after a short rest and some glasses of brandy, they were once again on the move.

In the late afternoon Kosciuszko and Niemcewicz followed the engineer's map with a troop of dragoons to scout the terrain ahead. They found Fersen's army stretched along the bank of the Wisla River as far as the eye could see. The setting sun reflected off the rifles and cannons, and they got close enough to hear neighing horses and the hum of the massive army. A Cossack troop chased the Poles away, and they retreated to find a place to stop for the night.

Kosciuszko and his officers found an abandoned stone manor belonging to the Zamoyskis that they chose for their headquarters. The Maciejowski family once owned it, giving the surrounding area its name, Maciejowice. Cossacks had ransacked the estate. The paintings of aristocrats, bishops, and generals had their eyes poked out and their faces slashed with swords.

Ever the poet, Niemcewicz looked through the old shelves and found some old newspaper that he read aloud to entertain his commander and the other officers. The army took a position in the field in front of the house, and on both sides were woods. Behind the house was a small river.

At this late stage Kosciuszko realized that he did not have enough troops to take on Fersen, but he decided to make a stand and sent a message to Poninski to march on their position "with the utmost urgency."[7]

The soldiers in the nearby Muscovite camp were much more optimistic, and on the night of October 9, a courier arrived with news from the Prussians. General Fersen was sitting around a campfire with his officers. In the dark around him the rest of his army was standing in rows with their rifles between their legs. The messenger told Fersen that as the bridge over the Wisla River would be burned, he would like to stay and witness the battle.

With the flickering light of the campfire dancing on his weather beaten face, Fersen replied, "I will allow it. But don't blame me if anything bad happens. The bones are already lying on the table."[8]

When the sun rose the next morning, a soldier rushed to tell Kosciuszko that the enemy was advancing in battle formations. The Russians opened with heavy artillery fire from the other side of the forest, and the Poles heard snapping branches as the cannonballs smashed through the forest and landed around them. A Russian marching band played military music as their infantry sloshed through the marshland.

The Poles were on a slight elevation above a village on their left flank. Kosciuszko ordered it set ablaze so the Russians could not hide behind it. Peasant women and children fled the flames screaming and crying to get out of the line of fire. The initial phase of the battle went well, as the Russians got stuck in the mud ahead of them. Kosciuszko manned one of the twelve-pound artillery pieces and pointed it at the enemy. But with thousands more behind them, they kept coming.

After a cannonball landed behind Sierakowski and some shrapnel hit him in the back, he rushed to Kosciuszko and said, "I think we still have time to retreat."

Kosciuszko replied to him, "There is no room here to retreat, this is the place to be buried, or be victorious."[9]

With bombs exploding around them, Niemcewicz described the scene as "a shower of balls of every size, grape shot, and grenades, spreading as they burst, death on all sides, overwhelmed us. One of those grenades burst right between General Kosciuszko, his aide-de-camp Fiszer, and myself, and its splinters passing over our heads, struck, at fifty paces, a gunner who fell dead on the spot."[10]

Col. Joseph Drzewiecki, standing nearby, saw the "cold-blooded" look on Kosciuszko's face when he looked at Niemcewicz and said, "We were lucky it wasn't closer. I was almost killed."[11]

The sound of whistling bullets and booming cannonballs terrified the horses and they began to grunt, whiney and buck as the earth and mud blew up around them. The Polish cannons fired on the attacking enemy for three hours, but in the early afternoon the guns stopped: They had run out of ammunition.

The Russian infantry charged in with their bayonets and stabbed the Polish soldiers and peasants. Kosciuszko bolted from one unit to the next, urging his men to fight on, promising that Poninski would arrive with reinforcements. But it was too late. The czarist troops jabbed away, stabbing and shooting thousands of Poles. Some dropped their rifles and fell to the ground pleading to surrender, but the Russians murdered them anyway, hollering, "That's for Warsaw, remember Warsaw!"[12]

All the czarina's officers were eager to win the reward money and notoriety for capturing Kosciuszko, but not knowing that he wore peasant robe tied with a green rope belt as a symbol of hope, they all searched for a fancy uniform like the top brass wore in their own army.[13]

The slaughter continued for three hours as four thousand Poles were killed or wounded. Even as some of his troops ran for their lives, Kosciuszko continued to fight like a madman, as if he wanted to die. He had three horses shot out from under him and was wounded several times, including a slash from a Russian sword across the top of his head, which sent blood gushing all over his face.

With most of his men killed, wounded, or on the run, he finally tried to leave the battlefield. He was chased by several Cossacks and fired at them with a pistol as he tried to gallop through a marshy field. His horse tripped, sending him flying facefirst into the mud. A Cossack caught Kosciuszko from behind and stabbed him in the back with a long pike. Another Cossack trotted up and rammed a second pike through his left hip, puncturing his sciatic nerve.[14]

Writhing in pain, spattered with mud, and blood oozing over his head and torso, Kosciuszko pulled out his pistol and put the barrel in his mouth. With his last drop of energy, he pulled the trigger. The gunbarrel was empty. He had used up all his bullets firing at the enemy. Dizzy from his wounds, he passed out in the mud.[15]

The Cossacks had no idea of the identity of the prisoner in the peasant robe as they stripped his body. They took his watch, the rings that he wore on his fingers to give out as medals to his soldiers, and even his shoes and pants.

Initially a rumor spread among the survivors of the Polish army that Kosciuszko had been killed. The Russians made the captured soldiers look at the faces of all of their dead officers in an effort to identify Kosciuszko, and finally someone recognized the bloody and muddy heap as their commander.

Colonel Drzewiecki, who had also been taken prisoner, cleaned up his commander's face and asked for water so he could take a drink. The Russians said vodka was better medicine and tried to pour it down Kosciuszko's throat through his clenched teeth.[16] An oxcart came to carry the bleeding commander off the field, but two Cossacks thought the beasts were undignified, even for an enemy general, so they made a stretcher out of lances and a long coat to carry the fallen leader from the field.

In an effort to destroy his legacy and discourage the Poles from rising up yet again, the Prussians spread a rumor that Kosciuszko had cried out the Latin words, *Finis Poloniae!* as he fell from his horse. Most of his countrymen did not believe that their commander in chief would utter such a phrase, much less in Latin to illiterate Cossacks who were ramming pikes through his torso. When he regained consciousness, Kosciuszko vehemently denied the claim, and it was seen for what it was, a ham-handed attempt by his enemies to ruin his reputation.

Kosciuszko was unconscious, and General Fersen had him taken back to the manor house at Maciejowice, where a Russian field surgeon treated his wounds. The mansion became a hospital and prison for the captured officers. Niemcewicz recalled that the cheerful Russian officers kept repeating, "We are not barbarians," as if to convince themselves of that as they carted off all the valuables in the home.[17]

When Kosciuszko awoke the next day Niemcewicz was at his side and explained that they were prisoners. With tears in his eyes the commander replied, "How happy I am to have such a friend in misfortune."[18] Kosciuszko had suffered a great loss of blood, and he could not stand because of the spears that had punctured his back and hip.

General Fersen visited the Polish commander to pay his respects, and allowed him to send letters to Warsaw. Kosciuszko asked his adjutant, Major Fiszer, to write to General Zajaczek, whom he had left in charge, asking that he send Peter Maignien, a French doctor who served as his army surgeon, along with his valet, Jean Lapierre, and his cook and servant, Stanislaw Balinski.[19]

Fersen wrote to King Stanislaw saying that now that the Polish army had been "destroyed," and the "commander of the 1794 revolution" was in custody, Russia demanded the release of all its prisoners of war and a restoration of its rights.[20]

The reply that was sent back was out of character for the usually timid Stanislaw, and most likely written by Kollontay and his revolutionaries. "While the defeat of a portion of the Polish army on Oct. 10, is painful," read the letter signed by the king, "especially to the loss of a respected man who initiated the independence movement in his fatherland, it has not shattered the determination of those who have sworn to die, or regain their freedom."[21]

After a few days to recuperate, Kosciuszko was put in a carriage, while Niemcewicz and three other wounded officers rode in another carriage to begin the long trek to prison in Russia. The rest of the prisoners, expecting to end up in Siberia, were forced to march behind wagons of luggage and plundered booty.

Dr. Maignien, caught up with the Russian army in the village of Kortnica. With him was Lapierre, who had brought Kosciuszko's personal belongings, and a letter proposing a prisoner swap: Kosciuszko in exchange for the three thousand Russian soldiers imprisoned in Warsaw. Lapierre also delivered three thousand ducats, three watches, a gold snuffbox, sheepskin blankets, fresh sheets, and clean underwear.[22] Twelve years earlier Kosciuszko tried to win the release of a wounded black soldier in a prisoner exchange for a captured British soldier. Ironically the situation had reversed, and a black man was trying to win the wounded Kosciuszko's freedom by delivering a similar proposition.

But Fersen, who had orders to link up with Suvorov, declined the prisoner trade, and kept marching. He detached General Alexei Khrushchev and two thousand Russian soldiers to escort Kosciuszko and the other prisoners to Russia, and he moved the rest of his army to join the attack on Warsaw. Lapierre climbed into the back of the carriage that was carrying Kosciuszko.[23]

Suvorov and Fersen attacked Praga, on the east bank of the Wisla, early in the morning on November 4, with a combined army of twenty-two thousand men. General Zajaczek, who Kosciuszko left in charge of the capital, was too preoccupied by Jacobin intrigue to prepare properly for the attack. Zajaczek, expecting another long siege, was unaccustomed to Suvorov's speedy attacks and could not hold off the Russians with his regular soldiers, who were supplemented by scythemen and Berek Joselewicz's fledgling Jewish cavalry.

Zajaczek was wounded and fled, leaving the Polish army without a leader. The Russian army killed thousands of his soldiers. The remaining soldiers retreated over the bridge into the main section of Warsaw. One of the survivors was Lt. Nicolas Chopin, whose son, Frédéric, would become Poland's greatest composer.

Suvorov allowed the Cossack horsemen to run wild like savages, slaughtering civilians, punishing Jews and burghers for taking part in the liberation of Warsaw. Most of Joselewicz's dragoons were killed, but he and a handful of his men managed to escape death and later fled the country.[24]

Hiding in the castle on the opposite bank of the river was Countess Anna Potocka, who recalled: "Nine thousand defenseless people where slaughtered in one night, with no other refuge nor tomb but their own dwellings reduced to ashes! The king's castle on the banks of the Wisla was all that separated us from the suburb of Praga, we distinctly heard the groans of the victims and the hurrahs of the butchers. It was even possible to distinguish the shrieks and the laments of the women and children, and the howls and imprecations of the fathers and husbands who were dying in defense of the dearest that man has. Profound darkness added to the horror of the scene. Against whirlwinds of fire exhaling a whitish smoke stood out infernal silhouettes of Cossacks, who, like devilish phantoms, tore hither and thither on horseback, their lances poised, with awful hisses urging themselves on in their murderous work."[25]

As the invaders carried off women and children, Szmul Zbytkower bought some of them back from the hands of the Cossacks. He had two barrels of coins in his house, and promised his neighbors one gold ducat for every rescued resident of Praga, whether they be Jewish or Christian, and a silver ducat for every dead body retrieved so they could receive a proper burial.[26]

Suvorov, who was proud of his work, sent a dispatch to Czarina Catherine: "The streets are covered with corpses; blood flows in torrents."[27] One Russian estimate was that twenty thousand people were murdered in the Praga massacre.[28]

Three days later King Stanislaw surrendered, and the remaining Polish soldiers fled Warsaw for western Europe.

Kosciuszko and the prisoners of war continued their long journey through Russia. The captured Polish officers had plenty of time to argue over who deserved the blame for their defeat at the Battle of Maciejowice. Poninski, who marched back to Warsaw, was put on trial and exonerated.

As they went from town to town through the Polish countryside, General Khrushchev barged into homes stealing valuables and the best horses and wagons, filling them with the spoils of war. The rapacious Khrushchev took furniture, china, paintings, bronze statues, curtains, and whatever else he could find.

General Suvorov sent Khrushchev a communiqué saying that the peasants were spreading a rumor that Kosciuszko had escaped at Maciejowice and that the czarina's army was taking an impostor back to Russia. To dispel the rumor Khrushchev would summon the lord in each town that they passed and bring him to see Kosciuszko as if he were a zoo attraction. "Men have been seen before this exhibiting ferocious animals," wrote Niemcewicz. "Now it was a ferocious animal that was exhibiting a man."[29]

As they continued their convoy, Polish noblemen with estates in the east sent food and supplies to ease the journey of their wounded soldiers. Kosciuszko's great love, Princess Louise, sent her young son with wine, clothes, and books.

On November 17 a messenger arrived with the news that Warsaw had fallen. The Russians changed course, sending the imprisoned soldiers farther east and taking Kosciuszko, Niemcewicz, Fiszer, and Lapierre to St. Petersburg.

They traveled for weeks across the cold steppes of Russia, arriving in St. Petersburg on December 10. Niemcewicz recalled the nightly journeys in which "the road was lighted only by the whiteness of the snow, upon which the aurora borealis reflected sometimes a blood-red color."[30]

The mind games and interrogations began as soon as they arrived. They were taken to the Peter and Paul Fortress on an island in the Neva River. Kosciuszko was separated from his officers, who were put in jail cells, while he was sent to a secluded part of the fort. On his first day in prison Niemcewicz found himself in an uncomfortable situation with Alexis Nikolaievich Samoilov, the grand procurator and head of secret affairs. "Let us talk in confidence," Samoilov said. "Let us say between us that your Kosciuszko is a stupid fellow."

Niemcewicz replied, "He has shown on many occasions that he is far from being what you say."

Trying to appeal to his prisoner's vanity, Samoilov said, "But it is you, Potocki and Kollontay who led him."[31]

Niemcewicz assured his interrogator that Kosciuszko was their commander and that they were simply advisers. The Russian interrogator pumped Niemcewicz for information about the revolutionaries, and when he did not cough up any secrets, Samoilov left in a huff, sending a list of questions and demanding a written reply under the threat of terrible consequences if he did not comply.

Despite having her men drag Kosciuszko's broken body hundreds of miles through the snow, she refused to meet with the rebel leader, writing to a friend, "He has been recognized as a fool in the full sense of the word, far beneath his task."[32]

Kosciuszko was given a list of twenty questions, asking for specific details about the insurrection, and ordered to answer them in writing. The probe focused on who was involved in the rebellion, what were its true goals, and what exactly did he do during his travels. His written reply did not jeopardize his compatriots because he mentioned little that was not already publicly known or reported in newspapers.

It was obvious from the questions that the elderly czarina and members of her court were still concerned about possible threats from France and Turkey, or a Jacobin uprising of serfs and dissenters in Russia against the rich land magnates. Kosciuszko wrote: "I did not express any plans to take any actions against the clergy and the aristocracy like the state of affairs in France."[33]

Aware of the political significance of arranged marriages and familial alliances, the Russian government's questions also probed into his personal affairs, asking specifically whether the Czartoryskis or other Polish aristocratic families had offered him the hands of their daughters, and about rumors that he carried a woman's portrait.

"As far as marriage is concerned," Kosciuszko replied, "neither the prince, nor the princess, under any circumstances or conditions, ever offered me to marry one of their daughters. And I never carried her portrait with me, or, that of any other woman in my entire life. . . . It was the voice of the people setting me up with five different women, with Miss Zamoyska, with the daughter of princess Czartoryska, with Miss Zurowska, with Miss Zakrzewska. In reality, I wanted to marry the widow Potocka."[34]

The secret police kept asking him more questions to try to trip him up and find out more about the revolution. He was so disgusted by the interrogations and life in captivity that he went on a hunger strike. Catherine softened her approach to see if he would open up. She viewed him as a pawn who was used by Kollontay and the conspirators. He had become dangerously thin and was constantly hunched over in pain, so on June 15, 1795, the czarina had him moved to the palace of a rich banker, explaining to a friend that since Kosciuszko was still very sick, "I moved him into Stegelman's house where he can spend time in the garden."[35]

The wounded prisoner still could not walk so Catherine asked a Scottish doctor named Samuel Rogerson to treat him. Dr. Rogerson's diagnosis was that Kosciuszko's intestines had twisted, and he began treating him with medicine. Kosciuszko enjoyed the Scotsman's company, and eventually, as his condition improved, he was allowed to go for rides through the city in a guarded carriage.[36] His valet, Lapierre, was with him throughout his incarceration. The Russians confiscated Kosciuszko's money and used it to pay Lapierre seven red zlotys per month and Kosciuszko's cook six zlotys per month.[37]

While his commander was living in a comfortable home, Niemcewicz was growing paranoid from spending so much time in a cell. His greatest pleasure was reading the books circulated through the prison cells, such as works by Horace, Swift, and Voltaire. After getting the right to use a pencil, he bribed a guard to sneak a note to Kosciuszko. It took a few months for Kosciuszko to find a way to respond, but he too was growing paranoid, and told Niemcewicz that rather than put his messages on paper, he should send them verbally through Lapierre.

After a few months in the Stegelman house, Kosciuszko was moved to the Marble Palace of the Orlov family. It was not, as it turned out, to benefit the czarina's sick prisoner but to try to win the respected hero over to her side.

The czarina had signed a pact with Prussia and Austria, dividing up the territory in central Europe and wiping Poland off the map altogether. Yet before the ink on the treaty was even dry, indigestion set in for these three powers as they tried to swallow their new territories, and soon they began sniping and tried to turn the Poles on one another. Catherine wrote to her friend Baron von Grimm that if the portly Prussian king Frederick William II did not meet her terms, "I will unleash my wretched beast, Kostiouchko. . . . He is as gentle as a lamb, but I gather that he would be willing to be unleashed on fatso!"[38]

It never came to be. Nearly two years after Kosciuszko arrived in St. Petersburg, on November 17, 1796, Catherine the Great died. She was sixty-seven. Even her Russian guards were relieved that the tyrant who had murdered her husband to take the throne was finally dead. Her son Paul, who had always hated his mother, succeeded her as czar.

Ten days later the door to Kosciuszko's room in the Marble Palace swung open, and a short, thin man strutted in with his head up and his shoulders arched back. An entourage of generals, aristocrats, and his son Grand Duke Alexander followed him in. The forty-two-year old Czar Paul had blond hair, a wide face, and a broad, flat pug nose. One of the men who accompanied him on the visit, Sergei Gagarin, left as soon as the meeting was over and wrote down the conversation to the best of his recollection.

"I have come my general," said the czar, "to restore your freedom."[39]

Kosciuszko was stunned and speechless. Seeing that the sickly general was moved by the news, Paul sat by his side and said, "I always pitied your fate, but under the rule of my mother, I could not help you. Now I can as the first act of my rule restore to you Sir, freedom. You are now free."

Kosciuszko nodded his thanks and said, "Your Royal Highness, I never grieved for my own fate, but I will never stop grieving the fate of my fatherland."

The czar replied, "Forget about your fatherland, Sir. Her turn has come as with some many other states, of which only their memory remains in history, in which you will always be beautifully remembered."

The dejected hero replied, "I would rather be forgotten and have my fatherland remain free."

Czar Paul said that Poland's demise was its own fault, because it infringed on the rights of its neighbors. The monarch said that the territories of the Greek and Roman empires were also carved up, and that if there were more patriots who loved their country like Kosciuszko, Poland would still be free.

Excited by the audience with the czar, Kosciuszko spoke up: "I know how some have tried to give your royal highness a false and bad impression of our nation, seen in the eyes of the world as a horde of restless scoundrels, impatient with government and laws, and therefore unworthy of existence. Virtuous and universal zeal for the betterment of one's country and rising up against oppression and chaos were called rebellion. The best desires of good citizens were regarded as faults and seen as the result of riotous Jacobinism, not only against injustice, but against Russia."

Kosciuszko continued, pleading Poland's case to the new czar, appealing to his "great and good heart . . . for the fate of our nation."

Turning around to his own generals, Czar Paul said, "Look at that intensity."

The czar told Kosciuszko to focus on his health and to let him know if he needed anything. "I am a real friend, Sir, and I hope that you will also be mine," Paul said. The czar excused himself and his guests, and Kosciuszko was told to rest.

The real business began during their next meeting, when Kosciuszko pleaded for the release of the twelve thousand Polish prisoners of war interned in Siberia and Russian prisons.

"They will be free, I give you my word," the czar said.[40]

But there was a catch. They all had to swear an oath of allegiance to the czar of Russia and promise not to organize any more rebellions. There were two Poles whom the czar's advisers did not want to free, Niemcewicz and Ignacy Potocki, who had also been captured. They were still considered enemies of the state.

Kosciuszko refused to leave these two collaborators in Russia. Their fate, as well as the future of twelve thousand Poles, fell on his shoulders. To free them he would have to acknowledge that Poland had been wiped off the map and ceased to exist as a country.

It was a conundrum that twisted Kosciuszko's intestines even more.

The weakened commander was allowed to meet with Potocki, who agreed that they had no choice but to take the oath and help free their countrymen. There was little they could do for their country from the inside of a prison cell.

While the Targowica traitors stabbed the Patriots in the back after the May 3 Constitution, some of them, who were living in St. Petersburg, urged Czar Paul to free Kosciuszko. One of them, Jerzy Wielhorski, devised a Faustian bargain with which to trap Kosciuszko to ensure that he would be beholden to Russia. At his suggestion the czar bequeathed one thousand indentured serfs to the peasant prince. Kosciuszko had refused many gifts of serfs, plantations, and money in the past, but to turn down the czar at a time when he was trying to negotiate the release of his men was tricky.[41]

Instead Kosciuszko politely declined the offer and said that he would like to share any gifts with his brothers-in-arms who needed them more than he did.

"I no longer see my fatherland in the country that I was born in," Kosciuszko told the czar, "but instead, the country in which I will die, America. For the freedom of both of these countries, I offered to sacrifice my life; at least the happy outlook of my second fatherland will cheer up the sorrow that fills my heart for the first."[42]

Kosciuszko asked for financial help to make the voyage back to America. He also gave the czar a list of prisoners who must be freed. Niemcewicz's name was at the top of the list. Czar Paul agreed to a general amnesty, and in exchange Kosciuszko agreed to sign the pledge.

Niemcewicz, who also agreed to take the pledge, was appalled. "The formula of the oath was terrible," he wrote. "We swore not only fealty and obedience to the emperor, but we promised to shed blood for his glory; we pledged ourselves to reveal all, that we ever should learn, dangerous to his person or empire; we declared, moreover, that in whatever corner of the world we might be, and with a single word of the emperor we would be obliged to drop everything and hasten to his person."[43]

The Polish prisoners were required to swear their allegiance to the czar and sign an affidavit in front of a Catholic priest in Saint Catherine's Church. By selling his good name to the czar, Kosciuszko won the freedom of more men than he realized. When the amnesty for Poles in Russian prisons was declared, it turned out there were 20,000 Polish political prisoners, 14,000 in Siberia alone. Catherine the Great had been arresting people in Poland dating back to the 1792 war, the period of the four-year Seym, and even to the days of Pulaski's Bar Confederation in the late 1760s.[44]

After two years of separation, Niemcewicz was allowed to visit Kosciuszko, who made hand gestures as if the walls had ears. "I found him lying upon his chaise lounge," Niemcewicz recalled, "with his head enveloped in bandages, and one leg entirely lifeless; but I was still more affected that his voice was almost gone, and there was great confusion in his ideas. He seemed struck with terror, spoke but in low tones, and whenever we raised our voices, he made signs with his finger to warn us that the servants in the corridor were listening, and that they were all spies."[45]

The two brothers-in-arms hugged and celebrated their liberation. Kosciuszko told Niemcewicz, "I know that you have suffered much, but you must complete your sacrifice; you must do me one favor, and promise to go with me to America."[46]

Niemcewicz's former commander was so frail and broken that he could not turn him down. As Kosciuszko could not walk and needed to be carried from his bed to a couch and to carriages, a strapping Polish officer named Lt. Libiszewski, Lapierre and his cook would join them on the voyage.

Czar Paul awarded Kosciuszko sixty thousand rubles for him and his staff to make the journey; twelve thousand was in cash, and the rest would be waiting for him in London. A large Siberian major, Ostaf Udom, who would escort them to Stockholm, would carry the money. The czar also had a special carriage made that allowed Kosciuszko to lie down for the voyage across Scandinavia. It came complete with cooking utensils, and a fine set of linen. Niemcewicz and Kosciuszko both received sable trimmed coats, sable hats, and fur-lined boots.[47]

The czar's wife, Empress Maria Feodorovna, asked if she could have the peasant's robe that Kosciuszko had worn during the war against Russia. When he went to the Winter Palace to deliver it and say farewell to Czar Paul and his wife, Kosciuszko was wearing his American general's uniform with white epaulets. He had been at war with Catherine the Great for many years, and ironically, her wheelchair was waiting for him when he arrived at her palace.[48]

The hero was wheeled through the halls of the Winter Palace to meet with the czar and the empress. She presented him with some expensive craftwork made on a lathe, and cameos with portraits of the royal family. He in turn gave her his peasant robe and a snuffbox that he had made. During her coronation celebration, she showed the snuffbox to Dr. Rogerson and said, "It reminds me of great feelings of morality."[49]

The next morning, December 19, 1796, Kosciuszko, Niemcewicz, Libiszewski, and Lapierre left St. Petersburg along the road through the frozen forests of Finland that led to Sweden. With the heavy snow and dark winter that cast little more than four hours of sunlight a day over Scandinavia, the trip took several weeks. Locals who heard that Kosciuszko was traveling past came out to greet them. Some of them helped by stomping with their bare feet on the ice that froze over the Gulf of Bothnia to see if it was solid enough for them to cross. For the first time Kosciuszko and Niemcewicz could talk openly about what had transpired during the two years they were incarcerated. Kosciuszko admitted to his friend that he had tried to commit suicide twice, once by putting the pistol in his mouth at Maciejowice, and then the hunger strike in prison.[50]

The Swedish newspapers reported the arrival of the "patriotic hero and national martyr," and crowds flocked to see him as he moved closer to the capital.[51] Throngs also turned out to see Lapierre, and Niemcewicz wrote that at one stop "the whole village ran to see his ebony face."[52]

By the time they reached Stockholm, Kosciuszko was tired and sick from the journey. With his left leg still paralyzed, he turned down invitations to have his portrait painted, and to visit Swedish king Gustav IV in his palace. (This would have angered the czar, and turned Kosciuszko into an entertainment attraction for the Swedish court.)

With the Russian escort, Major Udom, watching his every move, he was still paranoid about what he could say or do. By that point he realized that his dear friend Niemcewicz could not keep a secret—once a journalist, always a journalist. The general spoke only about music and art, keeping his thoughts on politics to himself. When Udom left for Russia, Kosciuszko relieved Lapierre and his cook, Stanislaw, of their duties and told them they could return to Poland, while he and Niemcewicz would cross Sweden to Gothenburg to find a ship to take them to England.[53]

In Gothenburg there were fewer eyes watching over him, and Kosciuszko started writing secret letters, keeping the contents hidden from Niemcewicz. Kosciuszko learned that General Dabrowski's cavalry had escaped to Italy where they joined the war against Austria as allies of the French. The commander was ecstatic that France was having success against the Austrian Empire, and with the help of Dabrowski, no less.

Dabrowski traveled to Paris to ask the government to help finance a separate Polish legion to fight alongside the French Army.[54] Kosciuszko had grudgingly sworn allegiance to the czar, but he tried to help Dabrowski with his mission to create a Polish army to fight on the western front.

"General Kosciuszko began corresponding with the French government," Niemcewicz wrote in his memoirs.[55] It seems that he was also writing to a twenty-seven-year-old French general who was having success against the Austrians. France had conquered Holland, and the historian Jan Dihm wrote, "most likely Kosciuszko wrote through a Dutch intermediary, not to the French government, but to General Bonaparte."[56]

Dabrowski tried to convince Napoleon Bonaparte to invite the Patriots, the exiled members of the Seym, to Lombardy, Italy, which was under French control, so that the Polish legions could protect them. And once their commander was released from prison, the Poles were abuzz that Kosciuszko would soon join them in Italy.

A group of Poles gathered in Paris to plan their next move. One of them wrote an article for the French newspaper *Le Moniteur Universel*: "The Czar may have given Kosciuszko rubles, but he cannot buy him. By giving back the present, Kosciuszko may yet stand at the head of an army. . . . From prison one can sometimes return to save the fatherland, but from death, never. So wait patiently Kosciuszko . . . because the fate of Europe is not yet doomed."[57]

Giving the money back would endanger the Poles whom Czar Paul had promised to release from Siberia. The commander was still too weak to ride a horse, much less lead an army, but he still planned to sail across the North Sea to France. Niemcewicz recalled that the secret "correspondence continued until we left for America. During this time, Kosciuszko wanted to send me to Copenhagen, so that I could arrange for a boat for him to sail to France."[58]

The general waited out the early spring in Gothenburg to hear back from France. He passed the time painting and listening to the local musicians who came to his hotel room to entertain him. Even though he couldn't walk, his reputation as a ladies' man still caused a stir. After a Mrs. G., "a being who possessed extraordinary talents" had visited Kosciuszko, her husband began to gossip and threaten his wife. Niemcewicz wrote to their friend Johan Toll in Stockholm, asking that as "a resourceful and fair knight," he defend the innocent Mrs. G.'s "downtrodden chastity."[59]

Russian and Prussian spies watched Kosciuszko's every move, and he never received any reply from Napoleon. By late April news of the armistice of Leoben between France and Austria had spread across Europe. The battle to liberate Poland had once again been put on hold. On May 10 a crestfallen Kosciuszko sailed for England, with plans to continue on to America.

The Italians and Poles who marched with Napoleon through Lombardy thought that *le petit caporal*'s patriotic rhetoric and camaraderie with the troops meant that he favored the rebirth of Italy and the restoration of Poland. Both nations were disappointed, and the Poles were upset that their commander in chief had been passed over.

"You didn't appreciate Kosciuszko's intellect," complained one Pole in France about Napoleon Bonaparte's snub of their leader, "Why do you let him set out on the seas? Why don't you keep him for Poland?"[60]

The time for Kosciuszko and Napoleon to size each other up was yet to come.

FOURTEEN

Kosciuszko Tries to Free Jefferson's Slaves

THE POLISH REBEL WAS NOT SURE HOW HE WOULD BE RECEIVED in England. After all, he had helped to eject Great Britain from its American colonies, and King George III was allied with Russia. Yet even though he was bitterly attacked by Tory newspapers such as the *Courier* and the *Post*, Kosciuszko was the toast of London.[1]

On May 30, 1797, the *Gentleman's Magazine* reported: "The gallant General Kosciuszko arrived in the river Thames on-board a Swedish vessel, attended by many Polish officers, who are going with him to America. He is incurably wounded in the head, has three bayonet-wounds in his back, and part of his thigh carried away by a cannon-shot; and, with the excruciating torments those wounds occasion, as he cannot move himself, he amuses his hours with drawing landscapes. He speaks with the most lively gratitude of the present Emperor of Russia; and complains that his wounds were long neglected after he was made prisoner."[2]

The room Niemcewicz rented for the Polish general in the Hotel de la Sablonniere in Leicester Square was soon packed with elite visitors and curiosity seekers.[3] Guests such as Francis Russell, the 5th Duke of Bedford; Earl Charles Grey; the statesman Charles James Fox; the playwright Richard Sheridan; and the Duchess of Devonshire all visited to pay their respects.

The general still had a black sash wrapped around his forehead to cover the saber wound, and refused requests to sit for paintings. But one of England's most talented artists, Richard Cosway, mingled with the crowd secretly sketching his features for a portrait that was completed later.[4] Another painter, the

American-born Benjamin West, also called on Kosciuszko and later produced a portrait of him from memory. Poets such as Keats and Byron, were inspired by the Polish revolutionary and praised him in verse.

Four days after his arrival a team of ten English doctors, led by King George's personal physician, examined Kosciuszko's wounds. Their diagnosis was that as he had no feeling on part of his scalp, the sword that struck his head "most probably divided the nerve upon the right side that supplies the posterior portion of the scalp," and that he had received "a concussion of the brain." The Cossack's pike, which "had penetrated deep so as to divide or injure extremely, the Sciatic Nerve near the place where it passes out of the grate Sciatic Notch," caused paralysis and bladder problems.[5]

Even one of his former enemies, legendary British dragoon leader Banastre Tarleton, who had battled Greene's army in the Southern campaign, came to see Kosciuszko and introduce him to the Whig Club. At a meeting in the Freemason's lodge at the Crown and Anchor Tavern, Tarleton made a motion, which passed unanimously: "That the Polish General Thaddeus Kosciuszko be requested by this club to accept a sword as a public testimony of their sense of his exalted virtues, and of his gallant, generous and exemplary efforts to defend and save his country."[6] The club commissioned an elegant gold-encrusted saber that cost two hundred guineas, inscribed, "The Whig Club of England to General Kosciuszko."[7]

Czar Paul ordered his representative in London, Semyon Vorontsov, to keep an eye on the released prisoner, and the Russian ambassador often dropped in under the guise of making sure that all Kosciuszko's needs were met. By the time he was in England, Kosciuszko regretted the pledge he had made to the czar and considered sending back the money he had received for traveling expenses. However, this would have jeopardized the release of the thousands of Poles still imprisoned in Siberia, so Niemcewicz talked him out of it.[8] They compromised by not drawing the funds that the czar had placed in a bank in London under Kosciuszko's name.

The spotlight on the rebel leader in London was even brighter than in Sweden, making it difficult for him to communicate with General Dabrowski's Polish legions in France. Worried about all of the attention he was getting in London, a week after arriving, Kosciuszko made arrangements to leave. He was introduced to the American merchant captain Frederick Lee, whose ship, the *Adriana*, was docked in Bristol and ready to sail to Philadelphia. The American consul in Bristol, Elias Vanderhorst, invited the Poles to stay at his home as they prepared for their voyage.[9]

Upon their arrival in Bristol the cavalry regiment of Col. Sir George Thomas greeted them, along with the American politician and diplomat Rufus King, and the soldier, painter, and former engineer at Fort Ticonderoga, John Trumbull.[10]

The City of Bristol presented Kosciuszko with a set of silver dishes engraved in his honor, and the residents feted him with parties before his departure. Each night crowds gathered in the square in the hopes of catching a glimpse of Kosciuszko while bands struck up concerts in front of the Vanderhorst house.

Rev. Richard Warner, who came to visit him, recalled: "I never contemplated a more interesting human figure than Kosciuszko, stretched out on his couch. His wounds were still unhealed, and he was unable to sit upright. He appeared to be a small man, spare and delicate. A black silk bandage crossed his fair and high, but somewhat wrinkled forehead. Beneath it, his dark eagle eye sent forth a stream of light that indicated the steady flame of patriotism, which still burned within his soul; unquenched by disaster and his wounds, weakness, poverty and exile. Contrasted with its brightness, was the paleness of his countenance, and the wan cast of every feature. He spoke very tolerable English, though in a low and feeble tone: but his conversation, replete with fine sense, lively remarks, sagacious answers, evinced a noble understanding and a cultivated mind."[11]

After their talk Warner rose and offered Kosciuszko his hand. Tears filled Warner's eyes as he muttered about "brighter prospects" and "happier days." With a warm clasp of Warner's hand, Kosciuszko replied, "Ah! Sir, he who devotes himself for his country, must not look for his reward on this side of the grave!"[12]

The day of his departure, British officers carried Kosciuszko in a sedan chair to the wharf. The English soldiers took off their helmets and carried them at their sides to honor the Polish rebel. Throngs of people waved hats and handkerchiefs and cheered as the general was carried to the water's edge. Several excited women jumped on board the ship as it sailed toward the ocean until it reached the mouth of the river, where they climbed down ropes onto the skiffs that were escorting the *Adriana*. Once the vessel pulled out of the mouth of the river Avon and into the portway heading out the sea, Captain Lee unfurled the Stars and Stripes and hauled it up the mast.[13]

The ship was also carrying Irish and Welsh farmers immigrating to America. While Captain Lee was able to provide Kosciuszko with comfortable quarters and fresh poultry to eat, Niemcewicz and the others subsisted on dry salted meat, crackers, and smelly water. On Sundays a Calvinist minister held religious services.

The *Adriana* sailed against the prevailing winds for the much of the journey, and Niemcewicz often took to the bridge to scan the blue ocean for sails on the horizon. The salty Captain Lee was always able to tell Niemcewicz where a ship was from, what it was carrying, and where it was headed. Occasionally they crossed paths with vessels full of slaves, sugar, and rum. When dolphins were spotted chasing schools of fish, the captain put out fishing poles, and the crews would boil water anticipating the catch of the day.[14]

One night Captain Lee woke his passengers at one o'clock in the morning to witness the pretty sight of a nighttime flotilla of merchant ships from Jamaica passing by with their white sails illuminated by lamps glowing on their decks. But when the helmsman on one of the ships got drunk and passed out, the rudder turned from its course, sending the vessel directly toward the *Adriana*. With little wind, the two ships were not able to change course and they collided, entwining their masts, cables, and sails.[15]

Women and children cried in terror as the two bobbing ships slammed together and the wooden hulls scraped alongside each other. Helpless in his chair, Kosciuszko watched calmly as the crews worked to untangle the masts. His calmness quieted the children. It was not as bad as his first sea trek to America, which ended with the vessel being smashed on the rocks in the Caribbean after a hurricane. This time, with a banged-up mast and a torn mainsail, the length of the voyage was stretched out to seventy days.

When they reached the coast of Newfoundland, spouts of water shot up the sides of the slow-moving vessel. A school of whales was swimming alongside, with fishing boats chasing them. As the giant mammals were feeding, Captain Lee handed out long poles with hooks and scraps of pork on the ends and told his passengers to start fishing. The hungry voyagers began pulling up cod and haddock. They saved the tongue of one fish, considered a delicacy, for General Kosciuszko.

In the autumn of 1776 Benjamin Franklin had put Kosciuszko to work building forts and obstructions in the Delaware River to block the British navy from attacking Philadelphia. The young Polish engineer made his troops cut down trees around the redoubts to get a better view of the soldiers who might approach from the land or the sea.

In the summer of 1797 a French engineer with one arm and two hundred men were working at Fort Mifflin under the command of Lt. Henry M. Muhlenberg.[16] They were in charge of monitoring the shipping channels in and out of Philadelphia, and at four o'clock in the afternoon on August 18, when they spotted the red, white and blue flag fluttering in the wind over the *Adriana* as it neared the fort, cannons fired a thirteen-gun salute to announce the arrival of the expected dignitary.

A crowd rushed to the docks as the boat pulled into the harbor. Henry Andrew Heins, president of the Emigrant Society, which assisted people coming to America from foreign countries, climbed into a whaleboat with a crew of eight sailors who rowed him out to the ship to greet the guest. Kosciuszko was lowered down from the deck of the *Adriana* to the boat as the ship's crew cheered, "Long Live Kosciuszko!"

The crowd on the docks picked up the chant, and Kosciuszko said to Heins, in French, "I look upon America as my second country and I am extremely happy when I return to her."[17]

The cheering people were so excited that when Kosciuszko landed, they untied the horse from the carriage sent to pick him up and pulled it themselves to Mrs. Lawson's hotel on Second Street.[18]

Newspaper reporters who witnessed the scene were stunned. There was so much animosity in American politics at the time that insults were constantly being hurled at Washington, who had just finished two terms as president, the new president, John Adams, and his vice president, Thomas Jefferson.

One reporter wrote that the crowd that pulled Kosciuszko's carriage acted like "cattle." And Noah Webster wrote in the *Herald*: "Men who can decline a common mark of genteel civility to the President can become beasts to a patriot. But the bait will not ensnare the hero of Poland. He will never be a sport of the party."[19]

Philadelphia had changed significantly since Kosciuszko had last seen it thirteen years earlier. The U.S. Congress had split into two antagonistic factions. The Federalists, led by Alexander Hamilton and the businessmen of New England, were Anglophiles and interpreted the U.S. Constitution as providing a strong central government. The Jeffersonian Republicans were Francophiles, who argued that states' rights were supreme. The free press fanned the flames of this dispute.

William Cobbett was an English pamphleteer who published *Porcupine's Gazette,* a pro-British Federalist newspaper in Philadelphia, writing under the pseudonym Peter Porcupine to push the limits of the new First Amendment in skewering rival newspapers and Jefferson's allies.

Even before Kosciuszko arrived in Philadelphia, Cobbett attacked the "savage and bloody Tarleton" for "presenting a token of respect to Kosciuszko!" He pointed out the Englishman's hypocrisy: "You have constantly been an advocate for the continuation of that traffic called the slave trade, while you are at the head of a liberty club; and you present the Polander with a sword, as a token of your present rank and pay to your having fought against him, having sought his destruction in that very cause!"[20]

Once the *Adriana* docked in Philadelphia, *Porcupine's Gazette* aimed its quills at Kosciuszko. Most Americans and newspapers welcomed Kosciuszko as a freedom fighter, while Cobbett attacked him as a "mercenary."

Claypoole's American Daily Advertiser reported that Kosciuszko was entitled to a land grant for serving in the American Revolution, and that a large sum of money was due to him from his service in the war. "We believe that with principal and interest," the *Advertiser* reported, "his pay will not amount to less than 18 or 20,000 dollars, as the General entered into the service as a Colonel of Engineers on October 1776, and remained until the end of the war. The land warrant, we are told the General presented to a Welsh farmer of the name of

Thomas, who was a passenger in the same ship and of whom he had conceived a high opinion."[21]

Even though it was not true that Kosciuszko had given away the land, Cobbett attacked the Welshman, writing, "I would lay fifty pounds that this high opinion man is a Jacobin. As to the General, whatever might be his views in crossing the Atlantic, it is certain that it has turned out no unprofitable voyage . . . If a man fights for the sheer love of Liberty, let him have the honor of it; but let him not enjoy this honor with the wages of a mercenary in his pocket. What does this man want with 20,000 dollars?"[22]

Cobbett made a comfortable living selling his popular pamphlet in Philadelphia and had no qualms about charging for the ink that he spilled onto paper to spread his thoughts on liberty. In the same vein Kosciuszko had no qualms about collecting the income he earned spilling his blood on the battlefield for American liberty, while refusing to pick up the blood money the czar left for him in London.

The peasant serfs had no voice in Poland, and Kosciuszko wanted to rescue them from oppression. But the sight of black slaves reminded him that there were those who were worse off. Even Niemcewicz wrote in his diary, "The first time I put my foot on land in the New World, I was most struck by the smell of cedar wood and the large number of Negroes."[23]

Niemcewicz also viewed serfdom and slavery as evil and was surprised when he saw with his own eyes the crime against humanity that would later become known as "America's original sin." Kosciuszko cared deeply about Niemcewicz, but as he was a chatty and entertaining writer who often called attention to himself, the rebel leader had to keep the poet in the dark about his diplomatic efforts to help Poland.

Kosciuszko spent his first day after returning to Philadelphia writing letters to his friends and acquaintances, such as Gates, Washington, and President Adams, apprising them of his arrival. He discreetly asked a member of Congress to act as intermediary and invite the French consul, Philippe-Henri Joseph Letombe, to sneak into the hotel to visit him. Kosciuszko's message to the French was clear—he wanted to meet Napoleon.

"He is only here to mislead his enemies," Letombe wrote to the French foreign minister, Charles Delacroix, after visiting Kosciuszko in his hotel. "The same Member of Congress came to tell me that General Kosciuszko desired to speak with me, so I went to the general last night. He wants to go to France. He will go there immediately via a safe route. He is observed here. This Martyr of liberty cannot speak or act, but only with the greatest precaution."[24]

After his stint in a Russian prison, the Polish rebel had grown suspicious of anyone he didn't know and always thought that people were listening in on his conversations and covertly reading his correspondence. He even asked his friends to burn his letters after they read them. One of those friends was Dr. Rush, who had served as the Continental Army's chief physician, and whom the British doctors praised as the best doctor in America.

Rush came to visit Kosciuszko to warn him about an outbreak of yellow fever in Philadelphia. People throughout the city were hunched over with abdominal cramps and vomiting, some bleeding through the mouth and nose. Hundreds began to die. As the highly contagious disease, which was spread by mosquitoes, often led to kidney failure, and because Kosciuszko was having bladder problems caused by his battle wounds, Dr. Rush ordered him to leave the city until the epidemic passed.

Kosciuszko would have been a welcomed guest at the homes of any of his former officers. Washington wrote to him from Mount Vernon: "Having just been informed of your safe arrival in America, I was on the point of writing you a congratulatory letter on the occasion, welcoming you to the land whose liberties you had been so instrumental in establishing. . . . I beg you to be assured that, no one has a higher respect, and veneration for your character than I have; or one who more sincerely wished, during your arduous struggle in the cause of liberty and your country, that it might be crowned with Success."[25]

But rather than visit Washington's slave plantation, he chose to visit his old friend Horatio Gates. Kosciuszko was happy to learn that Gates freed the slaves on his Virginia plantation and moved to New York. His first wife, Elizabeth, died after the war, and Gates married a wealthy widow, Mary Valance. They settled on an estate called Rose Hill, in the lower half of Manhattan, just north of what was then New York City.

At six o'clock in the morning on August 30, Kosciuszko, Niemcewicz, and a servant named Stanislaw Dabrowski left Philadelphia in a two-horse carriage they had rented for thirty-two dollars. They passed through farmland with corn and wheat fields and rows of apple, pear, and peach trees.[26]

After they left, Dr. Rush wrote to Gates letting him know that his friend was on the way. "His wounds are all healed," Dr. Rush wrote. "One of them on his hip has left his thigh & leg in a paralytic State. Time has done a little towards restoring it. I do not despair of his being yet able to walk. He will always limp— but what then? To use an ancient play upon words, every step he takes will remind him of his patriotism and bravery."[27]

It is not known how much Kosciuszko shared with Dr. Rush about his ability to walk, but Kosciuszko later admitted to Polish friends that he had been exaggerating the severity of his long healing process to fool his enemies into thinking he would no longer be able to lead an army into battle.

Along the way the Polish travelers were invited to stay in New Brunswick, New Jersey, at the home of Gen. Anthony Walton White, with whom Kosciuszko served in the Southern campaign. There was not much the Pole could do in the middle of the country in New Jersey so he "spent all his time reclining on a sofa, sketching with a pencil, and painting in water-colors, and India-ink." Mrs. White, who idolized Kosciuszko and considered him second only to George Washington, gathered up the pieces and gave them out to her friends.[28]

On September 6 Kosciuszko wrote to Gates informing him that he planned to leave for New York in three days. "I have only one friend and one servant with me," he wrote to his former commander, "and with such army I will attack your house." The genuine affection that he had for Gates came across in the letter because he also joked, "Unless you will set your dogs at me, and by force throw me out from your house."[29]

The Poles continued their carriage ride north and made it to Hoboken across the Hudson River from New York City, where they found a place for the night. Niemcewicz wrote, "We found the inn filled with sailors and other gentlemen, vagabonds, all a little drunk and in very good spirits. They were dancing in a room below. I saw a dance absolutely identical to that of our Polish Jews."[30]

The next morning Niemcewicz looked across the river in amazement at "the towers of the city of New York" as they crossed in a sailboat. They made their way to Gates's farm, which had "200 acres, a magnificent house, orchards, vegetable fields" and six cows, three horses, and everything they could need. Kosciuszko was pleased that Gates had given jobs to freed black people in New York, and Niemcewicz recalled, "The rest of the household consists of a Negro, a woman cook, and a Negro woman servant, all free, however, Gen. Gates having freed all his slaves."[31]

New York was then compacted in Lower Manhattan. Gates's house was north of the city line, on what would become the corner of Twenty-fourth Street and Second Avenue. The host invited many veterans from the Revolution to visit their friend Kosciuszko, and held dinner parties every night to entertain the guests.

One of those who came to see Kosciuszko at Gates's house was the Duc de la Liancourt. "Simple and modest, he even sheds tears of gratitude, and seems astonished at the homage he receives. He sees a brother in every man who is the friend of liberty," wrote the duke about Kosciuszko: "In a word, elevation of sentiment, grandeur, sweetness, force, goodness, all that commands respect and homage, appear to me to be concentrated in this celebrated and interesting victim of misfortune and despotism. I have met few men whose appearance so much excited me to that effect."[32]

When Agrippa Hull learned that his former commanding officer from West Point and the Southern campaign had come to New York, he rushed to visit him at Gates's house. As a free man "Grippy" worked as a butler for the Sedgwick family in Stockbridge, Massachusetts, a job that helped him to start a catering business that made him enough money to buy his own land and a house.

The Sedgwicks escorted Hull down to Manhattan to see Kosciuszko.[33] He still had the pistol from the Warsaw royal military academy that Kosciuszko gave him during the war.[34] Kosciuszko had always encouraged serfs, slaves, and all oppressed people to speak up for themselves, and Hull had learned to do just that. On one occasion Hull attended church with a haughty employer to hear a sermon given by "a distinguished mulatto preacher." After the services the employer said to Hull, "Well, how do you like nigger preaching?"

Without batting an eye, Hull replied, "Sir, he was half black and half white; I liked *my* half, how did you like yours?"[35]

While Kosciuszko was living in Poland trying to free the serfs, like-minded people in America were pushing to free American slaves. In 1787 John Jay, Alexander Hamilton, George Clinton, and several Quakers from the New York Manumission Society founded the African Free School to educate the children of former slaves. A white educator named Cornelius Davis began teaching black students, and the year before Kosciuszko arrived to visit Gates, the group bought land in Manhattan to put up a schoolhouse for black students.[36]

Given the progressive attitudes of most of the guests at Gates's house, it is quite likely that Kosciuszko heard about the school, because over the next few months he gave a good deal of thought to freeing and educating slaves.

Before yellow fever had forced him to leave Philadelphia, Kosciuszko had consulted with secretary of state, Timothy Pickering, about finally collecting the funds that America owed him. Pickering had also forwarded a letter to Kosciuszko in New York from President Adams, which said, "Give me leave Sir, to congratulate you on your arrival in America, where I hope, You will find all the consolation, tranquility and satisfaction you desire after the glorious efforts you have made on a greater Theatre. On my arrival in Philadelphia I hope to have the pleasure to receive you."[37]

With an autumn chill setting in, meaning an end to mosquito season, Kosciuszko and Niemcewicz crossed back over the Hudson on September 29, and began their journey south. They stopped in Elizabeth, New Jersey, and rented a room at the Indian Queen Tavern.

In addition to the correspondence from Adams, Kosciuszko received a letter from Washington while he was in New York, and in his room at the tavern, he finally had a chance to respond to his former commander in chief in Mount Vernon, Virginia.

"If the situation of my health would admit my traveling so far," Kosciuszko wrote, "I would immediately pay you my respects and my personal homage." He also politely asked Washington for his help in collecting the money that the United States owed him for the past thirteen years.[38]

Washington replied to Kosciuszko a week later: "I am sorry that the state of your health should deprive me of the pleasure of your company at this place— and I regret still more that the pain you feel from the wounds you have received—though glorious for your reputation—is the occasion of it." Washington added that he could only help with the treasury issues as "a private citizen," but that Congress would surely resolve the issue because, "Your rank and services in the American Army are too well known to require that testimony of your claim."[39]

The stay in Elizabeth dragged on for three weeks, in part because of the many visitors, and also because Kosciuszko introduced Niemcewicz to Susan Livingston-Kean, widow of John Kean of South Carolina, whom he had known during the Revolution. Niemcewicz became enamored of her, and a romance developed that would result in marriage several years later. The Polish writer accepted invitations to go duck hunting with the locals.

The publisher of the *New Jersey Journal*, Capt. Shepard Kollack, who named his son Shepard Kosciuszko Kollack, also came to visit the general. The Polish hero was so pleased at the sight of the little boy that he took him into his arms, kissed him, and affixed to the boy's coat the *Virtuti Militari* Medal that was awarded to him by King Stanislaw.[40]

After the first frosts of November the yellow fever had passed in Philadelphia, but not until it had taken hundreds of lives. People were returning to the nation's capital to bury the dead, and to get on with their business.

Kosciuszko and Niemcewicz returned to General White's house in New Brunswick and found that the whole town was in a flurry of activity because President John Adams, who was on his way back to Philadelphia, was expected to stop for a reception. Adams's stagecoach arrived early, and the president went into the kitchen to warm up, where a black woman was cooking for the guests. Niemcewicz wrote after witnessing the scene: "Nothing better depicts the simple weakness of America's customs than the fact that the first administration of this country did not employ a system of equal rights. How long will it take?"[41]

By that point Kosciuszko adhered to the politics of Jefferson and was opposed to the policies of Adams and the Federalists, whom he viewed as aristocrats and elitists. Adams was an Anglophile, and England was allied with Russia. Not one for feigning niceties, Kosciuszko begged off on the reception for Adams, sending Niemcewicz in his place.[42]

"I was presented to Mr. Adams. He was sitting reading a newspaper, facing the fireplace," Niemcewicz recalled. "I saw a dumpy little man, dressed wholly in gray, well-powdered hair and a long pigtail. His face appeared to me that of a good and honest man, touched nevertheless with a grain of malice. He received me civilly, and asked me news about General Kosciuszko and then Lafayette. I passed then into a room opposite where I found the true counterpart of Mr. Adams. It was his wife. Small, short and squat, she is accused of a horrible crime. It is said she puts on rouge. What is certain is that if her manner is not the most affable, her mind is well balanced and cultivated."[43]

While Adams criticized Washington's "Fabian strategy" during the Revolution, another Founding Father was invoking the name of the Roman general in his *Letters of Fabius*. In addition to being a member of the Continental Congress, John Dickinson served as president of Delaware and later president of Pennsylvania. Dickinson's *Letters* of 1788 rallied support for the Constitution, and his letters of 1797 warned about the deteriorating relations with France. The series caught Kosciuszko's attention because it also denounced "the catastrophe of Polish liberty closed in a partition of the whole republic between Russia, Austria and Prussia."[44]

The Quaker lawyer also authored "An Act for the Gradual Abolition of Slavery in Delaware."[45] Kosciuszko, whose writing always lacked clarity, was so impressed with Dickinson's clear prose, and the abolitionist stance of the Quakers, that on November 24 he sent him a letter that said: "The language of truth is the same in any shape whatsoever is dressed. I have not accustomate [sic] to express my ideas in so simple and comfortable manner to every man's understanding; yet I am of the same opinion . . . in my heart I am a kwaker too, will do anything for the happiness of Human kind."[46]

Once it was safe to return to Philadelphia, Kosciuszko sent Niemcewicz to find a cheap room to rent. Dr. Rush found them space in Mrs. Relf's boardinghouse for medical students on the corner of Third and Pine streets. Kosciuszko took a room on the second floor, which was only large enough to accommodate four visitors at a time. Niemcewicz was stuck in a cramped corner of the attic among the students.

Congress was back in session after the long break forced by the yellow fever epidemic, and many politicians came to visit Kosciuszko. One of them, Congressman John Dawson of Virginia, sponsored a resolution in the House of Representatives asking the Treasury Department to inquire into Kosciuszko's unpaid salary.[47] On December 28, 1797, Treasury Secretary Oliver Wolcott reported to Congress that Kosciuszko never received his base salary of $12,280.54, or the $2,947.33 in interest. By the time Congress calculated all the money it owed the Polish general, it amounted to $18,912. 03.[48] As a veteran of the war he was also promised a land grant of five hundred acres in Ohio.

Even more painful than the wounds he suffered was the anguish Kosciuszko felt over agreeing not to challenge Russia and the guilt over accepting the money—still sitting in a bank account in London—from Czar Paul. He felt that he had let his nation down and wanted to send the money back to the czar with a sweeping public gesture to instill new hope in his people for a free Poland.

"He'll take revenge on your countrymen," Niemcewicz told him. "Write a polite letter, saying that you have collected the debt that the United States owed to you, and that you don't want to be a burden on the czar, and ask that your funds be donated to support the devastated residents of Praga."[49]

The general's reaction to his friend's pacifist idea was silence. It was not the response he was looking for. The point was to give back the dirty money that had been made off the backs of peasants and collected from landed aristocrats as tax revenues by the czar. The rebel wanted his people to take up the fight once more.

As Kosciuszko and Niemcewicz drifted apart, the general became closer to Jefferson, who visited frequently. It was a curious friendship. Both were Francophiles, and both believed in radical principles and the spread of revolution to replace monarchies with true republics. Having lived in Paris, Jefferson was well versed in physiocracy and had his own vision of agrarian democracy. He never called himself a politician, referring to himself instead as a "farmer." He pushed for the rights of those who worked the land—up to a point. Jefferson said that he opposed slavery, yet he owned slaves. That is where the two friends parted ways—their personal commitment to abolishing slavery.

Jefferson did include a passage in the Declaration of Independence that would have forced the Founding Fathers to abolish the slave trade, criticizing the king of Great Britain who "determined to keep open a market where men should be bought and sold, he has prostituted his negative for suppressing every legislative attempt to prohibit or to restrain this execrable commerce."[50] Yet after members of Congress edited these words out, he continued to buy and sell slaves, even when he was president. He told friends that his first recollection in life was that of being carried on a pillow by a slave, and Kosciuszko's early memories as a child included watching the serfs slaving in the fields of his parents' plantation.[51]

By the time Jefferson and Kosciuszko became friends, the world had known of the vice president's *Notes on the State of Virginia,* in which he wrote that blacks were "in reason, much inferior, as I think one could scarcely be found capable of tracing and comprehending the investigations of Euclid; and that in imagination, they are dull, tasteless and anomalous." He added, "Their inferiority is not the effect merely of the condition of their life. . . . It is not their condition then, but Nature, which has produced the distinction. . . . Nature has been less bountiful to them in the endowments of the head."[52]

Kosciuszko vehemently disagreed. His black valet, Lapierre, was quite literate, and the general believed that there was no inherent difference between aristocrats and slaves, and that "we are all equals, riches and education constitute the only difference."[53]

The vice president did understand that slavery was immoral, and when South Carolina passed a temporary ban on the importation of slaves, Jefferson was pleased.

"I congratulate you," he wrote to Edward Rutledge. "This abomination must have an end, and there is a superior bench reserved in heaven for those who hasten it."[54]

Yet Jefferson did not reserve a space for himself on that bench.

The Polish rebel believed that education was the tool slaves needed to get ahead. Kosciuszko's vision for the revolution in Poland included rights for serfs, Jews, and Muslim Tatars. He argued that the United States should free its slaves and protect the rights of Native Americans.

"General Kosciuszko," Jefferson wrote to Gates, "I see him often, and with great pleasure mixed with commiseration. He is as pure a son of liberty as I have ever known, and of that liberty which is to go to all, and not to the few or rich alone."[55]

Jefferson and Kosciuszko also lamented the growing rift between France and the United States. The final stage of the French Revolution resulted in the executive powers of the country being put into the hands of a five-member council known as "the Executive Directory." The Directory was furious that the United States had signed the Jay Treaty on commerce with England, which France viewed as a violation of the alliance signed during the American Revolution.

The French navy boarded and seized three hundred American commercial vessels sailing to England, and a "quasi war" was fought on the open seas. Some members of Congress were unnerved by this act of national piracy and called for an official declaration of war on France. The mess was exacerbated further by a demand from French foreign minister Talleyrand for a bribe.

President Adams sent three of America's Founding Fathers, Charles Cotesworth Pinckney, John Marshall, and Elbridge Gerry, to talk sense into the Directory. Talleyrand could spare them only fifteen minutes, and then kept the envoys waiting for several weeks. Eventually the French foreign minister sent three agents to see the Americans with a demand that they pay a $250,000 *douceur*, or "sweetener," to Talleyrand, and provide a $10,000,000 loan to France.[56]

On March 19, 1798, Adams issued a report to Congress in which the names of the French agents were simply listed as "X, Y, and Z."[57] The quasi war was on the verge of breaking out into a full-scale conflict. A significant drawback for the United States was that it had no real navy to challenge the French fleet on the open seas.

Jefferson, the Francophile, was worried that the war would spiral out of control, and Kosciuszko was frustrated that France was fighting with the democratic United States rather than Poland's tyrannous enemies.

Two days after Adams issued the report on the "XYZ Affair" to Congress, Jefferson wrote to General Gates, "Kosciusko has been disappointed by the sudden peace between France and Austria. A ray of hope seemed to gleam on his mind for a moment, that the extension of the revolutionary spirit through Italy and Germany, might so have occupied the remnants of monarchy there, as that his country might have risen again."[58]

Another Revolutionary War veteran who fought Prussia and lost was

Lafayette. He spent five years in Prussian and Austrian prisons, and when he was released in late 1797, he wrote to the American Secretary of War, James McHenry. Hearing that the Polish revolutionary was in the United States, he said, "Remember me to Gen'l Kosciusko. I hope his health is better. My great regard for him makes me more affectionately partake in every thing that concerns him."[59]

However, this was not the Frenchman Kosciuszko was waiting to hear from. The young general Napoleon Bonaparte had shown skill in beating the Austrians and was a rising star in France, while Lafayette had little clout with the Directory. And according to Kosciuszko's close friend Gen. John Armstrong, the Polish rebel was jealous of all the attention Lafayette received during the American Revolution.[60] While Kosciuszko sweated and toiled in the corps of engineers, the French officers received all the glory and their pay as soon as they asked for it.

The friendship between Jefferson and Kosciuszko grew closer over the winter months of 1798, and the Pole felt more comfortable pointing out the hypocrisy that Jefferson, who wrote, "All men are created equal," was a slave owner.

The Polish rebel discussed using his American funds to buy black slaves and free them. Similar ideas on abolition were being discussed among members of the prestigious American Philosophical Society in Philadelphia. Kosciuszko had been a member for years, and with Jefferson's introduction, Niemcewicz was also invited to join.

While Niemcewicz was feted as a poet and became a man about town, attending various parties with congressmen, foreigners, and residents of Philadelphia, the general worried that his friend might be blabbing too much in public. Kosciuszko preferred to entertain guests whom he could trust with a pot of coffee or tea, and a game of backgammon, chess, or cards in his cramped room on Pine Street.

The visitors to that room were reported in the newspaper as the partisan Federalist editor of the *Gazette of the United States*, John Fenno, "watched Kosciuszko with an Argus eye."[61] But at least the conversations that took place there were private.

"It was fashionable among the young ladies to come visit Kosciuszko," Niemcewicz wrote, "and for some, he drew their portraits."[62]

It was also fashionable for champions of the oppressed to visit the hobbled Polish rebel. Chief "Me-She-Kin-No-Quah," or Little Turtle, of the Miami Ohio Indian tribe came to Philadelphia to ask President Adams to stop whiskey traffickers from peddling alcohol to his people. "Liquor," he told his tribe, "is to be more feared than the gun and tomahawk."[63]

After hearing about Kosciuszko's reputation as a supporter of human rights, Little Turtle visited the Pole to present him with a ceremonial peace pipe–tomahawk. At the end of the maple shaft was a piece of silver inlay with a hatchet blade on the bottom and a bowl to smoke tobacco on the top. The general was so pleased by the gift that when he saw his guest looking at his sleeveless wool Tatar cloak, he gave it to him as gift.

When Kosciuszko noticed that Little Turtle was squinting, the general gave his reading glasses, which were lying on the table, to the chief. As Niemcewicz recalled, "He could not conceive how it was done, nor tire of the pleasure of looking at objects grown larger by means of these glasses. 'You have given me new eyes!' he cried."[64]

Little Turtle, understanding what it meant to lose one's territory, was quite empathetic about his new friend's occupied country and grew agitated as he listened to the stories about Catherine the Great's systematic dismantling of Poland. After nervously walking back and forth across the room, he said to his host, "Let that woman yet beware," not realizing that the czarina had died. Then, as if thinking of a new strategy, he said to Kosciuszko, "You might have succeeded better in a love affair with her, especially, if she was handsome."

The Polish rebel was so delighted by Little Turtle's visit that when the chief got up to leave, Kosciuszko gave him his favorite pair of pistols, saying: "These pistols I have carried and used on many a hard-fought battlefield in defense of the oppressed, the weak, the wronged of my own race. I now present them to you with the injunction that with them you shoot dead the first man who ever comes to subjugate you or to despoil you of your country."[65]

His arms filled with gifts, the chief walked down the stairs and left the building on Pine Street to tell his people about his new friend, "Kotscho."[66]

Little Turtle also spent time with the Frenchman Constantin François Volney, who was considered a controversial figure by the Federalists because of his anticlerical views and belief that in the future all religions would be melded into one.[67] Niemcewicz had dinner with Volney and Jefferson on at least one occasion, and the association hurt the image of the Poles in the eyes of the Federalists.

Even though Volney was nothing more than a politician and historian dabbling in Native American archaeology, Adams considered him a spy sent by the French to colonize Louisiana. The Federalists began passing a series of bills known as the Alien and Sedition Acts to protect the country from citizens of enemy powers.

The witch hunt cast a shadow over all foreigners in Philadelphia, especially those with ties to France. Kosciuszko, who had been mistaken for a Frenchman during the American Revolution, and wrongly accused of being a Jacobin during the Polish revolution, was considered a suspicious character by some of Federalists. It didn't help that he openly supported Jefferson's Democratic-Republicans. "Kosciuszko threw himself into the opposition against President Adams and adhered totally to Jefferson," Niemcewicz wrote. "I did not want to take sides in a foreign country."[68]

The new nation's electoral process was tested after a Republican candidate, a popular Jewish tavern owner named Israel Israel, won a state senate seat in Pennsylvania by beating the Federalist candidate, a Quaker lawyer, Benjamin R. Morgan, by thirty-eight votes. The Federalists challenged the eligibility of some of Israel's voters, and demanded a new election, which was held.[69]

While Kosciuszko could not vote, he favored Israel because, as Niemcewicz described him, "He is what one calls here a rabid Democrat. He is said to be an honest man. He did much for the poor during the time of the yellow fever, and although he is a publican by trade, his mind and his manners are quite cultivated." Niemcewicz added that the choice was between "Democrats and Aristocrats."[70]

Jefferson was concerned about voter turnout when it started to snow on Election Day, and Niemcewicz bundled up to go out and watch the voting process.[71]

"From 10 in the morning until 10 in the evening, all the windows of the Court House were opened," he reported. "At each of these windows there was a table with an urn on top. The voter came up; a judge examined him on whether he had the right to vote. In order to have this right one must have been a citizen of the State for two years, take an oath of loyalty, renounce all allegiance to a foreign power, and pay the tax."

Niemcewicz was surprised that "the apostles of the parties were presenting ballots to the arrivals with the names of Morgan or Israel already written in." At the end of the day an army of Quakers showed up, and Morgan won by 357 votes.[72] Such was the civics lesson that the Poles witnessed in American democracy.

At the end of March, Kosciuszko received a package of mail from Europe. As he tore open the letters, one of them excited him so much that he jumped up off his couch and landed standing in the middle of the room. His servant was astonished by the hobbled general's sudden "recovery." Realizing that he was seen standing without his crutch, Kosciuszko asked his servant to help him back onto the couch.[73]

"I must return to Europe at once," he said to General White, who was a regular visitor to Kosciuszko's room. He did not explain why.[74]

(Ever since the Russians and Prussians had begun opening mail to and from Poland, Kosciuszko had burned all correspondence he did not want others to read. He later admitted to a friend in Paris that he had received an invitation for a personal consultation with the French Directory.[75])

The package also included an update on Kosciuszko's adroit cavalry commander, Gen. Dabrowski, who had joined forces with France and was with the army of Napoleon Bonaparte in Italy. The year before, from his camp in Milan, Dabrowski had issued a proclamation in Polish, French, German, and Italian to the Poles dispersed across Europe under the rallying cry "Freedom and Equality!"

The statement read: "My faithful fatherland, for whose freedom I fought until the last moment under the immortal Kosciuszko, has been conquered. We are left with nothing but the comforting memory that we spilled our blood for the land of our ancestors; and that we saw our victorious flags in Dubienka, Raclawice, Warsaw and Vilnius. Poles! A hope arises. . . . If France wins, she will fight for the cause of other nations! Let us try to weaken her enemies . . . let us fight for the cause of all nations, for freedom, under courageous Bonaparte, the conqueror of Italy."[76]

While there was a temporary truce between revolutionary France and the absolute monarchies of Europe, thousands of Poles flocked to Italy to join Dabrowski's legions.

Kosciuszko was eager to ride again.

The only person he trusted with his plans was Thomas Jefferson. Kosciuszko had to figure out a way to slip out of the country unnoticed. The bombastic and conspicuous Niemcewicz would have to be left behind.

The vice president arranged for a fake passport so that Kosciuszko could travel under an assumed name. Kosciuszko wrote the name "Mr. Kann" on the application, and Jefferson scribbled the letters *berg*, changing his friend's alias to "Thomas Kannberg."

It would not be the only editing of Kosciuszko's words done by the author of the Declaration of Independence. The Polish rebel thought the time for talk was over. He had decided to put his money where his mouth was and challenge Jefferson's ideas about the intellectual inferiority of black people. Kosciuszko decided that he could live off the interest and dividends from his American estate, and bequest the principal to be used for the manumission and education of African slaves.

Toward the end of April he scribbled notes on a piece of paper and gave it to the vice president.

It read: "I beg Mr. Jefferson that in case I should die without will or testament he should buy out of my money so many Negroes and free them, that the remaining sum should be sufficient to give them education and provide for their maintenence. That is to say each should know before, the duty of a citzen in the free Government, that he must defend his Country against foreign as well internal enemies who would wish to change the Constitution for the worst to enslave them by decree afterwards, to have good and human heart sensible for the sufferings of others, each must be married and have 100 acres of land, with instruments, cattle for tillage and know how to manage and govern it as well to know how to behave to neighbors, always with kindness and ready to help them—to them selves frugal, to their children give good education I mean as to the heart and the duty to the Country, in gratitude to me to make themselves happy as possible."[77]

It was signed, "Kosciuszko."

The general knew that he was not conversant with the law, so he asked the Founding Father to take a look at his draft, asking "whenever you will have a time in the daytime for a quarter hour, I beg you would grant me to finish what I have begun."[78]

By begging him "to finish what [he had] begun," Kosciuszko wanted Jefferson to take his awkward English and turn it into proper legalese so that the testament would comply with the laws of the United States. But he also hoped that the vice president would actually follow through on his request to use the money to free slaves. Jefferson took the time to revise the will and gave himself the power of attorney over Kosciuszko's estate.

The new document read: "I, Thaddeus Kosciuszko, being just in my departure from America, do hereby declare and direct that should I make no other testamentary disposition of my property in the United States thereby authorize my friend Thomas Jefferson to employ the whole thereof in purchasing negroes from among his own as any others and giving them liberty in my name in giving them an education in trades and otherwise, and in having them instructed for their new condition in the duties of morality which may make them good neighbors, good fathers or mothers, husbands or wives and in their duties as citizens, teaching them to be defenders of their liberty and country and of the good order of society and in whatsoever may make them happy and useful, and I make the said Thomas Jefferson my executor of this."[79]

The new version of the will not only gave Jefferson the authority to carry out the rebel's wishes, it made his slaves the beneficiaries of Kosciuszko's will. While it was the astute Virginia attorney who made the changes that potentially benefited his own plantation, by signing it Kosciuszko was telling Jefferson: Not only do I want to free slaves, I want to free *your* slaves.

Jefferson recommended his own banker, John Barnes, to handle Kosciuszko's financial matters. The Pole would leave his estate in the United States and live off the dividends. On April 25 Jefferson wrote a "memorandum to Tadeusz Kosciuszko," explaining that the "half yearly dividends" would be sent to Messrs. Nicolas & Jacob Van Staphorst & Hubbard bankers of Amsterdam. Barnes would safely invest the rest.[80]

As he wanted to travel light, Kosciuszko gave away most of his belongings. "Give me leave to present you a Fur," he wrote to Jefferson, offering him the sable that Czar Paul had presented to him upon his release from prison.[81] He also gave Jefferson a "Bear Skin as a Token of my veneration, respect and Esteem for you ever."[82]

The virtuous but inarticulate Kosciuszko was starting to resent his eloquent friend Niemcewicz because many people in Philadelphia were coming to view the writer as the general's guru. People thought that he "was my adviser or mentor, and I have to admit that this was getting boring," Kosciuszko told a friend.[83]

Niemcewicz was drawing too much attention to himself, as the Polish revolutionary was quietly trying to find ways to rekindle the rebellion. He kept his actions secret from Niemcewicz and everyone else. As vice president, Jefferson wanted someone to talk sense into the French before President Adams could persuade Congress to declare war on France. As Kosciuszko was already being invited by the Directory to talk about issues concerning Poland, he was the best choice for the assignment.

Kosciuszko confided to one of his officers in Paris that Niemcewicz was too conspicuous and that the diplomatic overtures to France had to be made quietly. "Since Jefferson thought that I would be the most effective intermediary with France," he told Colonel Drzewiecki, "I accepted the mission without an official authorization. I counted on the principles of my good friend Jefferson."[84]

The quasi war on the Atlantic complicated Kosciuszko's departure to Paris. The French were seizing ships bound for England, and the British were searching vessels bound for France. The Polish rebel told Jefferson that rather than cause an international incident, "I should prefer Lisbon to avoid being taken by the English."[85]

On the night of May 4, 1798, Niemcewicz returned to the boardinghouse on Pine Street after attending a meeting of the Philosophical Society at which Jefferson presented letters about "the discovery of bones of mammoths and other unknown animals" that were to be studied by scientists. Stanislaw Dabrowski, the general's servant, told Niemcewicz that his master would like to speak with him.

"I leave this night for Europe," Kosciuszko said. "I leave alone."[86]

The rebel left a hundred dollars for his servant and two hundred dollars for Niemcewicz, who was sworn to secrecy about Kosciuszko's departure. Niemcewicz refused the money and gifts from the general and gave them to Dabrowski, the servant.

"Stupefied, petrified at this confidence which came a bolt from the blue, I wanted, being recovered from my astonishment, to know the reason for this journey and the place to which he was going," Niemcewicz wrote.[87]

But the general did not offer him any details.

When they were imprisoned in St. Petersburg, Kosciuszko had begged Niemcewicz to accompany him to America. The roles reversed as Niemcewicz pleaded with Kosciuszko not to leave him alone without a source of income in a foreign land. The general refused.

Kosciuszko had often talked publicly about visiting the mineral baths in Virginia to treat his wounds, and Niemcewicz was instructed to say that his former commander had left for therapy at a Southern spa.

"You will leave Philadelphia in three days and you will go in that direction saying that it is to rejoin me," Kosciuszko said. The general packed a few things into a portmanteau and waited for his driver.[88]

At four o'clock in the morning, a covered stagecoach pulled up in front of the red brick boardinghouse on Pine Street. Thomas Jefferson was inside. Tears streamed down Niemcewicz's face as he watched the carriage bounce over the cobblestones toward the docks, where his friend would embark on a clandestine voyage.

Niemcewicz worried about how his limping commander would face the dangers on the open seas alone. Over the next few days he gathered the general's belongings and sent them to Jefferson's home for safekeeping. He heard that Congress had ordered the purchase of twelve battleships with cannons and had introduced a bill to raise an army of twenty thousand men. The Alien and Sedition Acts were also winding their way through Congress.

Ironically, more than a month after Kosciuszko set sail for Lisbon, to avoid being captured by the British, his gold-plated, engraved saber from the Whig Club of England finally arrived in Philadelphia on the *Adriana*, delivered by Captain Lee.[89] By that point Kosciuszko's ship was approaching the coast of Europe, while Niemcewicz was in Virginia, feeling humiliated that he had to spread the lie that Kosciuszko was recuperating at the mineral baths in Virginia.

Niemcewicz stopped in Georgetown, where he met George Washington in what was to become the new federal city. Washington graciously invited Niemcewicz to Mount Vernon, where he stayed as an honored guest for nearly two weeks.

The Polish writer recorded one of history's most vivid accounts of life at the Founding Father's plantation, describing the flower gardens, berry patches, mills, whiskey distillery, as well as fields of wheat, corn, peas, and various other crops all tended by the three hundred slaves that Washington owned along with his wife, Martha.

In the parlor was a painting of the Marquis de Lafayette and his family along with a gift from the French general, a small crystal lantern that housed the actual key to the Bastille in Paris.[90] In contrast, in the parlor at Monticello, Jefferson hung a portrait of Kosciuszko.[91] It was a reminder that while Jefferson had his favorite foreign officer from the American Revolution, Washington also had his.

FIFTEEN

Napoleon Comes Up Short

IT WOULD BE SIXTY YEARS BEFORE THE HEALING POWERS OF THE fountain of Lourdes would first mystify southern France, yet when Kosciuszko's ship docked nearby at the port of Bayonne on June 28, 1798, he cast aside his crutches and stood up on his own. Seagulls cawed as his schooner was moored to the landing pier. The rebel stepped onto the gangplank stretched over the swishing waves below. He walked down to the wharf with a limp, but he could walk.

It turned out that his game leg was not so game after all.[1]

Kosciuszko had pretended to be crippled as a cover for his plan to sneak back into Poland to resurrect the rebellion. Alone at night, he walked around in his room to exercise his leg. His departure from America had been kept secret for several months until a copy of the newspaper *Le Moniteur Universel* hailing his arrival reached the United States.[2]

Upon hearing the news, Jefferson wrote to Niemcewicz, who was worried about the fallout from the Alien and Sedition Acts: "I have no letter yet from our friend Gen. Kosciuszko, but find from the newspapers he is safely arrived in a country where a due value is set, even by those in power on his pure and republican zeal, however cold to that merit some in this country have been, I can assure you that the mass of our countrymen have the highest veneration & attachment to his character."

Jefferson expressed regret that Kosciuszko did not settle near him in Virginia, "This state would have felt a peculiar sensibility if he had thought proper to make it his residence." But understanding the rebel's burning desire to free his country, he wrote to Niemcewicz: "Should the war between France & Austria revive, I shall conceive great hope that your country will again rise into the map of the earth."[3]

The French understood these motives as well, and when the ship dropped anchor in Bayonne, the local magistrate knew that the "Thomas Kannberg" coming ashore was really Kosciuszko. The head of the Directory in Paris, Paul Barras, sent an officer to greet him with military honors.

The town of Bayonne was celebrating a crop festival, and as everyone knew of Kosciuszko's princely behavior toward peasants, farmers exchanged spades and plows with soldiers for their rifles and asked the general to review the troops.

"That's how it would be in Poland if fate had not deserted us," Kosciuszko said after walking past the soldiers standing at attention with spades and peasants who presented arms. Inspired by the welcoming committee, the general set out for Paris, with the French press reporting on Citizen Kosciuszko's trek north.[4]

"I have received a letter from Genl. Kosciuszko," Jefferson wrote later to Niemcewicz, "relating to some of his affairs here, & mentioning in general his good health. I learn through other channels that he is able to walk."[5]

Niemcewicz was enjoying himself in farm country in Elizabethtown, New Jersey, flirting with the wealthy widow Mrs. Livingston-Kean, to whom Kosciuszko had introduced him. Mrs. Kean told the Pole, "If you want it, this hand is yours."[6] Lucky in love, Niemcewicz was stunned by Jefferson's letter and still despondent over the departure of his friend. He replied to Jefferson that he, too, had received a letter from Kosciuszko, but "without mentioning a single word of his health, his mysterious & wonderful recovery, or any private political affairs."[7]

The political affairs of the Polish émigrés in Paris were hatched in a townhouse on the corner of the Rue de l'Échelle and the Rue Saint-Honoré. It was the home of Francis Barss, the attorney Kosciuszko had dispatched to Paris during the insurrection. It was in the center of town, two blocks from the Louvre Palace and the expansive lawns of the Tuileries Gardens. Barss gave the commander his room, with a balcony overlooking the palace of the Duc de Noailles.

Citizen Kosciuszko made the rounds visiting the members of the French Directory to discuss the issues facing his two countries, the United States and Poland.

"The celebrated Pole Kosciuszko has arrived in Paris," wrote Barras. "The hospitable soil of liberty should be proud of welcoming the new Washington."[8]

Kosciuszko admitted to a Polish colonel that while the comparisons to America's Founding Father "tickled" his vanity, he was frustrated because, "Washington and I had similar roles; his was blessed with happy results, mine failed."[9]

However, the Pole was able to use his goodwill with the French to push for the release of the American seamen and captured ships, and explain that the bribes demanded by Talleyrand's men during the XYZ Affair caused an uproar in the United States.

The French saw the party squabbling in Philadelphia as a chance to drive a wedge between the Americans. Yet even though Jefferson sent him, Kosciuszko also met with John Adams's Federalist representative in Paris, Elbridge Gerry. One Democratic-Republican, Sen. Jonathan Roberts, wrote in his memoirs: "Jefferson & the prominent men of the party had commissioned Kosciusko to make known to France, that if war ensued, there would be no division among the people of the U.S."[10]

Jefferson also dispatched other unofficial agents to Paris, such as Dr. George Logan and Constantin Volney, to talk sense into America's former ally. After having had time to ponder the last will and testament that the Pole had left with him, Jefferson gave Volney a letter to deliver to Kosciuszko, saying that his banker, Barnes, would handle the financial affairs, adding, "Your principles and dispositions were made to be honored, revered and loved. True to a single object, the freedom and happiness of man, they have not veered about with the changelings and apostates of our acquaintance."[11]

Kosciuszko, who had received false promises from revolutionary France during the Polish insurrection, told Logan not to believe the French until they "immediately give a pledge of their sincerity by a removal of the embargo."[12]

The Polish general had luck pushing the American cause, and wrote to Jefferson that the French want "to be in peace and in perfect harmony with America."

Some Americans in Paris who were losing business because of the quasi war agreed with his assessment. A Boston merchant in France, Richard Codman, wrote to a Federalist congressman from Massachusetts, Harrison Gray Otis, on August 26, 1798, reporting that the French government might be ready "to settle finally the existing differences . . . The directory have been induced to make this essential alteration in their conduct from the representations made to them by Dupont, Kosciusko, Volney & others lately from America."[13]

The American consul in Le Havre, Nathaniel Cutting, wrote to Jefferson: "General Kosciuszko likewise has, I am persuaded, improved every opportunity of pleading our cause at the Fountain-head of Power in this Country & with good effect."[14]

The secret diplomacy of Kosciuszko, Logan, Volney, and others bore fruit, and the American merchant ships and seamen held prisoner in French harbors were released.[15] When Logan sailed back to Philadelphia with the news, Kosciuszko wrote to Jefferson, "Write me as soon as possible of the effects which the news by Logan's arrival will produce in America, as well as by the Election of the members for Congress, you may rely upon my endeavors here but you must work in America with your friends and Republicans and state their real interest."[16]

Politics and diplomacy in revolutionary France were quite ruthless, and the Pole spent much of his political capital in Paris on American issues, making a few enemies in the process. By criticizing Talleyrand's request for a $250,000 "sweetener" from the United States, Kosciuszko angered the French foreign minister, who said, "This Pole is contemptuous, and so narrow minded toward everything that you can't advise him about anything."[17]

Back in Philadelphia, Logan's good deeds in Paris were denounced by the Adams administration. The angry Federalists passed the Logan Act, making it a crime for private citizens to meddle in relations with foreign countries. Ironically, the actions of Logan, who said up front that he did not speak for the government, helped ease the tensions between the United States and France. Nevertheless the vice president, who sent Logan and Kosciuszko to Paris, ended up with egg on his face.

"On politics I must write sparingly, lest it should fall into the hands of persons who do not love either you or me," Jefferson responded to Kosciuszko's letter. "The wonderful irritation produced in the minds of our citizens by the X.Y.Z. story, has in great measure subsided. . . . Mr. Gerry's communications, with other information, prove to them that France is sincere in her wishes for reconciliation."[18]

While Kosciuszko had luck in helping the United States avert war with France, he made less progress in persuading the French to help Poland. Europe had entered an era of frequent wars, where the maps of the continent were being redrawn every few years by monarchies with revolving loyalties and shifting alliances. In this game of musical chairs, Poland could not get a seat when the music stopped.

Jefferson knew that he could not help his friend with that part of his double mission, and expressed his hope to the Polish rebel that the United States would become "a model for the protection of man in a state of freedom and order. May heaven have in store for your country a restoration of these blessings, and you be destined as the instrument it will use for that purpose. But if this be forbidden by fate, I hope we shall be able to preserve here an asylum where your love of liberty and disinterested patriotism will be forever protected and honored, and where you will find in the hearts of the American people, a good portion of that esteem and affection which glow in the bosom of your friend who writes this."[19]

A biography of Catherine the Great appeared in Paris, and one of Kosciuszko's friends showed him a copy. As he flipped through the pages, he agreed with the accounts of the uprising that he led—until he got to a phrase that said the peasants were not yet suited to be free. Kosciuszko was outraged and said, "What blasphemy! If all of the Polish classes were like the peasants, who heroically performed miracles with their scythes, Poland would be independent and Europe would be judging us quite differently!"[20]

Kosciuszko's return caused quite a stir. In the name of the troops stationed in Italy, General Dabrowski wrote to welcome him back to Europe. The soldiers eagerly awaited the arrival of their chief to take the helm of the army to lead them back to Poland. Kosciuszko replied to Dabrowski, "Kiss each one of them from me and promise them that I too am attached to the fatherland and that together with them I am ready to lay down my life for the country as soon as the opportunity allows."[21]

Many soldiers felt that the time was right for revolution, and poet Joseph Wybicki composed an up-tempo mazurka with a nationalist call to arms urging Dabrowski to "march across Italian lands to Poland" to renew the fight. The hymn became Poland's national anthem, but the Poles still had too few soldiers to attack the three powerful monarchies that had sliced up their country.

"It's gratifying to hear that you, Citizen, a person who during the revolution gave proof of true citizenship, is now among the Polish legions," Kosciuszko responded to Wybicki after reading his lyrics. "I do not doubt your love for the fatherland, and the unwavering sentiment deep in your heart. . . . You know the effect of enthusiastic songs implanted in the souls of people that pant their breath for freedom. . . . We also need to draft a republican catechism for them that will replace superstition."[22]

It was a hint at his dissatisfaction with the church's influence from the pulpit over the serfs whose free labor the clergy took for granted. The successful separation of church and state in America had done much to advance democracy. But in Poland, where King Stanislaw's brother had been the primate of Poland, and government and church were intertwined, the commander would have to tread lightly.

Kosciuszko urged the troops to bide their time and issued a proclamation to his "Brother soldiers" that said: "The saddest moment of my life was when unfortunate circumstances forced me to part with you without expressing my gratitude for your acts of courage and love in the fight to protect your beloved country. Freed from Muscovite captivity and completely free, I send you, my beloved, the warmest expressions of my gratitude and respect." But "you are yet to be defeated," he told them. "I know you are waiting for a time to avenge your fatherland. My impatience is equal to yours . . . use this time to get ready."[23]

The rebel also did something Niemcewicz had tried to talk him out of: He repudiated Czar Paul's gift. It was an unwise move because it publicly revealed his plan of opposing Russia. He knew the Prussians would open his mail, so Kosciuszko sent it via French diplomatic courier to the Russian ambassador in Berlin. But the Prussians ignored the sanctity of the diplomatic pouch and made a copy of the letter before the czar had a chance to read it. By then the editors of

Le Moniteur Universel and *Ami Ides Lois*, whom Kosciuszko also sent it to, printed it in their newspapers.

The letter began: "I take advantage of the first moments of freedom that I can enjoy under the protection of laws of the greatest and most generous nation, to return your gift which gave the appearance of your benevolence, but was forced on me by your atrociously behaved ministers." He said that he only agreed to accept the present because of "the attachment that I have for my countrymen," who were imprisoned and "coerced by force" into agreeing to the pledge.[24]

The money was to be sent from the emperor's bankers, Thompson, Bonard & Co. in London to the Russian ambassador in Vienna.[25] But Czar Paul was furious and replied that he refused to "accept anything from a traitor."[26] The funds remained in the bank's vault under Kosciuszko's name.

It was all great fodder for *Porcupine's Gazette,* which wrote: "Now here is an impudent fellow! He very willingly received presents from the Emperor and his ministers, he comes afterwards, pleads poverty, and receives thousands of dollars from the ill-judging liberality of the American Congress; . . . Americans . . . this fellow was no friend of yours."[27]

Cobbett continued, saying, "It is evident that Kosciuszko is a mere tool in the hands of the Directory. He is, in fact, the 'Spurious Envoy' from Poland."

In another article Cobbett attacked Kosciuszko for taking the "cash . . . in his pocket" to France to "become the open enemy of those who had relieved him."[28]

Only Jefferson and his banker, Barnes, knew that the Polish rebel did not pocket the money. He left it in Philadelphia with the noble goal of freeing slaves, a plan Jefferson was not ready to make public.

Porcupine's Gazette continued its attacks on Kosciuszko and others, pushing freedom of the press to its limits. When Cobbett libeled Dr. Rush, the First Amendment proved too prickly even for *Porcupine's.* Rush sued Cobbett and won a libel judgment for five thousand dollars, forcing the *Porcupine* to go belly-up.[29]

But Cobbett was right about one thing, Kosciuszko had become a tool of the Directory, which had no intention of helping Poland, or any other country for that matter. For France, Poland was simply a second front against its enemies, Austria and Prussia. Kosciuszko and the émigrés in Paris naively swallowed the pap of universal *Liberté, Egalité,* and *Fraternité* as if they were baby chicks waiting with open mouths to feed on regurgitated food from the mother hen.

While Kosciuszko was in America, the Poles fawned over Napoleon to get him to support the Polish legions. "I love the Poles and attach great importance to them," Napoleon told them. "The partition of Poland was an unfair act that does not have the right to become permanent. After the conclusion of the hostilities in Italy, I will personally lead the French Army to force Russia to restore Poland. But, the Poles must not count on foreign help alone, they must arm themselves." He also warned them, saying, "Pretty words alone will lead to nowhere. A nation destroyed by its neighbors must take up arms herself."[30]

The French government agreed to fund a separate Polish legion that was small enough not to be a real threat, yet large enough to be a symbolic ally against Austria and Prussia. The Directory dressed the Poles in frilly uniforms with Italian epaulets, and French tricolors with revolutionary cockade ribbons. The Polish uniforms included an inscription in Italian, *Gli uomini liberi sono fratelli*, "Free men are brothers."[31]

The first unit of 3,600 Poles under General Dabrowski served as a fighting force in the French-occupied "Republic of Lombardy." Another unit was formed in Italy under General Zajaczek, and a third, the Danube legion of 6,000 men, led by Gen. Charles Kniaziewicz was posted on the German front.

One of the horsemen who rode into Milan to join Dabrowski was Berek Joselewicz, whose Jewish cavalry had been slaughtered by the Russians. Joselewicz told Dabrowski that he was "reporting for duty like all good Poles."[32]

At the Belgioioso Gardens near Milan, the French army feted the Polish and Italian soldiers and toasted "the illustrious but unhappy Kosciuszko, may he quickly return to his country to free it from tyrants."[33] The legions were hoodwinked by Napoleon's promise to "restore Poland" and thought that they would march across Europe to free their homeland. They would have to wait: The French were playing the Poles like a fiddle.

Napoleon was on his way to the Middle East when Kosciuszko arrived in Paris, so their meeting was deferred. When the minister of war held a banquet to celebrate Napoleon's capture of Malta, the writer Nicholas Bonneville raised his glass and gave a toast, not to the victorious French general, but to the Pole, saying, "Freedom recovered its defender when Kosciuszko arrived in Europe."[34]

Kosciuszko was moved to tears. He raised his glass and tried to make a toast, but the revelers clinked their wineglasses, and cheered, "To the tears of Kosciuszko!"

The commander was not the only emotional Pole in Paris during this period. Knowing that the Poles were big on pomp and circumstance, Napoleon handed them the perfect flag to wave as they marched with him.

When King John Sobieski freed Austria from the Ottoman army in 1683, he sent his sword and the flag of the Turkish grand vizier Kara Mustafa to the Vatican as a trophy for the pope to remember the victory against the Muslim invaders. When Napoleon "liberated" Italy, he gave the flag to Dabrowski, who proudly marched under the banner as a symbol of Poland's rekindled freedom. Dabrowski urged Kosciuszko "to be our Moses, who will lead us out of our slavery in Egypt."[35]

Sobieski's sword was sent to Paris and given to Kosciuszko as the new keeper of the flame.[36] The presentation of the saber of Poland's most successful king and general pleased Kosciuszko, and he wrote to General Kniaziewicz: "My esteemed general, the sword of Sobieski, which you have just sent me on behalf of our famous countrymen, who experienced many victories in Italy, I accept as proof of our friendship and ask you to extend to them my gratitude. If God allows us to join together to fight and defeat tyrants, we will put our swords together with Sobieski's saber in the temple of peace and freedom for the happiness of all of our compatriots."[37]

But the flame of liberty dimmed to a mere flicker as internal squabbles among the feuding émigrés nearly extinguished any chance to present a united front in liberating their nation. The Poles had broken into two factions, the Agency and the Deputation. The attorney Barss, who was part of the Agency, was accused of having clandestine ties to Russia. While the rumors were not true, to get rid of the distraction, Kosciuszko moved out of Barss's apartment and rented a small apartment on the Left Bank of the Seine, among the artists.

France was also facing problems because it was creating too many enemies. By 1799 Austria, Russia, and Great Britain had formed a coalition to push back at the expansionist desires of the French. Napoleon's expedition to Egypt and Syria to challenge England's communication routes with its colonies in India proved to be a mistake. While he was away Russia and Austria attacked the French troops stationed in northern Italy, killing thousands of them at the Battle of Trebbia. Thousands of Polish soldiers were slain fighting alongside the French.

This new alliance was a real threat to France, but during that summer Napoleon's army was marching across the hot sands of the Middle East. While he did bring archaeologists with him who discovered the Rosetta Stone, which provided valuable insight into hieroglyphics, Napoleon's men slaughtered thousands of Turkish prisoners, even when they cried for mercy. With the military setback at home and his ranks thinned by the bubonic plague, Napoleon was forced to return to France.

A relieved and cheering crowd greeted Napoleon when he returned to Paris on October 16. The next day he was on his way to meet with the five members of the Directory, but stopped on the way to surprise Kosciuszko in his Left Bank apartment on the Rue de Lille. Napoleon warmly greeted the Pole as if he were a brother-in-arms, saying, "I urgently wanted to meet the hero of the north."

Kosciuszko, who expected Napoleon to be an ally, replied, "And I am happy to see the conquerer of Europe, and the hero of the East."[38]

The meeting continued with all the niceties of diplomacy, but the Polish general sensed that something was not right. Having spent enough time in the company of double-crossers, he felt that Napoleon was hiding his real intentions. The egotistical French general was planning to make a power play, and he wanted Kosciuszko and the Poles on his side.

Afterward Kosciuszko cautioned the members of the French Directory "to keep a sharp eye on that young man, he might spoil your arrangement."[39]

It was a prescient warning.

On November 9, 1799, Napoleon staged a coup d'état and replaced the Directory with a troika known as the Consulate, naming himself first consul. The parliamentary and military powers of the nation were in the hands of one man, Napoleon Bonaparte.

Kosciuszko called Napoleon "the gravedigger of the republic."[40] But General Dabrowski disagreed, saying, "It's lucky for the French and for all of us that Bonaparte has become the head of the nation. He will not become a usurper, but the founder of a sure-footed government."[41]

Under the new status quo, the role of the fifty-four-year-old rebel evolved from that of commander to that of elder statesman. Kosciuszko wrote to Napoleon requesting that the fifteen thousand soldiers in the three Polish legions be combined into one unit so he could train them. He wanted to promote the officers based on experience and talent.[42] The French, however, sought to advance officers who were loyal to France. Kosciuszko was soon reduced to begging for bread, shoes, and guns for his troops.

Napoleon was concerned about Kosciuszko's popularity among the Poles and the French revolutionaries, and ordered his chief spy to keep track of him.

Joseph Fouché was a tight-lipped man, tall and skinny, with pale hair, a grayish blue complexion, and bloodshot eyes. His left eye was larger than his right, giving the appearance that he was squinting or peering through an "evil eye."[43]

"Intrigue," Napoleon said, "was to Fouché a necessity of life."[44]

The cruel and cunning Fouché was a bloodthirsty Jacobin during Robespierre's Reign of Terror and became known as a "de-Christianizer" who ransacked churches and denied the existence of the Holy Trinity.[45] His new job was as minister of police. Once Napoleon took control of the government, he began to manipulate Dabrowski's legions, and there was nothing Kosciuszko could do about it.

"I had once indulged in the hope of seeing the reestablishment of Poland, founded upon its liberty," Fouché wrote in his diary, "but Napoleon [was] repelling Kosciuszko, or at least endeavoring to draw him into a snare."[46]

The hairs stood on the back of Kosciuszko's neck at the mere mention of Napoleon's name, and ultimately his unwillingness to compromise and do business with the new French dictator hurt his cause. The situation came to a head when he was invited to an official banquet in the Luxembourg Palace. One of the ruling consuls, Charles-François Lebrun, was at Kosciuszko's table when Napoleon summoned him to talk.

A little while later Lebrun had a big smile on his face as he returned to

Kosciuszko, and in front of all of the guests at the feast said loudly, "Do you know, General, that the First Consul spoke of you?"

Kosciuszko turned his head away and curtly replied, "I never speak of him."[47]

Understandably Napoleon's demeanor toward the Polish commander also cooled. Yet, the Poles stubbornly pursued audiences with the first consul, lobbying for the Polish cause and asking for more assistance with the legions. General Kniaziewicz accompanied Kosciuszko to the meetings in the Luxembourg Palace and the royal residence at the Tuileries, but when Napoleon spoke he addressed the other Poles in the room, ignoring Kosciuszko's presence.[48]

The Polish rebel stopped attending Napoleon's lavish balls and spent most of his time with the political scribe Joseph Pawlikowski, who became his new secretary. Kosciuszko was never much of a writer, so he dictated his thoughts to Pawlikowski, who put them on paper and published an anonymous pamphlet that appeared in Paris in June 1800, "Can the Poles Win Their Independence?"[49]

It was a manual for guerrilla warfare.

"A nation that demands independence must believe in its own strength," it began.[50] Full of Kosciuszko's rhetoric, it demanded freedom for the peasants and criticized the nobility for not doing enough to support the revolution. It said Poland had all the manpower, horses, iron for weapons, and resources it needed to end foreign occupation.

One line said, "The American Revolutionaries did not have the support of one fourth of the nation, as testified by Franklin's life, whose steadfast mind pulled along the rest of the public."[51] It called on Poles to build redoubts, melt lead from windowpanes for cannonballs and bullets, and construct food storage magazines to hide wheat and enable them to starve out the enemy soldiers. It urged Ukrainians to rise up against Russia, and Hungarians to revolt against Austria.

Pawlikowski, an advocate for disenfranchised peasants, burghers, and Jews, wrote: "I see in Kosciuszko the genius and defender of fundamental human rights."[52]

Packages of the booklets were smuggled into Poland, and when a translated copy found its way into the hands of the French, all hell broke loose. The political treatise was critical of France, and a diplomat named Jean Bonneau, learning the identity of the author, wrote to Talleyrand: "A certain Pawlikowski, a longtime crazy demagogue and rabid revolutionary is an intimate and obliging creature of Kosciuszko."[53]

The French police ordered an immediate investigation. Copies of the pamphlet were confiscated, Pawlikowski was arrested, and Kosciuszko was warned not to cause trouble. The essay also caused friction between Kosciuszko and the legions because it mourned the ten thousand Poles who were killed fighting as part of the French army during the Italian campaigns, saying: "Why isn't this bravery used to push the occupying forces from our fatherland?"[54]

Pawlikowski was sent to jail, and Kosciuszko found another secretary, a twenty-three-year old captain from the legions named Francis Paszkowski, who took notes during the next several years for a biography he would write of his leader.

"During this time in Europe, there could not have been two more different souls than Kosciuszko and Bonaparte," Paszkowski wrote. "This new leader openly used the principles of Machiavelli."[55]

As a politician Kosciuszko was completely outmatched by the crafty Napoleon. A friend wrote about the Polish leader: "So much was finding its way to his mind that he was still easily deceived, a flaw he later corrected, instead becoming excessively cautious."[56]

After his return to Paris, France descended into tyranny and he became eccentric and paranoid. He felt most comfortable in the company of Americans. Having made enemies of the Russians, Prussians, and Austrians, he felt he was constantly being spied on, and soon the French also began keeping tabs on Kosciuszko.

Napoleon became the Machiavellian prince whom everyone feared, while Kosciuszko tried to be the peasant prince whom people loved. To many in France, Napoleon was a benevolent dictator who stabilized the country. However, the French royalists and revolutionaries did not feel the same way.

On Christmas Eve, 1800, Napoleon set out with his family to celebrate the holiday at the opera. As his horse carriage clopped over the cobblestones and out of the Tuileries toward the theater, a cart carrying a wine barrel packed with gunpowder and wrapped in iron rings was detonated as the dictator's coach passed by. The explosion hurled bits of iron and flaming splinters through the air, killing and injuring dozens of people. Napoleon survived the assassination attempt and ordered Fouché to clamp down on his political opponents. Surveillance on all dissidents was increased, including Kosciuszko.

Seeing that the chances of an independent Poland were dwindling, Jefferson encouraged Kosciuszko to settle in America, writing: "I have got your land warrant located and have received for you the patent for 500 acres to land on the Scioto River." President Adams signed the land grant for the Pole's property in Ohio as part of his compensation as a veteran of the Revolution. Kosciuszko's friend Armstrong scouted it out. The vice president also updated his friend on politics, expressing hope about the upcoming elections, adding, "An accommodation with France will entirely tranquilize our affairs."[57]

Instead of farming his new property Kosciuszko asked Jefferson if he could find a sharecropper to cultivate the land. He offered that a tenant could have it rent free for five years, and afterward continue at one percent below the market rate. The Pole would never see his land on the Scioto River, which would eventually become Columbus, Ohio. As for the invitation to return to the United States, Kosciuszko was optimistic that Jefferson would win the election, writing, "I hope you will be the same in that new station always, a good true American, a Philosopher and my Friend, it may happen under your helm I shall return to America, but not otherwise."[58]

The peace accord with France that Jefferson was looking for came when Napoleon concluded that it did not make sense to antagonize the Americans at a time when he was at war with Great Britain and much of continental Europe. France ended the quasi war that it started with the United States and signed the Treaty of Mortefontaine. For the occasion, Napoleon even trotted out Lafayette, whom he despised, and raised his glass before the assembled guests, toasting, "To the manes of the French and the Americans who died on the field of battle for the independence of the new world."[59]

Napoleon hated Lafayette because of his unwavering democratic principles. Once Kosciuszko realized this, he overcame his jealousy of Lafayette left over from the American Revolution, and the two became close. Both generals were vehemently opposed to slavery and serfdom. Lafayette later told an abolitionist in the United States, "I would have never drawn my sword in the cause of America, if I could have conceived, that thereby I was founding a land of slavery."[60]

Lafayette detested the "ancient system and ancient princes of the European continent," that had imprisoned the peasant masses and divided Poland, and he was a true republican who wanted to wipe out "bigotries of every kind." He attended a banquet held by the Poles to honor Kosciuszko.[61] Lafayette and Kosciuszko also attended a Fourth of July celebration held by the Americans in Paris. The feelings that Lafayette had for the Polish leader were obvious to anyone who visited his apartment. In his room Lafayette kept a bust of George Washington on a small cabinet. Hanging above it was a portrait of Kosciuszko.[62]

No longer having to worry about war with the United States, Napoleon shifted his focus to consolidating power. He exchanged friendly letters with Czar Paul of Russia, while at the same time leading the Poles on, letting them believe that an invasion of eastern Europe was imminent. Yet on February 9, 1801, France signed the Treaty of Luneville with Austria. The war was over.

It was a popular move with the French public, but the Polish legions were devastated that the treaty ignored the issue of Poland. The Poles had naively believed Napoleon when he said he would lead a multinational army across the continent to liberate Europe. Just as Catherine the Great had done before him, Napoleon broke up the Polish units and reassigned the soldiers to his own army. Some were ordered to police Italy. Many Polish soldiers resigned in disgust.

Eventually Napoleon showed his true colors when he forced 5,647 Poles onto battleships that sailed across the Atlantic to quash the slave revolt in the

French colony of Saint-Domingue, where Toussaint-Louverture had declared Haiti a free black republic.[63] Hundreds of Polish soldiers died in combat or from yellow fever. The Poles who volunteered in the French army to free their homeland were enraged that they were sent to fight black people who were trying to win their own freedom. Many changed sides and joined the Haitians. Fewer than four hundred Poles returned to Europe after the French failed to recapture the colony. Kosciuszko was appalled. Napoleon had become everything that he had despised, a tyrant and a slave driver.

The Polish rebel became a fixture at the gatherings in Paris of those who were opposed to Napoleon. He struck up a friendship with Thomas Paine at the dinner parties at the home of the writer Bonneville, where guests sat at an oblong table stacked with bronzes, globes, maps, books, and portraits discussing history and politics.[64] Kosciuszko clicked with Paine's circle of anti-Bonaparte friends, and they even threw a birthday party for the Pole. At one dinner gathering Joel Barlow called Napoleon, "the butcher of liberty, the greatest monster that Nature ever spewed."[65]

Paine was also an honorary citizen of France, and had published his *Agrarian Justice,* in which he talked about being "shocked by extremes of wretchedness" of the poor. Pointing out that neither the American Indians nor the shepherds in the Bible, like Abraham, owned land, he decried the "monopoly of natural inheritance" of land by the rich. He proposed the creation of a fund to help the poor and those who cultivate land, thus increasing its value.[66]

These ideas were in accord with Kosciuszko's efforts to help the peasants. And like Paine, the general also thought highly of the American Indians, whom he called noble and true to their word.[67]

Another satellite orbiting in Paine's social circle was Lewis Goldsmith, an English journalist of Portuguese-Jewish descent who initially came to Paris as a supporter of Napoleon but later founded the *Anti-Gallican Montitor*. Kosciuszko confided in Goldsmith about his frustration with the French.

"When the Revolution broke out in Poland in 1793," Goldsmith wrote, "its leaders were supported by France, and they had their agents in Paris, as soon, however as peace was signed at Basle between the King of Prussia and the Committee of Public Safety, the Polish agents were no longer recognized, and no further succor given to the Poles. This fact was told me by General Kosciuszko."[68]

Paine was also displeased with the failure of the Polish revolution. After the May 3 Constitution, he spoke highly of Poland, but the collapse of the democratic movements in Paris and Warsaw discouraged him.

In the spring of 1801 Congressman Dawson, who had sponsored the resolution to finally pay Kosciuszko's salary from the American Revolution, arrived in Paris from the new federal city of Washington, D.C., with a dispatch for the

French government: The big news was that Thomas Jefferson had been elected the third president of the United States.

Dawson also delivered a letter from the new president to Kosciuszko.

"I can now hail you with confidence on the return of our fellow citizens to the principles of '76 and to their thorough understanding of the artifices which have been played off on them and under the operation of which they were while you were here," Jefferson wrote to his Polish friend. "It would give me infinite pleasure to have you here a witness to our recovery, & to recognize the people whom you knew during the war. For the particulars, I refer you to Mr. Dawson." Jefferson also wrote that Kosciuszko should move to Virginia and that he could arrange to "buy the hundred acres of land for you in my neighborhood."[69]

Dawson conveyed the verbal news to Kosciuszko that Jefferson referred to in the letter, and the two men went to dine with Thomas Paine.[70] The witch hunt of the Alien and Sedition Acts had ended. Jefferson also wrote to Paine, explaining that as president he would provide for his safe return to America on the war sloop *Maryland*.

Kosciuszko was excited about the election of his friend. "I congratulate the United States of America on the choice they have made in your person for their President," he wrote to Jefferson. "I think I shall come this year to admire you and to leave my ashes in a land of liberty, where there are honest customs and justice."[71]

Paine took Jefferson's offer and sailed back to the United States, but the Pole, still hoping that his country could be freed, decided to stay in Europe.

As the days wore on, the loneliness of living by himself in Paris became more acute as Kosciuszko was shunned by Napoleon's court. He had met Peter Joseph Zeltner, the representative in Paris of the Swiss Republic of Helvetia, during negotiations to allow the Polish legions to camp in Switzerland. Kosciuszko was drawn to Zeltner, but even more so to his pretty French wife, Angelique. The Zeltners were renting a large townhouse at 43 Rue de Provence, and they invited the general to rent a room in their home so he could live in a family setting.

Zeltner was a gregarious animal whose political loyalties changed with the wind. When his diplomatic mission ended, Zeltner's career was adrift, but he inherited a struggling bank and a small farm in Berville, thirty-four miles south of Paris, near Fontainebleau. To help out his landlord Kosciuszko deposited his own meager funds in the bank and encouraged his friends to do the same.

The Zeltners had three children, and while the patriarch was friendly in public, he was an unemotional husband and father, leaving his family starved for attention and affection. Kosciuszko filled the void, spending several hours a day tutoring the children and becoming very close to Angelique. Once again there were rumors that Kosciuszko was having an affair with a married woman.[72] Captain Paszkowski described her as a "kindhearted, wise and pleasant woman; and, what is rare among women, she was capable of friendship without romantic inclinations, and without impositions."[73]

One of Kosciuszko's relatives who visited him in Paris, Lt. Joseph Sierakowski, was convinced that the general was pursuing Mrs. Zeltner, and wrote to one of his nephews, "The old man is wooing Zeltner's pretty wife."[74]

Domestic life with the Zeltners allowed Kosciuszko to remain out of the spotlight. Everyone knew that he refused to sit for paintings, but the officers of the Polish legions wanted a likeness of the Pole for posterity's sake. Zeltner came up with a sneaky plan.

The general loved music, so Zeltner bought a theater box so he could attend concerts anonymously. But Kosciuszko didn't know that his Swiss friend also purchased the adjoining box, so that a sculptor named Eggenschwiler could sit next to him to surreptitiously observe and sketch the occupant in the neighboring booth.

The sculptor was commissioned to create a statue of Kosciuszko and chiseled three marble busts of the commander in a toga. Kosciusko was a connoisseur of the arts, and when learned that a promising sculptor was working nearby, he asked Zeltner to take him to the studio. They walked in as Eggenschwiler was chipping away, and the general was shocked when he recognized his own likeness in stone. He exploded in anger and whacked two of the busts with his cane, sending the sculptures to the floor where they shattered. When he lifted his walking stick in the air and was about to bring it down on the third, the artist shielded his work and pleaded that it be spared.[75]

Kosciuszko lowered his cane and made the artist give his word of honor that no copies would be made. Zeltner and the Polish officers had their bust.

Many people vied for Kosciuszko's attention, and some went to great lengths just to get a glimpse of him. Lady Vera-Diana Kwilecka was a divorcée who traveled from Poland to Paris under the pretext of delivering a drawing to Kosciuszko. She knew he did not like people who fussed over him, so she sent a friendly but reserved letter, and he agreed to meet with her.

"He looked nothing liked the portraits I had seen," Lady Vera-Diana said. "He had the same features, but rather than thick and distinct, they were delicate and subtle, and slightly irregular. He had a face full of wrinkles, a wide mouth that was tightly closed, sparse teeth and an upturned nose. His eyes shined full of life and he had a thick crop of chestnut curls with a touch of gray that fell on his forehead and shoulders. The look on his face was focused. He was medium height and thin."[76]

She described his face as happy and witty. He spoke quickly but calmly. Lady Vera-Diana became the escort around town that Kosciuszko needed, and the two struck up a friendship. With a new social friend, Kosciuszko began attending parties, especially after Jefferson sent diplomats to Paris whom Kosciuszko knew. In the company of Americans, Kosciuszko "carried on with fatherly tenderness and brotherly love. He was always ready to help them with whatever they needed. In return, Americans treated him with the utmost respect belonging to a patriarch of the revolution."[77]

One evening after riding through the countryside in a horse and buggy, the general and Lady Vera-Diana stopped at the home of the new American ambassador, Robert Livingston, who turned out to be hosting a ball. Lady Vera-Diana refused to leave the carriage because she was not dressed in evening attire. Kosciuszko returned with a few young men and threatened that if she did not join the party, his friends would carry her inside.

"They are not French," he said. "But rather honest Americans. Please put aside your misgivings and be pleasant."[78]

Lady Vera-Diana had such a good time at the ball that she became a regular visitor to the Livingston affairs, even when Kosciuszko could not attend. She also became close to Mrs. Zeltner, but felt a rivalry for the general's affections.

"I tried to make the acquaintance with Mr. and Mrs. Zeltner, in whose home he [Kosciuszko] lived," Lady Vera-Diana wrote. "I especially searched for a chance to get close to the lady of the house, who was close to his heart. There was much gossip about this topic."[79]

It was even rumored that Kosciuszko was the father of the Zeltner's youngest daughter, Thaddea. She was named after the general, who was the baby's godfather. He tutored all the Zeltner children, but he often carried Thaddea in his arms and on his shoulders as if he were her father. It was not the first chatter about Kosciuszko and married women. Years earlier some officers gossiped that he had an affair with the wife of a Colonel Konarski, which produced a child.[80]

Women were always drawn to Kosciuszko, not just because he was a hero but also because he was not condescending and treated them as equals. "He was a friend to women and adored them," Paszkowski wrote. "They had a secret bond of tenderness, gentleness and modesty; they understood what he was capable of and they could appreciate his ordinary features, which were less understood by men."[81]

The worst thing a woman could do was to lavish him with attention. Kosciuszko was exasperated when Lady Vera-Diana invited him to her home, and there was "a chance" meeting with the writer Madame Germaine de Staël. He became uncomfortable when the pushy author, looking for new material, peppered him with questions.

"General, tell us something about your revolution," Madame de Staël asked.

"Madame, I was a soldier and I fought," he gasped.

Then, turning to his hostess, he said in Polish, "Please rescue me from this woman, or I am going to run away." The questions continued, and he got up and left.[82]

Kosciuszko was disgusted with the French for allowing the cult of personality to keep Napoleon in power. And, also tired of those who called him a hero, he tried to stay out of public places where he would be noticed. One night, while walking to a dinner party, he refused to take the shortest route through the Tuileries Gardens to avoid gawkers and suggested walking around the park. Lady Vera-Diana told him that his ego had gotten out of hand and said he wouldn't even be noticed. But as soon as they entered the gardens, people strolling by shouted his name and a crowd gathered and followed them all the way to the bridge over the Seine.[83]

Yet there was one group he always enjoyed hearing from. When a nobleman from Poznan rode into Paris on his horse with his servant and ordered the serf to return home to Poland, the peasant refused to leave until he had a chance to meet Kosciuszko. The aristocrat finally agreed, and the general was so touched by the serf's demand that he told him, "Thank you my brother that you wanted to see me." He asked the peasant if he had a wife and children, and inquired about the conditions of his life under feudalism. Kosciuszko hugged the man and told him that he was to hug all the serfs back home working in the fields.

"The peasant broke down and cried," Lady Vera-Diana wrote in her memoirs. "Kosciuszko was so moved he went pale, this was the only time I had ever seen him in such a state. He knew how to turn away from fawning social situations, but he could never resist the people who worked with nature."[84]

The attention he received in Paris became distracting, so Kosciuszko spent most of his time at the Zeltners' country estate. He noticed that Lady Vera-Diana had fallen in love with him, and she had become jealous of Mrs. Zeltner, whom she called "young, sweet, full of charm, a subtle Parisian."[85]

While Lady Vera-Diana had fallen for Kosciuszko, Major Fiszer, the general's former adjutant who was then in Paris, was smitten with her. The commander saw his solution to the situation by fixing up the lady with the major. Walking through a park near some aquatic hornwort plants growing in a pond, Kosciuszko whispered into Lady Vera-Diana's ear, "Don't let my young friend starve to death from hunger for love."[86]

The message was heard loud and clear, and Lady Vera-Diana Kwilecka became Mrs. Fiszer. The couple moved back to Poland, where they settled, and Kosciuszko wrote when he heard that they had finally gotten married, "I wish you as much happiness as is humanly possible and that your future satisfies all of your expectations." And always looking out for the serfs, he continued, "Take care of your servants and your peasants, so that they love you and that like you, they too can be happy."[87]

After the Fiszers returned to Poland, Kosciuszko often visited his colleague from the American Revolution, John Armstrong, whom Jefferson had appointed as the new ambassador to France. Armstrong had tried to persuade Kosciuszko to remain in America when he visited, and even found a beautiful farm for sale in the Hudson Valley of upstate New York, where the Pole could settle. The two veterans were so close that when the American had a son, he christened him Kosciuszko Armstrong and asked the Pole to be the boy's godfather.

His hair turning gray, and his chances for love and a free country slipping away, Kosciuszko began thinking about his legacy as historical accounts of his life appeared in Paris. One book written by Count Louis Segur called General Poninski a traitor because his late arrival at the Battle of Maciejowice sealed Kosciuszko's fate. When Poninski wrote to Kosciuszko asking him to set the record straight with Segur, the commander at first refused, and got so angry that he wanted to challenge Poninski to a duel. Talked out of it by other Polish officers, he eventually agreed to help Poninski clear his name, as the Poles would have lost the war with or without him.[88]

Another issue that cast a cloud over Polish history was the spurious claim that Kosciuszko uttered the Latin words *Finis Poloniae* when he fell from his horse at Maciejowice. The notion of what would be on his gravestone, and worse yet, that his name would be associated with the epitaph of his destroyed nation, depressed the commander greatly.

"Ignorance or malignity with fierce pertinacity have put the expression *Finis Poloniae* into my mouth," Kosciuszko purportedly wrote to Segur. "We the devoted soldiers of the country are mortal, Poland herself is immortal . . . those words . . . attributed to me a blasphemy against which I protest with all my soul."[89]

The legitimacy of the letter to Segur has been questioned, but the issue clearly caused Kosciuszko tremendous grief.[90] He was also annoyed that historians credited Prince Czartoryski with paying for all of his education. As the Seym funded the Knights' School in Warsaw, Kosciuszko told his friends that he was beholden to taxpayers and the nation, and that education was the key to providing serfs with the future they deserved.[91]

Retired and living in Berville, Kosciuszko was far from the intrigues of Paris, where Napoleon was planning to canonize himself and become emperor of France. In March 1803, Napoleon was once again scheming to take over more territory in Europe, and he asked Lewis Goldsmith to persuade Louis XVIII to renounce his claim to the French royal throne in exchange for being named the king of Poland. When Louis declined, Napoleon plotted to poison the true king of France, but that plan also failed.[92]

Foreign minister Talleyrand wanted to create an empire in North America that could rival the United States. But Napoleon was focused on conquering Europe, so he sold the Louisiana Territory to the Jefferson Administration for fifteen million dollars. With the extra money in his coffers and no more concerns about the New World, Napoleon had paved the way for his own coronation as emperor of France on December 2, 1804.

America's size doubled with the purchase of the Louisiana Territory, and Kosciuszko's funds in America were also growing, which meant that it would be possible for the Pole to free and educate even more slaves. Kosciuszko also felt strongly about the education of soldiers, and often spoke with Jefferson about the need for an American military academy such as those in France, Poland, and other European countries, ideas he frequently mentioned in his letters to Jefferson.

Jefferson established the U.S. Military Academy at West Point in 1802, in the fortress that Kosciuszko had designed during the Revolution. During a visit to Paris, Gen. William Davie had asked Kosciuszko to write a manual for the American Army on artillery warfare and the result was Kosciuszko's "Manoeuvres of Horse Artillery," which became one of the first textbooks used at West Point.[93]

When the first superintendent of the military academy, Jonathan Williams, sent the President a copy, Jefferson replied, "I thank you for the copy of Gen. Kosciuszko's treatise on the flying artillery. It is a branch of the military art which I wish extremely to see understood here to the height of the European level."[94]

Kosciuszko had long urged Jefferson to open a military academy, and in 1805 wrote to him in French that there should be a "military school in each state whose alumni upon graduating would be officers in the militia that through their knowledge and enlightenment will add even more peace to the lofty idea of being a virtuous republican." That was the only way, the Pole believed, that Jefferson could solidify the success of the Revolution after his death. "I love you," Kosciuszko wrote, "you are the sole hope of all humanity and I hope you will be an example to future ages."[95]

The Polish leader saw education as the best hope to improve the lives of the peasants in Europe as well. He read the works of Johann Heinrich Pestalozzi, a Swiss pedagogue who dedicated his life to reforming the educational system. After France conquered Switzerland, Pestalozzi went to see Napoleon to try to convince him to create a national department of education. But Napoleon, replied, "I have no time to bother with the alphabet."[96]

After Pestalozzi was shunned by Napoleon, he was invited to open a school in Philadelphia. He sent an associate, Joseph Neef, who sailed to America in 1806.

Kosciuszko wrote a letter of introduction for Neef to Jefferson, explaining that Pestalozzi's method of "elementary education of youth is to follow nature exactly, i.e. to speak to the eyes of the child, to give names of the objects which strike him, then to draw attention to their form, properties, uses, etc. In this way the child's judgment is formed and its memory enlarged. You will see from this that Pestalozzi's child in proportion to its intellectual powers may become versed in all the sciences."[97]

The lessons Kosciuszko provided for the Zeltner children were based on Pestalozzi's methods. But a peaceful retirement of teaching young children was not his final destiny. A strange twist of fate drew Kosciuszko back into the world of international politics against his will.

Czar Paul was assassinated, and his son Alexander took the throne, making his friend, Polish prince Adam Jerzy Czartoryski, the foreign minister of Russia. Prince Adam was raised as the son of Kosciuszko's mentor, the head of the Knights' School, Prince Czartoryski. But in reality, Prince Adam was the spawn of the affair that King Stanislaw urged Princess Isabella to have with Russian ambassador Repnin. Repnin was a pivotal figure in the partitions of Poland, and ironically his illegitimate son, Prince Adam, was secretly plotting to resurrect the county his father had helped dismantle.

Prince Adam was the architect of a *Mordplan,* code named the "Pulaski plan," to destroy Prussia and restore Poland under the tutelage of Czar Alexander.[98] In an attempt to give it an imprimatur of integrity, Kosciuszko was invited to return from Paris to take part in the new order. But in the vicious circle of European politics, Napoleon had his own plan to use Kosciuszko.

On July 12, 1806, the western Germanic states were forced into signing the Treaty of the Confederation of the Rhine, which essentially made them protectorates of France. After dawdling all summer over the situation, on September 26, Prussian king Frederick William III sent Napoleon an ultimatum giving him until October 8 to pull all his troops out of German territory. Napoleon's response was to march his army across Europe, destroying the Prussian army, and a month after the ultimatum he had captured Berlin.

The French emperor surprised even himself with how quickly he was able to storm across Europe. With his troops camped in Berlin, Napoleon pondered his next move. He sent for General Dabrowski and the writer Wybicki to draft a plea to the Poles to rise up. The same day Napoleon sent a letter to Fouché: "Send Kosciuszko here and tell him to take a stagecoach to meet with me, but secretly and not under his own name. . . . Give him as much money as he needs. And let the Poles who are with him to come too. I want this to all be carried out as discreetly as possible."[99]

The chief of police arrived at the Zeltners' country estate in Berville and told the general to gather his belongings because he was to accompany the French emperor on the expedition to Poland. The commander told Fouché he was upset that Napoleon had traipsed his countrymen through Italy, Egypt, Bavaria, Haiti, and other bitter battles and so far the Poles had nothing to show for their participation. Kosciuszko later relayed to friends that he told Fouché that he would not do anything for Napoleon unless there was a guarantee explaining what he would do for Poland.

"What kind of guarantees and security do you demand, General? Do you expect to be treated by the emperor like a state within a state?" Fouché replied.

"I am not a king, nor an authority of any country. I don't want anything," Kosciuszko said. "But let Emperor Napoleon declare that the time has come for Poland to arise, let him declare, in calling the Poles to arms, that he wants to dedicate himself to the resurrection of our country, giving it a proper constitution, declaring political equality of all residents without any differences, just like it is in France. Then the Poles will be loyal to him. . . . Under these conditions, not orders, but true and honest political advice, I will devote my body and soul."

The stunned Fouché, unused to people making demands of Napoleon, replied, "The emperor will never agree to any conditions. One needs to be blindly devoted and obedient to his will. He decides himself and based only on his wisdom and what circumstances suggest. His genius and power need no advice, exceptions or guarantees. I even have an order for you to sign this proclamation . . . and if you decide not to go along, then we will force you and declare it in your name."

Kosciuszko was outraged, and said, "If so, then I will publicly state that I am not free. . . . I will protest against any proclamation that does not come from me."

The police chief warned the general that France had censors in every territory that it controlled, and that his repudiation would not be published. The Polish general replied that such "lawlessness and injustice" would only lead to "a woeful collapse" for France.[100]

"I must confess General, that your answer or rather your questions, astonishes me," Fouché said. "His Majesty may command you to accompany him anywhere he may intend to make use of your services, and I think it to be neither in your own nor your countrymen's interest to refuse the desire of my august sovereign."

At age sixty Kosciuszko was not intimidated by anyone and replied, "I am perfectly aware of my position; I am residing in His Majesty's dominions, and am therefore at present his subject. His Majesty can dispose of me as he pleases, he can drag me with him, but I doubt whether by doing so either my nation or I can render him much service. But under reciprocal favors, both my nation and I are ready to aid him. May Providence forbid that your powerful master should once repent having disdained our good services."

Fouché was not accustomed to anyone turning down the emperor and responded, "I only wish general, that you may never repent your refusal."

Kosciuszko immediately answered, "It is in the highest interest of His Majesty to treat us as friends and allies."[101]

While Fouché was in Berville trying to persuade Kosciuszko to join the invasion, Napoleon's army pushed ahead and reached the western Polish city of Poznan, where a Count Xavier Dzialynski and representatives from Warsaw arrived to ask the French general to liberate Poland.

"I love the Poles," Napoleon told the count. "Their enthusiastic character pleases me; I should like to make them independent, but that is a difficult matter. Austria, Russia and Prussia have all had a slice of the cake; when the match is once kindled who knows where the conflagration may stop? My first duty is towards France, which I must not sacrifice to Poland; we must refer this matter to the sovereign of all things—Time; he will presently show us what we must do."[102]

Newspaper reporters were on hand and wrote accounts of the meeting.

"France has never recognized the dismemberment of Poland," Napoleon said to his guests. "If I shall see a Polish army of thirty to forty thousand men I shall proclaim in Warsaw your independence; and when I shall proclaim it, it will be inflexible. It is in the interest of France and that of all Europe, that Poland should have her free existence. Let internal strife cease. Your fate is in your own hands."[103]

Generals Dabrowski and Zajaczek and the other assembled Polish officers took Napoleon at his word and sent secret messages into their country for the soldiers to gather to back the French invasion.

Fouché also wasted no time after being rejected by Kosciuszko and forged a letter in his name that was sent to newspapers telling editors that the famous Pole supported Napoleon's cause. The pompous appeal said: "I soon shall again behold the paternal earth which my arm defended; those fields which I have bathed with my blood; and with tears of joy I embrace those unfortunate friends whom I was not permitted to follow to the grave. . . . I now return to restore you to freedom . . . and embrace you with a sacred mania."

The fake letter called Napoleon "a great man whose arm is extended to you."[104]

Once again the naive Poles put their faith in France as an ally that could help liberate them. Kosciuszko was furious when he read the ridiculous letter forged in his name and wrote to Fouché complaining about it.

Even Napoleon thought it a bit over the top. By New Year's Eve 1806 the French army had already crushed the Prussian armies in western Poland, and Napoleon was in the city of Pultusk, preparing to march triumphantly into Warsaw the next day. Napoleon wrote to Fouché: "I read the pretentious letter from Kosciuszko in *Le Publiciste*. These methods are terrible and do not deserve credit. Who serves the lie, when the truth is good? Why do we need Kosciuszko, if Kosciuszko wants to remain quiet? The people of Poland are not people who can be stirred up with proclamations. I have to confess that those whom I have seen from Warsaw are quite pitiful."[105]

Yet no sooner had he arrived in Warsaw than Napoleon's opinion of the Poles was turned around, this time by a blue-eyed brunette with dazzling white skin and a curvaceous figure. "She was a charming woman, and angel!" Napoleon said of the Polish beauty whom he met at a ball held by the nobility. "Her soul was as beautiful as her face."[106]

Maria Walewska, twenty-two, was married to a crotchety old man and the noblemen of Warsaw encouraged the young woman to sacrifice her body to Napoleon for the sake of Poland. After conquering Warsaw and Madame Walewska, Napoleon realized that he did not need Kosciuszko to win the hearts of the Poles.

Kosciuszko was losing the propaganda war with Napoleon among the Poles who saw the French leader as their savior. He had to make clear why he refused to serve under Napoleon, and he wrote to Fouché asking that the French guarantee Poland a constitutional monarchy similar to that of England, freedom for the peasants, and a restoration of Poland's borders to what it was before the three partitions.[107]

The demands were unrealistic. The Poles were in no position to negotiate. Napoleon responded to Fouché: "I do not attach any importance to Kosciuszko; he does not enjoy the regard in his country that he believes he has; moreover, his conduct proves that he is an idiot. It is therefore important to let him do whatever he wants, without showing any engagement from our side."[108]

Napoleon's control over European affairs soon stretched from Paris all the way to the border of Russia. He signed the Treaty of Tilsit with Czar Alexander, but rather than reestablish Poland as a republic or a kingdom, he created the Duchy of Warsaw as a satellite of France. Once again the Poles had been duped.

Seeing that he had no chance to liberate Poland under the current state of affairs, Kosciuszko found solace in his lessons with the Zeltner children, and working with the French peasants in the fields of Berville. The Poles continued to hold out hope that he would join them, and from time to time, some would visit the retired commander on the farm.

One such guest was Princess Anna Sapieha, nee Zamoyska, who had fallen in love with Kosciuszko when he visited Zamosc after the first failed war with Russia. The princess was living in Paris and remained close friends with the general, but when she rode out to Berville in her coach to try to coax Kosciuszko back to Poland, he was upset with her coquettish behavior and escorted her back to the carriage.

"Over this head, I have carte blanche," Kosciuszko said, referring to himself, "It is the first time in my life I have wished to shorten your visit; but you shall not make me think less respectfully of you than I now do."[109]

In the spring of 1808 a young Polish officer on leave, named Dezydery Chlapowski, traveled to see Kosciuszko. He found the general working in a field; dressed like a French peasant, in a serf jacket, short pants, heavy boots, and a straw hat. Some of his front teeth were loose, causing him to mumble.

The once-powerful commander welcomed his fellow soldier and answered his questions about the insurrection. When Kosciuszko spoke about the Battle of Raclawice he got so animated talking about the attack going "forward with faith" that he crushed his straw hat in his hand.

"It's good that you're serving and learning," Kosciuszko told the young man. "Learn eagerly and when there is a war, pay attention to everything and stay next to the emperor and you can learn and garner experience. Absorb as much as you can so that you can be of use to our unhappy fatherland."

But when it came to Napoleon, Kosciuszko told the officer: "He will not resurrect Poland—he thinks only of himself. He detests every great nation and especially the spirit of independence. He's a despot, and his only aim is personal ambition. He will not create anything durable, I am sure of it. But you, young man, don't let this bother you. Stay near him to acquire experience and learn strategy. He is a superb leader, and while he will not revive our fatherland, he can train many of our officers, without which things will be bad, even if God later sends us lucky circumstances. I repeat, learn from him, but he will not do anything for us."[110]

It would take the Poles a few years to figure out he was right.

During these trying times in Europe, Jefferson finished his second term as president and returned to Virginia, where he struggled to keep his neglected plantation afloat. He needed to borrow money and turned to Kosciuszko.

"I am retired to Monticello, where in the bosom of my family & surrounded by my books, I enjoy a repose to which I have long been a stranger," Jefferson wrote to Kosciuszko on February 26, 1810. "My mornings are devoted to correspondence. From breakfast to dinner to dark, I am in my shops, my garden, or on horseback among my farms; and friends; and from candlelight to early bedtime, I read."

Jefferson got down to business, admitting: "I must turn to another of unpleasant hue, and apologize to you for what has given me much mortification." He was in hock, and had borrowed $4,500 from Kosciuszko's funds to help pay off his debts. The retired president promised to pay back the loan at 8 percent interest.[111]

His English deteriorating after years away from America, Kosciuszko replied to Jefferson in French: "I approve all you have done with my fund, I have every confidence in you." Having felt the wrath of European dictators he commented that America's plan to call up young soldiers for military service was a good idea, but warned that the officers must be educated to guard against corruption.

"One must always fear the ambition of a president who, by using the influence of money and patronage, might easily want to change the state of things by attaching these regular corps to himself," Kosciuszko wrote. "Examples are not rare, and let us admit frankly a sad and hard truth; nearly all men can be corrupted; we love so passionately to be distinguished from others that we seize upon the slightest favor of fortune to raise ourselves above them. To guard against this difficulty, it seems to me that all you need is the military school, only increased to the number of 3,000, composed of young people . . . selected on the basis of an examination, individuals suited to be officers of the militia and the artillery corps."[112]

The despotic systems Kosciuszko lived under in Napoleon's France, Catherine the Great's Russia, and King Stanislaw's Poland depressed him, and he wrote that virtuous behavior should be rewarded with medals such as "a star of gold, silver or iron worn on the coat" to acknowledge "devotion to republican government, more justness, probity, disinterestedness, love of parents, discoveries in the arts, inventions in the sciences, and above all agriculture; and finally for all the social virtues and qualities which alone ought to distinguish some people from others."

Before he received Kosciuszko's reply, Jefferson wrote to his friend again, complaining about "the two great belligerent powers"—England and France, both "eager for mutual destruction"—that America was caught between. The United States chose not to "join in the maniac contest," instead "leaving the cannibals to mutual ravin."

But by remaining at peace America was "multiplying, improving, prospering beyond all example," Jefferson wrote. He was also hopeful that the revolts in "Spanish America" would help Spain's colonies to shake their oppressor: "If the obstacles of bigotry and priest-craft can be surmounted we may hope that common sense will suffice to do everything else. God send them a safe deliverance."

Kosciuszko and Jefferson believed in God, but as deists, they did not rely on miracles or the supernatural, instead believing that the Almighty gave people the ability to reason for themselves, and the ability to choose between right and wrong.

Jefferson felt comfortable enough with Kosciuszko's spirituality to complain about "priest-craft," those clergymen who rather than just pray, also prey on the religious concerns and insecurities of parishioners to gain wealth and power for themselves. In closing, Jefferson told his friend, "God bless you and give you many years of health and happiness, and that you may live to see more of the liberty that you love than present appearances promise."[113]

In addition to their similar outlook on liberty, Kosciuszko and Jefferson consoled each other during times of adversity, and once again war was on the horizon for both men. Jefferson knew what Kosciuszko was dealing with. He couldn't risk reprisals for Kosciuszko by criticizing Napoleon in letters sent to France, but he wrote to a friend in America, "Bonaparte is an unprincipled tyrant, who is deluging the continent of Europe with blood."[114]

With America on the verge of the War of 1812, Kosciuszko wrote to Jefferson calling him, "My dear Aristides," after the Greek statesman called "Aristides the Just" because he put aside personal glory for public service. The key to keeping America safe, Kosciuszko said, was to make sure that future generations of leaders had Jefferson's commitment to republicanism and social virtues. "If you reinforce these qualities with a strictly supervised education," he wrote, "then you will achieve your goal, and you will see your country produce as many heroes as Greece and more wise men than Rome."[115]

When war finally broke out with England, Jefferson wrote to Kosciuszko, "Our present enemy will have the sea to herself, while we shall be equally predominant at land, and shall strip her of all her possessions on this continent. She may burn New York, indeed, by her ships and congreve rockets, in which case we must burn the city of London by hired incendiaries."

Jefferson was so angry with the British, and the French, that he wanted to annex Canada and make it part of the United States. "I know your feelings on the present state of the world," he said to Kosciuszko, "and hope they will be cheered by the successful course of our war, and the addition of Canada to our confederacy. The infamous intrigues of Great Britain to destroy our government . . . and with the Indians to tomahawk our women and children prove that the cession of Canada, their fulcrum for these Machiavellian levers, must be a sine qua non at a treaty of peace."[116]

Even though Kosciuszko had been eager to capture Canada during the American Revolution, he tried to calm his friend and discouraged the invasion. "The just war which you have commenced with England should cause no anxiety," Kosciuszko wrote to Jefferson on May 30, 1813. "Your country is rich, large and populous, its inhabitants are good, energetic and brave. But do not be too ambitious to acquire the whole of Canada, too much security will make you soft."

Instead Kosciuszko suggested that the American border with "your line of demarcation should be from some point on the lake Champlain or the St. Lawrence and extend to the sea [Lake Ontario] in the south." The Polish general outlined military advice to his friend, telling him to make sure Congress provided for enough artillery, infantry, cavalry, and provisions. "Have your generals always attack the enemy first, and at two points if possible," Kosciuszko wrote.[117]

Unfortunately the initial phase of the war did not go well for the United States, at sea or on land. And England once again armed the Indians and urged them to slaughter any settlers who tried to move onto their tribal lands. It would take several years before the British would again be driven away, but in the meantime the English burned much of Washington, including the White House, and killed thousands of American soldiers.

"You have heard without doubt of the inauspicious commencement of our war by land," Jefferson wrote to Kosciuszko. "Our old officers of high command were all withdrawn by death or age . . . happy for us would it have been could we have followed your advice in appointing new generals."[118]

Jefferson also told his friend, "Your idea that our line of future demarcation should be from some point in Lake Champlain is a good one, because that would shut up all their scalp markets, but that of their entire removal from the continent is a better one."

After a long and detailed description of the events of the war to date, Jefferson told Kosciuszko: "I know that no native among us takes a livelier interest in them than you do. The tree, which you had so zealously assisted in planting, you cannot but delight in seeing watered and flourishing . . . from one man we can have but one life, and you gave us the most valuable and active part of yours, and we are now enjoying and improving its effects. Every sound American, every sincere votary of freedom loves and honors you . . . [119]

"God bless you under every circumstance, whether still reserved for the good of your native country, or destined to leave us in the fullness of time with the consciousness of successful efforts for the establishment of freedom in one country and of all which man could have done for its success in another. The lively sense I entertain of all you have done and deserved from both countries can be extinguished only with the lamp of life."[120]

⌒━━◆━━⌒

SIXTEEN

A Peasant Without a Country

T HE UNITED STATES WAS ONCE AGAIN AT WAR WITH ENGLAND, and Napoleon was again baiting the Poles to arms by calling his 1812 invasion of Russia the "Second Polish War." He led an army of 550,000 that captured Moscow by year's end, but the city was set on fire and, with little food or lodging, many French soldiers froze to death in the severe Russian winter. Napoleon abandoned his troops and fled through the snow back to Paris as most of his army was wiped out retreating across ice-covered battlefields. Napoleon's aggression united all of Europe against him, and by 1814 the armies of the autocratic monarchies converged on France.[1]

By springtime Cossacks were plundering their way through the outskirts of Paris. A Polish regiment in the czar's army pushed back the French troops in Troyes and marched out of the oak-and-pine forest toward Fontainebleau. With officers looking on, the hungry soldiers searched for food and were about to smash open the sluice gates holding back the water in stocked fishponds when a voice from the nearby fields cried out in Polish, "Stop, soldiers, stop!"

The marauding soldiers looked up and saw an elderly peasant. The old man in a farmer's hat looked at the officers and said, "When I had a command in the army of which your regiment is a part, I punished very severely such acts as you seem to authorize by your presence, and it is not on those soldiers but on you that punishment would have fallen."

Annoyed by the lecturing farmer who spoke Polish, the officers walked toward him. The peasants of the village took off their hats and formed a protective circle around the old man.

"And who are you to arrogate to yourself the right of rebuking us in this manner?" asked one of the officers.

In a half-stifled voice he replied, "I am Kosciuszko!"[2]

The stunned soldiers threw down their rifles and fell to the ground at his feet in an act of humble submission. The old commander walked back to his house and found Russian military guards protecting it.

Napoleon abdicated the throne on April 6, in Fontainebleau, not far from where Kosciuszko lived on the Zeltner estate. Czar Alexander arrived in Paris where he met the Polish émigrés and promised his protection if they returned home. Prince Adam Czartoryski convinced Kosciuszko that Poland's best chance for revival would be through Czar Alexander. Like Kosciuszko, Alexander was appalled by the deplorable condition of the serfs and wanted to reform feudalism.

Three days after Napoleon abdicated, Kosciuszko wrote to the czar: "Your Majesty—If, from my humble retreat, I venture to address a great monarch, it is because his generosity is well known to me. I ask three favors."

Kosciuszko asked Alexander to grant amnesty to the peasants drafted into the armies of the countries that divided Poland promising to abolish serfdom within ten years; to declare himself king of Poland under a constitutional monarchy like that of England, and to establish schools using government funds to educate the peasants.

"If my prayer is heard," Kosciuszko wrote, "I shall throw myself at Your Majesty's feet, thank you, and render homage to my sovereign. If my weak capacities may still be of any use, I will leave at once, to join my compatriots and faithfully serve my country and my king."[3]

The sixty-eight-year-old general was no longer much of a warrior, but he could still ride. The Knights' School alumnus who had been called "the Swede" by his fellow cadets jumped on his horse and rode to Paris and checked in to the Hotel de Suède (Sweden Hotel), on the Rue de Boulay, to await a response from the czar.

The next day the czar sent his own coach to pick up Kosciuszko.

Alexander was nineteen when he walked into Kosciuszko's room with his father, Czar Paul, who freed the Polish rebel. Twenty-one years had passed since then. The redheaded czar had a tall, balding forehead, and long auburn muttonchops framed his round face. He hugged and kissed the former commander in chief of Poland as if they were long-lost friends.

The czar said that as long as Kosciuszko was asking for favors, he would ask for one as well. The general had never touched the money that Czar Paul had deposited for him in an English bank, and Alexander finally persuaded Kosciuszko to accept it.[4]

Like Napoleon before him, Czar Alexander felt it was important to be publicly seen with the humble hero, and at a party in Paris escorted him arm in arm, say-ing, "Make room, make room, here is a great man."[5]

About forty Polish soldiers came to visit the Zeltner farm where Kosciuszko was staying and brought him a gray horse as a present. The old commander greeted them one by one. As they told him their names he realized that he had served with their fathers and grandfathers during the insurrection. Kosciuszko was moved when Colonel Madalinski's son showed him a ring that he had awarded to his father with the inscription, "For Defense of the Fatherland."[6]

There was still some fight left in these young Poles, and the czar had to figure out what to do with them. An adroit politician who knew how to tug on heart-strings, Alexander understood the significance of Constitution Day for the Poles, and on May 3, 1814, he sent Kosciuszko a vague letter promising the world:

"I feel a deep satisfaction, General, in answering your letter. Your dearest wishes are accomplished. With the aid of the Almighty I hope to realize the re-generation of the brave and worthy nation to which you belong. I have solemnly promised to do so . . . the Poles shall recover their country, their name, and I shall have the happiness of convincing them that, forgetting the past, one who they thought their enemy will be the man to fulfill their desires. What great pleasure, General, to have you at my right hand! Your name, your character, your talents will be my firmest support. Believe me, General, in fullest esteem, Alexander."[7]

The czar did not commit to any of Kosciuszko's requests, but Prince Adam Czartoryski assured the general that Alexander was someone they could trust and work with. Alexander set up a civil and military committee to start work on concepts for the new Polish legal code. Kosciuszko worked with the committee and wrote a memorandum that was a road map for gradually leading the serfs out of feudalism. He also worked with the military committee to plan an officer corps based on merit. It also planned to do away with the frilly French tricolor cockade ribbons that Napoleon made them wear, and bring back the blue uni-forms of the Polish republic.[8]

On May 30, 1814, the Treaty of Paris ended the state of war that had engulfed Europe for more than two decades. The Bourbon monarchy was restored in France, and King Louis XVIII was propped on the throne. The nations agreed to meet in Vienna in the fall to redraw the borders of Europe, which had moved several times.

Upon hearing the news of the peace treaty Jefferson wrote to Kosciuszko: "Great events, my dear friend, have happened in Paris. I hope and believe that they will be for the benefit of the world in general, and I especially wish they may be so to your country and to you yourself personally . . . but the transactions in Europe generally are too little known here to justify further observations or con-jectures."[9]

It was wishful thinking. In September representatives of the monarchs of England, Russia, Austria, Prussia, and France assembled at the Congress of Vienna. The monarchies fought over the borders, and once again Europe was on the brink of war, with England, Austria, and France on one side, and Russia and Prussia on the other.

The Poles were filled with dread as the powerful monarchies maneuvered against one another and rolled over Poland's ambitions for independence. Poznan would remain part of Prussia, Krakow was to be a free city controlled by the Austrians, and the center of the country would be called Congress Poland, under Czar Alexander's control, while the eastern Polish territories would remain part of Russia.

Complicating matters further, Napoleon escaped from exile on the island of Elba in the Mediterranean and returned to his army, which welcomed him in Grenoble, France.

Frustrated by the situation, Kosciuszko lamented to Jefferson about "European politics, which is nothing but the art of being better at deception."[10]

Kosciuszko also faced deception within his own ranks. A Polish journalist named Joseph Kalasanty Szaniawski, a Jacobin and a Mason, switched alliances and became a censor and hatchetman to serve the czar's brother. He forged a letter in Kosciuszko's name, hailing Alexander and claiming that the commander was ready to take up arms and follow the czar's orders.[11]

Czar Alexander was convinced that Kosciuszko would go along with the new borders if he understood what was happening in Vienna, so he summoned the general to the conference.

The former commander rode to Paris in mid-April 1815 to apply for a new passport. Once again he had to deal with Fouché, whom King Louis XVIII kept on as the chief of police. Fouché felt sorry for his former adversary, and with Napoleon's army once again on the rampage, he suggested that Kosciuszko use an assumed name.

Fouché issued Kosciuszko a passport under the name "Pole."[12]

Zeltner and his son joined Kosciuszko for the trip to Vienna, but even with the passport, and a former Swiss ambassador at his side, he was stopped at the border because he did not have a Swiss visa. They sneaked past the guards and traveled to Switzerland, but were again stopped as they tried to pass through Bavaria. It was not until he received special permission from the king of Bavaria that they were allowed to continue. It took more than a month to make the journey because of the heightened tensions during Napoleon's last gasp at restoring himself to the throne.

When Kosciuszko finally met with the czar near Vienna, Alexander could not answer specifics about the makeup of a new Poland, and the commander was sent to meet with Prince Czartoryski, who was to provide him with details.

The trip to Vienna was a waste of time. The czar wanted Kosciuszko to validate the creation of a buffer state between Russia and Europe to make sure that Moscow would never be invaded again. Kosciuszko reminded the czar that he had promised him in Paris that he would restore Poland. He wrote to Alexander complaining that he did not even know which country his own land in Lithuania now belonged to.[13]

Kosciuszko called Poland's diminished new borders "a joke" and informed Czartoryski that he could not support the new order in Europe. On June 18, 1815, Napoleon was finally defeated once and for all at Waterloo. Ten days earlier the powerful monarchies had agreed to Europe's new borders. The Congress of Vienna officially sanctioned the partitions of Poland.

The once-great "Citizen Kosciuszko" was reduced to being a peasant prince without a country. On June 19 he was given a Russian passport so that he could leave Austria.[14]

"I will not act without some guarantee on behalf of my country, nor will I be deluded by false hopes," Kosciuszko wrote to Czartoryski. "As I can no longer be of any service to my country, I shall take refuge in Switzerland."[15]

Prince Czartoryski was "blinded by illusion," Countess Potocka wrote in her memoirs. "An everlasting battle ensued between fiction and truth. . . . Alexander's plans were by no means what he had flattered himself they were going to be."[16]

Poland was no longer a sovereign nation.

Kosciuszko traveled with Peter Zeltner to Soleure, Switzerland, where they stayed at the home of Peter's brother, Francis Xavier Zeltner. There they learned that King Louis XVIII was engaged in a reign of revenge against the Bonapartists on the right and the French revolutionaries on the left. They also found out that Peter Zeltner's wife, Angelique, was dying. Returning to France was no longer an option for Kosciuszko.

Zeltner invited the exiled general to stay with him and his family in Soleure, a village surrounded by blue pine forests and vineyards in the Jura Mountains, just north of the snow-peaked Alps.

Back in Warsaw, Czartoryski pressed Alexander to establish a ministry of war and name Kosciuszko as its head, but the commander was not interested.

"Riding over the highest mountain tops and through the lowest valleys, has taught me to hold the middle of the road as much as possible," Kosciuszko wrote to the prince. "I want to follow this approach in my thoughts."[17]

The roles between a Czartoryski and Kosciuszko had reversed. It was now the white-haired old general who acted as sage to Prince Czartoryski, whose father had founded the Knights' School that educated an earlier generation of Polish leaders.

The seventy-year-old commander advised the prince, who had taken up the baton as the next leader who would try to restore Poland.

"It's clear to everyone that the blossoming of our nation depends on happiness for the largest number of people," Kosciuszko wrote to the prince, decrying the "barbarian use of beating peasants with whips and riding crops."[18]

A tyrannical system that relied on slave labor would never survive, Kosciuszko argued, telling Czartoryski that his government should order "estate owners to establish a school for peasants in each estate. In every town the government should establish a school for burghers and peasants teaching them mechanical crafts such as carpentry, smithery, lock smithing, tannery, etc."

People would work harder if they worked for themselves, Kosciuszko wrote, and the best way for the whole nation to prosper was to "gradually reduce the corvée, and hire paid workers with annual contracts to work the fields." Those who were "lazy, drunks or beggars" should be forced into "public works; to build roads, canals, paved roads, or cut or mow crops in the country side for a decent pay. To support our industry, to awaken indispensable activity in trading in our sole, and dying port in Gdansk, the government should establish textile factories, paper mills, steelworks, and glassworks."

He said that serfdom had turned the illiterate peasant into "a villain," and the only way to fix this was to educate them, and "apply these measures toward the peasants so that with time they could be freed from corvées and own their own land. Let's set a date. If I dare to suggest that in 20 years, everybody is free and owns land."[19]

In Soleure, Kosciuszko again took on the role of tutor to the Zeltner children, Xavier, eighteen; Emily, twelve; and Ursula, six. His landlord, Peter Joseph Zeltner, returned to Paris, and after the death of Angelique, he sent his youngest daughter, Thaddea, eleven, Kosciuszko's godchild, to live with the Zeltner family in Switzerland.[20] The children were always happy to see him because his pockets were usually filled with sugarplums for them and their friends who would come to visit.

Kosciuszko awoke early each morning to make coffee over a spirit lamp and drink it with white bread that he ate for breakfast. Afterward young Xavier would read the German and Italian newspapers to him, as Emily prepared for her lessons. She gave the general a pet bird, a bullfinch that would sit on his shoulder and eat hemp seeds from his hand. Kosciuszko spent two or three hours in the morning tutoring the children in history, math, and drawing, and then another two hours in the afternoon. In the springtime they went to pick strawberries.

The old general was ordered by his doctor to keep in shape, so he rode his horse through the neighboring towns. He made the rounds in an old blue suit with holes that were patched, and the ladies of the village kept him supplied with roses or violets that he wore on his lapel. Kosciuszko searched for poor people who had been befallen by tragedies such as fires, floods, or crop failures.

He asked local ministers and magistrates to guide him to the neediest people so he could help.

Despite the complications of Jefferson's loan from his American estate, Kosciuszko refused to touch the principal endowment he had left to free slaves, surviving on the occasional interest payments that Jefferson sent him. Jefferson finally repaid the loan in April 1815, after he sold his personal library to the Library of Congress to pay off some of his debts. On April 18 Jefferson wrote to his banker, Barnes, to pay back "4,500 dollars, the principal of Gen. Kosciuszko's money in my hands, and 360 dollars, one year's interest."[21] That money was to remain in the United States, and Jefferson instructed Barnes to find a "government loan of higher interst" for Kosciuszko.

Because he still refused to touch the czar's money, the interest from his American estate became crucial to the meager standard of living that the Pole decided to live on for the final years of his life, and most of that money Kosciuszko gave away to beggars. It got to the point that even his black pony stopped when it saw a pauper, and would not move again until Kosciuszko dropped the reins, opened his purse, and handed over a coin.

"When he took his daily ride, he had to first satisfy the poor, who surrounded his horse as it stood before the door," Xavier wrote. "When he had ridden away, the poor could tell, by the direction he took, by which gate he would leave the city; some tried the trick of running through other streets as fast as they could to the gate, which they reached long before Kosciuszko, who rode very slowly; then, passing out of the city, they would turn back and meet Kosciuszko coming through the gate; the horse would stand still, and Kosciuszko would again give them a present. He discovered the trick at last, but only laughed, shook his finger threateningly, and gave the money just the same."[22]

One day an old beggar knocked on the door of the Zeltner home, claiming to be a friend of Kosciuszko's. The man was let in, and after a short talk the commander gave him a coin. The visitor thanked him warmly and, turning toward the door, which Xavier had opened for him, he accidentally stepped on Kosciuszko's bird on the floor, killing it instantly.

Xavier described the look of deep dismay on the faces of both men. The old visitor turned pale and tried to speak, but nothing came out. Kosciuszko went to his desk, took out a gold piece, and gave it to the troubled man saying, "Here, my poor friend, something more for your pain," and then turned away to hide his own sorrow.[23]

After several decades of war, Europe was finally at peace. The war between the United States and England was also over, and when Jefferson wrote to Kosciuszko with the news that America had once again prevailed, the Pole responded that it gave him "great pleasure. . . . The names Madison and Jefferson are on everyone's lips and repeated thousandfold."

Kosciuszko updated Jefferson on the czar's broken promises to Poland: "I thought of good laws, the Emperor had promised me a constitutional, liberal, independent government, even the emancipation of our unfortunate peasants and granting them the land they worked on. That alone would have made him immortal. But everything went up in smoke." As for the great powers in Europe, he wrote that they are "doing injustice to other little states and behaving with their own people like wolves and sheep."[24]

The aging commander was also concerned that the church had treated peasants like sheep, by refusing to abolish feudalism. The church continued to exploit its own serfs, and Kosciuszko blamed the nobility and the clergy for not doing enough to help free Poland. Like Jefferson, he believed strongly in the separation of church and state, and was offended by priestcraft.

In fact Kosciuszko wrote that "men are natural imitators like monkeys," and many clergymen took advantage of this. Kosciuszko wrote to Prince Czartoryski that the clergy "fascinate the eyes of people by lies, the fear of hell, not of odd dogmas and the abstract and incomprehensible ideas beyond theology. The priests will always benefit from ignorance and superstitions of the people and will make use of religion as a mask, behind which they will conceal the hypocrisy and criminality of their actions."

The United States was the first country in the world to find a proper balance between freedom of religion and political liberty. "The nation should be the lord and master of its own fate," Kosciuszko told the prince, "and its rights should therefore be superior to those of the church; no religion should contravene them by appealing to divine law, but on the contrary, every religion should be obedient to the laws established by a given nation."[25]

While he was disillusioned with the Catholic Church for its role in perpetuating serfdom, Kosciuszko was a firm believer in prayer and showing respect to God. He even wrote his own prayer, in which he prayed for "the whole human race":

> Almighty God, who enlivens the world's millions with your Spirit,
> Who has ordered me to live in this valley of tears for designs hidden from
> me,
> Grant that I may wend my way through it over roads pleasing to You;
> Let me do good; keep me from evil; restrain the unruly impulses of my
> impetuosity;
> Let me come to know your genuine truth unmarred by any human error.
> Bless, O God, my country, my relatives, my friends, my benefactors, my
> countrymen—the whole human race.

And when my last hour comes, when my soul takes leave of my body, grant
that it may stand before Your countenance in the dwelling of the blessed and
comprehend the mystery of the world which today is beyond my comprehension.
Do not send me to eternal perdition; but permit me to stand before Your countenance in the abode of the blessed. I ask this through Jesus Christ our Savior.
Amen.[26]

Zeltner's eighteen-year-old son looked up to Kosciuszko, and the general
wrote him a letter about his philosophy of life. It said in part: "Rise at four in the
summer and six in the winter. Your first thoughts must be directed towards the
Supreme Being; worship Him for a few minutes."

There was a profound sense of morality in Kosciuszko's day-to-day actions,
and he told young Xavier to master a skill, preferably a science, and "always be
frank and loyal and always tell the truth. Never be idle but be sober and frugal
even hard on yourself while indulgent to others. Do not be vain nor an egotist.
Before speaking or answering on something, reflect. And consider well in order
not to lose your point and say something stupid. . . . If a secret is entrusted in
you keep it religiously."[27]

Many of the religious figures Kosciuszko met had disappointed him, so when
he heard that a Protestant minister had turned down an offer to live in a lucrative
parish, choosing instead to remain in his impoverished village in the Jura Mountains, the general rode into the hills and rushed into the parson's room while he
was shaving, and hugged him with tears of appreciation streaming down his face.
The commander became a regular visitor with the humble clergyman.

Kosciuszko also visited a convent where he heard a Polish woman lived within
the cloistered walls after fleeing her devastated country. The general visited her
incognito and began speaking Polish.

"You are Kosciuszko!" the shocked woman said. "When I was a young girl I
saw in Poland your portrait on the lockets which all the ladies wore on their
breasts."[28]

One of the women in Poland who held the memory of Kosciuszko close to
her breast was Princess Louise Lubomirska. She wrote to him, offering to come
to Switzerland to nurse him in his old age. Louise even offered finally to give him
her hand for their twilight years.[29]

The love of his life eventually stopped in Switzerland as she was passing
through on a trip to Italy.[30] "Her great powers of conversation, her amiability, and
sparkling gaiety shed a luster of happiness over the last days of his life," wrote a
journalist for *Harper's* magazine who visited Soleure and interviewed Emily Zeltner in her old age. After a few weeks Louise continued on to Italy and sent him a
souvenir, a ring with the inscription *L'amité de la vertu* (A friendship of virtue).[31]

It did not take much to make the old man happy, and he was willing to share everything he had, causing some people to take advantage of him. But at times the bitterness of losing his country made him prone to the "unruly impulses of impetuosity" that he struggled with. Such was the case with Peter Joseph Zeltner, who borrowed two large sums of money from Kosciuszko when he was his tenant in Paris. Zeltner never repaid the loans and kept asking for more. Zeltner wrote to the general again asking for money while he was renting a room from his brother in Soleure, but Kosciuszko unleashed his frustration over Zeltner's irresponsibility.

"I no longer believe in your promises," Kosciuszko wrote. "You possess great friendly features because you are pleasant, have lots of information, are full of humor, common sense and are thoughtful. But you have no head for business. You are stubborn, lazy, careless and inconsistent."

With Angelique dead, Kosciuszko spoke up in her name. "Don't think that I am the only one who sees your flaws, many people see them but won't tell as I will. Even your beloved wife saw them, and cried about it many times. I promised this beloved mother that I would extend my care over Thaddea and Carolina [another Zeltner daughter]. They will get something after my death."[32]

So that Zeltner could not get his hands on the money, Kosciuszko wrote a will distributing the 100,000 francs that he had in the Hottinger Bank in Paris. He left 60,000 of it to Thaddea, 35,000 to Carolina, and five thousand went to the notary.[33]

Even with the dividends Kosciuszko received from his American funds, by 1817 his estate in the United States had grown to more than $17,000. But he complicated matters when he was living in Paris by setting aside $3,704 of this estate for his godson, Kosciuszko Armstrong, the son of his Revolutionary War friend who became U.S. ambassador to France.[34] The balance was still dedicated for the manumission and education of slaves, and Kosciuszko was confident that Jefferson would carry out his wish.

To make sure that his sister's heirs understood that their inheritance was conditional on freeing the serfs, he issued another will regarding his estate in Poland, and sent copies of it to newspapers to create a public record and make a political statement. It began: "I deeply feel that serfdom is against the law of nature and the well-being of nations, I declare that I abolish it completely and forever at my estate in Siechnowicze in the Brest-Litovsk, on my behalf and that of its future owners. I recognize residents of the village that belong to this estate as free countrymen, unlimited by anything, as owners of the land they live on. I release them from all, with no exception, levees, corvées, and personal responsibilities to which they were subjected toward the owners of the estate. I only appeal to them, for their own and their country's sake, to try to establish schools and spread education."[35]

For Kosciuszko education was the road out of slavery for European serfs and American slaves. That's why his wills in Europe and the United States stressed the importance of proper schooling. And as a former cadet of the chivalrous Knights' School, he viewed military education, coupled with classes about ethics and politics, as the key to making sure that the gains of the American Revolution were not turned back the same way they were after the French Revolution.

Apparently still unsure that the U.S. Military Academy had become a reality at West Point, Kosciuszko wrote to the new President, James Monroe, in French, letting him know about the importance of opening an *École Militaire*.[36]

The Pole also wanted to improve the schools in Europe, and he became friends with Pestalozzi after Napoleon said that he had "no time for the alphabet." The teacher returned to Switzerland and established a school in Yverdon, and Kosciuszko traveled sixty miles with some friends to see the school, where he spent two days joining in and absorbing Pestalozzi's lesson plans in person. One of those who joined Kosciuszko was Marc Antoine Jullien, a French soldier and writer who opposed Jacobin terror, and Napoleon. They had much in common with Pestalozzi, who was also a firm believer in natural law and ending feudalism, and Kosciuszko returned to Soleure full of new ideas for applying these concepts to Poland.

Jefferson and Kosciuszko had not seen each other for nearly a decade, yet the sage of Monticello still had warm feelings for his enlightened friend. Jefferson often wore the fur that Kosciuszko had given him and even posed in it for his official portrait as president, painted by Rembrandt Peale. The third president was even sculpted in the fur coat for the statue at the Jefferson Memorial.

At a dinner party he was hosting, one of Jefferson's guests, Margaret Bayard Smith, came down with a fever, so he wrapped her in the fur cloak. She wrote: "Strange! thought, that an obscure individual in America, should be wrapped in the same mantle that once enveloped the Czar of Russia—that was afterwards long worn by the patriot hero of Poland, and now belongs to one of the greatest men alive! I wish the cloak could speak and tell me something of each of its possessors. Of the insane despot, to whom it belonged, it could tell me of no act of his life half so good as the one by which the cloak was transferred to the good Kosciuszko."[37]

After the failure of Poland to regain its independence, Jefferson once again invited Kosciuszko to come back to America: "Would you not, my dear friend, be now better here than at Soleure? That the society of Paris is better than ours we admitted: but we shall not yield that point to every European location. If you like city life, fix in the Quaker city of Philadelphia. If the country, I would say come to Monticello and be one of our family."[38]

At seventy-four, lamenting his advanced years, Jefferson wrote to Kosciuszko on June 15, 1817, updating the Polish engineer on the construction of the Erie Canal in "New York to bring the waters of Lake Erie into the Hudson, through a length of 353 miles and over a height of 661 feet." The "seat of empire" that

Washington had envisioned during the Revolution was finally becoming a reality in the Empire State.

Jefferson even told Kosciuszko that he would reserve a space for the Pole to be buried beside him: "Think seriously of this, my dear friend, close a life of liberty in a land of liberty. Come lay your bones with mine in the Cemetery of Monticello. This too will be the best way of placing your funds and yourself together, and will enable me to give in person those assurances of affectionate friendship and respect which must now be committed to the hazard of this letter."[39]

However, the aging Virginian was still uncomfortable with Kosciuszko's request to buy slaves and free them, and hinted in the letter that with the banker Barnes reaching eighty-seven, the question remained about who would carry out the Polish commander's wishes in terms of African Americans.

But Kosciuszko was adamant, and exactly one month before he died he wrote to Jefferson: "We are both getting on in years, and for that reason, my dear and respected friend, I am asking you to be so good (and having the title to do so) as to arrange that after the death of our worthy friend Mr. Barnes someone of equal probity should take his place, so that I may receive punctually the interest on my fund, the fixed designation of which after my death is known to you."[40]

He made it clear that the "fixed designation" meant that the balance was still to be used for his intended purpose, to free and educate slaves.

Also frustrated by the subjugation of his own country, he wrote: "I am the only true Pole in Europe, all the others have been rendered by circumstances the subjects of different powers."

It was too late for Kosciuszko to retire in Virginia, even though he envied America's progress, writing: "Your canal from Lake Erie to the Northern [Hudson] River has surprised everyone in Europe, but not me who knows your fellow citizens so well and has always seen them great in everything. You are more fortunate than the Europeans, thanks to your government, which is closer to the nature of man, and also thanks to your great distance from other powers. That does not prevent the establishment of a great civil military school in your country under the direction of supervision of a commission of Congress. Give my respects to your President, Mr. Monroe. I do not cease to repeat to him the absolute necessity of such a school."[41]

America's leaders understood this as well, and the U.S. Military Academy at West Point was on its way to becoming the most famous military school in history. Kosciuszko never learned that the military academy he had pushed for years would be placed in the fortress that he built.

On a trip to Lake Geneva, the old general was riding his horse down a mountain, and the horse stumbled on the descent, bruising the seventy-one-year-old rebel's battered body. He made it home but was overcome with fever. Feeling that he was close to death, he called for a notary. Having fulfilled his promise to

Angelique to leave something for her daughters, Kosciuszko decided to give away the money from Czar Paul that he had never touched. He drafted one last will in the company of the notary, bequeathing the funds in the London bank of Thomson, Bonard & Co. in equal shares to Francis Xavier Zeltner's daughter Emily, and his former adjutant, Gen. Francis Paszkowski.[42]

Kosciuszko also deducted payments to the notary and some servants, leaving his "personal effects," such as his horse and carriage, to the Zeltners, as well as two thousand francs for the poor and one thousand to pay for his funeral. Sobieski's sword was to be given back to the Polish nation to inspire future generations of freedom fighters, and he asked that his own sword be buried together with him. He asked that his personal papers in Polish be burned, leaving only the ashes of his innermost thoughts. As the clock struck 10:00 p.m. on October 15, 1817, Kosciuszko passed away, surrounded by the Zeltner family.[43]

The next day a Swiss undertaker performed a postmortem and found the corpse covered with old wounds and deep scars from the various battles Kosciuszko had fought in. Even his skull was scratched and indented with saber strokes. As the undertaker undressed the body, he found a white handkerchief on Kosciuszko's breast, which according to legend was the same one dropped by Louise when the couple tried to elope more than forty years earlier.[44]

An autopsy revealed that he had died from a stroke.[45] His organs were removed and buried and his body embalmed. Kosciuszko's heart was placed in a bronze urn, with instructions for it to be returned to his country only when Poland was free. Four days later six paupers carried his casket to the Jesuit sanctuary, Saint Ursus and Victor Church. The procession was led by a line of orphans in mourning scarves carrying his sword, hat, and Order of the Cincinnati on black velvet cushions. The beggars were given one thousand francs for carrying his casket to the funeral.

Several months later Czar Alexander sent a carriage to Switzerland to take Kosciuszko's body back to Krakow, where it was buried in the tombs of Wawel Castle in the company of Sobieski and Poland's other kings.

When news of his death in exile spread through Europe, funeral masses were held in Catholic, Lutheran, and Calvinist churches. Jewish synagogues and Muslim mosques also held services where worshippers prayed for Kosciuszko's soul.[46]

As soon as he heard of his friend's death, Jefferson began to waver on whether he could carry out Kosciuszko's wishes. On January 5, 1818, he wrote to the secretary of the treasury, William Crawford: "The death of Gen. Kosciuszko, which I see announced in the papers in a form no doubt, makes it a duty in me to trouble you with this letter." Jefferson explained that as executor of the will, he had "some doubts" about which court would execute it: "Although Gen. Kosciuszko in his last letter to me of Sept. 15 uses expressions that his purpose had not been changed, I shall withhold proving the will until I shall hear from the friends in his confidence who were about him at the time of his death."[47]

The same day he also wrote to his friend William Wirt, the United States attorney general. Without admitting that the will was to be used to free slaves, Jefferson said it was for "a particular course of charity," and as Kosciuszko had died in a foreign country he was not sure of his "qualification as executor," and perhaps the place of probate should be in "a foreign country."[48]

The matter of the will became more complicated when Gen. John Armstrong wrote to Jefferson explaining that Kosciuszko had left his son a portion of the funds. Jefferson replied that the will's "execution will call for a great many minute and continued attentions, and many more years to complete than I have to live."[49]

He was right. Within months, a number of Kosciuszko's relatives and friends, as well as con artists, began writing to Jefferson claiming that they were the real heirs to the Polish commander's fortune.

Kosciuszko wanted to keep his funds out of the hands of the "lazy and careless" Peter Zeltner, who had taken advantage of his generous loans in Paris, yet after the general's death Zeltner wrote to Jefferson touting his "special friendship with the illustrious deceased for twenty years," claiming that the general wanted to give the American estate to his daughters and nieces.[50] His brother, Francis Xavier Zeltner, in Soleure, also wrote to Jefferson, claiming that by leaving his "personal effects" to the Zeltners, and his money in Europe to their children, Kosciuszko meant them to inherit everything, including the estate in America.[51]

Obviously that was not Kosciuszko's intent. He had written four separate wills, each referring to a different pool of money that was destined for specific beneficiaries. And one month before his death he reminded Jefferson of the "fixed destination" of his American property.

The Frenchman Jullien began writing the first biography of Kosciuszko and wrote to Jefferson asking about his friendship with the general. On July 23 Jefferson responded to Jullien, writing: "The benevolence of his services during our Revolutionary War had been well known and acknowledged by all. When he left the United States in 1798, he left in my hands an instrument, giving, after his death, all his property in our funds, the price of his military labors here, to the charitable purposes of educating and emancipating as many of the children of bondage in this country as it should be adequate to. I am now too old to undertake the business. . . . I am therefore taking measures to have it placed in such hands as will ensure a faithful discharge of his philanthropic views."[52]

The same day Jefferson also got around to responding to Francis Xavier Zeltner, letting him know that Kosciuszko left a will dedicating his American funds to free slaves, and that he would place this money in "such hands" to carry out the general's wishes.[53]

The money Kosciuszko left in Jefferson's care continued to collect interest and was enough to free most of the Virginian's slaves. But Jefferson was uncomfortable with the idea of liberating his own slaves, or leading the fight on abolition against his neighbors. Zeltner provided him with the excuse he needed for resigning from his role as executor of Kosciuszko's estate. Jefferson asked his friend Gen. John Hartwell Cocke, a staunch opponent of slavery, to handle the matter for him.

"I propose to prove Kosciuszko's will in the district court on Monday and hope you will relieve me from that task," Jefferson wrote to Cocke on May 3, 1819.[54]

But that same day Cocke, who had looked into the logistics of Kosciuszko's request, wrote to Jefferson that he could not take on the task because of the "prejudices to be encountered in obtaining admission for Negroes" to schools and "the effect which might be produced on the minds of my own people."[55]

A year and a half after Kosciuszko's death, May 12, 1819, his trusted friend walked into the federal circuit court in Albemarle County, Virginia. The deputy clerk present, William Wertenbaker, wrote: "An illustrious man—then, as at all times, the observed of all observers, walked into the Court. The Judge, on perceiving that Thomas Jefferson, stately and erect was standing before him, bowed and invited him to take a seat on the bench. To this, Mr. Jefferson replied, 'As soon as your honor shall have leisure to attend to me, I have a matter of business which I wish to present to the Court.'"

All parties immediately agreed to drop what they were doing to hear what the former president had to say. He pulled a piece of paper out of his pocket. It was Kosciuszko's handwritten will, which Jefferson read aloud. He explained that he had been named executor, but that he was not able to carry out his duties. Judge Archibald Stewart took a sworn statement from the Founding Father and the will was admitted into the record.

"Nothing exhibits, more graphically or beautifully, the character of the man, than the short and simple paper," wrote the clerk, Wertenbaker, about Kosciuszko's will: "disinterestedness, universal philanthropy, and a heart bursting with desire for liberty, freedom and happiness to all mankind are pictured as in a mirror. Well did the poet say, 'And Freedom shrieked when Kosciuszko fell.'"[56]

Jefferson officially washed his hands of Kosciuszko's plan to free slaves.

The federal court in Washington, D.C., delegated an attorney named Benjamin L. Lear to handle the estate, leaving Jefferson to go back to the pressing issues on his struggling plantation. Jefferson, who knew that slavery was immoral, was afraid of what would happen to the union if slaves were liberated. The following year Jefferson wrote to a friend that the question of slavery breaking apart the union hit him "like a fire bell in the night, and awakened me with terror. . . . But as it is, we have the wolf by the ears; and we can neither hold him, nor safely let him go. Justice is in one scale, and self-preservation in the other."[57]

While Jefferson's fear dimmed Kosciuszko's legacy in the United States, on the outskirts of Krakow, Poles began building a memorial to honor their former commander in chief. Men, women, and children traveled from around Poland with wheelbarrows, buckets, and even handfuls of soil from Raclawice and other battlefields where Kosciuszko had fought for freedom. They began piling the dirt onto the "Kosciuszko Mound," which eventually towered higher than one thousand feet. Years later a brick citadel was built at its base, along with a neo-Gothic chapel.

Jefferson continued to face financial problems in his final years at Monticello, where he died on July 4, 1826. It was the fiftieth anniversary of the Continental Congress passing his Declaration of Independence. He was bankrupt, and his debts were passed on to his heirs.

Southern plantation owners arrived at Monticello on January 15, 1827, after the *Charlottesville Central Gazette* ran an advertisement proclaiming that "130 valuable Negroes . . . the most valuable for their number ever offered at one time in the state of Virginia," would be auctioned off in an "Executor's sale." Jefferson freed five of his slaves in his will, but that left 126 men, women, and children to be sold at auction along with horses, mules, cattle, vehicles, and farming tools. The Monticello historian Lucia Stanton wrote that those slaves accounted for 90 percent of the $31,400 appraised value of Jefferson's property at the plantation, not including the land and home furnishings.[58]

In addition to the five slaves that Jefferson freed in his will, he asked his daughter Martha Jefferson Randolph to give two more slaves "their time," meaning to free them discreetly without drawing attention to the act. One of these was Sally Hemings, with whom Jefferson had fathered several children. Putting Hemings in his last will would have acknowledged in writing the affair that Jefferson had been criticized for. Freeing her quietly allowed Jefferson to keep his legacy in tact.[59]

The other slave that Jefferson unofficially freed was Wormley Hughes, who had worked in his garden and dug his master's grave. On that cold January day the auctioneer banged his gavel and in a rapid-fire voice barked out the names of Jefferson's slaves and the prices that they would be sold for. Hughes watched as his wife Ursula and their eight children were auctioned off to three different white men for $2,125.[60]

Most of the Hughes family was later reunited on one plantation, but other families were not as lucky. Some black husbands were separated from their wives, and children, some as young as eight years old, were separated from their parents.

These were some of the very people that Kosciuszko had tried to liberate.

As the funds were not used for their intended purpose, teachers inquired whether they could use the money to educate former slaves. The board of a Pres-byterian church that had founded the African School of Parsippany, New Jersey, issued a request: "We have reason to hope, that the bequest made by Gen. Kosciuszko for the redemption and education of African Slaves, may be in some way applied for the enlargement and support of this school, and perhaps the name of his noble friend to a people whose friends have been few, shall be asso-ciated with an institution for their benefit, durable as the liberties or mountains of our country, and bright as the discoveries of Bacon."[61]

The court-appointed executor, Lear, favored giving the funds to a black school, and abolitionists tried to establish a "Kosciuszko School" in Newark, New Jersey. But the Zeltners, Kosciuszko Armstrong, Kosciuszko's heirs in Poland, and even several impostors sued to get the funds, and the legal entanglements dragged on for years.[62]

When Lear died in 1832, Col. George Bomford, a graduate of West Point, became executor of his estate, and thus the executor and administrator of the Kosciuszko estate. The various lawsuits concerning Kosciuszko's wills wound their way to the U.S. Supreme Court, which ruled in 1852 that the four wills were invalid, and that as far as the court was concerned, "General Kosciusko died intestate."[63]

At that point, Kosciuszko's estate was worth $43,504. But Col. Bomford had died in 1848, and only $5,680 of this could be found. Lewis Johnson, his succes-sor as administrator, reported to the court that Bomford had "wasted or con-verted to his own use" $37,924 of Kosciuszko's funds.[64] In the end, none of the money that Kosciuszko had set aide to free and educate slaves went for its in-tended purpose.

Two years after the court's decision, in 1854, during a debate in Congress on whether to allow slavery in Nebraska, Rep. Gerrit Smith stood up and said, "There was Kosciuszko, at whose fall 'Freedom shrieked,' and who provided by the will, written by himself, that his property in America should be used by his anti-slavery friend, Thomas Jefferson, in liberating and education of African slaves. Surely, he would not, with his eyes open, have fought to create a power that should be wielded on behalf of African slavery!"[65]

It would be more than a decade before slavery in the United States was fi-nally abolished, and more than a century until the Voting Rights Act of 1965, be-fore the scars of slavery in America would even begin to heal.

Israel Losey White, literary editor of the *Newark Evening News*, wrote in 1908, "This will is an unwritten chapter in American History. It is possible that if its suggestions had been followed, there might have been no Civil War in the United States, and the race problem of today would not be so perplexing to economists."[66]

The hard-to-pronounce name of the Polish general went down in American history because of his role in the Battle of Saratoga and for building West Point, but his greatest actions—his attempts to free serfs and slaves—were buried along with the abolitionist movements that did not achieve success until many decades later.

In the fall of 1910, the African American educator and former slave Booker T. Washington traveled to Poland and visited Krakow, the birthplace of Kosciuszko's insurrection. "I knew from my school history what Kosciuszko had done for America in its early struggle for independence," Washington wrote, "I did not know, however, until my attention was called to it in Krakow, what Kosciuszko had done for the freedom and education of my own people."

Washington climbed down the stairs to the tombs below Wawel Cathedral and walked through the dungeonlike corridors filled with the memorials to the princes and kings of Poland. "Kosciuszko lies in a vault beneath the marble floor of the cathedral," he wrote in his memoirs. "As I looked upon his tomb, I thought how small the world is after all, and how curiously interwoven are the interests that bind people together. Here I was in this strange land, farther from my home than I had ever expected to be in my life and yet, I was paying my respects to a man whom the members of my own race owed one of the first permanent schools for them in the United States. When I visited the tomb of Kosciuszko I placed a rose on it in the name of my race."[67]

Unfortunately Kosciuszko's American funds never made it to their "fixed destination." Ending slavery with the stroke of a pen, even if it was only Jefferson's slaves, proved to be a controversial idea ahead of its time. The Polish rebel's hope that he could simply will away slavery and serfdom by writing testaments on two continents that dealt with different portions of his estate left legal loopholes for people to exploit after his death. The French historian Jules Michelet called Kosciuszko "the last knight, but the first citizen in Slavic lands with a modern understanding of brotherhood and equality."[68]

Serfdom continued to choke European peasants well into the nineteenth century, while several generations of revolutionaries sparked failed uprisings to restore Poland's freedom in the name of Kosciuszko. The Polish revolutionary and writer Joachim Lelewel wrote that Kosciuszko was "a man who had his weaknesses, but was immaculate when it came to the rights of citizens."[69]

It was Lelewel who took the phrase that Kosciuszko spoke to the Russian clergy: "We fight for our freedom and yours," and turned it around. "For your freedom and ours!" was painted on banners in Polish and Russian as the Poles went to war with czarist armies manned by peasants. Unfortunately, as Kosciuszko had pointed out for years, the peasants could not read, so they did not get the message.

Feudalism was gradually phased out in Europe, but it was not until after World War I that Poland's national freedom was restored. When that happened the Poles finally brought the bronze urn containing Kosciuszko's heart back to Poland.

The peasant prince had finally returned.

Endnotes

ONE: *Broken Hearts and Greek Role Models*

1. Lucyan Siemieński, *Żywot Tadeusza Kościuszki* (Kraków: Drukarnia "Czas" W. Kirchmayer, 1866), p. 37. (Kosciuszko and his friends from the knight school worked out a plan to find a carriage, fast horses, and a priest so he could elope with Ludwika [Louise] Sosnowska.) *Foreign Quarterly Review*, (London: Adolphus Richter & Co., 1835), vol. 15, p. 113. This is a review and translation of sections of Karl Falkenstein, *Thaddaus Kościuszko, nach seinem offentlichen und hauslichen Leben geschildert* [*Thaddeus Kosciuszko, Delineated in His Public and Domestic Life*] (Leipzig: 1834), pp.111–113. (Falkenstein was the royal Saxon librarian. "From Kosciuszko's own lips Falkenstein thus heard many details . . .") The account of the elopement is on p. 113.
2. Julian Ursyn Niemcewicz, *Pamiętniki czasów moich* [*Memoirs of my times*] (Warsaw: Państwowy Instytut Wydawniczy, 1957), p. 72. (Kościuszko's confidant wrote in his memoirs that he tried to elope with Ludwika, but they were caught before they could "cross the border.")
3. Tadeusz Korzon, *Kościuszko, biografia z dokumentów wysnuta* [*Kosciuszko, a biography derived from documents*] (Kraków: G. Gebethner i Spółka, 1894), p. 98 ("pigeons are not meant for sparrows . . .").
4. James Thacher, *A Military Journal During the American Revolutionary War, from 1775 to 1783; Describing Interesting Events and Transactions of This Period; with Numerous Facts and Anecdotes* (Boston: Cottons & Barnard, 1827), pp. 138–139. (Dr. Thacher spent time with Kościuszko in his garden at West Point in 1778 and wrote that Kościuszko sheathed his sword so that he would not hurt Lord Sosnowski. As Kościuszko told Thacher of his failed elopement three years later, it clearly had an impact on him.) Falkenstein, *Thaddaus Kościuszko,* p. 113 ("Kosciuszko draws his sword . . .").
5. Falkenstein, *Thaddaus Kościuszko,* pp. 113. p. 140. (Attempted elopement, handkerchief.)
6. Historians have downplayed Kościuszko's failed elopement. Most have missed the fact that in addition to a romantic link there was an intellectual bond with Louise, who was also

interested in freeing the serfs and translated a book from French on physiocracy, *Sokrates wiesniak albo opisanie życia gospodarskiego y cnotliwego filozofa rolą bawiącego się," [The rural Socrates, or memoirs of a virtuous philosophical farmer]*. (Warsaw: 1770). See Stefan Bratkowski, *Tadeusz Kościuszko, Z czym do nieśmiertelności [Ways to immortality]* (Katowice: Wydawnictwo, Slask, 1977), p. 203. Falkenstein's telling of the elopement, published in Leipzig, has been criticized as romanticized. While Falkenstein (who interviewed Kościuszko) did make mistakes, Dr. Thacher (who also knew Kościuszko) published his journal in Boston and it was probably not known to Falkenstein. And Niemcewicz (Kościuszko's closest aide) wrote that he tried to elope with Ludwika, but her father caught them before they crossed the border. Falkenstein, Thacher, and Niemcewicz, none of whom knew each other, all had similar versions, with different details, of the elopment. Another clue is found in Korzon, *Kościuszko,* footnote 240, pp. 592–593, which says that Sosnowski gave a man named Wojewodzki a house and land "for intervening in the elopment of Lady Louise and Kosciuszko." Clearly, Kościuszko's rejection by Lord Sosnowski was the pivotal moment of his life.

7. Korzon, *Kościuszko,* p. 65 (Peasants could be hung for infractions and were at the mercy of the landlord.)

8. Bartłomiej Szyndler, *Tadeusz Kościuszko, 1746-1817* (Warsaw: Wydawnictwo Bellona, 1991), p. 103. (Kościuszko's exact birth date is not known, but the twelfth is generally used. Szyndler examines the theories of Kościuszko's birth date.)

9. Korzon, *Kościuszko,* p. 55 (the Kościuszko family had thirty-one families of serfs.)

10. Ibid., p. 65 (treatment and legal status of serfs).

11. Ibid., p. 70 (as a child, Kościuszko played on a huge rock near his home.)

12. G. A. J. Rogers, *Locke's Philosophy: Content and Context* (Oxford: Clarendon Press, 1994), p. 241. (Konarski, the Piarist, in 1740 founded the Collegium Nobilium in Warsaw. A careful reading of the school prospectus reveals that the shape of education prescribed was that of John Locke. He is mentioned three times as the author of manuals of instruction.)

13. Wacław Sobieski, *Młode lata Kościuszki [Kościuszko's early years]* (Kraków: 1917), pp. 13–14 (Kościuszko was fascinated with Timoleon because he overthrew tyrants, set up republics, and never demanded power for himself).

14. Jacek Jędruch, *Constitutions, Elections and Legislatures of Poland 1493–1993* (New York: Hippocrene Books, 1998), pp. 33–34, 84 (Henrician Articles and the Articles of Agreement).

15. Simon M. Dubnow, *History of the Jews in Russia and Poland: From the Earliest Times Until the Present Day* (Philadelphia: Jewish Publication Society of America, 1916), p. 15. Also see Abraham Leon Sachar, *A History of the Jews* (New York: Alfred Knopf, 1930), p. 223. (Jews who ran Polish mints put Hebrew characters on some of the coins.)

16. Heinrich Hirsch Graetz, *History of the Jews,* vol. 4 (Philadelphia: Jewish Publication Society of America, 1974, originally published in 1898), p. 419 (the collecting of the tolls was in the hands of the Jews).

17. Adam Zamoyski, *The Polish Way* (New York: Hippocrene Books, 1987), p. 27 (Tatars in Poland). Stephen Turnbull, *Mongol Warrior 1200–1350,* (Oxford: Osprey Publishing, 2003), p. 20, (Jean Sire De Joinville, 1224–1319, is the source for the famous mention of steak tartare, the Mongol culinary technique of placing meat between a saddle and saddle blanket).

18. William Richard Morfill, *Poland: The Story of the Nations* (New York: G. P. Putnam's Sons, 1893), p. 176 ("under the Saxon king . . .").

19. Jędruch, *Constitutions, Elections and Legislatures,* pp. 123–124 (*liberum veto*).

20. Mark Cruse and Hilde Hoogenboom, *The Memoirs of Catherine the Great: A New Translation* (New York: Modern Library, 2005), p. 146 ("while watching Count Poniatowski dance . . .").

ENDNOTES 287

21. Sarah Knowles Bolton, *Famous Leaders Among Women* (New York: Thomas Y. Cromwell & Company, 1895), p. 60 (Chevalier d'Eon quote).

22. Joan Haslip, *Catherine the Great* (New York: G. P. Putnam's Sons, 1978), p. 72 (Catherine as predator).

23. Adam Zamoyski, *The Last King of Poland* (London: Phoenix Giant, 1992), pp. 1–2 (the first liaison between Catherine and Poniatowski).

24. Dominique Maroger ed., *The Memoirs of Catherine the Great* (New York: Macmillan, 1955), p. 159 (Catherine, "blue as a plum").

25. Stanisław Augustus Poniatowski, *Mémoires secrets et inedits de Stanislas Auguste, comte Poniatowski, dernier roi de Pologne* [*Secret and unpublished memoirs of Stanislas Auguste, Count Poniatowski, last king of Poland*] (Leipzig: W. Gerhard, 1862), p. 7 (she made "one forget the very existence of Siberia").

26. Maroger, *Memoirs of Catherine*, p. 285 (Count Poniatowski incognito as the Grand Duke's musician).

27. Cruse and Hoogenboom, *Memoirs of Catherine*, p. 156 (Bolognese dog).

28. Stanisław Augustus Poniatowski, *Mémoires de roi Stanislas-Auguste Poniatowski*, edited by A. S. Lappo-Danilevskii and S. M. Goriainov, Vol. 1 (St. Petersburg: 1914), pp. 156–157 (a mouth that begged to be kissed).

29. Poniatowski, *Mémoires secrets*, p. 8, and *Mémoires de roie Stanislas-Auguste Poniatowski*, p. 7 (arbiter of my destiny).

30. Maroger, *Memoirs of Catherine*, p. 341, letter from the czarina to Poniatowski, August 2, 1762. ("I am sending at once Count Keyserling as Ambassador to Poland to declare you King after the death of the present monarch.")

31. Zamoyski, *The Last King of Poland,* pp. 125–126 (details of Poniatowski's various love affairs).

32. Roman Kaleta, *Oświeceni i sentymentalni: Studia nad literaturą i życiem w Polsce w okresie trzech rozbiorów* [*The enlightened and the sentimental: A study of literature and life in Poland in the period of the three partitions*] (Wrocław: Zakład Narodowy im. Ossolińskich, 1971), p. 224 (the popularity of erotic books and theater in Poland).

33. Jacques Casanova, *The Memoirs of Jacques Casanova de Seingalt: The Rare and Unabridged London Edition of 1894,* translated by Arthur Machen (London:, p. 32 ("all Europe seemed to have assembled at Warsaw").

34. Giacomo Casanova, *History of My Life. Volumes 9 and 10,* translated by Willard R. Trask (Baltimore: Johns Hopkins University Press, 1970) ("a peasant girl who came into my room pleased me . . .").

35. Charles Lee, *Lee Papers* (New York: New York Historical Society, 1874), p. 350 (Ounewaterika, "boiling water," or "the spirit that never sleeps").

36. Ibid., p. 219 (Lee gives Cromwell's sword to Poniatowski).

37. Korzon, *Kościuszko*, pp. 1–5 (family background and explanation of the name).

38. Ibid., p. 32 ("Sword-bearer of Brest").

39. Ibid., p. 26 (the ceremonial reenactments of Hussar Knights).

40. Ibid., pp. 55–57 (description of Kościuszko plantation).

41. Jan Dihm, *Kościuszko nieznany* [*The unknown Kościuszko*] (Wrocław: Ossolineum, 1969), pp. 23–27; Kamilla Mrozowska, *Szkoła Rycerska Stanisława Augusta Poniatowskiego (1765–1794)* [*Stanisław August Poniatowski's knight school (1765–1794)*] (Warsaw: Ossolineum, 1961), pp. 82, 93–94, 192–222 (planetary machine from Britain and the scholars and curriculum at the knight school).

42. Korzon, *Kościuszko,* p. 85 (tying a string to his hand in bed).

43. Ibid., p. 85 (the Swede).

44. Katarzyna Jedynakiewicz, *Osobowość i życie codzienne Tadeusza Kościuszko* [*The personality and daily life of Thaddeus Kościuszko*] (Łódź: Wydawnictwo Uniwersytetu Łódzkiego, 1996), p. 80 (the Royal Cadets exposed to erotic times, prostitution, etc.).

45. Henri Martin, *The Decline of the French Monarchy* (Boston: Walker, Fuller and Company, 1866); Charles Francois Dumouriez, *Mémoires et correspondance inedits* (Paris: 1834) (Dumouriez denounces Poniatowski).

46. M. A. Jullien, *Notice biographique sur le général polonais, Thadée Kościuszko* [Paris: 1818], pp. 3–4; Stef Bratkowski, *Tadeusz Kościuszko,* pp. 94–136; Wlodzimierz A. Dzwonkowski, *Młode lata Kościuszki,* vol. 4 (Biblioteka Warszawska: 1911), pp. 32 and 42 (Kosciuszko's studies in Paris).

47. Bratkowski, *Tadeusz Kościuszko,* p. 96 (Kosciuszko's fondness for coffee).

48. Ibid., p. 202 (Kościuszko exposed to Quesnay and physiocracy).

49. Archiwum Główne Akt Dawnych w Zbiory Popielów [Central Archives of Historic Documents from the Popielów Collection]; Dihm, *Kościuszko nieznany,* p. 36 (letter from Kosciuszko to Czartoryski from Paris).

50. Bogdan Grzeloński, *Jefferson/Kościuszko Correspondence* (Warsaw: Interpress Publishers, 1978), p. 11 (Kościuszko quote).

51. David Jayne Hill, *A History of Diplomacy in the International Development of Europe* (New York: Longmans, Green & Co. 1907), p. 675 (King George's response to King Stanislaw).

52. Edward H. Lewiński-Corwin, *The Political History of Poland* (New York: Polish Book Importing Company, 1917), p. 357 (French response).

53. Karol Falkenstein, *Tadeusz Kościuszko, czyli dokladny rys jego zycia* [*Thaddeus Kosciuszko, a precise outline of his life*] (Wrocław: Wilhelm Bogumil, 1827), p. 20 (Kosciuszko first meets Ludwika).

54. Bratkowski, *Tadeusz Kościuszko,* pp. 203, 417 (Ludwika and sister translated book on physiocracy).

55. Lucyan Siemieński, *Żywot Tadeusza Kościuszki* [*The life of Thaddeus Kosciuszko*] (Kraków: Drukarnia "Czas" W. Kirchmayer, 1866), p. 36 (Kościuszko visits Prince Czartoryski to talk about Ludwika Sosnowska).

56. Niemcewicz, *Pamiętniki czasów moich,* p. 72. (Kościuszko's physical description).

57. Siemieński, *Żywot Tadeusza Kościuszki,* p 37. Also in Korzon, *Kościuszko,* p. 592, footnote 240 (king warned Sosnowski about elopement plans).

58. Korzon, *Kościuszko,* p. 101 (marriage arranged through card game).

59. Bratkowski, *Tadeusz Kościuszko,* p. 227 (Lord Sosnowski would have been able to get the death sentence for Kosciuszko for *raptus puellae,* ravishing of the girl, or rape).

60. "Pamiętnik Jerzego Soroki," *Tygodnik Ilustrowany* ["Memoirs of Jerzy Soroka," *The Illustrated Weekly*] 12 (1881): 197; Wiktor Malski, *Amerykańska wojna Pułkownika Kościuszki* [*Colonel Kosciuszko's American War*] (Warsaw: Ksiazki i Wiedza, 1977), pp. 32–35. (The meeting between Kościuszko and Czartoryski in the village of Slawatycze comes from the memoirs of Jerzy Soroka, who witnessed the meeting. Korzon also references Soroka, who wrote that Kościuszko said Pulaski and other Poles were already in America. Pulaski did not arrive in the United States until a year later, but Kościuszko was not aware of this and probably *did* think that the Bar confederate was already in America.)

61. Author's note: One groundbreaking book about Kościuszko was Miecislaus Haiman's *Kościuszko in the American Revolution* (New York: Kościuszko Foundation, 1975, first published in 1943 by the Polish Institute of Arts and Sciences in America). However, it contains some mistakes. This appears to be the case in the belief that Kościuszko had a letter of recommendation from Prince Czartoryski to Gen. Charles Lee. This hypothetical letter was first mentioned in Władysław Kozlowski, "Pierwszy rok służby amerykańskiej Kościuszki [The first year of Kościuszko's American service]," *Przegląd Historyczny,* vol. 4 (Warsaw: 1909), pp. 310–314. Haiman then followed this scenario as likely and other historians have picked it up. Yet Kościuszko denied that he had any letters of recommendation. That is what he told Józef Pawlikowski, who was his secretary during the Polish insurrection and his exile in Paris (Józef Pawlikowski, "Weteran Poznański" [Poznań: W. Decker i Spółka,

March 1825], p. 118. As Haiman does not cite Pawlikowski in his bibliography, he may have not known about the "Weteran Poznański" articles. The following book also said that Kościuszko had no letter of recommendation: Charles Neilson, *An Original, Compiled and Corrected Account of Burgoyne's Campaign, and the Memorable Battles of Bemis Heights,* (Albany, NY: J Nunsell, 1844), p. 117. (Neilson writes: "This celebrated engineer came to this country utterly unprovided with letters of recommendation, or introduction, and nearly penniless, and offered himself as a volunteer in the American cause.")

62. Malski, *Amerykańska wojna Pułkownika Kościuszki,* p. 20 (the full text of the letter from Kosciuszko to Jerzy Wandalin Mniszech that Kosciuszko wrote when he left Poland, October 19, 1775).

63. Elizabeth S. Kite, *Beaumarchais and the War of American Independence* (Boston: Gorham Press, 1918), p. 49 (Beaumarchais letter to the king about slavery and the partition of Poland).

64. James S. Pula, *Thaddeus Kościuszko: The Purest Son of Liberty* (New York: Hippocrene Books, 1999), p. 34. (Circumstantial evidence suggests that Kościuszko received assistance and encouragement from Beaumarchais. Pula argues convincingly that Princess Sanguszko was probably the link between Kościuszko and Beaumarchais.)

65. M. Le Duc De Levis *Souvenirs de Felicie, par Mme de Genlis, suivi des souvenirs et portraits,* with foreword and notes by M. F. Barriere (Paris: Librairie de Firmin-Didot et C, 1879), p. 362. (Sanguszko was a beautiful and controversial divorcée, drawn to artists, freethinkers, and mercenaries).

66. Kite, *Beaumarchais,* p. 66. (Lee: "We need arms, powder and above all engineers").

67. Ibid., p. 67, and George Edouard Lemaitre, *Beaumarchais* (New York: A. A. Knopf, 1949), p. 184 (Beaumarchais quote about gunpowder and engineers).

68. Kite, *Beaumarchais,* p. 82 (one million livres to the cause).

TWO: *A Rebel Joins the Cause*

1. Siemieński, *Żywot Tadeusza Kościuszki,* p 47. (Kościuszko saved himself from the sinking ship by clinging to the mast. Siemieński quotes a letter written by Kosciuszko to Czartoryski. It was printed in a newspaper, *Nowiny,* in Warsaw on April 24, 1777.)

2. Adam Skałkowski, *Kościuszko w świetle nowszych badań* [*Kosciuszko in the light of new research*] (Poznań: 1924), p. 21. (The survivors of the wreckage swam to Martinique. From there they took a small fishing boat to the United States.)

3. Józef Pawlikowski, *Weteran Poznański* [*The Poznań veteran*] (Poznań: W. Decker i Spółka, March 1825), pp. 118–120. (Kościuszko's personal secretary, Pawlikowski revealed the details of Kościuszko's meeting with Franklin. This was six and a half years after Kościuszko's death.)

4. Ibid. (The quotes from Franklin and Kosciuszko are from Pawlikowski's article, as relayed to him by Kosciuszko.)

5. Brooke Hindle, *David Rittenhouse,* (New York: Arno Press: 1980), p. 164. (The board on which Rittenhouse served "lent the services of the Polish engineer, Thaddeus Kosciuszko.")

6. Paul K. Walker, *Engineers of Independence: A Documentary History of the Army Engineers in the American Revolution, 1775–1783* (Washington, D.C.: Historical Division, U.S. Army Corps of Engineers, 1977), p. 127 (Kermorvan complains about the workers and returns to France).

7. Willard Sterne Randall and Nancy Nahra, *Forgotten Americans: Footnote Figures Who Changed American History* (Reading, MA: Perseus Books, 1998), pp. 72–73 (Kościuszko worked with Benjamin Franklin on the master plan for Philadelphia defenses).

8. Ibid., pp. 72–73; Christopher Ward, *The War of the Revolution* (New York: Macmillan, 1952), p. 373; J. Thomas Scharf and Thompson Westcott, *History of Philadelphia, 1609-*

1884, vol. 2 (Philadelphia: L. H. Everts & Co., 1884), p. 1025 (Kościuszko designed fort at Billingsport, Fort Mercer, and the chevaux-de-frise).

9. *Journals of the Continental Congress,* Friday, October 18, 1776 (Kościuszko's appointment as an engineer in the service of the United States, with the pay of sixty dollars a month and the rank of colonel).

10. Haiman, *Kościuszko in the American Revolution,* p. 10 (fifty pounds for Kościuszko). Also, Jeffery M. Dorwart, *Fort Mifflin of Philadelphia: An Illustrated History* (Philadelphia: Pennsylvania University Press, 1998), p. 173 (Pennsylvania paid Kościuszko "as a reward for his services in laying out a plan of fortification at Billingsport").

11. Letter from Washington to John Hancock, December 9, 1776. Library of Congress.

12. Haiman, *Kościuszko in the American Revolution,* pp. 10–11 (Armstrong letter to the Board of War, December 9 1777).

13. Randall and Nahra, *Forgotten Americans*, p. 73 (Fort Mercer project).

14. Washington to John Hancock, December 20, 1776, Library of Congress.

15. Barry K. Wilson, *Benedict Arnold: A Traitor in Our Midst* (Montreal: McGill–Queen's University Press, 2001), pp. 131–132 (Gates takes credit for Arnold's fleet on Lake Champlain).

16. *New York Historical Magazine*, April 1859, p. 131, quoted in Beamish Murdoch, *A History of Nova Scotia or Acadie*, vol. 2 (Halifax: James Barnes, 1866), p. 624 (Gates was the "son of a housekeeper").

17. Max M. Mintz, *The Generals of Saratoga: John Burgoyne and Horatio Gates* (New Haven: Yale University Press, 1990), p. 15 (Gates was possibly the illegitimate son of a duke).

18. George Washington Greene, *The Life of Nathanael Greene: Major-General in the Army of the Revolution,* vol. I (Boston and New York: Houghton, Mifflin and Company, 1890), p. 293 (letter from Lee to Gates, December, 13, 1776).

19. Eric Donald Hirsch, Joseph F. Kett, and James S. Trefil, *The New Dictionary of Cultural Literacy* (New York: Houghton Mifflin, 2002), p. 201 ("Yankee Doodle").

20. John Trumbull, *Autobiography, Reminiscences and Letters of John Trumbull* (New Haven: B. L. Hamlen, 1841), pp. 29–31 (plan to defend Sugar Loaf Hill).

21. William Henry Smith, *The St. Clair Papers: The Life and Public Services of Arthur St. Clair* (Cincinnati: Robert Clarke & Co., 1882), p. 75. (Trumbull's idea laughed at).

22. Gen. James Wilkinson, *Memoirs of My Own Times, In Three Volumes,* (Philadelphia: Abraham Small, 1816), p. 162 (Gates sent Wilkinson "with instructions to examine and regulate the chain of communication Ticonderoga).

23. Armstrong memorial, Jared Sparks, ed., *Correspondence of the American Revolution: Being Letters of Eminent Men to George Washington, from the Times of His Taking Command of The Army to the End of His Presidency* (Boston: Little, Brown and Company, 1853), edited from the original manuscripts, Ser. 49, vol. 1, p. 70 (Gates' instruction to Kościuszko on Sugar Loaf Hill).

24. George Bancroft Papers, New York Public Library, vol 3, p. 111 (Gates letter introducing Kusiusco (*sic*) to Gen. Paterson).

25. Robert Leckie, *George Washington's War: The Saga of the American Revolution* (New York: HarperCollins, 1992), p. 383; Willard Sterne Randall, *Benedict Arnold, Patriot and Traitor* (New York: Barnes and Noble Books, 1990), p 340. (Randall calls Baldwin "incompetent," and both point out that Baldwin ridiculed the idea of fortifying Sugar Loaf Hill.)

26. Jeduthan Baldwin, *The Revolutionary Journal of Colonel Jeduthan Baldwin 1775–1778* (Bangor, ME: The De Burians, 1906), p. 104 (Baldwin's resentment of Kosciuszko's plans).

27. Kościuszko to Gates from Fort Ticonderoga, May 1777, Gates Papers, New York Historical Society (original in French).

28. Kościuszko to Gates, May 18, 1777, Gates Papers, New York Historical Society (original in French).

29. Haiman, *Kościuszko in the American Revolution,* pp. 16–17 (Armstrong's explanation of Kosciuszko's findings).
30. Andrew Carroll, ed., *Behind the Lines, Powerful and Revealing American and Foreign War Letters—and One Man's Secret to Find Them* (New York: Scribner, 2005), p. 226 (Kościuszko's quip about the pronunciation of "Knickerbocker" and "Schenectady").
31. Wilkinson, *Memoirs,* p. 164 (Wilkinson letter to Gen. Gates, May 22, 1777).
32. Ibid., p. 171 (Wilkinson to Gates, May 23, 1777).
33. Gates letter to Gen. Paterson, May 28, 1777, Papers of the Continental Congress, Library of Congress.
34. Baldwin, *The Revolutionary Journal of Col. Jeduthan Baldwin,* p 104 (". . . I hope will never be finished as Staked now").
35. Undated letter from Kościuszko to Gates, most likely sent from Fort Ticonderoga in early June 1777, Gates Papers, New York Historical Society (original in French).
36. Wilkinson, *Memoirs,* p. 172 (letter from Wilkinson to Gates, June 10, 1777).
37. Ibid., p. 174 (Schuyler admits he read Wilkinson's letter to Gates).
38. Jared Sparks Papers, ser. 49, vol. I ff. 34; Haiman, *Kościuszko in the American Revolution,* p. 18 (Schuyler's reasoning for not fortifying Sugar Loaf Hill).
39. John Fiske, *The American Revolution* (Boston: Houghton, Mifflin and Company, Riverside Press, 1891), p. 269. "Where a man can go . . .": Several historians have used variations of this quote. The earliest reference I have been able to find comes from Gen. William Heath's *Memoirs of the American War: Reprinted from the Original Edition of 1798* (New York: A. Wessels Company, 1904, p. 131), in which Heath writes that the British "should have recollected what had been said by the late King of Prussia, as to such positions—that 'where a goat can go, a man may go; and where a man can go, artillery can be drawn up.'"
40. Wilkinson, *Memoirs,* p. 184 (the British "fired at a vessel which lay in the strait").
41. James Macauley, *The Natural, Statistical, and Civil History of the State of New York* (Albany, NY: Gould & Banks, 1829), p. 185; Pula, *Thaddeus Kościuszko,* p. 61; Hoffman Nickerson, *The Turning Point of the Revolution: Or, Burgoyne in America* (Boston: Houghton Mifflin Company, 1928), p. 146 (the drunken Fermoy sets fire to buildings at Fort Ticonderoga).
42. Barbara Graymont, *The Iroquois in The American Revolution* (Syracuse: Syracuse University Press, 1972).
43. Jeanne Winston Adler, ed., *Chainbreaker's War: A Seneca Chief Remembers the American Revolution* (Hensonville, NY: Black Dome Press, 2002) (from an interview given by the chief in 1845), pp. 54 and 62 (British offer to pay for scalps, get Indians drunk on rum).
44. Letter from Schuyler to Kościuszko, July 16, 1777, "Orderly Book of Gen. Philip Schuyler," June 26–August 18, 1777, American Antiquarian Society, Worcester, Massachusetts, p. 53 (Schuyler puts Kościuszko in charge of covering the rear).
45. *Orderly Book of Henry B. Livingston, July 19, 1777,* American Antiquarian Society, Worcester, Massachusetts, p. 52 ("the fatigue party, till further orders . . . is to proceed . . . and receive orders from Colo. Kosciusko, Engineer").
46. John Armstrong to Thomas Jefferson, July 1, 1818. This handwritten letter, titled "Kosciuszko Biography," in which Armstrong relays events that he witnessed during the Revolution, as well as firsthand accounts told to him by Kościuszko of his later life, is in the Library of Congress. A published version is in H. A. Washington, ed., *The Writings of Thomas Jefferson, Being His Autobiography, Correspondence, Reports, Messages Addresses, and Other Writings, Official and Private. From the Original Manuscripts,* vol. 8 and subsequent volumes (New York: Derby & Jackson, 1859). For more on Kosciuszko's role in the retreat see: Haiman, *Kościuszko in the American Revolution,* p. 22.; Francis Casimir Kajencki, *Thaddeus Kościuszko: Military Engineer of the American Revolution* (El Paso, TX: Southwest Polonia Press, 1998), pp. 27–28; and Smith, *The St. Clair Papers,* pp. 81–82.

47. Thomas Anburey, *With Burgoyne from Quebec: An Account of the Life at Quebec and the Famous Battle of Saratoga*, edited by Sydney Jackman (Toronto: Macmillan of Canada, 1963), p. 152 (Anburey's description of the British delay due to the downed bridges and felled trees), originally published in 1789 as volume 1 of *Travels Through the Interior Parts of North America*.

48. Pula, *Thaddeus Kościuszko*, p. 71; Robert Leckie, *The Wars of America*, vol. 1 (New York: Harper & Row, 1968), p. 170 ("trees as plenty as lampposts upon a highway about London").

49. Walker, *Engineers of Independence*, 111. (Kościuszko's diversionary tactics worked, it took the British army twenty days to move twenty-two miles.)

50. Wilkinson, *Memoirs*, p. 200 ("Kosciusko was at that time our chief engineer, and for months had been the companion of my blanket . . .").

51. Letter from John Armstrong to Thomas Jefferson, July 1, 1818, from Armstrong's "Kosciuszko Biography" ("in the retreat of the American army, Kosciuszko was distinguished . . .").

52. Smith, *The St. Clair Papers*, p. 430 (letter from General St. Clair to General Washington, July 17, 1777).

THREE: *Turning Back the British Tide: The Battle of Saratoga*

1. Kościuszko to St. Clair undated: Haiman, *Kosciuszko in the American Revolution*, pp. 22–23; Martin I. J. Griffin, *Catholics and the American Revolution*, vol. 3 (Philadelphia: Published by the Author, 1911), p. 148.

2. Some historians have mistakenly credited Benedict Arnold with choosing Bemis Heights as the spot to make a stand against the British. Yet those who fought in the battle said it was Kościuszko's decision. Among them were General Gates and Colonels Lewis, Hay, and Wilkinson. Another was General Glover, in William P. Upham, *Memoir of General John Glover* (Salem: Charles W. Swasey, 1863), p. 30 (Gates by the advice of Kościuszko, an engineer in the service, moved the army up the river as far as Bemis Heights, four miles above Stillwater, where they encamped and prepared to resist the further advance of the British).

3. William Dunlap, *History of the New Netherlands, Province of New York, and State of New York, to the Adoption of the Federal Constitution* (New York: Carter & Thorp, 1840), p. 117. (Lewis recalled that Kościuszko said, "From Yonder Hill, on the left, your encampment may be cannoned by the enemy, or from that on our right they may take aim at your shoe-buckles.")

4. Ibid., p. 118. (Lewis said that "arrived on Behmus's Heights, the Polander rode rapidly around part of the hill and exclaimed, 'This is the spot!' ").

5. Robert H. Wilson, *Thaddeus Kościuszko and His Home in Philadelphia*, (Copernicus Society of America, 1976), p. 7 (Morgan Lewis quote on Kościuszko's choice of Bemis Heights).

6. Dunlap, *History*, p. 118 ("every division, brigade and regiment was placed . . .").

7. *The Writings of Thomas Jefferson*, vol. 8, p. 496 (Colonel Hay's letter about morale and Kościuszko's choice of Bemis Heights).

8. James Wilkinson, *Memoirs*, p. 232 (Kosciuszko has selected this ground).

9. John Church Hamilton, *History of the Republic of the United States of America: As Traced in the Writings of Alexander and His Contemporaries* (Philadelphia: J. B. Lippincott & Co., 1864), p. 311 (Burgoyne calls Gates "an old midwife").

10. William Dunlap, *Diary of William Dunlap, 1766–1839; the Memoirs of a Dramatist, Theatrical Manager, Painter, Critic, Novelist, and Historian* (New York: Collections of the New York Historical Society, 1930), p. 339; Miecislaus Haiman, *Poland and the American Revolutionary War* (Chicago: Polish Roman Catholic Union of America, 1932), p. 21. ("Kościuszko is the only pure republican I ever knew. He is without any dross").

11. *Lord Dunmore's Proclamation,* November 7, 1775, Manuscripts and University Archives, Special Collections Department, University of Virginia Library, Charlottesville.

12. George Washington, November 12, 1775, General Orders, George Washington Papers, 1741–1799, Library of Congress.

13. John Wood Sweet, *Bodies Politic: Negotiating Race in the American North, 1730–1830* (Baltimore: John Hopkins University Press, 2003), p. 204. (Ashley tried to take back his slave Gilliam; Gates quote: "slaves who have or will assist us in securing our freedom at the risk of their own lives.")

14. *The Anti-Slavery Record,* vol. 3, for 1837 (New York: American Anti-Slavery Society, R. G. Williams, 1839), p. 173. (An account in the *Baltimore Paper,* September 8, 1790, in which Gates freed his slaves. "A few days ago, passed through this town, the Hon. General Horatio Gates and lady, on their way to take possession of their new and elegant seat on the banks of the East River. The General, previous to leaving Virginia, summoned his numerous family and slaves about him, and amidst their tears of affection and gratitude, gave them their freedom; and what is still better made provision that their liberty should be a blessing to them.")

15. Samuel White Patterson, *Horatio Gates: Defender of American Liberties* (New York: Columbia University Press, 1941), p. 392. (At Gates' funeral, a former slave named Uncle Robert threw himself on the coffin as it was being lowered into its grave and honored "with grateful tears the author of his liberty and happiness.")

16. Charles Lee, *The Lee Papers, Vol. I, 1754–1776* (New York Historical Society, 1872), p. 125 (Gates letter to Lee: quote about Indians).

17. Richard Ketchum, *Saratoga: Turning Point of America's Revolutionary War* (New York: Henry Holt and Company, 1997), p. 291 (drinking champagne).

18. Randall, *Benedict Arnold,* p. 355 (Burgoyne's affair with Madame Rousseau).

19. James Graham, *The Life of General Daniel Morgan, of the Virginia Line of the Army of the United States, with Portions of His Correspondence, Compiled from Authentic Sources* (New York: Derby & Jackson, 1856), p. 28. (Morgan was whipped five hundred times and his skin hung down in tags.)

20. Randall, *Benedict Arnold,* p. 354. (Arnold wanted to "march out and attack.")

21. Metchie J. Budka, ed., *Autograph Letters of Thaddeus Kościuszko in the American Revolution,* Collections of the Polish Museum in America (Chicago: Polish Museum of America, 1977), p. 45. (Kościuszko on Arnold: "I will always Esteem him.")

22. Col. Troup to Timothy Pickering, October 12, 1824, Pickering Papers Massachusetts Historical Society, vol. 2, no. 110, pp. 7–8. (Troup writes that Kościuszko was "constantly about General Gates person" in the Saratoga campaign and calls him "a gross flatterer.")

23. Benson John Lossing, *The Life and Times of Philip Schuyler* (New York: Sheldon & Company, 1873), p. 349. (Gates spent much of the day of the battle in his tent drinking.)

24. Ceane O'Hanlon-Lincoln, *County Chronicles: A Vivid Collection of Fayette County Pennsylvania Histories* (Chicora, PA: Mechling Bookbindery, 2004), p. 37. (Comparison of the rifles, and origin of the phrase "can't hit the side of a barn." The Pennsylvania rifle was sometimes mistakenly called the Kentucky rifle, probably because of the legend of Daniel Boone.)

25. Randall, *Benedict Arnold,* p. 357 ("come on, boys. Hurry up, my brave boys!").

26. Lossing, *The Life and Times of Philip Schuyler,* p. 350, footnotes (Gates held Arnold back because his army was about to run out of ammunition).

27. William Hamilton Drummond, *Autobiography of Archibald Hamilton Rowan, Esq.* (Dublin: Thomas Tegg and Co., 1840), p. 320. (Kościuszko: Arnold was "rash" and "drunken" and should be ordered "out of the field.")

28. Isaac Newton Arnold, *The Life of Benedict Arnold,* (Chicago: Jansen, McClurg, 1880), p. 194 (Gates was irritating, arrogant, and vulgar; Arnold, indiscreet, haughty, and passionate).

29. Ibid., p. 193 (letter from Gen. Schuyler to Col. Varick, September 25, 1777).

30. James Phinney Baxter, *The British Invasion from the North: The Campaigns of Generals Car-leton and Burgoyne, from Canada, 1776–1777, with the Journal of Lieut. William Digby of the 53D, or Shropshire Regiment of Foot* (Albany, NY: Joel Munsell's & Sons, 1887), p. 246 (Lt. William Digby's description of the wolves and concern over the spread of the plague; wolves also mentioned in Anburey, *With Burgoyne from Quebec,* on p. 220).

31. Gates to his wife, October 17, 1777, Gates Papers, New York Historical Society.

32. Haiman, *Kościuszko,* p. 29; Armstrong's memorial, Sparks Papers, ser. 49. vol. 1, fol. 71 (Gates gives credit for victory at Saratoga to Kościuszko's battle plans).

33. Bernard Knollenberg, *Washington and the Revolution, a Reappraisal of Gates, Conway, and the Continental Congress* (New York: Macmillan, 1940, p. 95 (Jonathan L. Austin arrived in Paris with the news that Burgoyne's army had been captured).

FOUR: *French Egos and Colonial Conspirators*

1. Elizabeth S. Kite, *Brigadier General Louis Legeque Duportail, Commandant of Engineers in the Continental Army* (Institut Français de Washington) (Baltimore: Johns Hopkins Press/Philadelphia: Dolphin Press, 1933), pp. 12–13 and 24–28; Walker, *Engineers of Independence,* p. 12; Kajencki, *Thaddeus Kościuszko,* pp. 61 and 63 (the French engineers continuously demanded promotions).

2. Walker, *Engineers of Independence,* p. 14. (James Lovell letter to George Washington on July 24, 1777, says the four engineers were upset that Coudray was "exalted four ranks.")

3. Papers of the Continental Congress, microfilm roll 51, Memorial of Louis Duportail to Congress, Fall 1777. (Duportail demands horses, servants, etc., that are "absolutely necessary for our service.")

4. Charles Francis Adams, *Familiar Letters of John Adams and His Wife Abigail Adams During the Revolution* (New York: Hurd and Houghton, 1876), pp. 304–305 (John Adams "Fabian" letter, September 2, 1777).

5. Washington Irving, *The Life of George Washington,* vol. 3 (New York: G. P. Putnam & Co., 1857), p. 336 (Gates heads an enlarged Board of War meant to challenge Washington's authority).

6. Amos Blanchard, *American Military Biography: Containing the Lives, Characters, and Anecdotes of the Officers of the Revolution, Who Were Most Distinguished in Achieving Our National Independence,* (Printed for Subscribers, 1825), p. 45. ("Heaven has been determined to save your country, or a weak General and bad counselors would have ruined it.")

7. James Kirby Martin, *Benedict Arnold: Revolutionary War Hero, an American Warrior Reconsidered* (New York: New York University Press, 1997), p. 407 (Wilky meandered through the woods and went to see his girlfriend before going to see Congress).

8. Benson John Lossing, *The Life and Times of Philip Schuyler* (New York: Sheldon & Co., 1873), p. 387 (Wilkinson's proclamation before Congress).

9. Ibid., p. 387 (the gold medal for Gates).

10. Frank Moore, *Diary of the American Revolution: From Newspapers and Original Documents* (New York: Charles Scribner, 1860), p. 106, notes (*Rivington's Royal Gazette,* December 19, 1777).

11. Robert Leckie, *George Washington's War: The Saga of the American Revolution* (New York: HarperCollins, 1992), p. 445 (the Conway cabal).

12. Thomas Coffin Amory, *The Military Services and Public Life of Major-General John Sullivan of the American Revolutionary Army* (Boston: Wiggin and Lunt, 1868), p. 65, notes (Conway's declaration about the disparaging letter).

13. Wilkinson, *Memoirs,* pp. 386–388 (the duel that wasn't; Gates was in tears and told Wilky, "I injure you, it is impossible, I should as soon think of injuring my own child").

14. Washington to Continental Congress, November 10, 1777, Library of Congress: "Cosieski, I think his name is, is a Gentleman of science and merit. From the character I have had of him he is deserving of notice too."

15. Kościuszko to Col. Troup, January 17, 1778, the Gates Papers, New York Historical Society.

16. Budka, *Autograph Letters* (memorandum of agreement between Colonel Kościuszko and Captain Jedidiah Thayer, December 7, 1777).

17. Haiman, *Kościuszko*, pp. 35–36 (Kościuszko letter to Mrs. Gates, original in the Gates Papers, in French).

18. Ibid., p. 197 (letter from Kościuszko to Washington, January 17, 1778).

19. William Alexander Duer, ed., *Memoirs, Correspondence and Manuscripts of General Lafayette* (London: Saunders and Otley, 1837), p. 148 (Lafayette letter: "Count De Pulaski was much affronted by the decision of a court martial entirely acquitting Colonel Molens. . . .").

20. John Fiske, *The American Revolution* (Cambridge: Houghton, Mifflin and Company, 1896), pp. 40–43 (an account of the failed invasion of Canada).

21. Ibid., p. 42 ("the deep silence became still deeper. . . .").

22. Martin, *Benedict Arnold,* p. 406. (Arnold called Gates "the greatest poltroon in the world.")

23. "Letter from Marquis de Lafayette to Henry Laurens, President of Congress, February 19, 1778," *South Carolina Historical Magazine,* 1906, pp. 189–193.

24. Benjamin Franklin to George Washington, May 29, 1777, Franklin Papers.

25. Clarence A. Manning, *Soldier of Liberty, Casimir Pulaski* (New York: Philosophical Library, 1945), p. 212 (Pulaski's riding stunts).

26. Paul Bentalou [told to Louis Hue Girardin], *Pulaski Vindicated from an Unsupported Charge: Inconsiderately or Malignantly Introduced in Judge Johnson's Sketches of the Life and Correspondence of Major Gen. Nathaniel Green* (Baltimore: John D. Toy, 1824), pp. 23–24 (a firsthand account by Captain Bentalou, who witnessed Pulaski's role at the Battle of Brandywine).

27. Mark S. Hoffman, *The World Almanac and Book of Facts* (New York: World Almanac Education Group, Facts on File, Newspaper Enterprise Association, Robert Famighetti, 1923), p. 192 (Washington called New York "the seat of empire" after a tour of the state).

28. Joseph Nelson Larned and Augustus Hunt Shearer, *The New Larned History for Ready Reference, Reading and Research: The Actual Words of the World* (Springfield, MA: C. A. Nichols Publishing Company, 1922), p. 1393 (Washington's vision for a canal).

29. In a letter to David Humphrey on July 25, 1785 (*Washington's Papers*), Washington said that he was working on "a project which I think big with great political, as well as commercial consequences to these States . . . extending the inland navigation of our rivers, to bring the States on the Atlantic in closed [*sic*] connexion with those forming to the west." He even mentions the "Country of California," suggesting that the United States get to it before some other country does.

30. Letter from Washington to General Putnam, December 2, 1777, Library of Congress.

31. Haiman, *Kościuszko,* p. 42 (on the possible meeting between Pulaski and Kościuszko).

32. Simon Wolf, *American Jew as Patriot, Soldier and Citizen A Sketch of Haym Salomon: From An Unpublished MS in the Papers of Jared Sparks,* contributed by Herbert B. Adams, Ph.D., professor in the Johns Hopkins University, with notes by J. H. Hollander (Philadelphia: Levytype Company, 1895), p. 15 (Salomon is called an "intimate associate" of Pulaski and Kosciusko); Madison Clinton Peters, *Haym Salomon: The Financier of the Revolution, an Unwritten Chapter in American History* (New York: Trow Press, 1911), p. 11 (Salomon's friendship with Pulaski and Kościuszko).

33. Haym Salomon's contribution to the Revolution has been disputed by some Jewish scholars and praised by others. The debate surrounds hundreds of thousands of dollars that he

funneled to the rebels. At issue is how much of it was a loan or gift from Salomon and how much was from other sources. Much of what is known comes from *An Unpublished Manuscript in the Papers of Jared Sparks,* which was written by Salomon's son, *The Papers of Robert Morris,* the first Superintendent of Finance of the United States, and *Haym Salomon and the Revolution,* which was written in 1930 by Pulitzer Prize–winning biographer Charles Edward Russell. Max Kohler, a lawyer and member of the American Jewish Historical Society, criticized Russell's book in a letter to Congress, claiming it was an "exaggeration," saying: "I seriously doubt if he deserves a monument." While Salomon's son probably overstated his father's legend to be reimbursed for outstanding loans, Kohler's letter goes overboard and includes mistakes. For example, according to Haym M. Salomon (the son), his father was "an intimate associate" of Kościuszko and Pulaski, an assertion that Russell and other historians also made. Kohler wrote: "There isn't a particle of evidence to substantiate the claim" that he knew the Polish generals. However, on page 246 Russell cites a receipt for $142 that Salomon lent to Kościuszko, so clearly the two men knew each other. Salomon's brother-in-law, Col. Frank, was forage master at West Point for two years during Kościuszko's tenure there. Frank would have told the Polish engineer that his brother-in-law was also from Poland.

Kohler claimed that Pulaski could not have known Salomon because the cavalryman was in South Carolina when Salomon came to Philadelphia in August 1778. This is incorrect. Pulaski did not go to South Carolina until the following year, in May 1779. Until then, Pulaski spent most of his time in and around Philadelphia trying to raise money for his cavalry and trying to transfer some of his own funds from Poland through French banks. It was during this time that Pulaski was training his horsemen in an orbit around Philadelphia that included Baltimore; Bethlehem, Pennsylvania; and Trenton, New Jersey. During this time Pulaski visited Philadelphia several times. He would have heard about the famous Pole running a bank out of coffee shop on Front Street. See Leszek Szymański, *Casimir Pulaski: A Hero of the American Revolution* (New York: Hippocrene Books, 1979), pp. 199–200. Pulaski wrote in a letter on September 17, 1778, that he spent $16,000 of his own money to pay for the legion. Also, on September 30, 1778, he is in Philadelphia.

34. Avner Falk, *A Psychoanalytic History of the Jews* (Madison, NJ: Fairleigh Dickinson University Press, 1996), p. 660 (Salomon flees from the Russians).

35. Henry Samuel Morais, *The Jews of Philadelphia: Their History from the Earliest Settlements to the Present Time* (Philadelphia: Levytype Company, 1894), p. 37 (notes about Salomon's in-laws, the Franks).

36. Peter Wiernik, *History of the Jews in America* (New York: Jewish Press Publishing Company, 1912), p. 89 (Salomon's brother-in-law, Isaac Franks, was forage master at West Point from January 1778 until February 22, 1781); Madison C. Peters, *The Jews Who Stood by Washington: An Unwritten Chapter in American History* (New York: Trow Press, 1915), p. 12 (Rachel Franks was the sister of Colonel Isaac Franks, a Revolutionary officer of distinction); Issac Markens, *The Hebrews in America: A Series of Historical and Biographical Sketches* (New York: Published by the Author, 1888), p. 73 (Salomon's brother-in-law, Isaac Franks, was later named judge in the Supreme Court of Pennsylvania).

37. Wolf, *American Jew as Patriot, Soldier and Citizen,* p. 15 (Maj. [later Col.] David S. Franks was one of Arnold's aides); ibid., p. 16 (Maj. [Isaac] Franks was Salomon's brother-in-law).

38. Leonard Gansevoort to Gen. Philip Schuyler, June 12, 1776, Schuyler Papers, New York Public Library, Manuscript Division.

39. Peters, *The Jews Who Stood by Washington,* p. 24. On January 1, 1785, the *Pennsylvania Weekly Advertiser* ran a description of Salomon's business on Wall Street ("every species of merchandise . . . and every branch of business.").

40. Charles Edward Russell, *Haym Salomon and the Revolution* (Freeport, NY: Books for Libraries Press, 1930), p. ix (Morris preferred brokers of his own religion, but eventually his records showed seventy-five notations referring to business with Haym Salomon).
41. *Magazine of American History with Notes and Queries,* Illustrated (Martha J. Lamb, Editor) 21 (January–June 1889): 70 (John Paul Jones and Degrasse dropped off three thousand vessels from the English merchant marine with the Americans).
42. Gaillard Hunt, ed., *The Writings of James Madison: Comprising His Public Papers and His Private Correspondence* (New York: G. P. Putnam's Sons, 1900) p. 228 (letter from Madison to Edmund Randolph, August 27, 1782: "I have for some time been a pensioner on the favor of Haym Salomon, a Jew broker").
43. Ibid., p. 242 (letter from Madison to Randolph, September 30, 1782: "The kindness of our little friend in Front street . . .").
44. Russell, *Haym Salomon,* p. 246 (Salomon lent Kociuszko $142).
45. Morris U. Schappes, "Excerpts from Robert Morris" "Diaries in the office and Finance, 1781–1784, Referring to Haym Salomon and other Jews," *American Jewish Quarterly* 67, nos. 1 and 2 (September–December 1977): 15 (many of Salomon's records were lost in a fire when the British burned the Capitol in Washington).
46. Morais, *The Jews of Philadelphia*, p. 24 notes (the 1850 U.S. Senate Report honoring Haym Salomon).

FIVE: *Washington's West Point Architect*

1. Troup to Gates, March 26, 1778, Gates Papers, New York Historical Society; Haiman, *Kosciuszko in the American Revolution*, p. 42.
2. Philip Lee Philips, *Notes on the Life and Works of Bernard Romans* (Florida State Historical Society, 1924), p. 60. (Lord Stirling to Washington: "Upon the whole, Mr. Romans has displayed his genius at a very great expense and to very little publick advantage.")
3. David Humphreys, *An Essay on the Life of the Honorable Major-General Israel Putnam* (Hartford: Hudson and Goodwin, 1788), p. 177 (Humphrey's quote).
4. Putnam to Washington, January 13, 1778, Washington Papers, Library of Congress.
5. Ibid.
6. Kite, *Brigadier-General Louis Lebegue Duportial,* p. 86 (Radiere's letter: "It was resolved to fortify a place called West Point . . .").
7. George Bancroft, *The History of the United States of America, from the Discovery of the Continent [to 1789]* (New York: D. Appleton and Company, 1885), p. 432 ("four years before, Washington had sailed between the Highlands, and had marked with his eye the positions best adapted to command the passage").
8. George Washington to La Radiere, January 25, 1778, Washington Papers, Library of Congress ("we shall lose the winter").
9. Gen. Samuel H. Parsons to George Washington, March 7, 1778, Washington Papers, Library of Congress.
10. *Public Papers of George Clinton, First Governor of New York,* vol. 2 (New York and Albany: Published by the State of New York, Wynkoop Hallenbeck Crawford Co., State Printers, 1900), pp. 711–712 (Clinton letter, February 5, 1778).
11. Ibid., pp. 847–848 (Board of War reigns in Radiere and sends Kościuszko to West Point).
12. Ibid., p. 85. (Clinton letter introducing Kościuszko to Parsons).
13. Theodore J. Crackel, *West Point: A Bicentennial History* (Lawrence: University Press of Kansas, 2002), p. 14 (Parsons and Kościuszko worked well together).
14. Some of the descriptions of the redoubts are from the West Point Fortifications Staff Ride

Note Cards, prepared by former West Point professor Jim Johnson and others, January 1994, modified 1998, United States Military Academy, History Department, 2d edition, March 1998.

15. Lincoln Diamant, *Chaining the Hudson: The Fight for the River in the American Revolution* (New York: Fordham University Press, 2004), p. 154 (Captain Machin and Kościuszko work on the Constitution Island capstan).

16. Humphreys, *An Essay* (Humphreys' opinion of Radiere).

17. John Fellows, *The Veil Removed: Or, Reflections on David Humphrey's Essay on the Life of Israel Putnam* (New York: James D. Lockwood, 1842), p. 210 (Jared Sparks quote about Kościuszko).

18. Washington to McDougall, April 6, 1778, Washington Papers, Library of Congress.

19. Gen. Parsons letter to McDougall, March 28, 1778, Alexander McDougall Papers, New York Historical Society.

20. Diary entry for April 10, 1778, Alexander McDougall Papers, New York Historical Society.

21. Palmer, *The River and the Rock,* p. 159 (the arrival of Rufus Putnam).

22. McDougall to Parsons, April 11, 1778, Alexander McDougall Papers, New York Historical Society ("the hill which Col. Putnam is fortifying is the most commanding and important of any that we can now attend to . . .").

23. Gen. McDougall to Washington, April 13, 1778, Washington Papers, Library of Congress.

24. Washington to McDougall, April 22, 1778, Washington Papers, Library of Congress.

25. McDougall Diaries, April 2 and 3, 1778 ("Marquis de Lafayette arrived here at 5 P.M. with 7 horses. And four Domestics . . .").

26. *Public Papers of George Clinton,* vol. 2, p. 708–709 (Articles of Agreement with Townsend; the chain would cost £440 per ton); Diament, *Chaining the Hudson,* p. 146. (Diament converted the cost of the chain to $92,000 with wartime inflation.)

27. Col. Troup to Gen. Gates, April 18, 1778, Gates Papers, New York Historical Society.

28. Gov. Clinton to Gov. Trumbull, May 1, 1778, *Public Papers of George Clinton, First Governor of New York,* vol. 3 (New York and Albany: Published by the State of New York, Wynkoop Hallenbeck Crawford Co., State Printers, 1901) (the works were "in good forwardness").

29. Thacher, *A Military Journal,* p. 132 (description of West Point).

30. Hugh Hughes to James Clinton, May 1, 1778, in William Abbatt, New York: *The Magazine of History, with Notes and Queries* (1935), p. 111 (Kościuszko invited to celebration of France's alliance with America).

31. Palmer, *The River and the Rock,* p. 164. (Palmer makes a convincing case that McDougall named the fort after Benedict Arnold to spite Gates).

32. Gen. McDougall to Washington, April 13, 1778, Washington Papers, Library of Congress. (The letter praised Kościuszko's work).

33. McDougall to Gov. Clinton, May 11, 1778, *Public Papers of George Clinton,* p. 294. (McDougall turns on Kościuszko after Arnold arrives: "I am far from being pleased with Mr. Korsuasco's constructing the Batteries.")

34. Isaac Q. Leake, *Memoir of the Life and Times of General John Lamb, an Officer of the Revolution, Who Commanded the Post at West Point at the Time of Arnold's Defection, and His Correspondence with Washington, Clinton, Patrick Henry, and Other Distinguished Men of His Time* (Albany, NY: Joel Munsell, 1850), pp. 208–209 ("the consequence of this predilection of Gates . . .").

35. McDougall Diaries, May 26, 1778 ("4½ gallons of rum").

36. Leake, *Memoir of the Life and Times of General John Lamb,* p. 207 (letter from Col. Malcom to Lamb, August 2, 1778, where Malcom writes: "The works are not worth a farthing").

37. Duportail to Gates, Gates Papers, New York Historical Society.

38. Budka, *Autograph Letters,* pp. 26–27 (Gates letter to Glover, July 2, 1778).

39. Haiman, *Kosciuszko in the American Revolution*, p. 51; National Archives, Muster Rolls, Revolutionary War Papers (artisans sent to West Point).

40. Upham, *A Memoir of General John Glover*, p. 44 (Glover's orders on the hours of work and orders for supplies).

41. Historical Society of Pennsylvania, *The Pennsylvania Magazine of History and Biography* (Philadelphia: Publication Fund of the Historical Society of Pennsylvania, 1890), p. 355 (*Thatcher's Military Journal*).

42. Washington to William Malcom, July 27, 1778, Library of Congress ("Colo. Kosciuszko was left at the Fort as Acting Engineer and I have always understood is fully competent to the Business").

43. William Henry Smith, *The St. Clair Papers: The Life and Public Services of Arthur St. Clair, Soldier of the Revolutionary War; President of the Continental Congress; and Governor of the North Western Territory, with His Correspondence and Other Papers* (Cincinnati: Robert Clarke & Co., 1882), p. 515, notes (it was a favorite scheme of Lafayette to reconquer Canada and restore the power of the monarchy).

44. George Washington Papers at the Library of Congress, George Washington to Henry Laurens, November 14, 1778 (the proposed invasion of Canada "had its birth in the Cabinet of France and was put into this artful dress, to give it the readier currency").

45. Artur P. Watts, "A Newly Discovered Letter of Brigadier-General Duportail: Introduction and Translation," *Pennsylvania History*, 1, (April 1934): 103–106 ("... her commerce in consequence will pass to France . . . [Americans] hate the French more than they do the English").

46. Kościuszko to Gates, August 3, 1778, Gates Papers, New York Historical Society (encouraging an attack on Canada). The word "Habilitus" in French and Polish universities, as in "Doctor Habilitus," signifies someone who has credentials higher than a doctorate. In this case, Kościuszko is using it to say that Gates would add to his "qualifications."

47. Elkanah Watson, *Men and Times of the Revolution; Or, Memoirs of Elkanah Watson* (New York: Dana and Company, 1856), p. 74 (D'Estaing sent Sullivan daily assurances that the French fleet would enter the harbor).

48. Pontgiband, *A French Volunteer*, p. 95 (Sullivan and D'Estaing almost fought a duel).

49. William Cutter, *The Life of General Lafayette* (New York: George F. Cooledge & Brother, 1849), p. 74 (D'Estaing "was more punctilious than wise and, as the result proved, sacrificed the whole expedition to a point of etiquette").

50. Fiske, *The American Revolution,* p. 80 (a riot broke out between French and American sailors on the wharves of Boston).

51. Historical Society of Pennsylvania, *The Pennsylvania Magazine of History and Biography* (Philadelphia: Publication Fund of the Historical Society of Pennsylvania, 1890) p. 357 (Washington letter to John Augustine Washington, September 23, 1778: "there are but two capital objects, which they [the enemy] can have . . .).

52. Kite, *Duportail,* p. 111 (Radiere letter to Congress demanding a promotion to brigadier general).

53. *Papers of the Continental Congress,* August 27, 1778 (Duportail letter demanding that Kościuszko follow Radiere's orders).

54. Washington to the President of Congress, August 31, 1778, Washington Papers, Library of Congress (Kościuszko will not be subordinate to any engineer except Gen. Duportail).

55. Washington to Duportail, August 27, 1778, Washington Papers, Library of Congress.

56. Kite, *Duportail,* p. 59 (the "cold and reserved" Duportail was not popular with the troops).

57. Walker, *Engineers of Independence,* p. 216 (Duportail's animosity towards Kościuszko).

58. Palmer, *The River and the Rock,* p. 174 (Duportail's report was "marred by the thread of pettiness running through it).

59. Walker, *Engineers of Independence,* p. 216 (quote from Duportail's report).

60. Haiman, *Kosciuszko in the American Revolution,* pp. 57–59 (the first hand account of Major Lansing and Col. Morris of the confrontation between Kościuszko and Carter).

61. For a detailed account of the duel and the Carter affair, see Haiman, *Kosciuszko in the American Revolution,* pp. 56–68; Pula, *Thaddeus Kościuszko,* pp. 107–115; and Kajencki, *Thaddeus Kościuszko,* pp. 217–221.

62. *Collections of the New York Historical Society for the Year 1880* (New York: Printed for the Society, 1881), pp. 58–61 (transcript of Kościuszko's testimony at St. Clair's court-martial).

63. Gates to Washington, September 11, 1778, Library of Congress.

64. Washington to Gates, September 10, 1778, Library of Congress. (One of the dates on these previous two letter must be a typographical error, because Washington's response is dated a day before Gates's request).

65. Letter from Kościuszko to Gates, September 12, 1778, Gates Papers, New York Historical Society.

66. Col. Malcom to Gov. Clinton, November 20, 1778, *Public Papers of George Clinton,* vol. 4, pp. 301–302 (Malcom justifies his use of Tories as free laborers).

67. Kościuszko to John Taylor, September 14, 1778, in Budka, *Kościuszko Letters in the American Revolution,* 28.

68. Thacher, *A Military Journal,* p. 61. (Thacher wrote in his diary: "Many of the officers from the South are gentlemen of education, and unaccustomed to that equality which prevails in New England . . . we too frequently hear the burlesque epithet of Yankee." As Dr. Thacher spent time with Kościuszko in his garden and the Pole trusted the doctor enough to tell him about his failed love affair with Sosnowska (pp. 138–139) it is reasonable to surmise that the two also talked about their thoughts about equality and the revolution).

69. *The New England Historical and Genealogical Register,* vol. 30 (Boston: Published at the Society's House, 1876), p. 319 (letter from Gates to Gov. Jonathan Trumbull, August 5, 1778).

70. Washington to Duportail, September 19, 1778, Library of Congress (Washington's reaction to Duportail's report).

71. While Kościuszko's letter to Gates (note 72) shows that the Pole thought he won the dispute, Palmer (*The River and the Rock,* p. 178) makes the point that "each [Kościuszko and Duportail] believed he had won the argument."

72. Kościuszko to Gates, October 6, 1778, Gates Papers, New York Historical Society.

73. Ibid.

SIX: *A Rock, an African Prince, and America's Traitor*

1. Władysław Mieczysław Kozłowski, *Washington and Kościuszko* (Chicago: Polish Roman Catholic Union of America, 1942), p. 44 (Kościuszko lived in West Point at the house of Mrs. Warren).

2. Thacher, *A Military Journal,* p. 138 (Thacher quote about garden).

3. Korzon, *Kościuszko, Biografia z Dokumentów Wysnuta,* p. 601, note (years later an Australian helped a Pole with yellow fever because he was told that a Pole named Kosciuszko gave his grandfather some bread).

4. Haiman, *Kosciuszko in the American Revolution,* p. 97 (Van Rennsselaer sent Kościuszko a bed).

5. Samuel Richards, *Diary of Samuel Richards, Captain of Connecticut Line, War of the Revolution, 1775–1781* (Philadelphia: Leeds & Biddle Co., 1909), p. 55 ("I quartered a considerable time with Kosciuszko in the same log hut . . .").

6. Thomas Egleston, *The Life of John Patterson: Major General in the Revolutionary Army* (New York: G. P. Putnam's Sons, 1894), pp. 308–310.

7. Egleston, *The Life of John Patterson,* pp. 309.

8. Egleston, *The Life of John Patterson*, p. 309. (Hull tries on Kościuszko's dress uniform and throws a party).
9. Catherine Maria Sedgwick, *The Power of Her Sympathy: The Autobiography and Journals of Catharine Maria Sedgwick* (Boston: 1993, first published in 1822), p. 69 (the description of the alcohol Hull was forced to drink).
10. "Kościuszko's Pistol," *Polish Heritage*, 46, no. 1 (Spring 1995).
11. Kościuszko to Gates, December 28, 1778, Gates Papers, New York Historical Society; Haiman *Kosciuszko in the American Revolution*, p. 73, note 21 asserts that while the letter is dated 1779, its topic makes it clear that it was written in 1778.
12. McDougall to Gov. Clinton, December 15, 1778, *Public Papers of George Clinton, First Governor of New York, 1777–1795, 1801–1804,* vol. 4 (Albany, NY: James B. Lyon State Printer, 1900), pp. 383–387.
13. Palmer, *The River and the Rock,* p. 183 (McDougall to Gouvion: "What would be your plan . . .").
14. McDougall to Gouvion, December 31, 1778, Washington Papers, Library of Congress (McDougall sends Gouvion to Kings' Ferry).
15. Washington to McDougall, Februrary 9, 1779, Washington Papers, Library of Congress (asking if Kościuszko is "still at West Point").
16. Haiman, *Kosciuszko in the American Revolution,* p. 78 (notes) (the "Notes of Col. Houski-aso" from the McDougall Papers outlining some of Kościuszko's projects).
17. Kościuszko to McDougall, February 6, 1779, McDougall Papers, New York Historical Society (blueprints to build redoubt on Rocky Point).
18. McDougall to Washington, April 15, 1779, Washington Papers, Library of Congress ("Colo. Kusciasco has been undisturbed in his Line . . .").
19. Pula, *Son of Liberty,* p. 134 (number of workers shrank to five officers and 105 men).
20. Kościuszko to McDougall, December 28, 1778, McDougall Papers, New York Historical Society.
21. Malcom to Washington, November 5, 1778, Washington Papers, Library of Congress.
22. Washington to Malcom, November 8, 1778, Washington Papers, Library of Congress.
23. Palmer, *The River and the Rock,* p. 181 (Palmer quote about the "personality problems").
24. Kościuszko letter to Gates, March 3, 1779, Gates Papers, New York Historical Society ("I supposed to be myself at this time more than half a Yankee").
25. Patterson, *Horatio Gates,* p. 287 (Gates, who was called brother Arahoiktea by the Oneidas).
26. Gates to Washington, March 16, 1779 ("the Man who undertakes . . .").
27. Worthington Chauncey Ford, ed., *The Writings of George Washington* (New York: G. P. Putnam's Sons, 1889), p. 54 (notes) (Indian chief Cornplanter dubbed Washington "Town Destroyer").
28. Kościuszko to John Armstrong and his friends in Boston, March 3, 1779, Budka, *Autograph Letters,* p. 31. Most American historians who have written about Kosciuszko left out the last part of this ribald letter, and Polish historians have sanitized the sexual reference by changing the word "clap" to "katar," which means "cold," as in "be careful not to catch a cold."
29. Palmer, *The River and the Rock,* p. 188 ("two large coils of cable and one sloop").
30. William Graham Sumner, *The Financier and the Finances of the American Revolution* (New York: Dodd, Mead, and Company, 1892), p. 218 (Deane's "proceedings and his interests became really the sport of parties in Congress").
31. Martin I. J. Griffin, *General Thaddeus Kościuszko*, vol. 6 (Philadelphia: American Catholic Historical Researches, April 1910), p 166 (letter to Henry Wells: "My best compliments to all my friends of the Yankee species").
32. Duportail to John Jay, President of Congress, May 11, 1779, in Walker, *Engineers of Independence,* p. 221 (the Frenchman once again attacks Kościuszko).

33. George Washington to Alexander McDougall, May 28, 1779 ("ground opposite the Fort . . . Can it be possessed by us to advantage?").

34. Haiman, *Kosciuszko in the American Revolution* p. 82, originally from Joseph Johnson, *Traditions and Reminiscences, Chiefly of the American Revolution* (Charleston, SC: 1851), p. 415 (text of the poster about Washington's lost spur).

35. John R. Spears, *Anthony Wayne, Sometimes Called "Mad Anthony"* (New York: D. Appleton and Company, 1903), p. 148 ("killed every dog within 3 miles").

36. Henry Phelps Johnston, *The Storming of Stony Point on the Hudson, Midnight, July 15, 1779: Its Importance in the Light of Unpublished Documents* (New York: James T. White & Co., 1900), p. 74 (McLane arrested "the Widow Calhoun . . .").

37. *New Hampshire Gazette,* July 27, 1779, quoted in *Public Papers of George Clinton, First Governor of New York, 1777–1795, 1801–1804,* vol. 5, (Albany, NY: James B. Lyon State Printer, 1901), p. 154.

38. George Washington, General Orders June 30, 1779, Washington Papers, Library of Congress, 1741–1799: Series 3g Varick Transcripts.

39. George Washington to William Heath, March 21, 1781, Washington Papers, Library of Congress (Washington calls West Point "the most important Post in America").

40. Kościuszko to Washington, July 1779, Washington Papers, Library of Congress.

41. Letter from Washington to Gen. Wayne, July 20, 1779, Washington Papers, Library of Congress ("I propose either this evening or tomorrow to pitch my Tent some where near West Point").

42. Washington letter to Gen. St. Clair, July 20, 1779, Washington Papers, Library of Congress, ("the long Hill . . .").

43. Ibid ("the possession of this Hill . . .").

44. Palmer, *The River and the Rock,* p. 204 ("General Duportail might have seen a smirk flash across Colonel Kościuszko's face when Washington made that decision").

45. Frank Moore, *Diary of the American Revolution: From Newspapers and Original Documents,* vol. 2 (New York: Charles Scribner, 1850), p. 200 (New York Packet, August 17, 1779).

46. McDougall to Gov. Clinton, in *Public Papers of George Clinton,* vol. 4, pp. 383–386 (cattle eating their mangers).

47. Washington to Kościuszko, September 9, 1779, Washington Papers, Library of Congress ("I have ordered the Commy Genl. to procure a supply of Rum . . .").

48. Charles Cotesworth Pinckney, *Life of General Thomas Pinckney* (Boston and New York: Houghton, Mifflin and Company, 1895), p. 64 (French flee to the woods).

49. Bentalou, *Pulaski Vindicated,* p. 29 (eyewitness description of Pulaski's attempt to rally French).

50. Franklin Benjamin Hough, *The Siege of Savannah: By the Combined American and French forces, under the Command of Gen. Lincoln, and the Count D'Estaing, in the Autumn of 1779* (Albany, NY: J. Munsell, 1866), p. 41 (description of Casimir Pulaski's death).

51. Bentalou, *Pulaski Vindicated,* p. 19 (Ramsay quote about Pulaski).

52. George Washington, General Orders for Nov. 17, 1779, Washington Papers, Library of Congress, ("Pulaski" and "Poland").

53. George Washington, General Orders for Nov. 21, 1779, Washington Papers, Library of Congress.

54. Edward Field, ed., *Diary of Colonel Israel Angell, Commanding the Second Rhode Island Continental Regiment During the American Revolution, 1778–1781,* transcribed from the original manuscript) (Providence, RI: Preston and Rounds Company, 1899), p. 96 ("the American Gibraltar . . .").

55. Budka, *Kościuszko letters,* p. 38 (Kościuszko to Varrick, November 30, 1779).

56. Haiman, *Kosciuszko in the American Revolution,* p. 85; Pula, *Thaddeus Kościuszko,* p. 142; Edward C. Boynton, *History of West Point and Its Military Importance During the*

American Revolution (New York: D. Van Nostrand, 1863), pp. 85–86 (the winter of 1780).

57. Matthew Wilson, by the Rev. Mathew Wilson of Lewis, Dated 22d June 1780, "Observations on the Severity of the Winter 1779, 1780," *Transactions of the American Philosophical Society* 3 (1793): 326–328.

58. Kościuszko to Gen. Nathanael Greene, January 28, 1780, in *Correspondence Relating to the American Revolution of Maj. Gen. Nathanael Greene,* vol. 1 (Philadelphia: American Philosophical Society).

59. Kościuszko to Col. Richard K. Meade, March 23, 1780, Washington Papers, Library of Congress.

60. Col. Meade to Kościuszko, March 30, 1780, Washington Papers, Library of Congress.

61. Kościuszko to Philip Schuyler, May 12, 1780, Papers of the Continental Congress, item number 78, publication number M247.

62. Philip Schuyler to Benedict Arnold, June 2, 1780, in William B. Reed, *The Life and Correspondence of Joseph Reed, Military Secretary of Washington, at Cambridge; Adjutant General of the Continental Army; Member of the Congress of the United States; and President of the Executive Council of the State of Pennsylvania,* vol. 2. (Philadelphia: Lindsay and Blakiston, 1847), p. 276.

63. Palmer, *The River and the Rock,* p. 233; Carl Van Doren, *Secret History of the American Revolution: An Account of the Conspiracies of Benedict Arnold* (New York: Viking Press, 1941), pp. 266–267. (Howe recalled that Arnold "spoke so particularly of the Rocky Hill work [Redoubt No. 4] and with what ease it would be taken as struck me oddly even then, though I had not the least suspicion of him.")

64. Benedict Arnold to Major André, June 16, 1780, Clinton Papers, William L. Clements Library, University of Michigan.

65. Arnold to André, July 15, 1780, Clinton Papers, William L. Clements Library.

66. Budka, *Kościuszko Letters,* p. 42 (Gates letter to Washington, June 21, 1780).

67. H. A. Washington, *The Writings of Jefferson, Being His Autobiography, Correspondence, Reports, Messages, Addresses, and Other Writings, Official and Private, from the Original Manuscripts,* vol. 8 (Washington, DC: Taylor & Maury, 1854), p. 496 (Gates letter to Major John Armstrong).

68. Kościuszko to Washington, July 30, 1780, Washington Papers, Library of Congress.

69. Walker, *Engineers of Independence,* p. 233 ("only Kościuszko appears to have recognized Vauban's flexibility.")

70. Col. Dave R. Palmer, "Fortress West Point: 19th Century Concept in an 18th Century War," *Military Engineer* 68 (1976): 171–174. (Kościuszko created "a splendid prototype for the system of fortifications which were to be built in Europe in the next century.")

71. George Bancroft, *The History of the United States of America, from the Discovery of the Continent [to 1789]* (New York: D. Appleton and Company, 1885), p. 432 (quote about West Point).

72. Monica M. Gardiner, *Kościuszko, a Biography* (London: George Allen & Unwin, 1920), p. 25 (Kościuszko's idea to put military academy at West Point). Also, in several letters that are cited in later chapters, it is clear that Kosciuszko continually prodded Thomas Jefferson to open a military school at West Point.

73. Washington to Kościuszko, August 3 1780, Washington Papers, Library of Congress.

74. Washington to Benedict Arnold, August 6, 1780, Washington Papers, Library of Congress (. . . "if Genl. Howe has not left you a plan of the Works, Maj. Villefranche will be able to furnish you with one").

75. Washington to Gates, August 12, 1780, Washington Papers, Library of Congress.

76. Coded letter from Joseph Stansbury, July 7, 1780, Clinton Papers, William L. Clements Library, University of Michigan (a "drawing of the works on both sides of the river done by the French engineer").

77. Benjamin J. Lossing, *The Pictorial Handbook of the Revolution; Or Illustrations by Pen and Pencil, of The History, Biography, Scenery, Relics and Traditions of the War for Independence, Vol. II,* (New York: Harper & Brothers, 1852), p. 153 (Villefranche's memo on "Number of Men necessary to Man the Works at West Point").

78. Boynton, *History of West Point,* p. 76 (Arnold ordered a link from the chain removed).

79. Palmer, *The River and the Rock,* p. 259 (Arnold peddled "wine and meat").

80. Major Bauman to Alexander Hamilton, August 13, 1780, 1, Alexander Hamilton, *Official and Other Papers of the Late Major General Alexander Hamilton* (New York and London: Wiley & Putnam, 1842), p. 422. ("a Tartar's camp").

81. Lossing, *The Pictorial Handbook of the Revolution* p. 153 (Villefranche's memo).

82. Robert Bolton, *A History of the County of Westchester, from Its First Settlement to the Present Time,* vol. 1, (New York: Alexander S. Gould, 1848), p. 218 (Arnold's Artillery Orders at West Point, September 5, 1780, "in case of an alarm," only three men would be stationed on Redoubt No. 4).

83. Major Sebastian Bauman to Alexander Hamilton, from West Point, August 13, 1780, in Hamilton, *Official and Other Papers,* p. 421-24 ("engineer is transferred . . .").

84. Mary C. Doll Fairchild, ed., *Memoirs of Colonel Sebastian Beauman and His Descendants: With Selections from His Correspondence* (Franklin, Oh: Editor Pub. Co., 1900), pp. 18–19 (September 8, 1780, letter from Richard D. Varick to Major [Bauman] Beauman).

85. Budka, *Kościuszko Letters,* pp. 45–47, (Kościuszko to Richard Varick, August 10, 1780).

86. The documents found in Major André's boot are in the collections of the New York State Archives in Albany, New York.

87. John C. Dann, ed., *The Revolution Remembered: Eyewitness Accounts of the War for Independence* (Chicago: University of Chicago Press, 1980), p. 58 (Parkhurst: "A great rumbling and trampling of horses . . .").

88. Washington to Gen. William Heath, October 31, 1780, Washington Papers, Library of Congress.

89. Heath Papers, Massachusetts Historical Society, ser. 7, vol. 5 (1905), pp. 126–127 ("Mrs. Warren says upon the detection of Arnold, she burnt the plans").

90. Josiah Quincy, *The Journals of Major Samuel Shaw: The First American Consul at Canton* (Boston: WM. Crosby and H. P. Nichols, 1847), pp. 80–81 (Major Shaw letter to Rev. Eliot).

SEVEN: *A Polish Yankee Goes South*

1. *Journals of the American Congress from 1774–1788,* vol. 3 (Washington: Way and Gideon, 1823), p. 505 (Clajon's back pay and rations).

2. William Clajon to Gen. Gates, August 20, 1780, *The State Records of North Carolina,* vol. 14, p. 565 ("Col. Kosciusko intends to visit Traveller's Rest").

3. Mintz, *Generals of Saratoga,* p. 44 ("Hard Hand of Power").

4. Irving, *Life of Washington,* pp. 95–96; Fiske, *The American Revolution,* pp. 196–197 (Battle of Camden).

5. Hamilton, *The Official and Other Papers,* p. 205 (Hamilton's quote on Gates' flight).

6. Andrew Lipscomb, ed., *The Writings of Thomas Jefferson, Containing His Autobiography, Notes on Virginia, Parliamentary Manual, Official Papers, Messages and Addresses and Other Writings, Official and Private,* vol. 4 (Washington DC: Thomas Jefferson Memorial Association, 1904), pp. 104–106 (Jefferson letter to Gates, September 23, 1780). ("I enclose a certificate acknowledging satisfaction for the money furnished by Colonel Kościuszko.")

7. Thomas Jefferson, *The Writings of Thomas Jefferson,* vol. 3 (New York: G. P. Putnam Sons, 1894), p. 36 ("slaves are by the laws excluded . . .").

8. Robert Wilson Gibbes, *Documentary History of the American Revolution: Consisting of Let-*

ters and Papers Relating to the Contest for Liberty, Chiefly in South Carolina, from Originals in the Possession of the Editor, and Other Sources (New York: D. Appleton & Co., 1857), p. 267 (Kościuszko makes kind mention of Billy in a letter to Dr. Read).

9. Haiman, *Kosciuszko in the American Revolution,* p. 103 (Kościuszko orders a pair of shoes for Agrippa Hull).

10. Gibbes, *Documentary History,* p. 276 (Kościuszko and Dr. Read had to share Gen. Isaac Huger's cloak as their only form of bedding).

11. George Washington Greene, *The Life of Nathanael Greene: Major-General in the Army of the Revolution,* vol. 3 (New York: Hurd and Hougton, 1871), p. 58 (Greene letter to Washington about "water transportation").

12. Ibid., p. 83 (Greene orders Kościuszko to scout the Pedee River, December 8, 1780).

13. Budka, *Kościuszko Letters,* p. 50 (Greene to Polk, December 15, 1780).

14. Theodore Thayer, *Nathanael Greene: Strategist of the American Revolution* (New York: Twayne Publishers, 1960), p. 298 (the strategic significance of Cheraw Hill).

15. Greene, *The Life of Nathanael Greene,* p. 131 (Greene letter to Washington, December 28, 1780: "Kosciuszko is employed building flat-bottomed boats to be transported with the army").

16. Greene to Kościuszko, January 1, 1781, Nathanael Green Letter Book, Jan.–Feb., pp. 11–12, Nathanael Greene Papers Library of Congress.

17. Pula, *Thaddeus Kościuszko,* p. 164 ("Kościuszko appeared to be everywhere . . .).

18. Alexander Garden, *Anecdotes of the Revolutionary War in America* (Charleston: A. E. Miller, 1822), p. 60 (the rebels "would hold the bridle of their horse with one hand . . ." with "a piece of bacon stuck on the point of a stick").

19. William Johnson, *Sketches of the Life and Correspondence of Nathanael Greene: Major General of the Armies of the United States, in the War of the Revolution, Compiled Chiefly from Original Materials,* vol. 1 (Charleston: A. E. Miller, 1822), p. 431 (Kosciusko rejoined Greene at Guilford).

20. Boatner, *Encyclopedia of the American Revolution,* p. 461 (Greene considered making a stand at Guilford before he retreated to the Dan River).

21. Johnson, *Sketches of the Life and Correspondence of Nathanael Greene,* p. 431 (Kościuszko threw up breastworks on the Dan River to cover the passage of his army).

22. Greene, *The Life of Nathanael Greene,* p. 174 (Greene letter to Jefferson, "almost fatigued to death").

23. Budka, *Kościuszko Letters,* p. 59 (Greene's orders to Kościuszko, February 16, 1781).

24. Jared Sparks, ed., *Correspondence of the American Revolution: Being Letters of Eminent Men to George Washington, from the Time of His Taking Command of the Army to the End of His Presidency,* vol. 3 (Boston: Little, Brown and Company, 1853), p. 235 (Greene letter to Washington, February 15, 1781).

25. Haiman, *Kosciuszko in the American Revolution,* p. 110 (Kościuszko letter to Greene, February 19, 1781).

26. Ibid., p. 107 (Kościuszko's map of Halifax made for Greene).

27. George W. Greene, *The Life of Nathanael Greene: Major-General in the Army of the Revolution* (Boston: Charles C. Little and James Brown, 1846), p. 204 ("another such victory would ruin the British Army").

28. Jacob Abbott, *Pyrrhus* (New York and London: Harper & Brothers, 1901), p. 156 ("another such victory, and I shall be undone").

29. Howard Henry Peckham, *The War for Independence: A Military History* (Chicago: University of Chicago Press, 1958), p. 136 (the "ugliest man in England").

30. Richard Brandon Morris and Henry Steele Commager, *The Spirit of 'Seventy-six: The Story of the American Revolution As Told by Participants* (Indianapolis: Bobbs-Merrill, 1958), p. 423 ("the fair nymphs of this isle . . .").

31. Dann, *Revolution Remembered,* p. 220 (Greene in the thick of battle).
32. Ibid., p. 221 ("Kościuszko . . .").
33. Sparks, *Correspondence,* p. 299 (Greene: "We fight, get beat, rise . . .").
34. Washington to Lafayette, April 8, 1781, Library of Congress.
35. Kajencki, *Thaddeus Kościuszko,* p. 147 (Kościuszko's men used a rolling shield).
36. Mark M. Boatner III, *Encyclopedia of the American Revolution,* p. 806 (the rebels fired flaming "African Arrows" into the fort).
37. Morris and Commager, *The Spirit of 'Seventy-six,* p. 1183 (Mackenzie reported that Kościuszko was wounded in "the seat of honour").
38. Pula, *Thaddeus Kościuszko,* p. 178; Lynn Montross, *The Story of the Continental Army, 1775–1783* (New York: Barnes & Noble, 1967), p. 441 (". . . neither the pain nor the customary ribald jests kept him from duty").
39. Stanley A. South, *An Archaeological Evolution* (New York: Springer, 2005), p. 249 (the six hundred pounds of powder never arrived from Augusta).
40. Thayer, *Nathanael Greene,* p. 360; Benson John Lossing, *The Pictoral Field-book of the Revolution: Or, Illustrations, by Pen and Pencil, of the History, Biography, Scenery, Relics and Traditions of the War for Independence, Vol. II* (New York: Harper & Brothers, 1860), p. 486 (a rider raced into the gates of Ninety Six). Note: There are two versions of this book.
41. South, *An Archaeological Evolution,* p. 246; Kajencki, *Thaddeus Kościuszko,* p. 152; (Lee took Fort Holmes after British had already abandoned it).
42. Haiman, *Kosciuszko in the American Revolution,* pp. 111–115, (excerpts from the Otho Holland Williams Papers in the Maryland Historical Society, "Notes by My Friend Colo. Kościuszko Relative the Siege of 96," a seven-page manuscript written by Kościuszko in 1783 or 1784).
43. Henry Lee, Jr., *Memoirs of the War in the Southern Department of the United States* (Washington, DC: Peter Force, 1827), p. 252, notes ("his [Kościuszko's] blunders cost us Ninety Six").
44. Haiman, *Kosciuszko in the American Revolution,* p. 117 (Greene's Orderly Book of June 20, 1781, says 96 was "on the eve of surrender" and that Kościuszko's approaches "were judiciously design'd").
45. Ibid., p. 117 (Otho Williams letter).
46. Kościuszko to Gates, July 29, 1781, Gates Papers, New York Public Library.
47. Lee, *Memoirs,* p. 264 (the men ate frogs and alligators).
48. Theodorus Bailey Myers Collection, New York Public Library, Myers document 1294, located on microfilm reel 3. 1781, Kościuszko letter to Dr. Reed ("I cannot live without Coffee").
49. New Jersey Journal, August 1, 1781, "Frank" in Moore, *Diary of the American Revolution: From Newspapers and Original Documents,* p. 461 (Arnold on his possible capture).
50. Gen. Greene to Thomas Burke, August 12, 1781, *North Carolina State Records,* vol. 15 p. 606, reproduced in Budka, *Kościuszko Letters,* pp. 62–65.
51. George Washington Greene, *The Life of Nathanael Greene: Major-General in the Army of the Revolution,* vol. 3 (New York: Hurd and Hougton, 1871), p. 426 (Greene learned that 120,000 of South Carolina's 248,139 people were black).
52. Greene to Rutledge, December 9, 1781, Greene Papers, William Clements Library.
53. Thayer, *Nathanael Greene,* p. 391 (Lewis Morris, "disgrace of human nature").
54. Benjamin Quarles, *The Negro in the American Revolution* (Chapel Hill: University of North Carolina Press, 1961), p. 61 (Henry and John Laurens).
55. Ibid., p. 61 (Henry Laurens letter, August 1775).
56. Thayer, *Nathanael Greene,* p. 391 (John Laurens: "I have long deplored . . .").
57. Ibid., p. 288 ("fine girls").
58. Kościuszko to Williams, March 12, 1782, Otho Holland Williams Papers, Maryland Historical Society ("everybody is in love").

59. Kościuszko to Williams, from March 1782, Otho Holland Williams Papers, Maryland Historical Society (a long letter about the social life of Williams' former brothers in arms).

60. Kościuszko to Greene, undated, in *Memorial Exhibition: Thaddeus Kościuszko, Collection of Letters and Relics of Dr. Alexander Kahanowicz, Exhibited in the Anderson Galleries* (1927), p. 5 (stripping of Laurens possessions was "mean, low thinking . . .").

61. Kościuszko to Greene, September 2, 1782, in Budka, *Kościuszko Letters,* pp. 77–78; Kahanowicz Collection, p. 3 ("two negroes . . . their skin can bear as well as ours good things).

62. Budka, *Kościuszko Letters,* p. 88 (Kościuszko letter to Gates, September 15, 1782) (Petrie informs them where the British are hiding their livestock).

63. Ibid., p. 97 (Kościuszko letter to Gates, September 20, 1782) (Kościuszko warns Greene of the coming attack on Marion and plans his own attack on James Island with the help of a slave named Prince).

64. Thayer, *Nathanael Greene,* p. 408 (Leslie's corps of Negro dragoons went after deserters).

65. William Seymour, *A Journal of the Southern Expedition, 1780–1783: The Pennsylvania Magazine of History and Biography,* vol. 7, (Philadelphia: Historical Society of Pennsylvania, 1883), p. 393 (Negro Horse skirmish).

66. Garden, *Anecdotes,* pp. 91–92 (Kościuszko received intelligence from a slave; in the battle, the Pole's clothes were pierced by gunfire).

67. John Markland, "Revolutionary Services of Captain John Markland," *Pennsylvania Magazine of History and Biography* 9 (1885) 110–111 (Kościuszko leads charge on James Island, last battle of the Revolution).

68. Budka, *Kościuszko Letters,* p. 148 (Kościuszko letter to Gen. Leslie).

69. Ibid., p. 148; W. Dansey replies on November 25, 1782 (mulatto soldier is dead).

70. Kahanowicz Collection, p. 12, and replicated in Budka, *Kościuszko Letters,* p. 143 (letter from Kościuszko to Greene, December 9, 1782).

71. Haiman, *Kosciuszko in the American Revolution,* p. 138 (the celebratory ball).

72. Ebenezer Denny, *A Military Journal Kept by Major E. Denny, 1781 to 1795: Memoirs of the Historical Society of Pennsylvania* (Philadelphia: J. B. Lippincott & Co., 1860), pp. 255–256 (life on James Island, party and fireworks).

73. Haiman, *Kosciuszko in the American Revolution,* p. 141 (fireworks on April 23).

74. Kościuszko to O. H. Williams, February 11, 1783, Otho Holland Williams Papers, Maryland Historical Society.

75. George Washington Greene, *The Life of Nathanael Greene: Major-General in the Army of the Revolution,* vol. 1 (Boston and New York: Houghton Mifflin and Company, 1890), p. 409 (letter from Greene to Congress, May 28, 1777).

76. John Armstrong to Jared Sparks, Red Hook, New York, Sparks Manuscripts, ser. 49, vol. 1, p. 72, Houghton Library, Harvard College (Greene letter to Irvine about Kościuszko).

EIGHT: *Love and Rockets*

1. James Schouler, *History of the United States of America, Under the Constitution, Vol. I, 1783–1801* (New York: Dodd, Mead & Company, 1880), p. 22 (mutiny).

2. St. Clair Papers, p. 115 (Howe sent to quash mutiny).

3. Kościuszko to Williams, July 2, 1783, Otho Holland Williams Papers, Maryland Historical Society.

4. Budka, *Kościuszko Letters,* pp. 161–162 (Kościuszko letter to Williams, August 15, 1783 "I would marry her, and beg parents pardon").

5. Haiman, *Kosciuszko in the American Revolution,* p. 151, (Jackson letter quoted).

6. Greene letter to Boudinot, July 10, 1783, in *The Magazine of History with Notes and Queries,* vol. 6: July (New York: William Abbatt, 1907), p. 363.

7. Ibid., p. 363 (Washington's handwriting: "in favor of Kościuszko").

8. Haiman Kosciuszko in the American Revolution, p. 154 (Lincoln letter).

9. Pula, Thaddeus Kościuszko, p. 205 (Washington, Greene, and Kościuszko dined with Boudinot).

10. Washington to Congress, October 2, 1783, Washington Papers, Library of Congress; The Magazine of History, p. 363 ("it is a historical fact that almost the last of Washington's official acts was to intercede with Congress in favor of Kościuszko").

11. Washington to Kościuszko, October 3, 1783, Washington Papers, Library of Congress.

12. Journals of the American Congress from 1774–1788; vol. 4 (Washington, DC: Way and Gideon, 1823), p. 292 (Kościuszko's promotion by brevet).

13. Ibid., (Kościuszko's "meritorious services").

14. Thacher, A Military Journal, p. 340.

15. Pula, Thaddeus Kościuszko, p. 205 (Morris cites 1781 law but acknowledges "Kościuszko's merit").

16. Budka, Kościuszko Letters, p. 160 (receipt of Kościuszko's pay for March 31, 1783).

17. Russell, Haym Salomon, p. 246 (Salomon was feeding some of the hungry delegates; Salomon lent Kościuszko $142).

18. Budka, Kościuszko Letters, p. 150. (Kościuszko letter to Greene, June 18, 1783).

19. American State Papers, March 4, 1789–March 3, 1823, Legislative and Executive of the United States, (Washington, DC: Gales and Seaton, 1834), p. 207 (Kosciuszko's salary for serving in the American Revolution).

20. Haiman, Kosciuszko in the American Revolution, p. 158, note 29 (Washington's gifts to Kościuszko).

21. David Ramsay, The Life of George Washington: Commander in Chief of the Armies of the United States of America (New York: Hopkins & Seymour, 1807), p. 197 (Fraunces Tavern speech).

22. The Magazine of American History with Notes and Queries, by Martha Joanna Lamb, Nathan Gillett Pond, 1832, John Austin Stevens 1880, (New York and Chicago; A. S. Barnes & Company), p. 158; de Giradot, Cadre Americain de Cincinnatus en France, by 1860; Pula, Thaddeus Kościuszko, p 208. (the cameo ring).

23. Budka Kościuszko Letters, pp. 167–174, (Williams letter to Greene, January 14, 1784).

24. Haiman, Kosciuszko in the American Revolution pp. 155–56 (Wegerski).

25. Anne D'Estko to Benjamin Franklin, December 19, 1783, Papers of Benjamin Franklin, Yale University Library.

26. Count de Murinais to Franklin, February 25, 1784, Papers of Benjamin Franklin, Yale University Library.

27. Jakob Gordon, Przechadzki po Ameryce, [A Stroll Through America] (Berlin and Poznań: Ksiegarnia B. Behr'a, 1866), pp. 79–86 (Ludwika's letter).

28. Kościuszko to Major Evan Edwards, July 4, 1784, Archives of the Polish Museum in Rapperswil, Switzerland.

29. Budka, Kościuszko Letters, pp. 177–180 (Kosciusko letter to Greene, July 14, 1784).

30. Frank Landon Humphreys, Life and Times of David Humphreys: Soldier—Statesman—Poet, Beloved of Washington, (New York: G. P. Putnam's Sons, 1917), p. 307 (Kościuszko on Courrier de l'Europe).

31. Ibid., p. 314 (carriage ride to Paris).

32. January 20, 1786, Greene Papers, Huntington Library, HM 8056; Haiman, Kosciuszko in the American Revolution, p. 113 (Kościuszko letter to Greene about prejudice).

NINE: *Fiddling Lords and Enslaved Hordes*

1. Waleryn Kalinka, *Ostanie lata panowania Stanisława Augusta, [The final years of Stanislaw August's rule]* (Kraków: Nakładem Księgarni Spółki Wydawniczej Poskiej, 1891), pp. 267–270; J. I. Kraszewski, *Polska w czasie Trzech Rozbiorów, 1772–1799 [Poland in the time of the Three Partitions]* (Warsaw: Gebethnera I Wolffa, 1902), pp. 322–326; R. Nisbet Bain, *The Last King of Poland and His Contemporaries* (London: Methuen, 1909), pp. 135–137; Zamoyski, *The Last King of Poland*, pp. 284–286 (details of the Dogrumova affair).

2. *"Weteran Poznański"* (Poznań: W. Decker i Spółka, 1825), p. 175; Szyndler, *Kościuszko 1746–1817*, p. 103 (Kościuszko's audience with the king).

3. Bain, *The Last King of Poland*, p. 253 ("methinks this inscription savors somewhat of fanaticism").

4. *Memoirs of the Duc de Lauzun (Armand Louis de Gontaut, Duc de Biron)*, translated by E. Jules Meras (New York: Sturgis & Walton, 1912), p. 95 (the duke's physical description of Izabela).

5. W. H. Zawadzki, *A Man of Honour: Adam Czartoryski as a Statesman of Russia and Poland, 1795–1831* (Oxford: Clarendon Press, 1993), p. 18, notes (the lineage of Izabela's children).

6. Kraszewski, *Polska w czasie Trzech Rozbiorów*, pp. 324–325 (the events of the night of January 16, 1785).

7. Zamoyski, *The Last King of Poland*, p. 286.

8. "Pamiętnik Jerzego Soroki [*The memoirs of Jerzy Soroka*], *1772–1822,*" *Tygodnik Ilustrowany [Illustrated Weekly]*, no. 2 (1881), 212 (description of Kościuszko's homestead; Soroka was Prince Czartoryski's stable master).

9. Norman Davies, *God's Playground: A History of Poland*, vol. 1, (New York: Columbia University Press, 1982), p. 243 (a dungeon, together with chains, shackles, stocks, hooks, and instruments of torture, was part of the regular inventory).

10. Korzon, *Kościuszko*, p. 196 (Kościuszko on serfdom in a letter to Zaleski).

11. Miecislaus Haiman, *Kościuszko, Leader and Exile* (New York: Kościuszko Foundation, 1977 first published in 1946 by the Polish Institute of Arts and Sciences), p. 3; Nathanael Greene Papers, 1775–1786, Huntington Library (Kosciusko letter to Greene).

12. Lucyan Siemieński, ed., *Listy Kościuszki do jenarala Mokrońskiego i innych osób pisane [Kościuszko's letters to General Mokroński and others]* (Lwów: Gubrynowicz i Schmidt, 1877), p. 43; Korzon, *Kościuszko*, p. 195 (Kościuszko to Zaleski).

13. Siemieński, *Listy Kościuszki*; Korzon, *Kościuszko*, p. 195 (continuation of Kościuszko letter to Zaleski).

14. *Anonima listów kilka [Letters by an anonym]*, later revealed to be written by Hugo Kołłątaj, translation from Krystyna M. Olszer ed., *For Your Freedom and Ours: Polish Progressive Spirit, from the 14th Century to the Present* (New York: Frederick Ungar Publishing Co., 1981), pp. 44–46. Author's note: I transcribe "Kołłątaj" as "Kollontay," as some British historians have done, to make it easier for English readers.

15. Wojciech Mączyński, (Jozef Mączyński, ed.), "Kościuszkowskie Czasy, wypisane z księgi wspomnień Wojciecha Mączyńskiego, Pułkownika Komendanta Milicji Rzeczpospolitej Krakowskiej [Kosciuszko's times, taken from the diaries of Wojciech Maczynski, colonel commandant of the republic's militia in Krakow], "Czas": Dodatek miesieczny, Tom. VII, Lipiec, Sierpień, Wrzesień, Kraków: Czas, 1857 in *Time* (July, August, September); 432 (Kollontay offers Kosciuszko lecturer's post at Jagiellonian University).

16. Korzon, *Kościuszko*, p. 196 (Kościuszko letter to Zaleski).

17. Ibid.

18. Hugo Kołłątaj, *Listy Anonima, i Prawo polityczne narodu polskiego*, (Anonymous letters and Political Law of the Polish Nation), ed. Bogusław Leśnodorski i Helena Wereszycka, (Warsaw: Państwowe Wydawn. Naukowe, 1954) (Kollontay quote).

19. Thomas Jefferson to John Adams, November 13, 1787, Library of Congress.

20. Evgeny Dobrenko, *Political Economy of Socialist Realism,* translated by Jesse M. Savage (New Haven: Yale University Press, 2007), p. 46. (While some historians cast doubt on the existence of Potemkin villages, Dobrenko has found that Potemkin did use theatrical sets for his "villages.")

21. Zamoyski, *The Last King of Poland,* pp. 292–298 (Poniatowski visits Catherine on Dnieper).

22. Davies, *God's Playground,* p. 22 (Catherine denied Poniatowski's request to expand his military).

23. Ibid., p. 529 ("whilst the Russian cat was away . . .").

24. Robert Howard Lord, *The Second Partition of Poland: A Study in Diplomatic History* (Cambridge: Harvard University Press, 1915), p. 22, originally from *Histoire philosophique et politique des Etablissmens des Europiens dans les Indes,* vol. 10, p. 52 (Raynal quote).

25. Antoni Jan Ostrowski, *Żywot Tomasza Ostrowskiego, ministra rzeczypospolitej, [The life of Thomas Ostrowski, minister of the republic]* (Lwów: U. F. H. Richter, 1873), p. 73 (the Sejm was called under rules of confederation, so the liberum veto did not apply).

26. Jan Suchorzewski's speech in the Seym, October 16, 1788. Dyaryusz seymu ordynaryinego pod związkiem konfederacyi Generalney oboyga narodów w Warszawie rozpoczętego roku pańskiego 1788. Tom I. Część I. w Warszawie w Drukarni Nadworney JKMci i P. Komissyi Eduk: Narodowey (Diary of the Seym for 1788).

27. Julian Ursyn Niemcewicz, *Pamiętniki czasów moich, [Memoirs of my times],* vol. 1 (Warsaw: Panstwowy Insytut Wydawniczy, 1957), p. 287 (Lucchesini had "one large black eye, the other having been lost in a chemistry experiment).

28. Kalinka, *Sejm Czteroletni,* vol. I [*Four-Year Sejm*], p. 154 (Lucchesini's initial meeting with King Frederick).

29. Julian Ursyn Niemcewicz, *Pamiętniki czasow moich,* vol. 54 (Lipsk: F. A. Brockhaus, 1868), p. 102 (Lucchesini's wife told Niemcewicz that her husband disguised himself as a jeweler to hand out bribes in the Vatican).

30. Kalinka, *Ostatnie lata panowania,* p. 430 (letter from Lucchesini to Frederick William).

31. Ibid., p. 430 (letter from De Cache, Austrian charge d'affaires in Warsaw).

32. Zamoyski, *The Last King of Poland,* pp. 310–314 (the political stunts, i.e., ribbons, balloons, and maneuvering, during the first months of the Great Seym).

33. Korzon, *Kościuszko,* p. 199; Glos Sapiehy w Dyaryuszu, 1788 urzedowym, I., str. 303 (Brest Sejmik requests military commission for Kościuszko).

34. Korzon, *Kościuszko,* p. 200 (Princess Lubomirska's letter to the king about Kościuszko).

35. Budka, *Kościuszko Letters,* p. 185 (Kościuszko letter to Haskell, May 15, 1789, "rain falls heavy from my eyes . . .").

36. Ibid., p. 190 (Kościuszko letter to Haskell, August 10, 1789).

37. John Paul Jones, *John Paul Jones' Memoir of the American Revolution Presented to King Louis XVI of France,* translated by Gerard W. Gawalt (Honolulu, HI: University Press of the Pacific, 1979), p. 35. (The memoir provides a detailed explanation of the legendary words uttered by Jones. What Jones actually said was condensed into this sound bite by historians.)

38. Lincoln Lorenz, *The Admiral and the Empress: John Paul Jones and Catherine the Great* (New York: Bookman Associates, 1954), p. 21 (Russian minister contacts Jefferson hiring John Paul Jones).

39. Cyrus Townsend Brady, *Commodore Paul Jones* (New York: D. Appleton and Company, 1900), p. 380; Samuel Eliot Morison, *John Paul Jones: A Sailor's Biography* (Boston: Little, Brown and Company, 1959), p. 392 (Paul Jones' naval battles against Turks).

40. Mrs. Reginald (Anna) De Koven, *The Life and Letters of John Paul Jones,* vol. 2 (New York: Charles Scribner's Sons, 1913), pp. 344–345 (letter from Potemkin to Catherine, October 1788, "the sleepy Admiral Paul Jones . . .").

41. John T. Alexander, *Catherine the Great, Life and Legend* (New York: Oxford University Press, 1989), p. 269 (Jones charged with rape).

42. Korzon, *Biografia,* pp. 611–612, footnotes (letter from Princess Ludwika to Kościuszko, May 21, 1789).

43. Jan Dihm, *Kościuszko nieznany [The unknown Kościuszko]* (Wrocław: Ossolineum, 1969), p. 375, quoting from J. U. Niemcewicz, "Notice sure le General Kościuszko," *Le Polonais Journal de interets de la Polonge,* vol. 3 (Paris: 1854) (the chance meeting between Kościuszko and Louise; this story is relayed by Niemcewicz, Kościuszko's inseparable traveling companion in his travels through Russia, Sweden, England, and the United States).

44. De Koven, *The Life and Letters of John Paul Jones,* p. 370 (letter from Jones to Chevalier Bourgoing).

45. Augustus C. Buell, *Paul Jones: Founder of the American Navy, a History* (New York: Charles Scribner's Sons, 1906), p. 247 (an intimate friendship developed between Kościuszko and Jones).

46. Ibid., p. 247 (Potemkin sent spies to Poland to follow Jones).

47. John Paul Jones, *Memoirs of Paul Jones: Late Rear-Admiral in the Russian Service,* vol. 2 (London: Henry Washbourne, 1843), p. 197 (John Paul Jones letter to Kościuszko, November 2, 1789).

48. Kościuszko letter to Jones, February 15, 1790, in *Edinburgh Magazine, and Literary Miscellany; A New Series of the Scots Magazine, Vol. I., August–December, 1817* (Edinburgh: George Ramsay and Co., 1817), p. 20 (fight against oppression and tyranny).

TEN: *Europe's First Constitution and the Polish Revolution*

1. Tadeusz Korzon, *Wewnetrze dzieje Polski, za Stanisław Augusta [A domestic history of Poland under Stanislaw Augustus],* vol. 2 (Kraków: L. Zwoliński, 1897), pp. 379–382 (the United Cities Act and Black March of the Burghers).

2. Ks. Waleryan Kalinka, *Sejm czteroletni [The four-year Seym]* vol. 1 (Lwów: Ksiegarnia Seyfartha i Czajkowskiego, 1884, reprint, 1991), p. 449 (the Burgher march was called "impertinent").

3. Ibid., p. 452 (letter from Lucchesini to Frederik William).

4. Ibid., p. 452 (letter from Frederik William to Lucchesini).

5. Kołłątaj to Kościuszko, July 18, 1793, in Lucyan Siemieński, *Listy Hugona Kołłątaja, pisane z emigracyi, 1792, 1793, 1794 [The letters of Hugo Kołłątaj, Written in Exile, 1792, 1793, 1794],* vol. 2 (Poznań: Jan Kostanty Żupański, 1872), pp. 84–85 ("my own heart and way of thinking").

6. Hugo Kołłątaj, *Prawo polityczne narodu polskiego [Political law of the Polish nation],* 1790, translation from Olszer, *For Your Freedom and Ours,* pp. 47–48.

7. *Korespondencja i papiery Tadeusza Kościuszko [The correspondence and papers of Thaddeus Kościuszko],* PAN, 1171, Bibilioteka Naukowa, PAN w Krakówie, microfilm *rkps* 1171, k. 3. (This essay in Kościuszko's handwriting about raising a militia is simply dated 1789.)

8. Tadeusz Korzon, *Wewnętrzne dzieje Polski, za Stanisława Augusta [A domestic history of Poland under Stanislaw Augustus],* vol. 1 (Kraków: L. Zwoliński, 1897), p. 320 (chart of Poland's population in 1791).

9. *Korespondencja i papiery Tadeusza Kościuszko [The correspondence and papers of Thaddeus Kościuszko],* PAN, 1171 (the Jews and peasant class will each "be fighting for its own property, legal rights and happiness").

10. Kalinka, *Seym,* p. 440 (ten thousand serfs fled to Prussia).

11. Jacek Jędruch, *Constitutions, Elections and Legislatures of Poland 1493–1993* (New York: Hippocrene Books, 1998), p. 141 (a state within a state).

12. Simon M. Dubnow, *History of the Jews in Russia and Poland: From the Earliest Times Until the Present Day [1915]* (Philadelphia: Jewish Publication Society of America, 1918), pp. 46–47 (Kahals and Jewish self-government).

13. Abraham Leon Sachar, *A History of the Jews* (New York: Alfred Knopf, 1930), p. 223; Gunnar S. Paulsson, *Secret City: The Hidden Jews of Warsaw, 1940–1945* (New Haven: Yale University Press, 2002), p. 37 (Polish Jews called their country Canaan, the Promised Land).

14. Arthur Szyk, *Statut Kaliski [Jus Polonicum—jura judaeis] By Boleslav, Prince of Poland* (Paris: Éditions de la Table ronde, 1932) (the Statute of Kalisz).

15. Sachar, *History of the Jews,* p. 225 (Magna Carta of Jewish self -government).

16. Dubnow, *History of the Jews,* p. 128 (quote on Jewish commerce).

17. Ibid., p. 128 (quote on taverns).

18. Orest Subtelny, *Ukraine: A History,* 3d ed. (Toronto: University of Toronto Press, 2000), pp. 124–128; Adam Zamoyski, *The Polish Way* (New York: Hippocrene Books, 1987), pp. 166–167; Gershon David Hundert, *Jews in Poland-Lithuania in the Eighteenth Century: A Genealogy of Modernity* (Berkeley: University of California Press, 2006) p. 15; Maria Kowalska, ed., *Ukraina w polowie XVII wieku w relacji arabskiego podroznika Pawla, syna Makarego z Aleppo* (Warsaw, 1986), p. 19; Dubnow, *History of the Jews,* pp. 69–71 (Bohdan Khmelnytsky's massacre in the Ukraine).

19. Leo Rostein, *The Joys of Yiddish* (New York: Pocket Books, 1970), pp. 373–375. (Rostein describes shtetls as "Ashkenazi incubators . . . medieval in texture.")

20. Glenn Dynner, *Men of Silk: The Hasidic Conquest of Polish Jewish Society* (New York: Oxford University Press, 2006 (description of Hasidism).

21. Bernard Dov Weinryb, *The Jews of Poland* (Philadelphia: Jewish Publication Society of America, 1973), p. 175 (Solomon Maimon quote).

22. Davies, *God's Playground,* p. 241 (Jews expelled from Prussia and Austria deeper into Poland); Dubnow, *History of the Jews,* p. 137 (Austria and Prussia limited Jewish marriages).

23. Dubnow, *History of the Jews,* p. 125 (Czarina Elizabeth calls Jews "the enemies of Christ").

24. Andrzej Zahorski, *Warszawa w postaniu Kościuszkowskim [Warsaw in the Kosciuszko uprising]* (Warsaw: Wiedza Powszechna, 1985), p. 197 (in the eighteenth century, Jews paid a tax to spend the night in Warsaw).

25. Mateusz Topory Butrymowicz, *Sposób uformowania Żydów Polskich w pożytecznych krajowi obywatelów [A way to constitute Polish Jews as useful citizens of the nation]* (Warsawa: W Drukarni Wolney, 1789); Władysław Smoleński, *Stan i sprawa Żydów Polskich w XVIII wieku [The state and issues of Polish Jews in the eighteenth century]* (Warsaw: Nadkladem Ksiegarnia Celsa Lewickiego i Spółki, 1876) (Butrymowicz on Polish-Jewish relations).

26. Hundert, *Jews in Poland-Lithuania,* p. 223 (Butrymowicz quote on Jews).

27. Jacob Goldberg, "The Changes in the Attitude of Polish Society toward the Jews in the 18th Century," *Polin, a Journal of Polish-Jewish Studies* vol. 1 (1986): 42 (Pawlikowski quote).

28. Jędrzej Kitowicz and Władysław Zawadzki, *Pamiętniki Ks. A. Kitowicza, [The memoirs of Rev. Kitowicz],* vol. 3 (Lwów: Gubrynowicz and Schmit, 1882), pp. 82–83 (more than ten thousand Jews set up shop along Senator Street in Warsaw).

29. Ibid., p. 84 (burghers marched on city hall).

30. Ibid., p. 85; Hilary Nussbaum, *Historyja Żydów od Mojżesza do epoki obecnej, [The history of Jews from Moses to the Current Epoch], vol. 5.* (Warsaw: I. Mayzner, 1890), p. 361 (the riot caused by Fox).

31. Kołłątaj, *Political Law of the Polish Nation.*

32. Nussbaum, *Historyja Żydów,* p. 335 (Commission on Jewish Rights).

33. Smoleński, *State and Issues of Polish Jews,* p. 73 (Jezierski's statement in the Seym, December 30, 1791).

34. Nancy Sinkoff, *Out of the Shtetl: Making Jews Modern in the Polish Borderlands* (Providence, RI: Brown Judaic Studies, 2004), p. 75 (the opinions on reforms of Jewish leaders ranged from calls for full integration into Polish society to a rejection of any change of the status quo of Jewish life whatsoever).

35. Lord, *The Second Partition of Poland,* p. 391 (the first partition cost Poland 29 percent of its land, 36 percent of its population).

36. William S. Walsh, *Handy-Book of Literary Curiosities* (Philadelphia: J. B. Lippincott Company, 1893), p. 790 (German saying about Poland).

37. Stanisław to Philip Mazzei, Warsaw, March 17, 1790, in Margherita Marchione, ed., *Philip Mazzei: Selected Writings and Correspondence, Agent for the King of Poland During the French Revolution,* vol. 2 (Italy: Cassa di Risparmi e Depositi di Prato, 1983), p. 297 (Lucchesini's threat).

38. Korzon, *Kosciuszko,* p. 207 (letter from Kościuszko to his sister Anna).

39. Szymon Askenazy, *Książe Józef Poniatowski, [Prince Józef Poniatowski, 1763–1813]* (Warsaw: Gebehner i Wolf, 1905), p. 22 (Prince Józef made Kościuszko his deputy).

40. Edward Raczyński, *Obraz Polaków i Polski w XVII Wieku, zbiór pamiętników, dyaryuszów, korespondencyj publicznych i listów prywatnych, podroży i opisów zdarzeń sczegółowych, służących do wyjaśnienia stanu Polski w wierku wspomionym, wydany z rękopisów [A picture of Poles and Poland in the eighteenth century: A collection of memoirs, diaries, public correspondence and private letters, travelogues and descriptions of specific events, serving to elucidate the Polish state, from handwritten manuscripts]* (Poznań: Ksiegarnia Nowej, 1842). (This includes "Kościuszko's manuscript" outlining the 1792 campaign; on p. 108 is the quote "The American Revolution serves as an example.")

41. Siemieński, *Listy,* p. 163 (letter from Orlowski to Kościuszko).

42. Józef Chwalibóg, Prosper Chwalibóg, and Tadeusz Kościuszko, *Pisma Józefa Chwaliboga, listy Jenerala Kościuszki do Tekli Zurowskiej, pisane w roku 1791 w Miedzybozu [Writings of Joseph Chwalibóg, letters of General Kościuszko to Tekla Zurowska, written in 1791 from Miedzyboza,]* (Lwów: Tłoczono w Drukarni Stauropigiańskiej, 1849), pp. 416 (Kościuszko's letters to Tekla).

43. Ibid., pp. 414–415 (Kościuszko letter to Tekla asking for a pearl).

44. Ibid., p. 418, (Kościuszko letter to Tekla, "my sprinkled tears").

45. Korzon, *Kosciuszko,* p. 615, footnote 417 (letter from Kościuszko to Poniatowski asking for a leasehold).

46. *Letters to Tekla,* p. 430 (Kościuszko to Zurowski, "My God! . . .").

47. Ibid., p. 432 (Kościuszko to Tekla's mother).

48. Korzon, *Kosciuszko,* p. 218 (Kościuszko would rather "be brave in battle . . .").

49. Stanisław Macheta, *Hugo Kołłątaj* (Warsaw: Wiedza Powszechna, 1973), p. 29 (choice between a "noble revolution, or a mob, rabble revolution").

50. Zygmunt Gloger, *Ksiega rzeczy Polskich [Book of Polish Works]* (Lwów: Nakładem Macierzy Polskiej, 1896), p. 393 (number of legislators doubled).

51. Korzon, *Kosciuszko,* p. 223 (Kościuszko to Zaleski, "you demand tolerance . . .").

52. Filippo Mazzei, *Memoirs of the Life and Peregrinations of the Florentine Philip Mazzei 1730–1816,* translated by Howard Rosario Marraro (New York: Columbia University Press, 1942), p. 302 ("Jefferson assured me to the contrary . . .").

53. Adam Jerzy Czartoryski, *Żywot J.U. Niemcewicza [The life of J.U. Niemcewicz]* (Berlin: Ksiegarnia B. Behra, 1860), Annex, pp. 270–272 (Niemcewicz's speech before the Sejm on April 2, 1791).

54. Zamoyski, *The Last King of Poland,* p. 336; Boguslaw Lesnodorski, *Dzieło Sejmu Czteroletniego [History of the four-year Seym], 1781–1792* (Wrocław: Ossolineum, 1951), p. 130 (Ignacy Potocki: "Birth can produce a nobleman, but only property turns him into a citizen").

55. Letter from Piattoli to Mazzei, Warsaw, May 4, 1791, in *Philip Mazzei,* p. 539 ("the glory above all of the Polish youth").

56. Niemcewicz, *Pamietniki,* p. 330 (some legislators "never left the table without winning 200 or 300 red zloties").

57. Hugo Kołłątaj, *Wybór pism politycznych, [Chosen political writings]*, edited by Boguslaw Lesnodorski (Wrocław: Zadkaw Norodywy Imienia Ossolińskich, 1952), pp. 195–204 (Kołłątaj's eyewitness version of May 2 and 3, 1791).

58. Leon Wegner, *Dzieje dnia trzeciego i piątego maja 1791 [History of the days of May 3 and 5, 1791]* (Poznań: Nakładem Towarzystwa Przyaciol Nauk Poznańskiego, 1865), p. 121; Kazimierz Bartoszewicz, *Konstytucja 3 Maja, Kronika dni kwietniowych i majowych w Warszawie w r. 1791 [The May 3 constitution, a chronicle of the days of April and May in Warsaw in 1791]* (Warsaw: A. T. Jerzierski, 1906), pp. 46–47 (Prince Poniatowski's cavalry, army, and cannons circle the castle).

59. Stanisław Małachowski, *Pamiętniki Stanisława hr. Nałęcz Małachowskiego [Memoirs of Stanisław Malachowski]*, edited by Wincenty Łoś (Poznań: J. K. Żupański, 1885), pp. 72–73 (description of the chamber on May 3, 1791).

60. *New Constitution of the Government of Poland, Established by the Revolution, the Third of May, 1791* (London: J. Debrett, 1791), p. 11 (quote from the constitution, article 4).

61. Jędruch, *Constitutions, Elections and Legislatures of Poland 1493–1993*, p. 175 (analysis of the new rights for burghers).

62. *Constitution*, p. 97, section 2 (Neminem Captivabimus).

63. Ibid., pp. 9–11, article 4 ("This agricultural class of people . . .").

64. Hundert, *Jews in Poland-Lithuania*, p. 230. Professor Gershon David Hundert, professor of Jewish studies and history at McGill University, wrote that the Seym did not fully integrate Jews into middle-class society because of "the combination of the conservatism of most of the Jewish representatives, the opposition of the burgher plenipotentiaries and the refusal of the aristocrats to countenance any diminution of their authority over their own holdings."

65. *Constitution*, pp. 5–6, article 1 (religious freedom).

66. Zamoyski, *The Last King of Poland*, p. 338; Lesnodorski, *Dzielo Sejmu*, p. 66 (Malachowski quote).

67. Kołłątaj, *Wybór pism politycznych*, p. 204 (King Stanisław quote).

68. Piattoli to Mazzei, Warsaw, May 4, 1791, in *Philip Mazzei*, p. 543 (quoting Stanisław: "I lost my hat").

69. Washington to David Humphreys, July 20, 1791, Washington Papers, Library of Congress.

70. Edmund Burke, ed., *The Annual Register: A Review of Public Events at Home and Abroad* (London: Rivingtons, 1878), p. 53 ("a glory to humanity").

71. Edmund Burke, *The Works of the Right Honorable Edmund Burke*, vol. 6 (London: F. C. and J. Rivington, 1815), p. 246 (comparison of the French and Polish revolutions).

72. *Times* (London), May 20, 1791, quoted in Samuel Fiszman, *Constitution and Reform in Eighteenth Century Poland, the Constitution of 3 May 1791* (Bloomington: Indiana University Press, 1997), p. 475.

73. Horace Walpole, *The Letters of Horace Walpole: Fourth Earl of Orford*, edited by Peter Cunningham (Edinburgh: John Grant, 1906), p. 324, also quoted in Zamoyski, *The Last King of Poland*, p. 346 (Poland ought to make the French blush).

74. *Gazette de Leyde*, May 10, 1791, Indiana University. Lilly Library.

75. Ibid.

76. *Dunlap's American Daily Advertiser*, August 23, 1791, Library of Congress; Miecislaus Haiman, *The Fall of Poland in Contemporary American Opinion* (Chicago: Polish Roman Catholic Union of America, 1935), p. 53.

77. *Korespondencja i papiery Tadeusza Kościuszko [The correspondence and papers of Thaddeus Kościuszko]*, PAN, (letter and poem from David Humphreys, October 1, 1791).

78. Zamoyski, *The Last King of Poland*, p. 351 (Jefferson sent Stanisław a copy of *Notes on Virginia*).

79. Humphreys letter continued.

80. Askenazy, *Książe Józef Poniatowski,* p. 23 (four Russian officers in civilian clothes watched the Polish army maneuvers).

81. Siemieński, *Żywot Tadeusza Kosciuzki,* p. 103 (copies of the maps Kościuszko sent to Warsaw were made for the Russians).

82. Jerzy Łojek, ed., *Rok nadziei i rok kleski, 1791–1792; z korespondencji Stanisława Augusta z poslem polskim w Peterburgu Augustynem Deboli [The year of hope and defeat, 1791–1792; correspondence between Stanislaw August and the Polish representative in Petersburg, August Deboli]* (Warsaw: Czytelnik, 1964 (letter from Stanisław to Deboli, November 18, 1791).

83. Smoleński, *Ostatni rok Sejmu Wielkiego,* p. 270 (Kościuszko letter to Prince Józef).

84. Kitowicz, and Zawadzki, *Pamiętniki,* pp. 136–137 (description of the May 3 parade).

85. Artur Eisenbach, Jerzy Michalski, Emanuel Rostworowski, and Janusz Woliński, ed., *Materiały do dziejów Sejmu czteroletniego [Materials pertaining to the history of the four-year Seym],* vol. 6 (Wrocław: Instytut Historii Polskiej Akademii Nauk, 1969), pp. 480–483 (the Hebrew Hymn to celebrate the first anniversary of the May 3 constitution).

86. Friedrich Schultz, *Podroze inflantczyka z Rygi do Warszawy i po Polsce w latach 1791–1793 (Travels of a Livonian from Riga to Warsaw and through Poland in the years 1791–1793)* (Warsaw: Czytelnik, 1956), p. 176 ("hordes of the king's officers could be seen in the windows of bordellos").

87. Katarzyna Jedynakiewicz (*Osobowość i życie codzienne Tadeusza Kościuszko,* p. 97) quotes Seweryn Bukar, *Pamiętniki z końca XVIII i początków wieku XIX [Memoirs of the late eighteenth and early nineteenth centuries]* (Dresden: J. I. Kraszweski, 1871), p. 80 ("a flock of ladies to dance with").

88. Ibid., p. 80 (Col. Szyrer's wife "entertained" Kościuszko "pretty vigorously").

89. Donata Ciepieńko-Zielińska, *Królewięta na Tulczynie [Kings of Tulczn]* (Warsaw: Ksiażka i Wiedza, 1962), pp. 51, 110, and 117 (Sophia the Greek).

90. Jerzy Łojek, *Dzieje pięknej Bitynki [History of the beautiful Bitynka]* (Warsaw: Pax, 1970), p. 87–88 (Stanisław paid Witt's rent so that he could have sex with his wife).

91. Jedynakiewicz, *Osobowość i życie codzienne Tadeusza Kościuszko,* p. 79, quoting Bukar, *Pamiętniki* (Kościuszko "popped in for a little relaxation").

92. Siemieński, *Żywot,* p. 103, quoting Bukar, *Pamiętniki* (Kościuszko writing the note in his book).

93. Lord, *The Second Partition of Poland,* p. 527 (original letter in French); translated by Oscar Halecki in *The Third of May, Kościuszko, and Polish Democracy,* bulletin of the Polish Institute of Arts and Sciences in America, July 1944, pp. 925–926 (letter from Felix Potocki to Potemkin, May 14, 1791).

ELEVEN: *The "Noble" Traitors*

1. Jerzy Łojek, *Misja Debolego w Petersburgu, w latach 1787–1792 [The mission of Deboli to Petersburg in the years 1787–1792],* (Wrocław: Ossolineum, 1962), p. 137, footnote 55; also in Łojek, *The Year of Hope and Defeat,* p. 115 (letter from Deboli to Stanisław, March 5, 1792, quoting Catherine; "This will lure most of the peasants of Byelorussia to Poland . . .").

2. Korzon, *Kosciuszko,* 224 (Kościuszko, "The Muscovite regiments . . .").

3. Niemcewicz, *Pamiętniki czasów moich,* vol. 2, p. 16 (Lucchesini and Bulhalkov seen visiting each other).

4. Korzon, *Kosciuszko,* p. 227 (Kościuszko's letters to Prince Joseph).

5. Adam Wolański, *Wojna Polsko-Rosyjska 1792 R [The Polish Russian war of 1792]* (Kraków: E. E. Freidlein, 1906), p. 34 (Russian forces).

6. Kraszewski, *Polska w czasie Trzech Rozbiorów, 1772–1799*, pp. 202–203 (Lubomirski put in charge of ammunition reserves).
7. Korzon, *Kosciuszko*, p. 234 (Stanisław cancels trip due to lack of "decent cuisine").
8. Raczyński, *Kościuszko Manuscript*, p. 103 (Kościuszko's troops lacked bread).
9. Korzon, *Kosciuszko*, p. 231 (Kościuszko laments the failure to capture eight thousand of Russia's best soldiers).
10. Piotr Bańkowski, ed., *Tadeusza Kościuszki, Dwie Relacje o Kampanii Polsko-Rosyjskiej 1792 Roku [Thaddeus Kosciuszko, two dispatches about the Polish-Russian campaign of 1792]* (Warsaw: Panstwowe Wydawnictwo Naukowe, 1964), p. 55. (This is Kościuszko's daily "Journal" of the war of the campaign of 1792, herein marked "Journal." On July 4, the prince gave out tobacco.)
11. Ibid., p. 57 (Kościuszko mentions the *karczma* and the brewery).
12. Franciszek Paszkowski, *Książe Józef Poniatowski [Prince Joseph Poniatowski]* (Kraków: Spółka Wydawnicza Polska, 1898), p. 34 (Prince Joseph: "Every step backwards my heart is breaking and God knows I'm not hallucinating").
13. Bańkowski, *Tadeusza Kościuszki Journal*, p. 54 (Lubomirski ordered the arsenal sent to his palace so "the Muscovites won't take it").
14. Kraszewski, *Polska w czasie Trzech Rozbiorów*, p. 203; Kalinka, *Ostatnie lata panowania Stanisława Augusta*, p. 229 (Lubomirski hides the ammo for the Russians).
15. Raczyński, *Kościuszko Manuscript*, p. 103, Bańkowski, *Tadeusza Kosciuszki*, pp. 78–79 (quotes from Kościuszko's manuscript about the plundered supplies).
16. Letter from King Stanisław to Francis Bukaty, July 14, 1792, in Kalinka, *Ostanie lata panowania Stanisława Augusta*, vol. 2, p. 228, ("our excellent Kościuszko").
17. Kraszewski, *Polska w czasie Trzech Rozbiorów*, p. 188 (quote from an eyewitness in *The National Gazette* about Kościuszko).
18. Raczyński, *Kościuszko Manuscript*, p. 106 (the Russian cannons).
19. Bańkowski, *Tadeusza Kościuszki Journal*, p. 60 (he ordered the bridge to be burned).
20. Raczyński, *Kościuszko Manuscript*, p 106 (Kościuszko notes the bravery of a Russian cavalry soldier).
21. Jan Dihm, *Kościuszko Nieznany [The unknown Kościuszko]*, (Wrocław: Ossolineum, 1969), p. 117 (Bukar: "It was not until the Palembach attack . . .").
22. Niemcewicz, *Pamiętniki*, vol. 2, p. 35 (the meeting with Stanisław).
23. Szyndler, *Tadeusz Kościuszko*, p. 153 (Kachowski report to Prince Zubov).
24. Korzon, p. 235 (quote from Prince Joseph's report of July 8, 1792, about Kościuszko's "foresight").
25. Raczyński, *Kościuszko Manuscript*, p. 108 (quote from *Kościuszko Manuscript* about King Stanisław "sitting calmly in his walled-in bathroom").
26. Zamoyski, *The Last King of Poland*, p. 380 (the graffiti and offer to "assassinate" the king).
27. Korzon, *Kosciuszko*, p. 246 (Prince Joseph Poniatowski's letter to the king, originally in Poniatowski's *Moje Wspomnienia o Kampanii 1792 [My recollections of the campaign of 1792]*).
28. Szymon Askenazy, *Nowe Czasy [New times]* (Warsaw: Gebethner i Wolff, 1910), p. 35 (Princess Isabella proposed kidnapping the king).
29. Korzon, *Kosciuszko*, pp. 247–248 (Kościuszko letter to Princess Isabella).
30. Ibid., p. 249 (Kościuszko's resignation letter to Stanisław).
31. Ibid., pp. 249–250 (Kościuszko letter to Princess Isabella).
32. Askenazy, *Nowe Czasy*, pp. 156–157 (Fiszer quote on king sending women asking Kościuszko to stay).
33. Korzon, *Kosciuszko*, p. 250 (Kościuszko letter to Isabella explaining the king's efforts to persuade him to stay in the army).
34. Szyndler, *Tadeusz Kościuszko*, p. 157 (on August, 5 Kościuszko watched as the Russians pitched their camp in Praga).

35. Siemieński, *Żywot Tadeusza Kosciuszki*, p. 145 (letter from Kościuszko to Potocki, September 6, 1792).

36. Ibid., pp. 146–147 (letter from Potocki to Kościuszko).

37. Ibid., p.148 (newspaper quotes from *Correspondent*).

38. Jerzy Łolek, *Polska Inspiracja Prasowa w Holandii i Niemczech w Czasach Stanisława Augusta [Polish press inspiration in Holland and Germany in the Times of Stanislaw August]* (Warsaw: Panstwowe Wydawnicto Naukowe, 1969), p. 246 (The *Gazette de Leyde* "praised Kościuszko's courage to the heavens").

39. Kościuszko to his sister Anna Estko, September 15, 1792, *PAN* no. 189.

40. Korzon, *Kosciuszko*, p. 255 (letter from Kościuszko to Princess Isabella).

41. Ibid., p. 257 (letter from Kościuszko to his sister Anna).

42. Czartoryski to Mazzei, September 5, 1792, in Mazzei, *Writings,* vol. 3, p. 44.

43. The sketch of Kościuszko drawn by Maria Czartoryski is in the Czartoryski Museum in Kraków.

44. Siemieński, *Żywot Tadeusza Kościuszki,* p. 149 (women in Lwów cut off Kościuszko's buttons and locks of his hair as souvenirs).

45. Szyndler, *Tadeusz Kościuszko,* p. 167 (Constance Zamoyska offers her daughter's hand to Kościuszko, but Staszic disapproved of the marriage).

46. Leon Sapieha, *Wspomnienia: Z Lat od 1803 do 1863 r. [Recollections: Of the years 1803 to 1863]* (Lwów: A. Altenberg, 1913), p. 6 ("Kościuszko always recalled his first love, Hetman Sosnowski's daughter, Louise).

47. Kajetan Koźmian, *Pamiętniki Kajetana Koźmiana, Obejmujace Wspomnienia od Roku 1780 do Roku 1815 [The memoirs of Kajetan Koźmian, encompassing recollections from the years 1780 to 1815]* (Poznań: J. K. Żupański, 1858), pp. 225–226 (a Russian soldier shot into the darkness and said Kościuszko transformed himself into a cat).

48. Szyndler, *Tadeusz Kościuszko,* p. 167 (Staszic and Kościuszko discuss politics in Zamosc).

49. Wiktor Hahn, *Stanisław Staszic: Życie i Dzieła [Stanisław Staszic: His life and work]* (Lublin: Gebethner i Wolff, 1926), p. 55 (Stasicz: "we need someone like Sulla").

50. Simieński, *Żywot Tadeusza Kościuszki,* pp. 150–151 (quote from the *Korespondent Warszawski*, December 8, 1792).

51. Kościuszko's first letter to Princess Isabella, using the pseudonym "Monsieur Barron Bieda" (Mr. Baron Misery), December 17, 1792, is in the Czartoryski Museum in Kraków.

52. Alphonse De Lamartine, *History of the Girondists: Or, Personal Memoirs of the Patriots of the French Revolution, from Unpublished Sources,* vol. 2, Translated by H. T. Ryde (New York: Harper & Brothers, 1848), p. 435 (the French promise "fraternity and succor").

53. Mączyński, *Diaries,* p. 450 ("life on the cross").

54. Alexandra Kraushar, *Barss: Palestrant Warszawski, jego misya politiczna we Francyi, (1793–1800), ze Zrodel Archiwalnych [Barss: Warsaw's barrister and political mission in France (1793–1800), from Archival Material]* (Lwów: Naklad Przewodnika Naukowego i Literackiego, 1903), p. 13 (letter from Parandier to Roland, January 16, 1793).

55. Jan Stanisław Kopczewski, *Tadeusz Kościuszko w historii i tradycji [Tadeusz Kościuszko in history and tradition]* (Warsaw: 1968), p. 39 (Polish Revolution memorandum).

56. Bartlomiej Szyndler, *Powstanie Kościuszkowskie 1794 [The Kościuszko uprising, 1794]* (Warsaw: Anchor, 2001), p. 29 (Kościuszko meets with Dumouriez and shares his plans).

57. Korzon, *Kosciuszko,* p. 267 (Kołłątaj reference to Jonah and the whale).

58. Szymon Askenazy, *Upadek Polski a Francya [France and the fall of Poland]* (Warsaw: Biblioteka Warszawski, 1913), p. 20 (the French revolutionaries whom Kościuszko met with).

59. Lord, *The Second Partition of Poland,* p. 450 (letter from Lebrun to Parendier, February 28, 1793).

60. John Keane, *Tom Paine: A Political Life* (Boston: Little Brown and Company, 1995), p. 446 (Paine considered applying for Polish citizenship).

61. Joel Barlow to King Stanisław, February 20, 1792, in Miecislaus Haiman, *The Fall of Poland in Contemporary American Opinion* (Chicago: Polish Roman Catholic Union of America, 1935), pp. 60–61.

62. Tadeusz Kościuszko, edited by Henryk Mościcki, *Pisma Tadeusza Kościuszki [Writings of Tadeusz Kosciuszko],* (Warsaw: Panstwowe Zakłady wyd. Szkolnych), 1947, p. 74 ("abolish royal power" and "abolish higher clergy").

63. Siemieński, *Żywot Tadeusz Kosciuszki,* pp. 164–165 (Chrétien makes plate of Kościuszko).

64. Kołłątaj, p. 274 (spies locked people in basement of the Russian embassy).

65. Kołłątaj to Kościuszko, July 18, 1793, in Lucyan Siemieński, *Listy Hugona Kołłątaja, pisane z emigracyi, 1792, 1793, 1794 [The letters of Hugo Kołłątay, written in exile, 1792, 1793, 1794],* vol. 2 (Poznań: Jan Kostanty Żupański, 1872), pp. 84–85.

66. Korzon, *Kosciuszko,* p. 276 (Kołłątaj: "The whole nation was pointing to Kościuszko").

67. Franciszek Paszkowski, *Dzieje Tadeusza Kościuszki, Pierwszego Naczelnika Polaków [History of Thaddeus Kosciuszko, first commander of the Poles]* (Kraków: D. E. Friedlein, 1872), p. 53. (Kościuszko travels as "Milewski.")

68. Józef Pawlikowski, "Pamiętnik o Przygotowaniach do Insurekcji Kościuszkowskiej [A memoir of the preparations for the Kosciuszko insurrection]", edited by Lucjan Siemieński, *Przeglad Polski [Polish review]* 10, no. 7 (1876) ("Warsaw is not all of Poland").

69. Korzon, *Kosciuszko,* pp. 276–277 (Kościuszko renews call for militias).

70. Karol Wojda, *O rewolucji Polskiej w roku 1794 [About the revolution in Poland, in the year 1794]* (Poznań: J. K. Żupański, 1867), p. 70 ("Kościuszko's greatest wish . . ."). Wojda's memoirs were originally published in German in Zurich in 1796, as *Versuch einer Geschichte der lezten polnischen Revolution vom Jahr 1794,* by Karol Fryderyk Wojda.

71. Krzysztof Bauer, *Wojsko koronne powstania Kościuszkowskiego [The Crown's army in the Kosciuszko uprising]* (Warsaw: Ministry of Defense, 1981), p. 21 (the number of Polish troops available for the insurrection).

72. Pawlikowski, *Pamiętnik* ("I will not fight only for the nobility. . . .").

73. Siemieński, *Żywot Tadeusza Kościuszki,* p. 172 (the Russians found out Kościuszko was in Poland).

74. Niemcewicz, *Pamiętniki, (1957),* p. 65 (Kościuszko). (note: Niemcewicz's papers were published several times in the 1800s. Some editions published in the communist era censor some references, for example those to Jesus Christ.)

75. Mazzzei, *Memoirs,* p. 377 (Kościuszko tells Mazzei that he does not want to be seen as a mercenary and Mazzei suggests that he settle in America).

76. Niemcewicz, *Pamiętniki,* pp. 155–156 (Jelski quotes).

77. Jan Lubicz-Pachoński, *Kościuszko na ziemi Krakowskiej [Kosciuszko on the ground in Kraków]* (Warsaw: Panstwowe Wydawnictwo Naukowe, 1984), p 65. (Pachoński cites an exchange of letters between King Stanisław and Cardinal Antici, which say that Kosciuszko would have been named the head of the pope's army if not for his participation in the American Revolution.)

78. Kopczewski, p. 40 (Kościuszko's letter from Rome sending instructions to the Polish rebels).

79. Kraushar, *Barss: Palestrant Warszawski,* pp 47–29 (Barss' memorial).

TWELVE: *Kosciuszko's Rebels: Peasant Scythemen, a Burgher Militia, and a Jewish Cavalry*

1. Kopczewski, *Tadeusz Kościuszko,* pp. 128–132, excerpts from Filip Lichocki, *Pamiętnik Filipa Lichockiego, Prezydenta Miasta Krakowa w 1794 [Memoir of Philip Lichocki, Mayor of Kraków in 1794]* (Poznań: 1862), (eyewitness account of the events of March 24, 1794).

2. Generał Józef Sułkowski, *Życie i pamiętniki [Life and memoirs]* (Poznań: J. K. Żupański, 1864), p. 87 (Kościuszko crossed the bridge the night before with his horse behind him).

3. Wacław Sobieski, *Dzieje Polski [Polish history]* (Warsaw: Zorza, 1938), p. 92, footnotes (Kościuszko wanted the "country to be formed on the same model as the American republic").

4. *The Act of the Uprising*, Archiwum Główne Akt Dawnych, (AGAD) (Central Archives of Historical Records), Warsaw, Poland, Zbiór Popielów, nr. 374, k. 1.

5. Szyndler, *Powstanie Kościuszkowskie,* p. 53 (number of soldiers).

6. Kopczewski, *Tadeusz Kościuszko,* pp, 129–130 (Wodzicki criticizes Lichocki).

7. Pachoński, *Kościuszko na ziemi Krakowskiej,* p. 71 (rebel plan to disguise themselves as peasants to attack during fuel shipment).

8. Kopczewski, *Tadeusz Kościuszko,* p. 130 (Lichocki's recollection of conversation with Kościuszko).

9. Ibid., p. 130 (sashes with slogans).

10. Ibid., p. 130 ("guillotine for the mayor!").

11. Kościuszko, *The Writings of Tadeusz Kościuszko,* p. 78 (Kościuszko's oath).

12. Ibid.

13. Wojciech M. Bartel, *O Kosciuszce i O jego spotkaniach z Krakowem [About Kosciuszko and his meetings with Kraków]* (Kraków: Towarzystwo Miłośników Historii i Zabytków Krakowa, 1969), p. 31 ("Long Live Poland! Long Live Kościuszko!").

14. Korzon, *Kościuszko,* p. 297 (they left the king's portrait on the wall).

15. Pachoński, *Kościuszko na ziemi Krakowskiej,* p. 99; Szyndler, *Kościuszko,* p. 184 (copies of the act were sent to foreign governments and newspapers).

16. Ludwik Nabielak, ed., *Tadeusz Kościuszko, jego odezwy i raporty, [Thaddeus Kosciuszko, his proclamations and reports],* vol. 1 (Paris: Ksiegarnia Luxemborg, 1871), pp. 48–49 (appeal to the army).

17. Ibid., pp. 50–52 (appeal to citizenry).

18. Ibid., pp. 52–56 (appeal to clergy).

19. Ibid., pp. 57–58 (appeal to women).

20. *Mowa Hirsh Dawida Lewi miana w dniu 16. Października 1820 Roku. Do ludu zebranego z okazyi obchodzoney w tymże Dniu uroczystości założenia Pomnika Tadeusza Kościuszki* [A speech by Hirsh David Lewi, rabbi of the Kazimierz District, on the day of October 16, 1820, to the people gathered on this day to celebrate the establishment of a monument to honor Tadeusz Kosciuszko], translated from Hebrew by Samuel Baum, in Kraków, 1820 (Kościuszko, as quoted by Rabbi Lewi), p. 4; Jacob Shatzky, *Kościuszko a Żydzi [Kosciuszko and the Jews]* (Warsaw: F. Hoesick, 1917), p. 3. (The exact date of Kościuszko's meeting with Rabbi Lewi is not known. Shatzky points out that it had to have taken place between March 23 and March 28, 1794, when Kosciuszko was still in Kraków.) The Old Synagogue in Kraków (built in 1557) has a plaque commemorating Kościuszko's 1794 visit and his appeal to the Jewish community.

21. Korzon, *Kościuszko,* pp. 300–301 (commission passes a draft and income tax).

22. Szyndler, *Tadeusz Kościuszko,* p. 187 (Gabriel Taszycki's contribution).

23. Niemcewicz, *Pamiętniki* (1957), vol. 2 (the Czartoryskis and Bishop Turski sent thousands of zlotys).

24. Korzon, *Wewnętrzne Dzieje Polski,* vol. 3, p. 419 (the gold cross in the Kraków Cathedral was sold for 180,000 zlotys).

25. Pachoński, *Kościuszko na ziemi Krakowskiej,* p. 132 (Manget sends four wagons of guns to Kraków).

26. Ibid., p. 137 (850 regulars, two hundred cavalry volunteers, and four hundred scythemen).

27. Polish historians and memoirs of participants in the Battle of Raclawice have given various estimates about the number of men in the Polish forces. Pachoński, in *Kościuszko na ziemi Krakowskiej* (p.141), has a chart of the various estimates. From the sources that I have read, it's safest to say that it was about five thousand. Most likely there were about fifty-five hundred

Russians at the battle. Pachoński has a chart on p. 144 with estimates ranging up to eight thousand.

28. Korzon, *Kościuszko,* p. 304, (King Stanisław: they're "behaving like criminals, like muti- neers ignoring the rigors of the law").

29. Korzon, *Kościuszko,* p. 309 (Kościuzko: "My boys, take that artillery!").

30. Ibid. (the capture of the cannons).

31. Ibid. (Kościuszko estimates of dead and wounded); for a longer explanation of the various estimates of the death toll at Raclawice, see Pachoński, *Kościuszko na ziemi Krakówski,* pp. 176–180.

32. Kazimierz Bartoszewicz, *Dzieje insurekcji Kościuszkowskiej [History of the Kosciuszko insur- rection]* (Vienna: F. Bondy, 1909), p. 175. (Kościuszko sat on a bench under three large oak trees.)

33. Kopczewski, *Tadeusz Kościuszko,* pp. 48–50 (The "Report of Tadeusz Kościuszko to the Pol- ish Nation of the Victory at Raclawice").

34. Bartoszewicz, *Dzieje insurekcji Kościuszkowskiej,* p. 175 (lords arrived at Polaniec to take back their serfs, claming that they did not have permission to join the army).

35. Korzon, *Kościuszko,* p. 332 (letter from Jozef Maximilian Ossolinski to Johann Amadeus Thugut, Austrian minister of foreign affairs, May 1, 1794).

36. Korzon, *Kościuszko,* p. 314 (Kościuszko's appeal to the town of Sandomierz).

37. Benedikt de Cache, *Powstanie Kościuszkowskie w swietle korespondencji posła Austriackiego w Warszawie [The Kosciuszko uprising as seen in the correspondence of the Austrian repre- sentative in Warsaw]* (Warsaw: Pax, 1985), pp. 83–85 (letter from Cache to Johann Amadeus Thugut, Austrian minister of foreign affairs, April 19, 1794).

38. Johan Christopher Toll, *Powstanie Kościuszkowskie, w świetle korespondencji posła Szwedzkiego w Warszawie [The Kosciuszko uprising, as seen in the correspondence of the Swedish representative in Warsaw]* (Warsaw: Państwowe Wydawnictwo Naukowe, 1989), p. 94 (Toll to Prince Charles, April 19, 1794).

39. Andrzej Krzysztof Kunert and Andrzej Przewoźnik, *Żydzi Polscy w służbie rzeczpospolitej [Polish Jews in the service of the republic]* (Warsaw: Rada Ochrony Pamięci Walk i Męczeństwa, 2002), p. a reprint of *Żydzi bojownicy o niepodległość Polski [Jewish fighters for Polish independence],* edited by Norbert Getter (Lwów: Lwówski Institut Wydawniczy, 1939), p. 29 (Jews contributed 80,450 zlotys and a doctor recruited 40 soldiers.)

40. Ibid., p. 34 (Salmon Polonus' appeal).

41. Zamoyski, *The Last King of Poland,* p. 416 (Kołłątaj upset that king was not killed).

42. Szymon Askenazy and Włodzimierz Dzwonkowski, *Akty powstania Kościuszki [Acts of the Kosciuszko uprising],* vol. 2 (Kraków: Gebethner and Wolff, 1918), pp. 92–93 (letter from Kościuszko to Mokronowski, April 25, 1794).

43. Nabielski, *Kościuszko's Speeches and Reports,* vol., pp. 14–16 (Kościuszko's order to the Catholic Church, April 30, 1794).

44. Księcia (Prince) Eustachego Sanguszki, *Pamiętnik [Diary], 1786–1815* (Kraków: Drukarnia Uniwersytetu Jagiellońskiego, 1876), pp. 28–29 ("substantial contributions").

45. Mościcki, *The Writings of Tadeusz Kościuszko,* pp. 114–115 (copy of the Proclamation of Polaniec).

46. "*Odezwa do duchowienstwa polskiego, Grecko-Orientalnego, Nieunickiego, Tak Zakonnego, Jako i Swieckiego, Dan w obozie pod Polancem, dnia 7 maja 1794, roku*" (Kościuszko's speech to the clergy of various faiths at Polaniec, May 7), in Nabielak, *Kościuszko's Proclamations and Reports,* vol. 5, p. 37 ("join your hearts with the Poles, who defend our freedom and yours").

47. Korzon, *Kościuszko,* p. 316 (Kościuszko to Sapieha, May 12, 1794).

48. Szyndler, *Tadeusz Kościuszko,* p. 211, quotes: Hanna Dylągowa, *Duchowieństwo Katolickie wobec sprawy narodowej [The Catholic clergy's attitudes toward national affairs], (1764–1864)*

(Lublin: 1981), p. 38 ("the parish priests, who possessed their own land and serfs, were interested in keeping the old relationship of the corvée and did not wish to be tied with Kościuszko's reforms").

49. Korzon, *Wewnętrzne dzieje,* vol. 1, pp. 472–473, *(The Peasants' Voice).*

50. Bogusław Lesnodorski, *Polscy Jakobini [Polish Jacobins]* (Warsaw: Ksiażka i Wiedza, 1960), p. 396 (the hangings of Bishop Kossakowski, et al.).

51. Bartoszewicz, *History of the Kościuszko Insurrection,* p. 245 (Stanisław summoned Prince Joseph to Warsaw).

52. Korzon, *Kościuszko,* pp. 327–328 (Kościuszko letter in which he reassured the king of his "deep respect").

53. Mościcki, *The Writings of Kościuszko,* p. 117 (Kościuszko letter to King Stanisław, June 7, 1794).

54. Bartoszewicz, *History of the Kościuszko Insurrection,* p. 245 (Kościuszko: "What do you want, prince?").

55. Korzon, *Kościuszko,* p. 650, footnote 593, from the archives of the Czartoryski Museum in Kraków (Kościuszko letter to Princess Isabella).

56. Kopczewski, *Tadeusz Kościuszko,* p. 59 (signs and countersigns).

57. Szyndler, *Powstanie Kościuszkowskie,* p. 184 (number of soldiers in the three armies at the Battle of Szczekociny).

58. Stanisław Wodzicki, *Wspomnienia z przeszłości od r. 1768 do r. 1840 [Recollections of the past from 1768 to 1840]* (Kraków: A Nowolecki, 1873) p. 365 (Wodzicki: "I can see Prussians").

59. Ibid., p. 366 (Gen. Wodzicki: "don't take a step back until I say so").

60. Nabielak, *Kościuszko's Proclamations and Reports,* vol. 6, p. 46 (in his report on the Battle of Szczekociny , Kościuszko quotes Sergeant Derysarz's dying words: "Brothers! Defend the fatherland!").

61. Sanguszko, *Diary,* pp. 30–31 (Kosciuszko wounded at Szczekociny).

62. Kraushar, *Barss: Warsaw's Barrister and Political Mission in France,* p. 118 (the French Triumvirate wanted to hear that the Poles would get a guillotine and put "aristocrats" and "clergy" in their place); Korzon, *Kościsuzko,* p. 369 (Barss discussed setting up the guillotine in Warsaw).

63. Archiwum Główne Akt Dawnych (Central Archives of Historical Records) Warszawskie Archiwum Królestwa Polskiego, AKP (Archives of the Kingdom of Poland), AGAD, AKP, 323, k. 344 (Stanisław quotes the lyrics of the mob song "We Krakowians . . ." in a letter to Kościuszko.)

64. AGAD, AKP, 323, f. 353.

65. Korzon, *Kościuszko,* pp. 380–381 (Kościuszko's statement to the city of Warsaw after the unauthorized hangings).

66. Ibid., p. 381, (Jaźwiński and Kiliński gather recruits for Kościuszko's army).

67. Toll, *The Kościuszko Uprising in Correspondence,* p. 77 (letter from Toll to Prince Charles, April 2, 1794, "Gen. Kościuszko is . . . like Washington").

68. Kraushar, *Barss,* p. 120 (French reaction to Koscisuzko's ban on Jacobins).

69. Chrystian Piotr Aigner, *Krótką naukę o kosach i pikach [A short lesson on scythes and pikes]* (Warsaw: Piotr Zawadzki, 1794).

70. Korzon, *Kościuszko,* p. 386 (the Prussians and Russians had forty-one thousand soldiers).

71. Ibid., p. 388 (the Polish forces).

72. Szyndler, *Tadeusz Kościuszko,* p. 234 (Stanisław: "If I still had diamonds . . .").

73. Henryk Mościcki, ed., *Na schyłku dni rzeczpospolitej: Kartki z pamiętnika Michała Starzeńskiego [The closing days of the republic: Pages from the diary of Michael Starzeński]* (Warsaw: Gebethner i Wolff, 1914), p. 114 ("all of Warsaw was buzzing with activity. . . .").

74. Ibid., p. 123 (Starzeński diary).
75. Korzon, *Kościuszko,* p. 394 (Kościuszko gives out jewelry as medals).
76. Zofia Borzymińska and Rafal Zebrowski, *Polski słownik Judaistyczny [The Polish encyclopedia of Judaism]* (Warsaw: Prószyński, 2003), pp. 560–561 (short biography of Szmul Zybtkower).
77. Zahorski, *Warszawa w postaniu,* p. 27 (Zybtkower's factory requistioned).
78. Korzon, *Kościuszko,* p. 409 (all the fabrics that are usable should be picked up from the churches).
79. Zahorski, *Warszawa w postaniu,* p. 167 (Kościuszko's statement on the Jewish poll tax).
80. Korzon, *Kościuszko,* p. 411 (Kościuszko slept in a tent and drank wine and coffee).
81. Tadeusz Korzon, *Kim i czem był Kościuszko* (Warsaw: G. Gebethner, 1907), p. 147 (Kościuszko's black aide during the siege of Warsaw); Jan Lubicz Pachoński, *Kościuszko po insurekcji [Kosciuszko after the insurrection] 1794–1817* (Lublin: Wydawnictwo Lubelskie, 1986), pp. 201–202, footnote 65; his name was Jean Lapierre and a painting of him called *A portrait of Domingo, Kosciuszko's servant* is in the archives of the Polish Military Museum in Warsaw. The artist was Jan Jozef Sikorski (1804–1887).
82. Henryk Mościcki, "Około legendy Maciejowickiej [*The legends of Maciejowica*]," *Tygodnik Illustrowany,* July 9, no. 28 (1921): 446 (Lapierre was Radziwill's bookkeeper).
83. Kazimierz Władysław Wójcicki, *Pamiętniki dziecka Warszawy I inne Wspomnienia Warszawskie, [Journal of a child of warsaw and other warsaw memories]* (Warsaw: Państwowy Instytut Wydawniczy, 1974), p. 78 (the memoirs of Wojcicki, who met and described Lapierre).
84. *Journal of the Royal Asiatic Society of Great Britain & Ireland* (Cambridge: Cambridge University Press, 1834), p. 171; Korzon, *Kościuszko,* p. 406 (during the Kościuszko insurrection of 1794 there were six Tatar cavalry regiments); Kunert, *Jewish Warriors,* p. 34 (some units were 20 percent Jewish).
85. Korzon, *Kościuszko,* p. 394 ("Kościuszko, we won't surrender").
86. Ibid., p. 398 (Zajaczek: "What beautiful music . . .").
87. Mościcki, *Starzeński Diary,* p. 123.
88. *Gazeta Rządowa [Government gazette],* September 6, 1794.
89. James Monroe, *The Writings of James Monroe, Including a Collection of His Public and Private Papers and Correspondence,* vol. 2 (New York: G. P. Putnam's Sons, 1899), p. 52 (letter from Monroe to Jefferson, September 7, 1794).
90. Korzon, *Kościuszko,* pp. 418–419 (the Skarszewski verdict).
91. Mościcki, *Starzeński Diary,* p. 116.
92. Niemcewicz, *Pamiętniki, (1868),* p. 164 (Kołłątaj wrote to Kościuszko saying that he was dragging his feet to benefit the aristocracy).
93. Szyndler, *Tadeusz Kościuszko,* p. 250 (Taszycki quote).
94. Korzon, *Kościuszko,* p. 415 (fifty villages were burned).
95. Kunert and Przewoźnik, *Żydzi Polsky,* p. 30 (Joselewicz received three thousand zlotys from the treasury).
96. *Gazeta Rządowa,* September 17, 1794.
97. *Gazeta Rządowa,* October 1, 1794.
98. Kunert and Przewoźnik, *Żydzi Polsky,* p. 30 (the names of the first Jewish cavalrymen).
99. Ibid., p. 32 (Joselewicz's cavalry numbered five hundred). For more on Joselewicz see Ernest Luniński, *Berek Joselewicz i jego syn: Zarys historyczny [Berek Joselewicz and his son, a historical outline]* (Warsaw: S. Orgelbrand, 1909), and, Majer Bałaban, *Album Pamiątkowy ku Czci Berka Joselewicza pułkownika wojsk Polskich [Memorial album of Berek Joselewicz, colonel of the Polish military]* (Warsawa: 1934).

THIRTEEN: *Poland Is Wiped Off the Map*

1. Korzon, *Kościuszko*, p. 663, note 687 (reward for the capture of Kościuszko).
2. Władysław A. Serczyk, *Katarzyna II, carowa Rosji [Catherine II, czarina of Russia]* (Wrocław: Ossolineum, 1974), p. 278 (letter from Catherine to Gen. Suvrov: "I am sure you know about the rebel Kościuszko . . .").
3. Bruce W. Menning, "Train Hard, Fight Easy: The Legacy of A. V. Suvorov and His 'Art of Victory,' " *Air University Review,* November–December 1986 (Suvorov's motto).
4. Julian Ursyn Niemcewicz, *Notes of My Captivity in Russia, in the Years, 1794, 1795, and 1796,* translated by Alexander Laski (Edinburgh: William Tate, 1844), pp. 6–8 (Niemcewicz and Kościuszko attended a dinner party and then snuck out of Warsaw).
5. Korzon, *Kościuszko*, p. 438 (number of troops).
6. Niemcewicz, *Notes of My Captivity*, p. 11 (Niemcewicz recalls the march and the talk about "Livy").
7. Korzon, *Kościuszko*, p. 440 ("the utmost urgency").
8. Ibid., p. 441 ("the bones are already lying on the table").
9. Józef Drzewiecki, *Pamiętniki Józefa Drzewieckiego (1772–1852) [The memoirs of Józef Drzewiecki]* (Kraków: Gebethner i sp., 1891), p. 30 ("there is no room here to retreat").
10. Niemcewicz, *Notes of My Captivity*, p. 18 ("a shower of balls of every size").
11. Drzewiecki, *Pamiętniki*, p. 30 ("we were lucky it wasn't closer").
12. Korzon, *Kościuszko*, p. 444 ("remember Warsaw").
13. Ibid., p. 663, footnote, 687 (they looked for "expensive looking uniforms").
14. Stanisław Kosmowski, *Pamiętniki Stanisława Kosmowskiego z końca XVII wieku, [Memoirs of Stanisław Kosmowski from the end of the 18th century]* (Poznań: J. K. Żupański, 1867), p. 47 (Kościuszko fires on the Cossacks with his pistol).
15. Julian Ursyn Niemcewicz, *Podróż z Petersburga do Szwecyi, w drodze do Ameryki, w roku 1796, dziennik mojej podroży [A journey from St. Petersburg to Sweden, on the Road to America, in the year 1796, diary of my journey]* (Poznań: J. K. Żupański, 1858), p. 4 (Kościuszko put his pistol in his mouth and pulled the trigger).
16. Drzewiecki, *Pamiętniki*, p. 30 (Russians try to give him vodka).
17. Niemcewicz, *Notes of My Captivity*, p. 27 ("we are not barbarians").
18. Ibid., p. 32 (Kościuszko awakes).
19. Pachoński, *Kosciuszko po Insurekcji*, p. 25 (Fiszer wrote to Zajonczek saying that when he regained consciousness Kościuszko asked for Maignien, Lapierre, and his cook).
20. Korzon, *A History of Poland under Stanisław August,* vol. 6, p. 295 (Fersen to King Stanislaw, arriving in Warsaw October 14).
21. Ibid., p. 296 (the "king's" reply, October 15, 1794).
22. Szyndler, *Tadeusz Kościuszko*, p. 273 (the supplies sent to Kościuszko).
23. Jan Lubicz Pachoński, *Kościuszko w niewoli carskiej, 1794–1796 [Kosciuszko in czarist imprisonment], 1794–1796* (Kraków: Wydawnictwo Głównego Komitetu Kościuszkowskiego w Krakowie, 1947), p. 31 (Lapierre rode in the back of the carriage carrying Kościuszko).
24. Nussbaum, *History of Jews,* p. 365 (almost all of Joselewicz's cavalry was killed defending Praga).
25. Anna Potocka, *Memoirs of Countess Potocka,* edited by Casimir Stryieński, authorized translation by Lionel Stracey (New York: Doubleday & McClure Co., 1901), p. 9 (Potocka's description of the Praga Massacre).
26. Nussbaum, *The History of Jews,* p. 370 (Zbytkower offers rewards).
27. Alfred Rambaud, *History of Russia* (Boston: C. F. Jewett Publishing Co., 1882), pp. 243–244 ("the streets are covered with corpses; blood flows in torrents").
28. Zamoyski, *The Last King of Poland*, p. 429 (one Russian estimate had twenty thousand murdered).
29. Niemcewicz, *Notes of My Captivity*, p. 54 ("a ferocious animal exhibiting a man").

30. Ibid., p. 93 ("the aurora borealis reflected sometimes a blood-red color").
31. Ibid., 108 (conversation with Samoilov).
32. Korzon, *Kościuszko*, p. 469 (letter from Catherine to Baron von Grimm, December 26, 1794, calling Kościuszko "a fool").
33. Korzon, *Kościuszko,* p. 466 (quotes from Kościuszko's interrogations in St. Petersburg).
34. Ibid., p. 463.
35. Korzon, *Kościuszko,* p. 469 (letter from Catherine to Grimm, September 30, 1795; Kosciuszko moved to Stegelmen's house).
36. Pachoński, *Kościuszko po insurekcji,* p. 76 (Dr. Rogerson's treatment).
37. Pachoński, *Kościuszko w niewoli carskiej* (Russians used Kosciuszko's money to pay Lapierre seven zlotys per month).
38. Korzon, p. 469 ("my wretched beast").
39. Korzon, *Kościuszko,* pp. 471–473 (Korzon reproduces Gagarin's reconstruction of the conversation between Czar Paul and Kościuszko, along with accounts that Niemcewicz was able to put together after interviewing Kościuszko).
40. Ibid., continuation.
41. Niemcewicz, *Pamiętniki,* (1957), vol. 2, p. 192 (Wielhorski's plan to buy Kościuszko with one thousand serfs).
42. Pachoński, *Kosciuszko po Insurekcji,* p. 99, (Quoting the Gagarin transcript).
43. Niemcewicz, *Notes,* 224 (disgusted by the oath).
44. Szyndler, *Tadeusz Kościuszko,* p. 290 (the numbers from Russian prison).
45. Niemcewicz, *Notes,* p. 222 (a reunion after two years).
46. Ibid., p. 222 (". . . go with me to America").
47. Ibid., p. 249 (the presents from the czar).
48. Korzon, *Kościuszko,* p. 478 (Kościuszko wearing his American uniform).
49. Korzon, *Kościuszko,* p. 479 ("it reminds me of great feelings of morality").
50. Julian Ursyn Niemcewicz, *Podróż z Petersburga do Szwecyi,* p. 4 (Kościuszko's suicide attempts).
51. Korzon, *Kościuszko,* p. 483 (Swedish newspapers).
52. Niemcewicz, *Podróż z Petersburga do Szwecyi,* p. 22, (". . . village ran to see his ebony face").
53. Ibid.
54. Szymon Askenazy, *Napoleon a Polska [Napoleon and Poland],* vol. 2 (Warsaw: Towarzystwo Wydawnicze W Warszawie, 1918), pp. 163–164 (Dabrowski talks to Napoleon about the Poles).
55. Niemcewicz, *Pamiętniki,* p. 246 (Kościuszko wrote to French government).
56. Jan Dihm, *Kościuszko nieznany,* p. 247 (Kościuszko wrote through a Dutch intermediary to General Bonaparte).
57. Pachoński, *Kościuszko po Insurekcji,* pp. 120–121 (the article in *Le Moniteur Universel*).
58. Niemcewicz, *Pamiętniki,* p. 247 (Kościuszko's correspondence with the French continued until he left for America).
59. Korzon, *Kościuszko,* p. 670, footnote 727 (Niemcewicz letter to Johan Toll, March 10, 1797, about the honor of Mrs. G.).
60. Askenazy, *Napoleon a Polska,* 236 ("why don't you keep him for Poland?").

FOURTEEN: *Kosciuszko Tries to Free Jefferson's Slaves*

1. E. Little, *Little's Living Age* (Boston: E. Litttell & Company, 1851), p. 475 ("the tory press alone was hostile" to Kościuszko's arrival in London).
2. *Gentleman's Magazine* 67, part 2 (*1797*): 609 (Domestic Occurrences, Tuesday, May 30: "The gallant General Kosciuszko . . .").

3. Niemcewicz, *Pamiętniki,* (1868), p. 248, (Sablonnniere hotel).

4. Szyndler, *Tadeusz Kościuszko,* p. 295; Haiman, *Kościuszko, Leader and Exile,* p. 33.

5. Miecislaus Haiman, *Kościuszko, Leader and Exile* (New York: Kościuszko Foundation, 1977, first published in 1946 by the Polish Institute of Arts and Sciences in America), pp. 135–136 ("Appendix B: Diagnosis of Kościuszko's Physical Condition by British Physicians, Rush Paper, Ridgway Library, Library Company of Philadelphia).

6. William Cobbett, *Porcupine's Works,* vol. 7 (London: Cobbett and Morgan, 1801), p. 4 (Tarleton's motion at the Crown and Anchor Tavern).

7. Letter from Jefferson to Kościuszko, June 18, 1798, Jefferson Papers, Library of Congress, (the saber from "The Whig Club of England to General Kościuszko" cost two hundred guineas).

8. Korzon, *Kościuszko,* p. 671, note 736 (Niemcewicz talked Kościuszko out of sending the money back to the czar).

9. Niemcewicz, *Pamiętniki,* p. 249–251 (Kościuszko and Niemcewicz stay with Vanderhorst and sail from Bristol).

10. Charles R. King, ed., *The Life and Correspondence of Rufus King* (New York: G. P. Putnam's Sons, 1895), p. 189 (Kościuszko letter to King, June 16, 1797, thanking him for his hospitality).

11. Rev. Richard Warner, *Literary Recollections,* vol. 2 (London: Longman, Rees, Orme, Brown and Green, 1830), p. 135 (recollection of Kościuszko).

12. Ibid., p. 136 (Kościuszko's response).

13. Evans, *Memoir of Thaddeus Kościuszko,* pp. 21–22 (British officers greeted Kościuszko and carried him in a "sedan chair" to the ship).

14. Niemcewicz, *Pamiętniki* (1957), p. 211.

15. Ibid., p. 214 (tangled masts and fishing poles).

16. Jacob Cox Parsons, ed., *Extracts from the Diary of Jacob Hiltzheimer of Philadelphia, 1765–1798* (Philadelphia: Wm. F. Fell & Co., 1893), p. 255 (Muhlenberg and the workers at Fort Mifflin).

17. Korzon, *Kościuszko,* p. 489 (a French reporter recorded Kościuszko's words to Heins).

18. Niemcewicz, *Pamiętniki* (1868), p. 253 (the people of Philadelphia were so excited to see Kościuszko they untied his horse and pulled the carriage themselves).

19. Haiman, *Leader and Exile,* p. 43 (John Fenno of the *Gazette of the United States* called the crowd "cattle," and Webster in the *Herald* wrote: "Men who can decline common a mark of genteel civility . . .").

20. *Porcupine's Gazette* 7: 5 (to General Tarleton).

21. *Porcupine's Gazette* 7: 113 (quotes *Claypoole's American Daily Advertiser*).

22. Ibid., p. 114 (Cobbett's attack on Kościuszko and the "Jacobin").

23. Niemcewicz, *Pamiętniki,* p. 253 ("struck . . . by the large number of Negroes").

24. F. J. Turner, *Correspondence of the French Ministers to the United States, 1791–1797, Annual Report of the American Historical Association, for the Year 1903,* vol. 2 (Washington, DC: U.S. Government Printing Office, 1904), pp. 1068–69 (letter from Letombe to Charles Delacroix, August 20, 1797).

25. Jared Sparks, *The Writings of George Washington,* vol. 11 (Boston: Russell, Shattuck and Williams, 1836), p. 213 (letter from Washington to Kościuszko, August 31, 1797).

26. Julian Ursyn Niemcewicz, *Under Their Vine and Fig Tree, Travels Through America in 1797–1700, 1805 with Some Further Account of life in New Jersey,* translated and edited by Metchie J. E. Budka (Elizabeth, NJ: Grassman, 1965), p. 5 (they left Philadelphia August 30 . . .).

27. Dr. Rush to Gates, September 3, 1797, Gates Papers, New York Historical Society.

28. Anthony Walton White Evans, *Memoir of Thaddeus Kościuszko: Poland's Hero and Patriot, an Officer in the American Army of the Revolution, and Member of the Society of Cincinnati*

(New York: For the Society, 1883), p. 23 (Kościuszko "spent all his time reclining on a sofa, sketching with a pencil . . .").

29. Kościuszko to Gates, September 6, 1797, Gates Papers, New York Historical Society.

30. Niemcewicz, *Travels Through America,* p. 12 ("we found the inn . . .").

31. Ibid., p. 13 (Gates freed his slaves and employed free black people).

32. Duke de la Rochefoucault Liancourt, *Travels through the United States of North America, the Country of the Iroquois, and Upper Canada, in the Years 1795, 1796, and 1797,* vol. 2 (London: R. Philips, 1799), pp. 468–469, pp. 333–334 (Duc de la Liancourt called Kościuszko "simple and modest . . .").

33. Winnifred King Rugg, "Agrippa Hull of Stockbridge," *Christian Science Monitor,* April 11, 1950 (the Sedgwicks escorted Grippy to New York to meet with Kościuszko).

34. Wallace M. West, "Is This Kościuszko's Pistol?" *Polish Heritage Quarterly,* Spring 1995 (Hull later sold Kościuszko's pistol to a local Stockbridge historian).

35. Electa F. Jones, *Stockbridge, Past and Present, Or, Records of an Old Mission Station* (Springfield, MA: Samuel Bowles & Company, 1854) (Hull attends mass with a haughty employer to hear "a distinguished mulatto preacher").

36. *Examination Days,* New York African Free School Collection, New York Historical Society (the history of the Africa Free School).

37. John Adams to Kościuszko, September 4, 1797, Archives of the Czartoryski Foundation, Kraków.

38. Kościuszko to Washington, October 8, 1797, Library of Congress.

39. Washington to Kościuszko, October 15, 1797, Archives of the Czartoryski Foundation, Kraków.

40. Haiman, *Kosciuszko in the American Revolution,* p. 58; *The Magazine of American History with Notes and Queries,* vol. 6 (New York: A. S. Barnes & Co., 1881), p. 383 (Kościuszko gives his medal to Capt. Kollock's son).

41. Niemcewicz, *Pamiętniki,* p. 255 (Adams in the kitchen with the black cook).

42. Ibid., p. 256 (Kościuszko was opposed to Adams and clung to Jefferson).

43. Niemcewicz, *Travels Through America,* p. 29 (presented to Adams).

44. John Dickinson, *The Letters of Fabius, in 1788, on the Federal Constitution; and in 1797 on the Present Situation of Public Affairs* (Wilmington: W. C. Smyth, 1797), p. 163 ("the catastrophe of Polish liberty").

45. Charles J. Stille, *The Life and Times of John Dickinson, 1732–1808* (Philadelphia: J. B. Lippincott Co., 1891), p. 424, appendix 8 (act to abolish slavery).

46. Haiman, *Kosciuszko, Leader and Exile,* p. 59 (Kościuszko letter to Dickinson, November 24, 1797).

47. Ibid., pp. 70–72 (Dawson sponsored a resolution in Congress on Kościuszko's claim on December 22, 1797).

48. Ibid., p. 72.

49. Niemcewicz, *Pamiętniki,* p. 256, ("he'll take revenge on your countryman").

50. *Journals of the Continental Congress, 1774–1789* (Washington, DC: U.S. Government Printing Offfice, 1906), p. 498.

51. Henry Stephens Randall, *The Life of Thomas Jefferson* (Philadelphia: J. B. Lippincott & Co., 1871), p. 11 (Jefferson carried on a pillow by a slave).

52. Thomas Jefferson, *Notes of the State of Virginia* (Richmond, VA: J. W. Randolph, 1853), pp. 150, 152, and 154 ("in reason, much inferior").

53. Kościuszko to his sister Anna Estko, September 15, 1792, PAN 189.

54. Jefferson to Edward Rutledge, July 14, 1787, Jefferson Papers, Library of Congress.

55. Thomas Jefferson to Gen. Horatio Gates, February 21, 1798, Jefferson Papers, Library of Congress ("he is as pure a son of liberty . . .").

56. David McCullough, *John Adams* (New York: Simon & Schuster, 2001), p. 495 (the XYZ Affair).

57. J. F. Watts and Freid L. Israel, ed., *Presidential Documents: The Speeches, Proclamations, and Policies That Have Shaped the Nation from Washington to Clinton* (New York: Routledge, 1999), pp. 25–26 (President John Adams' report to Congress on the XYZ Affair, March 19, 1798).

58. Thomas Jefferson to Gen. Horatio Gates, February 21, 1798, Jefferson Papers, Library of Congress.

59. Bernard C. Steiner, *The Life and Correspondence of James McHenry, Secretary of War Under Washington and Adams* (Cleveland: Burrow Brothers Company, 1907), p. 288 (Lafayette letter to McHenry, December 26, 1797).

60. Niemcewicz, *Travels Through America*, p. 199 (Armstrong told Niemcewicz that Kościuszko did not like Lafayette and was jealous of him).

61. Haiman, *Kosciuszko in the American Revolution*, p. 62 (Fenno "watched Kościuszko with an Argus eye").

62. Niemcewicz, *Pamiętniki*, p. 259 ("it was fashionable among the young ladies . . .").

63. Calvin Young, *Little Turtle, (ME-SHE-KIN-NO-QUAH): The Great Chief of the Miami Indian Nation, Being a Sketch of His life Together with That of William Wells and Some Noted Descendents* (Greenville, OH: HBC, 1917), p. 149 (Little Turtle's fear of liquor).

64. Niemcewicz, *Travels Through America*, p. 45 (Little Turtle gave Kościuszko a tomahawk, and the Pole gave the chief his cloak and glasses). A replica of the tomahawk and Kościuszko's room is at the U.S. National Park Service museum on the corner of Third and Pine in Philadelphia.

65. Young, *Little Turtle,* pp. 146–147 (Kościuszko and Little Turtle quotes from their meeting in Philadelphia).

66. Robert Walsh, Eliakim Littell, and John Jay Smith, *The Museum of Foreign Literature and Science, Vol. XXVII, July to December, 1835* (Philadelphia: E. Littell, 1835) p. 146 (Little Turtle pronounced his new friend's name "Kotscho").

67. C. F. Volney, *View of the Climate and Soil of the United States of America* (London: J. Johnson, 1804), pp. 397–437 (Volney with Little Tortoise).

68. Niemcewicz, *Pamiętniki*, p. 256 ("Kościuszko threw himself into the opposition").

69. Harry Marlin Tinkcom, *The Republicans and Federalists in Pennsylvania, 1790–1801: A Study in National Stimulus and Local Response* (Philadelphia: Pennsylvania Historical and Museum Commission, 1950) pp. 176–179 (the Israel-Morgan election).

70. Niemcewicz, *Travels Through America,* p. 45 (Niemcewicz praises Israel, who was "Jewish in origin," as an "honest man" and "a rabid Democrat").

71. Jefferson to James Madison, February 22, 1798, Jefferson Papers, Library of Congress (Jefferson frustrated by the snow on Election Day).

72. Niemcewicz, *Travels Through America*, p. 46 (description of the election process).

73. Evans, *Memoir,* pp. 25–26 (Kosciusko jumps up after receiving letters).

74. Ibid., p. 26 (Kościuszko tells White, "I must return at once to Europe").

75. A. M. Skałkowski, ed., *Pamiętniki damy polskiej o Kosciuszce, "Przeglad Historyczny" [Memoirs of a Polish lady concerning Kościuszko, "Historical Review"),* 1934, p. 253 (Lady Wirydianna Kwilecka Fiszer recalled that Kościuszko was summoned by the French; hereafter "Fiszer memoirs").

76. Leonard Chodzko, *Histoire des legions Polonaises en Italie [History of the Polish legions in Italy]* (Paris: J. Barbezat: 1829), pp. 207–208 (Dabrowski's appeal to Polish troops).

77. First draft of Kościuszko's American will, April 20, 1798, Jefferson Papers, Massachussetts Historical Society.

78. Kościuszko to Thomas Jefferson, undated, before May 5, 1798, in *The Papers of Thomas Jefferson, January 1798 to January 1799,* edited by Barbara B. Oberg (Princeton, NJ: Princeton University Press, 2004), p. 331 ("I beg you . . . to finish what I have begun").

79. Ibid., pp. 332–333 (will of Tadeusz Kosciuszko [revised by Jefferson], fifth day of May 1798).

80. Ibid., p. 292, *Memorandum to Tadeusz Kościuszko,* April 25, 1798.
81. Kościuszko to Jefferson in 1798, exact day unclear, Jefferson Papers, Massachussetts Historical Society ("give me leave to present you a Fur").
82. Haiman, *Kosciuszko in the American Revolution,* p. 79, ("Bear skin . . .").
83. Drzewiecki, *Pamiętniki,* p. 152 (Kościuszko: "that this was getting boring").
84. Ibid., p. 152 ("Jefferson thought that I would be the most effective intermediary with France").
85. Kościuszko to Jefferson, undated, Jefferson Papers, Massachusetts Historical Society ("I should prefer Libson . . .").
86. Niemcewicz, *Travels Through America,* p. 65 (the events of May 4, 1798, and conversation with Kościuszko, "I leave this night for Europe").
87. Ibid.
88. Ibid.
89. Letter from Jefferson to Kościuszko, June 18, 1798, Jefferson Papers, Library of Congress, (saber arrived on Lee's *Adriana*).
90. Niemcewicz, *Travels Through America,* pp. 95–108 (Niemcewicz's stay at Mount Vernon).
91. Susan R. Stein, *The Worlds of Thomas Jefferson at Monticello* (New York: Harry N. Abrams), p. 120 (Kosciuszko's portrait hung in the parlor of Monticello).

FIFTEEN: *Napoleon Comes Up Short*

1. Fiszer memoirs, p. 249 (Fiszer said that after his departure from St. Petersburg and during his stay in America, Kościuszko "pretended that he could not walk" and that he kept it from his closest friends); Drzewiecki, *Pamiętniki,* p. 152 (Col. Drzewiecki wrote that Kościuszko told him that "at night I ran around in my room" so that no one would know that he could really walk).
2. Haiman, *Kosciuszko in the American Revolution,* p. 83 (Moniteur reports Kościuszko's arrival in France).
3. Letter from Jefferson to Niemcewicz, November 30 1798, Jefferson Papers.
4. Korzon, *Kościuszko,* p. 502 (Kościuszko's reception in Bayonne).
5. Jefferson to Niemcewicz, January 16, 1799, Jefferson Papers (Kościuszko can walk).
6. Niemcewicz, *Travels Through America,* p. 270 ("if you want it, this hand is yours").
7. Niemcewicz to Jefferson, January 19, 1799, Jefferson Papers.
8. Paul Barras, *Memoirs of Barras, Member of the Directorate,* vol.3, edited by George Duruy (New York: Harper & Brothers, 1896), p. 279 (welcome "the new Washington").
9. Drzewiecki, *Pamiętniki,* p. 152 ("Washington and I had similar roles").
10. Jonathan Roberts, "Memoirs of a Senator from Pennsylvania: Jonathan Roberts, 1771–1854," *Pennsylvania Magazine of History and Biography,* January 1938, p. 87.
11. Jefferson to Kosciuszko, May 30, 1798, Jefferson Papers, Library of Congress. The original handwritten text of this letter is dated May 30, but it is dated June 1, 1798, in Thomas Jefferson Randolph, ed., *Memoir, Correspondence and Miscellanies, from the Papers of Thomas Jefferson,* vol. 3, (Charlottesville: F. Carr and Co., 1829), p. 396.
12. Deborah Norris Logan, *Memoir of Dr. George Logan of Stenton* (Philadelphia: Historical Society of Pennsylvania, 1899), p. 65 (Kościuszko warns Logan).
13. Samuel Eliot Morison, *The Life and Letters of Harrison Gray Otis, Federalist, 1765–1848* (Boston and New York: Houghton Mifflin, 1913), p. 168 (letter from Codman to Otis, August 26, 1798).
14. Cutting to Jefferson, August 27, 1798, Library of Congress.
15. Logan, *Memoir,* p. 79, note (French released American ships and prisoners).

16. Kościuszko to Jefferson, (undated) Massachusetts Historical Society. From the text of the letter it had to have been sent after September 9, 1798, when Logan set sail for Philadelphia.

17. Askenazy, *Napoleon and Poland,* vol. 3, p. 43 ("this Pole is contemptuous").

18. Thomas Jefferson, *Memoir, Correspondence, and Miscellanies from the Papers of Thomas Jefferson,* vol. 2 (Charlottesville: F. Carr, 1829), p. 422 (Jefferson to Kościuszko, February 21, 1799).

19. Ibid., Jefferson to Kościuszko.

20. Kopczewski, *Tadeusz Kościuszko,* p. 162 (Kościuszko reacts to czarina's biography).

21. Adam M. Skałkowski, ed., *Z korespondencji Kosciuszki urzendowej i prywatnej:1790–1817 [The official and private correspondence of Kościuszko, 1790–1817]* (Kornik: Nakładem Fundacji Zaklawy Kornickie, 1946), p. 36 (Kościuszko letter to Dabrowski, July 22, 1798).

22. Ibid., p. 37 (Kościuszko letter to Wybicki, August 22, 1798).

23. Ibid., p. 38 (Kościuszko's proclamation to "Brother Soldiers," August 22, 1798).

24. Korzon, *Kościuszko,* p. 504 (Kościuszko's letter to Czar Paul, August 4, 1798).

25. Xavier Zeltner, "Personal Reminiscences of Kościuszko," *The United States Service Magazine, Vol. IV., August, 1865* (New York: Charles B. Richardson, 1865), p. 145 (the czar's bankers were Thompson, Bonard & Co.).

26. Korzon *Kościuszko,* p. 506 (Czar Paul refused to take the money back from a "traitor").

27. Cobbett, *Porcupine's Works,* vol. 10, pp. 88–89 (attack on Kościuszko).

28. Ibid., p. 83 ("cash . . . in his pocket").

29. John Holmes Agnew and Walter Hilliard Bidwell, *The Eclectic Magazine of Foreign Literature, Science, and Art, Sept. to Dec. 1854* (New York: W. H. Bidwell), p. 417 (libel judgment against *Porcupine's Gazette*).

30. Michel Ogiński, *Memoires sur la Pologne et le Polonais, depuis 1788 jusqu'a la fin 1815 [Memoirs of Poland and the Roles, up to the end of 1815],* vol. 2, (Paris: 1826), pp. 229–230 (Napoleon: "I love the Poles . . .").

31. Piotr S. Wandycz, *The Lands of Partitioned Poland, 1795–1918* (Seattle: University of Washington Press, 1974), p. 29 ("free men are brothers").

32. Jan Pachoński, *Legiony Polskie, prawda i legenda, 1804–1807 [The Polish legions, truth and legend, 1804–1807],* vol. 2. (Warszawa: Wydawnictwo Ministerstwa Obrony Narodowej, 1976), p. 153 (Joselewicz to Dabrowski).

33. Korzon, *Kościuszko,* p. 510 (toast in Belgioioso).

34. Dihm, *Kościuszko nieznany,* p. 335 (Bonneville toast).

35. Askenazy, *Napoleon and Poland,* vol. 3, p. 205 ("be our Moses").

36. Leonard Chodźko, *Histoire des legions Polonaises en Italie [History of the Polish legions in Italy]* (Paris: J. Barbezat, 1829), pp. 68–69 (Sobieski's sword and Mustafa's flag given to Dabrowski).

37. Kościuszko to Kniaziewicz, December 18, 1799, in A. M. Skałkowski, ed., *Archiwum Wybickiego [The Wybicki Archives],* vol. 1 (Gdańsk: Nakładem Towarzystwa Przyjaciół Nauki i Sztuki, 1948), p. 447 (original in French).

38. Drzewiecki, *Pamiętniki,* p. 146 (quotes from first meeting of Napoleon and Kościuszko); Korzon, *Kościuszko,* p. 514. In his footnotes, Korzon quotes Gen. Kniaziewicz, who also witnessed the meeting.

39. Franciszek Paszkowski, *Dzieje Tadeusza Kościuszki [The history of Tadeusz Kościuszko]* (Kraków: Uniwersytet Jagielloński, 1872), p. 200 (Kościuszko about Napoleon: keep an eye "on that young man"). Captain (later General) Paszkowski was Kościuszko's personal secretary for three years starting in 1801 and had the first draft of this book ready in 1819, two years after Kościuszko's death. But it was not published until fourteen years after Paszkowski's death, by his nephew.

40. Jerzy Topolski, *Zarys dziejów Polski [A Study of Polish history]* (Warsaw: Interpress, 1986), p. 146; Pachoński, *The Polish Legions,* p. 158 ("gravedigger of the republic").
41. Askenazy, *Napoleon and Poland,* vol. 3, (Dabrowski on Napoleon).
42. Korzon, *Kościuszko,* p. 515 (Kościuszko's note to unite the Polish troops, which soon numbered fifteen thousand).
43. Claude-Francois Meneval, *Memoirs of Napoleon Bonaparte, the Court of the First Empire* (New York: P. F. Collier & Son, 1910), p. 139 (Napoleon's physical description of Fouché; several paintings of Fouché show his left eye larger).
44. Emmanuel de Las Cases, *Memoirs of the Life, Exile, and Conversations of the Emperor Napoleon,* vol. 2 (New York: H. W. Hagemann, 1894), p. 66 ("intrigue . . .").
45. Louis Madelin, *The French Revolution* (New York: G. P. Putnam's Sons, 1916), p. 408 (Fouché was a "deChristianizer").
46. Joseph Fouché, *Memoirs of Joseph Fouché, Duke of Otranto, Minister of the General Police of France* (London: Gibbings, & Co., 1894), p. 297 (Napoleon wanted to "draw Kościuszko into a snare").
47. Paszkowski, *Dzieje Tadeusza Kościuszki,* p. 201 (Kościuszko, "I never speak of him").
48. Ibid. (Napoleon ignored Kościuszko at the audiences with the Poles).
49. Emanuel Halicz, ed., *Czy Polacy wybić sie moga na niepodległość? [Can the Poles win their independence?]* (Warsaw: Wydawnictwo Ministerstwa Obrony Narodwej, 1967), a reprint of Kościuszko's original pamphlet from 1800 with an introduction by Halicz.
50. Ibid., p. 69 ("a nation that demands independence . . .").
51. Ibid., p. 76 ("the American revolutionaries . . .").
52. Ibid., p. 97 ("defender of human rights").
53. Bonneau letter to Talleyrand, November 27, 1800, in A. M. Skałkowski, *O kokarde legionow [About the legion's Cokades],* (Lwów: Ksiegarni Gubrynowicza, 1912), pp. 136–137.
54. Halicz, *Czy Polacy,* p. 113 ("why isn't this bravery . . .").
55. Paszkowski, *Dzieje Tadeusza Kościuszki,* p. 204 (Napoleon was Machiavellian).
56. Fiszer memoirs, p. 253 (Kościuszko was "Easily deceived" in Paris).
57. Jeffferson to Kościuszko, May 7, 1800, Jefferson Papers.
58. Kościuszko to Jefferson, August 14, 1800, Jefferson Papers, Massachusetts Historical Society.
59. *The Reports of Committees of the Senate of the United States, for the First Session of the Thirty-eighth Congress* (Washington, DC: U.S. Government Printing Office, 1864), p. 21 (Lafayette was present to hear Napoleon's toast).
60. Gerrit Smith, *Speeches of Gerrit Smith in Congress [1853–1854]* (New York: Mason Brothers, 1855), p. 133 (the Lafayette quote is from the 1846 edition of "The Liberty Bell," as relayed by the abolitionist Thomas Clarkson).
61. Lafayette to Jefferson, November 16, 1806, Jefferson Papers, Library of Congress (Lafayette: "the anniversary of Kościuszko, who himself was there"; Lafayette also detested the "ancient system" and "bigotries of every kind").
62. M. Jules Cloquet, *Recollections of the Private Life of General Lafayette,* vol. 2 (New York: Leavitt, Lord & Co., 1836), pp. 70 and 76 (portrait of Kościuszko, and the Fourth of July dinners).
63. Korzon, *Kościuszko,* p. 516 (Napoleon forced 5,647 Poles onto ships bound for Haiti).
64. Keane, *Tom Paine,* p. 447, (Kościuszko was a good friend of Paine's); Thomas Paine, *The Writings of Thomas Paine, Edited by Moncure Daniel Conway,* 4 (New York: G. P. Putnam's Sons, 1896), p. xvii (Charles Nodier's description of the parties at Bonneville's).
65. John Goldworth Alger, *Paris in 1789–94: Farewell Letters of Victims of the Guillotine,* (London: George Allen, 1902), p. 88 ("butcher of liberty").
66. Thomas Paine, *Life and Writings of Thomas Paine* (New York: Vincent Parke and Company, 1908), pp. 9 and 18 (excerpts from *Agrarian Justice*).

67. Pachoński, *Polish Legions*, vol. 3, p. 584 (Kościuszko saw the American Indians as noble and true to their word).

68. Lewis Goldsmith, *The Secret History of the Cabinet of Bonaparte* (London: J. M. Richardson, 1810), p. 39 ("when the Revolution broke out in Poland . . .").

69. Jefferson to Kościuszko, March 14, 1900, Jefferson Papers. Some published versions cite this letter as saying: "I cannot hail you . . ." While the original handwritten letter is slightly smudged, it says "can now." The context of the rest of the letter is clearly optimistic.

70. Pachoński, *Kościuszko After the Insurrection*, p. 172 (Kościuszko visited Paine when Dawson arrived with a letter from Jefferson).

71. Kosciuszko to Jefferson, undated, but content suggests that it was from spring 1801, Massachusetts Historical Society.

72. Szyndler, *Tadeusz Kościuszko*, p. 335 (rumors of Kościuszko's affair with Angelique).

73. Paszkowski, *Dzieje Tadeusza Kościuszki*, p. 218 (quote about Angelique).

74. Korzon, *Kościuszko*, p. 689 (letter from Sierakowski to Stanislas Estko, undated, from 1801).

75. Zeltner, *"Personal Reminiscences,"* p. 137 (Kościuszko smashes the statues with his cane).

76. Fiszer memoirs, p. 249 (Kościuszko's physical description).

77. Ibid., p. 260 (brotherly love).

78. Ibid., p. 261 (Livingston party).

79. Szyndler, *Tadeusz Kościuszko*, p. 335 (Fiszer quote about gossip).

80. Jedynakiewicz, *The Personality and Daily Life of Thaddeus Kościuszko*, p. 89 (rumor about Kościuszko and Mrs. Konarski.)

81. Paszkowski, *Dzieje Tadeusza Kościuszki*, p. 249 (about women).

82. Fiszer memoirs, p. 249 (meeting with Madame de Staël).

83. Ibid., p. 18 (Tuileries Gardens).

84. Ibid. (meeting with the peasant).

85. Pachoński, *Polish legions*, vol. 3, (Fiszer quote about Mrs. Zeltner, "young, sweet . . .").

86. Fiszer memoirs, p. 251 ("hunger for love").

87. Ibid., p. 276 (Kościuszko letter to Fiszers).

88. Korzon, *Kościuszko*, p. 446 (Kościuszko wanted to challenge Poniński to a duel).

89. Kościuszko to Segur, October 30, 1803, from the archives of the Segur family, translation in *Fraser's Magazine* XIII, *Jan. to June 1876* (London: Longmans, Green, and Co., 1876) pp. 728–729.

90. Szyndler, *Tadeusz Kościuszko*, p. 263. (According to Szyndler, the letter was fabricated.)

91. *"Weteran Poznański,"* March 1825, p. 14 (Kościuszko said he was beholden to the nation because the Seym funded the Knight's School).

92. Goldsmith, *The Secret History of the Cabinet of Bonaparte*, pp. 145–151 (the plot to make Louis XVIII king of Poland).

93. Tadeusz Kościuszko, *Manoeuvres of Horse Artillery* (New York: U.S. Military Philosophical Society, 1808).

94. Jefferson to Jonathan Williams, October 28, 1808, Jefferson Papers.

95. Kościuszko to Jefferson (in French), undated but received by Jefferson November 15, 1805, Massachusetts Historical Society.

96. Elbridge Streeter Brooks, *The Story of the Nineteenth Century of the Christian Era* (Boston: Lothrop Publishing Co., 1900), p. 127 ("I have not time to bother with the alphabet").

97. Kościuszko to Jefferson, March 10, 1806, Massachusetts Historical Society.

98. Zawadzki, *A Man of Honour*, pp. 127–128 (Mordplan).

99. Napoleon to Fouché, October 27, 1806, Wybicki Archives, vol. 2, p. 33.

100. Kościuszko, *Pisma Tadeusza Kościuszko*, pp. 215–217 (Kościuszko meeting with Fouché).

101. Zeltner, *"Personal Reminiscences,"* pp. 144–145 (second part of Kościuszko's talk with Fouché, starting with "I must confess general . . .").

102. Louis Antoine Fauvelet de Bourrienne (His Private Secretary), *Memoirs of Napoleon Bonaparte,* vol. 3 (New York: Charles Scribner's Sons, 1892), p. 93 ("I love the Poles. . . .").

103. Lewiński Corwin, *The Political History of Poland,* p. 373 (Napoleon: "France has never recognized . . .").

104. Goldsmith, *The Secret History,* pp. 485–486 (the forged Kościuszko appeal).

105. Napoleon Bonaparte, *Correspondance de Napoleon I, Tome Quatorzieme* (Paris: Henri Plon, 1863), p. 126 (Letter from Napoleon to Fouché, December 31, 1806).

106. Arthur Levy, *The Private Life of Napoleon,* vol. 1, (New York: Charles Scribner's Sons, 1894), p. 261 (quoting *Memoirs de Lucien Bonaparte:* "an angel").

107. Kościuszko to Fouché, January 22, 1807, in Paszkowski, *Dzieje Tadeusza Kościuszki,* pp. 231–214.

108. Napoleon, *Correspondance,* p. 315 (Napoleon to Fouché, February 20, 1807).

109. John Armstrong to Thomas Jefferson, July 1, 1818, in "Kosciuszko Biography" (Kosciuszko's brush-off of Princess Saphieha).

110. Dezydery Chłapowski, *Pamiętniki, Wojny Napoleońskie, 1806–1813, [Memoirs of the Napoleonic Wars,* 1806–1813] (Poznań: Nakładem Synow, 1899), pp. 29–30 (Kościuszko's opinion of Napoleon).

111. Letter from Jefferson to Kościuszko, Jefferson Papers, Library of Congress.

112. Letter from Kościuszko to Jefferson, March 1, 1811, Massachusetts Historical Society.

113. Letter from Jefferson to Kościuszko, April 16, 1811, Jefferson Papers. For more on Kościuszko's deism see Andrzej Walicki, *The Enlightenment and the Birth of Modern Nationhood: Polish Political Thought from Noble Republicanism to Tadeusz Kościuszko,* translated by Emma Harris, (Notre Dame: University of Notre Dame Press, 1989), pp. 99–102; Józef Żuraw, *Myśl filozoficzna i społeczna Tadeusza Kościuszki: Tradycje i współczesność [The philosophical and social ideas of Thaddeus Kościuszko: In tradition and modern times]* (Warsaw: Wydawnictwo Ministerstwa Obrony Narodowej, 1979), pp. 56, 69, and 87; and Jedynakiewicz, *Osobowość i życie codzienne Tadeusza Kościuszko,* p. 162.

114. Jefferson to Thomas Leiper, January 1, 1814, Jefferson Papers, Library of Congress.

115. Kościuszko to Jefferson, February 1, 1812, Massachusetts Historical Society.

116. Jefferson to Kościuszko, June 28, 1812, Jefferson Papers, Library of Congress.

117. Kościuszko to Jefferson, May 30, 1813, in Bogdan Grzeloński, *Jefferson, Kościuszko Correspondence,* (Warsaw: Interpress Publishers, 1978). *(The Original letter, in French, is in Kościuszko Papers Archives and Museum of the Police Roman Catholic Union.)*

118. Jefferson to Kościuszko, November 30, 1813, Jefferson Papers, Library of Congress.

119. Ibid.

120. Ibid.

SIXTEEN: *A Peasant Without a Country*

1. R. H. Horne ed., *The History of Napoleon,* vol. 2 (London: Robert Tyas, 1841), p. 173 (Napoleon: "The second Polish war is commenced").

2. Helen Maria Williams, *A Narrative of the Events Which Have Taken Place in France, from the Landing of Napoleon Bonaparte on the First of March, 1815, till the Restoration of Louis XVIII* (Philadelphia: Moses Thomas, 1816), pp. 96–97; Theodore Johnson, "Last Years of Kosciuszko," *Harper's New Monthly Magazine* 37 (September 1868) V: 479 ("I am Kosciuszko!").

3. Kosciuszko to Czar Alexander, April 9, 1814, Biblioteka Naradowa w Warszawie (Archives of the National Library of Warsaw, Manuscripts).

4. Zeltner, *"Personal Reminiscences,"* p. 138 (czar asks Kosciuszko to finally accept the money left for him in England).

5. Korzon, *Kościuszko,* p. 528 ("make room . . .").
6. Szyndler, *Tadeusz Kościuszko,* p. 348 (the gray horse and Madalinski's ring).
7. Korzon, *Kościuszko,* p. 529 (letter from czar to Kosciuszko, May 3, 1814).
8. Paszkowski, *Dzieje Tadeusza Kościuszki,* pp. 285–294 (Kosciuszko's memorandum on serfdom).
9. Jefferson to Kościuszko, June 28, 1814, Massachusetts Historical Society.
10. Kościuszko letter to Jefferson, March 14, 1815 (original in French), Massachusetts Historical Society.
11. Szyndler, *Tadeusz Kościuszko,* p. 351 (the forged Szaniawski letter).
12. Korzon, *Kościuszko,* p. 530 (Fouché issues a passport under the name "Pole").
13. Kosciuszko to Alexander, June 13, 1815, in Paszkowski, *Dzieje Tadeusza Kościuszki,* pp. 234–235.
14. Russian passport issued in Kościuszko's name, June 19, 1815, Kościuszko papers, PAN, Krakow.
15. Korzon, *Kościuszko,* p. 533 (letter from Kosciuszko to Czartoryski, June 25, 1815).
16. Potocka, *Memoirs,* p. 230, ("blinded by illusion").
17. Tadeusz Kościuszko, *Lettres de Soleure de Tadeusz Kosciuszko, 1815–1817, Facsimiles et textes [Letters from Soleure to Tadeusz Kosciuszko, 1815–1817, facsimiles and texts],* edited by Dr. J. A. Konopka (Geneva: Imprimeries de Versoix, 2000), p. 41 (letter from Kosciuszko to Prince Czartoryski, July 18, 1815).
18. Tadeusz Kościuszko, *Pisma Tadeusza Kościuszki, [The writings of Tadeusz Kościuszko],* edited by Henryk Moscicki (Warsaw: Panstwowe Zakłady Wyd. Szkolnych, 1947), pp. 129–132 (Kosciuszko to Czartoryski, December 1815).
19. Ibid.
20. Zeltner, *"Personal Reminiscences,"* p. 139 (Kosciuszko's goddaughter came to live with him).
21. Jefferson to Barnes, April 18, 1815, Jefferson Papers, Library of Congress.
22. Zeltner, *"Personal Reminiscences,"* p. 143 (Kosciuszko's horse rides).
23. Ibid., p. 142 ("something more for you pain").
24. Kosciuszko to Jefferson, April 1816, Massachusetts Historical Society.
25. Tadeusz Kościuszko, "O kościele, religii i wolnej myśli [On the church, religion and free-thinking]," *Kwartalnik Historyczny [Historical Quarterly]* 72, no. 4 (1965); Walicki, *The Enlightenment and the Birth of Modern Nationhood,* p. 101 (Kosciuszko's letter to Czartoryski about priests). According to Professor Walicki, this text "seemed to several generations of Polish historians so flagrant in its excessive radicalism and anticlericalism that it was not published until 1965."
26. Teodor Taczak, *Kazanie: W setna rocznice zgonu, Tadeusza Kościuszki, wygłosił w Archikatedrze Gnieziewskiej, Dnia 15-go Października 1917 roku [Homily: On the hundredth anniversary of the death of Tadeusz Kosciuszko, delivered in the archcathedral in Gniezno, October 15, 1917]* (Gniezno: J. B. Lange, 1917), p. 12, Tadeusz Kosciuszko's prayer. (Kosciuszko gave this prayer that he wrote to Michal Czacki, brother of Tadeusz Czacki, the educator, historian, and politician who worked for the emancipation of Jews in Poland.)
27. Budka, *Kosciuszko Letters,* p. 195 (Kosciuszko's advice to Xavier Zeltner).
28. *Harper's,* "Last Years of Kosciuszko," p. 482 ("I am Kosciuszko!").
29. Jozafat Ohryzko, *Pismo zbiorowe [Collected writings]* (Petersburg: Jozafat Ohryzko Printers, 1859), p. 195 (Louise wrote to Kosciuszko in Switzerland).
30. Jules Michelet, *Légendes démocratiques du Nord [Democratic legends of the North]* (Paris: Levy, 1899), p. 57 (Louise came to visit Kosciuszko).
31. "Last Years of Kosciuszko," *Harper's,* p. 482 (the ring from Louise).
32. Korzon, *Kościuszko,* pp. 536–537 (letter from Kosciuszko to Zeltner, March 4, 1816).
33. Ibid., pp 537–538 (Kosciuszko left money to Thaddea and Carolina).

34. Richard Peters, *Reports of the Cases Argued and Adjudged in the Supreme Court of the United States, January Term, 1834* (New York: Banks Law Publishing, 1903), p. 56 (codicil leaving Kosciuszko Armstrong $3,704).

35. Moscicki, *Kosciuszko Letters,* pp. 139–149 (Kosciuszko's will, April 2, 1817).

36. Letter from Kosciuszko to James Monroe, March 5, 1817, Jefferson Papers, Library of Congress.

37. S. G. Goodrich, ed., *The Token and Atlantic Souvenir: A Christmas and New Year's Present* (Boston: Gray and Bowen, 1833), p. 342 (the fur cloak).

38. Tadeusz Kościuszko and Thomas Jefferson, *Korespondencja [Correspondence],* edited by Izabella Rusinowa (Warsaw: Panstwowy Instytut Wydawniczy, 1976), pp. 141–143 (letter from Jefferson to Kosciuszko, June 15, 1817).

39. Ibid.

40. Kosciuszko to Jefferson, September 15, 1817.

41. Ibid.

42. Kosciuszko last will, dated October 10, 1817, Item Number, 224, Archives of the Czartoryski Foundation, Kraków (Kościuszko's allocation of czar's funds).

43. Ibid. ("personal effects to the Zeltners . . .").

44. "Last Years of Kosciuszko," p. 482 (undertaker's postmortem).

45. Szyndler, *Tadeusz Kościuszko,* p. 366 (cause of death was a stroke).

46. Joachim Lelewel, *Polska Odradzajanca Sie, Czyli, Dzieje Polskie Od Roku 1795,* (Brussels: P. J. Vogleta, 1836), p. 38 (when Kościuszko died in 1817, services were held in Catholic, Lutheran, and Calvinist churches, as well as in Jewish synagogues and Muslim mosques).

47. Jefferson to William Crawford, January 5, 1818, Jefferson Papers, Library of Congress.

48. Jefferson to William Wirt, January 5, 1818, Jefferson Papers, Library of Congress.

49. Jefferson to Gen. John Armstrong, January 17, 1818, Jefferson Papers, Library of Congress.

50. Joseph Peter Zeltner to Jefferson, undated, in Peters, *Reports of the Cases Argued and Adjudged in the Supreme Court,* p. 70.

51. Francis Xavier to Jefferson, October 29, 1817, Massachussets Historical Society.

52. Jefferson to Marc Antoine Jullien, July 23, 1818, Jefferson Papers, Library of Congress.

53. Jefferson to Zeltner, July 23, 1818, Massachussets Historical Society.

54. Jefferson to Gen. Cocke, May 3, 1819, Jefferson Papers, Library of Congress.

55. Gen. Cocke to Jefferson, May 3, 1819, Jefferson Papers, Alderman Library, University of Virginia.

56. *The Historical Magazine and Notes and Queries Concerning the Antiquities, History and Biography of America,* vol. 5 (Morrisania, NY: Henry B. Dawson, 1869), p. 55 (Jefferson's visit to court and statement of William Wertenbaker).

57. Jefferson to John Holmes, April 22, 1820, Jefferson Papers; John Chester Miller, *The Wolf by the Ears: Thomas Jefferson and Slavery* (Charlottesville: University Press of Virginia, 1991).

58. Lucia C. Stanton, *Free Some Day: The African-American Families of Monticello* (Charlottesville: Thomas Jefferson Foundation, 2000), p. 141 (executor's sale).

59. Annette Gordon-Reed, *The Hemingses of Monticello: An American Family,* (New York: W.W. Norton and Company), 2008, pp. 657-659 (Jefferson freed Sally Hemings, discretly to protect his legacy).

60. Stanton, *Free Some Day,* p. 144 ($2,125 paid for Hughes family.)

61. United States Congress, *Hearings, Ninety-second Congress, Second Session, on H.R. 256 on the Thaddeus Kosciuszko Home National Historic Site, Committee on Interior and Insular Affairs, Subcommittee on National Parks and Recreation* (Washington, DC: U.S. Government Printing Office, 1972), p. 22 (the African School asked if it could use Kosciuszko's funds).

62. For more details on Kosciuszko's will, see: Pula, *Kosciuszko,* pp. 287–289; Haiman, *Leader and Exile,* 119–130; Louis Ottenberg, "A Testamentary Tragedy: Jefferson and the Wills of

General Kosciuszko," *American Bar Association Journal,* January 1958, and "Gary B. Nash and Graham Russell Gao Hodges, *Friends of Liberty: Thomas Jefferson, Tadeusz Kosciuszko and Agrippa Hull* (New York: Basic Books, 2008).

63. B.R. Curtis, *Decisions in the Supreme Court of the United States,* Vol. XX, (Boston: Little Brown and Company, 1870), p. 262, (Kosciuszko died intestate).

64. Ottenburg, "A Testamentary Tragedy" (Bomford had "wasted or converted to his own use" $37,924.40 of this estate).

65. Gerrit Smith, *Speeches of Gerrit Smith in Congress [1853–1854]* (New York: Mason Brothers, 1855), p. 133 (Smith before Congress about Kosciuszko).

66. *Journal of American History* 2, no. 3 (1908) (Losey quote.)

67. Booker T. Washington, *My Larger Education: Being Chapters from My Experience* (Garden City, NY: Doubleday, Page & Company, 1911), pp. 240–241 (quotes about Kosciuszko).

68. Michelet, *Légendes démocratiques du Nord.*

69. Joachim Lelewel, *Polska dzieje i rzeczy jej [Poland's history and her affairs],* vol. 7 (Poznań: J. K. Żupański, 1859), p. 34 (Kosciuszko was "a man who had his weaknesses").

Bibliography

Manuscripts and Archives

American Philosophical Society, Philadelphia

Archiwum Główne Akt Dawnych (AGAD) (Central Archives of Historical Records), Warsaw
Archiwum Królestwa Polskiego (Archives of the Kingdom of Poland), Zbiory Popielów (Popielow Collection)

Bibilioteka Polskiej Akademii Nauk, PAN, w Krakowie (Library of Polish Academic Sciences in Kraków), Korespondencja i papiery Tadeusza Kościuszko (Correspondence and Papers of Tadeusz Kościuszko)

Biblioteka Narodowa w Warszawie (Archives of the National Library of Warsaw), Manuscripts

Biblioteka Czartoryskich w Krakowie (Czartoryski Foundation Archives)

Archives of the Polish Museum in Rapperswil, Switzerland

George Bancroft Papers, New York Public Library

Dickinson College Archives

Jared Sparks Papers, Harvard University

Journals of the American Congress from 1774–1788. Washington, D.C.: Way and Gideon, 1823.

Clinton Papers, William L. Clements Library, University of Michigan

Public Papers of George Clinton, First Governor of New York. Vol 2. New York and Albany: Wynkoop Hallenbeck Crawford Co., 1900.

Horatio Gates Papers, New-York Historical Society

Lee Papers, New-York Historical Society

*Collections of the New-York Historical Society for the Year 1880: Revolutionary and Miscella-
neous Papers,* Vol. 3. New York: New-York Historical Society, 1881.

Alexander McDougall Papers, New York Public Library

Pickering Papers, Massachusetts Historical Society

Philip Schuyler Papers, New York Public Library

George Washington Papers, Library of Congress

New England Historical and Genealogical Register. Vol. 30. Boston: New England Historical Society, 1876.

Nathanael Greene Papers, 1775–86 Huntington Library

Gen. Nathanael Greene's Orderly Book, Huntington Library

Otho Holland Williams Papers, Maryland Historical Society

Papers of the Continental Congress

Pennsylvania Colonial Records

Pennsylvania History

Przegląd Polski (Polish Review), 1876

Orderly Book of Philip Schuyler, American Antiquarian Society, Worcester, Massachusetts

Orderly Book of Henry B. Livingston, American Antiquarian Society, Worcester, Massachusetts

Orderly Book of Nathan Savage, Connecticut State Library, Hartford

Manuscripts and University Archives, Special Collections Department, University of Virginia
Library, Charlottesville

*Memorial Exhibition: Thaddeus Kościuszko, Collection of Letters and Relics of Dr. Alexander Ka-
hanowicz.* Exhibition catalog. New York: Anderson Galleries, 1927

Anti-Slavery Record. Vol. 3, *For 1837.* New York: Published by American Anti-Slavery Soci-
ety/R. G. Williams, 1839.

Edinburgh Magazine, and Literary Miscellany: A New Series of the Scots Magazine. Vol. 1, *Aug.–
Dec. 1817.* Edinburgh: George Ramsay and Co., 1817.

Magazine of History with Notes and Queries 6 (July 1907).

"Memoirs of a Senator from Pennsylvania: Jonathan Roberts, 1771–1854." *Pennsylvania Magazine of History and Biography* (Jan. 1938).

Czartoryski Museum, Kraków

Wolność, Całość i Niepodległość, 1794, Powstanie Kościuszkowskie w dokumencie archiwalnym
[Freedom, Integrity, and Independence, 1794, the Kościuszko Uprising in Archive Docu-
ments] Warsaw: Wydawnictwo Ministerstwa Obrony Narodowej (National Ministry of Defense), 1985.

New Constitution of the Government of Poland, Established by the Revolution, the Third of May, 1791. London: J. Debrett, 1791.

American State Papers, Claims, Feb. 5, 1790–March 3, 1823, Legislative and Executive, of the Congress of the United States. Washington: Gales and Seaton, 1834 (pp. 207–8, *Claims of General Kosciusko for Military Services*, Oliver Wolcott, Secretary of the Treasury, Dec. 28, 1797.

Thaddeus Kościuszko National Memorial Furnishings Plan. Robert Lewis Giannini III, Associate Curator, Independence Hall National Historical Park, September 1988.

U.S. Congress. Senate. *Reports of Committees of the Senate of the United States, for the First Session of the Thirty-eighth Congress,* Washington, DC: U.S. Government Printing Office, 1864.

U.S. Congress. Committee on Interior and Insular Affairs, Subcommittee on National Parks and Recreation. *Hearings on H.R. 256 on the Thaddeus Kosciuszko Home National Historic Site*. 92nd Congress, 2nd sess., 1972.

Diaries, Journals, Letters, Memoirs, and Published Archival Material

Adams, Charles Francis. *Familiar Letters of John Adams and His Wife Abigail Adams During the Revolution*. New York: Hurd and Houghton, 1876.

Aigner, Chrystian Piotr. *Krótką naukę o kosach i pikach* [A short lesson on scythes and pikes]. Warsaw: Piotr Zawadzki, 1794.

Amory, Thomas Coffin. *The Military Services and Public Life of Major-General John Sullivan of the American Revolutionary Army*. Boston: Wiggin and Lunt, 1868.

Anburey, Thomas. *With Burgoyne from Quebec: An Account of the Life at Quebec and the Famous Battle of Saratoga*. Edited by Sydney Jackman. Toronto: Macmillan of Canada, 1963.

Askenazy, Szymon, and Włodzimierz Dzwonkowski. *Akty powstania Kościuszki* [Acts of the Kościuszko Uprising]. Vol. 2. Kraków: Gebethner and Wolff, 1918.

August, Stanisław, King of Poland, and Augustyn Antoni Dęboli. *Rok nadziei i rok klęski, 1791–1792; z korespondencji Stanisława Augusta z posłem polskim w Petersburgu, Augustynem Dęboli* [The year of hope and defeat, 1791–1792; correspondence between Stanisław August and the Polish representative in Petersburg, August Deboli]. Warsaw: Czytelnik, 1964.

Bańkowski, Piotr. *Tadeusza Kościuszki dwie relacje o kampanii polsko-rosyjskiej 1792 roku* [Thaddeus Kościuszko, two dispatches about the Polish-Russian campaign of 1792]. Warsaw: Państwowe Wydawnictwo Naukowe, 1964.

Baldwin, Jeduthan. *The Revolutionary Journal of Colonel Jeduthan Baldwin 1775–1778*. Bangor, ME: The De Burians, 1906.

Barras, Paul. *Memoirs of Barras, Member of the Directorate*. Edited by George Duruy. New York: Harper & Brothers, 1896.

Baxter, James Phinney. *The British Invasion from the North: The Campaigns of Generals Carleton and Burgoyne, from Canada, 1776–1777, With The Journal of Lieut. William Digby of the 53D, Or Shropshire Regiment of Foot*. Albany, NY: Joel Munsell's & Sons, 1887.

Bentalou, Paul. *Pulaski Vindicated from an Unsupported Charge: Inconsiderately Or Malignantly Introduced in Judge Johnson's Sketches of the Life and Correspondence of Major Gen. Nathaniel Greene* [Told to Louis Hue Girardin]. Baltimore: John D. Toy, 1824.

de Biron, Armand Louis de Gontaut. *Memoirs of the Duc de Lauzun (Armand Louis de Gontaut, Duc de Biron).* Translated by E. Jules Meras. New York: Sturgis & Walton, 1912.

Blanchard, Amos. *American Military Biography: Containing the Lives, Characters, and Anecdotes of the Officers of the Revolution, Who Were Most Distinguished in Achieving Our National Independence.* N.P.: Printed for Subscribers, 1825.

Bonaparte, Napoleon, *Correspondance de Napoleon I, Tome Quatorzième.* Paris: Henri Plon, 1863.

Bukar, Seweryn. *Pamiętniki z konca XVIII i początków wieku XIX* [Memoirs of the late eighteenth and early nineteenth centuries]. Dresden: J.I. Kraszweski, 1871.

Cache, Benedikt de. *Powstanie Kościuszkowskie w świetle korespondencji posła austryjackiego w Warszawie* [The Kościuszko Uprising as seen in the correspondence of the Austrian representative in Warsaw]. Warszaw: Pax, 1985,

Casanova, Giacomo. *History of My Life. Volumes 9 and 10.* Translated by Willard R. Trask. Baltimore: Johns Hopkins University Press, 1970.

Casanova, Jacques. *The Memoirs of Jacques Casanova de Seingalt: The Rare and Unabridged London Edition of 1894.* Translated by Arthur Machen. London: 1894.

Chlapowski, Dezydery. *Pamiętniki, Wojny Napoleońskie, 1806–1813* [Memoirs of the Napoleonie Wars 1806–1813]. Poznan: Nakladem Synow, 1899.

Ciepieńko-Zielińska, Donata. *Królewięta na Tulczynie* [*Kings of Tulczyn*]. Warsaw: Ksiazka i Wiedza, 1962.

Cloquet, M. Jules. *Recollections of the Private Life of General Lafayette.* Vol. 2. New York: Leavitt, Lord & Co., 1836.

Cruse, Mark, and Hoogenboom, Hilde. *The Memoirs of Catherine the Great: A New Translation.* New York: Modern Library, 2005.

Czartoryski, Adam Jerzy. *Żywot J. U. Niemcewicza* [The Life of J. U. Niemcewicz, including his letters ands speeches]. Berlin: B. Behr, 1860.

Dann, John C., ed. *The Revolution Remembered: Eyewitness Accounts of the War for Independence.* Chicago: University of Chicago Press, 1980.

De Koven, Mrs. Reginald (Anna). *The Life and Letters of John Paul Jones.* Vol. 2. New York: Charles Scribner's Sons, 1913.

De Lamartine, Alphonse. *History of the Girondists: Or, Personal Memoirs of the Patriots of the French Revolution, From Unpublished Sources.* Vol. 2. Translated by H. T. Ryde. New York: Harper & Brothers, 1848.

De Levis, M. Le Duc. *Souvenirs De Felicie, Par Mme de Genlis, Suivi des Souvenirs et Portraits.* With foreword and notes by M. F. Barriere. Paris: Librairie de Firmin-Didot et C, 1879.

Denny, Ebenezer. *A Military Journal Kept By Major E. Denny, 1781 to 1795: Memoirs of the Historical Society of Pennsylvania.* Philadelphia: J.B. Lippincott & Co., 1860.

Dickinson, John. *The Letters of Fabius, in 1788, on the Federal Constitution; and in 1797 on the Present Situation of Public Affairs.* Wilmington: W. C. Smyth, 1797.

Drummond, William Hamilton. *Autobiography of Archibald Hamilton Rowan, Esq.* Dublin, Ireland: Thomas Tegg and Co., 1840.

Drzewiecki, Józef. *Pamiętniki Józefa Drzewieckiego (1772–1852)* [Memoirs of Józef Drzewiecki]. Kraków: Gebethner i sp., 1891.

Duer, William Alexander, ed. *Memoirs, Correspondence and Manuscripts of General Lafayette.* London: Saunders and Otley, 1837.

Dumouriez, Charles Francois. *Mémoires et Correspondance inedits.* Paris, 1834.

Dunlap, William. *Diary of William Dunlap, 1766–1839: the Memoirs of a Dramatist, Theatrical Manager, Painter, Critic, Novelist, and Historian.* New York: Collections of the New-York Historical Society, 1930.

Eisenbach, Artur, Jerzy Michalski, Emanuel Rostworowski, and Janusz Wolinski, ed., *Materiały do Dziejów Sejmu Czteroletniego* (Materials pertaining to the history of the Four-Year Seym). Vol. 6. Wroclaw: Instytut Historii Polskiej Akademii Nauk, 1969.

Fairchild, Mary C. Doll, ed. *Memoirs of Colonel Sebastian Beauman and His Descendants: With Selections from His correspondence,* Franklin, Ohio: Editor Pub. Co., 1900.

Field, Edward, ed. *Diary of Colonel Israel Angell, Commanding the Second Rhode Island Continental Regiment during the American Revolution, 1778–1781.* Transcribed from the original manuscript. Providence, RI: Preston and Rounds Company, 1899.

Ford, Worthington Chauncey, ed. *The Writings of George Washington.* New York: G.P. Putnam's Sons, 1889.

Fouché, Joseph. *Memoirs of Joseph Fouché, Duke of Otranto, Minister of the General Police of France.* London: Gibbings, & Co., 1894.

Gibbes, Robert Wilson. *Documentary History of the American Revolution: Consisting of Letters and Papers Relating to the Contest for Liberty, Chiefly in South Carolina, From Originals in the Possession of the Editor, and Other Sources.* New York: D. Appleton & Co., 1857.

Glover, Zygmunt. *Księga Rzeczy Polskich* [Book of Polish Works]. Lwów: Nakładem Macierzy Polskiej, 1896.

Gordon, Jakob. *Przechadzki po Ameryce* (A stroll through America). Berlin and Poznan: Ksiegarnia B. Behr'a, 1866.

Greene, George Washington, *The Life of Nathanael Greene: Major-General in the Army of the Revolution.* Boston: Charles C. Little and James Brown, 1846.

———. *The Life of Nathanael Greene: Major-General in the Army of the Revolution.* Vol. 3. New York: Hurd and Hougton, 1871.

———. *The Life of Nathanael Greene: Major-General in the Army of the Revolution.* Vol. 1. Boston and New York: Houghton Mifflin and Company, 1890.

Griffin, Martin, I.J., *General Thaddeus Kościuszko.* Philadelphia: American Catholic Historical Researches. Vol. VI, April 1910.

———. *Catholics and the American Revolution*. Vol. 3. Philadelphia: Published by the Author, 1911.

Grzelonski, Bogdan. *Jefferson, Kościuszko Correspondence*, Warsaw: Interpress Publishers, 1978.

Hamilton, Alexander. *The Official and Other Papers of the Late Major General Alexander Hamilton*. New York and London: Wiley & Putnam, 1842.

Hamilton, John Church. *History of the Republic of the United States of America: As Traced in the Writings of Alexander Hamilton and His Contemporaries,* Philadelphia: J.B. Lippincott & Co., 1864.

Heath, William. *Memoirs of Major-General Heath containing anecdotes, details of skirmishes, battles, and other military events, during the American war*. Boston: Printed by I. Thomas and E.T. Andrews, 1798.

Humphreys, Col. David, *An Essay on the Life of the Honorable Major-General Israel Putnam*. Hartford, CT: Hudson and Goodwin, 1788.

Hunt, Gaillard, ed. *The Writings of James Madison: Comprising His Public Papers and His Private Correspondence*, New York: G.P. Putnam's Sons, 1900.

Jefferson, Thomas. *Memoir, Correspondence, and Miscellanies from the Papers of Thomas Jefferson*. Vols. 2 and 3. Charlottesville, VA: F. Carr, 1829.

———. *The Writings of Thomas Jefferson*. Vol. 3. New York: G.P. Putnam's Sons, 1894.

———. *Notes of the State of Virginia*. Richmond, VA: J.W. Randolph, 1853.

———. *The Writings of Thomas Jefferson, Being His Autobiography, Correspondence, Reports, Messages Addresses, and Other Writings, Official And Private. From the Original Manuscripts*. Edited by H. A. Washington. Vol. 8: New York: Derby & Jackson, 1854.

———. *The Writings of Thomas Jefferson*, Edited by Andrew A. Lipscomb. Vols. 13 and 18. Washington, DC: Thomas Jefferson Memorial Association, 1905 and 1903.

Johnson, Joseph. *Traditions and Reminiscences, chiefly of the American Revolution*, Charleston, SC: 1851.

Johnson, William. *Sketches of the Life and Correspondence of Nathanael Greene: Major General of the Armies of the United States, In the War of the Revolution, Compiled Chiefly from Original Materials*. Vol. 1. Charleston: A. E. Miller, 1822.

Jones, John Paul. *Memoirs of Paul Jones: Late Rear-Admiral in the Russian Service*. London: Henry Washbourne, 1843.

———. *John Paul Jones' Memoir of the American Revolution Presented to King Louis XVI of France*. Translated by Gerard W. Gawalt. Honolulu: University Press of the Pacific, 1979.

King, Charles R., ed. *The Life and Correspondence of Rufus King*, New York: G. P. Putnam's Sons, 1895.

Kitowicz, Jędrzej, and Zawadzki, Władysław, eds. *Pamiętniki Ks. A. Kitowicza* [The memoirs of Rev. Kitowicz]. Vol. 2. Lwów: Gubrynowicz and Schmit, 1882.

Kołłątaj, Hugo, *Listy Anonima, i Prawo polityczne narodu polskiego*, (Anonymous letters and Political Law of the Polish Nation,) ed. Bogusław Leśnodorski i Helena Wereszycka, Warsaw: Państwowe Wydawn. Naukowe, 1954.

Kołłątaj, Hugo. *Wybór Pism Politycznych* [Chosen Political Writings]. Edited by Bogusław Lesnodorski. Wrocław: Zakład Narodowy Imienia Ossolińskich, 1952.

Kościuszko, Tadeusz. *Pisma Józefa Chwaliboga, Listy Jenerała Kościuszki do Tekli Żurowskiej, Pisane w Roku 1791 w Międzybożu*. Lwów: Tłoczono w Drukarni Stauropigiańskiej, 1849.

———. *Autograph Letters of Thaddeus Kościuszko in the American Revolution*. Edited by Metchie J. Budka. Chicago: Polish Museum of America, 1977.

———, and Jefferson, Thomas. *Korespondencja* [Correspondence]. Edited by Izabella Rusinowa. Warsaw: Państwowy Instytut Wydawniczy, 1976.

———. *Listy, Odezwy, Wspomnienia* [Letters, proclamations, Recollections]. Edited by H. Mościcki. Warszaw: Gebethner i Wolff, 1917.

———. *Pisma Tadeusza Kosciuszki* [Writings of Tadeusz Kościuszko]. Edited by Henryk Moscicki. Warszaw: Panstwowe Zakłady Wyd. Szkolnych, 1947.

———. *Manoeuvres of Horse Artillery*. New York: U.S. Military Philosophical Society, 1808.

———. (Dr. J. A. Konopka, Editor), *Lettres de Soleure de Tadeusz Kościuszko, 1815–1817, Facsimiles et textes* [Letters from Soleure, facsimiles, and texts]. Geneva: Imprimeries de Versoix, 2000.

Kosmowski, Stanisław. *Pamietniki Stanisława Kosmowskiego z konca XVIIwieku* [Memoirs of Stanisław Kosmowski from the end of the eighteenth century]. Poznań: J.K. Żupański, 1867.

Kopczewski, Jan Stanisław. *Tadeusz Kościuszko w Historii i Tradycji* [Kościuszko in history and tradition]. Warsaw: Panstwowe Zakłady Wydawnictw Szkolnych, 1968.

Koźmian, Kajetan. *Pamiętniki Kajetana Koźmiana, obejmujące wspomnienia od roku 1780 do roku 1815* [Memoirs of Kajetan Koźmian, encompassing recollections from the years 1780 to 1815]. Poznań: J.K. Żupański, 1858.

Larned, Joseph Nelson, and Augustus Hunt Shearer, *The New Larned History for Ready Reference, Reading and Research: The Actual Words of the World*. Springfield, MA: C.A. Nichols Publishing Company, 1922.

Leake, Isaac Q. *Memoir of the life and times of General John Lamb, an officer of the revolution, who commanded the post at West Point at the time of Arnold's defection, and his correspondence with Washington, Clinton, Patrick Henry, and other distinguished men of his time*. Albany, NY: Joel Munsell, 1850.

Lee, Henry. *Memoirs of the War in the Southern Department of the United States*. Washington, DC: Printed by Peter Force, 1827.

Lewi, Rabbi Hirsh Dawid. *Mowa Hirsh Dawida Lewi miana w dniu 16. Października 1820 Roku. Do Ludu zebranego z okazyi obchodzoney w tymże Dniu uroczystości założenia Pomnika Tadeusza Kościuszki*. [A Speech by Hirsh David Lewi, rabbi of the Kazimierz District, on the day of Oct. 16, 1820, to the people gathered on this day to celebrate the establishment of a monument to honor Thaddeus Kosciuszko]. Translated from the Hebrew by Samuel Baum. Kraków, 1820.

Liancourt, Duc de La Rochefoucault. *Travels Through the United States of North America, The Country of the Iroquois, and Upper Canada, in the Years 1795, 1796, and 1797*. London: R. Philips, 1799.

――――. *Travels Through the United States of North America, The Country of the Iroquois, and Upper Canada, in the Years 1795, 1796, and 1797*. Vol. 2. London: R. Philips, 1799.

Lichocki, Filip, *Pamietnik Filipa Lichockiego, prezydent miasta Krakowa in 1794, (Memoir of Philip Lichocki, Mayor of Kraków in 1794)*, Poznań: 1862.

Logan, Deborah Norris, *Memoir of Dr. George Logan of Stenton*, Philadelphia: Historical Society of Pennsylvania, 1899.

Łojek, Jerzy, (ed.), *Rok nadziei i rok klęski, 1791-1792; z korespondencji Stanisława Augusta z posłem polskim w Peterburgu Augustynem Dęboli, (The Year of Hope and Defeat, 1791-1792; Correspondence between Stanisław August and the Polish Representative in Petersburg, August Dęboli,)* Warszawa: Czytelnik, 1964.

Małachowski, Stanisław, and Wincenty Łoś, eds. *Pamiętniki Stanisława hr. Nałęcz Małachowskiego* [Memoirs of Stanisław Malachowski]. Poznań: Księgarnia J. K. Żupański, 1885.

Maroger, Dominique, ed. *The Memoirs of Catherine the Great*. New York: The Macmillan Company, 1955.

Mazzei, Filippo. *Memoirs of the life and peregrinations of the Florentine Philip Mazzei, 1730–1816*. Translated by Howard Rosario Marraro. New York: Columbia University Press, 1942.

――――. *Selected Writings and Correspondence*. vols. 2 and 3. *Agent for the King of Poland during the French Revolution*. Edited by Margherita Marchione. Prato, Italy: Cassa di Risparmi e Depositi, 1983.

Mączyński, Wojciech. Edited by Jozef Mączyński. *Kościuszkowskie Czasy, wypisane z księgni wspomnien Wojciecha Mączynskiego, Pułkownika Kommendant Milicji Rzeczpospolitej Krakowskie, "Czas": Dodatek miesieczny, Tom. VII, Lipiec, Sierpien, Wrzesien* [Kosciuszko's Times, taken from the diaries of Wojciech Maczynski, Colonel Commandant of the Republic's Militia in Kraków, in the Monthly Time, Vol. 7, July, Aug. Sept.] Kraków: Czas, 1857.

Meneval, Claude-François. *Memoirs of Napoleon Bonaparte, The Court of the First Empire*. New York: P. F. Collier & Son, 1910.

Monroe, James. *The Writings of James Monroe, Including a Collection of his Public and Private Papers and Correspondence*. Vol. 2. New York: G.P. Putnam's Sons, 1899.

Moore, Frank. *Diary of the American Revolution: From Newspapers and Original Documents*. New York: Charles Scribner, 1860.

Morris, Richard Brandon, and Commager, Henry Steele. *The Spirit of 'Seventy-Six: The Story of the American Revolution as Told by Participants*. Indianapolis: Bobbs-Merrill, 1958.

Moscicki, Henryk ed. *Na Schyłku Dni Rzeczpospolitej: Kartki z pamiętnika Michała Starzeńskiego* [The closing days of the republic: pages from the diary of Michael Starzeński]. Warszaw: Gebethner i Wolff, 1914.

Nabielak, Ludwik, ed. *Tadeusz Kościuszko, jego odezwy i raporty* [Thaddeus Kosciuszko, his proclamations and reports]. Vols. 1–8. Paris: Księgarnia Luxemborg, 1871.

Niemcewicz, Julian Ursyn. *Notes of My Captivity in Russia, in the Years, 1794, 1795, and 1796.* Translated by Alexander Laski. Edinburgh: William Tate, 1844.

———. *Pamiętniki czasów moich* [Memoirs of my times]. Lipsk: F.A. Brockhaus, 1868.

———. *Pamiętniki Czasów Moich* [Memoirs of my times]. Vol. 1. Warsaw: Państwowy Instytut Wydawniczy, 1957.

———. *Podróże po Ameryce, 1797–1807. Z rękopisu wydała, wstępem i objaśnieniami opatrzyla Antonina Wellman-Zalewska, pd red. Emila Kipy* [Travels through America, 1797–1807, from handwritten notes published and edited by . . .]. Wrocław: Zakład Narodowy im Ossolinskich, 1959.

———. *Podroz z Petersburga do Szwecyi, w Drodze do Ameryki, w roku 1796, Dziennik Mojej Podróży* [A journey from St. Petersburg to Sweden, on the road to America, in the year 1796, Diary of my journey]. Poznań: J.K. Żupański, 1858.

———. *Under Their Vine and Fig Tree, Travels through America in 1797–1700, 1805 with some further account of life in New Jersey.* Translated and edited by Metchie J. E. Budka. Elizabeth, NJ: Grassman Publishing, 1965.

Oginski, Michel. *Mémoires sur la Pologne et le Polonais, depuis 1788 jusqu'à la fin 1815.* Vol. 2. Paris, 1826.

Olszer, Krystyna M., ed. *For Your Freedom and Ours: Polish Progressive Spirit, From the 14th Century to the Present.* (Excerpts from old documents and historical writings.) New York: Frederick Ungar Publishing Co., 1981.

Parsons, Jacob Cox, ed. *Extracts From the Diary of Jacob Hiltzheimer of Philadelphia, 1765–1798.* Philadelphia: Wm. F. Fell & Co., 1893.

Pawlikowski, Józef, Tadeusz Kościuszko (anonymously), and Emanuel Halicz, eds. *Czy Polacy Wybić Się Moga Na Niepodległość?* [Can the Poles win their independence?] Warsaw: Wydawnictwo Ministerstwa Obrony Narodowej, 1967. Originally published as a pamphlet in Paris in 1800.

Paul Jones, John. *Memoirs of Rear-Admiral Paul Jones.* Vol. 1. London: Simpkin & Marshal, 1830.

Peters, Richard. *Reports of the Cases Argued and Adjudged in the Supreme Court of the United States, January Term, 1834.* New York: Banks Law Publishing, 1903.

Poniatowski, Stanisław Augustus. *Mémoires secrets et inedits de Stanislas Auguste, comte Poniatowski, dernier roi de Pologne.* Leipzig: W. Gerhard, 1862.

———. *Mémoires de roi Stanislas-Auguste Poniatowski.* Edited by A. S. Lappo-Danilevskii and S. M. Goriainov. Vol. 1. St. Petersburg, 1914.

Pontgiband, Chevalier de. *A French Volunteer of the War of Independence.* Translated by Robert B. Douglas. New York: D. Appleton and Company, 1898.

Potocka, Anna. *Memoirs of Countess Potocka.* Edited by Casimir Stryienski. Authorized Translation by Lionel Stracey. New York: Doubleday & McClure Co., 1901.

Quincy, Josiah. *The Journals of Major Samuel Shaw: The First American Consul at Canton.* Boston: WM. Crosby and H. P. Nichols, 1847.

Raczyński, Edwards. *Obraz Polaków i Polski w XVII Wieku, Zbiór Pamiętników, Dyaryuszów, Korrespondencyj Publicznych i Listów Prywatnych, Podróży i Opisów Zdarzeń Szczególnych, służacych Do Wyjaśnienia Stanu Polski W Wierku Wspomnionym, Wydany Z Rękopisów* [A Picture of Poles and Poland in the eighteenth century: A collection of memoirs, diaries, public correspondence and private letters, travelogues, and descriptions of specific events, serving to elucidate the Polish state from handwritten manuscripts]. Poznan: Ksiegarnia Nowej, 1842. (Includes Thaddeus Kościuszko's handwritten manuscript outlining the campaign against the Muscovites in 1792.)

Reed, William B. *The Life and Correspondence of Joseph Reed, Military Secretary of Washington, at Cambridge; Adjutant General of the Continental Army; Member of the Congress of the United States; and President of the Executive Council of the State of Pennsylvania.* Vol. 2. Philadelphia: Lindsay and Blakiston, 1847.

Richards, Samuel. *Diary of Samuel Richards, Captain of Connecticut Line, War of the Revolution, 1775–1781.* Philadelphia: 1909.

Sanguszki, Księcia (Prince) Eustachego. *Pamiętnik 1786-1815.* [Diary] Kraków: Drukarni Uniwersytetu Jagiellonski, 1876.

Sapieha, Leon. *Wspomnienia: z lat 1803 do 1863 r.* [Recollections: of the years 1803 to 1863]. Lwów: A. Altenberg, 1913.

Sedgwick, Catherine Maria. *The Power of Her Sympathy: The Autobiography and Journals of Catharine Maria Sedgwick*, Boston, Massachusetts Historical Society, 1993. First published in 1822.

Seymour, William. *A Journal of the Southern Expedition, 1780–1783: The Pennsylvania Magazine of History and Biography.* Vol. 7. Philadelphia: Historical Society of Pennsylvania, 1883.

Siemienski, Lucyan. *Listy Hugona Kołłątaja, Pisane z Emigracyi, 1792, 1793, 1794,* [The letters of Hugo Kollatay, written in exile, 1792, 1793 and 1794]. Vol. 2. Poznań: Jan Kostanty Żupański, 1872.

———. *Listy Kościuszki do jenarala Mokrońskiego i innych osób pisane* (Kościuszko's letters to General Mokroński and others). Lwów: Gubrynowicz i Schmidt, 1877.

Skałkowski, A. M. *Pamiętnik damy polskiej o Kościuszce, "Przegląd Historyczny"* [Memoirs of a Polish lady concerning Kościuszko, "Historical Review"], 1934.

———, ed. *Z Korespondencji Kościuszki Urzędowej i Prywatnej: 1790–1817* [The official and private correspondence of Kościuszko, 1790–1817]. Kornik: Nakładem Fundacji Zakłady Kornickie, 1946.

———. *Archiwum Wybickiego* [Wybicki archives]. Vol. 1. Gdańsk: Nakładem Towarzystwa Przyjaciól Nauki i Sztuki, 1948.

Smith, Gerrit. *Speeches of Gerrit Smith in Congress [1853–1854],* New York: Mason Brothers, 1855.

Smith, William Henry. *The St. Clair Papers: The Life and Public Services of Arthur St. Clair.* Cincinnati: Robert Clarke & Co., 1882.

Sparks, Jared. *The Writings of George Washington*. Vol. 11. Boston: Russell, Shattuck and Williams, 1836.

———. *Correspondence of the American Revolution: Being Letters of Eminent Men to George Washington, From the Time of His Taking Command of The Army to The End of His Presidency*. Vol. 3. Boston: Little, Brown and Company, 1853. (Edited from the original manuscripts)

Sobolowa, Barbara, ed. *Wolność, Całość i Niepodległość, 1794, Powstanie Kościuszkowskie w dokumencie archiwalnym* [*Liberty, Unity, and Independence, the Kościuszko uprising of 1794 in archive documents*]. Warszaw: MON, 1985,

Soroka, Jerzy. "Pamiętnik Jerzego Soroki." *Tydgodnik Ilustrowany* 12 (1881), 197 ["Memoirs of Jerzy Soroka." *Illustrated Weekly*].

Sułkowski, Generał Józef. *Życie i Pamiętniki* [*Life and memoirs*]. Poznań: J.K. Żupański, 1864.

Thacher, James. *A Military Journal During the American Revolutionary War, from 1775 to 1783; Describing Interesting Events and Transactions of This Period; with Numerous Facts and Anecdotes*. Boston: Cottons & Barnard, 1827.

Toll, Johan Christopher. *Powstanie Kościuszkowskie, w swietle korespondencji posła szwedzkiego w Warszawie* [*The Kościuszko uprising as seen in the correspondence of the Swedish representative in Warsaw*]. Warsaw: Państwowe Wydawnictwo Naukowe, 1989.

Trumbull, John. *Autobiography, Reminiscences and Letters of John Trumbull*. New Haven: B. L. Hamlen, 1841.

Turner, F. J., *Correspondence of the French Ministers to the United States, 1791–1797, Annual Report of the American Historical Association, For the Year 1903*. Vol. 2. Washington, DC: U.S. Government Printing Office, 1904.

Upham, William P. ed. *Memoir of General John Glover*. Salem: Charles W. Swasey, 1863.

Volney, Constantin François. *View of the Climate and Soil of the United States of America*. London: J. Johnson, 1804

Warner, Rev. Richard. *Literary Recollections*. Vol. 2. London: Longman, Reees, Orme, Brown and Green, 1830.

Washington, Booker T. "My Larger Education: Being Chapters from My Experience," Garden City, NY: Doubleday, Page & Company, 1911.

Watson, Elkanah. *Men and Times of the Revolution; Or, Memoirs of Elkanah Watson*. New York: Dana and Company, 1856.

Watts, J. F., and Freid L. Israel, eds. *Presidential Documents: The Speeches, Proclamations, and Policies That Have Shaped the Nation from Washington to Clinton*. New York: Routledge, 1999.

Wilkinson, Gen. James. *Memoirs of My Own Times, In Three Volumes*. Vol. 1. Philadelphia: Printed by Abraham Small, 1816.

Williams, Helen Maria. *A narrative of the events which have taken place in France, from the landing of Napoleon Bonaparte on the First of March, 1815, Till the Restoration of Louis XVIII*. Philadelphia: Moses Thomas, 1816.

Wilson, Matthew. "Observations on the Severity of the Winter 1779, 1780, by the Reverend Mathew Wilson of Lewis, Dated 22d June 1780." *Transactions of the American Philosophical Society* 3 (1793), pp. 326–328.

Wodzicki, Stanisław. *Wspomnienia z przeszłości od r. 1768 do r. 1840. [Recollections of the past from 1768 to 1840]*. Kraków: A Nowolecki, 1873.

Wójcicki, Kazimierz Władysław. *Pamiętniki dziecka Warszawy I inne wspomnienia warszawskie, tom 1* Warszaw: Panstwowy Instytut Wydawnicy, 1974.

Wojda, Karol. *O Rewolucji Polskie; w roku 1794 [About the revolution in Poland, in the year 1794]*. Poznan: J.K. Żupanski, 1867. These memoirs were originally published in German in Zurich, in 1796, as *Versuch einer Geschichte der lezten polnischen Revolution vom Jahr 1794*, by Karol Fryderyk Wojda.

Wolf, Simon. *American Jew as Patriot, Soldier and Citizen, A Sketch of Haym Salomon: From An Unpublished MS in the Papers of Jared Sparks*. Contributed by Herbert B. Adams, Ph. D., Professor in the Johns Hopkins University, with Notes by J. H. Hollander. Philadelphia: Levytype Company, 1895. (The Salomon sketch begins on p. 14.)

Zeltner, Xavier. "Personal Reminiscences of Kościuszko." *United States Service Magazine* 4 (Aug. 1865).

Books and Historical Periodicals

Abbott, Jacob. *Pyrrhus*. New York and London: Harper & Brothers, 1901.

Adler, Jeanne Winston. *Chainbreaker's War: A Seneca Chief Remembers the American Revolution*. Hensonville, NY: Black Dome Press Corp., 2002.

Alexander, John T. *Catherine the Great, Life and Legend*. New York: Oxford University Press, 1989.

Alger, John Goldworth. *Paris in 1789–94: Farewell Letters of Victims of the Guillotine*. London: George Allen, 1902.

Arnold, Isaac Newton. *The Life of Benedict Arnold*. Chicago: Jansen, McClurg, 1880.

Askenazy, Szymon. *Książę Józef Poniatowski, 1763–1813*. Warszaw: Gebethner i Wolff, 1905.

———. *Nowe czasy [New times]*. Warszaw: Gebethner i Wolff, 1910.

———. *Upadek Polski a Francya [France and the fall of Poland]*. Warszaw: Biblioteka Warszawska, 1913.

———. *Napoleon a Polska*. 3 vols. Warszaw: Towarzystwo Wydawnicze w Warszawie, 1918.

Bałaban, Majer. *Album Pamiątkowy ku czci Berka Joselewicza pułkownika wojsk polskich [Memorial album of Berek Joselewicz, colonel of the Polish military]*. Warszaw: 1934.

Bancroft, George. *The History of the United States of America, from the Discovery of the Continent [to 1789]*. New York: D. Appleton and Company, 1885.

Bartel, Wojciech M. *O Kościuszce i o jego Spotkaniach z Krakowem [About Kościuszko and his meetings with Kraków]*. Kraków: Towarzystwo Milośników Historii i Zabytków Krakowa, 1969.

Bartoszewicz, Kazimierz. *Konstytucya 3 Maja, Kronika dni kwietniowych i majowych w Warszawie w r. 1791* [*The May 3 Constitution, a chronicle of the days of April and May in Warsaw in 1791*]. Warszaw: A. T. Jezierski, 1906.

———. *Dzieje Insurekcji Kościuszkowskiej* [History of the Kościuszko insurrection]. Vienna: F. Bondy, 1909.

Bauer, Krzysztof. *Wojsko koronne powstania Kościuszkowsiego* [*The crown's army in the Kościuszko uprising*]. Warszawa: Ministry of Defense, 1981.

Boatner, Mark M. *Encyclopedia of the American Revolution*. New York: David McKay Company, Inc. 1966.

Bolton, Robert. *A History of the County of Westchester, From Its First Settlement to the Present Time*. Vol. 1, New York: Alexander S. Gould, 1848.

Bolton, Sarah Knowles. *Famous Leaders Among Women*. New York: Thomas Y. Cromwell & Company, 1895.

Borzymińska, Zofia, and Rafał Żebrowski. *Polski Slownik Judaisztyczny* [*The Polish encyclopedia of Judaism*]. Warsaw: Prószynski, 2003.

Bourrienne, Louis Antoine Fauvelet de. *Memoirs of Napoleon Bonaparte*. Vol. 3. New York: Charles Scribner's Sons, 1892. (Bourrienne was Napoleon's private secretary.)

Boynton, Edward C. *History of West Point and Its Military Importance During the American Revolution*. New York: D. Van Nostrand, 1863.

Brady, Cyrus Townsend. *Commodore Paul Jones*. New York: D. Appleton and Company, 1900.

Brandt, Clare. *The Man in the Mirror: A Life of Benedict Arnold*. New York: Random House, 1994.

Buell, Augustus C. *Paul Jones: Founder of the American Navy, A History*. New York: Charles Scribner's Sons, 1906.

Bratkowski, Stefan. *Tadeusz Kościuszko, Z czym do nieśmiertelnosci* [*Traces of Immortality*]. Katowice: Wydawnictwo, Slask, 1977.

Butler, Samuel. *Hudibras*. New York: D. Appleton & Company, 1856.

Carroll, Andrew, ed. *Behind the Lines, Powerful and Revealing American and Foreign War Letters—and One Man's Secret to Find Them*. New York: Scribner: 2005.

Chodzko, Leonard. *Histoire des Légions Polonaises en Italie* [*History of the Polish legions in Italy*]. *Vols. 1 and 2*. Paris: J. Barbezat: 1829.

Crackel, Theodore J. *West Point: A Bicentennial History*. Lawrence: University Press of Kansas, 2002.

Cobbett, William. *Porcupine's Works*. Vol. 7. London: Cobbett and Morgan, 1801.

Cutter, William. *The Life of General Lafayette*. New York: George F. Cooledge & Brother, 1849.

Davies, Norman. *God's Playground: A History of Poland, in Two Volumes*. New York: Columbia University Press, 1982.

Diamant, Lincoln. *Chaining the Hudson: The Fight for the River in the American Revolution*. New York: Fordham University Press, 2004.

Dihm, Jan. *Kościuszko Nieznany [The unknown Kościuszko]*. Wroclaw: Ossolineum, 1969.

Dobrenko, Evgeny. *Political Economy of Socialist Realism*. Translated by Jesse M. Savage. New Haven: Yale University Press, 2007.

Dorwart, Jeffery M. *Fort Mifflin of Philadelphia: An Illustrated History*. Philadelphia: Pennsylvania University Press, 1998.

Dubnow, Simon M. *History of the Jews in Russian and Poland: From the Earliest Times Until the Present Day [1915]*. Philadelphia: Jewish Publication Society of America, 1918.

Dunlap, William. *History of the New Netherlands, Province of New York, and State of New York, to the Adoption of the Federal Constitution*. New York: Carter & Thorp, 1840.

Dzwonkowski, Włodzimierz A. *Młode lata Kościuszki [Kosciuszko's early years]*. Biblioteka Warszawska, 1911.

Falk, Avner. *A Psychoanalytic History of the Jews*. Madison, NJ: Fairleigh Dickinson University Press, 1996.

Falkenstein, Karol. *Tadeusz Kościuszko, czyli Dokładny Rys Jego Życia [Thaddeus Kościuszko, a precise outline of his life]*. Wrocław: Wilhelm Bogumił, 1827.

Egleston, Thomas. *The Life of John Patterson: Major General in the Revolutionary Army*. New York: G.P. Putnam's Sons, 1894.

Evans, Anthony Walton White. *Memoir of Thaddeus Kościuszko: Poland's Hero and Patriot, An Officer in the American Army of the Revolution, and Member of the Society of Cincinnati*. New York: Printed for the Society, 1883.

Falkenstein, Karl. *Thaddäus Kościuszko, nach seinem offentlichen und hauslichen leben geschildert [Thaddaus Kosciuszko, depicted through his public and private life]*. Translated by Adam Waldie. Philadelphia: Museum of Foreign Literature and Science, 1835.

Fiske, John. *The American Revolution*. Boston: Houghton, Mifflin and Company/Riverside Press, 1891.

Fiszman, Samuel, *Constitution and Reform in Eighteenth Century Poland, The Constitution of 3 May 1791,* Bloomington: Indiana University Press, 1997.

Fellows, John. *The Veil Removed: Or, Reflections on David Humphrey's Essay on the Life of Israel Putnam*. New York: James D. Lockwood, 1842.

Garden, Alexander. *Anecdotes of the Revolutionary War in America*. Charleston: A.E. Miller, 1822.

Gardiner, Monica M. *Kościuszko, A Biography*. London: George Allen & Unwin, Ltd., 1920.

Goodrich, S. G., ed. *The Token and Atlantic Souvenir: A Christmas and New Year's Present*. Boston: Gray and Bowen, 1833.

Gordon-Reed, Annette, *The Hemingses of Monticello: An American Family*. New York: W. W. Norton & Co., 2008.

Graetz, Heinrich Hirsch. *History of the Jews*. Vol. 4, Philadelphia: Jewish Publication Society of America, 1974. Originally published in 1898.

Graham, James. *The Life of General Daniel Morgan, of the Virginia Line of the Army of the United States, With Portions of his Correspondence, Compiled From Authentic Sources*. New York: Derby & Jackson, 1856.

Griswold, Rufus Wilmot Griswold. *The Republican Court, or American Society in the Days of Washington.* New York: D. Appleton and Company, 1856.

Haiman, Miecislaus. *Kościuszko in the American Revolution.* New York: Kościuszko Foundation, 1975. First published in 1943 by the Polish Institute of Arts and Sciences in America.

———. *Kościuszko, Leader and Exile.* New York: Kościuszko Foundation, 1977. First published in 1946 by the Polish Institute of Arts and Sciences in America.

———. *Poland and the American Revolutionary War.* Chicago: Polish Roman Catholic Union of America, 1932.

———. *The Fall of Poland in Contemporary American Opinion.* Chicago: Polish Roman Catholic Union of America, 1935.

Halecki, Oscar. "The Third of May, Kościuszko, and Polish Democracy." *Bulletin of the Polish Institute of Arts and Sciences in America* (July 1944).

Hahn, Wiktor. *Stanisław Staszic: życie i dzieła [Stanisław Staszic His Life and Work].* Lublin: Gebethner i Wolff, 1926.

Haslip, Joan. *Catherine the Great.* New York: G.P. Putnam's Sons, 1978.

Hill, David Jayne. *A History of Diplomacy in the International Development of Europe.* New York: Longmans, Green & Co., 1907.

Hindle, Brooke, *David Rittenhouse,* New York: Arno Press, 1980.

Hirsch, Eric Donald, Joseph F. Kett, and James S. Trefil. *The New Dictionary of Cultural Literacy.* New York: Houghton Mifflin Books, 2002.

Hirschfeld, Fritz. *George Washington and Slavery: A Documentary Portrayal.* Columbia and London: University of Missouri Press, 1997.

Hoffman, Mark S. *The World Almanac and Book of Facts.* New York: World Almanac Education Group, Facts on File, Inc., Newspaper Enterprise Association, Robert Famighetti, 1923.

Horne, R. H., ed., *The History of Napoleon, Vol. II.* London: Robert Tyas, 1841.

Hough, Franklin Benjamin. *The Siege of Savannah: By the combined American and French forces, under the command of Gen. Lincoln, and the Count D'Estaing, in the Autumn of 1779.* Albany, NY: J. Munsell, 1866.

Humphreys, Frank Landon. *Life and Times of David Humphreys: Soldier—Statesman—Poet, "Belov'd of Washington."* New York: G.P. Putnam's Sons, 1917.

Hundert, Gershon David. *Jews in Poland-Lithuania in the Eighteenth Century: A Genealogy of Modernity.* Berkeley: University of California Press, 2006.

Irving, Washington. *The Life of George Washington.* Vol. 3, New York: G.P. Putnam & Co., 1857.

Jedruch, Jacek. *Constitutions, Elections and Legislatures of Poland 1493–1993.* New York: Hippocrene Books, Inc., 1998.

Jedynakiewicz, Katarzyna. *Osobowość i życie codzienne Tadeusza Kościuszko [The personality and daily life of Thaddeus Kosciuszko].* Łódz: Wydawnictwo Universytetu Łódzkiego, 1996.

Johnston, Henry Phelps. *The Storming of Stony Point on the Hudson, Midnight, July 15, 1779: Its Importance in the Light of Unpublished Documents.* New York: James T. White & Co., 1900.

Jones, Electa F. *Stockbridge, Past and Present, Or, Records of An Old Mission Station.* Springfield, MA: Samuel Bowles & Company, 1854.

Jullien, M. A. *Notice biographique sur le general polonais, Thadée Kościuszko.* Paris, 1818.

Kajencki, Francis Casimir, *Thaddeus Kościuszko: Military Engineer of the American Revolution.* El Paso, TX: Southwest Polonia Press, 1998.

Kaleta, Roman. *Oświeceni i sentymentalni: studia nad literaturą i życiem w Polsce w okresie trzech rozbiorów* [*The Enlightened and the Sentimental: A study of literature and life in Poland in the period of the three partitions*]. Wrocław: Zakład Narodowy im. Ossolińskich, 1971.

Kalinka, Ks. Waleryn. *Ostatnie Lata Panowania Stanisława Augusta* [*The final years of Stanislaw Augustus's rule*], 2 vols. Kraków: Nakładem Księgarni Spółki Wydawniczej Poskiej, 1891.

Keane, John. *Tom Paine: A Political Life.* Boston: Little Brown and Company, 1995.

Ketchum, Richard. *Saratoga: Turning Point of America's Revolutionary War.* New York: Henry Holt and Company, 1997.

Kite, Elizabeth S. *Beaumarchais and the War of American Independence.* Boston: Gorham Press, 1918.

Kite, Elizabeth S. *Brigadier General Louis Lebegue Duportail, Commandant of Engineers in the Continental Army* (Institut Français de Washington). Baltimore: John Hopkins Press/Philadelphia: Dolphin Press, 1933.

Knollenberg, Bernard. *Washington and the Revolution, A Reappraisal of Gates, Conway, and the Continental Congress.* New York: Macmillan Company, 1940.

Kohler, Max. *Haym Salomon, the Patriot Broker of the Revolution: His Real Achievements and their Exaggeration, An Open Letter to Congressman Celler.* New York: American Jewish Historical Society, 1931.

Korzon, Tadeusz. *Kościuszko, Biografia z Dokumentów Wysnuta* [*Kosciuszko, a biography derived from documents*]. Kraków: G. Gebethner i Spolka, 1894.

———. *Kim i czem byl, Kościuszko* [*Who and what was Kościuszko*]. Warsaw: G. Gebethner, 1907.

———. *Wewnętrzne Dzieje Polski, za Stanisława Augusta* [*A domestic History of Poland under Stanislaw August*]. 6 Vol. Kraków: L. Zwolinski, 1897–98.

Kozłowski, Wladyslaw. *Pierwszy Rok Służby Amerykanskiei Kosciuszki* [*The first year of Kościuszko's American Service*]. Warsaw: Przegląd Historyczny, IV, 1909.

Kozłowski, Władysław Mieczysław. *Washington and Kościuszko.* Chicago: Polish Roman Catholic Union of America, 1942.

Kraszewski, J. I., *Polska W Czasie Trzech Rozbiorow, 1772–1799* [*Poland in the time of the three partitions*]. Warsaw: Gebethnera I Wolffa, 1902.

Kunert, Andrzej Krzysztof, and Andrzej Przewoźnik. *Żydzi polscy w służbie Rzeczpospolitej* [*Polish Jews in the service of the republic*]. Warsaw: Rada Ochrony Pamięci Walk i Męczeństwa, 2002. Reprint of *Zydzi bojownicy o niepodleglosc Polski* [*Jewish fighters for Polish independence*]. Lwów: Lwowski Instytut Wydawniczy, 1939.

Leckie, Robert. *George Washington's War: The Saga of the American Revolution*. New York: HarperCollins, 1992.

———. *The Wars of America*. Vol. 1. New York: Harper & Row, 1968.

Lelewel, Joachim. *Polska Odradzajanca Się, Czyli, Dzieje Polskie Od Roku 1795*. [*Poland Resurrecting itself, or History of Poland from the year 1795*] Brussels: P.J. Vogleta, 1836.

———. *Polska dzieje i rzeczy jej* [*Poland's history and its affairs*]. Vol. 7. Poznań: J.K. Żupański, 1859.

Lesnodorski, Boguslaw. *Dzieło Sejmu Czteroletniego* [*The work of the four-year Sejm*]. Wrocław, 1951.

———. *Polscy Jakobini* [*Polish Jacobins*]. Warszaw: Ksiażka i Wiedza, 1960.

Lewinski-Corwin, Edward H., *The Political History of Poland*. New York: Polish Book Importing Company, 1917.

Levy, Artur. *The Private Life of Napoleon, Vol. I*, New York: Charles Scribner's Sons, 1894.

Little, E. *Little's Living Age*. Boston: E. Litttell & Company, 1851.

Lord, Robert Howard. *The Second Partition of Poland: A Study in Diplomatic History*. Cambridge, MA: Harvard University Press, 1915.

Lorenz, Lincoln. *The Admiral and the Empress: John Paul Jones and Catherine the Great*. New York: Bookman Associates, 1954.

Lossing, Benjamin J. *The Pictorial Handbook of the Revolution; Or Illustrations, By Pen And Pencil, Of The History, Biography, Scenery, Relics And Traditions Of The War For Independence, Vol. II*. New York: Harper & Brothers, 1852.

———. *The Pictoral Field-book of the Revolution: Or, Illustrations, By Pen And Pencil, Of The History, Biography, Scenery, Relics And Traditions Of The War For Independence, Vol. II*, New York: Harper & Brothers, 1860. (There are two versions of this book, this one dated 1860.)

Lossing, Benson John. *The Life and Times of Philip Schuyler*. New York: Sheldon & Company, 1873.

Łojek, Jerzy. *Misja Debolego w Petersburgu, w latach 1787–1792* [*The Mission of Deboli to Petersburg in the years 1787–1792*], Wrocław: Ossolineum, 1962.

———. *Polska inspiracja prasowa w Holandii i Niemczech w czasach Stanisława Augusta* [*Polish press inspiration in Holland and Germany in the Times of Stanislaw August*]. Warsaw: Państwowe Wydawnictwo Naukowe, 1969.

———. *Dzieje Pięknej Bitynki* [*History of beautiful Bitynka*]. Warsaw: Pax, 1970.

Łuninski, Ernest. *Berek Joselewicz i Jego Syn: Zarys Historyczny* [*Berek Joselewicz & His Son: Historical Outline*]. Warsaw: S. Orgelbrand,1909.

Macauley, James. *The Natural, Statistical, and Civil History of the State of New York.* Albany, NY: Gould & Banks, 1829.

Macheta, Stanisław. *Hugo Kołłataj.* Warszawa: Wiedza Powszechna, 1973.

Madelin, Louis. *The French Revolution.* New York: G.P. Putnam's Sons, 1916.

Malski, Wiktor. *Amerykańska Wojna Pułkownika Kościuszki [Colonel Kosciuszko's American War].* Warsaw: Książki i Wiedza, 1977.

Manning, Clarence A. *Soldier of Liberty, Casimir Pulaski.* New York: Philosophical Library, Inc., 1945.

Martin, Henri. *The Decline of the French Monarchy.* Boston: Walker, Fuller and Company, 1866.

Martin, James Kirby. *Benedict Arnold: Revolutionary Hero, An American Warrior Reconsidered,* New York: New York University Press, 1997.

Markens, Issac. *The Hebrews in America: A Series of Historical and Biographical Sketches.* New York: Published by the Author, 1888.

McCullough, David. *John Adams.* New York: Simon & Schuster, 2001.

Michelet, Jules. *Légendes démocratiques du Nord [Democratic legends of the North].* Paris: Levy, 1899.

Miller, John Chester. *The Wolf by the Ears: Thomas Jefferson and Slavery.* Charlottesville: University Press of Virginia, 1991.

Mintz, Max M. *The Generals of Saratoga: John Burgoyne and Horatio Gates.* New Haven: Yale University Press, 1990.

Montross, Lynn. *The Story of the Continental Army, 1775–1783.* New York: Barnes & Noble Inc., 1967.

Morais, Henry Samuel. *The Jews of Philadelphia: Their History from the Earliest Settlements to the Present Time.* Philadelphia: The Levytype Co. 1894.

Morison, Samuel Eliot. *John Paul Jones: A Sailor's Biography.* Boston: Little, Brown and Company, 1959.

Mrozowska, Kamilla. *Szkoła Rycerska Stanisława Augusta Poniatowskiego (1765–1794). [Stanislaw August Poniatowski's knight school 1765–1794].* Warsaw: Ossolineum, 1961.

Murdoch, Beamish. *A History of Nova Scotia Or Acadie.* Vol. 2. Halifax: James Barnes, 1866.

Nash, Gary B., and Graham Russell Gao, Hodges. *Friends of Liberty: Thomas Jefferson, Tadeusz Kosciuszko and Agrippa Hull.* New York: Basic Books, 2008.

Neilson, Charles. *An Original, Compiled and Corrected Account of Burgoyne's Campaign, and the Memorable Battles of Bemis Heights.* Albany, NY: J. Nunsell, 1844.

Nickerson, Hoffman. *The Turning Point of the Revolution: Or, Burgoyne in America.* Boston: Houghton Mifflin Company, 1928.

Nussbaum, Hilary. *Historyja Żydów od Mojżesza do epoki obecnej, Tom V [The history of Jews from Moses to the current epoch,* Vol. V]. Warsaw: I. Mayzner, 1890.

Ohryzko, Jozafat. *Pismo zbiorowe [Collected writings].* St. Petersburg: Jozafat Ohryzko Printers, 1859.

Ostrowski, Antoni Jan. *Żywot Tomasza Ostrowskiego, ministra Rzeczypospolitej,* [*The life of Thomas Ostrowski, minister of the republic*]. Lwów: U.F.H. Richter, 1873.

Pachoński, Jan Lubicz. *Kościuszkow niewoli carskiej, 1794–1796* [*Kosciuszko in czarist imprisonment*]. Kraków: Wydawnictwo Głownego Komitetu Kościuszkowskiego w Krakowie, 1947.

———. *Legiony Polskie, Prawda i Legenda, 1804–1807* [*The Polish legions, truth and legend*]. 3 Vols. Warsaw: Wydawnictwo Ministerstwa Obrony Narodowej, 1976.

———. *Kościuszko na Ziemi Krakowskiej* [*Kosciuszko in Cracowian land*]. Warsaw: Państwowe Wydawnictwo Naukowe, 1984.

———. *Kościuszko po Insurekcji, 1794–1817* [*Kościuszko after the insurrection*]. Lublin: Wydawnictwo Lubelski, 1986.

Paine, Thomas. *The Writings of Thomas Paine,* edited by Moncure Daniel Conway. Vol. 4. New York: G.P. Putnam's Sons, 1896.

———. *The Life and Writings of Thomas Paine* (containing a biography by Thomas Clio Rickman). New York: Vincent Parke and Company, 1908.

Palmer, Dave Richard. *The River and The Rock: The History of Fortress West Point, 1775–1783.* New York: Greenwood Publishing Corporation, 1969.

———. "Fortress West Point: 19th Century Concept in an 18th Century War." *Military Engineer* 68 (1976).

Paszkowski, Franciszek. *Dzieje Tadeusza Kościuszki, pierwszego naczelnika Polaków,* [*History of Thaddeus Kosciuszko, first commander of the Poles*]. Kraków: Uniwersytet Jagielloński, 1872.

———. *Książe Józef Poniatowski* [*Prince Joseph Poniatowski*]. Kraków: Spółka Wydawnicza Polska, 1898.

Patterson, Samuel White. *Horatio Gates: Defender of American Liberties.* New York: Columbia University Press, 1941.

Paulsson, Gunnar S. *Secret City: The Hidden Jews of Warsaw, 1940–1945,* New Haven: Yale University Press, 2002.

Peckham, Howard Henry. *The War for Independence: A Military History,* Chicago: University of Chicago Press, 1958.

Peters, Madison Clinton. *Haym Salomon: The Financier of the Revolution, An Unwritten Chapter in American History.* New York: The Trow Press, 1911.

———. *The Jews Who Stood by Washington: An Unwritten Chapter in American History,* New York: The Trow Press, 1915.

Philips, Philip Lee. *Notes on the Life and Works of Bernard Romans.* Florida State Historical Society, 1924.

Pinckney, Charles Cotesworth. *Life of General Thomas Pinckney.* Boston and New York: Houghton, Mifflin and Company, 1895.

Pula, James S. *Thaddeus Kościuszko: The Purest Son of Liberty.* New York: Hippocrene Books, 1999.

Quarles, Benjamin. *The Negro in the American Revolution*. Chapel Hill: University of North Carolina Press, 1961.

Rambaud, Alfred. *History of Russia*. Boston: C.F. Jewett Publishing Co., 1882.

Ramsay, David. *The Life of George Washington: Commander in Chief of the Armies of the United States of America*. New York: Hopkins & Seymour, 1807.

Randall, Henry Stephens. *The Life of Thomas Jefferson*. Philadelphia: J.B. Lippincott & Co., 1871.

Randall, Willard Sterne. *Benedict Arnold, Patriot and Traitor*. New York: Barnes and Noble Books, 1990.

————. and Nancy Nahra. *Forgotten Americans: Footnote Figures Who Changed American History*. Reading, MA: Perseus Books, 1998.

Rosten, Leo. *The Joys of Yiddish*. New York: Pocket Books, 1970.

Russell, Charles Edward. *Haym Salomon and the Revolution*. Freeport, NY: Books for Libraries Press, 1930.

Sachar, Abraham Leon. *A History of the Jews*. New York: Alfred Knopf, 1930.

Sargent, Winthrop. *The Life and Career of Major John André*. Boston: Ticknor and Fields, 1861.

Scharf, J. Thomas, and Thompson Westcott. *History of Philadelphia, 1609–1884*. Vol. 2. Philadelphia, L.H. Everts & Co., 1884.

Schappes, Morris U. *American Jewish Quarterly* 67, nos. 1 and 2 (Sept. and Dec. 1977). "Excerpts from Robert Morris' 'Diaries in the Officer of Finance, 1781–1784,' Referring to Haym Salomon and Other Jews."

Schouler, James. *History of the United States of America, Under the Constitution, Vol. I, 1783–1801*. New York: Dodd, Mead & Company, 1880.

Schultz, Friedrich. *Podroze Inflantczyka Rygi do Warszawy i po Polsce w latach 1791–1793* [*Travels of the Livonian from Riga to Warsaw and through Poland in the years 1791–1793*]. Warsaw: Czytelnik, 1956.

Shatzky, Jacob. *Kościuszko a Zydzi* [*Kościuszko and the Jews*].Warsaw: F. Hoesick, 1917.

Siemienski, Lucyan. *Zywot Tadeusza Kosciuszki* [*The life of Thaddeus Kościuszko*]. Kraków: Drukarnia "Czas" W. Kirchmayer, 1866.

Sinkoff, Nancy. *Out of the Shtetl: Making Jews Modern in the Polish Borderlands*. Providence, RI: Brown Judaic Studies, 2004.

Skałkowski, A.M. *O Kokarde Legionów* [*About the legion's cockades*]. Lwów: Księgarnia Gubrynowicza, 1912.

————. *Kościuszko w Swietle Nowszych Badań* [*Kościuszko in the light of new research*], Poznań: 1924.

Smoleński, Władysław. *Stan i Sprawa Żydów Polskich w XVIII wieku* [*The State and issues of Polish Jews in the eighteenth Century*]. Warsaw: Nadkładem Księgarnii Celsa Lewickiego i Spółki, 1876.

————. *Ostatni Rok Sejmu Wielkiego* [*The final year of the great Sejm*]. Kraków: Gebethner I Wolff, 1897.

————. *Dzieje Narodu Polskiego, Wydanie Piąte* [*History of the Polish Nation, 5ᵗʰ Edition*]. Warsaw: Gebthner i Wolff, 1906.

Sobieski, Wacław. *Młode lata Kościuszki* [*Kościuszko: the early years*]. Kraków: 1917.

————. *Dzieje Polski* [*Polish history*]. Warsaw: Zorza, 1938.

South, Stanley A. *An Archaeological Evolution*. New York: Springer, 2005.

Sparks, Jared. *The Life and Treason of Benedict Arnold*. Boston: Hilliard, Gray & Co. London: Richard James Kennet, 1835.

Spears, John R. *Anthony Wayne, Sometimes Called "Mad Anthony."* New York: D. Appleton and Company, 1903.

Stein, Susan. R., *The World of Thomas Jefferson at Monticello*. New York: Harry N. Abrams, 1993.

Steiner, Bernard C. *The Life and Correspondence of James McHenry, Secretary of War Under Washington and Adams*. Cleveland: Burrow Brothers Company, 1907.

Stille, Charles J. *The Life and Times of John Dickinson, 1732–1808*, Philadelphia: J.B. Lippincott Co., 1891.

Subtelny, Orest. *Ukraine: A History*. 3rd ed. Toronto: University of Toronto Press, 2000.

Sumner, William Graham. *The Financier and the Finances of the American Revolution*. New York: Dodd, Mead, and Company, 1892.

Szymański, Leszek. *Casimir Pulaski: A Hero of the American Revolution*. New York: Hippocrene Books, 1979.

Szyndler, Bartłomiej. *Tadeusz Kościuszko, 1746–1817*. Warsaw: Bellona, 1991.

Taczak, Teodor. *Kazanie: w setna rocznice zgonu, Tadeusza Kosciuszki, Wyglosil w Archikatedrze Gnieziewskiej, Dnia 15-go Pazdziernika 1917 roku* [*Homily: on the hundredth anniversary of the death of Tadeusz Kosciuszko, delivered in the archcathedral in Gniezno, October 15, 1917*]. Gniezno: J.B. Lange, 1917.

Thayer, Theodore. *Nathanael Greene: Strategist of the American Revolution*. New York: Twayne Publishers, 1960.

Troyat, Henri. *Catherine the Great*. Paris: Flammarion, 1977.

Van Doren, Carl. *Secret History of the American Revolution: An Account of the Conspiracies of Benedict Arnold*. New York: Viking Press, 1941.

Walicki, Andrzej. *The Enlightenment and the Birth of Modern Nationhood: Polish Political Thought from Noble Republicanism to Tadeusz Kościuszko*. Translated by Emma Harris. Notre Dame: University of Notre Dame Press, 1989.

Walker, Paul K. *Engineers of Independence: A Documentary History of the Army Engineers in the American Revolution, 1775–1783.* Washington, DC: Historical Division, U.S. Army Corps of Engineers, 1977.

Walsh, Robert, Eliakim Littell, and John Jay Smith. *Museum of Foreign Literature and Science,* *Vol. XXVII, July to December, 1835.* Philadelphia: E. Littell, 1835.

Walsh, William S. *Handy-Book of Literary Curiosities.* Philadelphia: J.B. Lippincott Company, 1893.

Wandycz, Piotr. S. *The Lands of Partitioned Poland*, 1795–1918. Seattle: University of Washington Press, 1974.

Ward, Christopher. *The War of the Revolution.* New York: Macmillan Company, 1952.

Wegner, Leon. *Dzieje dnia trzeciego i piątego maja 1791* [*History of May 3 and 5, 1791*]. Poznań: Nakladem Towarzystwa Przyaciol Nauk Poznanskiego, 1865.

Węgrzynek, Hanna. *Historia i Kultura Żydow Polskich, Słownik* [*The History and Culture of Polish Jews,* A Dictionary]. Warsaw: Wydawnictwa Szkolne i Pedagogiczne, 2000.

Weinryb, Bernard Dov. *The Jews of Poland.* Philadelphia: Jewish Publication Society of America, 1973.

Wilson, Barry K. *Benedict Arnold: A Traitor in Our Midst.* Montreal: McGill–Queen's University Press, 2001.

Wilson, Robert H. *Thaddeus Kościuszko and His Home in Philadelphia.* Copernicus Society of America, 1976.

Wiernik, Peter, *History of the Jews in America.* New York: The Jewish Press Publishing Company, 1912.

Wolański, Adam. *Wojna polsko-rosyjska 1792 r* [*The Polish-Russian war of 1792*]. Kraków: E.E. Freidlein, 1906.

Wolf, Simon. *American Jew as Patriot, Soldier and Citizen. A Sketch of Haym Salomon: From An Unpublished MS in the Papers of Jared Sparks.* Contributed by Herbert B. Adams, Ph.D., professor in the Johns Hopkins University, with Notes by J. H. Hollander., Philadelphia: The Levytype Company, 1895.

Young, Calvin. *Little Turtle (ME-SHE-KIN-NO-QUAH): The Great Chief of the Miami Indian Nation, Being a sketch of his life together with that of William Wells and some noted descendents.* Greenville, OH: HBC, 1917.

Zahorski, Andrzej. *Warszawa W Postaniu Kościuszkowskim* [*Warsaw in the Kościuszko uprising*]. Warsaw: Wiedza Powszechna, 1985.

Zamoyski, Adam. *The Last King of Poland.* London: Phoenix Giant, 1992.

———. *The Polish Way.* New York: Hippocrene Books, 1987.

Zawadzki, W. H. *A Man of Honour: Adam Czartoryski as a Statesman of Russia and Poland, 1795—1831.* Oxford: Clarendon Press, 1993.

Żuraw, Józef. *Myśl filozoficzna i społeczna Tadeusza Kościuszki: tradycje i współczesność* [*The philosophical and social ideas of Thaddeus Kościuszko in tradition and modern times*]. Warsaw: Wydawnictwo Ministerstwa Obrony Narodowej, 1979.

Newspapers, Magazines, and Periodicals

County Chronicles: A Vivid Collection of Fayette County Pennsylvania Histories Magazine of American History with Notes and Queries

Magazine of American History with Notes and Queries, 21 (Jan.–June, 1889)

Dunlap's American Daily Advertiser

Gazette de Leyde, May 10 and 20, 1791, Indiana University, Lilly Library

Journal of the Royal Asiatic Society of Great Britain & Ireland, 1834

New York Historical Magazine, April 1859

New York Sun

New York Packet

Nowinny (Warsaw)

Pennsylvania Magazine of History and Biography

Pennsylvania Weekly Advertiser

Polish Heritage, published quarterly by the American Council for Polish Culture

South Carolina Historical Magazine

Rivington's Royal Gazette

Thatcher's Military Journal

Washington Spy

Tygodnik Ilustrowany [Illustrated Weekly], 1881

Weteran Poznański [Poznań Veteran], 1825

Johnson, Theodore. "Last Years of Kościuszko." *Harper's New Monthly Magazine* 37 (Sept. 1868.)

"Testamentary Tragedy: Jefferson and the Wills of General Kosciuszko" *American Bar Association Journal* (Jan. 1958)

Index